ArtScroll Tanach Series®

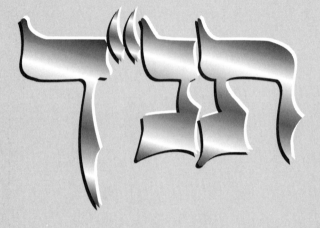

A traditional commentary on the Books of the Bible

Rabbi Nosson Scherman / Rabbi Meir Zlotowitz

General Editors

A PROJECT OF THE

Mesorah Heritage Foundation

Translation and Commentary by
Rabbi Eliezer Ginsburg

An Overview:
Wisdom of the Wisest
by
Rabbi Nosson Scherman

VOLUME I
CHAPTERS 1-15

mishlei

PROVERBS / A NEW TRANSLATION WITH A COMMENTARY
ANTHOLOGIZED FROM TALMUDIC, MIDRASHIC, AND RABBINIC SOURCES.

Published by

Mesorah Publications, ltd

FIRST EDITION
First Impression … November 1998
Second Impression … July 2001
Third Impression … May 2003
Fourth Impression … January 2004

Published and Distributed by
MESORAH PUBLICATIONS, LTD.
4401 Second Avenue / Brooklyn, N.Y 11232

Distributed in Europe by
LEHMANNS
Unit E, Viking Industrial Park
Rolling Mill Road
Jarow, Tyne & Wear, NE32 3DP
England

Distributed in Australia and New Zealand by
GOLDS WORLDS OF JUDAICA
3-13 William Street
Balaclava, Melbourne 3183
Victoria, Australia

Distributed in Israel by
SIFRIATI / A. GITLER — BOOKS
6 Hayarkon Street
Bnei Brak 51127

Distributed in South Africa by
KOLLEL BOOKSHOP
Shop 8A Norwood Hypermarket
Norwood 2196, Johannesburg, South Africa

THE ARTSCROLL TANACH SERIES®
MISHLEI / PROVERBS VOLUME 1
© *Copyright 1998, by* MESORAH PUBLICATIONS, Ltd.
4401 Second Avenue / Brooklyn, N.Y. 11232 / (718) 921-9000 / www.artscroll.com

ISBN:
1-57819-277-3 (hard cover)
1-57819-278-1 (paperback)

Typography by CompuScribe at ArtScroll Studios, Ltd.

Printed in the United States of America by Noble Book Press Corp.
Bound by Sefercraft, Quality Bookbinders, Ltd., Brooklyn N.Y. 11232

This volume is dedicated
as a memorial tribute to our parents,
who not only survived the horrors of the Holocaust,
but, with commitment, resolve and tenacity, rebuilt their lives,
creating and nurturing their contribution to the future of *Klal Yisrael*,
steeped in the tradition and foundations of their past.

ר׳ צבי יצחק ב״ר חיים ע״ה
Reverend Herschel Weintraub

A prominent pre-war *baal habayis,* profound *talmid chacham,* and fiercely observant Jew, he did not allow his enormous personal losses, the ovens of Auschwitz, nor the effects of his own captivity, to change his perspective or deter him from building a new life in his later years, with the same intense devotion to *kiyum hamitzvos.*

שרה בת שמואל ע״ה
Sarah Weintraub Basser

She invested her entire being in the welfare of her husband and the raising of her only child. Under the most difficult of circumstances, she exhibited a spirit of kindness, compassion, and uncompromising honesty. She was overjoyed wih *"Yiddishe nachas,"* as she shared in the accomplishments of her children and grandchildren.

מרדכי בן יהושע הלוי ע״ה
Max Basser

No father could have been more loving, devoted, or giving, then this gentle soul. He helped raise a family as if it were his own, and its growth remains a tribute to his character, loyalty, and generosity.

We, their children and grandchildren, thank Hashem Yisbarach for their shining example, and are grateful for this opportunity to express our admiration, for each of them exemplified the *middos tovos* of *Mishlei.*

Barry and Harriet Ray
Tzvi and Tybi Ray and family   **Shua and Devorah Ray and family**
Yanky and Huvie Feiler and family   **Shoshana Ray**

~§ Author's Preface

The works of such classic commentators as *Ramban* and *Rabbeinu Bachya*, as well as the most widely accepted volumes of the masters of *mussar* are filled with references to *Mishlei / Proverbs*. Indeed, the wisdom of the wisest of all men has been a beacon for succeeding generations for three thousand years. It has been a great challenge and privilege, therefore, for us to attempt to present the wisdom of Shlomo HaMelech as it has been understood by our Sages and teachers ever since he began presenting it to his nation.

Let us remember that when Shlomo acceded to his father's throne, his only request of God was for the wisdom he would need to judge Israel wisely and well. God granted his request. The Book of *Proverbs* is one product of that Divine blessing. Our teachers have found in it infinite lessons for the conduct of a proper and upright life.

In this work, we have attempted to mine the works and words of our classic commentators for insights into the Book and for anecdotes that illustrate how its teachings have molded the conduct of our people. We thank Hashem for affording us this honor; we have discharged this responsibility to the best of our ability and we pray that we have done some measure of justice to this awesome task. Nevertheless, however, the work presented here has only tapped the surface of the infinite treasures of wisdom and *mussar* embedded in the words of King Solomon.

We must thank the many people who made this finished product possible. If not for RABBI MEIR ZLOTOWITZ's great foresight and sense of responsibility to make Torah available to our English-speaking Jewish brethren; if not for RABBI NOSSON SCHERMAN's Torah knowledge and editorial skill; if not for REB AVROHOM BIDERMAN's prodding and organizational skill; if not for the graphics expertise of REB SHEAH BRANDER with the assistance of REB YAAKOV HERSH HOROWITZ, this work would not have come to fruition, and certainly not in its present beautiful form. We are deeply grateful to them all.

We express our appreciation to the entire staff of ArtScroll/Mesorah, and in particular to those who were involved in the production of this work: RABBI ASHER MARGOLIOT ע״ה and להבחל״ח RABBI MOSHE LIEBER, who did preliminary editing; and to the proofreaders and typists, who worked diligently and well.

We take this opportunity to thank our parents, Rabbi and MRS. MOSHE DAVID GOLDFINGER and REBBITZIN ZLATA GINSBURG שיחיו, whose ongoing guidance, encouragement, and influence have been our supporting pillars in all our undertakings. May Hashem bless them with continued good health, *nachas*, and joy.

Marcheshvan 5759 / November 1998
Rabbi Eliezer Ginsburg

לזכרון עולם ולמזכרת נצח

להאי שופרא דבלי בעפרא

ה״ה אבינו

הרב ר׳ לימא בן ר׳ נח צבי לוין ע״ה

למד ולימד תורה לעדרים

יסורים סבל והיה למופת לרבים

מוכתר במידות עליונות וטובות

אוהב את המקום ואוהב את הבריות

למד תורה מאת הגאון הגדול ר׳ אלחנן בונם וסרמן זצוק״ל הי״ד
בישיבת ברנוביץ ואח״כ בישיבת מיר הקד׳
וניצול בדרך נס עם הישיבה ובא לארצות הברית והעמיד משפחה
ונקטף בדמי ימיו ביום שבת קדש ה׳ תמוז תשי״ט.

המזכירים שמו, חתניו ובנותיו

משפחת גינזבורג   משפחת נוימאן

An Overview /
Wisdom of the Wisest

⊷§ An Overview /
Wisdom of the Wisest

I. The Choice

Solomon was only twelve years old when he was anointed as the successor to his great father David as king of Israel. Young though he was, only one thing mattered to him above all others. God appeared to him in a prophetic dream and said, "Request what I should give you." It was the young lad's great opportunity. Anything could have been his for the asking, and there was much that he needed. He knew full well that his half-brother Adonijah aspired to the throne and had tried to seize it; Israel was not truly secure from its surrounding enemies, who had often invaded even in the days of the mighty David; Solomon's fledgling reign had no guarantee of the prosperity that is important to the success of a leader.

It was the young lad's great opportunity. Anything could have been his for the asking, and there was much that he needed.

Solomon's Priority THE YOUNG KING TOOK FULL ADVANTAGE of the Divinely offered boon. He asked for the most precious thing in the world:

> You have done a great kindness with Your servant, David, my father, because he walked before You with truth and justice and with uprightness of heart with You; and You have preserved for him this great kindness and You have granted him a son who sits on his throne this very day. And now, HASHEM, my God, You have crowned Your servant in place of David,

*I am a young lad;
I do not know
how to go out and
how to come in.*

*my father, but I am a young lad; I do not know
how to go out and how to come in* [i.e., how to
lead]. *Your servant is in the midst of Your
people whom You have chosen, a large nation
that can neither be counted nor numbered
because of its abundance. May You grant Your
servant an understanding heart, to judge Your
people, to distinguish between good and evil; for
who can judge this formidable people of Yours?*
(*I Kings* 3:6-9).

*All he wanted
was the ability to
judge God's people
according to His
Torah.*

Solomon chose what was most important to *him*. All
he wanted was the ability to judge God's people
according to His Torah, so he ignored all his other needs
and asked only for wisdom.

God's answer is well known. He said that because
Solomon requested wisdom, instead of longevity, riches
or the life of his enemies, he would have all of these. God
promised him a long reign, riches, dominion, *and*, God
said: *Behold I have given you a wise and understanding
heart, such as there has never been anyone like you
before, nor will anyone like you ever arise.* Solomon
became the wisest man who ever lived (ibid. vs. 10-13).

Solomon awoke and realized that it had been a dream

*The dream had
been prophetic.*

— but not an ordinary one. The dream had been
prophetic. According to Rabbi Yitzchak, Solomon could
tell that the Divine promise of the dream had been
fulfilled because he was able to understand even the
braying of donkeys and the chirping of birds (*Shir
HaShirim Rabbah* 1:9).

*Three
Books*

IMMEDIATELY SOLOMON RETURNED TO JERUSALEM and
expressed his gratitude to God by bringing many
offerings and making a great feast for all of his servants
(*I Kings* 3:15). From this celebration, Rabbi Elazar derives
that one should make a feast upon completing a

*Just as Solomon
celebrated the gift
of Torah,
so should everyone
express his joy
upon learning a
section of Torah.*

significant portion of the Torah; for just as Solomon
celebrated the gift of Torah, so should everyone express
his joy upon learning a section of Torah knowledge.
Furthermore, R' Elazar continues, the Divine Spirit of
wisdom rested upon Solomon and he composed all three
of his Books that became part of the Holy Scriptures:

Mishlei / Proverbs; *Shir HaShirim* / Song of Songs; and *Koheles* / Ecclesiastes.

Rabbi Yonasan differs. He offers the familiar opinion that Solomon composed the three works at different stages of his life. When he was a young man enjoying the surge of God-given wisdom, he composed *Song of Songs*, the lyrical and passionate allegory of the love between God and Israel, the depiction of an ardor so lofty that Rabbi Akiva said of it, "All the songs of Scripture are holy, but *Song of Songs* is the holy of holies." [See the Overview to the ArtScroll edition of *Song of Songs*.] When Solomon was older, he wrote the Book of *Proverbs*, to convey his wisdom to all the world. And when he was advanced in years, he poured his disillusionment with the material world into *Ecclesiastes*. There are other opinions regarding the chronology of the three works (ibid.), but all agree that they represent not ordinary wisdom, but wisdom that was Divinely and uniquely given.

When Solomon was older, he wrote the Book of Proverbs, to convey his wisdom to all the world.

Everything and Everyone

SOLOMON WAS GIVEN THE DESCRIPTIVE NAME "Koheles," from the root קהל, *to congregate*. *Rashi* and *Ibn Ezra* interpret this as a reference to his wisdom: He "congregated" within himself all that there was to know. The Sages, however, interpret differently. Solomon "congregated" multitudes to hear his teachings (*Koheles Rabbah* 1:2), Jew and gentile alike (*I Kings* 8:1,14). He was not content to be wise; he wanted others to realize their own potential and he wanted to elevate all nations, not merely his own. Of course, Israel's responsibilities and role are not the same as those of the nations. The nation of Torah must place the highest value on the knowledge of the Torah and, as the Sages teach, Solomon used his vast understanding and his unmatched ability to compose proverbs that would make the depths of the Torah intelligible to his people. He explained every law of the Torah, the Sages say, in hundreds of ways, for maximum clarity. As we will see below, he communicated his wisdom in such a way that it had many layers of meaning, all of them true, and comprehensible to everyone according to his own

He communicated his wisdom in such a way that it had many layers of meaning, all of them true.

capacity to absorb it. [For a discussion of the Book of Ecclesiastes / *Koheles*, see the Overview to that Book.]

That, too, was a gift that was almost unique to Solomon; surely it was part of the Divine blessing that was conferred upon him. His proverbs and epigrams provided practical guidance to people who had never opened a book of Torah, but, for those capable of plumbing the depth of his intentions, they simultaneously illuminated the most profound areas of the Torah. In modern times, such a skill was often ascribed to the Chofetz Chaim, who spoke in apparently simple terms, but whose seemingly informal discourses captivated and instructed scholars and shoemakers alike.

For those capable of plumbing the depth of his intentions, they illuminated the most profound areas of the Torah.

Multi-Layered

A PRIME EXAMPLE OF THIS PHENOMENON is the last, and most familiar, chapter of *Proverbs*, which includes the twenty-two verses of אֵשֶׁת חַיִל [*Eishes Chayil*], *An Accomplished Woman*, or, in the better known translation, *A Woman of Valor*. (That chapter will be treated in volume 2 of this work.) Without question, the literal translation of its twenty-two verses stand on their own and have inspired countless people. The worth of such a woman is indeed *far beyond pearls* (31:10): her loyalty to her family, self-reliance, initiative, kindness, energetic performance of charity, faith and serenity and more are exemplary. Most appropriately, *Her children have risen and praised her; her husband and he extolled her* (31:28).

These praises of the *Eishes Chayil* are, of course, true in the literal sense; indeed, that is the only sense ever contemplated by the vast majority of Bible readers through the centuries. But *Eishes Chayil* includes far deeper meanings, which are discussed by the Sages and the classic commentators. An example, *Ramban* interprets the *Accomplished Woman* as a metaphor for the Torah. Her "husband" is the outstanding scholar; her "children" are the diligent and dedicated students; the "poor people" she helps are the masses who benefit from her teachings, and so on. Similarly, the rest of the Book of *Proverbs* must be understood on more than the obvious level. This is typical of the progression of Torah

Similarly, the rest of the Book of Proverbs must be understood on more than the obvious level.

interpretation, from simple meaning [פְּשַׁט] to allusion [רֶמֶז] to hermeneutic interpretion [דְּרוּשׁ] to the mysteries of the Torah [סוֹד]. So, too, the commentary in this volume will demonstrate the richness of the Book of *Proverbs*, although it must be understood that the most profound secrets of the Torah are the province of only the greatest Jews.

In the Introduction to his Commentary on the Torah, *Rabbeinu Bachya* cites another familiar verse from this Book: אֹרֶךְ יָמִים בִּימִינָהּ בִּשְׂמֹאולָהּ עֹשֶׁר וְכָבוֹד, *Length of days is at its [Torah wisdom's] right, at its left are wealth and honor (Proverbs 3:16).* Literally, the verse extols the benefits that come in the wake of wisdom. True, but again, there is a deeper meaning.

Torah, because it is God's own wisdom and because it was His blueprint for the creation of the universe, is the *If someone could* source of life itself, so much so that if someone could *interpret it to its* interpret it to its very essence, one could literally bring *very essence, one* could literally bring *the dead back to life (Midrash Tehillim,* ch. 3). Indeed, *bring the dead* there were Talmudic Sages who did so. We do not *back to life.* possess this skill, but the Torah's commandments and study are still our road to the eternal life of the World to Come. The "right" and "left" of the verse are similes for This World (the *left*) and the World to Come (the *right*). This temporal world is the portal to the eternal world; it is here that we can amass the Torah knowledge and good deeds that will open the gates of Paradise. The pursuit of wisdom in the here and now can bring one the *wealth and honor* that should be used as tools to perform the deeds that will elevate our lives and make us worthy of the eternal life of the spirit, the life of the *"right,"* the World to Come.

Those who read *Proverbs* without awareness of the two worlds and the true goal of life, people who live only for the temporal world, whether or not they acknowledge that there is another, higher life, will surely agree that wisdom is a precious commodity and *Those with a* that length of days, wealth, and honor are its hand- *deeper knowledge* maidens. But for them, it ends with the grave. Those *of God's plan* with a deeper knowledge of God's plan, however, know *know that life* *should be a* that life should be a progression, and man must use its *progression.*

gifts in this world as means to elevate himself and make himself worthy of life in the next.

II. The Good and the Futile*

Why Despair? The contrast between the transitory nature of This World and the eternity of the World to Come is at the root of *Ramban*'s response to a very perplexing problem. The Book of *Koheles*/Ecclesiastes is an almost unrelieved exercise in gloom. In it, Solomon refers to life as a *"futility of futilities,"* a refrain that he repeats no less than seven times, and there is hardly a human pursuit that Solomon does not put under that rubric.

How can King Solomon say that God created the universe in vain? At the time of Creation, God pronounced it as "very good." But, *Ramban* protests, how can King Solomon say that God created the universe in vain? At the time of Creation, God surveyed all that He had done and pronounced it as "very good." Three thousand years later, when the world was hardly in an ideal state, and Israel was on the verge of Babylonian conquest and the destruction of the First Temple, God still said such things as *I made the earth — with the man and the animal that are on the face of the earth — with My great strength and with My outstretched arm, and I gave it to whomever was fitting in My eyes (Jeremiah 27:5); . . . Raise your eyes on high and see Who created these [things] (Isaiah 40:26);* and many similar verses, where God takes pride in Creation. *Ramban* continues at length to wonder how Solomon can be so despairing. Surely he is not contradicting God; why does he see futility where God sees accomplishment?

God presents us with a universe that is indeed "very good," and it is up to us to use it wisely. *Ramban* explains that the physical world is like raw material in the hands of people. God presents us with a universe that is indeed "very good," and it is up to us to use it wisely, to perfect ourselves and our surroundings in accordance with His will, as expressed in His Torah and expounded by His wise counselors. When Noah's generation corrupted itself and even the very earth through its moral perversions and selfishness,

---

* *This section of the Overview is based on Ramban's "Derashah on Koheles."*

it was not *Creation* that God pronounced to be a failure; rather *HASHEM reconsidered having made Man on earth, and He had heartfelt sadness* (Genesis 6:6). It was not the earth — the raw material — that would be destroyed, but the artisan who abused it.

Man, not God, is at fault when his actions cause punishment and destruction.

Man, not God, is at fault when his actions cause punishment and destruction. As Jeremiah said, *Of what shall a living man complain? A man for his sins! Let us search and examine our ways and return to HASHEM. Let us lift our hearts with our hands to our Father in heaven* (Lamentations 3:39-42).

Meaning of "Hevel"

SOLOMON SEES FUTILITY NOT IN GOD'S HANDIWORK, but in man's. God's creation is permanent; man's is passing. This is why Solomon uses the word הֶבֶל to express *futility*. The word *hevel* also means *breath* or *air*, as in "the innocent breath [הֶבֶל] of young Torah students, in whose merit the world endures" (*Shabbos* 119b), and the stagnant air [הֶבֶל] at the bottom of a pit, which can suffocate an animal that falls into it (*Bava Kamma* 50b). *Ramban* likens the transitoriness of life to the sparks that are created when stones are rubbed together. They can start a fire, but they disappear in a split second. So, too, a person's breath on a cold day will become a mist that will soon be gone. In a powerful simile, *Ramban* says that the mist rising from putrefying garbage symbolizes the fleeting reality of misdeeds. Can there be a greater *futility of futilities?*

Ramban likens the transitoriness of life to sparks. They can start a fire, but they disappear in a split second.

Solomon laments man's misuse of God's gifts. It is destructive and essentially temporary. Significant though they may seem, his accomplishments are essentially futile — although the daily papers and the history books may not record this sad reality — until the ultimate redemption, when God's unity and sovereignty will be acknowledged by all mankind (*Zechariah* 14:9).

Proper Evaluation

IN A NOVEL AND TELLING HOMILETICAL interpretation, *Ramban* suggests that Solomon's theme הֲבֵל הֲבָלִים, *futility of futilities*, can be translated differently. The world הֲבֵל can be rendered in the imperative form, as an instruction from Solomon to us: "Consider futilities to

be futile." In other words, Solomon urges us to evaluate the world through God's lenses and to recognize that anything that conflicts with the Torah's scheme is of no value.

Thus, *Ramban* concludes, these are the themes of Solomon's three books: *Song of Songs* is ecstatic at Israel's loving relationship with God, the holiest of the holy. *Proverbs* charts the course that will lead people to the ultimate goal of eternal life. *Ecclesiastes* warns man away from the road to futility and oblivion.

III. The Wooden Ark*

וַיְהִי כְּכַלּוֹת שְׁלֹמֹה לִבְנוֹת אֶת בֵּית ה' וְאֶת בֵּית הַמֶּלֶךְ וְאֵת כָּל חֵשֶׁק שְׁלֹמֹה אֲשֶׁר חָפֵץ לַעֲשׂוֹת.
It happened when Solomon had finished building the Temple of HASHEM *and the king's palace, and every luxury [lit. desire] of Solomon that he wished to make (I Kings 9:1).*

Origin of Sin   The Holy Ark in the Temple and Tabernacle, which contained the Tablets of the Law, the Ten Commandments, was made of עֲצֵי שִׁטִּים, *acacia wood*, covered on the inside and outside with pure gold (*Exodus* 25:10-11). The Sages explain that the Ark consisted of three separate boxes: a golden one tucked inside the wooden one, which was, in turn, tucked inside another golden one (see *Rashi* ibid.). *Ibn Ezra* wonders, therefore, since the golden boxes were not merely a coating, but solid arks in their own right, why was there a need for the wooden ark at all; since the wood was not visible, either on the inside or outside, why should there not have been a single ark made of gold?

R' Tzaddok HaKohen cites *Midrash Tanchuma*

---

* *This section of the Overview is based the writings of R' Tzaddok HaKohen, in P'ri Tzaddik and Resisei Laylah.*

The shittim wood of the Ark was to atone for the sort of grievous sin that the Jewish people committed in "Shittim."

(*Parashas Terumah*) that the *shittim* wood of the Ark was to atone for the sort of grievous sin that the Jewish people later committed in a place called "Shittim," where a mass orgy of immorality led to a plague that took 24,000 lives (*Numbers* ch. 25). According to R' Yehoshua, Shittim is not a place name, but a description of the outrage that took place there: The people engaged in *sh'tus*, idiocy [שְׁטִים=שְׁטוּת] (*Bechoros* 5b). As the Tal-

A normal person does not sin unless a spirit of idiocy [רוּחַ שְׁטוּת] has come upon him.

mud states, a normal person does not sin unless a spirit of idiocy [רוּחַ שְׁטוּת] has come upon him (*Sotah* 3a).

Lust, the source of the abominable sin at Shittim, is truly foolish. How else can one understand how a rational human being can sacrifice his share in the World to Come for a pleasure that will be gone in but a few moments? At Shittim, this lust caused not only the sin of immorality, but also the worship of the idol of Peor, which is itself one of the basest forms of idolatry.

Balanced Inclinations

THE ARK WAS THE REPOSITORY OF THE TABLETS of the Testimony, which were testimony to the eternal and intimate relationship of God and Israel, and the *shittim*

The shittim wood was a reminder of the human capacity for foolishness, and of God's merciful readiness to accept repentance.

wood of which it was made was simultaneously a reminder of the human capacity for the basest sort of foolishness, and of God's merciful readiness always to accept Israel's repentance. It is noteworthy that this sin is symbolized by the Ark, the embodiment of Torah, because the Evil Inclination makes a special effort to subject Torah scholars to lust. In fact, the greater the person, the greater his Evil Inclination (*Succah* 52a).

As many commentators have explained, human spiritual existence is predicated on free choice. Man must be equally balanced between good and evil, and he must then make his choice. Only if his temptation is as

Only if his temptation is as strong as his conscience does he deserve to be rewarded for making the proper choice.

strong as his conscience does he deserve to be rewarded for making the proper choice. Conversely, because his own inner voice for good is as eloquent as the competing choir of temptation — if only he is willing to hear it — he deserves to be punished for choosing to hear the wrong siren song. It is understandable, therefore, that the greater the person, the greater his susceptibility to temptation.

Desire R' TZADDOK OFFERS ANOTHER REASON why the Torah
for scholar's Evil Inclination should be stronger than
Pleasure normal. The quintessential manifestation of this inclination is a powerful desire for pleasure, which is part of
human nature. As the Torah states, HASHEM *saw that*
the wickedness of Man was great upon the earth, and
that every product of the thoughts of his heart was but
evil, always (Genesis 6:5).

Such thoughts and desires fashioned the prelude to
In Noah's time the Deluge in Noah's time. The behavior of the people
the entire earth deteriorated, as described in *Genesis* 6:11. At first, *they*
"was corrupted," were corrupt — being guilty of immorality and idolatry
because man is — and they sinned covertly, only "before God." Later
the essence of the "earth had become filled with robbery" — which
Creation, and his was obvious to all. Then the entire earth "was
corruption affects corrupted," because man is the essence of Creation, and
everything else. his corruption affects everything else (*Zohar*).

Strong desire within man was created for a positive
purpose. Passivity is not the stuff of greatness; initiative
is. Those with powerful drives have the potential for
outstanding accomplishment — provided they have the
moral fortitude to channel their drives in the right
direction. God created passion so that people could
direct it toward an intensive study of Torah and a
creative and enthusiastic pursuit of good deeds. Teach-
Many of the most ers and parents can attest to the fact that many of the
uncontrollable most uncontrollable students became exemplary people
students became once they matured and steered their aggressiveness to
exemplary people constructive pursuits. As the Sages say, "If this repulsive
once they steered one [i.e., the Evil Inclination] comes upon you, drag him
their aggressive-
ness to construc- to the study hall (*Succah* 52b).
tive pursuits.
Many miracles will occur in Messianic times, as
Israel's enemies will fall and the dispersed people of God
will be returned to its land in unimaginable prosperity.
Among those miracles, *a spring will go out from the*
House of HASHEM and water the Valley of Shittim (Joel
The "Valley of 4:18). Joel's reference to the "Valley of Shittim" alludes
Shittim" alludes to to the powerful lusts that led to the mass immorality at
the powerful lusts
that led to mass Shittim cited above (*Numbers* ch. 25). When the world
immorality. is elevated to its ideal state in Messianic times, a spring
from God's Abode will bring a spirit of Torah and

sanctity that will overwhelm immorality and lead mankind to pursue good, rather than idle or evil pleasure.

The Lost and the Castaways IN A SIMILAR CLASSIC FORMULATION, *R' Tzaddok* explains the familiar verse . . . וְהָיָה בַּיּוֹם הַהוּא, *It shall be on that day that a great shofar will be blown, and those who are lost in the land of Assyria and those who are cast away in the land of Egypt will come, and they will prostrate themselves to HASHEM on the holy mountain in Jerusalem (Isaiah 27:13).* The prophet states that those in Assyria will return before those in Egypt, which hardly seems logical. The Assyrians are "lost," the Egyptians are merely "cast away"; it would seem that "lost" people would never come back to God, certainly they would not be the first to return.

It would seem that "lost" people would never come back to God, certainly they would not be the first to return.

R' *Tzaddok* explains the symbolism of the prophecy. The locales of Assyria and Egypt are not meant to be the actual places from which the exiles will come, certainly not in the hoped-for imminent coming of Messiah, when there are hardly any Jews left in either of these inhospitable countries. Rather, Assyria and Egypt represent two different kinds of people. Assyria, in present-day Iraq, is a mountainous, rocky land that is unkind to plows and planters. People must work very hard to wring a livelihood from its rugged soil. Ancient Egypt, on the other hand, was the very symbol of ease. The Nile brought irrigation, and farm life was leisurely. Men wore cosmetics and luxuriated in a slothful life.

Assyria symbolizes people who work hard to find the truth — their quest takes them through rocks and over mountains. Egypt symbolizes people who never bothered to search for it.

In spiritual terms, Assyria symbolizes people who work hard to find the truth — their quest takes them through rocks and over mountains — but they are "lost." Try though they may, they are far, far from the truth, because they have searched in the wrong places and adopted the wrong philosophies. Egypt, on the other hand, symbolizes people who have become "cast away" from the truth, because they never bothered to search for it. On the one hand, they are not actively opposed to it, as are the spiritual Assyrians, but on other hand, their lazy habits of mind have prevented them from escaping the enticements of pleasure that are a barrier to serious choice.

When the truth becomes revealed with the approach of the End of Time, the active, aggressive searchers of Assyria will realize that they were wrong. Their zeal for the truth will propel them to make an about-face and hurry to prostrate themselves to Hashem and embrace the Torah's way of life. But the spiritual Egyptians? They never exerted themselves as they slid into the quicksand of sin, and they will be equally slow to extricate themselves and find their way back to the holy mountain in Jerusalem.

The truth will propel them to make an about-face and hurry to embrace the Torah's way of life.

Solomon's Desire

SO, TOO, THE HIGH POINT OF SOLOMON'S life came when he completed the Holy Temple, his palace, וְאֵת כָּל חֵשֶׁק שְׁלֹמֹה אֲשֶׁר חָפֵץ לַעֲשׂוֹת, *and every luxury* [lit. *desire*] *of Solomon that he wished to make* (I Kings 9:1). This came after Scripture described his stature and accomplishments and his ecstatic celebration at the dedication of the Temple in several chapters. With feeling and eloquence, he had prayed that God should accept the offerings and prayers of those who would come to the Temple, even those of gentiles, and God had accepted his request, as long as Israel continued to obey the commandments of the Torah. This is followed by a lengthy account of his further successes, including the universal respect that he earned throughout the known world, as evidenced by the tribute paid Solomon by King Hiram of Tyre and the legendary Queen of Sheba.

The above verse refers to everything that he desired to build, a refrain that is repeated later in the chapter (ibid 9:19). The word חֵשֶׁק, the *luxuries*, the strong desire, the urge to gratify his wishes, is indicative of his greatness. He had a powerful urge to accomplish great things. Such strivings could have gone to gratify physical hunger, but Solomon sublimated them and used them to bring himself and his subjects to a spiritual peak that will not be duplicated until the coming of Messiah.

The strong desire, the urge to gratify his wishes, is indicative of his greatness. He had a powerful urge to accomplish great things.

To demonstrate the need for the spiritual to transcend the physical, the Holy Ark was composed of three separate arks, the middle one of *shittim* wood and the

inner and outer ones of gold. The Ark represents Torah
and its scholars. At the core of such people, there are
powerful urges, urges that can easily lead them to base
conduct and gratification of man's lowest instincts. But
such people *can* sublimate their desires and use their
initiative for good and constructive purposes. The
Talmud comments on the commandment that the Ark
have gold on its inside and outside, אָמַר רָבָא כָּל תַּלְמִיד
חָכָם שֶׁאֵין תּוֹכוֹ כְּבָרוֹ אֵינוֹ תַּלְמִיד חָכָם, *Rava said: Any
Torah scholar whose inside is not like his outside is not
a Torah scholar*, meaning that a Torah scholar must be
consistently sincere, both within and without (*Yoma*
72b). The Evil Inclination of *shittim* wood is always
present, but a scholar can use his immersion in Torah to
coat both his inner desires and his outward conduct
with the "gold" of exalted behavior — the conduct of
King Solomon.

*The Ark
represents Torah
and its scholars.
At the core of such
people, there are
powerful urges.*

*The Evil
Inclination of
shittim wood is
always present,
but a scholar can
coat both his inner
desires and his
outward conduct
with the "gold" of
exalted behavior.*

Solomon's Achievement

SOLOMON'S MISSION WAS TO SUBJUGATE his Evil
Inclination and accept God's will. His way of establish-
ing God's kingdom within himself was to bring
holiness into every aspect of luxurious living. Lavish
feasts were everyday occurrences. Beauty and ostenta-
tion were the rule of the day. His harem held seven
hundred wives and three hundred concubines. But
feasts, beauty, and wives did not affect him. Instead,
they were his vehicle to prove that holiness can conquer
every apparent manifestation of hedonism. Indeed,
Solomon used his experiences with such chimeras to
proclaim *Futility of futilities, all is futility* (*Ecclesiastes*
1:2).

*Solomon
surrounded his life
with luxury to
show that it was
meaningless —
except to serve
God and his
people.*

Solomon had no foreign enemies, and he conquered
his inner enemies. He surrounded his life with luxury to
show that it was meaningless — except to serve God
and his people. Superficially, he seemed immersed in
love — to prove, as in the lyricism of *Song of Songs*, that
all love should be devoted only to God. He provided
lavish feasts for his guests and courtiers — to show that
one should tender a feast to celebrate the completion of
the Torah. Far from the exercises in indulgence that are
portrayed by the misreaders of Scripture, Solomon's

extravagance was a celebration of Torah study, good deeds, and service of God. He *defeated* his Evil Inclination.

This is why *Song of Songs* is the holiest of all prophetic songs. Its author was a man who was able to descend to the depths of physical indulgence and remain complete, untouched, and unsullied. To Jews, *There is no such thing as a holy work produced by a profane person. Only a human holy of holies can write a holy of holies.* there is no such thing as a holy work produced by a profane person. Only a human holy of holies can write a holy of holies, and such holiness, by definition, means abstinence from lust. For Solomon to achieve such holiness while living as he did is eloquent testimony to the sort of person he was: a holy of holies.

Only a heart that has felt revulsion against extreme earthly darkness and the pseudo-pleasures of animal lust can best know that material necessity, reward, and joy are but a mirage, and that they have no meaningful existence whatsoever (*Resisei Laylah*).

The Light Returns

ACCORDING TO RABBI ELAZAR, WHEN GOD created light on the first day of Creation, it was of such an intense spiritual quality that God separated it from the rest of the universe and set it aside for the righteous to enjoy in the World to Come (*Chagigah* 12a; see *Rashi to Genesis* 1:4). Other Sages disagree, and maintain that the light of the first day was the same light that God emplaced in the heavenly bodies on the "fourth day." The *Vilna Gaon* maintains that the Sages agree with Rabbi Elazar *The primeval light was set aside. When they say that it was emplaced on the "fourth day," they refer to the fourth millennium from Creation.* that the primeval light *was* set aside. When they say that it was emplaced on the "fourth day," they refer to the fourth millennium from Creation, for it was on the threshold of that era, the year 2935 from Creation, that Solomon completed the Temple. Only then, the *Zohar* teaches, was the universe truly completed. Near the end of the fourth millennium (3830), however, when the Second Temple was destroyed, the great spiritual light *That Solomon, and only Solomon, was able to achieve the return of the primeval light is further testimony to his greatness.* of Creation was withdrawn again, and it awaits the coming of Messiah and the building of the Third Temple. That Solomon, and only Solomon, was able to achieve the return of the primeval light is further testimony to his greatness.

It is fitting that Solomon composed the Book of *Proverbs*, for, while the sayings of this Book — especially since it was composed with Divinely granted רוּחַ הַקֹּדֶשׁ, *the spirit of holiness* — are meaningful in their literal sense, they are also garments for many deeper meanings. As the commentary will show, the Sages and commentators find countless teachings in all the wise sayings of the Book. Rav Hamnuna goes so far as to say that Solomon composed as many as three thousand proverbs and parables to elucidate every statement of the Torah (*Eruvin* 21b). Such is the nature of the greatest teachers: They speak to everyone, and everyone willing to listen discerns the message meant for him.

Such is the nature of the greatest teachers: They speak to everyone, and everyone willing to listen discerns the message meant for him.

Solomon's teachings are saturated with fear of God. Even the apparent despair and cynicism of *Ecclesiastes*, whose sanctity was for a time questioned by the Sages, was redeemed by its closing proclamation, *The sum of the matter, when all has been considered: Fear God and keep His commandments, for that is man's whole duty* (*Ecclesiastes* 12:13). That was the proof that the underlying message of *Ecclesiastes* was one of loyalty to God and the Torah (see *Shabbos* 30b).

IV. Part of the Covenant

Prophecy and Spirit

The commentators disagree whether Solomon was a prophet or not, that is, whether God communicated with him directly or not. One thing, however, is undisputed: His three Books that are part of the Scriptural Writings — *Song of Songs, Proverbs,* and *Ecclesiastes* — are not prophecies, meaning that their texts were not given to him directly by God. Rather, they were composed by Solomon with the assistance of רוּחַ הַקֹּדֶשׁ, *the spirit of holiness*.

Succinctly, the difference between prophecy and *ruach hakodesh*, as explained by the commentators, is

Prophecy comes from God. The prophet does not know what the message will be nor does he contribute to its content.

that prophecy comes from God. Although the prophet must prepare himself for the Divine communication, and he may have prayed that God respond to his need for knowledge, guidance or inspiration, he does not know what the message will be nor does he contribute to its content.

Ruach hakodesh, on the other hand, is granted to a person who is using his own efforts and intelligence, and receives Divine help, guidance, and inspiration in order to enhance his accomplishment and save him from error. Thus, a prophet speaks the word of God, while someone with *ruach hakodesh* speaks his own word, but a word that is far superior than it could have been without God's help.

Someone with ruach hakodesh speaks his own word, but a word that is far superior than it could have been without God's help.

Solomon's proverbs, therefore, are more than the ideas of the wisest person who ever lived, although that alone would have made them more than worthy of our most intense study. The Book of *Proverbs*, like the other sacred Books of the Writings, are the product of Divinely guided intelligence. Beyond that, the writings that were included in the twenty-four Books of TaNaCH have an eternal relevance, a relevance that is as important to us as it was to the contemporaries of their authors.

The Torah repeatedly describes itself as the סֵפֶר הַבְּרִית, *the Book of the Covenant* between God and Israel. A covenant implies that the two parties to it are inextricably bound to one another: Hashem is our God and Israel is His people. It is in the nature of a שְׁטַר קִנְיָן, *bill of sale*, which confers ownership upon the purchaser, as opposed to a document that merely attests to an act that had already taken place [שְׁטַר רְאָיָה].

A covenant implies that the two parties to it are inextricably bound to one another: Hashem is our God and Israel is His people.

Contents of the Torah

BEFORE THE REVELATION AT SINAI, MOSES "*took the Book of the Covenant and read it in earshot of the people*" (Exodus 24:7). *Rashi* explains that the Book of the Covenant was the entire Torah, from the beginning of the Book of *Genesis* up to that point in history. Thus the Covenant at that time consisted primarily of the life stories of the Patriarchs and their offspring; there are few commandments or other direct revelations of God's

word in that portion of the Torah. Clearly the Covenant between God and Israel includes the lessons of behavior that God wants us to derive from the experiences of the spiritual giants of our people. When Israel accepted the Torah, it accepted it in its entirety, not only the commandments, but also the way of life exemplified by the narratives about the Patriarchs and other role models of the nation.

So, too, all the sacred Books became part of the Covenant, once they were included in Scripture, because all of them are part of God's message to Israel. The words of *Tehillim* / Psalms are David's and the words of *Mishlei* / Proverbs are Solomon's, but they are part of the Covenant, part of the Torah, which gives them a sacred status and an authenticity far above even the most profound products of human intelligence.

The challenge of the Jewish people is to bring the sanctity of the Torah into all areas of life. Judaism does not differentiate between "ordinary, private" affairs and the laboratory, stage, or synagogue. The Book of *Proverbs*, in a sense, continues the work of the Book of *Genesis*, in that it seeks to refine behavior. In the words of the *Zohar* and *Midrash Rabbah*, God peered into the Torah and created the world; if the Torah is the blueprint of Creation, then it must also be the life-force and ongoing plan for human activity. Indeed, the challenge of the Jewish people is to bring the sanctity of the Torah into all areas of life. Judaism does not differentiate between "ordinary, private" affairs and the laboratory, stage, or synagogue.

Appeals to All IN *PROVERBS* 1:20-25, SOLOMON ELOQUENTLY depicts how "wisdom," meaning the Torah, calls out in the streets and squares, urging those who reject it to hear its teaching and reproof. *Maharal* (*Nesiv HaTeshuvah ch.* 1) comments that the Torah encompasses all aspects of wisdom, and as such must speak to all sorts of people, from the best to the worst, from the wisest to the most ignorant, and that is why it cries out even to those who congregate in the streets and squares, far from the locus and atmosphere of the study hall.

The Torah cries out even to those who congregate in the streets and squares, far from the locus and atmosphere of the study hall.

The above passage appeals to three categories of people: (a) There are sinners who rush after their base, animal desires. Solomon calls them fools, because, as noted above, they ignore all that truly matters in life, in

favor of momentary gratification of their senses. (b) There are scoffers who waste their lives with worthless activities, cynically deriding moral and spiritual values. (c) Finally, there are wicked people who sin not because they are driven by sensual pleasure, but because they deny and even despise the Torah's truth and wisdom.

All these people are lacking in wisdom and even good sense, no matter how much they protest to the contrary. That deficiency makes it possible for man to repent. If his intelligence were not under attack by his animal nature and his Evil Inclination, a sinner would be so completely evil that he would not deserve the merciful opportunity to regret his ways and receive God's forgiveness. But man is far from perfect. His sins are the product of error and foolishness, so Wisdom appeals to him to relent, listen, think, and change. And because God created us to be balanced between good and evil, our repentance can be accepted if we err and then reconsider our waywardness.

Because God created us to be balanced between good and evil, our repentance can be accepted if we err.

Proverbs is filled with such calls. Sometimes Solomon speaks in clearly spiritual terms. Sometimes he garbs his message in pithy advice to farmers or gullible youths. Always, they are the product of a great man, a great mind powered by Divine guidance.

V. The Decline

Solomon's Error

It seems incomprehensible that someone as great, as God-fearing, as wise, as dedicated as Solomon could slide from the summit of holiness, but it happened. We have seen that despite the Ark's golden splendor internally and externally, it still had a core of *shittim* wood — the wood of foolishness — and so it can be with even the greatest of the great. The need for vigilance never ends, because the Evil Inclination never rests. Foolish people can be misled easily by its wiles, but wise people can be in even greater danger, because they may forget that while their wisdom is limited, God's is infinite.

Wise people may forget that while their wisdom is limited, God's is infinite.

אָמַר ר' יִצְחָק: מִפְּנֵי מָה לֹא נִתְגַּלּוּ טַעֲמֵי תוֹרָה?
שֶׁהֲרֵי שְׁתֵּי מִקְרָאוֹת נִתְגַּלּוּ טַעְמָן וְנִכְשַׁל בָּהֶן גָּדוֹל
הָעוֹלָם. כְּתִיב "לֹא יַרְבֶּה לוֹ נָשִׁים."
אָמַר שְׁלֹמֹה, "אֲנִי אַרְבֶּה וְלֹא אָסוּר." וּכְתִיב, "וַיְהִי
לְעֵת זִקְנַת שְׁלֹמֹה נָשָׁיו הִטּוּ אֶת לְבָבוֹ."

*R' Yitzchak said: Why were the reasons for
the Torah['s commandments] not revealed?
Because the reasons for two verses were
revealed and the great one of the world [i.e.,
Solomon] stumbled over them. It is written:
"And [the king] shall not have too many
wives" [so that his heart will not turn away
from God] (Deuteronomy 17:17). Solomon
said,"I will have many [wives]and I will not
turn away." But it is written: "So it was that
when Solomon grew old, his wives swayed
his heart"(I Kings 11:4). The passage continues that the Torah commands the king not to
have too many horses lest he send Jews back
to Egypt to deal in horses for him. Solomon
said that he would have large numbers of
horses and avoid Egypt, but he was wrong
(Sanhedrin 21b).*

In giving the laws of the Jewish monarch, the Torah
limited his powers. He was forbidden to take an
excessive number of wives lest they sway his heart, and
he was not to have an excessive number of horses for his
retinue lest he engage in commerce with Egypt, the
source of the finest horses. Solomon was certain that the
wisest of all men could surely avoid these clearly
spelled-out traps. Without doubt he had good reasons
for taking so many wives and for accumulating tens of
thousands of steeds, and he was confident that his
wisdom would prevent him from falling into the traps
that await lesser men. So he *did* take many wives — and
they *did* sway his heart. And he *did* fill his stables —
and he *did* flood Egypt with his emissaries.

*Solomon was
certain that the
wisest of all men
could surely avoid
these clearly
spelled-out traps.*

The Fifteenth Day

THE *VILNA GAON* COMMENTS THAT ISRAEL is likened to
the moon, which waxes to fullness and then wanes.
This symbolizes the history of the Jewish people. The

lunar month is twenty-nine full days; its fifteenth day is the time when it reaches the peak of its powers and then begins to recede. Solomon, the fifteenth generation from Abraham, reached the highest pinnacle in Jewish history; the first ten chapters of *I Kings* list his unprecedented greatness, wealth, power, and international stature. But on the fifteenth day of the month the moon begins to wane. And so did Solomon.

Chapter 11 of I Kings lists the seeds of Solomon's decline.

Chapter 11 of *I Kings* lists the seeds of Solomon's decline, which eventually led to the split of the Jewish people into two kingdoms after Solomon's death. It seems inconceivable that Solomon could be guilty of idolatry; did not the Sages say that sin can only stem from a spirit of idiocy? How can this be said of the wisest of men?

Yet Scripture states:

> *So it was that when Solomon grew old his wives swayed his heart after the gods of others [i.e., idols], and his heart was not as complete with HASHEM, his God, as had been the heart of his father David. Solomon went after Ashtoreth, the god of the Sidonians, and after Milcom, the abomination of the Ammonites. And Solomon did what was sinful in the eyes of HASHEM, and did not fulfill [his obligation of] following HASHEM as his father David had done (I Kings 11:4-6).*

Solomon did not fulfill [his obligation of] following HASHEM as his father David had done.

So serious was this transgression on its face, that the Men of the Great Assembly wanted to add Solomon to the list of three kings — Jeroboam, Ahab and Menashe — who lost their share in the World to Come. To show them that they should desist, three Heavenly signs came to them, but they persisted in their resolve. Finally a Heavenly voice rang out, with the words of *Job* 34:33, saying: *Is it from you that [punishment] is meted out, that you despise [Solomon]? Shall you choose and not I?* It took God himself to inform His great Sanhedrin that it was for Him alone to decide who would enter the World to Come. Despite Solomon's sin, he still remained Solomon (*Sanhedrin* 104b).

It took God himself to inform His great Sanhedrin that it was for Him alone to decide who would enter the World to Come.

A Higher THE TALMUD DECLARES THAT WHOEVER CLAIMS that
Standard Solomon sinned — that he literally worshiped idols —
is in error. It is noteworthy that the above passage
describes Solomon's sin as a failure to live up to
the example of David; that implies clearly that he
was not guilty of actual idolatry. He himself remained
totally loyal to God, but he did not prevent some
of his wives from erecting idols and worshiping
their gods, and for that Scripture condemns him as if
he himself had joined in their worship (*Shabbos* 56b).
For someone else, such negligence would be an unfortunate though understandable lapse; for someone as
great as Solomon, it was tantamount to the gravest of all
sins.

Unquestionably, Solomon fell short of his own lofty
standard and Scripture criticizes him in the harshest
terms. The Talmud continues that Solomon would
gladly have served as a groom to swine to prevent those
words from being written about him. Because he was so
great, because all the excess and luxury of his life did
The greatest not affect his essential purity, his lapses were so
people must hew unforgivable. Great people must hew to high standards;
to standards the greatest people must hew to standards unimagin-
unimaginably high ably high by ordinary standards.
by ordinary
standards.

In the words of R' S.R. Hirsch on *Proverbs*:
Solomon teaches "not to have reliance on
whatever God has already granted, but to
trust God, be confident about what he has in
store for us. It means to build our entire
future upon God, to be unshakeable in our
conviction that we can reach our goal in life
only with God, from God, and with God's
help. Hence we should ask ourselves at every
step whether the aims we seek and the means
by which we try to attain them are in
keeping with God's will, to such an extent
that we may hopefully expect his assistance.
This is the attitude which, according to
Mishlei, is fundamental to the *tzaddik's*
thinking.

Faith can sunder on the cliff of arrogance, it can be misled and misleading by its over-reliance on human understanding.

"Contrastingly, we are shown how faith can sunder on the cliff of arrogance, how it can be misled and misleading by its over-reliance on human understanding and by the thought that God's knowledge, teachings, and guidance — and consequently also His assistance — can be dispensed with.

"A lawless person thinks that his own intelligence and calculations make him able to do virtually anything at all; he 'lifts high his eyes'; and by raising, 'lifting high' his eyes, by putting his confidence entirely on his own qualifications, he lets his heart's desires roam far and wide."

Solomon was hardly a "lawless person," but even his lapses remain a constructive lesson for us, because they demonstrate the Jew's duty never to relax his striving to improve and his vigilance against backsliding. Ultimately, even the Men of the Great Assembly acknowledged that his greatness remained in place, because they were the ones who brought Solomon's works into Scripture, where his Books stand alongside the holies of all time (see *Shabbos* 30b).

The Men of the Great Assembly acknowledged that his greatness remained in place.

Mishlei / Proverbs is Solomon's road map of life. Its subtleties reach every level of man's experience and aspiration. Its levels are so many that every reading reveals new lessons and new inspirations. Let us begin.

Rabbi Nosson Scherman

Marcheshvan 5759 /
November 1998

✥ An Introduction to the Terms of Mishlei / Proverbs

Many terms appear over and over in this Book. Although, the nuances of these terms may vary according to the context and the views of the various commentators, it would be helpful to review their basic meanings before we begin the actual text of the Book.

❏ חָכְמָה — Chochmah / Wisdom

The attainment of *chochmah* is a major goal. *Rabbeinu Yonah* defines it as knowing the way of the righteous — truth and justice. According to *Meiri*, *chochmah* refers to perfection of the intellect.

Malbim elaborates that *chochmah* implies the proper choice between two opposite courses of action, such as cruelty and compassion, arrogance and humility, brazenness and shame, eating and fasting, holiness and impurity. The correct choice would be called *chochmah* and its opposite *sichlus, folly*. For instance, as a rule, to act with humility is wise, whereas arrogance is foolish, but there are exceptions. For example, when dealing with the wicked, it is wise to display some arrogance. *Chochmah* shows the person which path to choose — how, when, and how much to use each trait. Since man cannot deduce *chochmah* through his own intelligence, it follows that the only way to attain it is by studying the Torah and the teachings of the Sages.

❏ מוּסָר — Mussar

Depending on the context, *mussar* is translated as discipline, ethical teaching, or affliction. It is all or any of these. *Mussar* also refers to the perfection of מדות, *character traits*, which is inextricably linked to wisdom, for *mussar* cannot be attained without *chochmah*. Conversely, *Rabbeinu Yonah* and the *Vilna Gaon* comment that *chochmah* without *mussar* is repulsive to people; as the *mussar* masters teach, "*chochmah* without *mussar* is like a tent without ropes," lacking stability and permanence.

Malbim explains that *mussar* is derived from the root יסר, *to afflict*, and is related to the verb אסר, *to bind*. Since a person's natural tendencies are toward arrogance, jealousy, vengeance, cruelty, lust, passion, and the like, he must learn to afflict and restrict himself so that he remains bound to the dictates of *chochmah*.

One must have wisdom so that he will not be ensnared by the ra-

tionalizations of the Evil Inclination. One must also know *mussar* so that he can overpower the inevitable blandishments of the Evil Inclination (*Vilna Gaon*).

❑ בִּינָה — Binah / Understanding or Discernment

Binah refers to one's ability to deduce one thing from another [לְהָבִין דָּבָר מִתּוֹךְ דָּבָר]. Whereas *chochmah* is knowledge garnered from external sources, *binah* flows from within — as one analyzes, examines, and plumbs the depths to bring forth hidden perceptions.

A *navon* is a person who has *binah*; his wisdom is superior to that of a *chacham*, for he is able to derive one thing from another and thus adds to the teachings he has heard from others (*Rashi*).

In *Deuteronomy* (1:13, s.v. נבונים), *Rashi* quotes R' Yose, who illustrates the difference between a *chacham* and a *navon*. A *chacham* is like a money-changer. When people bring him coins, he inspects them; if not, he sits idle. Similarly, *chochmah* is static; a wise man has only his acquired knowledge. A *navon*, an understanding person, however, is like a merchant banker. If people bring him coins, he inspects them; if not, he goes out and solicits business. So, too, a *navon* increases his wisdom with new thoughts and ideas based on what he has already learned.

Tevunah follows *binah*; it means clearly comprehending *binah*, i.e., not only being able to deduce one thing from another, but also to understand how this new teaching was derived from the original *chochmah* (*Vilna Gaon*).

❑ מוּסַר הַשְׂכֵּל — Mussar Haskel

Wise discipline, מוּסַר הַשְׂכֵּל, is related to the term שֵׂכֶל, *intelligence*. A person must apply *mussar* precepts intelligently, not foolishly. For instance, if a friend makes a request, and the dictates of *mussar* would seem to obligate one to comply, one must still analyze the situation to see if granting the request in this particular case would be wise or foolish. For if it is wrong, one should refrain from doing it (*Meiri*)

According to *Malbim*, the difference between *mussar* and *wise* or *enlightened mussar* is based on a fundamental concept. There are two levels of fear of God. One is יִרְאַת הָעוֹנֶשׁ, *fear of Divine retribution*. The other, a more elevated form, is called יִרְאַת הָרוֹמְמוּת, which is reverence based on an understanding of the gaping chasm between God's sublimity and our limited existence. *Mussar* refers to the former while מוּסַר הַשְׂכֵּל, *enlightened mussar*, refers to the latter, for *intelligence* leads to fear of God through observation of His greatness in areas that are beyond human comprehension.

❑ פֶּתִי — Simpleton; לֵץ — Scoffer; כְּסִיל — Fool

These three uncomplimentary terms have different connotations. *Malbim* explains as follows: A פֶּתִי, *simpleton*, is easily swayed toward evil ways,

because he lacks the understanding to accept *chochmah* and reject the Evil Inclination. Later in *Mishlei*, we learn פֶּתִי יַאֲמִין לְכָל דָּבָר, *a credulous person believes everything* (14:15). A לֵץ, *scoffer*, mocks *chochmah* because it cannot be proven through logic, but he does not hate it. However, since he mocks anything that is based on faith alone, he lacks fear of God, the only key that can unlock the portals of Godly *chochmah*. A כְּסִיל, *fool*, knows *chochmah*; he is not deficient in his ability to understand it, but he rejects it because it demands that he not indulge his every desire. He is worse than a scoffer, because he despises *chochmah*.

According to the *Vilna Gaon*, the three groups represent the three main reasons that people do not study Torah: (1) *Simpletons* have been enticed by the evil impulse to abandon Torah in favor of worldly pleasure. They believe that this will always be the true good. (2) *Scoffers* neglect Torah because of their love for דְּבָרִים בְּטֵלִים, *idle talk* (jokes, stories, gossip, irony and the whole gamut of useless and harmful talk that comes under the heading of scoffing and mockery). Even though this affords them no physical pleasure, it is sweet to them and they covet it. (3) *Fools* resist the diligence needed to study Torah properly; they want Torah knowledge to be bestowed upon them spontaneously, without any effort on their part. When they see that they are not becoming "instant Torah scholars," they abandon their study, because they fail to appreciate the sweetness of learning.

Rabbeinu Yonah states that the *mitzvah* of giving תּוֹכָחָה, *reproof*, applies mainly regarding the פֶּתִי, *simpleton*, and the נַעַר, *youth*, but not to a לֵץ, *scoffer*, or a כְּסִיל, *fool*, because they are generally not open to accepting such constructive criticism.

❏ עָרְמָה — Shrewdness, Cleverness

An *arum* is a shrewd person who uses the art of persuasion to convince others to do wrong. There is also a positive aspect to an *arum*, if he is a good person who is shrewd enough to recognize someone else's evil designs. A פֶּתִי, *simpleton*, is easily persuaded, for he is תָּם, *straightforward*, and lacks shrewdness. The study of *Mishlei* will provide him with the cleverness necessary to withstand the wiles of the Evil Inclination and repulse them (*Vilna Gaon*).

❏ אֱוִיל — Skeptic

An אֱוִיל lacks fear of God. *Malbim* relates the term אֱוִיל to אוּלַי, *maybe*, denoting doubt, since doubters are skeptical about wise men and fear of Hashem. Their skepticism does not allow them to accept the teachings of *wisdom* and *discipline*, which are predicated on recognition and fear of Hashem, and which allow man to be open and responsive to His wisdom. It is not their lack of intelligence that stops them from arriving at truth, for even some great philosophers were skeptical of *chochmah*.

mishlei

מִשְׁלֵי שְׁלֹמֹה בֶן־דָוִד מֶלֶךְ יִשְׂרָאֵל: לָדַעַת א־ב

ג חָכְמָה וּמוּסָר לְהָבִין אִמְרֵי בִינָה: לָקַחַת

I

⊷ঃ Solomon's purpose

R' Saadyah Gaon describes *Proverbs* as סֵפֶר דְּרִישַׁת חָכְמָה, *the Book of the search for wisdom*. As the introductory verses of the Book set forth, it addresses all who search for wisdom and self-perfection, and teaches the best means of attaining these objectives.

Chapter 1 speaks about the importance of wisdom and the necessity to follow the path it prescribes. Verses 1-6 includes a general introduction to the entire Book, speaking about the author of the Book, its form, purpose and who will benefit from its study.

Note: Many terms appear throughout the Book, such as בִינָה, מוּסָר, חָכְמָה, *wisdom, discipline, understanding* and others. Such terms have meanings and nuances that cannot be captured in one-word translations. Indeed, the major commentators often discern a variety of definitions as the terms are used in this Book, and we sometimes vary the translation of a term according to the context of the individual verse. See the Introduction for a discussion of such terms and their various connotations.

1. מִשְׁלֵי שְׁלֹמֹה בֶן־דָוִד מֶלֶךְ יִשְׂרָאֵל — *The proverbs of Solomon, son of David, king of Israel*. All his words are examples and comparisons. For instance, Solomon compares Torah to a loyal wife, and idol-worship (i.e., heresy) to an adulteress (*Rashi*). As *Malbim* puts it, proverbs and parables are tools that make a deep, abstract concept understandable by clothing it in an easily grasped metaphor. Thus, while it may be hard for the average person to comprehend the value of Torah study and the harm of idolatry, everyone can associate with the inestimable benefits of a good and loyal wife and the destructiveness of an adulteress.

⊷ঃ Use of parables

Rambam (Introduction to *Moreh Nevuchim*) writes that parables and metaphors are primary educational tools that are used to present a message in such a way that both scholar and layman can absorb it, each according to his respective understanding, for an apt parable can add new dimensions to one's understanding.

The commentators (*Radak, Ralbag, Rabbeinu Bachya*, et al.) elaborate that our great prophets used the parable as a literary device to make difficult subject matter comprehensible to the listener or student. Through this medium, King Solomon will teach us how to inculcate the teachings of *chochmah* and *mussar* (see comm. to verse 2), as well as the ethical and intellectual

values enumerated in verses 3-6.

R' Bachya quotes the Sages to illustrate the function of parables. Someone lost a precious stone in a dark place. He knew that the stone was there, but was unable to see it. By lighting a small wick for just a second, he was able to find his precious jewel. Thus, a virtually worthless strand of cotton assumed great importance because it enabled someone to find a gem of great value. Similarly, without reference to the concept it illustrates, a parable is but a simple story of limited value; properly used, however, it is the means by which one may achieve understanding. Torah words are hidden in darkness to those who do not understand them, and that which is hidden may be compared to luminous jewels. Solomon used proverbs and parables as flashes of light to penetrate the darkness. This, too, is a commonly used methodology of Aggadic literature in both the Midrash and Talmud, which often speak in allegorical terms: "This may be likened to an earthly king, wealthy matron, etc." By clothing the deep meanings of the Torah in the familiar trappings of kings and matrons, the Sages enable us to plumb below the surface (*Kad HaKemach, Succah*).

Yalkut Shimoni notes that the first letter of the word מִשְׁלֵי, "מ," *mem*, is written large. *Mem* has the numerical value of forty, which alludes to the forty days that Solomon fasted, in order to merit the wis-

¹ The proverbs of Solomon, son of David, king of Israel: ² [In order] to make known words of wisdom and discipline; to make words of understanding discernible; ³ to accept

dom of the Torah. In this he paralleled Moses, who spent forty days and nights with God, neither eating nor drinking, while receiving the Torah (see *Exodus* 34:28).

The *Vilna Gaon* comments that human activity consists of four components: חוֹמֶר, *substance*; פּוֹעֵל, *agent*; צוּרָה, *form*; and תַּכְלִית, *purpose*. *Substance* is taken by an *agent*, who gives it *form* in order to achieve a desired *purpose*. In the case of our Book, proverbs, i.e., the wise sayings and parables, are the *substance* of the Book. Solomon is the *agent*. Its *form* is to teach *wisdom*, *discipline* and *understanding* (verse 2). Its *purpose* is to give practical application to these teachings (verse 3), for actual practice, not abstract study, is the goal of learning (see *Avos* 1:17).

שְׁלֹמֹה בֶן דָּוִד מֶלֶךְ יִשְׂרָאֵל — *Solomon, son of David, king of Israel.* One who studies a text must know the credentials of its author. If the author is very wise, his book will surely contain great wisdom; if he is outstanding in fear of God and in Torah, this will also be reflected in his writings.[1]

Solomon divided the Book of Proverbs into three sections — the first dealing with *chochmah* (generally translated as *wisdom*), the second with *mussar* (generally translated as *moral discipline*) and the third with Torah. The three descriptive statements in this verse correspond to the three sections. The first section, Chapters 1-9, is about *chochmah*. This introductory verse tells us that the author of the work is Solomon, about whom it is said: וַיֶּחְכַּם מִכָּל הָאָדָם, *He was wiser than all men* (*I Kings* 5:11).

The second section, Chapters 10-24, also begins with the words מִשְׁלֵי שְׁלֹמֹה, *The proverbs of Solomon*, and is concerned

with *mussar*. This introductory verse describes Solomon as a *son of David*. David was a very pious man (*Psalms* 86:2), and this verse testifies that Solomon was a loyal son who followed in his father's ways, and was therefore qualified to teach *mussar*.

The third section, Chapter 25 to the conclusion, opens with the words, גַּם אֵלֶּה מִשְׁלֵי שְׁלֹמֹה, *These too are the proverbs of* Solomon. Its subject is the Torah. This introductory verse describes him as *king of Israel*, alluding to the Torah, which is the source of all dominion (see 8:15), and which was a gift to the nation of Israel.[2] As their king, Solomon acquired the Torah in its entirety (*Vilna Gaon*).

Malbim offers a different reason for enumerating three descriptions of the author in this verse. Truth can be acquired in three ways, and Solomon utilized them all in his search for truth:

(1) Through *chochmah* or prophecy. The verse, therefore, states that the author of this work is Solomon, who was a great *chacham* and upon whom God's spirit rested.

(2) By transmission of tradition from father to son. As a son of David, Solomon was capable of imparting the knowledge he received from his fathers.

(3) Through experimentation and experience. Because he was king of Israel, a wise and discerning nation, and was surrounded by a retinue of scholars, Solomon could put his wisdom to the test in the laboratory of life. (See *Ecclesiastes* 7:23, כָּל זֹה נִסִּיתִי בַחָכְמָה, *all this I tested with wisdom*.)

2. לָדַעַת חָכְמָה וּמוּסָר לְהָבִין אִמְרֵי בִינָה — *To make known words of wisdom and discipline; to make words of understanding*

---

1. Having attained perfection in the areas of *chochmah*, *mussar* and Torah, Solomon is the most fitting author of such a work. Although this work was written with Divine inspiration [רוּחַ הַקֹּדֶשׁ], the level of Divine inspiration is linked to the author's own level of *chochmah* and *daas* (*Vilna Gaon*).

2. These three themes are alluded to in the verse וַיְדַבֵּר שְׁלֹשֶׁת אֲלָפִים מָשָׁל, *he [Solomon] spoke three thousand proverbs* (*I Kings* 5:12). Homiletically, the word אֲלָפִים is related to the word לְאַלֵּף, *to teach*. This verse can be understood to say that *Proverbs* is divided into three parts. Each of these parts is introduced with the word מִשְׁלֵי, *proverbs*. (See *Rashi*, ad loc.)

discernible. The translation follows *Rashi*, who explains לָדַעַת as לְהוֹדִיעַ, *to make known.* Solomon taught these proverbs to inform people that they should toil in Torah, which encompasses *chochmah*, *mussar* and *binah*, the three branches of wisdom mentioned in this verse.

Other commentators (*R' Yonah, Vilna Gaon*) explain לָדַעַת as: *to know [chochmah and mussar].* *R' Yonah* defines *chochmah* as knowing the way of the righteous — truth and justice — and *mussar* as denigrating the wicked, by making known the damage they cause through their actions. Many verses in *Proverbs* follow a dual track: They describe the character of the righteous and malign the traits of the wicked — thus by contrast emphasizing the difference between them.

Meiri defines these terms as King Solomon's instructions for acquiring perfection. *Chochmah* refers to perfection of the intellect, while *mussar* refers to perfection of מִדּוֹת, *character traits.* The two are inextricably linked, and one is impossible without the other. *Mussar* cannot be attained without *chochmah*, as our Sages teach: וְלֹא עַם הָאָרֶץ חָסִיד, *and an unlearned person cannot be scrupulously pious* (*Avos* 2:6). Yet *chochmah* without *mussar* is repulsive to people, as the masters of *mussar* comment, "*chochmah* without *mussar* is like a tent without ropes," lacking stability and permanence.

One must have wisdom so that he will not be ensnared by the rationalizations of the Evil Inclination.[1] One must also know *mussar* so that he can overpower the inevitable blandishments of the Evil Inclination (*Vilna Gaon*).[2]

לְהָבִין אִמְרֵי בִינָה — *To make words of understanding discernible.* *R' Yonah* defines לְהָבִין as *penetrating the true intention contained within the words.* אִמְרֵי בִינָה, *words of binah,* refers to the profound concepts whose true meaning cannot be fathomed unless the individual delves into the words, and subjects them to in-depth analysis.

According to the *Vilna Gaon*, this means that one should follow the ways of the Torah in his battle against the Evil Inclination, and not resort to pieties that have no basis in halachah. For instance, in attempting to curb excessive eating, one should not fast on the Sabbath, which is halachically forbidden.

Malbim explains *chochmah, mussar* and *binah* as follows:

The term *chochmah* implies the proper choice between two opposite courses of action, such as cruelty and compassion, arrogance and humility, brazenness and shame, eating and fasting, holiness and impurity. The correct choice would be called *chochmah* and its opposite סִכְלוּת, *folly.* For instance, to act with humility is *chochmah*, whereas arrogance is folly. However, this is not absolute. For example, when dealing with the wicked, it is wise to display some arrogance. In all cases where

---

1. A person must be cognizant of the Evil Inclination's shrewdness — and he must turn that same shrewdness against his adversary, as we are taught: *And with the crooked You act perversely* (*Psalms* 18:27). [Just as God acts perversely with "crooked" people, so should man act shrewdly with the Evil Inclination, which seeks to rob man's soul.] The Evil Inclination may suggest a course of action that appears to be a *mitzvah*, but after careful scrutiny the true sinful nature of the suggestion will become clear. *To know chochmah* means to understand the cunning of the Evil Inclination, as the Sages explain: *Man should constantly be cunning in his fear of Heaven* (*Berachos* 7a). By recognizing the duplicity of the Evil Inclination, one can avoid being ensnared in its net (*Vilna Gaon*).

2. The *Vilna Gaon* illustrates these points with a quotation from *Isaiah* (49:9): לֵאמר לַאֲסוּרִים צֵאוּ, לַאֲשֶׁר בַּחשֶׁךְ הִגָּלוּ, *To say to the prisoners, "Go out;" to those in the darkness, "Reveal yourselves."* **Prisoners** refers to those already trapped by the Evil Inclination. They can *go out* and escape its clutches through the study of *mussar. Those in the darkness* refers to those who do not recognize the Evil Inclination's persuasive tactics. Torah wisdom will illuminate the machinations of the Evil Inclination, causing its blandishments to be *revealed* as false and illusory.

the terms "good" or "bad" apply, *chochmah* shows the person which path to choose — how, when and how much to use each trait.[1]

It is impossible for a person to understand the ways of *chochmah* on his own. They are attainable solely from Hashem Himself, for He established the dictates of *chochmah* and taught them to man in the Written and Oral Law. Every mention of *chochmah* in *Tanach* is Divine. It is the Master's instruction, commanding man to follow a certain path and to avoid opposite courses of action. Since man cannot deduce *chochmah* through his own intelligence, it follows that the only way to attain it is by studying Hashem's Torah or by learning from the Sages.

Mussar is derived from the root יסר, *to afflict*, and is related to the verb אסר, *to bind*. Since a person's natural tendencies are toward arrogance, jealousy, vengeance, cruelty, lust, passion and the like, he must learn to afflict and restrict himself so that he remains bound to the dictates of *chochmah*, neither deviating toward folly nor toward excessive piety. Given man's natural tendency towards the negative, as the Torah states, כִּי יֵצֶר לֵב הָאָדָם רַע מִנְּעֻרָיו, *since the imagery of man's heart is evil from his youth* (Genesis 8:21), he needs *mussar*. Sometimes God brings hardship and pain upon an individual, causing him to restructure his course and return to the right path. Therefore, such hardships are

termed יִסּוּרִים, *afflictions*.[2] Sometimes, this restructuring is achieved through rebuke received from one's elders.

In the Book of *Proverbs*, *mussar* refers to יִרְאַת ה', *fear of God* (see 15:33, יִרְאַת ה', מוּסַר חָכְמָה, *the fear of* HASHEM *[is the] mussar [of] wisdom*). One who believes in God and realizes that the dictates of *chochmah* are Divine will be in awe of His greatness, judgment and punishment. This will bring about compliance with His commandments. Thus *mussar* acts as a "rope," forcing a person to remain within Divinely ordained bounds [אסר] and restraining his natural inclination to break loose.

Binah refers to one's ability to deduce one thing from another [לְהָבִין דָּבָר מִתּוֹךְ דָּבָר]. Whereas *chochmah* is knowledge garnered from external sources, *binah* flows from within — as one analyzes, examines and plumbs the depths to bring forth hidden perceptions.[3]

3. לָקַחַת מוּסַר הַשְׂכֵּל צֶדֶק וּמִשְׁפָּט וּמֵשָׁרִים — *To accept wise discipline. To accept* means that one must listen to and study *mussar* (*Ibn Ezra*). One must delve into the proverbs and parables of this Book in order to extract *mussar* from them (*Metzudos*).

R' Yonah explains that "accepting" means to put *mussar*'s precepts into practice, i.e., refining one's character traits to conform to the dictates of *mussar*.

מוּסַר הַשְׂכֵּל, *wise discipline*, is related to the term שֵׂכֶל, *intelligence*. A person must

1. The word for character traits, מִדּוֹת, literally means *measurements*. There are no good or bad traits *per se*. Through *chochmah*, one must measure the amount and intensity of any trait to be applied to life's situations in accordance with Torah values.

2. *Maharal* explains the relationship between *mussar* and affliction as follows: Human existence is a joint venture of body and soul. Each seeks to be the controlling partner. *Mussar* is the verbal and emotional affliction given the body, in order to subordinate it to the soul.

3. *Rashi* (*Exodus* 31:3) defines *chochmah* and *tevunah* as follows: *Chochmah* is what a person hears from outside sources. *Tevunah* is inductive and derivative; it is something new that is derived from knowledge that he had before.

In *Deuteronomy* (1:13, s.v. נְבוֹנִים), *Rashi* quotes R' Yose, who illustrates the difference between a *chacham* and a *navon*. A *chacham* is like a moneychanger. When people bring him coins, he inspects them; if not, he sits idle. [Similarly, *chochmah* is static; a wise man has only his acquired knowledge.] A *navon*, an understanding person, however, is like a merchant banker. If people bring him coins, he inspects them; if not, he goes out and solicits business. [So, too, a *navon* increases his wisdom by new thoughts and ideas based on what he has already learned.] (See *Sifre Devarim* 13.)

apply *mussar* precepts intelligently, not foolishly. For instance, if a friend makes a request, and the dictates of *mussar* would seem to obligate one to comply, one must still analyze the situation to see if granting the request in this particular case would be wise or foolish. For if it is wrong, one should refrain from doing it (*Meiri*).[1]

According to *Malbim*, the difference between *mussar* (in the previous verse) and *wise* or *enlightened mussar* is based on a fundamental concept. There are two levels of fear of God. One is יִרְאַת הָעוֹנֶשׁ, *fear of Divine retribution.* The other is a more elevated form and is called יִרְאַת הָרוֹמְמוּת, which is fear based on an understanding of the gaping chasm between God's sublimity and our limited existence. *Mussar* refers to the former while מוּסַר הַשְׂכֵּל, *enlightened mussar*, refers to the latter, for שֵׂכֶל leads to fear of God through observation of His greatness in areas that are beyond human comprehension, so that man's ability to reason and deduce does not come into play. For example, one can see God's greatness in the universe, but one can hardly pretend to *understand* His workings. Such comprehension of the greatness of the Creator leads to fear of transgressing the dictates of His *chochmah*.

צֶדֶק וּמִשְׁפָּט וּמֵשָׁרִים — *Righteousness, and*

justice and fairness. Rashi defines these three terms as follows: *Righteousness* is the giving of charity; *justice* refers to judging truthfully; and *fairness* means a compromise, a smooth and straight path, which achieves a sense of balance.[2]

Rabbeinu Yonah proposes a different explanation for these terms. צֶדֶק, *righteousness*, refers to going beyond the letter of the law (לִפְנִים מִשּׁוּרַת הַדִּין). There are times when it is appropriate to go beyond the exact letter of the law, as our Sages deduce from the verse: וְאֶת הַמַּעֲשֶׂה אֲשֶׁר יַעֲשׂוּן, *and the deeds that they should do* (*Exodus* 18:20). *And the deeds* refers to the letter of the law; *that they should do* refers to going beyond the letter of the law (see *Mechilta Yisro*). מִשְׁפָּט, *justice*, refers to following the exact letter of the law (שׁוּרַת הַדִּין). מֵשָׁרִים, *equity*, refers to acting with strong moral rectitude even in situations where the court has no jurisdiction (פָּטוּר בָּהֶם מִדִּינֵי אָדָם וְחַיָּב בְּדִינֵי שָׁמַיִם).[3]

According to *Metzudos*, these terms mirror the three areas of life. צֶדֶק, *righteousness*, refers to Divine service. מִשְׁפָּט, *justice*, must rule relationships between man and his fellow man. מֵשָׁרִים, *fairness*, is a reference to the way each individual relates to himself: his character traits and behavior.[4]

1. *Meiri* cites an example of this principle from the *mitzvah* of returning lost property. Though the Torah commands one to return lost property to its owner, Scripture implies that there are times when one may or even should refrain from doing so. *Sifri* and *Bava Metzia* 30a explain that if a lost animal is in a cemetery and was discovered by a Kohen who is forbidden to enter such a place, or by a distinguished person whose dignity does not allow him to lead even his own animal through the street, or if one would suffer a greater financial loss by returning the animal than it is worth, he is not obligated to return it (*Meiri*).

2. King David is praised as עֹשֶׂה מִשְׁפָּט וּצְדָקָה, *one who administered justice and charity* (II Samuel 8:15). The Talmud (*Sanhedrin* 6b) resolves the apparent conflict between *justice*, which implies strict application of the law, and *charity*, which indicates leniency and compassion, implying that the claims were not settled in compliance with the letter of the law. R' Yehoshua ben Korcha explains that this refers to a judge's obligation to attempt a compromise, which is justice tempered by charity.

3. See *Bava Kamma* 55b-56a, which discusses actions not subject to a court of law, yet about which one has a moral "heavenly" obligation to make restitution.

4. Proper development of character traits is alluded to in various verses in Torah, as we see from *Rashi*'s interpretation of לָלֶכֶת בְּכָל דְּרָכָיו, *to walk in all His ways* (*Deuteronomy* 11:22). Yet, there is no specific commandment in the Torah to develop one's character traits.

R' Chaim Vital, in *Shaarei Kedushah*, gives a reason for this. Character traits are the very foundation of the Torah. Without them, fidelity to Torah is impossible, as we are taught in the

According to the *Vilna Gaon*, the word הַשְׂכֵּל is related to the word מַשְׂכִּיל, *successful* (see *I Samuel* 18:14, וַיְהִי דָוִד לְכָל דְּרָכָיו מַשְׂכִּיל, *And David was successful in all his ways*). This verse states the purpose of *Proverbs*: that a person succeed in inculcating *mussar*. Success in *mussar* is measured by how well an individual integrates the traits of righteousness, justice and fairness into his character. צֶדֶק refers to showing kindness and *tzedakah* toward others. However, this is not yet מוּסַר הַשְׂכֵּל, *wise discipline*, since by itself it is not a successful formula for life. At times, a person must temper kindness with anger, which is considered מִשְׁפָּט, *justice*. This is often necessary when dealing with one's own Evil Inclination, so that one can control his Evil Inclination and not accede to its demands (see *Berachos* 5a). One must occasionally resort to anger when dealing with others; for example, when one is involved in a situation which halachically demands dispensing proper justice to the wicked. Usually, however, one must use מֵשָׁרִים, *fairness*, by balancing the two extremes to arrive at the straight, middle path. Only by using the proper mixture of all three traits will one succeed.[1]

4-5. Verses 4 and 5 explain that all types of people will benefit from studying this Book, from the wisest to the most foolish (*Malbim*).

4. לָתֵת לִפְתָאיִם עָרְמָה — *To provide simpletons with cleverness.* Solomon taught the maxims and parables of *Proverbs* to enable the simpletons to acquire clever wisdom (*Rashi*). [The word עָרְמָה can be either positive or negative, depending on how someone uses his cleverness. In this verse, it is a virtue, for it enables simple people to deal with the problems and temptations of life.]

A פֶּתִי, *simpleton*, is one who has not studied wisdom and therefore allows himself to be persuaded by his Evil Inclination. Later in *Proverbs*, we learn פֶּתִי יַאֲמִין לְכָל דָּבָר, *a simpleton believes anything* (14:15). (*Rabbeinu Yonah*)

The general category of *chochmah* has several subdivisions, two of which are represented by the *chacham* and the *arum*. A *chacham* is one who has studied and

Mishnah: אִם אֵין דֶּרֶךְ אֶרֶץ אֵין תּוֹרָה, *If there is no proper social conduct, there is no Torah* (*Avos* 3:21). Therefore, their development is self-evident, and it is not necessary for the Torah to explicitly mention character development or warn us about individual traits.

This may be illustrated with an example. A person contracted to have a house built for him. He and the builder agreed upon a price and the work was begun. Upon completion, the builder presented the purchaser with a bill. To his surprise, the purchaser noticed an additional fee tacked on for the foundation. "What!" he exclaimed, "A fee for the foundation? When we agreed upon a price, it was understood that the foundation was included. There is no need to state that specifically." Likewise, proper character traits are intrinsic to a person's spiritual life. Without them, it would be impossible to fulfill any Torah directives.

1. *Rambam* (Hilchos Deios 1:1,3,4) states that different people possess many different character traits. One person is hot tempered and tends toward anger, while another person is of a calmer temperament and is rarely angered. Whereas one person may be haughty, another might be humble. Similarly, one person may starve himself in order to amass more money, only begrudgingly spending even for his basic needs, while another knowingly wastes away his entire fortune.

Practically speaking, extremes in character traits are improper and should not be followed. One should follow the proper path, the median measure of each trait. One should remain equidistant from both extremes and constantly analyze his character traits, directing them towards this "middle road."

For instance, he should neither be quick tempered and easily angered nor without feelings. Rather, he should position himself in the middle. He should only get angry regarding important matters, where anger is necessary in order to assure that the wrong is not repeated. One should neither be excessively stingy, nor should he squander his money. He should give charity according to his means and lend money to the needy in a halachically correct fashion. This is the path of *chachamim*, and the individual who practices this type of moderation is deemed a *chacham*.

incorporated much knowledge. An *arum* is a shrewd person who uses the art of persuasion and sweet-talks others into doing wrong. There is also a positive aspect to an *arum*, if he is a good person who is shrewd enough to recognize someone else's evil designs. A פֶּתִי, *simpleton*, is easily persuaded, for he is תָם, *straightforward*, and lacks shrewdness. The study of *Proberbs* will provide him with the shrewdness necessary to withstand the wiles of the Evil Inclination and repulse them (*Vilna Gaon*).[1]

לְנַעַר דַּעַת וּמְזִמָּה — *A youth with knowledge and design.* According to *Rashi* and the *Vilna Gaon*, a נַעַר, *youth,* is one devoid of all *chochmah*, not yet having studied anything at all. These proverbs will provide him with knowledge and thoughts of counsel.

Metzudos notes that a youth acts without knowledge and forethought. Through these parables and maxims, even a youth will be exposed to greater understanding and will develop the ability to assess his projected activities before he undertakes them.

Rabbeinu Yonah explains this verse as the logical continuation of verses 2 and 3. After achieving a knowledge of *mussar* and giving it practical application in one's own life, one must extend its teachings to the uninitiated by offering them reproof. This follows the directive of the Sages, קְשׁוֹט עַצְמְךָ וְאַחַר כַּךְ קְשׁוֹט אֲחֵרִים, *first correct yourself and then correct others* (*Bava Metzia* 107b). As the Torah commands, הוֹכֵחַ תּוֹכִיחַ אֶת עֲמִיתֶךָ, *You shall reprove your fellow* (*Leviticus* 19:17). (See

Rambam, Hilchos Deios 6:7-10, for guidelines regarding this *mitzvah*.)

The *mitzvah* of giving תּוֹכָחָה, *reproof,* applies mainly regarding the פֶּתִי, *simpleton,* and the נַעַר, *youth,* but not to a לֵץ, *scoffer,* or a כְּסִיל, *fool,* who are not generally open to accepting such constructive criticism. As the Sages state (*Yevamos* 65b): כְּשֵׁם שֶׁמִּצְוָה עַל אָדָם לוֹמַר דָּבָר הַנִּשְׁמָע כָּךְ מִצְוָה שֶׁלֹּא לוֹמַר דָּבָר שֶׁאֵינוֹ נִשְׁמָע, *Just as it is a mitzvah for a person to say something that will be accepted, so it is also a mitzvah not to say something that will not be accepted.* (See also *Proverbs* 9:7-8.) A *k'sil* should not be reproved because he has become so accustomed to sinning over such a long period of time that it has become part of his nature. Reproof would only make him increase his sinful actions. However, if one is overwhelmed by his Evil Inclination and sins by chance, even if he sins intentionally, it is proper to rebuke him. Since such a sinner has not yet become accustomed to this sin, nor has he committed it repeatedly, in all likelihood, he will heed the rebuke. A simpleton is included among those who should be reproved, since it is credulity that allows the Evil Inclination to victimize him (הַמִּתְפַּתֶּה, בְּיִצְרוֹ, see *Eruvin* 19a).

A נַעַר, *youth,* should also be admonished. Even if he has become accustomed to sinning, he is still under the authority of his parents and may respond to parental reproof and punishment. Moreover, his youthfulness still gives us the hope that he will be able to control his impulses and desires and return to the Torah path (*Rabbeinu Yonah*).

[The study of *Proverbs* is not only of

---

1. Equating תָם and פֶּתִי seems incongruous. תָם is generally understood as a positive term; e.g., יַעֲקֹב אִישׁ תָּם, *Jacob was a straightforward man* (*Genesis* 25:27). פֶּתִי, usually translated as simpleton, appears to be a less complimentary term. Yet, as with all character traits, a trait which is generally negative may in fact become positive when properly applied. Straightforwardness is the positive side of simplicity. In fact, according to the Midrash (*Shemos Rabbah* 3), the verse, פֶּתִי יַאֲמִין לְכָל דָּבָר, *A simpleton believes anything* (14:15), refers even to Moses, our teacher, before the giving of the Torah, because he possessed a simple faith that was a prerequisite for the acceptance of the Torah. Had Aristotle or any of the great philosophers been offered the Torah, they would have brought countless "proofs" to demonstrate that it was not really a Godly revelation. Moses' straightforwardness was the trait required by his role at that time. Only afterwards did he learn Torah, which gave the simpleton cleverness (*R' Tzadok HaKohen*).

value to the credulous or those devoid of wisdom; it will also benefit those who have already acquired it, as the following verse states.]

5. יִשְׁמַע חָכָם וְיוֹסֶף לֶקַח וְנָבוֹן תַּחְבֻּלוֹת יִקְנֶה — *That a wise one may hear and increase [his] learning, and a discerning one may acquire strategies.* A *chacham* is one who has heard many teachings from others. He will hear these proverbs and add on additional teachings to his wisdom. A *navon's* wisdom is superior to that of a *chacham*, for he is able to derive one thing from another and thus adds to the teachings he has heard from others (*Rashi*).

[The definitions of the terms *chacham* and *navon* are based on *chochma* and *binah*, from which they are derived.]

לֶקַח is a general term for any teaching which is acquired from others (*Meiri*).

Malbim explains this verse as follows: Even a *chacham* who has already acquired a deep perception of Torah, either through the tutelage of others or his own Torah study, will enhance his Torah acumen through these parables, for he will now understand additional Torah principles which the Torah and Sages do not explicitly explain. These parables will also help the *discerning one*, who already possesses deductive powers and sees what is not evident to most, acquire *strategies* and intellectual "building blocks" with which to associate ideas in order to further expand his cognitive parameters.

The word תַּחְבֻּלוֹת, *strategies*, means counsel and thought (*Ibn Ezra*). It is related to the word חֶבֶל, a rope. The *Midrash* (*Genesis Rabbah* 93:3) employs the parable of a deep well filled with cool, refreshing water, which no one was able to enjoy until

someone came along and tied one rope to another, one string to another, and used them to draw up the waters and drink from them.

So, too, says *Meiri*, the *navon* combines one thought to another, and one concept of *chochmah* to another, and is thus able to access and utilize new thoughts and ideas. *Malbim* adds on to the parable, explaining that just as rope is fashioned from many strands wound together, the *navon* formulates his opinion using many strands of analogy and comparison.

6. לְהָבִין מָשָׁל וּמְלִיצָה — *To understand parable and epigram.* One must understand the verses of *Proverbs* in two ways: (1) מָשָׁל, the *object or concept which the metaphor seeks to represent*; and (2) מְלִיצָה, *the metaphorical term itself.*

The following example illustrates the dual levels implied by *parable and of epigram.* In 2:16, King Solomon teaches that *chochmah* will deliver one from a *strange woman.* The מָשָׁל, i.e., intent of the metaphor, is "idolatry" or "heresy." However, even the מְלִיצָה, the metaphorical term used to convey this idea (i.e., to avoid a strange woman), is specifically chosen to teach a lesson. Not only must one steer clear of heresy, which is the metaphorical meaning of *strange woman*, but even the woman herself must be avoided (*Rashi*).

Thus, each parable must be understood on more than one level.[1]

The *Vilna Gaon* and *Malbim* explain the word מָשָׁל refers to the actual *metaphor* that is used, while the word מְלִיצָה refers to the נִמְשָׁל, *the concept which is represented by the metaphor.*[2]

The *Vilna Gaon* explains that the מָשָׁל, *metaphor*, alludes to תּוֹרָה שֶׁבִּכְתָב, *the*

---

1. *I Kings* 5:12 states that King Solomon spoke three thousand proverbs. The Midrash notes that a careful appraisal of the verses in *Proverbs* yields only about eight hundred maxims. How, then, are we to understand the figure of three thousand? The Midrash (*Bamidbar Rabbah* 19:3) answers that there are different levels of understanding for each verse in *Proverbs*. This is borne out by our verse, which teaches that each parable must be understood in both its literal and metaphorical sense.

2. *Malbim* relates מְלִיצָה to the word מֵלִיץ, *interpreter*. He explains that the מְלִיצָה explains the metaphor and reveals the profound concepts contained within it just like a מֵלִיץ, *interpreter*, who reveals one person's thoughts to another.

ז דִּבְרֵי חֲכָמִים וְחִידֹתָם: יִרְאַת יְהוה רֵאשִׁית דָּעַת
חָכְמָה וּמוּסָר אֱוִילִים בָּזוּ:

Written Torah. Just as the superficial meaning of a metaphor is easily understood but also encompasses a corresponding hidden concept, so, too, the words of the Written Torah are superficially understandable, yet are merely the external clothing of profound hidden meanings. Thus, both the מָשָׁל — the superficial, literal meaning of the stories of the Torah — and the מְלִיצָה — its profound metaphorical interpretation — must be understood. Malbim cites the Biblical narrative of the Tree of Knowledge and the snake as examples of concepts which must be understood on both a literal and allegorical level.

דִּבְרֵי חֲכָמִים וְחִידֹתָם — The words of the wise and their enigmas. חִידָה is something hidden, which cannot be understood until interpreted (Ibn Ezra).

According to Rashi, this refers to the Sages' commentary on Torah, which explains why some words are written in full form while others are written with letters omitted (מִקְרָא מָלֵא, מִקְרָא חָסֵר). They also interpret the allusions of Biblical verses, its comparisons and enigmas.

According to the Vilna Gaon, חִידוֹת, enigmas, refers to the Aggadata, the non-halachic areas of the Talmud, especially to those stories and parables that seem incredible. They are often enigmatic and unintelligible to those who do not understand the underlying ideas upon which the statements are based. Only when their true intent is understood, can one penetrate the enigma. The words of the wise refers to the concept conveyed by the metaphor, while the phrase their enigmas refers to the metaphor itself. Malbim adds

that through learning the parables of this Book, one will be able to decipher these enigmatic words of the Sages.

Having defined the author and purpose, the introductory portion of the Book is concluded here (Vilna Gaon). Now the actual text of the Book begins (Rashi).

7. יִרְאַת ה' רֵאשִׁית דָּעַת — Fear of HASHEM is the beginning of knowledge. Fear of Hashem is the primary, choice component of knowledge[1] and its fundamental prerequisite. Chochmah must be predicated on fear of the Creator, which generates the desire to be engrossed in chochmah (Rashi).[2]

Yirah, fear, is to chochmah as a foundation is to an edifice. If there is any weakness in a building's foundation, the slightest stress will place the entire structure in danger of collapse. So, too, if a person's yirah is weak, even the slightest doubt will confuse him, causing his faith to collapse and overturn his entire belief system (Meiri).

Every area of wisdom is based on certain fundamentals. Science, for example, is based on experimentation and observation. However, the wisdom referred to in Proverbs is the chochmah of Torah and good character traits. Its fundamentals are not rationally accessible. This wisdom must be received from its source: Hashem. Therefore, it is impossible to truly acquire such wisdom without fear of Hashem. Fear of Hashem is the belief in Him and the unquestioning acceptance and fulfillment of His dictates (Malbim).

Shnos Chayim regards this statement as the motive for proper conduct and the

1. The Midrash explains רֵאשִׁית as תְּרוּמָה, earliest and choicest component, as in the verses, רֵאשִׁית דְּגָנְךָ, the choicest, first of your grain (Deuteronomy 18:4); רֵאשִׁית עֲרִסֹתֵכֶם, the first of your kneading (Numbers 15:20); and רֵאשִׁית בִּכּוּרֵי אַדְמָתְךָ, the choicest, first fruit of your land (Exodus 23:19) (Meiri).

2. One who receives a letter from the royal palace is so cognizant of its origin that he rereads it tirelessly, seeking to mine it for its full meaning. Similarly, those who fear Hashem desire tirelessly to hear the words of chochmah and mussar included in His Divine document (Orchos Tzaddikim, Shaar HaTorah).

the words of the wise and their enigmas.

    ⁷ Fear of HASHEM is the beginning of knowledge; skeptics scorn wisdom and discipline.

motto for *Proverbs*. As such, it is found at the beginning (1:7) and the end (9:10) of the discourse on *chochmah*.

To know about God and as a result of this knowledge to subordinate ourselves to Him is what is meant by *fear of Hashem*, and is the beginning of all knowledge (*R' Hirsch*).

חָכְמָה וּמוּסָר אֱוִילִים בָּזוּ — *Skeptics scorn wisdom and discipline*. Skeptics, who do not fear Hashem, scorn *chochmah* and *mussar* (*Rashi*).[1] Therefore, if one does not acquire the fear of Hashem first, what benefit will he derive from studying *chochmah*? He will only scorn and despise it! (*Metzudos*).

Skeptics scorn *chochmah* and *mussar* since they do not fear Hashem. Consequently, *chochmah* and *mussar* have no value to them. If *chochmah* is not precious to the individual, he will never succeed in its pursuit, nor will his *chochmah* endure. As R' Chanina ben Dosa teaches (*Avos* 3:11): כֹּל שֶׁיִּרְאַת חֶטְאוֹ קוֹדֶמֶת לְחָכְמָתוֹ חָכְמָתוֹ מִתְקַיֶּמֶת, *Anyone whose fear of sin takes priority to his chochmah, his chochmah will endure; but anyone whose chochmah takes priority to his fear of sin, his chochmah will not endure* (*Rabbeinu Yonah*).

The *Vilna Gaon* develops this point further: A person who is God fearing wants to study *chochmah* in order to ascertain the spiritual pitfalls he must avoid. Since he is searching for something which is important to him, when he

discovers *chochmah* he will hold it dear and observe its teachings. Hence, it will endure. On the other hand, one who lacks fear of Hashem and does not worry about avoiding sin will not attain wisdom even after repeated study. As he is not in search of *chochmah*'s corrective quality, his success in attaining *chochmah* is unimportant to him. Therefore, even if the skeptic, who lacks fear of Hashem, were to study *chochmah* and *mussar*, they will not endure, for he disdains them.[2]

Meiri notes that one tends to scorn that which he feels is unattainable. For instance, according to our Sages, one who cannot afford to buy meat scorns it by saying it is spoiled. It is for this reason that the אֱוִיל, *skeptic*, scorns *chochmah* and *mussar*.

Were an individual offered the opportunity to be as wise as Solomon, even the greatest fool would readily agree. However, wisdom is unlike a ready-made suit bought off the rack, which fits perfectly without any toil or labor. The acquisition of *chochmah* demands herculean effort. Once the skeptic realizes the amount of effort necessary to attain *chochmah*, he is unwilling to exert himself to achieve it. He then despairs of ever succeeding in this achievement and scorns it.

Meiri concludes that this is a warning to the individual who wishes to attain *chochmah*. Let him not become frustrated by the overwhelming effort needed. Let him rather continue to apply himself ever so

1. All commentators point out that an אֱוִיל lacks fear of God. Our definition of אֱוִילִים as *skeptics* follows *Malbim*, who relates the term אֱוִיל to אוּלַי, *maybe*, denoting doubt. These people are doubters, skeptical about wisdom and fear of Hashem. Their skepticism does not allow them to accept the teachings of *wisdom* and *discipline*, which are predicated on recognition and fear of Hashem and which allow man to be open and responsive to His wisdom. It is not their lack of intelligence that stops them from arriving at truth, for even some great philosophers were skeptical of *chochmah*.

2. *Rambam* (*Hilchos Deios* 2:1) instructs those who suffer from maladies of the soul to seek a remedy from our spiritual "doctors," the Sages. By teaching them appropriate wisdom, these "doctors" nurse the afflicted souls back onto the proper path to spiritual health. *Rambam* applies this dictum, חָכְמָה וּמוּסָר אֱוִילִים בָּזוּ, *skeptics scorn wisdom and discipline*, to those who recognize their faulty character yet fail to seek remedy with the Sages.

ח שְׁמַע בְּנִי מוּסַר אָבִיךָ וְאַל־תִּטֹּשׁ תּוֹרַת אִמֶּךָ:
ט כִּי | לִוְיַת חֵן הֵם לְרֹאשֶׁךָ וַעֲנָקִים לְגַרְגְּרֹתֶיךָ:

diligently to the pursuit of *chochmah,*
until slowly but steadily he attains it.

8. שְׁמַע בְּנִי מוּסַר אָבִיךָ וְאַל־תִּטֹּשׁ תּוֹרַת אִמֶּךָ
— *Hear, my child, the discipline of your
father, and do not forsake the teaching of
your mother.*

Metzudos explains this verse literally:
The child should accept his father's rebuke
and his mother's teachings, for they are
certainly offered for the child's benefit.
(תּוֹרָה is related to the word הוֹרָאָה, *instruction* or *teaching.*)

This verse, which speaks of honoring
one's parents, and the previous verse,
which speaks of fearing God, correspond
to the three partners involved in creating
each individual: Hashem, his father, and
his mother (see *Niddah* 31a) (*Vilna Gaon*).

שְׁמַע implies three meanings: physical
hearing with the ears; *understanding* with
the heart; and *obeying*, by accepting upon
oneself the yoke of *mitzvos* and *mussar*
(see *Deuteronomy* 11:13, וְהָיָה אִם שָׁמֹעַ
תִּשְׁמְעוּ אֶל מִצְוֹתַי) (*Rabbeinu Bachaye*).

The first *mussar* a person must accept is
that of his parents. They admonish him
and direct him from his early youth, and
their *mussar* will sensitize him to appreciate and receive *mussar* from the words of
Torah. Since parental *mussar* prepares one
for Torah *mussar*, death was decreed for a
בֵּן סוֹרֵר וּמוֹרֶה, *the wayward and rebellious
son* (*Deuteronomy* 21:18) (*Ralbag*). [Re-
pulsing parental reproof can lead to total
estrangement from the corrective quality
of Torah.]

In *Proverbs* we find repeated warnings
to the child to heed his parents' rebuke, as
well as warnings to parents regarding their
obligation to chastise their child. Parental
rebuke is extremely vital to the child. A
person's intelligence does not fully develop
in youth. Only when he reaches adulthood

do his intellectual faculties fully mature.
However, his Evil Inclination is with him
from birth: כִּי יֵצֶר לֵב הָאָדָם רַע מִנְּעֻרָיו, *since
the imagery of man's heart is evil from his
youth* (*Genesis* 8:21). Due to the immatu-
rity of youth, the benefit of full intelligence is not available to hold desires in
check and counteract negative tendencies.
This may have longlasting ramifications.
Once accustomed to acting in accordance
with one's desires, even the mature individual will experience extreme difficulty in
reforming his behavior, since these imma-
ture patterns of behavior have become
second nature to him. For this reason, it is
imperative that parents assist their child in
his development. Their admonition and
reproof counterbalance his entrenched
negativity. When parents direct their child
onto the correct path in youth, they assure
the proper molding of his nature in a
positive and enduring way (*Rabbeinu
Yonah*).[1]

The commentaries discuss the designa-
tion of paternal teachings as *mussar* and
maternal guidance as *teaching.* *Meiri* explains that the *mussar* of the father refers to
the paternal reproof generally given the
child to encourage him to study *chochmah.* The *teaching* of the mother refers to
maternal efforts to teach the child proper
behavior.

R' Saadyah Gaon points out that the
intention of the verse is not to limit
mussar to the father and *teaching* to the
mother, but rather to teach us to accept
both *mussar* and teaching from both
parents.

Other commentaries refer to the father's
natural parental role. He is the parent who
speaks harshly and strictly disciplines the
children. Therefore, Solomon, the wisest of
men, adjures us to "listen" and follow our
father's mussar. Mothers are generally

---

1. Life may be likened to a person standing in a thick forest with no path or road. Those who
traversed the area before him established signposts and landmarks and know the way. If it were
not for the ability of these veterans to serve as the eyes of the young, the uninitiated would slip
on the thorns and obstacles strewn throughout the terrain of life (*Chazon Ish: Collected Letters*
55).

⁸ *Hear, my child, the discipline of your father, and do not forsake the teaching of your mother.* ⁹ *For they are an adornment of grace for your head and chains for your neck.*

more soft spoken. Even when they admonish, they do so with a request or plea, and their children are more receptive listeners. The tutelage and methodology of mothers remains ingrained within the children. Therefore, King Solomon uses the phrase, *do not forsake the teaching of your mother* (*Likutei Yehudah*).

Chevel Nachalah points out that this verse refers to two approaches in serving Hashem, each of which must be utilized in the appropriate situation. At times, one must be as firm as a cedar tree, a trait which one learns through the *mussar* of his father. At other times, one must be as soft as a reed, a trait one absorbs from his mother's instruction, which is given in gentle terms (*cf.* 6:20).

Rashi interprets אָבִיךָ, *your Father*, as a reference to the Holy One, Blessed is He. *The mussar of your Father* thus consists of both the Written and Oral Law which Hashem gave to Moses. אִמֶּךָ, *your mother*, refers to אוּמָתְךָ, *your nation*, the nation of Israel. This refers to the enactments, innovations and additional protective "fences" which the Sages of the nation added to the Torah (Rabbinic decrees).[1]

The *Vilna Gaon* explains that *the mussar of your father* refers to the Written Torah, while *the teaching of your mother* refers to the Oral Torah (*cf. Midrash Mishlei*). The Written Torah is compared to the father's *mussar* since in it we find the general principles of the *mitzvos* without further definition. This corresponds to paternal instruction, which is general and sets the tone. Maternal guidance is more detailed, outlining steady progress through positive paths while simultaneously distancing the child from all the details of sin. This type of detailed instruction is the function of the Oral Torah, which is replete with all the minutiae of *mitzvah* observances.

Based on this verse, the Sages rule that one may not depart from his father's custom (see *Pesachim* 51a and *Shulchan Aruch Yoreh Deah* 214:1-2).

9. כִּי לִוְיַת חֵן הֵם לְרֹאשֶׁךָ וַעֲנָקִים לְגַרְגְּרֹתֶיךָ — *For they are an adornment of grace for your head and chains for your neck.* The Torah instruction and *mussar* mentioned in the previous verse will be charming decorations for your head and like the beads of a golden necklace on your neck. The throat is referred to in the plural (גַרְגְּרֹתֶיךָ) because the trachea is formed of many rings (*Rashi*).

Malbim explains that *head* symbolizes thought, while *neck* symbolizes speech. *Mussar* teachings will adorn an individual's thought and speech.

The *Vilna Gaon* explains the symbolism of this verse differently. In the days of the Talmudic Sages, it was customary to make jewelry for one's wife according to her qualities (see *Yerushalmi Shabbos* 6:1). A head ornament was created for a woman who possessed superior intelligence, while a necklace was made for one who performed good deeds. The head ornament was fashioned from one piece as a symbol of the שֵׂכֶל, *intelligence*, which is considered a single, inseparable entity. The neck ornament was comprised of many pieces, just as every good deed is a separate *mitzvah*. Similarly, Torah and *mitzvos* are a person's ornaments. Torah study is reflected in the singular form, *an adornment of grace*, for all its areas are essentially an interrelated totality that preoccupies the mind. The *mitzvos*, however, are symbolized by the plural *chains*, because they are separate actions performed at distinct times. They adorn the *neck*, which is representative of the body, the agent for their performance.

1. The Written Torah is a direct gift from Hashem, *your Father*, while the Oral Torah is the expression of Torah as it filters through the soul of the Jewish People, *your mother* or *nation* (see *Tzidkas HaTzaddik*).

יא בְּנִי אִם־יְפַתּוּךָ חַטָּאִים אַל־תֹּבֵא: אִם־יֹאמְרוּ
לְכָה אִתָּנוּ נֶאֶרְבָה לְדָם נִצְפְּנָה לְנָקִי חִנָּם:

R' Hirsch points out that parental teachings — a *father's mussar* and a *mother's instruction* (v. 8) — began before a child's formal education. When he approaches adulthood, he may easily think that he has become better educated and more intelligent than his mother and rebel against his father's demands. Therefore, he is advised always to accept his father's education and not to abandon his mother's lessons. An adult is considered a person of independent judgment whose head (רֹאשֶׁךָ) rests maturely on his neck (גַּרְגְּרֹתֶיךָ) — poetic imagery indicating the seat of mental ability (head) and the controlling factor of one's creative and active being (neck). Yet even an adult is obligated to follow his father's teachings. This applies to what one has learned from his father in both the past and the present. They should be a person's most precious ornament, complementing his own intellectual ability.

R' Yehoshua ben Levi (*Eruvin* 54a) expounds: One who is walking alone along the road should immerse himself in the study of Torah, as the verse states: *For they are an accompaniment of grace.* [לְוְיָה means an *accompaniment*, i.e., Torah will accompany and protect him.] If one's head or throat hurts, he should become engrossed in Torah study, as the verse states: *for your head, for your throat.* R' Yehoshua goes on to apply this dictum to a pain in any part of one's body, bringing relevant Biblical quotes for each organ. (*Cf.* 4:22.)

The Sages (*Devarim Rabbah* 6:3) liken the word רֹאשֶׁךָ, *your head*, to רֵשׁוּתֶךָ, *your poverty* (see 6:11), explaining that the words of the Torah always remain

an adornment of grace, for even when a man becomes old and is no longer able to support himself, he will be assisted by those who respect him for his learning.

R' Pinchas ben Chama explains that the verse refers to *mitzvos*, which accompany a person [לְוְיָה] wherever he goes and whatever he does. When he builds a house, he must build a fence around the roof; when he installs a door, he must affix a *mezuzah*; when he puts on new clothing, he is subject to the prohibition not to wear *shaatnez*, i.e., a mixture of wool and linen; and so on.

◆§ The blandishments of the wicked

10. בְּנִי אִם־יְפַתּוּךָ חַטָּאִים אַל־תֹּבֵא — *My child, if sinners* [lit. *sins*] *entice you, do not consent.* *Rashi* renders חַטָּאִים as חוֹטְאִים, *sinners*. *Metzudos* derives תֹּבֵא from the root אָבָה, *want* (cf. *Deuteronomy* 25:7).

Since man's natural inclination is to evil, he is susceptible to the enticements of those who advocate sin. Therefore, King Solomon warns his son: Should sinners seek to persuade you to join them and follow in their ways, do not consent, and do not listen to them (*Ralbag*).

The *Vilna Gaon* elaborates on this warning. Those who entice others to sin naturally paint the "benefits" of transgression in glowing terms, while ignoring the disgrace and ugliness of such a lifestyle. For this reason, it is futile even to enter into dialogue with such people. They will not discuss *mitzvos*, for they, themselves, do not observe a Torah lifestyle. It is certain that they seek only to involve others in sin.[1]

1. Even when a person knows that he is right and his adversary's position is absolutely false, he may still be adversely affected by hearing his counterpart's specious arguments. When Joseph and his brothers came to the Cave of the Patriarchs to bury our forefather Jacob, Esau claimed that the burial plot was rightfully his. The brothers responded that Jacob had in fact purchased the cave, but Esau demanded to see the deed. They sent the fleet-footed Naftali to Egypt to bring the deed, but meanwhile the burial was delayed. Chushim, Dan's deaf son, was unable to follow the conversation. He asked, "Why has the funeral procession stopped?" When he was made to understand, he exclaimed, "And until Naftali returns from Egypt, will our grandfather Jacob lie here in disgrace?" Immediately, he seized a stick and beheaded Esau (see *Sotah* 13a).

1/10-11   ¹⁰ *My child, if sinners entice you, do not consent.* ¹¹ *If they say, "Come with us; let us wait in ambush for bloodshed; let us lurk for an innocent one, without cause.*

These words of King Solomon parallel those of his father, King David (*Psalms* 1:1-2) first praises the individual who does not tread the path of the wicked, and only afterwards lauds the virtues of constant involvement in Torah study. Torah study can flourish only after a person distances himself from the company of sinners. [See *Rambam, Hilchos Deios* 6:1-2.] Following the same pattern, King Solomon first warns against bad company, and only then (2:1) does he speak of seeking *chochmah* (R' *Yonah*).

◆§ A scenario and a warning

In verses 11-14, King Solomon provides a script of the enticement used by sinners seeking compatriots for their crimes of murder and robbery, followed by a warning to avoid their ways (verse 15) and the disastrous consequences for one who joins them (verses 16-19). The commentators explain why Solomon addresses the sin of murder first. The *Vilna Gaon* expains that there are two general types of Evil Inclination: anger and lust. The Ten Commandments (*Exodus* 20:13) list murder — an outgrowth of anger — before adultery — an outgrowth of lust, and Solomon follows this pattern. Here he speaks of bloodshed, and later (see 2:16-19) about the allure of lust.

Malbim explains why Solomon began with the heinous crime of murder. When a father admonishes his son, he begins by citing an obvious and unquestionable truth that even a child can easily understand. For example, it is universally understood that joining a group of murderers

and robbers is evil. This is because murder is naturally repulsive to man, and because the danger inherent in this type of crime is obvious to all. Once such an example has been accepted, the parent can proceed to teach the child the danger of enticement inherent in any sin.

By resisting the blandishments of murder, one is deemed as if one had saved an entire world. Our Sages taught, "An individual who saves [even] one soul in Israel is considered to have saved an entire world." However, one who destroys one soul in Israel is as if he destroyed an entire world (*Yalkut Shimoni*).

11. אִם־יֹאמְרוּ לְכָה אִתָּנוּ נֶאֶרְבָה לְדָם — *If they say, Come with us; let us wait in ambush for bloodshed.* These criminals plan to kill innocent people and rob them of their wealth (*Rashi*). To entice someone to join them, they say: You need not participate in the murder. Merely join us, and *we* will wait in ambush for blood (*Vilna Gaon*).[1]

According to *Rabbeinu Yonah*, they plan to rob people, and our Sages have taught that robbery is tantamount to murder: *One who steals anything of value from his fellow man is deemed to be taking away his soul* (*Bava Kamma* 119a)

נִצְפְּנָה לְנָקִי חִנָּם — *Let us lurk for an innocent one, without cause.* Rashi notes that the word חִנָּם, *without cause*, is not said by the murderers. Rather, Scripture informs us that there is no excuse for their ambush.

Metzudos renders: We will hide in ambush waiting to spill the blood of an innocent person, even though he has done

Why was Chushim the only bystander to protest? R' *Chaim Shmulevitz* explains that the rest of the family was involved in the verbal exchange with Esau. Despite their vehement disagreement, once they heard his arguments, his lies left their mark upon them, and they could neither respond nor act. Chushim was deaf; he never heard Esau's lies. Only he, therefore, was not blinded to the truth and could take appropriate action.

The insidious power of evil can cause irreparable spiritual harm. Even if one's intention is to refute the arguments of evil, the mere exposure to it may be fatal.

1. In other words, the Evil Inclination does not initially ask man to actively participate in sin, for he is confident in the knowledge that exposure to evil will desensitize people. By merely going along with evildoers, man will eventually be trapped in their net.

[43]   *Proverbs*

יב נִבְלָעֵם כִּשְׁאוֹל חַיִּים וּתְמִימִים כְּיוֹרְדֵי בוֹר:
יג-יד כָּל־הוֹן יָקָר נִמְצָא נְמַלֵּא בָתֵּינוּ שָׁלָל: גּוֹרָלְךָ
טו תַּפִּיל בְּתוֹכֵנוּ כִּיס אֶחָד יִהְיֶה לְכֻלָּנוּ: בְּנִי
אַל־תֵּלֵךְ בְּדֶרֶךְ אִתָּם מְנַע רַגְלְךָ מִנְּתִיבָתָם:
טז כִּי רַגְלֵיהֶם לָרַע יָרוּצוּ וִימַהֲרוּ לִשְׁפָּךְ־דָּם:

no wrong.

R' Yonah has a different explanation for the seeming redundancy of the words *innocent* and *without cause*. *Innocent* refers to one who is without sin. Similarly, in the next verse, the intended victims are called תְּמִימִים, *wholehearted*. Evil people single out "the innocent" as their intended victim, which demonstrates their intense hatred for the righteous (see 29:10).[1] This corresponds to the diametric opposition of fire and water. Sinners hate the innocent more than anyone else. One who admonishes others must apprise his listeners of this prejudice. Whether young or old, they must learn not to believe the false and disgraceful claims with which the wicked besmirch the righteous.

12. נִבְלָעֵם כִּשְׁאוֹל חַיִּים — *Like the grave, let us swallow them alive.* We will swallow these innocent people alive, as the grave absorbs an entire dead body (*Rashi*).

By robbing the victims of their material wealth, we shall effectively make them as non-existent as the dead. This evil design corresponds to the function of the grave [*she'ol*], since poverty is tantamount to death (*Nedarim* 64b). These verses teach the severity of robbery by comparing it to murder (*R' Yonah*).

R' Chaim Shmulevitz comments that life is defined as the ability to give; poverty nullifies this vital life force.

וּתְמִימִים כְּיוֹרְדֵי בוֹר — [*While they are*] *whole — like those descending to the pit.* As used in this verse, תְּמִימִים does not mean righteous ones, but rather those who are complete in their wealth. The wicked

ones state: We will swallow them while they are "whole," much like one who falls into a pit while he is whole. They intend to kill their victims while they are still rich and inherit their possessions (*Rashi*).

According to *Meiri*, pit refers to the grave. The *Vilna Gaon* defines *she'ol* as a closed grave and pit as an open one.

13. כָּל־הוֹן יָקָר נִמְצָא נְמַלֵּא בָתֵּינוּ שָׁלָל — *We will find all precious wealth, we will fill our houses with booty.* We will find all of his precious wealth on his person and fill our houses with the spoils of our thievery (*Metzudos*).

Malbim explains that הוֹן, *wealth*, refers to gold and silver, and שָׁלָל, *booty*, to other possessions. The criminals will divide the booty for their own use, but the gold and silver will be deposited in a communal treasury (see next verse).

14. גּוֹרָלְךָ תַּפִּיל בְּתוֹכֵנוּ כִּיס אֶחָד יִהְיֶה לְכֻלָּנוּ — *Cast your lot among us; there will be one pouch for all of us!* The first part of the verse speaks of a division of the spoils, while the latter part describes a communal purse. *Rashi* explains it as two options. Either you can take a share of the spoils, or, if you wish, it will all become common property.

According to *Malbim*, the two parts of this verse correspond to the spoils and precious wealth of the previous verse. [In either case, however, the newcomer will be on equal footing with all the other criminals in enjoying this illicit wealth.]

This verse is a warning not to succumb to the blandishment of sinners because of a desire for spoils and profit (*R' Yonah*).

1. Quagmired in their shortcomings, the evil cannot countenance the elevated lifestyle of the innocent. Their hate is a reflection of their disappointment with themselves. The great sage R' Akiva said that when he was still an unlearned shepherd, his antipathy for a Torah scholar was such that "I would bite him like a donkey" [whose bite doesn't heal easily] (*Pesachim* 49b).

> [12] *Like the grave, let us swallow them alive, [while they are] whole — like those descending to the pit.* [13] *We will find all precious wealth, we will fill our houses with booty.* [14] *Cast your lot among us; there will be one pouch for all of us!"* [15] *My child, do not walk on the way with them; restrain your foot from their pathway.* [16] *For their feet run to evil and they hasten to spill blood.*

◈§ Avoid the wicked. Their blandishments are a dangerous trap.

15. בְּנִי אַל־תֵּלֵךְ בְּדֶרֶךְ אִתָּם מְנַע רַגְלְךָ מִנְּתִיבָתָם — *My child, do not walk on the way with them, restrain your foot from their pathway.* Do not go on the evil path they traverse, so as not to learn from their actions (*Metzudos*).

According to *R' Yonah*, this verse refers to two distinct situations. *Do not walk on the way with them* refers to the ambush suggested by the sinners — i.e., bloodshed and plunder. Do not join with them on this destructive course! *Restrain your foot from their pathway* warns that such people should be avoided even when they are involved in their seemingly legitimate businesses. Because they are sinners, they will entice you to join them whenever there is an opportunity to engage in harmful behavior, robbery or other forms of wickedness.[1] If you hear their evil plea and do not protest, you will be punished for associating with them.

Based on the Biblical injunction, הוֹכֵחַ תּוֹכִיחַ אֶת עֲמִיתֶךָ, *You shall reprove your fellow* (*Leviticus* 19:17), Maimonides rules that if one has the ability to protest his friend's incorrect behavior and does not do so, he is punished for that action (*Hilchos Dei'os* 6:7).

Moreover, points out *R' Yonah*, an individual will be punished for his association with the wicked, since their inclination is only to sin. Our Sages tell us that accomplices of transgressors will be punished like the transgressors themselves (*Sanhedrin* 9a). For example, when righteous King Jehosafat of Judah joined wicked King Ahaziah of Israel in a shipping venture, the prophet Eliezer ben Dodavahu foretold the failure of that venture: *As you joined with Ahaziah, Hashem has made your activities unsuccessful* (*II Chronicles* 20:37). Disassociating oneself from sinners is a hallmark of fear of God.

דֶּרֶךְ, *way*, is a wide paved road. נָתִיב, *pathway*, is a smaller conduit that leads to the main road. Not only should you not join the wicked on their main roads, but even when you walk alone, restrain your feet from treading on their small paths, for even those lead to the main road (*Vilna Gaon*).

According to *Midrash Mishlei*, this verse refers to the nations of the world, about whom the Torah commands: *Do not follow the traditions of the nation[s]* (*Leviticus* 20:23).[2]

Malbim explains this verse pragmatically. Do not go in their ways, for they will kill you as well as their intended victim.

16. כִּי רַגְלֵיהֶם לָרַע יָרוּצוּ וִימַהֲרוּ לִשְׁפָּךְ דָּם — *For their feet run to evil, and they hasten to spill blood.* Their paths are self-destructive, but they do not even realize it (*Rashi*).

Continuing the theme of the previous verse, Solomon explains why one should avoid not only the *deeds* of sinners, but also avoid associating with them in any of their activities: I warn you to disassociate yourself from them, since evil people are always poised to sin, rob or harm others. Even when not actively committing such crimes, their basic orientation is toward violent and crooked behavior, and when an opportunity to sin or steal presents

---

1. This warning can also be inferred from the vowelization of the word בְּדֶרֶךְ, literally *in a [i.e., any] way*, rather than בַּדֶּרֶךְ, *in the way*. There may be no need to warn a person not to join in *the way* of murder; rather this is a warning that once you know they are sinners, you should not associate in *any* of their ways (*Rabbeinu Yonah*).

2. The nations call for brotherhood, unity and equality, asking us to "be like them." In response, Solomon advises: *My child, . . . restrain your foot from their pathway.*

יז-יח כִּי־חִנָּם מְזֹרָה הָרָשֶׁת בְּעֵינֵי כָל־בַּעַל כָּנָף: וְהֵם
יט לְדָמָם יֶאֱרֹבוּ יִצְפְּנוּ לְנַפְשֹׁתָם: כֵּן אָרְחוֹת
כָּל־בֹּצֵעַ בָּצַע אֶת־נֶפֶשׁ בְּעָלָיו יִקָּח:
כ חָכְמוֹת בַּחוּץ תָּרֹנָּה בָּרְחֹבוֹת תִּתֵּן קוֹלָהּ:

itself, *their feet run to evil* (*R' Yonah*).

King Solomon warns against the blandishments of evildoers. Their actions contradict their sweet words of enticement. How can you be fooled into believing that their intention is really to benefit you, when you see that *their feet run to evil*? Should you rationalize that you will join them only long enough to amass wealth and then part company with them, remember that *they will hasten to spill blood* before you have a chance to leave (*Vilna Gaon*).

17. כִּי־חִנָּם מְזֹרָה הָרָשֶׁת — *For the net seems spread out with free [bait].* The birds who see wheat and legumes spread out on a net think it is free for the taking. Not realizing why the net was baited, the birds approach the net to eat (*Rashi*). According to *Metzudos*, the net itself, rather than the bait, seems spread out for no reason. The birds don't even "think" that this net may be used to trap them.

By thinking that the criminals want to help you get rich, you are like birds who imagine that the net was spread only to feed them. Surely you realize the fallacy of such a contention (*Vilna Gaon*).

R' Yonah explains *the net* as a metaphor for Divine justice, which will be meted out for all of man's actions (see *Avos* 3:20: *and a net is spread out over all the living*). Just as a hungry bird refuses to recognize that the net is there to entrap him, so a man under the spell of his desires stifles the realization that his actions are constantly observed and weighed by the Divine Judge. As soon as a person sins, he is ensnared, even if Hashem in His infinite mercy does not punish him immediately.[1]

18. וְהֵם לְדָמָם יֶאֱרֹבוּ יִצְפְּנוּ לְנַפְשֹׁתָם — *But they* [the hunters] *wait in ambush for their blood and lurk for their souls.* The hunters who spread out the net wait in ambush for the blood of the unsuspecting birds (*Rashi, R' Yonah*).

R' Yonah explains that robbers wait in ambush not only for the blood of their intended victims, but ultimately for their own blood, as well. Robbers lurking to kill others really lie in ambush for their own blood [because they become enmeshed in their own trap. Such behavior is symptomatic of the self-defeating quality of evil].

19. כֵּן אָרְחוֹת כָּל־בֹּצֵעַ בָּצַע אֶת־נֶפֶשׁ בְּעָלָיו יִקָּח — *Such are the ways of all despoilers; they take the soul of [wealth's] owners.* The robber may end by killing the person he robbed either to cover up his own crime or because of the victim's resistance (*Ralbag*).

The attitude of the thief is analogous to that of the birds. The item he robs is so alluring that he assumes it can be his for "free." Yet, ultimately it will take his life. The robber himself is termed the *owner* of the money he stole from his friend (*Rashi*).

Blinded by the pleasure he will derive from his theft, the robber forgets about justice and retribution. Robbery takes the life of the robber since, depending on the anguish and harm caused the victim, this sin may be punished by death at the hands of Heaven. While such a severe punishment is not explicitly stated in the Torah, it is alluded to in *Job* 27:8: *For what is the hypocrite's hope though he gains a profit, for surely God will cast away his soul* (see *Bava Kamma* 119a). The enormity of

1. The Talmud (*Sotah* 38b) gives a different interpretation of this verse. Even birds, either instinctively or because of the sparseness of the grain, sense the miserliness of the person who spread the net. Thus, *Maharsha* explains, unless the hunter has conditioned the birds to frequent this netted area, they will not partake of his miserly spread. Hence, he has baited his net in vain.

[17] *For the net seems spread out with free [bait], in the eyes of every winged creature,* [18] *but they wait in ambush for their blood and lurk for their souls.* [19] *Such are the ways of all despoilers; they take the souls of [wealth's] owners.*

[20] *Wisdom sings out in the street; it gives forth its voice in the*

destructiveness inherent in robbery may be seen in the Generation of the Flood. Though the populace had transgressed all types of sins, their fate was sealed because of robbery (*Sanhedrin* 108a). (*R' Yonah*).

Robbery is symptomatic of a total breakdown of human relations. When basic communication breaks down, nothing can be saved (*Maharal*).

The Sages teach that a person who steals anything of value from his fellow man is deemed to have taken away his very soul, such is the severity of his sin (*Bava Kamma* 119a).[1]

The *Vilna Gaon* explains these verses as a metaphor for the Evil Inclination, which tries to entice a person to sin by pretending to mean his own good. For example, it will convince the person that the trait of anger is good, for it is needed against the wicked; and coveting and procuring another's wealth will enable one to give more money to charity. But how can the Evil Inclination mean his good if its true intention is to annihilate its victim both in this world and in the World to Come?

◄§ God's message is everywhere — if you care to see it.

The balance of the chapter is comprised of the content of *chochmah*'s exhortation, and the consequences people will suffer for ignoring its call. Verses 23-32 are written in the first person, as if *chochmah* is directly addressing the sinners.

R' Yonah points out that these verses speak of punishment and retribution. A

person must constantly remind himself to fear Hashem and be cognizant of Divine retribution. This is a prerequisite to the study of *chochmah*. Therefore, these verses precede Chapter 2, which speaks of the importance of studying *chochmah* [reiterating the basic principle stated above: *Fear of HASHEM is the beginning of knowledge* (v. 7)].

20. חָכְמוֹת בַּחוּץ תָּרֹנָּה בָּרְחֹבוֹת תִּתֵּן קוֹלָהּ — *Wisdom sings out in the street; it gives forth its voice in the squares. The street* is the marketplace (*Targum, R' Yonah*).

In contrast to robbers who commit their crimes furtively (see verse 11), the Torah calls out its message in a loud, clear voice, neither fearful nor embarrassed (*Vilna Gaon*).

Chochmos, literally *wisdoms*, is in the plural form, while the verse continues in the singular form. *Meiri* explains that *Chochmos*, a synonym for Torah, is in the plural form to allude to each of the Torah's many commandments. Alternatively, the plural form alludes to the all-encompassing nature of the Torah, which incorporates every exalted trait, virtue and enlightened idea.

Alshich explains that the plural form refers to both the Written and Oral Torah. The verbs — *sings out, gives forth* — are in the singular since the two parts of Torah constitute a unified whole which guides its students along the correct path.

Meiri explains that these verses are preceded by the warning to avoid the

---

1. When the prophet Nathan presented King David with the hypothetical case of a rich man who robbed a poor man of his one and only ewe, David declared indignantly, "Any man who does this deserves to die!" (*II Samuel* 12:5). *Rashi* (ad loc.) comments that stealing from a pauper is tantamount to taking his life. Similarly, causing a person to lose his means of earning a livelihood is equated with murder. Accordingly, when King Saul ordered the execution of the priests of the city of Nob, he was regarded as if he had killed the Gibeonites (*II Samuel* 21:1), because they earned their livelihood as wood-choppers and water-carriers for the priests (see *Bava Kamma* 119a).

If causing a loss to someone, even indirectly, is tantamount in the eyes of Heaven to murdering that person and his family, how grave, then, is the sin of deceitful people who knowingly and willfully exploit and rob others! (*Chafetz Chaim*).

company of the wicked (verses 10-19), for that is an essential prerequisite for the study of wisdom. The pattern of separating oneself from evil prior to embarking on the correct path was set by Abraham, when he obeyed God's command to leave his homeland (*Genesis* 12:1). King David followed this pattern by beginning *Psalms* with *Praiseworthy is the man that walked not in the counsel of the wicked* (1:1), and only then following with, *but his desire is the Torah of* HASHEM (1:2).

Following *Midrash Tanchuma*, *Rashi* explains that *street*, the location of the marketplace, is a metaphor for the study halls of Torah [where scholars come "to trade" in the wisdom of Torah]. Similarly רְחוֹבוֹת, *squares* (lit. *broad places*), are places where the Torah is "broadened" [i.e., it is expanded upon by scholars who explain and interpret it, uncovering its true meaning through their study and discussions].[1]

R' Yonah renders: Those who give rebuke should make their words heard in the city squares, in the marketplace and in all places where people gather, in order that as broad an audience as possible will benefit from their reproof.[2]

R' Hirsch explains that the wisdom of Hashem's teaching embraces all of life's phenomena. This wisdom is not a spirited gift awaiting fruition in the seclusion of study and prayer, but rather seeks to animate the pulsating heartbeat of humanity and civilization. Its message must be proclaimed in the *streets* and in the *squares*, as it were — the centers of living and striving.

21. בְּרֹאשׁ הֹמִיּוֹת תִּקְרָא בְּפִתְחֵי שְׁעָרִים בָּעִיר אֲמָרֶיהָ תֹאמֵר — *It calls out at the head of noisy throngs, at the entrances of the gates, in the city it speaks its words.* In the places where it can be heard,[3] wisdom calls out the following statement (*Rashi*). Metaphorically, verses 20 and 21 teach that Torah is revealed to all and it exhorts everyone to heed it (*Metzudos*). Since the words of Torah and its commandments are well known and publicized everywhere and to everyone, no one may claim that its ways are concealed (*Meiri*).

The entrances of the [city] gates were where the elders would sit to judge and govern (*Rashi*) [see also 31:23]. These were the places where people would come and go (*Metzudos*).

1. The Talmud (*Moed Katan* 16a-b) relates that R' Yehudah HaNasi once decreed that it was forbidden to study Torah with disciples in the marketplace. Despite this decree, R' Chiya taught his two nephews in the marketplace. When R' Yehudah voiced his displeasure, R' Chiya replied that he did so "because it is written, חׇכְמוֹת בַּחוּץ תָּרֹנָּה, *wisdom sings out in the street*," which he interpreted to mean that the market is a proper place to learn Torah. R' Yehudah answered [according to *Maharsha*, loc. cit.]: "If you learned the written verse, you did not learn the Mishnah; and if you learned the Mishnah, you did not learn the *Gemara*; and if you learned the *Gemara*, it was not explained to you properly. The proper explanation of this verse is that *"whoever engages in the study of Torah within, his Torah will herald him on the outside."* Although Torah study requires the seclusion and modesty of an indoor setting, its effects are obvious in the external bearing and conduct of its scholars, whose wisdom will thus be acknowledged *outside*.

2. *R' Yonah* (*Shaarei Teshuvah* 3:72-73) comments that it is proper to appoint men of stature in each marketplace and neighborhood to supervise and honestly rebuke their neighbors for any wrongdoing, thus removing the evil from their midst. Otherwise, those who can offer reproof and fail to do so will be held responsible for the sins.

3. The root המה means to make noise, as in *Isaiah* 17:12. Since there is bound to be noise wherever crowds gather, the word for crowd, therefore, is הָמוֹן. The Patriarch Abraham was אַב הֲמוֹן גּוֹיִם, *the father of a multitude of nations* (*Genesis* 17:5), which implies that he was involved with throngs of people. As *Rambam* (*Hil. Avodah Zarah* 1:3) writes, Abraham gathered people by the tens and tens of thousands and addressed them about the existence of the One God.

squares. [21] *It calls out at the head of noisy throngs, at the entrances of the gates, in the city it speaks its words:* [22] *How long, O simpletons, will you love folly? and scoffers*

Alshich interprets the enumeration of these specific places metaphorically, as representative of various levels of learning and understanding Torah. There are four types who study Torah:

(1) one who engages only in its simple, superficial meaning;

(2) one who studies the plain meaning, but on a deeper level and with broader scope;

(3) one who is completely engrossed, engaging his mind and raising his voice night and day in the study of Torah;

(4) one who probes the depths of Torah and enters into its hidden inner meanings.

Alshich notes that the Torah's call is expressed in four ways in verses 20-21, which correspond to the four kinds of students. Torah has the power to diminish man's evil instinct through study: *I [Hashem] created the evil instinct and I created Torah as its antidote* (*Kiddushin* 30b), but its ennobling effect varies according to the degree of intensity and profundity of each individual's approach to his learning. To the student whose learning is superficial [בְּחוּץ], Torah's wisdom cries out on a level of תָּרֹנָּה, signifying a distant sound that arouses a vague desire for repentance. For the student who has broadened [בָּרְחֹבוֹת] his involvement in Torah learning, תִּתֵּן קוֹלָהּ, the Torah *gives forth its voice*; he hears not just a vague humming but an audible voice, and correspondingly feels a greater urge to forsake evil and turn to good. For the third one, who is בְּרֹאשׁ הוֹמִיּוֹת, constantly

raising his voice and taxing his mind in Torah study, תִּקְרָא, the Torah issues a clear, distinct call. His is a stronger, more clearly defined inner conviction to turn away from that which is against God's Will. But for the fourth one, בְּפִתְחֵי שְׁעָרִים בָּעִיר, who has *entered into the gates* and is *within the city* — in other words, he has arrived at the profound inner meaning of Torah — for him אֲמָרֶיהָ תֹאמֵר, the Torah *speaks precisely and unmistakably.* His commitment to return to Hashem is overwhelming and unequivocal.

Ralbag interprets these verses as referring to the wondrous revelation of Hashem's *wisdom*, which is manifest in the natural world. Once a person begins to reflect upon it, *chochmah* beckons him toward a recognition of the Creator.[1]

22. עַד־מָתַי פְּתָיִם תְּאֵהֲבוּ־פֶּתִי — *How long, O simpletons, will you love folly? Choch-mah* cries out: How long will those who are swayed by enticers and heretics enjoy such seductions? (*Rashi*). [On a subliminal level the "victim" of enticement enjoys being "victimized."]

R' Yonah explains that פְּתָיִם are people of weak intelligence who are easily led astray by seducers and demagogues. Also included under this heading are those with false ideas and opinions, as well as those whose desires confuse and mislead them. Their lack of intelligence and the weakness of their powers of reasoning let them be blinded by their lusts and desires, until they believe uncritically that whatever they want is good.

R' Yonah stresses a fundamental prin-

1. To heed this call of wisdom as manifested in God's Creation is, according to *Rambam*, the means of achieving יִרְאַת ה', *fear of Hashem*, which Solomon calls רֵאשִׁית דָּעַת, *the beginning* and the choicest *of knowledge* (see verse 7). "And what is the way to love and fear Him? When man contemplates His great and marvelous works and creatures and realizes His incomparable and infinite wisdom, he immediately loves, praises and glorifies Him and is overtaken with a great desire to know the Great God. As David said, *My soul thirsts for the Lord, for the living God* (*Psalms* 42:3). And when that man reflects on these same things, he is immediately overcome by fear and realizes that he is a lowly benighted creature, with a tiny insignificant intelligence, standing before the All Knowing, as David stated (ibid., 8:4-5), *When I behold Your heavens, the work of Your fingers . . . what is the son of mortal man that You should be mindful of him?*" (*Rambam*, Hil. *Yesodei HaTorah* 2:2).

כג לְצוֹן חָמְדוּ לָהֶם וּכְסִילִים יִשְׂנְאוּ־דָעַת: תָּשׁוּבוּ לְתוֹכַחְתִּי
כד הִנֵּה אַבִּיעָה לָכֶם רוּחִי אוֹדִיעָה דְבָרַי אֶתְכֶם: יַעַן

ciple in the Divine patterns of free will and reward and punishment. If people would not allow themselves to be controlled by their lusts, their thought processes would not be corrupted. Thus the Sages teach that an individual is responsible for his actions: כָּל הַמִּתְפַּתֶּה בְּיִצְרוֹ נוֹפֵל שָׁם, *Whoever is seduced by his evil impulse will fall [to Gehinnom]* (*Eruvin* 19a). The Almighty informed Cain of this fundamental concept after he killed his brother Abel: וְאֵלֶיךָ תְּשׁוּקָתוֹ וְאַתָּה תִּמְשָׁל בּוֹ, *Its* [the evil impulse's] *desire is toward you, yet you can conquer it* (*Genesis* 4:7). The Evil Inclination always lusts and demands that man give it whatever it desires. The Evil Inclination cannot satisfy itself, however, without the agreement of man's intelligent judgment. Therefore, if man succumbs to his baser instincts, he will be punished.

עַד־מָתַי — *How long.* The verse does not use the expression "why," but rather "how long." It is a child's nature to act immaturely and long for foolish things. But as he grows, his desires mature — ideally to thoughts of loving and fearing Hashem. But you, naive scoffers and fools, how long will you remain as children? When will you finally grow up? (*Yetav Panim*).

וְלֵצִים לָצוֹן חָמְדוּ לָהֶם — *And scoffers covet mockery for themselves?* This is a continuation of the question עַד מָתַי, *how long.* In other words, until when will scoffers covet scoffing? The same question applies to *fools*, the next category in the verse — how long will they hate knowledge? (*Metzudos*).

A לֵץ, *scoffer*, scorns everything, mocking people and speaking slanderously. This trait stems from two factors: the faulty character traits of cruelty and arrogance (see 21:24), and the complete renunciation of the yoke of Heaven. Since his heart is devoid of fear of God, it is readily susceptible to ridicule, mockery and scorn (*R' Yonah*).

A *scoffer* cannot concede importance to any person, idea, or concept. He seeks to undermine any possible value by distortion and scorn (*Pachad Yitzchak*).[1]

וּכְסִילִים יִשְׂנְאוּ־דָעַת — *And fools hate knowledge?* The fools of this verse, *k'silim*, are perpetrators of wicked deeds, who transgress in order to satisfy their desires for pleasure and enjoyment (*R' Yonah*).[2]

R' Hirsch translates כְּסִילִים as conceited fools.[3]

---

1. It is for this reason that לֵץ, *scoffer*, and צֵל, *shadow*, share the same letters. A shadow distorts the perception of reality, lending prestige to the insignificant, and belittling the important.

2. *R' Yonah* explains that these groups — פְּתָיִם, *simpletons*, לֵצִים, *scoffers*, and כְּסִילִים, *fools* — represent three functional divisions of the human soul: כֹּחַ הַצּוֹמֵחַ, *physical growth and bodily functions*; כֹּחַ הַמִּתְאַוֶּה, *desire and emotion*; and כֹּחַ הַמַּשְׂכֶּלֶת, *intelligence and reason.* Man shares the first function, pure physical growth, with plants and animals. The second force, emotional, is common to man and animals. It is the source of מִדּוֹת, *character traits* or instincts, which direct both man and animals toward the satisfaction of biological needs and desires, and the desire to conquer and do harm to others. The third and highest power, reason and intellect, is unique to man. *Simpletons* lack enough intelligence to make proper value judgments. The verb describing their deficiency — תֶּאֱהָבוּ, *love* — implies that they choose to believe that pursuit of their evil impulses is the "good life." *Scoffers* have bad character traits, which come from their flawed control over desires and emotions. Therefore, the verb used for them is חָמְדוּ, *covet.* *Fools* are overwhelmed by their base animal instincts, and contantly indulge their purely physical needs. They, least of all, are capable of properly using the powers of reason and fear of God to restrain their evil impulses. Therefore, they are described as hating wisdom. [For an alternative understanding of פְּתָיִם, לֵצִים and כְּסִילִים in the light of the three divisions of the human soul, see *Meiri.*]

3. Perhaps there is a connection between כְּסִיל, *fool*, and כֶּסֶל, *trust* or *security*, as in כִּי ה' יִהְיֶה בְכִסְלֶךָ, *for HASHEM will be your security* (3:26). A fool believes smugly that no matter what he does, no evil will befall him. This conceited security and the prudent caution of the wise man are contrasted

1/23-24   *covet mockery for themselves? and fools hate knowledge?*
²³ *Return to my reproof! Behold, I will express my spirit
to you; I will make my words known to you.* ²⁴ *But because*

Malbim differentiates between the verse's three categories — כְּסִיל, לֵץ and פֶּתִי — as follows: A פֶּתִי, *simpleton*, is easily swayed toward evil ways, because he lacks the understanding to accept *chochmah*. A לֵץ, *scoffer*, mocks *chochmah* because it cannot be proven through logic, but he does not hate it. However, since he mocks anything based on faith alone, he lacks fear of God, the only key that can unlock the portals of Godly *chochmah*. A כְּסִיל, *fool*, knows *chochmah*; he is not deficient in his ability to understand it. But he rejects it because it demands of him that he not indulge his every desire. He is worse than a scoffer, because he despises *chochmah*.

According to the *Vilna Gaon*, the three groups represent the three main reasons that people do not study Torah: (1) *Simpletons* have been enticed by the evil impulse to abandon Torah in favor of worldly pleasure. They believe that this will always be the true good. (2) *Scoffers* neglect Torah because of their love for דְּבָרִים בְּטֵלִים, *idle talk* (jokes, stories, gossip, irony and the whole gamut of useless and harmful talk which comes under the heading of scoffing and mockery). Even though this affords them no physical pleasure, it is sweet to them and they covet it. (3) *Fools* resist the diligence needed to study Torah properly; they want Torah knowledge to be bestowed upon them spontaneously without any effort on their part. When they see that they are not becoming "instant Torah scholars," they abandon their study, because they fail to appreciate the sweetness of learning.

23. תָּשׁוּבוּ לְתוֹכַחְתִּי — *Return to my reproof!* The translation follows *Meiri*. Alternatively *Meiri* relates תָּשׁוּבוּ to מְשׁוּבָה, *waywardness*, explaining this phrase as a continuation of the question posed in the previous verse: *How long will you rebel against my reproof.*

R' Yonah renders תָּשׁוּבוּ לְתוֹכַחְתִּי as: *Repent from your ways because of my reproof.*

הִנֵּה אַבִּיעָה לָכֶם רוּחִי — *Behold, I will express my spirit to you.* You have no excuse to claim that Hashem's ways are concealed from you, because *behold! I will express my spirit to you*. Just as hidden underground waters flow from their source [אַבִּיעָה is related to נַחַל נוֹבֵעַ, *a flowing stream*], so, too, does my hidden desire flow forth to you; i.e., the Torah's warning is laid out before you (*Meiri*).

אוֹדִיעָה דְבָרַי אֶתְכֶם — *I will make my words known to you.* According to *Malbim*, this refers to the words of punishment for those who forsake *chochmah*, which appear in the following verses.

The *Vilna Gaon* explains that the three parts of this verse constitute the remedy for the three types of people who distance themselves from Torah (see previous verse). A פֶּתִי, *simpleton*, who has been enticed to pursue worldly pleasures should *return to my reproof*, for words of rebuke and *mussar* will subjugate his desires.

A לֵץ, *scoffer*, gains pleasure from speaking words of scorn, even though it affords him no physical pleasure. The Torah addresses this scoffer, saying, הִנֵּה אַבִּיעָה לָכֶם רוּחִי, *Behold, I will express my spirit to you*. Through the Torah's spirit of holiness, one attains tremendous enjoyment, because the enjoyment derived from Torah's spirit will certainly far surpass all other pleasures, for תַּלְמוּד תּוֹרָה כְּנֶגֶד כֻּלָּם, *the study of Torah is equivalent to them all* (*Peah* 1:1). Such pleasure is greater than that of impurity, for it is an absolute, true pleasure.

The *Vilna Gaon* explains the scoffer's attraction to mockery. For every action, a person receives a corresponding רוּחַ, *heavenly spirit*, that propels him to perform similar actions, and rewards the person doing so with a sense of satisfaction. This applies both to a *mitzvah* and to a sin, as expressed by the dictum, "one mitzvah leads to another mitzvah and one sin leads to another sin" (*Avos* 4:2). The greater the sin, the greater the spirit it brings forth, and the greater the desire to continue sinning in this manner. Since idle chatter and mockery

כה קָרָאתִי וַתְּמָאֵנוּ נָטִיתִי יָדִי וְאֵין מַקְשִׁיב: וַתִּפְרְעוּ
כו כָל־עֲצָתִי וְתוֹכַחְתִּי לֹא אֲבִיתֶם: גַּם־אֲנִי בְּאֵידְכֶם
כז אֶשְׂחָק אֶלְעַג בְּבֹא פַחְדְּכֶם: בְּבֹא °כְשׁוֹאָה| פַחְדְּכֶם
כח וְאֵידְכֶם כְּסוּפָה יֶאֱתֶה בְּבֹא עֲלֵיכֶם צָרָה וְצוּקָה: אָז
יִקְרָאֻנְנִי וְלֹא אֶעֱנֶה יְשַׁחֲרֻנְנִי וְלֹא יִמְצָאֻנְנִי:

°כְשׁוֹאָה ק׳

are the opposite of Torah study, they bring the sinner greater pleasure than any sin. The tremendous spirit of impurity which results from these sins causes this heightened enjoyment. On the other hand, if the *mitzvah* is very great, then the heavenly spirit which results from it is also great. The individual now has a tremendous desire to perform similar *mitzvos* and he therefore derives an enormous satisfaction from this *mitzvah*. Since the study of Torah is the greatest of all *mitzvos*, the spirit that flows from it will afford a person the greatest pleasure of all.[1]

A כְּסִיל, *fool*, hates Torah because he finds it difficult to understand. To these people, the Torah says, אוֹדִיעָה דְבָרַי אֶתְכֶם, *I will make my words known to you*, and then you will see their sweetness and love them.

24. יַעַן קָרָאתִי וַתְּמָאֵנוּ נָטִיתִי יָדִי וְאֵין מַקְשִׁיב — *But because I have called and you refused; I have stretched forth my hand and no one listened.* I stretched out my hand to signal you to return to me, just as a person beckons his friend by stretching out his hand (*Rashi*), *and you refused* to pay attention to my call (*Metzudos*).

Meiri presents two interpretations of the outstretched hand. Either *chochmah* stretched out its hand to accept the sinner, or it stretched out its hand to afflict the sinner, to influence him to repent.

The verb, קָרָאתִי, *I have called*, applies

to someone who is leaving, but is still close enough to hear a call. However, once he is too far to hear, he can be signaled by a hand gesture. Thus *chochmah* declares, "I called you when were still close, but you refused to listen. Even when you distanced yourself, I still had mercy on you and stretched out my hand to signal you to come back, but you pretended not to see or hear" (*Vilna Gaon*).

25. וַתִּפְרְעוּ כָל־עֲצָתִי וְתוֹכַחְתִּי לֹא אֲבִיתֶם — *And you rejected my every counsel, and desired not my reproof.* You neglected my advice, which was intended to make you great in the world (*Rashi*).

Allegiance to the Torah raises the stature of Israel in the eyes of the nations, as the verse states: *You shall safeguard and perform* [the commandments], *for it is your wisdom and discernment in the eyes of the peoples, who shall hear all these decrees, and who shall say, "Surely a wise and discerning people is this great nation!"* (*Deuteronomy* 4:6).

A friend advises one which path to follow. If, subsequently, the person disregards this good advice and chooses the wrong path, his adviser will rebuke him for not listening. In this vein, the verse states *and you rejected my every counsel* to choose the correct path. Therefore, I rebuked you for going on the wrong path, but *you desired not my reproof* (*Vilna Gaon*).

later in *Proverbs*: חָכָם יָרֵא וְסָר מֵרָע וּכְסִיל מִתְעַבֵּר וּבוֹטֵחַ, *A wise man fears and turns away from evil, but a fool becomes enraged and is confident* (14:16).

1. It therefore follows that if a person performed an outstanding good deed, it must have resulted from the merit of a previously observed *mitzvah*. At the dedication celebration of Yeshivas Chachmei Lublin in prewar Poland, the Rebbe of Tchortkov praised the magnanimity of Shmuel Eichenbaum, the benefactor who had donated the plot of land on which the yeshivah was built. The Rebbe addressed him, saying, "Donating this property to the yeshivah is certainly a *mitzvah*, and for it you have earned great honor and recognition. What I want to know is what great *mitzvah* did you previously perform, by virtue of which you merited to become the donor of the property upon which this great yeshivah was erected?"

1/25-28 *I have called and you refused; I have stretched forth my hand and no one listened;* ²⁵ *and you rejected my every counsel, and desired not my reproof,* ²⁶ *I, too, will laugh at your misfortune; I will mock when your dread arrives.* ²⁷ *When your fear arrives as sudden darkness, and your misfortune comes like a storm; when affliction and oppression come upon you,* ²⁸ *then they will call me, but I will not answer; they will search for me, but they will not find me.*

26. גַּם־אֲנִי בְּאֵידְכֶם אֶשְׂחָק אֶלְעַג בְּבֹא פַחְדְּכֶם — *I, too, will laugh at your misfortune; I will mock when your dread arrives.* Since you ignored my attempts to help you, I will not have pity on you and I will laugh when your calamity comes (*Metzudos*).

27. בְּבֹא כְשׁוֹאָה פַחְדְּכֶם וְאֵידְכֶם כְּסוּפָה יֶאֱתֶה בְּבֹא עֲלֵיכֶם צָרָה וְצוּקָה — *When your fear arrives as sudden darkness, and your misfortune comes like a storm; when affliction and oppression come upon you.* *Metzudos* and *Malbim* render כְשׁוֹאָה as *sudden darkness*. *Rashi* renders *like a sudden cloud.*

The *Vilna Gaon* and *Malbim* differentiate between צָרָה and צוּקָה. צָרָה is an *external trouble* (such as an enemy coming to take away one's children and possessions). צוּקָה is *an internal trouble*, the distress of the soul (i.e., the despair and worry caused by the enemy's threats). *Malbim* adds that if the external trouble is accompanied by internal distress, the situation is very bitter, for then, one loses all hope and despairs completely.

28. אָז יִקְרָאֻנְנִי וְלֹא אֶעֱנֶה יְשַׁחֲרֻנְנִי וְלֹא יִמְצָאֻנְנִי — *Then they will call me, but I will not answer; they will search for me, but they will not find me.* Then, i.e., when the trouble comes (*Metzudos*).

In order to attain Torah knowledge, a person must do two things: 1) Seek it and delve into it with effort and toil; 2) pray for Divine assistance. This verse refers to both factors, saying: When you *call me* [in prayer], I will not answer. When you *search for me* — i.e., through your labor and toil in Torah — you will not find me. The punishment in this verse corresponds measure for measure to the actions described in verse 24. I called to them (יַעַן קָרָאתִי), but they refused; therefore, when they call to me, I will not answer. I stretched out my hand to them (נָטִיתִי יָדִי) with great effort, even when they were far away, but they did not pay attention. Therefore, when they expend great effort to seek me after distancing themselves from me, they will not find me. For, אם תַּעֲזְבֵנִי יוֹם יוֹמַיִם אֶעֱזְבֶךָ, *If you forsake Me for one day, I will forsake you for two* (*Vilna Gaon*).[1]

Ibn Nachmias explains that since they did not study Torah in their youth, they will not be able to study it in their old age. Alternatively, if they have not studied Torah in this world, it will be impossible for them to do so in the World to Come, for a person cannot do any good once he leaves this world, the world of deeds.

Meiri explains that although repentance always diminishes the punishment, and is always accepted, even from one who has been very rebellious, it does not always completely erase punishment in this world.

Hashem is so merciful that He even answers the cries of the individual who calls out to Him purely because of his distress. [See *Deuteronomy* 4:30-31: בַּצַּר לְךָ וּמְצָאוּךָ כֹּל הַדְּבָרִים הָאֵלֶּה . . . וְשַׁבְתָּ עַד־ה' אֱלֹהֶיךָ . . . לֹא יַרְפְּךָ וְלֹא יַשְׁחִיתֶךָ, *When you are in distress and all these things have befallen you . . . you will return unto Hashem . . . He will not abandon you nor*

---

1. The following example illustrates how this adage is practically applied. If two people start at a certain point and begin to travel in opposite directions, at the end of one day, there will be two days' distance between them. (See *Yerushalmi Berachos* 9:5, as well as *Sifri Eikev* 11:22, as quoted by *Rashi* to *Deuteronomy* 11:13.)

כט תַּחַת כִּי־שָׂנְאוּ דָעַת וְיִרְאַת יהוֹה לֹא בָחָרוּ:

ל-לא לֹא־אָבוּ לַעֲצָתִי נָאֲצוּ כָּל־תּוֹכַחְתִּי: וְיֹאכְלוּ

לב מִפְּרִי דַרְכָּם וּמִמֹּעֲצֹתֵיהֶם יִשְׂבָּעוּ: כִּי מְשׁוּבַת

פְּתָיִם תַּהַרְגֵם וְשַׁלְוַת כְּסִילִים תְּאַבְּדֵם:

destroy you.] In this case, however, He will not answer their outcry because He knows that their repentance is only temporary and not from the depths of their heart. They repent only while they are in danger, but as soon as the crisis passes, they will again reject His words. [See *Exodus* 7:3, where *Rambam* and *Sforno* apply this principle to Pharaoh.] (*R' Shmuel Uzidah*).

Rabbeinu Bachya ibn Paquda illustrates the penitent's situation by comparing him to a servant who has run away from his master. If he recalls the kind treatment his master always showed him, and if of his own free will he seeks forgiveness for having rebelled and fled, he deserves to be forgiven. Hashem's reply to such a penitent is the promise expressed by Jeremiah: *All nations shall bless themselves in Him and in Him shall they glory* (*Jeremiah* 4:2). But a servant who does not realize his mistake and thus forces the master to send a messenger to chastise him and discipline him for having run away is different. When he finally begs forgiveness, his master ignores his pleas; as the verse tells us, *When your misfortune comes like a storm . . . they will call me, but I will not answer.*

Most fortunate is the individual who returns to God on his own initiative. Less fortunate is one who doesn't repent until he has been rebuked by God. Even more unfortunate is one who doesn't repent until he is aroused by punishment inflicted on others. Least acceptable and most difficult to be readmitted into Hashem's favor is the person who does not repent until he himself is punished. Such an individual is furthest from Divine acceptance and forgiveness, and must repent by showing deep remorse and completely renouncing evil. He must demonstrate great earnestness in his thoughts, speech, deeds and all his actions. Only then is he considered worthy of having his repentance accepted and his evil deeds

overlooked (*Chovos HaLevavos, Shaar HaTeshuvah* 6).

29. תַּחַת כִּי־שָׂנְאוּ דָעַת וְיִרְאַת ה' לֹא בָחָרוּ — *Because they hated knowledge and did not choose fear of HASHEM.* Choice applies where there are two alternatives (see *Deuteronomy* 30:15, 19, רְאֵה נָתַתִּי לְפָנֶיךָ הַיּוֹם אֶת־הַחַיִּים וְאֶת־הַטּוֹב וְאֶת־הַמָּוֶת וְאֶת־הָרָע . . . וּבָחַרְתָּ בַּחַיִּים, *See — I have placed before you today the life and the good, and the death and the evil . . . and you shall choose life.* Not only do they fail to actively pursue the fear of Hashem, which is the the most vital thing of all, but even if it were one of two choices available to them, they would not choose it (*Vilna Gaon*).

30. לֹא־אָבוּ לַעֲצָתִי נָאֲצוּ כָּל־תּוֹכַחְתִּי — *They did not desire my counsel, they spurned all my reproof.* They did not even wish to hear my advice (*Metzudos*).

My counsel refers to the good advice beginning in verse 10 not to associate with those who entice you to join them in sin. *My reproof* refers to the reproof beginning in verse 22 (*Vilna Gaon*).

31. וְיֹאכְלוּ מִפְּרִי דַרְכָּם וּמִמֹּעֲצֹתֵיהֶם יִשְׂבָּעוּ — *They will eat from the fruit of their way and be sated with their own schemes.* Just as one who plants a tree ultimately eats from its fruits, so, too, sinners will be compensated according to their actions (*Metzudos*).

Rashi comments that they will eat the *fruit,* i.e., the minor part of the reimbursement, through the troubles that will befall them during their lives. The קֶרֶן, *principal* (i.e., the major part of the recompense), is preserved for them in *Gehinnom* (*Rashi*).[1]

1. The Talmud (*Kiddushin* 40a) explains that God has different systems of compensation for one's actions. For certain *mitzvos*, He pays both *principal* (i.e., the main reward) and *fruits* (i.e., additional reward). For most sins God pays only the principal, and no fruits. In other words, the sinner is not punished more than the extent of his wickedness (*Rashi* ibid.). If so, how are we to

²⁹ Because they hated knowledge and did not choose fear of
HASHEM, ³⁰ they did not desire my counsel, they spurned all my
reproof. ³¹ They will eat from the fruit of their way and be sated
with their own schemes. ³² For the waywardness of simpletons
will kill them, and the contentment of fools will destroy them.

32. כִּי מְשׁוּבַת פְּתָיִם תַּהַרְגֵם — *For the
waywardness of simpletons will kill them.*
Their heart was wayward (*Rashi*), as in .
. וַיֵּלֶךְ שׁוֹבָב בְּדֶרֶךְ לִבּוֹ, *He went waywardly
on the path of his heart* [Isaiah 57:17]
(*Vilna Gaon*).

Ralbag explains that a simpleton impulsively follows the dictates of his heart
without investigating what *chochmah*
prescribes. This is considered wayward, for
his conduct is inconsistent. He acts according to his whim at any given moment, at
times one way, and at other times in a
completely opposite manner. Such a trait
ultimately brings about his downfall,
since it is likely that he will often choose
evil.

According to *Metzudos*, מְשׁוּבַת is related to the word שׁוּבָה, *tranquility*, as
in בְּשׁוּבָה וָנַחַת תִּוָּשֵׁעוּן, *in tranquility
and peacefulness will you be saved*
(*Isaiah* 30:15). Their choice to sit quietly
without toiling under the yoke of Torah
will kill them, for they will be punished.

וְשַׁלְוַת כְּסִילִים תְּאַבְּדֵם — *And the contentment of fools will destroy them.* Since the
wicked feel that they are succeeding, they
continue their wickedness and do not repent. Thus their success will cause them to
perish (*Rashi, Meiri*).

Ibn Ezra quotes Jeremiah, who asks:
מַדּוּעַ דֶּרֶךְ רְשָׁעִים צָלֵחָה שָׁלוּ כָּל־בֹּגְדֵי בָגֶד,
*Why does the way of the wicked prosper;
and [why are] all the betrayers tranquil?*
(*Jeremiah* 12:1). Addressing this same situation, King Solomon explains that because
Hashem does not immediately punish the
wicked, they think there will be no retribution and are encouraged to perpetrate even
more evil. Since God is patient and does not
immediately punish even a persistent sinner, people assume that they can continue
sinning with impunity (*Ecclesiastes* 8:11-
12). Thus, לֵב בְּנֵי־הָאָדָם מָלֵא־רָע, *the heart
of man is full of evil* (ibid., 9:3), for he is
convinced that everything happens by
chance. However, there is Divine retribution, and ultimately sinners go to *Gehinnom.*[1]

Ibn Ezra also explains that the serenity
of the wicked will slay them, for when
they have serenity they commit evil. Thus
their tranquility and lack of misfortune
causes them to perish.

The *Vilna Gaon* explains that fools
choose to sit serenely; they desire neither to
labor in Torah and *mitzvos*, nor to relinquish the pleasures and tranquility of this
world. Therefore they will perish both in
this world and in the World to Come, for
they will not find satisfaction for their
desires in this world, and in the future they

understand this verse, which states that the sinners will be punished *from the fruit of their way*?
The Talmud explains that this applies to a sin that produces "fruit," i.e., by-products. As *Rashi*
illustrates: God's Name is desecrated when a respected person sins and, as a result, others learn
from his example and emulate his deed.

1. *R' Yosef Albo* (*Sefer Halkkarim*) explains that benefits may come to the wicked for their own
sake or for the sake of the righteous. For their own sake, they are sometimes treated well in order
to harden their hearts so that they will not repent, because they have sinned so much that they
have lost the privilege of repentance. This is what the Rabbis mean when they say that God
withholds repentance from the wicked. Or conversely, God is kind and prolongs their days to
allow them time to repent.

A wicked man may also be prosperous for the sake of the righteous. The reward of the
righteous is increased when they are not enticed by the success of the wicked. For if the wicked
were punished as soon as they sinned, righteous people would be suspected of serving God only
because they feared punishment.

לג וְשֹׁמֵעַ לִי יִשְׁכָּן־בֶּטַח וְשַׁאֲנַן מִפַּחַד רָעָה:

א בְּנִי אִם־תִּקַּח אֲמָרָי וּמִצְוֹתַי תִּצְפֹּן אִתָּךְ:

ב לְהַקְשִׁיב לַחָכְמָה אָזְנֶךָ תַּטֶּה לִבְּךָ לַתְּבוּנָה:

ג כִּי אִם לַבִּינָה תִקְרָא לַתְּבוּנָה תִּתֵּן קוֹלֶךָ:

---

will inherit *Gehinnom*.[1]

The *Chafetz Chaim* interprets this verse as follows: Because a person was wayward, it was decreed that he should eventually be slain. Therefore, Hashem lets him live serenely in this world so that he may be rewarded for all his merits. Thus, his serenity becomes the very cause of his eternal doom [שַׁלְוַת כְּסִילִים תְּאַבְּדֵם]. This is the fulfillment of the verse, *He repays His enemies in his lifetime to make him perish* (*Deuteronomy* 7:10). *Onkelos* interprets this verse as: *He repays His enemies for the good they did before Him during their lifetime, in order to make them perish [in the World to Come]*.[2]

Malbim explains that תַּהַרְגֵם means *will kill them* in this world, whereas תְּאַבְּדֵם means *will destroy them* both in this world and in the World to Come. The

simpletons sin unintentionally, for they do not know the dictates of *chochmah*, therefore they have a share in the World to Come. *Fools*, however, are aware of the dictates of *chochmah*, but knowingly forsake them because of their desires. They will perish both in this world and in the Hereafter.

33. וְשֹׁמֵעַ לִי יִשְׁכָּן־בֶּטַח וְשַׁאֲנַן מִפַּחַד רָעָה — *But he who listens to me will dwell securely, and will be undisturbed by fear of evil.* *Chochmah* ends its words saying: One who listens to me will be secure in the realization that no harm will befall him (*Metzudos*).

Rashi explains that he will *dwell securely* in this world and *be undisturbed* in the World to Come, translating מִפַּחַד רָעָה, *fear of evil*, as referring to the punishment of *Gehinnom*.

II

1. בְּנִי אִם־תִּקַּח אֲמָרָי — *My child: If you accept [lit. take] my words.* The conditional אִם, *if*, is to be understood as: You will be my child *if* you accept my words (*Rashi*).

וּמִצְוֹתַי תִּצְפֹּן אִתָּךְ — *And treasure my commandments with yourself*, i.e., if you make sure that you do not forget the commandments (*Metzudos*).

1. The tranquility enjoyed by the wicked becomes the very reason that they may ultimately perish (see *Psalms* 92:8). This may be compared to two paths. The first is straight and clear at first, but becomes filled with snakes, scorpions and beasts of prey. The second path begins with a steep mountain, but ends in a beautiful, fertile plain. If the first path were to begin with snakes and scorpions, would anyone be foolish enough to choose it? Such is the way of fools. They rejoice in their temporal success in this world and think that everything belongs to them, and fail to realize that they will end up as dust under the feet of the righteous! (*Vilna Gaon*).

2. The *Chafetz Chaim* illustrates this principle with a parable. Once a respected official committed a serious offense against the king. He was brought to trial and sentenced to death by hanging. Because of his high rank, however, he was given a special privilege. Before his hanging, the royal band would play before him. And so it was. Before the sinner was hanged, the royal musicians played joyful tunes until the whole city resounded with their music. Upon hearing this music, one of the observers remarked, "How fortunate this man is! They are playing for him with the very same instruments they used for the king's coronation. What a lucky fellow!"

A bystander turned to this observer and exclaimed, "What a fool you are! You think that this person is lucky?! Don't you know that this music is actually a hymn for his hanging? Just wait and see — as soon as the song is over, they will hang him!"

The *Chafetz Chaim* explains that a similar fate befalls the individual who leaves God's ways. Although he is given wealth, its purpose is merely to use up any merits he may still have. Afterwards, he will perish through the afflictions of *Gehinnom*.

[33] *But he who listens to me will dwell securely, and will be undisturbed by fear of evil.*

¹**M**y *child: If you accept my words and treasure my commandments with yourself,* ² *to make your ear attentive to wisdom, incline your heart to discernment.* ³ *[For] only if you call out to understanding [and] give forth your voice to discernment,*

According to the *Vilna Gaon*, אֲמָרַי, *my words*, refers to the study of Torah, which is obligatory at all times — day and night. The verse states תִּקַּח, *accept*, for the Torah must be studied constantly. Most commandments, however, can be performed only at specific times or when a particular opportunity arises [for example, one is commanded to eat matzah specifically on the fifteenth night of Nissan]. Therefore, regarding *mitzvos*, the instruction is תִּצְפֹּן, *treasure* them, i.e., safeguard them until the appropriate time to fulfill them.[1]

2. לְהַקְשִׁיב לַחָכְמָה אָזְנֶךָ — *To make your ear attentive to wisdom*, i.e., to be engrossed in [the study of] Torah (*Rashi*).

Chochmah refers to the knowledge one attains from a teacher through listening to him. As our Sages state (*Chagigah* 3b), עֲשֵׂה אָזְנֶיךָ כְּאַפַּרְכֶּסֶת, *make your ears like a mill-hopper*, a large funnel through which grain is channeled to the grinding area (*Vilna Gaon*). Genuine wisdom can be acquired only from a prophet or through Torah study; a person cannot arrive at it through his own intellectual probing. Therefore, this verse instructs us to be attentive to *chochmah* (*Malbim*).

תַּטֶּה לִבְּךָ לַתְּבוּנָה — *Incline your heart to discernment*. The term *tvunah* means לְהָבִין דָּבָר עַל בּוּרְיוֹ, *to understand something with clarity*. It may apply to *chochmah*, as in this verse, or to *binah*, as in the following verse. To truly comprehend *chochmah* i.e., the lessons of your teachers, תַּטֶּה לִבְּךָ, you must *incline your heart*, for it is the heart which is the source of understanding. [See *Berachos* 61a, לֵב מֵבִין, *a heart understands*] (*Vilna Gaon*).

[תְּבוּנָה, *tvunah*, and בִּינָה, *binah*, are related terms. One who has attained them is a נָבוֹן, *navon.*]

R' Yonah enumerates the five steps that are necessary to acquire *chochmah*:

(1) listening carefully to your teachers' words;

(2) concentrating your heart to the exclusion of all else;

(3) prayer to merit *chochmah*;

(4) effort and toil in its pursuit;

(5) love and enjoyment of *chochmah*.

He explains that the first two steps are discussed in this verse, as follows: (1) You must *be attentive* to the words of your teachers, without adding to or detracting from their teaching. People who are not precise in listening can err, and even think they have heard that the prohibited is permitted, and *vice versa*. (2) You must turn your heart away from all worldly desires in order to delve into the *chochmah* you have heard. Analyze the *chochmah* and try to fathom the reasons behind it, until you reach the level of *binah*, deducing one thing from another.

3. כִּי אִם לַבִּינָה תִקְרָא לַתְּבוּנָה תִּתֵּן קוֹלֶךָ — *[For] only if you call out to understanding [and] give forth your voice to discernment*. *Metzudos* renders כִּי אִם as כַּאֲשֶׁר, *when*, i.e., when you will call out to *binah*, to come close to it.

Targum Yonasan renders the word אִם as אֵם, a *mother*, explaining the phrase, "If you call *binah* your mother." *Minchas Shai* explains that this follows the Midrashic interpretation of the word. Torah is called the "mother" of those who study it, for just as a mother provides her

1. *Sfas Emes* comments that one should treasure a commandment even after he has performed it. The good deed should leave a Jew with an enduring sense of devotion and attachment to Hashem. We should not only *perform* the commandments, but cherish, treasure and safeguard their essential teachings.

ד אִם־תְּבַקְשֶׁנָּה כַכָּסֶף וְכַמַּטְמוֹנִים תַּחְפְּשֶׂנָּה:
ה אָז תָּבִין יִרְאַת יהוה וְדַעַת אֱלֹהִים תִּמְצָא:

children with the best of everything, so those who follow Torah's ways are rewarded with the best of everything (*Bamidbar Rabbah* 10:9, see *Eitz Yosef*).

Based on this verse, the Talmud (*Berachos* 57a) states that one who sees his mother in a dream should expect to attain *binah*.[1]

Continuing with his delineation of the prerequisites for *chochmah*, R' Yonah explains the third condition, prayer: תִקְרָא, *call out*, and תִּתֵּן קוֹלֶךָ, *give forth your voice*, are both expressions of prayer. You must pray in order to gain *chochmah*. The model for such prayer is King David: גַּל עֵינַי וְאַבִּיטָה נִפְלָאוֹת מִתּוֹרָתֶךָ, *Unveil my eyes that I may perceive wonders from your Torah* (*Psalms* 119:18).[2]

In this verse, *tevunah* follows *binah*, and therefore means clearly comprehending *binah*; i.e., not only being able to deduce one thing from another, but also to understand how this new teaching was derived from the original *chochmah* (*Vilna Gaon*).

4. אִם־תְּבַקְשֶׁנָּה כַכָּסֶף — *If you seek it as [you seek] money* [lit., silver]. According to R' Yonah, this is the fourth prerequisite for *chochmah*: Just as a person labors hard to earn money, so one must put effort and toil into the pursuit of *chochmah*.

Our Sages emphasize this point. R' Nehorai advises that one must exile himself to a place where Torah can be found (*Avos* 4:13). Reish Lakish warns that if a person does not pursue the words of Torah, they will not come to him. The comparison of Torah to money teaches us how necessary it is to guard one's Torah knowledge. Just as one makes a special effort to safeguard his money, so must he take care lest he lose his Torah knowledge. *Chochmah* is as hard to acquire as gold, but is equally as fragile as glass (*Yalkut Shimoni*).[3]

1. Our Sages teach that בִּינָה יְתֵרָה, *an extra measure of binah*, was given to woman, beyond that given to man (*Niddah* 45b); thus, the connection between a mother and *binah* (*Chevel Nachalah*). [This may also be understood as follows: *Binah* is having one idea give birth to another; hence the connection to "mother."]

2. The *Netziv* (R' Naftali Zvi Yehudah Berlin) once told R' Isser Zalman Meltzer that only on a day when he shed tears while reciting the prayer אַהֲבָה רַבָּה (the blessing for Torah knowledge, which precedes the morning *Shema*) did he feel that the wellsprings of *chochmah* were open to him.

The Maggid of Kozhnitz would always encourage people to study Torah directly after prayer. For, after asking the Almighty to "Endow us graciously from Yourself with wisdom, insight and discernment" (*Amidah*), we will see that we are now able to understand that which was previously unclear.

3. Elaborating on this metaphor, the *Chafetz Chaim* offers several examples to show how a person's attitude towards earning money should carry over to his pursuit of Torah knowledge. He explains that in earning his livelihood, a person is deterred neither by cold weather nor by late hours; he knows that some sacrifice is demanded of him in order to provide for his physical needs. How much more so, then, should he be willing to toil and sacrifice in order to provide for his spiritual needs. One's approach to Torah and *mitzvos* should reflect this attitude. And just as one always strives to improve his financial status, so should he never be complacent about his spiritual level. He should always try to advance in Torah knowledge and fear of Hashem. [Cf. אֹהֵב כֶּסֶף לֹא יִשְׂבַּע כֶּסֶף, *A lover of money will never be satisfied with money* (*Ecclesiastes* 5:9), which *Rashi* (ad loc.) applies to the love of *mitzvos*.]

A person who earns his living as a storekeeper knows that he will not realize a large profit from every customer; nevertheless, he cheerfully serves all who enter his store. An occasional loss does not induce him to abandon his business entirely. He is ready to travel if he must in pursuit of his livelihood. He is even prepared to suffer disgrace and embarrassment so that his venture will yield a profit.

The same sentiment should prevail in spiritual matters. If a person finds that performing a

⁴ *if you seek it as [you seek] money, and search for it [as you search for] hidden treasures. ⁵ Then you will understand the fear of HASHEM, and discover the knowledge of God.*

וְכַמַּטְמוֹנִים תַּחְפְּשֶׂנָה — *And search for it [as you search for] hidden treasures.* This is *R' Yonah's* fifth prerequisite for *chochmah.* A person must enjoy the quest for Torah just as he enjoys digging for a treasure that he knows will yield him instant wealth. He would pursue it eagerly, knowing that a great fortune awaits him. So, too, if one loves *chochmah,* he will not find its study burdensome. The more pleasant a person finds his toil in Torah, the more he will succeed in understanding and remembering its teachings. As King David said: שָׂשׂ אָנֹכִי עַל אִמְרָתֶךָ כְּמוֹצֵא שָׁלָל רָב, *I rejoice over Your word like one who finds abundant spoils* (Psalms 119:162). Success in Torah study is directly related to desire and eagerness to attain it.[1]

For this reason, the morning blessings of Torah study include the prayer *Please [Hashem] sweeten the words of Torah.* One can fulfill the *mitzvah* of *lulav* without enjoyment, but Torah *chochmah* is unattainable without enjoyment. Indeed, love of learning is an integral part of the commandment to study Torah (see Introduction to *Eglei Tal).*

5. אָז תָּבִין יִרְאַת ה' וְדַעַת אֱלֹהִים תִּמְצָא — *Then you will understand the fear of HASHEM, and discover the knowledge of God. Rashi* sees this verse as a continuation of verse 3: if you call out to *understanding,* then you will understand the fear of Hashem.

R' Moshe Chaim Luzzatto, stressing the necessity of toiling to acquire the fear of Hashem, quotes verses 4 and 5 of this chapter. He points out that Solomon does not say that seeking and searching will help one understand philosophy, medicine, laws, etc. Rather, *then you will understand the fear of HASHEM.* Unless one invests much effort and contemplation, he cannot succeed in his quest of true fear of God (preface to *Mesilas Yesharim).*

R' Yonah explains that this verse comes directly after the enumeration of the steps through which a person can attain *chochmah* (vs. 2-4), and speaks of the benefits derived from that accomplishment. In other fields of study, the primary benefit attained is honor and intellectual accomplishment. *Chochmah,* however, yields יִרְאַת ה', *the fear of God,* as its primary benefit; as our Sages state, אֵין לְהקב"ה בְּעוֹלָמוֹ אֶלָּא יִרְאַת ה' בִּלְבַד, *all that the Holy*

commandment involves difficulty, if he seems to suffer a loss from being generous, if he must leave home to study Torah, if he is the object of derision for his eagerness to advance spiritually, let him not be deterred. Financial success is highly unpredictable, but when one strives to acquire Torah knowledge, his efforts are guaranteed to succeed and bring him everlasting rewards.

1. To further illustrate this metaphor, the *Chafetz Chaim* tells of a rich man who was about to die. He called his children to his bedside and revealed to them that he had hidden 20,000 rubles at the foot of a certain mountain, in ten sacks of 2,000 coins each. After giving his sons the exact details of their location, he beseeched them to retrieve the money after his death and divide it among themselves so that his lifelong labors should not have been in vain.

When the father died, the sons rushed to the designated spot and began to search. They searched for several hours but found nothing. Yet they still continued to search, certain that a fortune was buried there.

After much toil, the sons succeeded in finding nine of the ten sacks. Despite the riches they had already attained, they certainly continue their search. Only a fool would walk away and leave the rest of the fortune buried in the earth.

In spiritual matters, the same attitude should prevail. Every Jew knows that his personal portion in Torah was given to him at Mount Sinai. He only needs to expend the effort to retrieve his treasure. That is why the Sages say: אִם יֹאמַר לְךָ אָדָם יָגַעְתִּי וְלֹא מָצָאתִי אַל תַּאֲמֵן, *if someone says to you, I have toiled but have not found, do not believe [him]* (Megillah 6b). Each person's portion of Torah is already present in this world. If he has not yet found it, it can only be attributed to his lack of effort. And even one who spends much of his time in the rewarding pursuit of Torah would be foolish not to spend additional time and have even more opportunities to uncover the endless wealth of Torah knowledge.

ו כִּי־יהוה יִתֵּן חָכְמָה מִפִּיו דַּעַת וּתְבוּנָה:
ז °וצפן לַיְשָׁרִים תּוּשִׁיָּה מָגֵן לְהֹלְכֵי תְם:
ח לִנְצֹר אָרְחוֹת מִשְׁפָּט וְדֶרֶךְ °חסידו יִשְׁמֹר:

°יִצְפֹּן ק'

°חֲסִידָיו ק'

One, Blessed is He, has in His world is fear of God (Shabbos 31b).

Verse 1:7 states that fear of God is the beginning of knowledge. The *mishnah* reiterates this point, stating, אִם אֵין יִרְאָה אֵין חָכְמָה, *If there is no fear [of God] there is no chochmah* (*Avos* 3:21). Since the *chochmah* of the Torah may be inimical to man's nature and it cannot be proven by rational means, only fear of God can enable a person to accept and absorb it. Concurrently, however, the prerequisite for acquiring fear of Hashem is *chochmah*, as the same *mishnah* states: אִם אֵין חָכְמָה אֵין יִרְאָה, *if there is no chochmah there is no fear [of God]* (ibid.). The only way a person can understand the majesty of God and thereby learn to fear Him is through studying His Torah, which reveals the infinite power of the Creator and Master of the universe. Through the pursuit of *chochmah* a person will come *to understand* [תָּבִין] the fear of Hashem; and fear of Hashem will lead him to greater levels of *chochmah*, until he attains דַּעַת אֱלֹקִים, *knowledge of God*, meaning the esoteric levels of spiritual knowledge, such as מַעֲשֵׂה בְּרֵאשִׁית, *the process of Creation*, and מַעֲשֵׂה מֶרְכָּבָה, *the process of the Heavenly Chariot*, i.e, the celestial spiritual realms. Thus, wisdom and fear of God work in tandem; each one propels the person to greater levels of the other (*Malbim*)

Even after much toil and effort, success in attaining *the knowledge of God* is dependent on Hashem's will. Your efforts are necessary, but ultimately success is a Heavenly gift, a *discovery*. Only if God wills it will you gain this knowledge (*Kiflayim L'sushiah*).[1]

6. כִּי־ה' יִתֵּן חָכְמָה מִפִּיו דַּעַת וּתְבוּנָה — *For HASHEM will grant wisdom; from His mouth are knowledge and discernment.* The very fact that *chochmah* is God given indicates its great value — a compelling reason why you should seek to acquire it (*Rashi*).

[*Chochmah* always refers to Divinely inspired wisdom (see 1:2). Thus, this verse stresses that God gives it.]

Hashem will reveal the hidden secrets of Torah to you; therefore, it is as if it emanates from His mouth (*Metzudos*).

The Talmud (*Niddah* 70b) quotes a question the people of Alexandria put to R' Yehoshua ben Chananya: What should a person do in order to acquire *chochmah*? R' Yehoshua advised them to devote much time to Torah study and minimize their business activities. They responded that many people have followed this advice and have not yet succeeded in attaining *chochmah*. R' Yehoshua then instructed them, "Ask for mercy from the Source of *chochmah*, as this verse states, כִּי־ה' יִתֵּן חָכְמָה, *For HASHEM will grant chochmah*, מִפִּיו דַּעַת וּתְבוּנָה, *from His mouth are knowledge and discernment.*"

Malbim comments that only after an intellectual struggle does a person arrive at his conclusions, and despite his effort, these conclusions may be faulty. But if a person is meritorious, he will receive true knowledge and understanding מִפִּיו, *from [God's] mouth*; then he can be assured that they are free of doubt or error.

Yalkut Shimoni uses a parable to point out the superiority of *daas* (knowledge) and *tevunah* (discernment) to *chochmah*. A king's son came home from school feeling very hungry. The king offered

1. Rabbi Isser Zalman Meltzer stressed this point, explaining that a person who finds something would not be foolish enough to claim, "I deserved this find." So, too, a person who invested toil and effort in his Torah study and succeeded in deriving an original Torah thought from his studies should realize that this is really a Divine gift, which far surpasses the amount of human effort invested in obtaining it.

⁶ *For HASHEM will grant wisdom; from His mouth are knowledge and discernment.* ⁷ *He will secure the eternal Torah for the upright; it is a shield for those who walk in innocence,* ⁸ *to safeguard the paths of justice, and He will protect the way of His devout ones.*

him some food from a pot. "No, Father, I want food only from your mouth." As an expression of his love, the king acceded to his son's request and gave him food directly from his mouth. Likewise, Hashem provides *chochmah*, but *daas* and *tevunah* come directly from His mouth. [See *Maharal, Nesiv HaTorah* 14 for elucidation of the *Midrash*.]

7. יִצְפֹּן לַיְשָׁרִים תּוּשִׁיָּה — *He will secure the eternal Torah for the upright.* The commentators offer several explanations as to why Torah is called תּוּשִׁיָּה. The word is related to the word יֵשׁ, *existent*, for Torah is everlasting (*Ibn Ezra*), and does not revert to nothingness, as do all other worldly things (*Metzudos*). R' Yonah relates the word to אֲשִׁיּוֹתֶיהָ, *its foundations* (*Jeremiah* 50:15), for the Torah is the foundation of the world. Our Sages [*Sanhedrin* 26b] offer a different explanation. They relate תּוּשִׁיָּה to מַתֶּשֶׁת, *weakening*. Torah physically weakens the strength of those who study it (*Metzudos*).[1]

Rashi explains the verse as follows: Hashem kept the Torah hidden with Him for twenty-six generations, until it was given to דּוֹר הַמִּדְבָּר, *the Generation of the Wilderness*, who are referred to here as *the upright*. Once revealed, the Torah serves as a shield [for those who observe it].

According to *Metzudos*, this verse refers to the secrets of Torah. They are kept hidden by God to be revealed only to those who are deserving.

מָגֵן לְהֹלְכֵי תֹם — *It is a shield for those who walk in innocence.* The Vilna Gaon explains the difference between the *upright* and the *innocent*. An upright person weighs all points of view, right and wrong alike, and after careful deliberation chooses the proper course. He will never stumble, for he acts with forethought, assessing every action carefully — but he needs Torah [תּוּשִׁיָּה] to provide him with proper guidance and to direct him on the right path, by weakening his desires and negative character traits. An innocent person single-mindedly follows the course set by the Torah. He refuses to give thought to alternative courses of deed or thought for he does not rely on his own intelligence. However, such a person can sometimes be misled unwittingly. Therefore, this verse promises that the Torah will be his shield and protect him from stumbling.

8. לִנְצֹר אָרְחוֹת מִשְׁפָּט וְדֶרֶךְ חֲסִידָיו יִשְׁמֹר — *To safeguard the paths of justice, and He will protect the way of His devout ones.* Through Torah, a person keeps the paths of justice. God, in turn, will protect the

1. This seems to indicate that *chochmah* may have a harmful effect on man, contradicting many verses of Torah and teachings of the Sages that promise physical benefit to those who devote themselves to Torah study. [See for example, וּלְכָל בְּשָׂרוֹ מַרְפֵּא, *a healing for all his flesh* (4:22).]

The Talmud (*Beitzah* 25b) states that the Torah was given to the Jewish people because they are עַזִּין, *bold* or *brazen*. *Rashi* comments that involvement in Torah study will weaken and subdue their brazenness. Such weakening is advantageous to the nation.

Rabbi Yechezkel Levenstein points out that certain physical strengths and character traits can be detrimental to the fulfillment of Torah commandments. These are the forces that are weakened by Torah observance. Thus, "weakening" is really a benefit to the individual who adheres to the Torah. A clear example of this is seen in the case of Reish Lakish. The Talmud (*Bava Metzia* 84a) recounts that R' Yochanan saw Reish Lakish, a bandit chieftain, spring across the Jordan in one jump. R' Yochanan promptly declared, "Let your strength be dedicated to Torah study!" As soon as Reish Lakish agreed, he was unable to jump back over the river. Once he had committed himself to a Torah life, his physical strength immediately waned (*Rashi*, ibid.) (see also 8:14).

טי אָז תָּבִין צֶדֶק וּמִשְׁפָּט וּמֵישָׁרִים כָּל־מַעְגַּל־טוֹב: כִּי־
יא תָבוֹא חָכְמָה בְלִבֶּךָ וְדַעַת לְנַפְשְׁךָ יִנְעָם: מְזִמָּה תִּשְׁמֹר
יב עָלֶיךָ תְּבוּנָה תִנְצְרֶכָּה: לְהַצִּילְךָ מִדֶּרֶךְ רָע מֵאִישׁ
יג מְדַבֵּר תַּהְפֻּכוֹת: הַעֹזְבִים אָרְחוֹת יֹשֶׁר לָלֶכֶת בְּדַרְכֵי־
יד חֹשֶׁךְ: הַשְּׂמֵחִים לַעֲשׂוֹת רָע יָגִילוּ בְּתַהְפֻּכוֹת רָע:

paths of the devout, so that they will not stumble (*Rashi*).

The *Vilna Gaon* explains that the two halves of the verse refer to those who study Torah and to those who fulfill *mitzvos* respectively. The word דֶּרֶךְ implies a *main, wide road*, whereas אֹרַח is a *small path*. מִשְׁפָּט, *justice*, refers to the study of Torah. Since few people devote themselves exclusively to Torah study, the verse refers to the *small path* of such study. Most people, however, even those not well versed in Torah knowledge, perform commandments, which the verse refers to as a *road*. To *safeguard* connotes a stronger form of care and defense than *to protect*. This stronger protection is afforded to those who study Torah, for they have a more powerful Evil Inclination. Our Sages state, וּבְתַלְמִידֵי חֲכָמִים יוֹתֵר מִכֻּלָּם, that the Evil Inclination *incites Torah scholars more than all others* (*Succah* 52a).

9. אָז תָּבִין צֶדֶק וּמִשְׁפָּט וּמֵישָׁרִים — *Then you will understand righteousness, and justice and fairness.* As a result of your search for *chochmah*, Hashem will help you develop a sense of what is right, just and equitable and the ability to discern the best course to choose (*Metzudos*). [For the definitions of צֶדֶק, מִשְׁפָּט, וּמֵישָׁרִים see 1:3.] As *Bartenura* comments on *Avos* 1:1, ethical values and judgment are rooted in the Torah and are not "situational."

כָּל־מַעְגַּל־טוֹב — *Every good course.* A מַעְגָּל is *a circuitous path*, for sometimes a person must detour from the main, straight road. Arrogance, cruelty and pride are generally negative qualities, but our Sages recommend resorting to them occasionally, when indicated for positive purposes, such as when dealing with the wicked. In this way they can be used positively, as a means to reach the correct path (*Malbim*).

10. כִּי־תָבוֹא חָכְמָה בְלִבֶּךָ — *When wisdom enters your heart.* With Divine assistance, a person may achieve a level where *wisdom* becomes second nature to him, to such an extent that his Evil Inclination will no longer battle with him, for all his illicit desires and bad character traits have been subdued. Such a person has wisdom in his heart; he will no longer suffer from inner strife and turmoil [cf. 10:8.] (*Malbim*).

וְדַעַת לְנַפְשְׁךָ יִנְעָם — *And knowledge will be pleasant to your soul*, i.e., your soul will long for *knowledge*, just as one longs for something pleasurable (*Metzudos*).

11. מְזִמָּה תִּשְׁמֹר עָלֶיךָ תְּבוּנָה תִנְצְרֶכָּה — *[A wise] design will protect you; discernment will safeguard you.* The Torah will watch over you (*Rashi*).

מְזִמָּה is *thoughts of Torah.* The word זִמָּה, as used in Torah, means *thoughts of immorality* (see *Leviticus* 18:17). It is the thoughts of Torah — מְזִמָּה — that will save a person from sinful thoughts (*Vilna Gaon*).

Verses 12-15 mention three areas wherein *chochmah* will save an individual from mishap. (1) Character traits; (2) deeds; and (3) Torah study. Verse 12-13 speak of a דֶּרֶךְ רָע, *the way of evil*, which refers to bad *character* traits. Verse 14 refers to those who do bad deeds. Verse 15 addresses crookedness in Torah study (*Vilna Gaon*).

12. לְהַצִּילְךָ מִדֶּרֶךְ רָע מֵאִישׁ מְדַבֵּר תַּהְפֻּכוֹת — *To rescue you from the way of evil, from a person who speaks duplicities.* The evil way is the way of מִינוּת, *heresy.* The person who speaks תַּהְפֻּכוֹת, *duplicities*, inverts [מְהַפֵּךְ] the words of Torah to comform to his own faulty understanding (*Metzudos*).

The *Vilna Gaon* differentiates between an evil way and being duplicitous: *An evil way* refers to those who are obviously evil in both word and intention. Those who

⁹ *Then you will understand righteousness, and justice and fairness, every good course.* ¹⁰ *When wisdom enters your heart and knowledge will be pleasant to your soul.* ¹¹ *[A wise] design will protect you; discernment will safeguard you —* ¹² *to rescue you from the way of evil, from a person who speaks duplicities,* ¹³ *[from those] who forsake paths of uprightness to walk in roads of darkness,* ¹⁴ *who are glad to do evil, who rejoice in the duplicities of evil,*

speak duplicities say the opposite of what they are actually thinking, i.e., they pay lip service to their friends' welfare, but harbor evil in their hearts.

Malbim explains this verse differently and connects the two phrases in the previous verse to this one. *A wise design* defends a person and protects him *from the way of evil.* He will thus be saved from the enticements of the Evil Inclination by the *wisdom* in his heart. *Discernment* will protect him *from someone who speaks duplicities* about faith in Hashem, denying basic tenets of faith with contrary, false and misleading calculations, because the discernment gained from Torah study provides one with the correct response to such heretics. (See *Avos* 2:19, וְדַע מַה שֶׁתָּשִׁיב לְאֶפִּיקוֹרוֹס, *and know what to answer a heretic.*) One can easily fall prey to heretical influences, and the consequences can be even more damaging than following evil temptations. Therefore, when referring to the danger of heresy, the verse states תְּבוּנָה תִנְצְרֶכָּה, *discernment will safegaurd you,* for *to safeguard* is a more forceful verb than לִשְׁמֹר, *to protect.*

The Midrash applies the appellation *a person who speaks duplicities* to Pharaoh. When he was afflicted with the Ten Plagues, he would summon Moses and promise to free the Jews, if only the plague were stopped. As soon as Moses prayed and brought an end to the plague, Pharaoh would renege on his promise and deny knowing Hashem (*Yalkut Shimoni*).

13. הַעֹזְבִים אָרְחוֹת יֹשֶׁר לָלֶכֶת בְּדַרְכֵי־חֹשֶׁךְ — *[From those] who forsake paths of up-*

rightness *to walk in roads of darkness,* i.e., those who leave the path of Torah and follow the ways of heresy (*Metzudos*).

In a comment similar to his teaching on v. 8, the *Vilna Gaon* explains that since there are only a small number of righteous people, their way is termed אֹרַח, *a small narrow path.*[1] As evildoers abound, their way is termed דֶּרֶךְ, *a wide, well-traveled road.*

14. הַשְּׂמֵחִים לַעֲשׂוֹת רָע — *Who are glad to do evil.* A person who believes in Divine reward and punishment feels remorse if he succumbs to the persuasions of his Evil Inclination, because he still fears Divine retribution. However, the happiness of wicked sinners is not diminished by remorse, for they do not believe in Divine retribution (*Metzudos*).

יָגִילוּ בְּתַהְפֻּכוֹת רָע — *Who rejoice in the duplicities of evil.* They are delighted when they can distort things according to their evil intentions (*Metzudos*).

Ibn Ezra and *Ralbag* explain רָע as *an evildoer* — i.e., sinners rejoice in the perversities of an evildoer.

The *Vilna Gaon* explains this verse as a continuing description of two types of evildoers mentioned in verse 12. Those who are evil both in heart and word are happy when doing wicked deeds [הַשְּׂמֵחִים לַעֲשׂוֹת רָע]. Those who utter sweet words when they actually harbor evil thoughts in their hearts will be rejoice [וְיָגִילוּ] when their duplicitous talk causes harm. The *Gaon* differentiates between the terms שִׂמְחָה [simchah] and גִילָה [gilah]. Simchah refers to the joy sparked by something new.

1. *Rashi* (Bereishis 2:4) explains that the World to Come was created with the letter yud — "י," — the smallest of all the letters, hinting that the number of righteous will be very small. This sentiment echoes R' Shimon Bar Yochai's statement "I've seen those who have attained spiritual heights — they are few" (*Succah* 45b).

טו אֲשֶׁר אָרְחֹתֵיהֶם עִקְּשִׁים וּנְלוֹזִים בְּמַעְגְּלוֹתָם:
טז לְהַצִּילְךָ מֵאִשָּׁה זָרָה מִנָּכְרִיָּה אֲמָרֶיהָ הֶחֱלִיקָה:
יז הַעֹזֶבֶת אַלּוּף נְעוּרֶיהָ וְאֶת־בְּרִית אֱלֹהֶיהָ שָׁכֵחָה:
יח כִּי שָׁחָה אֶל־מָוֶת בֵּיתָהּ וְאֶל־רְפָאִים מַעְגְּלֹתֶיהָ:
יט כָּל־בָּאֶיהָ לֹא יְשׁוּבוּן וְלֹא־יַשִּׂיגוּ אָרְחוֹת חַיִּים:
כ לְמַעַן תֵּלֵךְ בְּדֶרֶךְ טוֹבִים וְאָרְחוֹת צַדִּיקִים תִּשְׁמֹר:

Gilah refers to the happiness evoked by something already present which recurs constantly. The wicked person will feel *simchah* when he commits a new evil, for the deed is new to him. However, one who masks his evil intentions with sweet words will feel *gilah* when his wicked plans materialize, for the evil is not new; it was in his heart earlier and is only now reaching his desired conclusion.

15. אֲשֶׁר אָרְחֹתֵיהֶם עִקְּשִׁים — *Whose ways are crooked.* Their Torah study lacks clarity and straightforwardness (*Metzudos*).

וּנְלוֹזִים בְּמַעְגְּלוֹתָם — *And who are perverse in their courses*, i.e., crooked in their corrupt ways (*Rashi*).

A wise traveler may take a מַעְגָּל, *circuitous course*, in order to avoid danger, such as robbers, but eventually he will return to the main road and reach his destination. Similarly, spiritual perfection sometimes demands that one diverge from what is ordinarily the righteous course. For example, though cruelty is a negative trait, it can be foolhardy and dangerous to show mercy to the wicked. [An example of this is King Saul, who lost his kingdom for being "merciful" towards Amalek (see *I Samuel* 15).] Similarly, one must be brazen with those who mock the service of God. Such a detour will actually enable a person to return to the straight road (see v. 10). Our verse, however, speaks of sinners who follow a circuitous course away from the right path, leading them totally astray (*Malbim*).

16. לְהַצִּילְךָ מֵאִשָּׁה זָרָה מִנָּכְרִיָּה אֲמָרֶיהָ הֶחֱלִיקָה — *To rescue you from a strange woman, from the foreign woman, whose words are glib* [lit. *who makes her words glib*]. The

strange woman is a married Jewess; the *foreign woman* is not Jewish. Both are forbidden. Metaphorically the *strange woman* refers to the sin of חֶמְדָה, *coveting*, and the *foreign woman* to the sin of תַּאֲוָה, *lust* (*Vilna Gaon*).

Rashi interprets the metaphor to refer to the dangers of idolatry or heresy. This verse cannot be understood only literally, i.e., as referring exclusively to forbidden women, for it would be demeaning to suggest that the Torah's protection is limited to these sins alone. Hence, it must mean that Torah protects a person from heresy, a sin which is tantamount to casting off all the *mitzvos*.

17. הַעֹזֶבֶת אַלּוּף נְעוּרֶיהָ וְאֶת־בְּרִית אֱלֹהֶיהָ שָׁכֵחָה — *Who forsakes the husband* [lit. *master*] *of her youth and forgets the covenant of her God.* The covenant refers to a woman's obligation to keep God's commandments and not betray her husband (*Metzudos*).

God inserts His Holy Name in the partnership of man and woman — the letter *yud* of God's name is in אִישׁ, *man*, and the letter *hei* is in אִשָּׁה, *woman*. Once [loyalty to] His Name is, God forbid, removed from them, then only *aleph* and *shin* — אֵשׁ, *fire* — remain between them and consume them (*Ibn Ezra*).

According to the *Vilna Gaon*, the verse speaks metaphorically about those who leave the Torah to pursue their desires and lusts. אַלּוּף נְעוּרֶיהָ refers to the Torah, as the word אַלּוּף is related to the word וַאֲאַלֶּפְךָ, *I will teach you* (see *Job* 33:33).

18. כִּי שָׁחָה אֶל־מָוֶת בֵּיתָהּ וְאֶל־רְפָאִים מַעְגְּלֹתֶיהָ — *For her house declines toward death and her courses toward the lifeless.* According to *Metzudos*, רְפָאִים means

¹⁵ *whose ways are crooked and who are perverse in their courses;* ¹⁶ *to rescue you from a strange woman, from the foreign woman, whose words are glib,* ¹⁷ *who forsakes the husband of her youth and forgets the covenant of her God,* ¹⁸ *for her house declines toward death, and her course toward the lifeless.* ¹⁹ *All who come to her do not return, nor do they attain the paths of life.* ²⁰ *In order that you may walk in the way of the good and keep the paths of the righteous.*

those who are weak; here it refers to the dead, who have lost all strength. One who goes to the house of the forbidden woman will end up losing his life.

Rashi connects this verse to verse 16. A man who goes to her house will find himself on an incline sliding down toward death. Only the Torah can save you from this drastic fall; thus, the Torah will benefit You greatly. רְפָאִים are people who are negligent about proper conduct, and therefore are left without support, eventually falling into *Gehinnom*.

19. כָּל־בָּאֶיהָ לֹא יְשׁוּבוּן וְלֹא יַשִּׂיגוּ אָרְחוֹת חַיִּים — *All who come to her do not return, nor do they attain the paths of life.* Heresy is like a forbidden woman. Once one becomes involved in it, it is extremely difficult to detach oneself and repent (*Rashi, Metzudos*).[1]

Malbim explains that לֹא יְשׁוּבוּן can mean either *will not return,* or *will not repent* (from the word תְּשׁוּבָה, *repentance*). Once a person becomes involved in heresy, he will find it very hard to fully repent, and even if

he does attempt repentance, he may not regain the path of life, because remnants of his earlier ideas will cling to him. Heretical thoughts act like שְׂאוֹר שֶׁבְּעִיסָה, a leavening agent in dough, constantly affecting a person's mind, making it almost impossible for him to regain true faith in God.

20. לְמַעַן תֵּלֵךְ בְּדֶרֶךְ טוֹבִים וְאָרְחוֹת צַדִּיקִים תִּשְׁמֹר — *In order that you may walk in the way of the good and keep the paths of the righteous.* Rashi sees this verse as the continuation of verse 12: *Chochmah* will save you from the evil way in order to lead you onto the proper road.

The *Vilna Gaon* explains the difference between the two parts of this verse. *Good people* are those who do not do bad to another person, even when it is sanctioned by Torah law. *The righteous* are those who maintain an even higher level of good — they act charitably even to undeserving people. Since only rare individuals attain this level, their way is referred to as an אֹרַח, *a narrow path,* traversed only by the select few.[2]

1. The Sages say about the powerful sway of heresy, שָׁאנִי מִינוּת דְּמָשְׁכִי, *heresy differs in that it attracts,* i.e., heresy envelops its followers and one must be exceedingly careful not to be drawn after it (*Avodah Zarah* 27b).

2. The Talmud (*Bava Metzia* 83a) relates an incident that illustrates this awesome degree of righteousness:

Rabbah bar Bar Chanah once hired workers to transport a barrel of wine, and they broke it. He took their cloaks as collateral for the damages they owed him. When the workers complained to Rav, he ordered Rabbah bar Bar Chanah to return the cloaks. Rabbah asked Rav if this was the law [for he knew that he was entitled to be reimbursed for his loss]. Rav responded by quoting our verse, לְמַעַן תֵּלֵךְ בְּדֶרֶךְ טוֹבִים, *in order that you may walk in the way of the good —* in other words, return it to them because one should do more than the letter of the law demands [לִפְנִים מִשּׁוּרַת הַדִּין] (*Rashi*).

When Rabbah returned the clothes to the workers, they were still unhappy. They said that they were very poor and had worked the whole day and were now hungry. When Rav ordered Rabbah bar Bar Chanah to pay their wages, he once again asked Rav if this was the law. Rav answered by quoting the second half of the verse, וְאָרְחוֹת צַדִּיקִים תִּשְׁמֹר, and [you should] keep the paths of the righteous.

[The Torah teaches וְעָשִׂיתָ הַיָּשָׁר וְהַטּוֹב, *You shall do what is fair and good* (Deuteronomy 6:18). The Sages understand this to mean one should do more than the strict requirements of the

ב/ כא-כב כִּי־יְשָׁרִים יִשְׁכְּנוּ־אָרֶץ וּתְמִימִים יִוָּתְרוּ בָהּ: וּרְשָׁעִים
כא-כב מֵאֶרֶץ יִכָּרֵתוּ וּבוֹגְדִים יִסְּחוּ מִמֶּנָּה:
ג/א-ג א-ב בְּנִי תּוֹרָתִי אַל־תִּשְׁכָּח וּמִצְוֺתַי יִצֹּר לִבֶּךָ: כִּי אֹרֶךְ יָמִים
ג וּשְׁנוֹת חַיִּים וְשָׁלוֹם יוֹסִיפוּ לָךְ: חֶסֶד וֶאֱמֶת אַל־יַעַזְבֻךָ

21. כִּי־יְשָׁרִים יִשְׁכְּנוּ־אָרֶץ וּתְמִימִים יִוָּתְרוּ בָהּ
— *For the upright will dwell [in the] land [forever], and wholehearted ones will remain in it.* The upright will dwell in the land forever, and *the wholehearted ones will remain in it* when the wicked are driven out (*Metzudos*).

Rashi explains that *upright ones will*

dwell in the land in the World to Come, while the wicked descend to *Gehinnom*.

22. וּרְשָׁעִים מֵאֶרֶץ יִכָּרֵתוּ וּבוֹגְדִים יִסְּחוּ מִמֶּנָּה
— *But the wicked will be cut off from the land, and the faithless uprooted from it.* The wicked will be cut off from the land, whereas the wholehearted ones will remain there (see previous verse) (*Meiri*).

III

1. בְּנִי תּוֹרָתִי אַל־תִּשְׁכָּח — *My child, do not forget My Torah.* Speaking in God's Name, King Solomon says: Israel, you are as dear to Me as a child is to a parent; therefore, I caution you not to forget My Torah (*Metzudos*).

וּמִצְוֺתַי יִצֹּר לִבֶּךָ — *And let your heart guard My commandments.* A Jew is obligated to study Torah at all times (see Joshua 1:8, וְהָגִיתָ בּוֹ יוֹמָם וָלַיְלָה, *You should contemplate it day and night*). Therefore, with reference to Torah study, the verse stipulates אַל־תִּשְׁכָּח, *do not forget* — at any time. Most commandments, however, can be performed only at specific times; therefore, the verse states יִצֹּר לִבֶּךָ, *let your heart guard* them until the time arrives to perform them (cf. 2:1). *My commandments* is in the plural, because it refers to both positive and negative commandments (*Vilna Gaon*).

2. כִּי אֹרֶךְ יָמִים וּשְׁנוֹת חַיִּים וְשָׁלוֹם יוֹסִיפוּ לָךְ
— *For they add to you length of days and years of life and peace.* My Torah and My commandments will add these to you

(*Rashi*) for they will defend you and mention your merits (*Metzudos*). *Length of days* refers to the number of years; *years of life* refers to the quality of life — i.e., years of tranquility and peace (*Metzudos*), years of health and good (*Rabbeinu Yonah*).[1]

Length of days, and years of life and *peace* are the rewards that correspond to the items mentioned in the previous verse: *Torah* and *commandments*, positive and negative. *Length of days* is the reward for heeding positive commandments, as the Torah states: אֲשֶׁר יַעֲשֶׂה אֹתָם הָאָדָם וָחַי בָּהֶם, *which man shall carry out and by which he shall live* (*Leviticus 18:5*). *Years of life* results from heeding the negative commandments. Sin brings Heavenly retribution. Scrupulous behavior regarding the negative commandments or repentance for misdeeds changes the quality of one's life from bad to good, for the prosecuting angels now turn into his friends. *Peace* is a result of Torah study, as verse 17 states: וְכָל נְתִיבֹתֶיהָ שָׁלוֹם, *and all its* [i.e., Torah's] *byways are peace.* Just as Torah study is

law.] The *Vilna Gaon* explains: When Rabbah bar Bar Chanah surrendered the workers' cloaks, he was *walking in the way of the good* for he was forgiving the damage, even though halachically, the workers were liable to pay for it. When Rabbah paid them their wages, he was keeping *the paths of the righteous*, for he gave them his money even though halachically they owed him money

Rav said that this ruling applied only to a man of Rabbah bar Bar Chanah's stature. [See *Rambam Hilchos Deios*, ch. 5 for the special code of behavior expected of Torah scholars.]

1. See *Yoma 71a*: "Are there years of life and years of non-life? R' Eliezer says this refers to those years that change from bad to good."

משלי [66]

2/21-22 [21] *For the upright will dwell [in the] land [forever], and whole-hearted ones will remain in it.* [22] *But the wicked will be cut off from land, and the faithless uprooted from it.*

3/1-3 [1] **M**y child, do not forget My Torah, and let your heart guard My commandments, [2] for they add to you length of days and years of life and peace. [3] Kindness and truth should not forsake

equivalent to all the *mitzvos* — (וְתַלְמוּד תּוֹרָה כְּנֶגֶד כֻּלָם, *and the study of Torah is equivalent to all of them (Peah 1:1)* — and is the harbinger of all good deeds (שֶׁהַלְמוּד מֵבִיא לִידֵי מַעֲשֶׂה, *learning Torah brings one to the performance of mitzvos — Megillah 27a)*, so too, its reward שָׁלוֹם, *peace*, includes all other blessings; as the Sages state: "God found no better receptacle of blessing for Israel than peace" (*Uktzin 3:12*) (*Vilna Gaon*).

3. חֶסֶד וֶאֱמֶת אַל־יַעַזְבֻךָ — *Kindness and truth should not forsake you*, i.e., do not let them forsake you; hold onto them (*Metzudos*).

King Solomon now starts to spell out the "spiritual prescription" needed to serve Hashem, beginning with the two virtues of kindness [*chessed*] and truth [*emes*]. *Chessed* includes many of the noble character traits, and *emes* includes the virtues of the intellect.

Chessed is characterized by the desire and effort to benefit and help others, whether monetarily or by physically exerting oneself on their behalf. It is the concrete expression of a desire to bring pleasure to others, seek their good and certainly avoid harming them, in deed or speech. *Chessed* proscribes such traits as cruelty, stinginess, hatred and jealousy.

Everyone, even a person of limited means, can easily perform acts of *chessed*. In addition to charity, *chessed* includes such kind deeds as visiting the sick, comforting mourners, speaking words of encouragement to the poor, helping the downtrodden and being the eyes of the blind and the feet of the lame. Even a person lacking wealth should yearn to relieve the plight of the impoverished. He should praise those who are able to give charity and help others, delight in their good deeds, and strengthen them in their efforts. He should never forgo involvement in *chessed*, whether physical, verbal, or emotional.[1]

Emes entails not calling what is bad, good, nor what is good, bad; not flattering others, but being zealous for the truth and rejoicing in the honor of the righteous and the downfall of the wicked. It includes judging others truthfully and avoiding favoritism, as well as scrutinizing trial witnesses carefully. In any dispute, one should seek to exonerate the righteous party and condemn the wicked. Should he be involved in a dispute and he realizes that truth is on the side of his opponent, *emes* demands that he admit he is wrong. *Emes* would proscribe believing slander, for its truth is suspect. *Emes* demands that a person reject all false theories, and study with intellectual honesty and in pursuit of truth. He should be constantly wary not to be led astray emotionally by false ideas and premises.

Emes is a trait so beloved and sought after by Hashem that a person should strive to be especially exacting about it, even beyond the literal demands of the law. For instance, when one strives for perfection in attaining fear of God, *emes*

1. *Acts of kindness* [גְּמִילוּת חֲסָדִים] are greater than charity [צְדָקָה] in three ways:
   (1) A person gives charity with his money, but he can perform kind deeds in any number of ways.
   (2) Charity can be given only to the poor, but kindness can be done for both the poor and the wealthy (i.e., monetary loans or lending of property, or ordinary helpfulness).
   (3) Charity can be given only to the living, but both the living and the dead can be the beneficiaries of kindness (*Succah* 49b).

ד קָשְׁרֵם עַל־גַּרְגְּרוֹתֶיךָ כָּתְבֵם עַל־לוּחַ לִבֶּךָ: וּמְצָא־
חֵן וְשֵׂכֶל־טוֹב בְּעֵינֵי אֱלֹהִים וְאָדָם:

would dictate that he not only fulfill his written and verbal commitments, but even those which he had only thought about in his heart (*R' Yonah*).[1]

The *Vilna Gaon* defines the terms *chessed* and *emes* differently, and he applies both to man's conduct towards his fellow man and his conduct toward God. In interpersonal relationships, any undeserved goodness bestowed upon others voluntarily is termed *chessed*.[2] *Emes*, conversely, is when someone acts nicely to his benefactor to reciprocate for the

chessed done to him. *Chessed* is distinguished by its quality rather than quantity, since it is done voluntarily; even if the extent or monetary value of the service is small, it is still an act of kindness, especially since there was no prior obligation to do it. *Emes*, on the other hand, should be commensurate with the kindness it reciprocates; its quantity is important. Therefore, our verse instructs: Do *chessed* even to those to whom you owe nothing, and do it in as great a quantity as if it were *emes*. In this manner, we

1. We find examples in the Talmud of the high standard of truth that is required of the devout. R' Oshiya (*Bava Basra* 88a, see *Rashi*) rules that once such a person selects vegetables from a seller, he is responsible to set aside tithes from the purchase, even though he has not yet made a *kinyan* [formal act of acquisition] and has the legal right to return it. This illustrates the higher standard of honesty expected of a God-fearing person.

Rav Safra exemplified this standard of *emes*, for he fulfilled the precept of וְדֹבֵר אֱמֶת בִּלְבָבוֹ, *and he speaks truth in his heart* (*Psalms* 15:2). Once, while he was reciting the *Shema*, a man approached with an offer to buy his merchandise for a specific price. When Rav Safra did not reply, the man assumed that the offer was too low. He kept raising his bid, finally offering a very hefty price. When Rav Safra finished praying, he addressed the buyer: "I will accept your initial low bid, for in my heart I had already agreed to sell it to you at that price!" (*Makkos* 24a, *Rashi*, ibid. See also *Shitah Mekubetzes*, *Kesubos* 18 on אנוסים היינו מחמת ממון.)

Such scrupulousness in the trait of *emes* in recent times is beautifully illustrated by the following two anecdotes.

Rabbi Yechezkel [Chatzkel] Levenstein, *Mashgiach* of the Ponevezh Yeshivah, was scheduled to speak at the *shloshim* memorial service for R' Isaac Sher. Before the eulogy was to be given, Rabbi Levenstein informed the organizers that he would be unable to speak. They protested that posters had already been put up announcing his participation, and the audience would expect to hear the *Mashgiach*. Against his will, he consented to speak, but in contrast to his usual tearful and moving eulogy, he was unemotional.

Afterwards, one of his students questioned his uncharacteristic lack of emotion. R' Chatzkel explained, "Last night I received the tragic news that my young grandson in America had passed away. I feared that if I were to cry when eulogizing R' Isaac Scher, those tears would stem from my own personal anguish at the loss of a grandchild, rather than at the passing of the *tzaddik*. Such tears would be שֶׁקֶר, *false!*" (Retold by a grandson).

R' Zelig Reuven Bengis, Rabbi of Yerushalayim, was among the leaders of the battle against the Israeli law drafting women into the army. The leading Torah authorities of the time composed a proclamation vehemently protesting the law. When the proclamation was brought to R' Reuven for his signature, he did not immediately sign it. First he studied its contents for a time and then became visibly upset and was moved to tears. Only then did he sign the document.

His apparent hesitation in signing puzzled the bystanders. Hadn't Rabbi Bengis himself been one of the leading opponents of this very bill? He explained that what concerned him were two words at the end of the document which stated הַחוֹתֵם בְּדֶמַע, *one who is signing tearfully*. That being the case, how could he truthfully sign this document unless he was actually moved to tears? (retold by Rabbi Avraham Pam).

2. *Rambam* (*Moreh Nevuchim* 3:53) defines *chessed* as going beyond established requirements; it is the ability to go beyond one's own parameters and reach out to others, in contrast to man's nature to be egotistical and selfish. For this reason one who goes more than the law demands is called a *chassid*.

emulate God, Who is described as וְרַב־חֶסֶד וֶאֱמֶת, *and abundant in kindness and truth* (*Exodus* 34:6), for even when He bestows undeserved good upon man [kindness], He bestows it abundantly. Moreover, when He rewards man's good [truth], He repays an even greater amount for if His *chessed* is abundant, how much more so is His *emes*! Man should do the same in his dealings with his fellows.

In man's conduct toward God, the concepts of *chessed* and *emes* apply to one's attitude toward Torah study: Does he learn only for himself, or does he accept the responsibility to teach others, as well? To dedicate oneself to Torah study is *emes*, because one is obligated to study the Torah to the full extent of his ability. But to go further and teach others is *chessed* (see *Succah* 49b).

קָשְׁרֵם עַל־גַּרְגְּרוֹתֶיךָ — *Bind them on your neck*, i.e., constantly speak and think of them (*Metzudos*).

When someone speaks constantly about *chessed* and *emes*, it will add splendor to him, like a garland around his neck. Continuous mention of these traits will remind one to be scrupulous in fulfilling them. Constant discussion of these traits will benefit others, as well, by providing instruction in proper behavior patterns, and by lending prestige to those who practice them. And by disparaging negative traits, one will deter his listeners from behaving that way (*R' Yonah*).

כָּתְבֵם עַל־לוּחַ לִבֶּךָ — *Inscribe them on the tablet of your heart*. Constantly concentrate your thoughts on these traits in order to devise ways of implementing them in action and deed (*R' Yonah*).

Alshich defines *chessed* as *acts of kindness* and *emes* as *the study of Torah*. He sees this verse as a continuation of the previous one: By pursuing Torah and kindness, one will merit not only a reward in the World to Come, but also longevity and good years in this world.

This point was illustrated in the lives of the Talmudic sages Abaye and Rava, who were descendants of the house of Eli, the High Priest in the Tabernacle at Shiloh. Because Eli's sons abused their offices as priests, God decreed various misfortunes upon their descendants (*I Samuel* 2:32-33). One such misfortune was that their male descendants would die young (see *Sanhedrin* 14a). Rava, who involved himself in Torah study, merited an additional twenty years of life; Abaye, who was deeply involved in acts of kindness in addition to his Torah study, was reprieved for forty extra years (see *Rosh Hashanah* 18a).

Another key to lengthening one's life is suggested by the words *bind them on your neck*, i.e., teach Torah to others and do so in public. One who does so will merit longevity even in this world, as we find with Rav Preida, who was rewarded with four hundred extra years of life for having reviewed his teachings four hundred times with a student who was very slow to grasp (*Eruvin* 54b).

In order for a person's Torah teachings to have the proper effect on his listeners, they must emanate from his heart. Words uttered externally by the mouth alone do not have the power to penetrate the listener's heart. Therefore, the verse instructs, כָּתְבֵם עַל־לוּחַ לִבֶּךָ, *inscribe them on the tablet of your heart*, i.e., Torah should be engraved deeply in your heart so that when you teach others it is as if you are reading the words of Torah from the inscription in your heart.

According to the *Vilna Gaon*, the three phrases of this verse refer to deed, speech and thought. In deed, do not forsake kindness and truth; *bind them on your neck* by verbalizing them; make them the constant preoccupation of your thoughts and emotions by *inscrib[ing] them on the tablet of your heart*.

4. וּמְצָא־חֵן וְשֵׂכֶל־טוֹב בְּעֵינֵי אֱלֹהִים וְאָדָם — *And you will find favor and goodly sense in the eyes of God and man*. A kind

ה בְּטַח אֶל־יהוה בְּכָל־לִבֶּךָ וְאֶל־בִּינָתְךָ אַל־
ו תִּשָּׁעֵן: בְּכָל־דְּרָכֶיךָ דָעֵהוּ וְהוּא יְיַשֵּׁר אֹרְחֹתֶיךָ:

person will find *favor* in the eyes of both God and people. Our Sages state that whoever is merciful to others is the recipient of Heavenly mercy (*Shabbos* 151b), and it is obvious that a person's acts of kindness endear him to people as well. One who practices truth will find *good sense* in the eyes of both God and man for, by vindicating the righteous and condemning the wicked, he displays sensible judgment, rather then misconceptions (*R' Yonah*).

The *Vilna Gaon* explains that חֵן, *favor*, is derived from the term חִנָּם, *undeserved*, because it need not be related to one's actions.[1] [That is why Scripture always speaks of "finding" favor, as in the phrase, אִם מָצָאתִי חֵן, *If I have found favor* (*Exodus* 32:12, *Numbers* 11:15, etc.).] He renders שֵׂכֶל as *success*, as in *David succeeded* [מַשְׂכִּיל] in all his ways (*I Samuel* 18:14). For *chessed*, an undeserved act of kindness, one will be rewarded with חֵן, *undeserved favor*. As a reward for *emes*, one will be granted success.

According to *Meiri*, וּמְצָא can be understood as a command: Behave in such a manner that you will find favor in the eyes of God and man, and will be considered sensible and wise.

The Sages (*Yerushalmi, Shekalim* 3:2) state that just as a person is obligated to make his actions pleasing in the eyes of Heaven, so, too, must his actions be pleasing in the eyes of people. This is inferred from the verse וִהְיִיתֶם נְקִיִּם מֵה' וּמִיִּשְׂרָאֵל, *and you shall be vindicated from Hashem and from Israel* (*Numbers* 32:22), as well as from this verse.

Therefore, the Kohen who was sent to the Temple chamber to bring coins to purchase animals for offerings was not permitted to wear the sort of clothing where he could be suspected of concealing money. If he were subsequently to become poor, people would assume that it was because he stole Temple funds; and if he were to become wealthy, people would say he got rich from the wealth of the Temple.

Thus, a person must be careful not to act in such a manner that people suspect that he is committing a sin, even though he is actually not sinning (*Kitzur Shulchan Aruch* 29:20).

The Sages praised the Garmo family for adhering to this principle. They were experts in baking the shewbread for the Temple. They never fed their children bread of fine flour, so that people should not suspect that they were eating shewbread. The Sages also praised the Avtinas family, who were experts in preparing the spices for the incense offering in the Temple. No bride in their family, daughters or daughters-in-law ever wore perfume, lest people exclaim, "Oh, they are perfuming themselves with the spices of the incense offering" (*Yoma* 38a).

This higher standard is expressed by *Rambam* (*Hilchos Yesodei HaTorah* 5:11): If a person, outstanding in Torah and recognized for his piety, acts in a manner that causes people to criticize his actions, even though he has not committed a sin, he has desecrated God's Name. This includes a Torah scholar who buys merchandise and does not pay for it immediately [in a place where credit transactions are not customary]; who engages in merrymaking with people ignorant in Torah; who does not speak pleasantly to others; who does not greet others with a smiling countenance; or who is argumentative and easily angered. Commensurate with the greatness of the individual is his obligation to see that his actions comply with standards even higher than those demanded by the letter of the law.

On the other hand, a Torah scholar who speaks pleasantly with others and who is well liked by people, who accepts insults without insulting others, who honors others, who conducts his business honestly, who is constantly seen engrossed in Torah study and who goes beyond the letter of the law, thus causing others to praise him, love him and be desirous of his good deeds,

1. This explanation is borne out by the Talmudic understanding of Hashem's formulation of forgiveness after the Sin of the Golden Calf, וְחַנֹּתִי אֶת אֲשֶׁר אָחֹן, *I shall show favor when I choose to show favor* (*Exodus* 33:19), even though the recipient is not worthy (*Berachos* 7a).

⁵ *Trust in* HASHEM *with all your heart and do not rely upon your own understanding.* ⁶ *In all your ways, know Him and He will smooth your paths.*

has sanctified Hashem's Name and is praised by the verse: *And He said to me, "You are My servant, Israel, in whom I take pride"* (Isaiah 49:3) (see also *Yoma* 86a).[1]

5. בְּטַח אֶל־ה' בְּכָל־לִבֶּךָ וְאֶל־בִּינָתְךָ אַל־תִּשָּׁעֵן — *Trust in Hashem with all your heart and do not rely upon your own understanding.*

Rashi applies this to the study of Torah. *Trust in Hashem*, and spend extravagantly in search of a teacher; do not depend exclusively on your own understanding.

This trait was personified by Hillel the Elder, who gave away half of his minimal daily wages for the privilege of entering the Torah study hall (*Yoma* 35b).

Metzudos renders: Do not assume, "I will certainly succeed, since I acted intelligently," for everything is in Hashem's hands, not in the hands of man's intelligence.

R' Yonah states: A person is obligated to trust in Hashem with his whole heart, fully and without reservation. Complete trust in Hashem precludes relying on others or on one's own strength, abilities, or intelligence. The verse specifies not relying on one's *binah*, for people are more prone to rely on their own understanding than on wealth or strength. Furthermore, reliance on wealth and strength is predicated on relying on one's understanding. A person will trust in the latter two only when

his intelligence indicates that they are reliable. Even when one's own sense and understanding clearly indicate that the action he has undertaken is certain to succeed according to his plans, even then, he should not rely on them, for ultimately, everything is dependent on the Will of Heaven. Thus, King Solomon teaches: *There are many thoughts in a man's heart, but it is* HASHEM's *plan that will stand* (19:21), and *The arrangements of the heart are man's, but the response of the tongue is from* HASHEM (16:1). If even the reply of one's tongue is not in his own hands, how much more so is one's actions!

The *Vilna Gaon* interprets אַל תִּשָּׁעֵן, *do not rely*, in the sense of מִשְׁעֶנֶת, *a crutch*. One may be tempted to rely on his intelligence as a supplement to his trust in God. Therefore, the verse teaches us: *Do not rely* [i.e., use as a crutch] *on your own binah*; put your full trust in HASHEM.

Ralbag points out that an attitude of self-reliance causes a person to forfeit the Divine assistance which he would normally receive. Hashem's will is that man be cognizant of Divine Providence. One who relies on his own intelligence, however, indicates his own feeling that Divine assistance is unnecessary.

R' Bachya ibn Paquda (*Chovos HaLevavos, Shaar HaBitachon* 7) lists ten progressive levels of human trust:

(1) A newborn infant trusts in his mother's breasts, for they are his sustenance and lifeline.

1. The author once visited R' Moshe Feinstein, and the Rebbetzin served tea. When the visit was over and R' Moshe accompanied the guests to the door, he remarked, "The tea was hot. I drank it too slowly to be obligated to recite the blessing following food." Lest his guests suspect that he was negligent regarding the blessing, the leading Torah sage of the generation felt obligated to explain why he had not recited it.

R' Naftali Porush was the moving force behind the construction of the Shaarei Chessed neighborhood in Yerushalayim. He arranged that poor families could purchase houses there by paying only $5 a month, until the mortgage would be paid off. One day, while he was in *shul*, he overheard two people discussing his project. "Did you hear about R' Naftali's plan to build houses in Shaarei Chesed?" remarked one. "Sure," replied the other. "It's a wonderful idea. But I'm sure R' Naftali will be left with two houses for himself."

Upon hearing that, R' Naftali shelved the project for two years. When he finally restarted it, he vowed never to even *buy* a house for himself, a promise that he kept for the rest of his life.

(2) As he grows and begins to sense reality, he transfers his trust to his mother, because she cares for him devotedly.

(3) When he observes that his mother depends on his father for her own protection, he transfers his trust to his father.

(4) When he becomes able to earn his own livelihood, he transfers his trust to his own strength and skill.

(5) If his livelihood depends on others, he places his trust in them.

(6) As his understanding grows, man recognizes human deficiencies and realizes his need of the Creator. At first he transfers his trust to God only in matters where he knows he is helpless, trusting Him to provide rains for crops, or salvation from storms at sea, robbers, and wild animals in a desert.

(7) A more complete level of trust entails reliance on God even in areas where he himself is not completely helpless. He gives up perilous or exhausting occupations, and trusts that God will provide other ways to earn a livelihood.

(8) Eventually, he will trust God in all his affairs, difficult and easy, and direct all his efforts to Hashem's service and the observance of His commandments.

(9) When he reaches a higher realization of Divine mercy, a person happily accepts the Divine Will, desiring only what God desires for him — life or death, poverty or wealth, illness or health.

(10) When man's knowledge of God becomes still stronger, he understands why he was created and realizes the enduring value of the World to Come. His joy in his love of God will cause him to turn away from worldly pleasures. This is the very high level of בִּטָחוֹן, *trust*, in God attained by the "treasured ones," who are illuminated by His glory.

6. בְּכָל־דְּרָכֶיךָ דָעֵהוּ וְהוּא יְיַשֵּׁר אֹרְחֹתֶיךָ — *In all your ways, know Him and He will smooth your paths.* In all that you do, know Hashem. Create a "mindset" that the purpose of whatever you do is the fulfillment of God's will. Then He will direct your path and you will succeed (*Metzudos*).

Bar Kapara regards this verse as *a short chapter that encapsulates all the main ideas of Torah* (*Berachos* 63a). The entire Torah is a guide to the application of God's Will to life and human behavior. To know Him in all your ways — even the seemingly mundane — is the exhortation of this verse.

This point is echoed in the *mishnah*: וְכָל מַעֲשֶׂיךָ יִהְיוּ לְשֵׁם שָׁמַיִם, *And all your deeds should be for the sake of Heaven* (*Avos* 2:17). When eating, one should be cognizant of the great Divine wisdom involved in the creation of foodstuffs and the digestive mechanism, which allows man to benefit from food (*Ralbag*). One should not live to eat but rather eat to live a life of service to the Creator.[1] Instead of resting just because he is tired and craves sleep, a person should think that sleep will restore his energies for the important tasks of life — the pursuit of Torah and *mitzvos*. A healthy body and a fresh mind are primary tools in the efforts necessary for spiritual growth.

1. When Rebbetzin Nechama Kook, the grandmother of Rabbi Simcha Kook, Rav of Rechovot, was well advanced in years, she became ill and weak. When she was told that the *halachah* forbade her to fast on Yom Kippur due to her ill health, she broke down and cried. Her grandchildren tried to comfort her, saying, "You know that just as others have a *mitzvah* to fast on Yom Kippur, you have a *mitzvah* to eat. You shouldn't feel bad about it, because this is Hashem's desire of you now."

"You misunderstand why I am crying," responded Reb. Kook. "Let me explain. All my life I have been trained to eat for the sake of heaven. When I was a child, I ate so that I could have strength to help my mother. When I got married, I ate in order to be able to be a good wife to my husband and mother to my children. Now, however, my husband is gone and my children are grown up. What purpose is there for my eating? I then consoled myself with the thought I will eat during the year so that I will be strong enough to fast on Yom Kippur. However, now that I am not permitted to fast on Yom Kippur anymore, what purpose will there be for my eating year round? It is for this that I cry!" (Retold by R' Mendel Weinbach).

Earning a living should never be confused with amassing wealth. One's intention should be to support his family, give charity, raise his children and enable them to study Torah.

A person who considers each of his actions carefully, trying to determine that whatever he does will contribute to the service of God, will be serving Him all his life, in every minute of human existence. (See *Rambam, Hilchos Deios* 3:2-3; *Kitzur Shulchan Aruch* 31; *R' Bachya* to *Exodus* 20:9, s.v. שֵׁשֶׁת יָמִים תַּעֲבֹוד; and *Pachad Yitzchak, Kuntres HaShabbos*.)

The *Chafetz Chaim* comments that one infuses spirituality into and earns rewards even for one's working hours, as long as his Torah study is of primary importance to him. He elaborates that with a mere thought or statement, a person can infuse holiness and spirituality into his ordinary workday, just as man can confer sanctity on a piece of wood or stone or an animal by designating it for the Temple service. In the same way, one can infuse his eating and drinking and all his seemingly mundane affairs with holiness by utilizing them to serve God.[1]

This is so even when the major part of a person's day is spent working, and only a few hours are devoted to Torah study. In the case of Torah study, the litmus test of this primacy is his being uncompromising about his daily designated time for Torah study. It must be immutable under all circumstances. Regarding such a person, our verse assures that *He will straighten your paths*, i.e., Hashem in His kindness will consider even the working hours upright and straight, and reward him for

them. However, this is true only when he devotes his spare time, especially on Shabbos, to the study of Torah, thus proving that he uses his free moments for learning and works because he must earn a livelihood. But if he wastes his free time on frivolous things, not only will he lose the reward he could have earned during those hours, he will also lose the reward for all his working hours, for he will have made it obvious that he was not working for the sake of Heaven.

Meiri adds that this is the meaning of וְאָהַבְתָּ אֵת ה' אֱלֹהֶיךָ בְּכָל לְבָבְךָ, *And You shall love Hashem, your God, with all your heart* (*Deuteronomy* 6:1). The Sages (*Berachos* 54b) explain that the letter *beis* appears twice in the word לְבָבְךָ, *your heart*, to allude to two inclinations — the Good and the Evil; both of them must be impressed into the service and love of God. Even those parts of life generally associated with the Evil Inclination can be harnessed for good by the intention of using them for the love of Hashem.

R' Yonah explains that this verse is a continuation of the previous one, referring to the trait of בְּטָחוֹן, *trust*. There are people who generally trust in Hashem. They believe that everything is ordained by Him and do not rely on human strength or intelligence. However, this is their *modus operandi* only in matters of "great" concern. They do not apply this trust to the details of their day-to-day actions. Therefore, this verse teaches us *Know Hashem in all your ways*, i.e., in every detail of every action.

For instance, there are people who turn to God before a huge or dangerous under-

1. We cite two examples of how the proper intention can transform the mundane into the Divine. The Torah tells us: וַיִּתְהַלֵּךְ חֲנוֹךְ אֶת־הָאֱלֹהִים, *and Enoch walked with God* (*Genesis* 5:22). *Midrash Talpios* expounds that Enoch was a cobbler and with each stitch, he was מְיַחֵד יִחוּדִים לְקוֹנוֹ, *thinking profound thoughts for the sake of his Creator*. R' Yisrael Salanter explains the words of the *Midrash*. Surely Enoch's mind was not occupied with thoughts of the Divine while he was sewing shoes; it would have been halachically prohibited for him to divert his thoughts to God while engaged in work he had been paid to do. Rather, his devotion to God was indicated by his sincere intention to make sure that every stitch in the shoe would be to the customer's satisfaction. Thus, Enoch was zealous to avoid cheating his customers — an act of devotion to God (*Michtav MeEliyahu* vol. 1, *Kuntres HaChessed* ch. 3).

During a hospital stay, R' Yechezkel Levenstein was treated with great kindness by his doctor. R' Yechezkel took the doctor's hand in his, and with great earnestness advised him: "When you practice medicine, don't do it only for mercenary reasons. When you treat your patients, have in mind that you are doing it as a *chessed* for them. Then the reward you earn for the practice of medicine will be immeasurable."

ז אַל־תְּהִי חָכָם בְּעֵינֶיךָ יְרָא אֶת־יהוה וְסוּר
ח מֵרָע: רִפְאוּת תְּהִי לְשָׁרֶּךָ וְשִׁקּוּי לְעַצְמוֹתֶיךָ:

taking, such as a crucial business trip, but do not think of Him in their "small" undertakings. They are certain they will succeed, and even if they were to fail, they would not suffer any great loss. It is regarding such cases that Solomon instructs *In all your ways, know Him,* whether they be big or small. Should someone succeed in his undertaking without thinking that he needs God's assistance, he will have fallen short of his spiritual obligation. One should also realize that the reward for trusting in Hashem far surpasses any benefits he may stand to gain from the success of the undertaking itself.

R' Yonah continues that not only will you be rewarded immeasurably for your trust in Hashem, your trust will also bring you success: *and He will smooth your paths.*

In summary, R' Yonah derives four teachings from this verse:
(1) Regarding all of life's paths, place your trust in God;
(2) your goal should be to know, serve and honor Hashem, by doing everything לְשֵׁם שָׁמַיִם, *for Heaven's sake;*
(3) never let pursuit of a livelihood or any other worldly goal drown out the Divine message;
(4) prior to any pursuit, make sure that it is in accord with God's wishes and goals; whatever you do, know Him and reckon with His values and priorities.

Malbim explains the verse based on his definition that דְּרָכִים are *main highways* and אֳרָחוֹת are *small paths* that branch out from them. The small paths of Torah are endless, for they deal with so many myriads of details that it would be impossible for a person to know how to react to every situation. Therefore, the verse instructs: *In all your ways, know Him,* i.e., in general modes of behavior, such as humility, compassion and generosity, know Him and emulate His ways. Then you will merit Divine assistance so that even *your paths,* the particulars of daily life, will be straight

and correct. For instance, if you follow the main road of generosity, Hashem will help you know when, how much and to whom to give.

R' Hirsch comments that we must base our entire future on such trust, in the unshakeable conviction that we can reach our goals only with God, from God and by God's help. We should always ask ourselves whether our plans are in keeping with God's will to such an extent that we may hopefully expect His assistance.

7. אַל־תְּהִי חָכָם בְּעֵינֶיךָ — *Do not be wise in your own eyes;* i.e., do not be unreceptive to reprimand (*Rashi*). *Ibn Ezra* considers this phrase to be a continuation of verse 6. Thus, he renders: Do not be wise in your eyes and say that with your own wisdom you will gain the straight path.

R' Yonah explains: Once Hashem smooths your ways and grants you success and wealth, do not credit this good fortune to your own wisdom, as the wealthy often do (see 28:11, חָכָם בְּעֵינָיו אִישׁ עָשִׁיר, *a rich man is wise in his own eyes*). We find this concept in the Torah's warning, פֶּן־תֹּאכַל וְשָׂבָעְתָּ... וְאָמַרְתָּ בִּלְבָבֶךָ כֹּחִי וְעֹצֶם יָדִי עָשָׂה לִי אֶת הַחַיִל הַזֶּה, *Lest you eat and be satisfied ... and you say in your heart, "My strength and the might of my hand made me all this wealth"* (*Deuteronomy* 8:12-17). Verse 5 prescribes the proper approach *before* taking any action: Rather than relying on your own intelligence for success, turn to Hashem for help. This verse refers to a person's attitude *after* having achieved success. Do not attribute it to your own prowess, but rather realize that everything results only from the Almighty's decree.

יְרָא אֶת־ה' וְסוּר מֵרָע — *Fear Hashem and turn away from evil.* R' Yonah explains that fear of God is inextricably linked to בִּטָּחוֹן, *trust* in God, the theme of the two previous verses. A person can attain such fear by recognizing that everything is from Heaven and by constantly anticipat-

⁷ *Do not be wise in your own eyes; fear* HASHEM *and turn away from evil.* ⁸ *It will be health to your navel and marrow to your bones.*

ing His assistance and focusing all his aspirations on Him, rather than on mortals.

In general, *Proverbs* deals with the improvement of character traits [תִּקּוּן הַמִּדּוֹת]. This chapter, however, begins with the importance of rectifying one's thinking [תִּקּוּן דִּבְרֵי הַשֵּׂכֶל], by developing trust in God, rather than relying on human intelligence, for if one's שֵׂכֶל, *intelligence*, is proper, one will be able to go on to correct character traits. If one's intelligence is warped, however, for one is deficient in his belief and trust in God, and he considers himself to be wise, he will refuse to accept rebuke or instruction. If so, how can he hope to perfect his character?

According to *Metzudos*, the verse refers to one's attitude toward a גָּדֵר, *fence*, i.e., a prohibition that serves like a protective boundary in order to prevent transgression of a law of the Torah. Do not be dismissive of such "fences" in the mistaken belief they are unnecessary for someone as wise as you. Rather *fear God*, and realize that despite your wisdom, you may stumble.[1] *Turn* away *from evil* by distancing yourself from it and putting up a "fence," to avoid any contact with it.[2]

According to *Ibn Ezra*, this phrase in-

troduces verse 8: Fear Hashem and turn away from bad deeds, then He will preserve your health.

8. רְפָאוּת תְּהִי לְשָׁרֶּךָ וְשִׁקּוּי לְעַצְמוֹתֶיךָ — *It will be health to your navel and marrow to your bones.*

Chochmah is a cure to your navel and marrow to your bones (*Rashi*, see *Eruvin* 54a)[3] (cf. 4:22).

Meiri explains that the navel represents the entire body, for it is the conduit through which a fetus receives its nourishment.

Like a mother nourishing her fetus, the Torah will heal the bad character traits and faulty ideologies of those who have begun to nourish themselves from it and to strive for perfection. However, even after a person has attained perfection in *chochmah*, he must constantly maintain it through his continued attachment to Torah. Just as human bones constantly need marrow to strengthen them, so, too, a person's level of perfection needs constant reinforcement from its life source — *chochmah* (*Ralbag*).

The Torah's *chochmah* is foreign to man's desires; therefore, someone might feel that its dictates — such as its restrictions on food — would have a detrimental

---

1. King Solomon himself erred by relying on his wisdom (see 30:1, *Rashi* ad loc.). Assuming that his unprecedented wisdom would protect him from going astray, he thought he was not bound by the prohibitions against a king having too many wives, too much wealth, or too many horses (see *Deuteronomy* 17:16-17).

2. The connection between erecting protective "fences" around the *mitzvos* and attaining fear of Hashem is apparent from the words of R' Yonah in *Shaarei Teshuvah* (3:7). He explains that fear of Hashem is the foundation of all *mitzvos*: וְעַתָּה יִשְׂרָאֵל מָה ה' אֱלֹהֶיךָ שֹׁאֵל מֵעִמָּךְ כִּי אִם־לְיִרְאָה אֶת־ה', *Now, O Israel, what does Hashem, your God, ask of you? Only to fear Hashem* (*Deuteronomy* 10:12). The protective ordinances of the Sages and their "fences," which are precautions against transgressing Torah prohibitions, are fundamental ways to acquire this fear [יְסוֹד לְדֶרֶךְ הַיִּרְאָה]. Just as a farmer erects fences around his valuable property, so one erects barriers to distance himself from the prohibited. The Sages captured the special quality of these "fences" with their statement: "The words of the scribes [Sages] are more beloved than the wine of Torah" (*Avodah Zarah* 35a). By erecting barriers one shows the extent to which he fears transgressing Hashem's will.

3. *Rashi* explains the verse, *Any of the diseases I placed upon Egypt I will not bring upon you, for I am Hashem your Healer* (*Exodus* 15:26), to mean that God has given us a preventative medicine, i.e., Torah and *mitzvos*, against all sicknesses. If the Torah has the power to heal, it can certainly prevent a malady from coming (*Sifsei Chachamim*, ad loc. 15:26). This is the thrust of this verse, *it will be a healing to your navel.*

ט כַּבֵּד אֶת־יהוה מֵהוֹנֶךָ וּמֵרֵאשִׁית כָּל־
י תְּבוּאָתֶךָ: וְיִמָּלְאוּ אֲסָמֶיךָ שָׂבָע וְתִירוֹשׁ יְקָבֶיךָ
יא יִפְרֹצוּ: מוּסַר יהוה בְּנִי אַל־תִּמְאָס וְאַל־

effect on his health. In truth, however, these restrictions on a person's desires and physical pleasures will serve to strengthen his bones,[1] and not weaken them, as is the case with worldly indulgence (*Malbim*).

9. כַּבֵּד אֶת־ה' מֵהוֹנֶךָ וּמֵרֵאשִׁית כָּל־תְּבוּאָתֶךָ — *Honor Hashem with your wealth and with the first of all your produce.*

Recognize that your success is from Hashem by honoring Him from your wealth and the first of your produce (*Meiri*).

To *honor Hashem with your wealth* means setting some of it aside for charity (*Metzudos*). *The first of all your produce* refers to *terumah*, the portion of the produce which was set aside and given to the Kohanim, and *maaser*, tithes — the tenths of the produce that were given to the Levites, and to the poor, or eaten in Jerusalem (*Metzudos*).

By giving the first of your possessions to Hashem you acknowledge *that it was He who gave you strength to make wealth* (Deuteronomy 8:13) (*Sifsei Daas*).

R' Yonah points out that when a person uses his wealth for *mitzvos* and charity, he demonstrates his בִּטָּחוֹן, *trust*, in Hashem. These verses teach a person to trust that God will bless him for his generosity and cause his possessions to increase. The more one depletes, the more Hashem increases; as the Jerusalem proverb expressed it, מְלַח מָמוֹן חֶסֶר, *to salt money, diminish it*, i.e., the way to preserve money is to give a great deal to charity (*Kesubos* 66b; cf. 10:2).

This can be compared to a nursing mother. As long as the infant nurses, her milk increases. Once he is weaned, her milk dries up (*Sifsei Daas*).

[Material possessions make it possible for us to advance the aims which God has entrusted to human care. If we faithfully put our material possessions to the use ordained by God, we may look forward to receiving His lasting blessing. If we give priority to God's honor and His purpose, he will appoint us as custodians of His goods and increase our wealth.]

The beneficial effect of taking tithes from personal wealth is illustrated by the following incident. R' Levi told of a man who was always scrupulous to separate tithes properly. His field produced one thousand measures; he would give all the tithes and support his family from the remainder. Before his death, he instructed his son to continue the practice. The first year after his father's death, the son did so, but the second year he regretted giving so much of his crop away and decreased each hundred measures by ten. The field, in turn, reduced its yield by one hundred measures. Each successive year, as the son lessened his tithe, the field reduced its produce proportionally, until the field produced only one tenth of its original yield. His friends and relatives said to him, "Until now you were the master of the field and God was like the Kohen [who took only a small measure]. Now, however, you have become the Kohen [who is left with only a small percentage] and God is the master of the field" (*Pesikta D'Rav Kahana*).

As the Sages expound, עַשֵּׂר תְּעַשֵּׂר אֵת כָּל־תְּבוּאַת זַרְעֶךָ, *You shall surely tithe [the entire crop of your planting]* (Deuteronomy 14:22), as עַשֵּׂר בִּשְׁבִיל שֶׁתִּתְעַשֵּׁר, *tithe so that you should become wealthy* (Shabbos 119a).

Homiletically, *Rashi* renders מֵהוֹנֶךָ, *with your wealth*, as מִכָּל מַה שֶּׁחָנַנְךָ, *with*

---

1. The righteous seem to be endowed with superhuman strength in the area of *mitzvah* observance and fear of God. Rabbi Yechezkel Levenstein's devotion in prayer was especially evident during Rosh Hashanah and Yom Kippur. Even when he was well into his 80s, a thin and frail man, he would stand motionless throughout the *Shemoneh Esrei* prayer and focus his whole being on its words. On Yom Kippur, by the time he would finish his *Shacharis Amidah*, the congregation would already be at the beginning of the *Mussaf Amidah*. His *Mussaf Amidah* would extend until *Minchah*, and so on. Thus, this elderly, frail sage remained on his feet for almost the entire fast day!

whatever He favored you. מֵהוֹנֶךָ may also be understood as מִגְּרוֹנֶךָ, *with your throat*, meaning that if you have a pleasant voice, you should use even that to serve God. As *R' Bachya* comments, when using his voice, one's intention must for the sake of heaven, not to show off and be admired, for then his voice will be despised by Hashem.

The severity of not using one's voice to honor Hashem is illustrated by the case of Naboth the Jezreelite (*I Kings* 21). When he made the pilgrimage to Jerusalem, all of Israel would gather to hear his sweet voice. One year, he decided not to go to Jerusalem. That was the year Queen Jezebel plotted to get Naboth's vineyard for herself and her husband, King Ahab. She hired witnesses to testify falsely against Naboth and have him executed. Although Jezebel's intention was to have Ahab gain Naboth's vineyard, this tragedy was actually caused by Naboth himself, because he did not grace the festival with his God-given talent (*Yalkut Shimoni*). [Since he did not use his voice positively, the "voice" of false testimony was put into effect against him.]

The Sages also employ this verse to teach the importance of honoring one's parents. The same form of command is used here in reference to honoring God (כַּבֵּד אֶת ה') as the Torah uses in reference to honoring one's parents (כַּבֵּד אֶת־אָבִיךָ וְאֶת־אִמֶּךָ — *Exodus* 20:12). This is only fitting, for all three — God, father, and mother — are partners in the creation of the child. R' Chiya bar Abba points out that Hashem gives even greater importance to honoring one's parents than to honoring Himself. In speaking of honoring Hashem, the verse states מֵהוֹנֶךָ, *with your wealth*; poverty frees one from many *mitzvah* obligations. However, the Torah states nothing about wealth in connection with the commandment to honor

parents. Therefore, even the poor or destitute are obligated to perform this *mitzvah* (*Yalkut Shimoni*).

10. וְיִמָּלְאוּ אֲסָמֶיךָ שָׂבָע וְתִירוֹשׁ יְקָבֶיךָ יִפְרֹצוּ — *Then your storehouses will be filled with plenty, and the wine of your vats will burst forth.*

Not only will you not lack anything because of your charity, your produce will be blessed and increase, as will the wine in the vats (*Metzudos*).

The translation of יִפְרֹצוּ as *will burst forth* follows *Meiri* and *Ibn Ezra* who explain that this is related to the meaning of לִפְרֹץ as *to break* (e.g., לִפְרֹץ גָּדֵר, *to breach barriers*). There will be such plenty that the wine will burst forth from its vats.

The Torah prohibits testing of Hashem: לֹא תְנַסּוּ אֶת־ה', *You shall not test Hashem* (*Deuteronomy* 6:16). The Jewish people have neither the right to doubt Hashem or test His prowess. A person may not say, "I will perform this commandment in order to succeed financially." The commandments of giving charity and separating tithes, however, are exceptions to this prohibition. Regarding tithes, the verse states: הָבִיאוּ אֶת־כָּל־הַמַּעֲשֵׂר . . . וּבְחָנוּנִי נָא . . . בָּזֹאת, *Bring all the tithes . . . and test me in this . . .* (*Malachi* 3:10), and see if I do not shower you with endless blessing (see *Taanis* 9a). Verses 9 and 10 refer to this permissible test (*R' Bachya*).

R' Yonah comments that this verse gives the outcome of the previous verse's urging that one should dedicate one's wealth and faculties to God's honor. This verse calls for faith that such devotion will be rewarded with full storehouses and bursting vats.

11. מוּסַר ה' בְּנִי אַל־תִּמְאָס — *My child, do not despise* HASHEM'*s discipline.* If suffering comes upon you, cherish it (*Rashi*). If you despise afflictions, you will not

יב 'תָּקֹץ בְּתוֹכַחְתּוֹ: כִּי אֶת אֲשֶׁר יֶאֱהַב יהוה
יג יוֹכִיחַ וּכְאָב אֶת־בֵּן יִרְצֶה: אַשְׁרֵי אָדָם

receive the benefits they were to have brought (Ralbag).[1]

וְאַל תָּקֹץ בְּתוֹכַחְתּוֹ — And do not be disgusted with His reproof. Do not say, "How could I deserve such a punishment?" It is God's way to be very exacting with the righteous. Precise punishment indicates Hashem's special concern: You alone did I know from among all the families of the earth; therefore I will hold you to account for all your iniquities [Amos 3:2] (Meiri).

מוּסָר, discipline, refers to corporal afflictions; תּוֹכָחָה to verbal rebuke (Vilna Gaon).

According to R' Yonah, this verse refers to someone who has achieved an outstanding level of בְּטָחוֹן, trust, in Hashem. When such a person gives charity and performs good deeds, yet does not attain wealth or success, or even suffers afflictions, he does not despise such Divine chastisements. Rather he strengthens his trust in God, realizing that they are of greater benefit to him than success and wealth, for through them, Hashem purifies him and cleanses him of sin, thus increasing his reward in the World to Come. Tranquility in this world is of little value, for a person's life is transitory and fleeting. Yet, with respect to the World to Come, our Sages teach: וְיָפָה שָׁעָה אַחַת שֶׁל קוֹרַת רוּחַ בָּעוֹלָם הַבָּא מִכֹּל חַיֵּי

הָעוֹלָם הַזֶּה, and better one hour of spiritual bliss in the World to Come than the entire life of this world (Avos 4:22). The individual himself does not know what is good for him; only Hashem knows where his true benefit lies — whether in tranquility or suffering.

Menoras HaMaor (HaNer HaChamishi 3:1) teaches that if someone looks upon afflictions as happenstance, his destiny will be left to chance and Divine protection will be removed from him. (See Leviticus 26:23-24.) He must realize that the afflictions are either to arouse him to repentance and atone for his sins, or to afford him the opportunity to earn more reward in the World to Come (see Berachos 5a). Our Sages explain (Pesikta D'Rav Kahana 25) that if a person committed a sin for which he is liable to death by the hand of Heaven, and instead of his imminent death, his ox dies, his rooster is lost, his utensil breaks, or his finger is hurt, then the partial loss he has endured is considered as if he had actually suffered the death penalty. Therefore, one should be thankful for God's mercy in bringing upon him a rather mild punishment in this world, instead of a more severe punishment in the World to Come.

Afflictions are particularly beloved to the righteous, who appreciate their true value. The Talmud (Sanhedrin 101a) recounts that when R' Eliezer became ill, four sages visited him. The first three praised his virtues, but R' Akiva said, חֲבִיבִין יִסּוּרִים, afflictions are beloved, for they are an atonement for you

---

1. R' Avrohom of Slonim rendered the verse homiletically. What is Hashem's chastisement (מוּסָר ה')? That you are my son (בְּנִי), a child of royalty; as such, do not make yourself disgusting (אַל תְּמָאֵס). Do not do things that are improper for someone of your station and dignity.

R' Yonah (Shaarei Teshuvah 2:3,4) emphasizes the benefits of God's chastisements. They atone for sins, for the suffering of a person's body heals the illness of his soul [i.e., his sins]. Moreover, chastisements are a constant reminder that one should repent. If an individual does not accept the lesson of this mussar, he will have suffered the affliction yet not atoned for his sins. As a result, his punishment will now be doubled. On the other hand, one who accepts Hashem's mussar and improves his ways should accept his afflictions with joy, since they will benefit him greatly. He should thank Hashem for them as he would for successes. For the Psalmist tells us: I will raise the cup of salvation and the Name of HASHEM I will invoke (Psalms 116:13), and The pains of death encircled me; the confines of the grave have found me, trouble and sorrow I would find. Then I would invoke the name of HASHEM (Psalms 116:3-4).

Maharal explains how suffering can heal the soul. Suffering minimizes an individual's corporeal concerns and makes him more aware of his spiritual senses and needs. Through the anguish of physical pain, his physicality is placed in proper perspective and his soul is given an opportunity to develop and flourish. As a result, his value judgments enable him to be more open to his spiritual needs (Introduction to Derech Chaim).

(*Rashi*, ad loc.). It was the words of R' Akiva which R' Eliezer found most comforting.

12. בִּי אֶת אֲשֶׁר יֶאֱהַב ה' יוֹכִיחַ — *For Hashem admonishes the one He loves.* If someone cares for another, he admonishes him to prevent him from taking the wrong path. So, it is with God; when He admonishes a person, it is only because He loves him (*Vilna Gaon*).

וּכְאָב אֶת־בֵּן יִרְצֶה — *And like a father He mollifies a child.* God treats us like a loving father, who appeases his child after being forced to punish him. Similarly, the good we receive after the punishment will be most pleasant (*Rashi*). *Metzudos* adds: It is like a father who hits his son only to reprove him and improve his actions — not to take revenge.

According to the *Vilna Gaon*, this phrase refers to verbal rebuke (תוֹכָחָה — יוֹכִיחַ), whereas this part of the verse refers to מוּסָר, i.e., physically afflicting a person in order to improve his ways. God's verbal rebuke shows love and concern. If He inflicts physical suffering, that indicates an even greater degree of closeness — that of a loving father. If a wayward child disregards his father's verbal rebuke, the father will continue to admonish him,

even resorting to corporal punishment. Since a concerned father is pained by his child's errors and longs for his improvement, he punishes only for the sake of the child. Proof of this is that as soon as the punishment is over, the father tries to console his child. Therefore, do not despise Heavenly afflictions, for it is an indication of your preciousness in Hashem's eyes. Eventually He will placate you and fulfill your desires, like a father (cf. 27:5).[1]

R' Yonah renders: *as a father rebukes a child whom he desires.* If a father has special affection for one of his children, he will rebuke that child the most, to make him realize his full potential. In the same way, Hashem rebukes those whom He loves more than ordinary people; צַדִּיק ה' יִבְחָן, *Hashem examines the righteous one* (*Psalms* 11:5), i.e., He specifically chastises and tests the righteous.[2]

The Sages infer the concept of "affliction of love" from this verse. Such afflictions are visited upon the righteous not as a punishment from sin, but solely to serve as an opportunity for them to increase their reward in the Hereafter (see *Rashi, Berachos* 5a). The Talmud explains (ibid.) that if a person sees that afflictions come

1. If a speeding car is about to strike a child, his father will grab him and violently cast him out of the vehicle's path. The child may be injured or bruised, but his life has been saved. This is the nature of *mussar*. It appears to be injurious, but, in reality, it saves one from spiritual death.

The name of the month in which the Temple was destroyed is *Av*, which means father. The *Kotzker Rebbe* explained that if an adult caresses a child, it does not indicate that the adult is his father, but if he slaps the youngster, you can be sure he is the father. Similarly, the Divine retribution inflicted with the destruction of the Temple was an indication of our father's love for us. For this reason the month is called *Av*.

This principle also applies to the entire Nation of Israel, as the Torah states: וְיָדַעְתָּ עִם־לְבָבֶךָ כִּי כַּאֲשֶׁר יְיַסֵּר אִישׁ אֶת־בְּנוֹ ה' אֱלֹהֶיךָ מְיַסְּרֶךָ, *You should know in your heart that just as a father will chastise his son, so Hashem, your God, chastises you* (*Deuteronomy* 8:5). *Or HaChaim* (ibid.) explains that human nature is such that a person will not rebuke or chastise anyone other than his own child. He is pedantic and meticulous when his son does wrong, and he will even curse him and punish him for his wrongdoing. Such is not the case when his friend's son does wrong. For then he is not as fastidious and does not act as such a strict disciplinarian.

The same is true in Hashem's relationship with the nations. When other nations behave abominably, God is not as exacting with them as He is with Israel. Since Israel bears His name, He chastises them for every improper thing that they do.

2. *Rashi* (*Psalms* 11:5) likens this to a flax maker, who, when he knows that the flax is strong and durable, beats it vigorously. However, when it is not strong, he refrains from beating, lest it shred and fall apart.

יד מָצָא חָכְמָה וְאָדָם יָפִיק תְּבוּנָה: כִּי טוֹב סַחְרָהּ

טו מִסְּחַר־כֶּסֶף וּמֵחָרוּץ תְּבוּאָתָהּ: יְקָרָה הִיא

טז °מִפְּנִיִּים וְכָל־חֲפָצֶיךָ לֹא יִשְׁווּ־בָהּ: אֹרֶךְ יָמִים

°מִפְּנִינִים ק׳

upon him, יְפַשְׁפֵּשׁ בְּמַעֲשָׂיו, *he should examine his deeds*. If he does not find any fault in his deeds that would account for this suffering, then he should assume that the afflictions are a result of his wasting time instead of studying Torah. If, however, he finds himself not guilty of this, then these afflictions must be יִסּוּרִים שֶׁל אַהֲבָה, *afflictions of love*; as the verse states: כִּי אֶת אֲשֶׁר יֶאֱהַב ה׳ יוֹכִיחַ, for Hashem rebukes the one whom He loves.[1]

13. אַשְׁרֵי אָדָם מָצָא חָכְמָה — *Praiseworthy is a person who has found wisdom*. The verse employs the verb *found* because a person cannot deduce *chochmah* through his own reasoning. He must hear it from his teacher or find it in sacred books (*Vilna Gaon*).

וְאָדָם יָפִיק תְּבוּנָה — *And a person who gives forth understanding*. He has studied *chochmah* and has become so fluent in it that he expresses it verbally (*Rashi*).

A person deduces תְּבוּנָה with his own intellectual resources. He extracts it [יָפִיק] through logical deduction, from the data he has already processed (*Malbim*).

Verses 13-18 speak of the praises and virtues of *chochmah*. They are connected to verses 11 and 12, which teach the value of afflictions. Suffering will arouse a person to examine his deeds and repent.

Should he find no sin to account for his suffering, then surely the cause was his lack of Torah study (see citation from *Berachos* 5a above) and he will then apply himself to Torah study, which is the ultimate goal of man and the source of all success (*Meiri*).

Ibn Ezra connects the verses as follows: Praiseworthy is one who has found *chochmah*, for it will protect him from sinning and, as a result, spare him from affliction.[2]

Chochmah, the wisdom derived from Hashem's world, and *tevunah*, the resulting understanding of the precise relationships and man's duties in the world, stamp us with the ultimate imprint of humanity (*R' Hirsch*).

14. כִּי טוֹב סַחְרָהּ מִסְּחַר־כָּסֶף — *For its commerce is better than the commerce of silver*. In any commercial venture, there is an exchange: The buyer takes the merchandise and the seller takes the payment. However, where Torah is concerned, one says to his friend, "Teach me your chapter and I will teach you mine" (i.e., they "trade" their Torah knowledge), but ultimately each one gains the knowledge of both chapters (*Rashi*).[3]

וּמֵחָרוּץ תְּבוּאָתָהּ — *And its produce [is better] than fine gold*. The "produce" of wisdom is what one deduces from the *chochmah* he has learned (*Metzudos*).

1. The extent to which the righteous are exacting in examining their deeds is illustrated by the following incident. When R' Moshe Feinstein became ill in his later years, he searched through all of his deeds to find the reason for his suffering. However, he was unable to pinpoint the action which could have accounted for such an affliction, until he reached far back into his youth. When still a young child in *cheder*, he recalled, his *rebbi* had posed a difficult question to the class. He and a friend had both suggested answers, but the *rebbi* had praised, "Moshele's" answer as the correct one. "My feeling of superiority over my friend is the reason I deserve the pain I am suffering today," declared R' Moshe.

2. The Torah's power to protect its students from afflictions is evident from the Talmud (*Berachos* 5a), which states: Afflictions separate themselves from anyone who occupies himself with Torah study.

3. This is exemplified by Reb Chiya's educational methodology, which he devised in order to ensure that Torah learning would not be forgotten. He wrote down the Five Books of Moses for five children; he taught the Six Orders of the Mishnah to six children. Then he instructed each child to teach others what he had been taught (*Kesubos* 103b).

*who has found wisdom, and a person who gives forth understand-
ing. ¹⁴ For its commerce is better than the commerce of silver, and its
produce [is better] than fine gold. ¹⁵ It is more precious than pearls,
and all of your desires cannot compare to it. ¹⁶ Length of days*

Possessions such as merchandise and
gold are not lasting, nor do they become
an integral part of a person. *Chochmah*
and *tevunah*, however, are eternal and
continually enrich a person's soul (*Malbim*). (See 4:2 citation from *Yalkut Shimoni*.)

To occupy ourselves with the Torah,
which gives us this wisdom, is far more
profitable than the pursuit of any other
promising venture: The entire inventory of
all our other acquisitions cannot be compared to the Torah's worth (*R' Hirsch*).

15. יָקְרָה הִיא מִפְּנִינִים — *It is more precious
than pearls.* The Chafetz Chaim draws a
parallel between the value of Torah and
the value of pearls. As the size of the pearl
increases, its value increases manifold —
far more than the proportionate increase in
size. Larger pearls are unusually rare, and
their value may thus be ten or twenty
times greater than smaller pearls. For
example, an 8mm. pearl is worth much
more than double the price of a pearl half
its size. The same principle applies to the
study of Torah. If one person toils and
masters one chapter of Torah, and his
friend toils longer and masters two chapters, the value of the latter's achievement is
incomparably greater than the former's.
Should a third person study three chapters,
his level would far surpass those of his
friends, as if he had attained an entirely
different realm of understanding and
sanctity.[1]

Our Sages (*Horayos* 13a) interpret this verse
homiletically to teach that the merit of a Torah

scholar — even if he is a *mamzer*, i.e., one who
is forbidden to marry a fellow Jew — is
even greater than that of a Kohen Gadol who
enters the Inner Sanctuary [לִפְנַי וְלִפְנִים] on
Yom Kippur. [Homiletically, the word מִפְּנִינִים
is interpreted as לִפְנַי וְלִפְנִים, *the Inner Sanctuary.*

וְכָל־חֲפָצֶיךָ לֹא יִשְׁווּ־בָהּ — *And all of your
desires cannot compare to it.* All things
that you desire are not equal to the worth
of *chochmah* (*Rashi*).

A person tries to acquire something for
one of two reasons — either because it is
an item which is of rare beauty and worth,
or it is something he needs, such as bread.
A person should strive to acquire Torah
for both reasons: It is rarer than pearls, and
it is so necessary that no other desire can
compare to it. Torah is life — and what
can be more vital to a person than life
itself? (*Vilna Gaon*).

Pearls are valuable for they are found in
a non-human environment; not on land
where man can live, but in the sea. The
same is true of Torah wisdom, which is
also not found in the material world and
cannot be derived purely from man's
intellect, which is bound by physical
constraints. Rather, *chochmah* is spiritual
and must be attained from Heaven; it is
Divine wisdom, farther removed from
man than even the depths of the sea.
Though one must give up physical desires
and pleasures to attain *chochmah*, all
man's desires cannot possibly compare to
Torah (*Malbim*).

An almost identical verse is found in

---

1. A similar idea is expounded in the Talmud (*Chagigah* 9b), based on the verse: וְשַׁבְתֶּם וּרְאִיתֶם בֵּין
צַדִּיק לְרָשָׁע בֵּין עֹבֵד אֱלֹהִים לַאֲשֶׁר לֹא עֲבָדוֹ, *Then you shall return and see the difference between the
righteous and the wicked, between one who serves God and one who does not serve Him* (*Malachi*
3:18). Hillel explains the difference between *one who serves God* and *one who does not* in terms
of Torah study. The Talmud tells us: אֵינוֹ דוֹמֶה שׁוֹנֶה פִּרְקוֹ מֵאָה פְּעָמִים לְמִי שֶׁשּׁוֹנֶה פִּרְקוֹ מֵאָה וְאֶחָד, *A
person who has reviewed his studies one hundred times cannot be compared to one who has
reviewed his studies one hundred and one times* (*Chagigah* 9b). The *Chafetz Chaim* explains that
although the latter studied the chapter only one time more than the former, this small amount of
additional Torah study allowed him to attain a higher level — so much so, that by comparison
to him, the former is likened to one who does not serve Hashem.

יז בְּיָמִינָהּ בִּשְׂמֹאולָהּ עֹשֶׁר וְכָבוֹד: דְּרָכֶיהָ דַרְכֵי־
יח נֹעַם וְכָל־נְתִיבֹתֶיהָ שָׁלוֹם: עֵץ־חַיִּים הִיא
לַמַּחֲזִיקִים בָּהּ וְתֹמְכֶיהָ מְאֻשָּׁר:

8:11, with a slight variation: Whereas our verse speaks of *your desires*, 8:11 speaks of *desires*. The Sages (*Bereishis Rabbah* 35:4) explain that *your desires* refers to precious jewels, whereas *desires* refers to *mitzvos* and good deeds. Thus, King Solomon declares that nothing — neither wealth nor *mitzvos* — can compare to the importance of even one word of Torah study. The Talmud declares emphatically that the study of Torah is equivalent to them all (*Shabbos* 127a).

The Midrash (ibid.) relates that Artavin, a Persian king, once sent Rebbe Yehudah HaNasi a priceless jewel as a gift. Rebbe sent him a *mezuzah* in return. Artavin said, "I sent you something priceless, and you are sending me something worth but a coin!" Rebbe responded, "Your desirable things and my desirable things cannot compare to the Torah. And not only that, but you sent me an item which I must guard, whereas I sent you an item which protects you."

16. אֹרֶךְ יָמִים בִּימִינָהּ בִּשְׂמֹאולָהּ עֹשֶׁר וְכָבוֹד — *Length of days is at its right; at its left, wealth and honor.* Through Torah, a person will attain long life, wealth and honor (*Metzudos*). The "right side" of Torah refers to those who study it לִשְׁמָהּ, *for its own sake* — i.e., purely for the sake of

Heaven. ("Right" always represents the stronger side, and "left" the weaker.) They will merit long life, and most certainly wealth and honor as well (for even those on the "left side" of the Torah merit the latter). The "left side" of Torah refers to those who are involved in its study, שֶׁלֹּא לִשְׁמָה, *not for its own sake* [i.e., they study in order to attain wealth or honor (*Vilna Gaon*)]. Nevertheless, they *will* have wealth and honor (*Rashi*).

According to *Rabbeinu Bachya*, the "right side" of Torah refers to the World to Come; the "left side" to this world. An individual who performs commandments with the intention of earning reward in the World to Come will merit length of days for eternity, for the World to Come is eternal. If his intentions are for reward in this world, then he will merit wealth and honor, which are not eternal.

The Midrash explains that Torah asked the Holy One, Blessed is He: "It says that 'at its left [are] wealth and honor'; why, then, are my children poor?" The Holy One, Blessed is He, responded, *I have what to bequeath [to] those who love Me* (8:21). Why then are they poor in this world? So that they will not get involved in earthly matters and forget the Torah (*Yalkut Shimoni*).[1]

1. The following story illustrates the relationship between wealth and Torah scholarship. In the time of Rabbi Chaim of Volozhin, there was an extremely wealthy family that was famous for its philanthropy. The head of the family, R' Moshe Soloveitchik, owned vast forests, and year after year sold his timber at rich profits. Then Reb Moshe lost his vast properties one after the other, and went bankrupt. Because he had been so well known for his open home and generous *tzedakah*, everyone wondered how to account for his sudden change of fortune.

The change was so quick and striking that R' Chaim set up a special *beis din* to investigate whether R' Moshe had committed a serious transgression for which he had been punished. The *beis din* concluded that R' Moshe had done everything according to the *halachah*, except that he had sometimes given away more than one fifth of his wealth. But apart from disregarding this one guideline, the judges could find nothing that he had done wrong.

Meanwhile, since R' Moshe had much more free time, he and his sons went to the study hall and learned with much energy and concentration. Before long the name Soloveitchik came to represent greatness in Torah, just as previously it had stood for great wealth and *tzedakah*. R' Moshe was appointed rabbi in the new community of Kovno. His brilliant son Yosef became the son-in-law of the *gadol hador*, Rav Chaim of Volozhin. And Yosef's son, Reb Yitzchak Zev of Kovno, also an outstanding scholar, was the father of the *Beis HaLevi*, Rabbi Yosef Dov

17. דְּרָכֶיהָ דַרְכֵי־נֹעַם — *Its ways are ways of pleasantness.* The ways of Torah are pleasant; it does not burden or impose difficulties upon the individual. On the contrary, the *mitzvos* are beneficial, bringing both physical and spiritual health and well-being (*Ralbag*).[1] The ways of Torah teach the person neither to overindulge in the pleasures of life nor to suffer unnecessarily. For instance, the Torah commands a person to enjoy himself on the Sabbath and festivals, and to partake in a festive meal on many occasions (*Ibn Nachmias*). [This is in stark contrast to many nations that consider it a higher level of divine service to don sackcloth, deprive themselves of food and drink, and seclude themselves in mountain or forest retreats.]

וְכָל־נְתִיבֹתֶיהָ שָׁלוֹם — *And all its byways are peace.* The Holy One, Blessed is He, wished to give the Torah to the Jewish people as soon as they left Egypt, but there were disputes among them as they traveled from Succos to Eisam (*Exodus* 13:20). It was only when they came from Refidim that they became united, as the verse states: וַיִּחַן שָׁם יִשְׂרָאֵל, *and Israel camped there* [i.e., in Sinai] (ibid., 19:2). The Torah does not say, וַיַּחֲנוּ, *and they camped*, in the plural, but rather וַיִּחַן, *[Israel] encamped*, in the singular; they were like a single person, with a single desire [כְּאִישׁ אֶחָד בְּלֵב אֶחָד] (see *Rashi*, ibid.). God said, "The entire Torah is peace. To whom shall I give it? To a nation

that loves peace!" (*Yalkut Shimoni*).

18. עֵץ־חַיִּים הִיא לַמַּחֲזִיקִים בָּהּ — *It is a tree of life to those who hold fast to it*, i.e., one who eats from its fruits will live long (*Ibn Ezra*).

R' Huna states: If one transgressed a sin for which he was liable to death at the hands of Heaven, what should he do in order to live? Involve himself in Torah study. If he usually reads one page, let him read two; if he usually studies once, let him study twice (*Yalkut Shimoni*).

R' Nachman bar Yitzchak explains why the Torah's words are compared to a tree. Just as small pieces of wood ignite the larger pieces, so, too, junior Torah scholars sharpen the senior scholars (with their constant questioning, *Rashi* ibid.). In this vein, R' Chanina said, "I have learned much from my teachers, and from my colleagues even more than from my teachers, וּמִתַּלְמִידַי יוֹתֵר מִכֻּלָּם, *but from my students more than from them all*" (*Taanis* 7a).[2]

וְתֹמְכֶיהָ מְאֻשָּׁר — *And its supporters are praiseworthy.* *Rashi* renders תֹּמְכֶיהָ as *those who come close to it*, for תְּמִיכָה means *grasping on to something.*

Metzudos explains תֹּמְכֶיהָ as *those who support Torah by adding fences* (גְּדָרִים וּסְיָיגִים) *to it* — i.e., they add provisions to safeguard against transgression.

The Midrash (*Bamidbar Rabbah* 13) states that *It is a tree of life to those who hold fast to it* refers to the tribe of Issachar,

Soloveitchik. Thus, a dynasty of many generations of Torah greatness descended from a man who suddenly went bankrupt.

Some years after the Soloveitchik's financial catastrophe, R' Chaim of Volozhin commented: "Now I understand why the family suddenly lost so much money. They had done so much good that Hashem wanted to reward them with not only one son who would be a great Torah scholar, but with a dynasty of such people. But greatness in Torah cannot come together with great wealth; before R' Moshe could receive his reward, the family had to lose most of its money."

1. The *Rambam* states that illness prevents a person from enjoying the taste of food. The same principle applies in spiritual matters. A person whose soul is ill cannot appreciate the pleasantness of a *mitzvah*, nor can he realize the dangers inherent in what the Torah warns us to avoid (*Kol Omeir K'ra*).

2. Rabbi Akiva Eiger wrote to his son that he never asked a student to bring him a book, because he wasn't sure who learned more from whom — his student from him, or he from his student.

which devoted itself to Torah study; *and its supporters are praiseworthy* refers to the tribe of Zebulun, whose businessmen supported Issachar.

One who supports Torah scholars is credited with the merit of their Torah study. *Yalkut Shimoni* cites the case of a ruling quoted in the name of Shimon, the brother of Azaryah (*Zevachim* 2a). Azaryah's name is mentioned when quoting Shimon's halachic ruling, because Azaryah was a businessman whose support enabled his brother to study Torah. Therefore, Shimon's ruling is credited to Azaryah. Similarly, when Moses blessed the tribes (*Deuteronomy* 33:18), he mentioned Zebulun before Issachar, even though Issachar was older. The tribe of Zebulun was to engage in maritime commerce and support the scholars of Issachar, who devoted themselves to Torah study as teachers, judges and cultivators of the spiritual treasure of the people (see *I Chronicles* 12:32). Therefore Zebulun is mentioned first because it made Issachar's Torah study possible (*Midrash Tanchuma*).

The *Vilna Gaon* explains that there are two types of Torah supporters: those who support Torah scholars with money, and those who support them with physical assistance.

The *Chafetz Chaim* explains why this verse states that Torah will be a tree of life *to those who hold fast to it*, rather than לַמַּחֲזִיקִים אוֹתָהּ, *to those who uphold it*. The merit of Torah study upholds the world (see *Jeremiah* 33:25; *Nedarim* 32a); one who supports Torah should realize that in essence, Torah is upholding him, as

well as all of creation. [The same was true of the priests who carried the Ark. Though to all appearances it was the priests who were carrying the Ark, for this is what they were commanded to do, in reality, the Ark carried those who were carrying it, and they merely grasped on to it. (See *Sotah* 35a).]

Therefore, the verse suggests that the Torah is a tree of life to those who realize that by supporting it, they are really grasping onto it and being strengthened by it. However, even those who assume that they are giving support to the Torah (תֹמְכֶיהָ) are *praiseworthy*.

Several commentators remark on the change in voice, with the word תֹמְכֶיהָ, [the Torah's] *supporters* in the plural form, and the word מְאֻשָּׁר, *praiseworthy*, in the singular. Numerous people may support one Torah scholar, for none of them individually can provide for all his needs. Nevertheless, each of them will be credited with the complete reward, as if he had supported the Torah scholar singlehandedly (*Zechus Avos*).[1]

The *Vilna Gaon* enumerates seven gifts, mentioned in verses 16-18, which the Holy One, Blessed is He, gave Israel through Torah: (1) long life; (2) wealth; (3) honor; (4) wisdom — which is referred to as *pleasantness*, for wisdom is pleasant to the soul (see 2:10); (5) children — who are referred to as *a tree of life* (see 11:30); (6) favor [חֵן] (v. 18 states *praiseworthy*, i.e., through Torah one will be praised); (7) peace.

By plucking the fruits of the Tree of Knowledge against God's will, Adam and Eve forfeited the Tree of Life. By giving us

---

1. When R' Eliezer (Lazer) Gordon of Telshe was married, his father-in-law undertook to support the young couple for the first ten years of their marriage, so that R' Lazer could devote himself full time to Torah study. As the ten years ended, his mother-in-law said to her husband, "Perhaps it is time for R' Lazer to seek a position to be able to become self-supporting." Her husband responded, "Who knows who has been supporting whom until now!"

Of course, R' Lazer acceded to his in-law's request and due to his stature as a Torah scholar, he was able to attain a position as a rav in another city. The day arrived for his departure, and R' Lazer and his family were taking leave of his in-laws. However, just as his father-in-law returned from his morning prayers and re-entered the house, he collapsed and died. It was then that everyone tearfully recalled his now-prophetic words: "Who knows who has been supporting whom!"

His Torah, granting *chochmah* and *tevu-nah*, Hashem, in effect, granted us a com-bination of the tree of knowledge and the tree of life. If we tend it lovingly and faithfully, we may earn both the fruits of knowledge and the fruits of eternal life. When a community gathers in support of this tree of life, they are united with God's spiritual and moral support, and are *praiseworthy*, as one harmonious unit. Should the Torah, this single beam of support, be lacking, then every society becomes a mere pretense, being held to-gether only outwardly, while inwardly divided by the diverging interests of sepa-rate pluralities (*R' Hirsch*).

19. ה' בְּחָכְמָה יָסַד־אָרֶץ כּוֹנֵן שָׁמַיִם בִּתְבוּנָה — *Hashem founded the earth with wisdom, He establishes heavens with understand-ing.*

Chochmah, tevunah and *daas* (next verse) all refer to Torah; thus, Hashem created the world according to Torah (*Rashi, Metzudos*).

The Sages explain that Torah was the tool through which Hashem fashioned the world (see 8:30). It was the blueprint for

the creation of the world: הִסְתַּכֵּל בְּאוֹרַיְתָא וּבָרָא עוֹלָם, *The Holy One, Blessed is He, looked into the Torah and created the world* (*Bereishis Rabbah* 1:2).[1] Accord-ingly, nothing exists in this world that does not have its place in the Torah. We cannot explain any phenomenon without Torah. The Sages of the Mishnah teach: There is nothing without its "place" (*Avos* 4:3). This means that everything in our existence has a *place* in the Torah. We should not explain things devoid of their meaning in the perspective of the Torah (*Sfas Emes*).

It follows, then, that if people do not heed the Torah's commandments, the world will revert to its original state of תֹהוּ וָבֹהוּ, *astonishing emptiness*. Adherence to the Torah's dictates is the condition for the continued existence of the world (*Chevel Nachalah*) [cf. 8:22-30].[2]

From this verse, our Sages derive that the whole world and everything in it was created solely in the merit of Torah (*Bereishis Rabbah* 1:6). This is inferred from the words, ה' בְּחָכְמָה יָסַד אָרֶץ, which can also be rendered: *Hashem founded [the] earth for the sake of chochmah* — i.e., Torah (*Eitz Yosef*, ibid.). Similarly, the

1. Every creation in the world has but one *raison d'être*, one purpose for its existence: Torah. Torah laws were not promulgated as instruction and guidelines for mankind; mankind, as well as every other form of creation in the universe, was created in conformance with the dictates of Torah. The *Beis HaLevi* (*Parashas Bo*) notes that the commandment to eat matzah was a part of Torah not only before the Egyptian exile, but even before Creation. The redemption from Egypt took the specific form it did — that of a departure so hurried that there was no time for the dough to rise — only in order to conform to the Torah's commandment of eating matzah as a remembrance of the Exodus from Egypt.

Rabbi Yaakov Kamenetsky answered a seemingly perplexing question according to this principle. How was our forefather Abraham able to keep all the commandments of the Torah even before it was given? He likens Abraham to a master architect, who can study a building and understand how the original blueprint must have looked. Since every aspect of the universe is a manifestation of the Divine blueprint which was Torah, it was possible for Abraham to look at the world and understand the Divine will. Thus he was able to fulfill all the commandments without ever having been given the Torah.

2. After describing the sixth day of Creation, the Torah states: וַיְהִי־עֶרֶב וַיְהִי־בֹקֶר יוֹם הַשִּׁשִּׁי, *and there was evening and there was morning,* **the** *sixth day* (*Genesis* 1:31). The verse adds the definitive article ה, *the*, before the word *sixth*, which is not the case for the other days of Creation. *Rashi* (ibid.) explains that this is a reference to the Five Books of Torah, for ה numerically equals 5. When Hashem completed all of Creation, He stipulated that their existence is conditional on Israel's future acceptance of the Five Books of the Torah. Alternatively, the sixth day is a reference to the sixth day of the month of Sivan, the day the Torah would be given to Israel.

כא כְּ תְּהוֹמוֹת נִבְקָעוּ וּשְׁחָקִים יִרְעֲפוּ־טָל: בְּנִי אַל־יָלֻזוּ
כב מֵעֵינֶיךָ נְצֹר תֻּשִׁיָּה וּמְזִמָּה: וְיִהְיוּ חַיִּים לְנַפְשֶׁךָ וְחֵן
כג לְגַרְגְּרֹתֶיךָ: אָז תֵּלֵךְ לָבֶטַח דַּרְכֶּךָ וְרַגְלְךָ לֹא תִגּוֹף:
כד אִם־תִּשְׁכַּב לֹא־תִפְחָד וְשָׁכַבְתָּ וְעָרְבָה שְׁנָתֶךָ:
כה אַל־תִּירָא מִפַּחַד פִּתְאֹם וּמִשֹּׁאַת רְשָׁעִים כִּי תָבֹא:

בְּרֵאשִׁית בָּרָא אֱלֹהִים, *In the beginning of God's creating* (Genesis 1:1), are interpreted midrashic as בִּשְׁבִיל הַתּוֹרָה שֶׁנִּקְרָאָה רֵאשִׁית דַּרְכּוֹ, *For the sake of the Torah which was called the beginning of His "way,"* Elokim created the [heavens and earth] (see Rashi, ibid.).

The term *understanding* applies to the complex pattern of the orbits of the heavenly bodies, a system that is beyond human calculation (*Ibn Yachya to Psalms 136:5*).

20. בְּדַעְתּוֹ תְּהוֹמוֹת נִבְקָעוּ וּשְׁחָקִים יִרְעֲפוּ־טָל — *Through His knowledge, the depths were cleaved, and the heavens drip dew.* The *depths* refers to the underground wellsprings. The emergence of underground water and the dripping of dew from the heavens are both according to *knowledge* of Torah (*Metzudos*).

Malbim differentiates between the role played by *chochmah, tevunah* and *daas* [wisdom, understanding and knowledge] in Creation. The creation of אֶרֶץ, *earth* (v. 19), corresponds to the foundation of an edifice. The establishment of the *heavens* (v. 19) signifies the completion of the edifice, just as a roof completes a structure. The *depths* and *dew* (v. 20), which fill the world with blessing and good, correspond to furnishing the rooms in the completed building with beautiful utensils (cf. 24:3-4).

Creation is specifically associated with *wisdom*, because the initial creation was יֵשׁ מֵאַיִן, *ex nihilo*, just as the source of wisdom is the Creator Himself, and is not found within the person.

Understanding, on the other hand, is derived from the principles of *chochmah*. The establishment of the heavens, i.e., the completion of creation, was a process of יֵשׁ מִיֵּשׁ, *continuous creation from existing matter*, and thus corresponds to understanding.

The Divine Providence which controls the world from its inception onward is symbolized by the opening of the deep waters and the showering of dew. These are associated with *knowledge*, for the management of the world and its needs are factors of Divine *daas*.

The Midrash states that just as the world was created by means of three traits — *chochmah, tevunah* and *daas* — so, too, was the מִשְׁכָּן, *Tabernacle*, constructed by means of these same three traits. For the verse describing Bezalel (who constructed the Tabernacle) states: וָאֲמַלֵּא אֹתוֹ רוּחַ אֱלֹהִים בְּחָכְמָה וּבִתְבוּנָה וּבְדַעַת, *I have filled him with a Godly spirit, with chochmah and tevunah and daas* (Exodus 31:3). The Sages (*Berachos 55a*) deduce that Bezalel knew how to form the combinations of letters through which heaven and earth were created, for the verse in *Exodus* attributes *chochmah, tevunah* and *daas* to him, just as verses 19-20 here associate Creation with those same three traits. The Holy Temple was also made with these three traits. The Third Temple, too, will be built with these traits, and then they will be given to Israel; as stated by verse 2:6: *For Hashem* יִתֵּן, *will give, chochmah; from His mouth come daas and tevunah.* The verse does not say נָתַן, *He gave* in the past tense, but יִתֵּן, *He will give*, in the future (*Yalkut Shimoni*).

21. בְּנִי אַל־יָלֻזוּ מֵעֵינֶיךָ — *My child, do not let them stray from your eyes.* The aforementioned *chochmah, tevunah* and *daas* [representing the Torah] should not be removed from you, especially now that you realize their great significance, and understand that it was through them that heaven and earth were created (*R' Yonah*).

נְצֹר תֻּשִׁיָּה וּמְזִמָּה — *Safeguard the eternal Torah and [its] wise design.* Heed the

the depths were cleaved, and the heavens drip dew.[21] My child, do not let them stray from your eyes; safeguard the eternal Torah and [its] wise design. [22] They will be life to your soul and a graceful [ornament] for your neck. [23] Then you will walk on your way securely, and your foot will not stumble. [24] When you lie down you will not fear; you will lie down and your sleep will be pleasant. [25] You will not fear sudden terror, nor the holocaust of the wicked when it comes.

Torah in both deed and thought (Metzudos). (Cf. 2:7 for elaboration on תושיה.)

22. וְיִהְיוּ חַיִּים לְנַפְשֶׁךָ — They will be life to your soul, for Torah is a tree of life (see verse 18) (Rashi).

וְחֵן לְגַרְגְּרֹתֶיךָ — And a graceful [ornament] for your neck, for the Torah is praised as an ornament for the neck (see 1:9) (Rashi).

If you heed the Torah, your words will be accepted when you admonish others. This is the favor for your neck. We find that the Sages (Bava Metzia 107b) advise: קְשׁוֹט עַצְמְךָ וְאַחַר כָּךְ קְשׁוֹט אֲחֵרִים, lit., Decorate [i.e. correct] yourself first, and afterwards — only then — decorate others (R' Yonah).[1]

23. אָז תֵּלֵךְ לָבֶטַח דַּרְכֶּךָ — Then you will walk on your way securely. אָז, then, implies a condition: If you heed all of the Torah, then you will walk securely. However, should you transgress even one Torah commandment, then there is reason for you to be fearful (R' Yonah).[2]

וְרַגְלְךָ לֹא תִגּוֹף — And your foot will not stumble. The translation of תִגּוֹף follows Rashi. Metzudos explains it as striking, i.e., your feet will not be struck by stones

strewn on the road, i.e., no evil will befall you.

24. אִם־תִּשְׁכַּב לֹא־תִפְחָד וְשָׁכַבְתָּ וְעָרְבָה שְׁנָתֶךָ — When you lie down you will not fear; you will lie down and your sleep will be pleasant. Your sleep will be pleasant for you will not fear a sudden terror (verse 25) (Rashi).[3]

25. אַל־תִּירָא מִפַּחַד פִּתְאֹם וּמִשֹּׁאַת רְשָׁעִים כִּי תָבֹא — You will not fear sudden terror, nor the holocaust of the wicked when it comes. When darkness comes upon the wicked, you need not fear it, for it will not harm you (Metzudos).

Malbim explains that verses 23-25 each refer to the same two aspects of Divine Providence:

(1) A person will trust in Hashem and therefore not be frightened.

(2) Because Hashem will protect him, no harm will befall him. Verse 23 speaks of the dangers faced by a traveler: He will walk securely, and Hashem will protect him from stumbling. Verse 24 refers to vulnerability during sleep. A person who trusts Hashem will not be afraid, and his sleep will be sweet for Hashem will protect him from nightmares and danger. Verse 25 refers to the time when he arises from his sleep.

1. Most people are blind to their own faults; they see the splinter in someone else's eye, but not in their own. As the saying goes, "Physician, heal yourself!"

2. According to Sfas Emes, the verse refers to our forefather Jacob. Rebecca instructed him to "flee" to Laban's house and seek refuge from Esau (Genesis 27:43). Yet, when Jacob actually left, the Torah does not use the word "fled," but rather, "Jacob departed" (ibid., 28:10). This was because Jacob had בִּטָּחוֹן, trust, in Hashem, and was able to walk on [his] way securely.

3. The Midrash (Bereishis Rabbah 68:1) applies verses 23 and 24 to our forefather Jacob. Although he had to flee from Beer Sheba to Charan, he went securely and did not fear Esau and Laban. He lay down securely and slept (see Rashi to Genesis 28:11) even though one who is pursued usually is too frightened to sleep peacefully (Eitz Yosef ad loc.).
Your heart will be so secure that even dreams will not frighten you (R' Yonah).

כו כִּי־יהוה יִהְיֶה בְכִסְלֶךָ וְשָׁמַר רַגְלְךָ מִלָּכֶד:

כז אַל־תִּמְנַע־טוֹב מִבְּעָלָיו בִּהְיוֹת לְאֵל °יָדְיך לַעֲשׂוֹת: °יָדְךָ ק׳

כח אַל־תֹּאמַר °לְרֵעֶיךָ לֵךְ וָשׁוּב וּמָחָר אֶתֵּן וְיֵשׁ אִתָּךְ: °לְרֵעֲךָ ק׳

He will not be frightened by sudden terror, and will be saved from harm. [These verses indicate an assurance combining trust in Hashem and belief in His protection, a combination of an emotional and physical sense of security found in Hashem's protection.]

26. כִּי־ה׳ יִהְיֶה בְכִסְלֶךָ — *For Hashem will be* [lit. *in*] *your security.* Hashem is the One in Whom you place your confidence and hope (*Rashi, Metzudos*).[1]

Malbim explains this verse as the achievement of complete serenity. With your trust in Hashem and observance of His commandments, you have no need to fear, and no need to take special measures to guard yourself from danger. God guarantees you complete protection.

Rashi cites an alternative explanation from *Talmud Yerushalmi*: בְכִסְלֶךָ refers to matters in which you are a כְּסִיל, *fool* [I.e., God will assist you in areas in which you are foolish, or know not how to behave.][2]

וְשָׁמַר רַגְלְךָ מִלָּכֶד — *And He will guard your feet from entrapment.* This verse is a continuation of the previous one. The righteous who are free of sin and who trust in Hashem will be miraculously saved, even when everything around them is destroyed. *He will guard your feet from entrapment,* i.e., from being ensnared and punished because of the sins of the wicked (cf. *Genesis* 19:15). In the merit of heeding Torah and trust in God (v. 21), God will protect the righteous from misfortune (*R' Yonah*).

The *Vilna Gaon* points out that a person can be ensnared by the Evil Inclination as a result of two factors: either he lacks knowledge, or he is overcome by his desire.

Therefore, this verse states that even in matters *in which you are a fool,* i.e., you lack knowledge, God will keep your feet from stumbling. He will protect you so that the Evil Inclination does not overcome you.

27. אַל־תִּמְנַע־טוֹב מִבְּעָלָיו בִּהְיוֹת לְאֵל יָדְךָ לַעֲשׂוֹת — *Do not withhold good from its rightful recipient, when you have the power to do it.* After the warning in the previous verses to heed all the principles of Torah, these next verses stress the importance of avoiding bad character traits. The trait of begrudging others is mentioned first, for if someone needs a favor, one is obligated by God's command to help him. As the Torah commands (*Deuteronomy* 15:7), *you shall not harden your heart or close your hand against your destitute brother* (*R' Yonah*).

The Sages teach that one who turns a blind eye to the needy is considered as if he worships idols (*Kesubos* 68a) (*R' Yonah*).

בְּעָלָיו — *Its rightful recipient* refers to one who needs the favor (*Metzudos*) or a poor person requesting alms. *If you have the power to do it,* do not withhold it, for there may come a time when you will not be able to give (*Rashi*).

The person requesting the favor is labeled *its rightful recipient,* because one who has the means to fulfill the request becomes obligated to do so (*Meiri*). Thus, *R' Hirsch* points out, the Torah grants the needy the "legal" right to claim help from those who are able to give.

Ralbag explains בְּעָלָיו as *someone who is deserving.* Do not withhold good from someone who is deserving of it if you have it in your power to do this good. This warning also applies to the teaching of

1. *R' Mendel of Kotzk* used to quote this verse to people in time of despair. *For Hashem will be your confidence;* rely on Him *always,* but especially in times of despair, and He will prevent you from feeling helpless.

2. See *Radak* to *Psalms* 116:6, שֹׁמֵר פְּתָאִים ה׳.

 ²⁶ *For HASHEM will be your security, and He will guard your feet from entrapment.*

²⁷ Do not withhold good from its rightful recipient, when you have the power to do it. ²⁸ Do not tell your fellow, "Leave and come back; tomorrow I will give it," when it is [already] with you.

Torah. Do not withhold its knowledge from one who asks you to teach him and is worthy of learning.

Rashi interprets: If you see that your friend wants to help the needy, and *you have it in your power* to stop him, do not stand in his way.[1]

Malbim explains this verse metaphorically: Do not withhold good from yourself, i.e., do kindness to your soul by doing God's will.

בְּהְיוֹת לְאֵל יָדְךָ לַעֲשׂוֹת — *When you have the power to do it.* You do not know how long your wealth will remain with you, so as long as you can afford to give charity — do it! As the Sages teach (see *Shabbos* 151b), עֲשֵׂה עַד שֶׁאַתָּה מוֹצֵא וּמָצוּי לְךָ, *perform the commandments of charity as long as you find someone in need and you have money available* [see *Rashi*, ibid.] (R' Yonah).[2]

28. אַל־תֹּאמַר לְרֵעֲךָ לֵךְ וָשׁוּב וּמָחָר אֶתֵּן וְיֵשׁ אִתָּךְ — *Do not tell your fellow, "Leave and come back; and tomorrow I will give it," when it is [already] with you.* If a poor person requests alms (*Rashi*) or someone needs a favor — and you can comply immediately — do not tell the person to come back another time (*Metzudos*).

If you vowed to give someone a gift, you should fulfill your words as quickly as possible. Telling your friend, "Go away and return," is a sign of reluctance or resentment in the giver, and it aggravates the would-be recipient with a prolonged wait for his expectations to be fulfilled. It can also cause you to sin by humiliating your friend (R' Yonah).

The Talmud (*Bava Metzia* 110b) interprets this verse as a warning against delaying payment of wages to a hired hand [שָׂכָר שָׂכִיר] (*Rashi*). The Torah (*Leviticus* 19:13, *Deuteronomy* 24:15) stipulates that a worker must be paid his wages within a 12-hour period, a day or a night, after he completes his work. If a person has not paid his worker by the first morning the wages are due, he transgresses, *You shall not withhold a worker's wage with you until morning* (*Leviticus*, ibid.). For any subsequent days, he transgresses this verse (R' Yonah).[3]

Malbim interprets this verse metaphorically: Do not delay in doing good for your soul by pushing it off for the next day. Our Sages teach: וְאַל תֹּאמַר לִכְשֶׁאֶפָּנֶה אֶשְׁנֶה שֶׁמָּא לֹא תִפָּנֶה, *And do not say, "When I am free I will study," for perhaps you will not become free* (*Avos* 2:5).

1. Among the four types of donors to charity enumerated in *Avos* (5:16) there is one who wishes to give himself, but wants others not to give. Regarding such a person the *mishnah* states that *his eyes are evil with regard to others,* i.e., he begrudges others the merit that they could earn through this *mitzvah*; or, he begrudges the needy the extra charity. The *mishnah* continues that one who does not give himself and also does not want others to give is labeled רָשָׁע, *wicked.*

2. The Sages state that wealth is like a revolving wheel — it can touch everyone sooner or later. A person should ask for Heavenly mercy that poverty should not strike him, for it is very likely that in time either he or his children or his grandchildren will be poor.

3. The *Chafetz Chaim* was once seen running through the streets of Warsaw on Friday afternoon, as the time of candle lighting approached. People were shocked to see this, until they found out the reason for his haste. One of the workers in the printing house where the *Chafetz Chaim's* books were printed had hurried home before he could be paid. The *Chafetz Chaim* was running to this worker's home in order to pay him his wages before the day was over so that he would not transgress the prohibition of לֹא תָלִין, *You shall not withhold ...* (*Chafetz Chaim Al HaTorah, Maasai L'Melech, Parashas Kedoshim.*)

כט אַל־תַּחֲרֹשׁ עַל־רֵעֲךָ רָעָה וְהוּא־יוֹשֵׁב לָבֶטַח
ל אִתָּךְ: אַל־°תָּרוֹב עִם־אָדָם חִנָּם אִם־לֹא גְמָלְךָ
לא רָעָה: אַל־תְּקַנֵּא בְּאִישׁ חָמָס וְאַל־תִּבְחַר בְּכָל־
לב דְּרָכָיו: כִּי תוֹעֲבַת יְהוָה נָלוֹז וְאֶת־יְשָׁרִים סוֹדוֹ:
לג מְאֵרַת יְהוָה בְּבֵית רָשָׁע וּנְוֵה צַדִּיקִים יְבָרֵךְ:

°תָּרִיב ק'

29. אַל־תַּחֲרֹשׁ עַל־רֵעֲךָ רָעָה וְהוּא־יוֹשֵׁב
לָבֶטַח אִתָּךְ — *Do not devise* [lit. *plow*] *evil
against your fellow, one who dwells
securely with you.* Your friend trusts you
— why, then, should you plot evil against
him? (*Metzudos*).

Rashi relates אַל־תַּחֲרֹשׁ to the literal
meaning of the word לַחֲרֹשׁ, *to plow.* Just
as one who plows prepares a place for the
time of sowing, so, too, one who thinks
evil thoughts prepares a place in his heart
for strategies on how to execute his evil
designs.

R' Yonah explains that this verse surely
does not mean that you are permitted to
devise schemes against someone who is
not loyal to you. Rather, it means that to
plot against one who trusts in you is not
only despicable, it is doubly sinful. If
someone caused you distress, do not plot
evil against him while he still trusts you,
for this would be dishonest. First let him
know that you feel hatred towards him
because of what he did, so that he will
know not to trust you.

This verse may also refer to a case
where one is permitted to plot against
another person in self-defense. Even then,
one should first inform the other person of
one's hard feelings, so that he should not
continue his unjustified trust.

Meiri comments that if your friend
trusts you, you should give him the
benefit of the doubt; do not think badly
about him by suspecting him of doing
something evil against you.

Metaphorically speaking, the verse
teaches that it is improper to allow our
physical forces to plot evil against our

spiritual forces, for Hashem has endowed
our physical body with spirituality for its
benefit and ultimate good (*Malbim*).

30. אַל־תָּרוֹב עִם־אָדָם חִנָּם אִם־לֹא גְמָלְךָ רָעָה
— *Do not quarrel with any man without
cause, if he has done you no evil.* R'
Yonah explains that *if he has done you no
evil* is the explanation of *without cause.*
In other words, quarreling with someone
for no cause refers to someone who has
spoken against you, but whose words
have not caused you harm (cf. *Ecclesiastes*
7:21, גַּם לְכָל־הַדְּבָרִים אֲשֶׁר יְדַבֵּרוּ אַל־תִּתֵּן
לִבֶּךָ, *Moreover, pay no attention to everything* [*men*] *say*). To quarrel is ignoble;
therefore, despite your anger, try to be
calm; do not overreact to what others say.

Rashi renders that you should not complain about someone who has done you
no wrong, even though he does not display the love commanded by וְאָהַבְתָּ לְרֵעֲךָ
כָּמוֹךָ, *You shall love your fellow as yourself* (*Leviticus* 19:18). But it is permitted to
hate someone who is actually wicked.

The word גְּמוּל usually connotes repayment
in kind for some act. *Metzudos*, however,
points out that it can also refer to the initial
stage of action, as used in *Joel* 4:4.

Kiflayim L'sushiah states: Should someone harm you, you should realize that the
harm was ordained by God and the perpetrator was merely His agent. Therefore, do
not quarrel with him, for the evil did not
emanate from him (*Me'am Loez*).[1]

31. אַל־תְּקַנֵּא בְּאִישׁ חָמָס וְעַל־תִּבְחַר בְּכָל־דְּרָכָיו
— *Do not envy a man of violence and do not
choose any of his ways.* Do not follow his
ways, even though you see his success
(*Rashi*), and do not envy the success of a

---

1. King David exemplified this attitude toward tribulation. When he was cursed by Shimi ben
Gera, David's loyal follower Avishai ben Zeruyah insisted on avenging the king's honor, but
David would not permit it. In his humility David asserted, *"He is cursing because HASHEM has said
to him, 'Curse David'"* (see *II Samuel* 16:5-12).

29 *Do not devise evil against your fellow, one who dwells securely with you.* 30 *Do not quarrel with any man without cause, if he has done you no evil.* 31 *Do not envy a man of violence and do not choose any of his ways.* 32 *For one who deviates is an abomination to* H*ASHEM*; *and His counsel is with the upright.* 33 H*ASHEM's blight is upon the house of the wicked, but He blesses the abode of the righteous.*

violent person (*Metzudos*).

וְאַל־תִּבְחַר בְּכָל־דְּרָכָיו — *And do not choose any of his ways,* even the good ones. Do not say, "I will learn only from his good ways, and I will not accept the evil." Our Sages teach us that even the goodness of the wicked is evil to the righteous (see *Yevamos* 103b) (*Vilna Gaon*).[1]

It is forbidden to join the wicked in any undertaking (see II *Chronicles* 20:37, כְּהִתְחַבֶּרְךָ עִם־אֲחַזְיָהוּ פָּרַץ ה' אֶת־מַעֲשֶׂיךָ, *Because you have allied yourself with Ahaziah, H*ASHEM *has wrecked your undertakings*). One is prohibited from joining with the wicked, even for the sake of a *mitzvah*, for this verse teaches us not to choose **any** of his ways (*R' Yonah, Shaarei Teshuvah* 3:51).

According to the Midrash, *a man of violence* refers to Esau. When the Jewish people will be subjugated and oppressed under the rule of Esau, they will complain that their Divine service seems to be in vain, for it is the wicked who succeed (*Malachi* 3:14-15). Therefore, Solomon prophetically exhorts us not to envy the wicked Esau's tranquility, nor to act as he does. Rather, Solomon tells us to look at the outcome, for the day will come when God will despise all who are crooked in commandments (see the next verse), for אִישׁ דָּמִים וּמִרְמָה יְתָעֵב ה', H*ASHEM abhors a bloodthirsty and deceitful man (Psalms* 5:7). On the other hand, one who straightens his ways will be among those who are privy to Hashem's secrets (see the next verse) (*Bamidbar Rabbah* 11).

32-36. Verses 32-36 describe four types of righteous people and their antitheses. This verse contrasts the deviant with the upright. Whereas the former are abhorrent to

God, the latter are so beloved to Him that He reveals His secrets to them (*Vilna Gaon*).

32. כִּי תוֹעֲבַת ה' נָלוֹז — *For one who deviates is an abomination to* H*ASHEM.* נָלוֹז is one who is twisted in his ways (*Rashi*); someone who strays from the straight path (*Metzudos*); one who divests himself of moral ties (*R' Hirsch*).

וְאֶת־יְשָׁרִים סוֹדוֹ — *And His counsel is with the upright.* God reveals His secret counsel to the upright, whom He loves. For example, when He prepared to destroy Sodom, He said, הַמֲכַסֶּה אֲנִי מֵאַבְרָהָם אֲשֶׁר אֲנִי עֹשֶׂה, *Shall I conceal from Abraham what I do?* (*Genesis* 18:17), and revealed His plan to Abraham (*Metzudos*). The word סוֹד denotes an intimate relationship known only to the person involved (*R' Hirsch*).

33. מְאֵרַת ה' בְּבֵית רָשָׁע — H*ASHEM's blight is upon the house of the wicked. Metzudos* explains that wealth in the house of a wicked person is actually a curse, for ultimately it will be the cause of misfortune (cf. *Ecclesiastes* 5:12).

וּנְוֵה צַדִּיקִים יְבָרֵךְ — *But He blesses the abode of the righteous.* God will bless whatever is in the abode of the righteous, for they use their bounty to help the poor, and will, therefore, be rewarded for their actions (*Metzudos*).

The dwelling of a wicked person is termed a בַּיִת, *house,* i.e., a permanent abode, because the wicked regard this world as their permanent home. A righteous person, on the other hand, views this world as but a נָוֶה, *abode,* i.e., a temporary dwelling. God's curse will be even upon the wicked person's "permanent home" in this world, and all the more so in the World to Come. The

1. The Talmud (ibid. 104a) cites the case of Laban, who pursued Jacob with the intention of harming him. God warned Laban, הִשָּׁמֶר לְךָ פֶּן־תְּדַבֵּר עִם־יַעֲקֹב מִטּוֹב עַד־רָע, *Beware lest you speak with Jacob either good or bad* (*Genesis* 31:24). Laban's "good" would inevitably be evil for the righteous Jacob.

לד-לה אִם־לַלֵּצִים הוּא־יָלִיץ °וְלַעֲנִיִּים יִתֶּן־חֵן: כְּבוֹד
חֲכָמִים יִנְחָלוּ וּכְסִילִים מֵרִים קָלוֹן:
ד/א-ב א שִׁמְעוּ בָנִים מוּסַר אָב וְהַקְשִׁיבוּ לָדַעַת בִּינָה:
ב כִּי לֶקַח טוֹב נָתַתִּי לָכֶם תּוֹרָתִי אַל־תַּעֲזֹבוּ:

°וְלַעֲנָוִים ק׳

righteous person, who looks at this world as but a transitory dwelling place, will enjoy Hashem's blessing even in his "temporary abode," and certainly in the Hereafter (*Vilna Gaon*).[1]

34. אִם־לַלֵּצִים הוּא־יָלִיץ וְלַעֲנָוִים יִתֶּן־חֵן — *If [one is drawn] to the scoffers, he will scoff; but [if one is drawn] to the humble, one will find favor.* The translation, which suggests that a person is influenced by his companions, follows *Rashi*. A person drawn after scoffers will become one. But if he joins humble people, he will be influenced by them and eventually his deeds will win the favor of other people.

Metzudos renders: Hashem repays each person according to his actions. He will cause scorners to be mocked and scorned at the time of their own downfall. On the other hand, God grants favor to humble people who honor others, and He sees to it that others appreciate them, and hold them in high esteem.

For those who, in frivolous concert, degrade any God-willed sanctity and seek to make a mockery of it in the minds of men, Hashem has ruin in store: *He prepares scorn for the scorners.* They and their ideas will ultimately be exposed as such futile nonsense that they will not escape the laughter of the world. On the other hand, people who subordinate themselves humbly to God's will and sacred values shall, through their ability and the integrity of their conduct, gain חֵן, *gracious favor*, not

only in God's eyes, but also in the eyes of men (*R' Hirsch*).

A לֵץ, *scoffer*, is the opposite of an עָנָו, *humble person*. Even when insulted by others, a humble person will not respond in kind; when he is disgraced by others, he does not answer. A scoffer, on the other hand, disgraces and mocks everyone (*Vilna Gaon*).

Malbim explains the two opposites as follows: A scoffer mocks *chochmah*, for he does not comprehend the logic behind it. In his haughtiness, he concludes that anything he cannot understand cannot be true. A humble person, on the other hand, realizes that a human being is incapable of fully comprehending Divine *chochmah*. Therefore, he does not dispute it.

The Sages (*Shabbos* 104a and *Yoma* 38b) deduce from this verse that בָּא לִיטַמֵא פּוֹתְחִין לוֹ, *If one wishes to do something impure* [i.e., to be wicked] *he is given the opportunity to do so* — i.e., Heaven will not interfere to hinder him from impurity (*Rashi*, ibid.). Conversely, however, בָּא לִיטַהֵר מְסַיְיעִים אוֹתוֹ, *If one wishes to do something pure he is assisted from On High.*

This teaching is implicit in the verse: *If one goes to the scoffers, he will scoff* — if he wishes to join the scorners, he will be afforded the opportunity to scorn on his own, and will neither be impeded nor assisted by Heaven. However, if he *joins the humble ones*, יִתֶּן־חֵן, *He [i.e., Hashem] will give him favor*; he will be Divinely assisted (*Rashi* ibid.).

1. The homes of the righteous personify their perspective on life. An American woman, who was a renowned supporter of worthy causes, went to Radin in the course of a trip, to visit the saintly *Chafetz Chaim*. When she entered the latter's house she was taken aback by the simplicity of his "furnishings." Aside from an old wooden table and several well-worn chairs and bookcases, the room was bare. Unable to contain her shock, she blurted out, "Where is your furniture?"

The *Chafetz Chaim* responded with a question of his own, "And where is yours?"

"Why, mine is at home, of course," she answered. "I am only passing through Radin temporarily, during a trip. I don't carry my furniture with me."

"The same is true of my furniture," explained the *Chafetz Chaim*. "I am just passing through this world temporarily. I don't need my furniture with me here. My possessions are all in my permanent home — the one I am building in the World to Come."

³⁴ *If [one is drawn] to the scoffers, he will scoff; but [if one is drawn] to the humble, one will find favor.* ³⁵ *The wise inherit honor, but fools generate disgrace.*

¹ **H**ear, children, the Father's discipline, and be attentive to know understanding: ² For I have given you a good teaching, do not forsake My Torah.

The Torah, the Prophets and the Holy Writings all reiterate the principle that: בְּדֶרֶךְ שֶׁאָדָם רוֹצֶה לֵילֵךְ בָּהּ מוֹלִיכִין אוֹתוֹ, *A person is led in the way he wishes to go.* This verse is one of the sources for this principle (*Makkos* 10b).

35. כְּבוֹד חֲכָמִים יִנְחָלוּ — *The wise inherit honor,* i.e., they will be honored by everyone (*Meiri*). Not only will the wise themselves enjoy honor, but they will also pass it on as an inheritance (יִנְחָלוּ) to their children (*Vilna Gaon*).

וּכְסִילִים מֵרִים קָלוֹן — *But fools generate disgrace* as their portion. The word מֵרִים is derived from תְּרוּמָה, lit., *raised up or separated*, the portion of a crop that is separated from the rest and given to the Kohen. Thus, in contrast to wise people whose personal portion is honor, the fool can look forward to disgrace (*Rashi, Metzudos*).

The word קָלוֹן, *disgrace*, is derived from the term קָלוּי בָּאֵשׁ, *parched over fire* (Leviticus 2:14), for when a person is shamed, his face reddens as if it were burnt by fire (*Metzudos*).

The *Vilna Gaon* explains that when God gives honor to the wicked, it is in order to "raise up," i.e., increase, their subsequent disgrace [מֵרִים קָלוֹן]. Such was the case of

Haman — had he not risen to a position of pomp and honor, his downfall and disgrace would not have been so great.

R' Yonah (Shaarei Teshuvah 3:147 and 191) renders this phrase as *a disgraceful person* (אִישׁ קָלוֹן) *elevates fools,* honoring and praising them. Tremendous benefit results from honoring the wise, and immense harm results from respecting the wicked. When wise people are held in high esteem, their teachings are accepted, and others are inspired to emulate them, and Torah knowledge increases. Even those whose hearts are in a stupor become aroused at witnessing the honor accorded the Torah. They recognize Torah's virtues; the desire for Torah permeates their hearts; and they immerse themselves in the sincere study of Torah for the sake of Heaven.

Thus, it is understandable that our Sages explain (*Sanhedrin* 99b) that one who scorns a Torah scholar has no share in the World to Come, even if he has Torah and good deeds to his credit, for by scorning Torah scholars, he mocks Hashem's word. A servant cannot love his master if he respects his master's enemies and has a close relationship with those his master has distanced.

IV

1. שִׁמְעוּ בָנִים מוּסַר אָב — *Hear, children, the Father's discipline.* The father is God (*Rashi*), and the discipline is His Torah (*Ralbag*).

Ibn Ezra explains that after warning his own son [to heed his reproof], King Solomon admonishes other children to heed the reproof of their parents. Accordingly, our verse addresses *children*, in the plural, whereas the previous chapters speak to *my child*, in the singular.

וְהַקְשִׁיבוּ לָדַעַת בִּינָה — *And be attentive to know understanding.* The *Vilna Gaon* explains that the word שִׁמְעוּ in the first half of

the verse has three connotations: 1) accepting; 2) understanding; and 3) literally, it means listening. The word הַקְשִׁיבוּ, in the second half, also refers to listening, but it implies a greater concentration on hearing and understanding what is being said. Thus, this verse exhorts children to accept their Father's discipline and also to *be attentive*, and listen with great concentration in order to derive *understanding* from the *chochmah*.

2. כִּי לֶקַח טוֹב נָתַתִּי לָכֶם תּוֹרָתִי אַל־תַּעֲזֹבוּ — *For I have given you a good teaching, do not forsake My Torah.* King Solomon speaks in

ג־ד כִּי־בֵן הָיִיתִי לְאָבִי רַךְ וְיָחִיד לִפְנֵי אִמִּי: וַיֹּרֵנִי
ה וַיֹּאמֶר לִי יִתְמָךְ־דְּבָרַי לִבֶּךָ שְׁמֹר מִצְוֹתַי וֶחְיֵה: קְנֵה
חָכְמָה קְנֵה בִינָה אַל־תִּשְׁכַּח וְאַל־תֵּט מֵאִמְרֵי־פִי:

the first person, as if Hashem had said this directly (*Rashi*).

The *Vilna Gaon* relates לֶקַח to לָקַחַת, *to take* (see 10:8, חֲכַם־לֵב יִקַּח מִצְוֹת). This refers to the commandments that are to be "taken" and performed at their appropriate times. Unlike other *mitzvos*, however, Torah study is a perpetual obligation, regarding which the verse warns אַל תַּעֲזֹבוּ, *do not forsake [it]*, even for a moment (*Vilna Gaon*).

Only through immersion in Torah study and the performance of its commandments can one appreciate the beauty of its way. But once a person distances himself from the Torah, his Evil Inclination makes him perceive God's service as a burden and a hardship, thus preventing him from returning to His way. Therefore, this verse warns: *do not forsake My Torah*, for only then will you see that it is a *good teaching* (*Chevel Nachalah*).[1]

The Midrash (*Yalkut Shimoni*) interprets לֶקַח טוֹב to mean *good merchandise*, and elaborates with the tale of several merchants traveling at sea with their wares. They asked one passenger, who appeared to have no baggage at all, "Where is your merchandise?" He responded, "It is hidden. When we reach our destination I will show it to you." The merchants searched the entire ship but found no trace of this fellow's wares and began to mock him. A short while later, customs officials came aboard and impounded the ship's entire contents. The bewildered merchants disembarked at their destination bereft of all their posses-

sions. Meanwhile, the passenger who had been the object of their derision made his way to the local study hall and began teaching the public from the wealth of his Torah knowledge, whereupon the merchants contritely approached him to intercede with the local citizenry on their behalf. To their chagrin, they had been taught the value of his "merchandise" as opposed to theirs. [See *Shemos Rabbah* 33:1, for further elaboration of the superiority of Torah over other acquisitions.][2]

3. כִּי־בֵן הָיִיתִי לְאָבִי רַךְ וְיָחִיד לִפְנֵי אִמִּי — *For I was a son to my father, a tender and only son before my mother.* To demonstrate that his admonitions against such enticing activities as robbery and immorality are not motivated by misanthropy, King Solomon recalls his parents' love for him. His parents showered great love upon him, but despite that, they reproved him whenever necessary to give him instruction, and King Solomon is passing on their instruction to us (*Rashi* quoting R' Yosef Kara).

Alternately, the "Father" in this verse refers to God, Who granted Divine inspiration to Solomon. This interpretation finds support in *II Samuel* 7:14, where God declares, *I will be a Father to him and he will be a son to Me*. The "mother" of this verse is the Jewish nation, to whom King Solomon was as beloved as an only son. Because of these special relationships, Hashem taught Solomon the following words of *mussar* (*Rashi*).

1. This verse refers to Torah as לֶקַח, based on the term לִקּוּחִין, *betrothal*, and implores the Jew not to sever his bond with God, just as a married woman remains faithful to her husband (*Zechus Avos*).

2. The *Chafetz Chaim* explains that טוֹב, *good*, is a very subjective description. What may be "good" to a pauper would be worthless to a wealthy man, whereas the rich man's "good" may be meaningless to a king. Similarly, people have widely varying tastes regarding what they enjoy and what they consider good, depending on their education and background. However, it is the King of all kings, in Whose eyes everything He created is insignificant, Who tells us that the Torah is the ultimate "good." Only the Master of the Universe, Who knows the full depths of Torah's wisdom, can tell man that Torah is the absolute "good.'

³ *For I was a son to my father, a tender and only son before my mother.* ⁴ *He taught me, and said to me, "Let my words sustain your heart; observe my commandments and live.* ⁵ *Acquire wisdom; acquire understanding. Do not forget and do not stray from the words of my mouth.*

Though Solomon was not his father David's only child, he was his primary offspring by virtue of his ascension to the throne, which ensured the continuity of the Davidic dynasty. To his mother, Bathsheba, he was literally an only son, and as a result of David's deep affection for Bathsheba, he considered Solomon like an only son. This confirms that the *mussar* Solomon received from his father was very precious, for a father will discipline his children, all the more so the child who is most beloved to him, and for whom he reserves the most special and lofty concepts (*Malbim*).

4. וַיֹּרֵנִי וַיֹּאמֶר לִי — *He taught me, and said to me.* King David *taught* his son through personal example, for Solomon observed how David fulfilled the Torah's precepts throughout his life. In addition to being a role model, David also *said to me*, i.e., he taught his son verbally (*Malbim*).

יִתְמָךְ־דְּבָרַי לִבֶּךָ שְׁמֹר מִצְוֹתַי וֶחְיֵה — *Let my words sustain your heart; observe my commandments and live.* Man's heart vacillates in its constant struggle to remain faithful to the truths perceived by his intellect. King Solomon's admonitions are intended to support and strengthen the heart's resolve to prevail over the Evil Inclination (*Malbim*).

A person may mistakenly assume that since commandments are so valuable, he should concentrate on them instead of Torah study. To dispel the notion that Torah study has no independent value

apart from serving as a vehicle to know the commandments, Solomon refers to the Torah as that which sustains the heart, and serves as the mainstay of man's spiritual diet, much as bread is the staple of bodily sustenance. Just as the body must be nourished constantly, so the study of Torah must be ongoing. The commandments are analogous to spiced dishes and medicinal herbs, of which one partakes intermittently as dietary supplements or culinary additives. Therefore, this verse first stipulates, *let my words support your heart,* i.e., first study the words of my Torah, which will sustain your heart, and only afterwards *keep my commandments* at their proper time *and live* (*Vilna Gaon*).[1,2]

5. קְנֵה חָכְמָה קְנֵה בִינָה — *Acquire wisdom; acquire understanding.* The word קְנֵה, *acquire,* also means *buy.*[3] Its use in this verse indicates that if one cannot find someone willing to teach him Torah free of charge, he should be prepared to hire a teacher (*Vilna Gaon*). [Just as someone is willing to pay for food since it is a necessity of life, so, too, one must be ready to pay for Torah, which is the "food" of the soul.]

אַל־תִּשְׁכַּח וְאַל־תֵּט מֵאִמְרֵי־פִי — *Do not forget and do not stray from the words of my mouth.* Beware of forsaking the Torah, either through forgetfulness or through your surrender to the desires of your Evil Inclination (*Malbim*). Beware that when acquiring *chochmah* and *binah*, you do not *forget* the teachings of *mussar* nor *turn away* from them in practice. Make sure

1. Despite the primacy of Torah study in and of itself, one must also study with a view towards achieving mastery over the practical details of how to perform the commandments.

2. The Talmud derives from this verse that an unborn child is taught the entire Torah during its gestation, only to forget it all upon birth (*Niddah* 30b).

3. In its discussion of dream symbolism, the Talmud (*Berachos* 56b) states: One who sees the word קְנֵה, *acquire,* in his dream (see *Maharsha*) should anticipate the acquisition of wisdom as our verse states, קְנֵה חָכְמָה, *acquire wisdom.* That the word קְנֵה portends wisdom echoes another Talmudic statement: דָּא קְנִי מַה חָסֵר, דָּא לֹא קְנִי מַה קְנִי, *If one acquires it* [i.e., wisdom], *what does he lack? If one fails to acquire it, what does he possess?* (*Nedarim* 41a).

רז אַל־תַּעַזְבֶהָ וְתִשְׁמְרֶךָּ אֱהָבֶהָ וְתִצְּרֶךָּ: רֵאשִׁית

ח חָכְמָה קְנֵה חָכְמָה וּבְכָל־קִנְיָנְךָ קְנֵה בִינָה: סַלְסְלֶהָ

ט וּתְרוֹמְמֶךָ תְּכַבֵּדְךָ כִּי תְחַבְּקֶנָּה: תִּתֵּן לְרֹאשְׁךָ

י לִוְיַת־חֵן עֲטֶרֶת תִּפְאֶרֶת תְּמַגְּנֶךָ: שְׁמַע בְּנִי וְקַח

יא אֲמָרָי וְיִרְבּוּ לְךָ שְׁנוֹת חַיִּים: בְּדֶרֶךְ חָכְמָה הֹרֵתִיךָ

that your engrossment in wisdom does not cause you to neglect your efforts at perfecting your character traits. The *mishnah* states: וְלֹא הַמִּדְרָשׁ אֶלָּא הַמַּעֲשֶׂה, *not study but practice is the main thing (Avos 1:17) (Rabbeinu Yonah).*

6. אַל־תַּעַזְבֶהָ וְתִשְׁמְרֶךָּ אֱהָבֶהָ וְתִצְּרֶךָּ — *Do not forsake [the Torah], and it will protect you; love it, and it will safeguard you.* Do not forsake the Torah, and it will protect you from all obstacles (*Metzudos*). One who does not abandon Torah even when motivated by pragmatic considerations will be protected by it [שְׁמִירָה], but one who goes to a higher level and actually loves Torah for itself will enjoy נְצִירָה, *safeguarding,* a correspondingly higher level of security (*Malbim*).

7. רֵאשִׁית חָכְמָה קְנֵה חָכְמָה — *The beginning of wisdom [is to] acquire wisdom.* The initial stage of wisdom is to learn from others and to study with a teacher (*Rashi*).

וּבְכָל־קִנְיָנְךָ קְנֵה בִינָה — *From your every acquisition acquire understanding.* Once a person has absorbed wisdom from his teachers, he should use his own deductive powers to derive the reasons for what he has learned and seek new applications of his wisdom (*Rashi*).[1]

According to *Ibn Nachmiash* this verse provides us with the proper sequence to follow in the study of Torah: First, one must accumulate knowledge of Torah;

only afterwards can he delve into understanding the reasoning behind it (see *Shabbos* 63a).

R' Bachya renders the verse: *and with all your possessions, acquire understanding.* First and foremost you must acquire wisdom, but this acquisition is incomplete without also acquiring understanding. Therefore, a person must use *all his possessions* — כָּל קִנְיָנֶךָ — if necessary, in order to acquire *understanding,* for that is true wealth.

Malbim notes that *chochmah* — i.e., the wisdom of the Torah — is based solely on what was received from God Himself; one must accept the principles taught by God as its basis. Thus, the beginning of *chochmah* is only *chochmah* itself; there is no other source of wisdom — only the principles of the Torah. *Binah,* however, is attained through logical and inductive processes, based on previously acquired Torah wisdom and general knowledge. Therefore, the verse continues: In all the fields of knowledge you have already acquired, use your inductive processes to attain *understanding.*

8. סַלְסְלֶהָ וּתְרוֹמְמֶךָ — *Search for it and it will uplift you.* The translation follows *Rashi,* who adds, review it, over and over again, examining it with precision, as one examines the shoots in a vineyard to find the clusters ready for harvest [cf. כְּבוֹצֵר עַל סַלְסִלּוֹת (*Jeremiah* 6:9)].

1. The Talmud (*Gittin* 67a) relates that Isi ben Yehudah praised R' Akiva as being an אוֹצָר בָּלוּם, a *storehouse with compartments. Rashi,* citing *Avos D'Rav Nosson,* explains that R' Akiva's approach to the study and teaching of Torah was akin to one who enters a field and harvests barley, wheat, peas and beans. As he harvests, he places all of these varieties in his basket, and then assorts them in separate bins upon his return home. Similarly, R' Akiva absorbed and reviewed his teachers' lessons in the Scriptures, Halachic discourses, Midrashic interpretations, and Aggadic portions. Only when he began teaching Torah to others did he classify his teachings into the distinct categories of knowledge — אַגָּדוֹת, הֲלָכוֹת, סִפְרָא, סִפְרֵי — to facilitate his students' comprehension, just as different varieties of food are compartmentalized in a storehouse.

⁶ *Do not forsake [the Torah], and it will protect you; love it, and it will safeguard you.'*

⁷ *The beginning of wisdom [is to] acquire wisdom! From your every acquisition acquire understanding.* ⁸ *Search for it and it will uplift you. It will honor you when you embrace it.* ⁹ *It will set an adornment of grace upon your head. It will bestow a crown of splendor upon you.*

¹⁰ *Hear, my child, and take my words; and they will add years of life to you.* ¹¹ *I instructed you in the way of wisdom;*

Ibn Ezra and *Malbim* render סַלְסְלֶהָ as *lifting up* and *extolling wisdom*, holding it in high esteem. In return, wisdom will exalt you.[1]

Ralbag explains it to mean, *Tread in its path*.

Metzudos renders as constantly *caress* wisdom.

תְּכַבֵּדְךָ כִּי תְחַבְּקֶנָּה — *It will honor you when you embrace it*. To *embrace* wisdom is to study the Torah assiduously (*Ibn Ezra*).

9. תִּתֵּן לְרֹאשְׁךָ לִוְיַת־חֵן — *It will set an adornment of grace upon your head*. Your words will be accepted and heeded (*Rabbeinu Yonah*) [cf. 1:9]).

עֲטֶרֶת תִּפְאֶרֶת תְּמַגְּנֶךָּ — *It will bestow a crown of splendor upon you*. A Torah scholar who is favored and esteemed by others would do well to realize that he achieves such acclaim only by dint of his Torah study. It was in this vein that R' Yose would exclaim each year on Shavuos (*Pesachim* 68b): "Were it not for this day [on which the Torah was given] there are many Yoses in the marketplace [from

whom I would be indistinguishable]" (*Chevel Nachalah*).

10. שְׁמַע בְּנִי וְקַח אֲמָרָי וְיִרְבּוּ לְךָ שְׁנוֹת חַיִּים — *Hear, my child, and take my words; and they will add years of life to you*. *My child* is a term of endearment. It is because you are so dear to me that I wish to correct your ways, and add good and peaceful years to your life (*Metzudos*). (See also 3:2.)

11. בְּדֶרֶךְ חָכְמָה הֹרֵתִיךָ הִדְרַכְתִּיךָ בְּמַעְגְּלֵי־יֹשֶׁר — *I instructed you in the way of wisdom; I led you in courses of fairness*. One's goal in character development should be to travel upon *the way of wisdom*, by adopting the median position between the extremes of each character trait, e.g., by being generous rather than miserly or profligate.[2] To achieve this goal, a well-balanced individual must have הוֹרָאָה, i.e., proper instruction. At times, however, it may be necessary for the person to use a מַעְגָּל, a *circular course*, by veering towards one extreme to counteract his natural inclination towards the opposite extreme. Thus, one who is stingy must force himself to be a spend-

1. The sixth chapter of *Pirkei Avos* enumerates the special qualities merited by someone who studies Torah לִשְׁמָהּ, *for its own sake*. It concludes: וּמְגַדַּלְתּוֹ וּמְרוֹמַמְתּוֹ עַל כָּל הַמַּעֲשִׂים, *[the Torah] makes him great and exalts him above all things.* "Torah study for its own sake" is characterized by a searching inquiry born of a thirst to uncover ever more of its depths. Thus, this verse enjoins the Torah student to study with סִלְסוּל, an ongoing quest for in-depth understanding, through which he will merit the exalted position reserved for those who study Torah for its own sake (*Nefesh HaChaim*).

2. The classic text of this concept is *Rambam's Hil. Deios* (1:4). He counsels that one should avoid extremes and search for the middle course, and he gives several examples. One should be neither quick to anger nor completely passive; rather, one should become angry only to insure that harmful conduct not be repeated. One should curb eating except for foods that are needed for survival. One should aspire only to as much wealth as is needed for a decent livelihood. One should avoid both stinginess and profligacy, but should give charity according to his means and lend money to those who need funds. Finally, *Rambam* says that one should be neither overly jolly nor morbidly depressed; rather, one should always be cheerful and pleasant.

יב הַדְרַכְתִּיךָ בְּמַעְגְּלֵי־יֹשֶׁר: בְּלֶכְתְּךָ לֹא־יֵצַר צַעֲדֶךָ
יג וְאִם־תָּרוּץ לֹא תִכָּשֵׁל: הַחֲזֵק בַּמּוּסָר אַל־תֶּרֶף
יד נִצְּרֶהָ כִּי־הִיא חַיֶּיךָ: בְּאֹרַח רְשָׁעִים אַל־תָּבֹא
טו וְאַל־תְּאַשֵּׁר בְּדֶרֶךְ רָעִים: פְּרָעֵהוּ אַל־תַּעֲבָר־בּוֹ
טז שְׂטֵה מֵעָלָיו וַעֲבוֹר: כִּי לֹא יִשְׁנוּ אִם־לֹא יָרֵעוּ
יז וְנִגְזְלָה שְׁנָתָם אִם־לֹא °יכשולו: כִּי לָחֲמוּ לֶחֶם

°יַכְשִׁילוּ ק׳

thrift for a time, in order to imbue himself with a general spirit of generosity (see *Rambam, Hil. Deios* 1:4, 2:2).[1] When taking such a circuitous route, however, there is a danger that one may become mired in the extreme toward which one has veered. To prevent this, one requires הַדְרָכָה, *to be led* and guided along this circular path, so that the temporary detour will lead back to the straight path (*Malbim*).

12. בְּלֶכְתְּךָ לֹא־יֵצַר צַעֲדֶךָ — *When you walk, your steps will not be constricted.* Someone who walks in a narrow place where he cannot stride freely is likely to fall (*Rashi*).

וְאִם־תָּרוּץ לֹא תִכָּשֵׁל — *And when you run, you will not stumble.* This verse warns about two potential pitfalls to avoid: When one "walks" on the path of Torah, fulfilling the obligations incumbent upon him, he must be careful not to be slothful in the performance of *mitzvos*. This is the meaning of not constricting his footsteps.

At times, however, one may wish to "run" along this same path with great enthusiasm, progressing rapidly upward through the levels of spirituality, adopting ever increasing stringencies, practicing unusual piety. Under such circumstances, one must always be vigilant not to stumble by overstepping his current spiritual capabilities. This occurred to Elisha ben Avuyah (*Chagigah* 15a) the *tanna*, who delved prematurely into the mystical realm of Torah and emerged a heretic. As a result,

he was shunned by his former colleagues and was known as *Acher*, or "The Other." Therefore, the verse warns that one must be careful not to stumble when advancing quickly on the path of Torah (*Malbim*).

To successfully advance in Divine service, a person must proceed gradually and restrain the urge to exceed his current spiritual level. The *Vilna Gaon* interprets this verse as an assurance (rather than a warning) to one who attempts to accelerate his spiritual ascent by "running" from one level to the next. The Torah will protect him so that he will not stumble and fall.

13. הַחֲזֵק בַּמּוּסָר אַל־תֶּרֶף — *Hold fast to discipline; do not let go.* Hold onto the Torah (*Rashi*). Do not weaken your grasp on *mussar* (*Metzudos*). Grasp onto the discipline of *mussar* and strengthen yourself in it. Do not let yourself weaken even for a moment (*Vilna Gaon*).

Man's natural inclinations tend toward evil. (See 1:2, *Malbim's* definition of *mussar*.) Therefore, in man's ongoing struggle for mastery over his logical facilities and his natural inclinations, only *mussar*, i.e., fear of Heaven, can provide the spiritual fortitude to restrain passion and allow the intellect to prevail. Thus, one must cling mightily to discipline lest it elude one's grasp for even a moment and dissipate. The term הַחֲזֵק, *hold fast*, implies that the object in one's grasp is trying to separate itself from the person, i.e., *mussar* is a concept that is not natural to the person, so

1. The Yeshiva of Kelm emphasized תִּיקוּן הַמִּדּוֹת, *perfection of character traits*. When Rabbi Yechezkel Levenstein was a student there, he was considered too shy. Even though shame is a trait that merits Paradise [see *Avos* 5:24], as with every other trait, it must be measured and balanced so that it does not interfere with other facets of serving God. The "prescription" to cure his excessive shyness was the following exercise: R' Chatzkel had to stand up on a chair in front of the packed study hall and wind up the big clock hanging on the wall.

I led you in courses of fairness. ¹² *When you walk, your steps will not be constricted and when you run, you will not stumble.* ¹³ *Hold fast to discipline; do not let go. Guard it, for it is your life.* ¹⁴ *Do not come to the path of the wicked, and do not walk in the way of evildoers.* ¹⁵ *Reject it; do not pass on it — veer away from it and move away.* ¹⁶ *For the [wicked] cannot sleep if they do not do evil, and their sleep will be robbed [from them] if they do not cause others to stumble.* ¹⁷ *For they eat the bread*

he must forcefully grasp onto it and not weaken even for a moment (*Malbim*).

The Talmud (*Shabbos* 31a,b) compares a person who has Torah knowledge but lacks fear of Heaven to a גִּזְבָּר, *treasurer*, who has the keys to a safe, but not the keys to the building. Therefore, says the *Chafetz Chaim*, if a Torah scholar lacks *mussar*, his Torah will not endure. He likens such a person to a traveler buffeted by storm winds. If he does not wrap his clothing tightly around himself, the winds may rip all his clothing from him. So, too, with the winds of heresy blowing in society, a person must wrap a cloak of *mussar* around his Torah learning to protect it from damage.

נִצְּרֶהָ — *Guard it.* Constantly add safeguards to your discipline to prevent yourself from weakening (*Vilna Gaon*).

כִּי־הִיא חַיֶּיךָ — *For it is your life.* God grants man the gift of life so that he may improve any character traits that he has not yet perfected. Therefore, a person must always intensify his efforts in *mussar*, for if not, לָמָּה לּוֹ חַיִּים, *for what purpose does he have life?* (*Vilna Gaon*).

14. בְּאֹרַח רְשָׁעִים אַל־תָּבֹא וְאַל־תְּאַשֵּׁר בְּדֶרֶךְ רָעִים — *Do not come to the path of the wicked, and do not walk in the way of evildoers.* רְשָׁעִים, *the wicked*, refers to those who sin only against God, while רָעִים, *evildoers*, connotes those who sin against their fellow man and, thereby, against God, as well. The Talmud notes that most people are guilty of a degree of theft [either directly or indirectly, through withholding profits or wages, or not giving full value for money received, etc.] (*Bava Basra* 165a). Since there is a proliferation of people acting wrongly toward

their fellows, the term דֶּרֶךְ, meaning a broad, well-traveled road, is used in conjunction with those who perpetrate evil against man, while a narrow, less frequented path, termed אֹרַח, is associated with the *wicked* who sin against God (*Vilna Gaon*).

15. פְּרָעֵהוּ אַל־תַּעֲבָר־בּוֹ שְׂטֵה מֵעָלָיו וַעֲבוֹר — *Reject it; do not pass on it — veer away from it and move away.* *Ralbag* renders: If you can nullify the way of the wicked by preventing them from completing their evil, do it and do not pass on their way by agreeing with them. If you are unable to stop them, veer away from them; avoid them and have no part in their evil.

According to the *Vilna Gaon*, this verse counsels that base desires can be subjugated only gradually; a person who "jumps" immediately to the opposite extreme in an attempt to completely uproot his desires will fail. Rather than trying to uproot his passions immediately, one should first stop indulging as a matter of unbridled habit [*reject it*]; then one should strive to refrain from even chance indulgences [*do not pass on it*]; and ultimately, he should stop even activities that remotely connected with such desires [*veer away and move away*].

16. כִּי לֹא יִשְׁנוּ אִם־לֹא יָרֵעוּ — *For the [wicked] cannot sleep if they do not do evil.* Those who have integrated sin into their very natures cannot even sleep without first indulging in sin (*R' Saadyah Gaon*). [In comparison to the restlessness of evildoers, the innocent man's sleep is sweet (see 3:24).]

וְנִגְזְלָה שְׁנָתָם אִם־לֹא יַכְשִׁילוּ — *And their sleep will be robbed [from them] if they do not cause others to stumble.* Even after the

יח רֶשַׁע וְיֵין חֲמָסִים יִשְׁתּוּ: וְאֹרַח צַדִּיקִים כְּאוֹר

יט נֹגַהּ הוֹלֵךְ וָאוֹר עַד־נְכוֹן הַיּוֹם: דֶּרֶךְ רְשָׁעִים

כ כָּאֲפֵלָה לֹא יָדְעוּ בַּמֶּה יִכָּשֵׁלוּ: בְּנִי

כא לִדְבָרַי הַקְשִׁיבָה לַאֲמָרַי הַט־אָזְנֶךָ: אַל־יַלִּיזוּ

כב מֵעֵינֶיךָ שָׁמְרֵם בְּתוֹךְ לְבָבֶךָ: כִּי־חַיִּים הֵם

wicked have satisfied their sinful appetites, they cannot sleep comfortably; they view their sleep as "stolen" if they haven't led others to sin (*Malbim*).

17. כִּי לָחֲמוּ לֶחֶם רֶשַׁע וְיֵין חֲמָסִים יִשְׁתּוּ — *For they eat the bread of wickedness, and they drink the wine of violence*. They obtained their bread and wine through violence and theft (*Metzudos*).

This verse explains why the wicked cannot sleep: To them, evil and sin are like bread. Just as someone who is hungry cannot fall asleep, so, too, they cannot sleep until they have committed evil (*Vilna Gaon*).

18. וְאֹרַח צַדִּיקִים כְּאוֹר נֹגַהּ הוֹלֵךְ וָאוֹר עַד־נְכוֹן הַיּוֹם — *The path of the righteous is like the glow of sunlight, growing until high noon.* Sunlight is a metaphor for Torah scholars, who attain continuously higher levels of Torah comprehension, just as the day becomes progressively brighter until it reaches its zenith at noon. High noon is the time when the light is established [נְכוֹן] in its completeness (*Metzudos*).

The Sages (*Bereishis Rabbah* 66:4) teach that the righteous undergo suffering in this world, but ultimately experience tranquility in the next [תְּחִלָּתָן יִסּוּרִין וְסוֹפָן שַׁלְוָה]. Accordingly, *Alshich* explains that the path of the righteous is termed an אֹרַח, a narrow, shaded path which, however, ultimately turns into a broad, sunny road. It

is comparable to the light of dawn, which initially is very dim, but grows and brightens until it shines forth in its full strength. So, too, the righteous initially suffer in this world, but this very suffering is the reason for the great light they will merit in the Hereafter.

19. דֶּרֶךְ רְשָׁעִים כָּאֲפֵלָה לֹא יָדְעוּ בַּמֶּה יִכָּשֵׁלוּ — *[But] the way of the wicked is like darkness; they do not know upon what they stumble.* Someone walking in darkness [whether physical or spiritual] cannot avoid the obstacles in his path, for he cannot see them. This refers specifically to those who are led astray by their false ideologies and do not know of what to be wary and what to avoid (*Metzudos*).

The way of the wicked is described as a דֶּרֶךְ, *wide road*, reflecting the Midrashic teaching (*Bereishis Rabbah* 66:5) that תְּחִלָּתָן שַׁלְוָה וְסוֹפָן יִסּוּרִין, *their beginning is tranquility, but their end is suffering*. Despite the benefits the wicked achieve at first, they will eventually stumble and fall.[1] *Alshich* explains that their initial success is to their detriment. It is darkness to them, for just as darkness blinds a person to the obstacles in his way and causes his downfall, so, too, the success of the wicked in this world renders them oblivious to the ultimate consequences of their wicked ways; sooner or later they will fall.[2]

1. *Rashi* (Genesis 27:29) explains that the righteous, who experience suffering at first and enjoy tranquility at the end, commence with a curse and end with a blessing [אֹרְרֶיךָ אָרוּר וּמְבָרְכֶיךָ בָּרוּךְ]. The wicked, however, who enjoy ease at first and suffering at the end, commence with blessing and end with curse [מְבָרְכֶיךָ בָּרוּךְ וְאֹרְרֶיךָ אָרוּר].

2. The pattern of תְּחִלָּתָן יִסּוּרִין וְסוֹפָן שַׁלְוָה, *their beginning is suffering but their end is tranquility*, applies not only to the overall life of the righteous, but also to individual acts of righteousness, i.e., initially the performance of a *mitzvah* may involve hardship and difficulty, but it ultimately affords tranquility and reward to the one who performs it. Conversely, committing a sin seems to offer the perpetrator pleasure and gain, but eventually it will cause him harm [see *Koheles Rabbah* 1:35]. This pattern may also help a person evaluate an action: If it seems unduly

of wickedness, and they drink the wine of violence.

18 The path of the righteous is like the glow of sunlight, growing until high noon. 19 [But] the way of the wicked is like darkness; they do not know upon what they stumble.

20 My child, be attentive to my speech; incline your ear to my words. 21 Let them not depart from your eyes; safeguard them in your heart. 22 For they are life

Koheles Rabbah (1:35) tells of two paths branching off from a crossroads. One is initially straight but ends up full of thorns and thistles, and the other begins with thorns and thistles but ends up straight and smooth.

20. — בְּנִי לִדְבָרַי הַקְשִׁיבָה לַאֲמָרַי הַט־אָזְנֶךְ *My child, be attentive to my speech; incline your ear to my words.* According to *Malbim*, דְּבּוּר, *speech*, refers to the full elaboration of the teaching, including all the relevant laws. אֲמִירָה, *words*, refers to the language of the text itself and what the words imply.

The *Vilna Gaon* comments that the דְּבּוּר [דְּבָרַי] of Torah refers to the literal words of the verses. The אֲמִירָה [אֲמָרַי] is its inner essence — its meaning, its reasons and its purpose. Therefore, when referring to the words of Torah, King Solomon instructs

his son to be attentive to the speech, as it is. However, to understand the inner significance of the words, you must *incline your ear*, because a greater effort than mere "listening" is needed to fathom the deeper significance of the Torah's words.[1]

21. אַל־יַלִּיזוּ מֵעֵינֶיךָ — *Let them not depart from your eyes.* In all your actions, make sure that words of Torah stand before your eyes, i.e., that all your actions follow its dictates (*Malbim*).

שָׁמְרֵם בְּתוֹךְ לְבָבֶךָ — *Safeguard them in your heart.* Constantly focus your thoughts on the Torah (*Malbim*). This verse specifies the eyes and the heart because these two organs lead a person to sin, as the Sages state: הָעַיִן רוֹאָה וְהַלֵּב חוֹמֵד, *the eye sees and the heart desires* (*Chevel Nachalah*).

appealing, perhaps that is a warning signal of its inherent spiritual danger, whereas if it seems difficult or even insurmountable, that is all the more reason to suspect that it is the Evil Inclination's attempt to deter the person from a tremendous opportunity of spiritual gain.

This principle is evident from the following incident. Rabbi Eliyahu Chaim Meisel, Rav of Lodz, was once approached by someone who desperately pleaded for money. His wife and children were being held captive by bandits who threatened to kill them if a large ransom was not paid at once. After verifying the facts, Rabbi Meisel set out to collect the funds necessary to perform this great *mitzvah* of פִּדְיוֹן שְׁבוּיִים, *the ransom of captives*. In a short time, he was able to collect all the money demanded by the bandits.

Returning home, the rabbi summoned the father into his room, and angrily demanded, "Scoundrel! Admit the truth or I will call the police and have you arrested!" The man broke down and admitted that the kidnaping had really been staged in order to extort money from the community.

As soon as he left the room, the stunned observers of the exchange turned to R' Eliyahu Chaim and asked wonderingly, "How did you realize that this man was lying?" The rabbi replied, "I never was able to raise such a large sum of money in such a short time, no matter how worthy the cause. When this money came in so easily I became suspicious — why was the Satan not interfering with the execution of this great *mitzvah*? Perhaps it is not a *mitzvah* at all! And as you see, my suspicions turned out to be correct!"

1. The *Vilna Gaon* uses this principle to explain the frequently repeated verse, וַיְדַבֵּר ה' אֶל מֹשֶׁה לֵּאמֹר, *HASHEM spoke to Moses, saying.* When addressing Moses, God merely had to convey the actual words of the Torah, and Moses was able to fathom the full depth and nuances of their meaning. But when Moses repeated these same words to the Children of Israel, he had to explain them in full to the people.

כג לְמֹצְאֵיהֶם וּלְכָל־בְּשָׂרוֹ מַרְפֵּא: מִכָּל־מִשְׁמָר נְצֹר
כד לִבֶּךָ כִּי־מִמֶּנּוּ תּוֹצְאוֹת חַיִּים: הָסֵר מִמְּךָ עִקְּשׁוּת

22. כִּי־חַיִּים הֵם לְמֹצְאֵיהֶם וּלְכָל־בְּשָׂרוֹ מַרְפֵּא
— *For they are life to him who finds them,
and healing for all his flesh.* Just as there
are two aspects to Torah — its "outer" and
"inner" facets (see verse 20) — so, too,
there are two aspects of the person — his
body and his soul. Study of the secrets of
Torah, its inner essence, provides vitality
to one's inner self, i.e., the soul; while study
of the outer words of Torah in its revealed
state provides physical healing to the external encasement of the soul, i.e., the body.
Thus, the 248 words of the *Shema* correspond to and provide a healing for each of
man's 248 bodily organs (*Vilna Gaon*).

The commandments are both a source
of life for the soul and a remedy that heals
the body. By contrast, foods proscribed by
the Torah are both injurious to physical
health and they invoke a cruel and ill-
spirited nature in those who eat them
(*Rabbeinu Bachya*).

This verse specifies that the words of
Torah will be a source of life to *one who
finds them*, i.e, to one who toils and labors
until he succeeds in attaining them. One
cannot expect to attain something without
investing time and effort.[1] This verse
implies that a person must avoid the trait
of עַצְלוּת, *laziness*, if he is to succeed. The
Talmud teaches that if a person tells you
יָגַעְתִּי וְלֹא מָצָאתִי, *I labored in the study of
Torah but did not succeed,* or לֹא יָגַעְתִּי
וּמָצָאתִי, *I have not labored in the study of
Torah and have succeeded,* do not believe
him! Only if he says, יָגַעְתִּי וּמָצָאתִי, *I have*

toiled and I have found, can you believe
him (*Megillah* 6b) (*R' Yonah*).

The Talmud (*Eruvin* 54a) suggests another interpretation: מֹצְאֵיהֶם can be read
מוֹצִיאֵיהֶם, *those who enunciate them*
(מוֹצִיא meaning *to take out, express, verbalize*). One who studies Torah audibly is
far more likely to retain what he learns
than one who studies silently, and he will
also merit long life.[2] The Talmud (ibid.)
recounts the case of one of R' Eliezer's
students who studied Torah silently, and
after three years, forgot what he had
learned.[3]

The Talmud (*Eruvin* 54a) cites this verse
in recommending Torah study to one suffering from a bodily ailment. Indeed, the
Talmud notes that the tonic of Torah
study remedies the entire body [וּלְכָל־בְּשָׂרוֹ
מַרְפֵּא], unlike conventional medicines,
which cure one malady but may also cause
side effects.

23. מִכָּל־מִשְׁמָר נְצֹר לִבֶּךָ כִּי־מִמֶּנּוּ תּוֹצְאוֹת
חַיִּים — *More than you guard anything,
safeguard your heart, for from it are the
sources of life.* More than anything he
protects, a person must be careful to guard
his heart from improper thoughts, for one
cannot contemplate using the heart, the
very vortex of life, to harbor thoughts that
are inimical to life (*Metzudos*).

The physiological centrality of the
heart, as "king of the body" that distributes man's lifeblood, symbolizes its
preeminent role as the source of spiritual

1 R' Chaim Volozhiner recalled that the *Vilna Gaon* merited having an angel come to teach him
hidden aspects of Torah knowledge. However, the *Gaon* refused to avail himself of this
opportunity, for he preferred Torah knowledge achieved through toil and labor.

2. The Torah is a source of life to those who recite its words aloud, for this allows the Torah they
have studied to endure and not be forgotten. They will thereby be saved from the punishment
for one who forgets something of his Torah studies, which is כְּאִילּוּ מִתְחַיֵּיב בְּנַפְשׁוֹ, *it is as if he
bears guilt for his soul* [*Avos* 3:10] (*Maharsha* ad loc.)

3. The study halls of Torah throughout the ages bear eloquent testimony to this Talmudic
teaching. Even a brief visit to a yeshiva leaves one with a sense of the enthralling effect of the
sounds of Torah, resonating throughout the hall. These seemingly cacophonous sounds — in one
corner an excited, high-pitched debate, in another the mellifluous repetition of a Talmudic
passage — merge to form a harmonious cascade of sound that renews the spirit and uplifts the
soul.

to him who finds them, and healing for all his flesh. ²³ *More than you guard anything, safeguard your heart, for from it are the sources of life.* ²⁴ *Remove from yourself distortion of*

life in the Hereafter, for it inculcates Torah thought and commitment to the service of God. This leads each of the person's limbs to perform its specific commandment. Realizing its importance, one must be careful to guard his heart well (*Alshich*).

The heart [i.e., thought] plays a pivotal role in eradicating one's negative character traits. One must uproot these traits by guarding the heart from thoughts of cruelty, anger, and the like, and refocusing one's thoughts on the negation of bad traits and the desire to develop positive ones (*R' Yonah*).

The heart especially needs to be protected from evil, for the results of life are primarily determined by the heart, as our Sages (*Sanhedrin* 106b) teach: רַחֲמָנָא לִבָּא בָּעֵי, *the Merciful One wants the heart* (*Malbim*).[1]

Rashi, citing *Midrash Tanchuma*, explains this verse differently. מִכָּל-מִשְׁמָר, *from whatever Torah told you to beware of*, whether it is a "minor" commandment or a "major" one, נְצֹר לִבֶּךָ, *guard your heart* [from transgressing], כִּי-מִמֶּנּוּ, *for from it* — from the very *mitzvah* that seems minor to you — the results are life, and you will receive a great reward for fulfilling it. [See *Avos* 2:1, "Be as scrupulous in performing a minor *mitzvah* as in a major one, for you do not know the reward given for the respective *mitzvos*."]

The Midrash explains that the 248 positive commandments in Torah correspond to the 248 bodily organs, each of which cries out to the person: "Use me as the medium to perform a *mitzvah* so that you may merit long life." The 365 negative

commandments correspond to the 365 days in a solar year. From sunrise to sunset, each day cries out to man, decreeing that he not use that day to sin, so that this day, together with the entire world, will not be deemed guilty.

Every commandment has its commensurate reward; why then does the Torah not reveal the reward for each *mitzvah*? Because God wants people to fulfill His commandments for their own sake, thereby earning an even greater reward.

Antigonus, leader of Socho, teaches this point (*Avos* 1:3): אַל תִּהְיוּ כַּעֲבָדִים הַמְשַׁמְּשִׁין אֶת הָרַב עַל מְנָת לְקַבֵּל פְּרָס, *Be not like servants who serve the master for the sake of receiving a reward*, אֶלָּא הֱווּ כַּעֲבָדִים הַמְשַׁמְּשִׁין אֶת הָרַב שֶׁלֹּא עַל מְנָת לְקַבֵּל פְּרָס, *instead be like servants who serve the master not for the sake of receiving a reward* (*Yalkut Shimoni*).

The Midrash illustrates the reward for *mitzvos* with a parable. A king once hired workers to plant a field without informing them what they would be paid for their services. Only at the end of the day was each worker who had planted one tree given a golden coin. Those who had planted many trees remarked, "If someone who planted only one tree received a golden coin, how much more will we receive for the many trees we have planted." Thus, if the Torah promises long life as the reward for sending a mother bird away from her nest (*Deuteronomy* 23:6-7), we can imagine what a great reward awaits someone who performs a *mitzvah* which entails a financial loss or which results in the saving of lives.

1. The Talmud (*Nazir* 23a) compares two people who roasted their *pesach* offerings. One ate it for the sake of performing the *mitzvah*, and the other ate it purely out of gluttony. Describing the former, the Talmud quotes the verse, כִּי יְשָׁרִים דַּרְכֵי ה' וְצַדִּיקִים יֵלְכוּ בָם, *for the ways of Hashem are straight; the righteous walk in them*. To the glutton, they apply the second half of the same verse, וּפֹשְׁעִים יִכָּשְׁלוּ בָם, *and sinners will stumble over them* (*Hosea* 14:10).

Abarbanel (ad loc.) explains that commandments must be performed with the proper intention to fulfill God's will; lacking that, they have no substance. In this they differ from good character traits, which are praiseworthy independent of intent.

כה פֶּה וּלְזוּת שְׂפָתַיִם הַרְחֵק מִמֶּךָ: עֵינֶיךָ לְנֹכַח
כו יַבִּיטוּ וְעַפְעַפֶּיךָ יַיְשִׁרוּ נֶגְדֶּךָ: פַּלֵּס מַעְגַּל רַגְלֶךָ
כז וְכָל־דְּרָכֶיךָ יִכֹּנוּ: אַל־תֵּט־יָמִין וּשְׂמֹאול הָסֵר
רַגְלְךָ מֵרָע:

24. הָסֵר מִמֶּךָ עַקְשׁוּת פֶּה וּלְזוּת שְׂפָתַיִם
הַרְחֵק מִמֶּךָ — *Remove from yourself distortion of the mouth, and distance perversity of lips from yourself.* Beware of acting in a manner that will cause others to twist their mouth or widen their mouths concerning you, i.e., to speak badly of you (*Rashi*).

The previous verse's noble intentions of the heart cannot suffice when others perceive your behavior as ignoble, for that results in a desecration of God's Name. Therefore, even when your intentions are pure, avoid acting in a manner which may arouse suspicion of wrongdoing on your part (*Malbim*).

According to the Midrash, *distortion of the mouth* refers to gossip, which can cause such harm that it is comparable to murder. *Perversity of lips* refers to *duplicitous speech*, treating one's fellow in an outwardly friendly manner while inwardly harboring animosity towards him (*Yalkut Shimoni*).

25. עֵינֶיךָ לְנֹכַח יַבִּיטוּ וְעַפְעַפֶּיךָ יַיְשִׁרוּ נֶגְדֶּךָ —
Let your eyes look ahead, and your eyelids will straighten your path before you. Your

eyes should look for truth and for uprightness in order to find the proper path (*Rashi*).[1]

Metzudos renders: A person should contemplate well the consequences of an action he plans to perform, for then his eyes guide him on the true path.

R' Hirsch relates עַפְעַפַּיִם to עָף, *fly*, for the eyelids are constantly flapping up and down like wings. (See ArtScroll *Tehillim* 11:4, and *R' Hirsch* commentary, ad loc.)

According to *Malbim*, עֵינֶיךָ denotes open eyes, whereas עַפְעַפֶּיךָ refers to the eyes when the eyelids are closed. In spiritual matters, a person's eyes should be open to observe God's deeds and the manifestations of His greatness, and to enable one to walk in His ways. This is the directive of the first part of the verse. However, one's eyes should be closed to his physical temptations. By covering one's eyes, his eyelids [עַפְעַפֶּיךָ] will lead one along the straight path [יַיְשִׁרוּ] in matters pertaining to himself [נֶגְדֶּךָ] and will guide one to behave properly regarding his physical needs and desires.[2]

1. That to which a person exposes his vision can be an extremely potent factor in his spiritual ascent or, God forbid, his decline. The sight of a Torah scholar has a great positive effect that can even enhance the observer's ability to advance in Torah study. This is illustrated by the Talmud (*Eruvin* 13b) which quotes Rebbe, who attributes his attainment of a greater depth of understanding in Torah than his colleagues to the fact that he saw R' Meir from the back. [When Rebbe was R' Meir's student, he sat behind him (*Rashi* ibid.).] Had he merited to see R' Meir's face, he would have reached even greater heights in Torah scholarship, as the verse states, וְהָיוּ עֵינֶיךָ רֹאוֹת אֶת־מוֹרֶיךָ, *your eyes will behold your teachers* (Isaiah 30:20).

Conversely, the Torah often warns against the deleterious effect on an observer's spiritual standing of viewing immoral behavior. A telling example of this is conveyed by the Torah's juxtaposition of the laws of a *sotah*, a suspected adulteress, with those of a nazarite. According to the Talmud (*Sotah* 2a), one who witnesses the punishment of a *sotah* should take the nazarite vow of abstention from wine. Even though the observer had seen the death throes of an adulteress, there is still a real psychological danger that the sight may tempt the viewer toward such a sin. To counteract the danger, the Torah implies that he should take a precaution to protect himself from its effects. In this light, we can understand the spiritual danger of an attractively packaged sin portrayed as a societal norm. Realizing how great an effect vision has on a person's soul, we can appreciate the exhortation of this verse to look only at what is true and just, so that we will be influenced by it.

2. Rabbi Isser Zalman Meltzer, Rosh Yeshiva of Yeshiva Etz Chaim in Jerusalem and formerly

the mouth, and distance perversity of lips from yourself. ²⁵ *Let your eyes look ahead, and your eyelids will straighten your path before you.* ²⁶ *Weigh the course of your foot, and all your ways will be established.* ²⁷ *Do not deviate right or left; remove your foot from evil.*

26. פַּלֵּס מַעְגַּל רַגְלֶךָ וְכָל־דְּרָכֶיךָ יִכֹּנוּ — *Weigh the course of your foot and all your ways will be established.* Weigh the "loss" incurred in performing a *mitzvah* against its reward, and the "reward" of a sin against its loss, and then all your ways will be established (*Rashi*) (cf. *Avos* 2:1).

Ibn Ezra explains that the *weighing* is done on the scales of a person's thoughts, where he must consider and decide on the right path.

Metzudos renders פַּלֵּס as *align.* (The balance bar of a scale is called פֶּלֶס, for it aligns the scale.) Before a person acts, he must straighten his path — i.e., plan a straightforward course of action — rather than act in a haphazard and ad hoc fashion.

The *Vilna Gaon* divides character traits into two categories: inborn traits, which are referred to as one's דֶּרֶךְ, *way*, and acquired traits which are called רֶגֶל, for they have become second nature to the person through הֶרְגֵּל, *habit*. When correcting a negative trait acquired through habit (רַגְלֶךָ), the person is advised to remove it gradually from his nature. This is similar to a פֶּלֶס, *balance weight*, where the plumb bob must be moved slowly in order for it to reach its destination. So, too, a person must train himself gradually until the desired trait becomes second nature to him. He should not swing suddenly to the other extreme (see v. 15, *Vilna Gaon's* commentary). Such personal character development will affect even one's inborn traits: וְכָל־דְּרָכֶיךָ יִכֹּנוּ, *all your ways* [i.e., your inborn traits] *will be established*, for even one's innate positive

tendencies are not secure until he has perfected the rest of his character. Character traits are comparable to a strand of pearls — if it is knotted at the end, then all the pearls are secure; if not, all of them are lost. (See *Chovos HaLevavos* 9:5.)

The *Malbim* explains that a דֶּרֶךְ is the median road whereas a מַעְגַּל is a circular path that digresses from the main road [see v. 11]. To ensure that the *magal* will return to the main road, one must use a פֶּלֶס, a balance tool which measures this circular path and determines the necessary degree of digression. Ideally, a person should strike a balance between the extremes of each character trait, but if he has veered toward an extreme, a radical corrective shift to the opposite extreme is necessary. The extent and duration of the shift must be calibrated to ensure a timely return to the "middle of the road." For instance, if a person has been too arrogant, he must train himself to be excessively humble until he achieves the medium way of humility.[1]

27. אַל־תֵּט־יָמִין וּשְׂמֹאול הָסֵר רַגְלְךָ מֵרָע — *Do not deviate right or left; remove your foot from evil.* Do not deviate from the proper balance (*Rashi*). Though the previous verse teaches the methods to correct one's course and regain the medium road, ideally a person should have been careful not to veer right or left off this road. In this way he will have removed his foot from evil (*Malbim*).

In every area, do not veer right of left from the median course. Regarding evil, however, remove yourself from it entirely (*Metzudos*).

Rav of Slutzk, explained this verse a little differently. לְנֹכַח can also mean *toward yourself*. A person should direct his eyesight inward, searching for his own faults rather than the faults of others. R' Isser Zalman would keep a piece of paper in front of him with this verse inscribed on it, in order to avoid feeling pride when visitors streamed in to see him. Years after his passing, his daughter would show visitors the sugar bowl that had been on her father's table. On it was etched this verse.

1. See *Rambam, Hilchos Deios* 2:2 and *Kitzur Shulchan Aruch* 29:7 for the way to correct faulty character traits.

בְּנִי לְחָכְמָתִי הַקְשִׁיבָה לִתְבוּנָתִי הַט־אָזְנֶךָ: א

לִשְׁמֹר מְזִמּוֹת וְדַעַת שְׂפָתֶיךָ יִנְצֹרוּ: כִּי נֹפֶת ב־ג

תִּטֹּפְנָה שִׂפְתֵי זָרָה וְחָלָק מִשֶּׁמֶן חִכָּהּ:

וְאַחֲרִיתָהּ מָרָה כַלַּעֲנָה חַדָּה כְּחֶרֶב פִּיּוֹת: ד

רַגְלֶיהָ יֹרְדוֹת מָוֶת שְׁאוֹל צְעָדֶיהָ יִתְמֹכוּ: אֹרַח ה־ו

חַיִּים פֶּן־תְּפַלֵּס נָעוּ מַעְגְּלֹתֶיהָ לֹא תֵדָע:

V

1. בְּנִי לְחָכְמָתִי הַקְשִׁיבָה לִתְבוּנָתִי הַט־אָזְנֶךָ — *My child, be attentive to my wisdom, incline your ear to my understanding.* According to *Metzudos*, the first six verses of this chapter continue King David's teachings to his son Solomon [which began in the preceding chapter]. In verse 7, Solomon addresses these teachings to the nation of Israel, the children of God.

Verse 20 of the preceding chapter, בְּנִי לִדְבָרַי הַקְשִׁיבָה לַאֲמָרַי הַט־אָזְנֶךָ, *My child, be attentive to my speech, incline your ear to my words*, is very similar to this one. That verse introduces concepts whose benefits are readily apparent. The present verse introduces the subject of withstanding temptation, an area where man's quest for pleasure blinds him to the dangerous consequences of such a course of action. Only with farsighted understanding — through wisdom and understanding — can one withstand the demands of the senses for immediate gratification (*R' Saadya Gaon*).

2. לִשְׁמֹר מְזִמּוֹת וְדַעַת שְׂפָתֶיךָ יִנְצֹרוּ — *To heed [wise] designs and let your lips safeguard knowledge.* Be careful to keep thoughts of wisdom in your heart, and speak words of wisdom with your lips (*Metzudos*).

3. כִּי נֹפֶת תִּטֹּפְנָה שִׂפְתֵי זָרָה וְחָלָק מִשֶּׁמֶן חִכָּהּ — *For the lips of a strange woman drip honey and her palate is smoother than oil.* *Metzudos* renders נֹפֶת as an abbreviated form of the phrase וְנֹפֶת צוּפִים, *and drippings from [honey] combs* (Psalms 19:11); hence, the connotation of sweetness. The זָרָה, *strange woman*, is a metaphor for heresy (*Rashi*). [See 2:16, where a *strange woman* is a married Jewess, who is forbidden to another man.] The sense of the metaphor is not to be enticed by this woman [i.e. heresy], whose words are sweeter than honey and whose palate is smoother than oil (*Metzudos*).

Choosing honey, a kosher product of the non-kosher bee, as a metaphor for heresy teaches that even seemingly innocuous works written by heretics may subtly convey attitudes and ideas that are antithetical to the Torah, and therefore are to avoided (*Chevel Nachalah*).

R' Saadyah Gaon views the strange woman as a symbol for all of life's temporal pleasures.

The *Vilna Gaon* explains that there are two stages of difficulty which the Evil Inclination imposes on a person performing a *mitzvah*: (1) The Evil Inclination tries to deter a person before he does the *mitzvah* by making it seem very difficult. (2) Even when he is performing the *mitzvah*, the Evil Inclination tries to prevent the person from deriving full pleasure from it in this world. The two statements in this verse contrast this with the sweetness of sin. (1) The forbidden woman's lips drip sweetness as she entices a person before he actually sins. (2) While he is transgressing, the sin seems as smooth as oil to the sinner, who enjoys great pleasure from his deed (see 9:17). Therefore, a person must exercise wisdom and understanding very well (verse 1), for they will protect him from this "strange woman" (*Vilna Gaon*).

4. וְאַחֲרִיתָהּ מָרָה כַלַּעֲנָה חַדָּה כְּחֶרֶב פִּיּוֹת — *But her end is as bitter as wormwood, as sharp as a double-edged sword.* The re-

¹ **M**y child, be attentive to my wisdom, incline your ear to my understanding. ² To heed [wise] designs and let your lips safeguard knowledge. ³ For the lips of a strange woman drip honey and her palate is smoother than oil. ⁴ But her end is as bitter as wormwood, as sharp as a double-edged sword. ⁵ Her feet descend to death; her footsteps come near to the grave. ⁶ Lest you liken the path of life [to her's] — her courses wander [astray]; you cannot know.

sults of these enticements are as bitter as wormwood and as lethal as a double-edged sword to those who succumb to them (*Metzudos*).

A double-edged sword is doubly lethal; likewise, involvement with an adulteress leads to death in this world, and to the loss of one's eternal share in the World to Come (*Midrash Mishlei*).

The bitter wormwood in this verse contrasts with the honey in the preceding verse; the double-edged sword contrasts with the smoothness of oil (*Vilna Gaon*).

This verse continues to warn people to be very cautious regarding what they read. Just as *wormwood*, once consumed, tortures a person with its bitterness (לַעֲנָה is derived from עָנָה, *torture*), so, too, harmful reading material may seem very enjoyable, but cause immeasurable spiritual torture. Even when one attempts to be selective, one may err and, like someone trying to grab the blade of a double-edged sword, will be cut, no matter where he touches it (*Chevel Nachalah*).

5. רַגְלֶיהָ יֹרְדוֹת מָוֶת שְׁאוֹל צְעָדֶיהָ יִתְמֹכוּ — *Her feet descend to death; her footsteps come near to the grave.* The translation follows *Rashi*, who interprets יִתְמֹכוּ as an expression of *nearness*. According to *Metzudos*, her steps "support" and hold up *sheol* [*the grave*], so that anyone who listens to her persuasions fall into it (*Metzudos*).

Alshich explains these verses as a warning to beware of the Evil Inclination. Like the forbidden woman, the Evil Inclination comes as a friend, concerned with his victim's welfare, and entices him with promises of happiness and pleasure. The truth is quite the opposite. He is man's bitter enemy. The Sages teach: הוּא שָׂטָן הוּא יֵצֶר הָרַע, הוּא מַלְאַךְ הַמָּוֶת, *he is the Satan, he is man's Evil Inclination, he is the Angel of Death* (*Bava Basra* 16a). The very same force that misleads a person to sin, goes before God and indicts the sinner, and then obtains God's permission to kill him.

6. אֹרַח חַיִּים פֶּן־תְּפַלֵּס נָעוּ מַעְגְּלֹתֶיהָ לֹא תֵדָע — *Lest you liken the path of life [to her's] — her courses wander [astray]; you cannot know.* A person should not weigh and compare the way of Torah against the ways of the forbidden woman saying: "Which should I choose, the former or the latter?" The course of the adulteress moves towards the grave — but if a person even begins to consider the evil ways of the forbidden woman, he will not know how to beware until he wanders off and falls (*Rashi*).

Metzudos renders לְפַלֵּס as *to align* (see 4:26) and explains this verse as a warning against attempting to *align* — i.e., compare — the wisdom of the Torah with that of the forbidden woman, i.e., heresy. Her course diverges totally from that of the Torah; there is no basis of comparison between the two.

According to *Malbim*, the metaphor of this verse warns against philosophical attempts to prove God's existence. Just as a detour past the house of the forbidden woman moves completely away from the straight path, and the individual who follows it becomes lost and cannot find his way back, so too, philosophical speculation may leave one confused. Rather than helping one find a firm foundation of belief, it may entrap one in skepticism, and make it difficult or impossible to find the

ז וְעַתָּה בָנִים שִׁמְעוּ־לִי וְאַל־תָּסוּרוּ מֵאִמְרֵי־פִי:
ח הַרְחֵק מֵעָלֶיהָ דַרְכֶּךָ וְאַל־תִּקְרַב אֶל־פֶּתַח
ט בֵּיתָהּ: פֶּן־תִּתֵּן לַאֲחֵרִים הוֹדֶךָ וּשְׁנֹתֶיךָ לְאַכְזָרִי:
י פֶּן־יִשְׂבְּעוּ זָרִים כֹּחֶךָ וַעֲצָבֶיךָ בְּבֵית נָכְרִי:
יא וְנָהַמְתָּ בְאַחֲרִיתֶךָ בִּכְלוֹת בְּשָׂרְךָ וּשְׁאֵרֶךָ:

true path of God.[1]

Rashi, citing *Midrash Tanchuma*, explains that the Torah does not specify rewards for performing various commandments, so that a person will not choose to perform only the ones that will earn a large reward, and neglect others. This verse would then be understood as follows: Lest a person weigh the paths of Torah, attempting to choose which ones to follow and which ones to ignore, God did not explain the Torah's paths nor reveal its ways to us.

The Midrash compares this to a king who hired workers to plant an orchard without revealing the wages for tending different plants. He feared that if the pay scale would be known, workers would choose to plant only the plants that would bring them a higher income, while the other plants in the orchard would be neglected. So too, if the reward for *mitzvos* was known, people might do only those that carry a great reward and neglect the others (cf. 4:23).[2]

7. וְעַתָּה בָנִים שִׁמְעוּ־לִי — *And now, [my] children, listen to me.* Now, while you are

still considered "my children," before I reject you for your misdeeds, listen to me and do not turn away from my words (*Alshich*).

Before a person sins, he is so blinded by the pleasures with which the Evil Inclination entices him that he is impervious to rebuke. But, my children, *now* that you have experienced the bitter consequences of sin (verses 4-5) and you are receptive to reprimand, listen to me and do not remain with your sinful ways (*Kiflayim L'Sushiah*).

8. הַרְחֵק מֵעָלֶיהָ דַרְכֶּךָ וְאַל־תִּקְרַב אֶל־פֶּתַח בֵּיתָהּ — *Distance your way from her and do not come near the door of her house.* Do not pass near the forbidden woman; and even if she is not home, avoid her house. Metaphorically, this is a warning not only to stay away from actual idolatry and heresy, but even to avoid comparisons and analogies that may lead to heretical thinking, justifying them as a means to strengthen oneself in Torah (*Malbim*).

This is an admonition to keep one's distance from places of heresy and promiscuity (*Avodah Zarah* 17a).[3]

1. The *Chassid Yavetz* notes that Jews who faced the tortures of the Spanish Inquisition with an ingrained faith and an unquestioning acceptance of God were the ones who retained their faith in the face of the worst horrors. However, those whose belief in God was based on a philosophical and analytical scholarship were the ones who succumbed when confronted with the fiery specter of the *auto-da-fe*.

2. In two cases, the Torah does specify the reward for a *mitzvah*: for the קַלָּה שֶׁבְּקַלּוֹת, *the easiest of the easy* — שִׁלּוּחַ הַקֵּן, *sending away the mother bird before taking its eggs or its baby birds*, and for חֲמוּרָה שֶׁבַּחֲמוּרוֹת, *the hardest of the hard* — כִּבּוּד אָב וָאֵם, *honoring of father and mother*. The Torah states that the reward for both of these commandments is אֲרִיכוּת יָמִים, *long life*, thus confirming that human intelligence is incapable of evaluating the relative importance of *mitzvos*.

3. The Sages repeatedly stress that there is a tremendous spiritual danger inherent in being in the proximity of evil, because a person cannot rely on himself to withstand the influence of such an environment. One's only recourse is to physically remove oneself from such a potentially damaging surrounding. Thus, the Sages counsel that disengagement is preferable to confrontation, and certainly to accommodation. Illustrating this point, R' Chaim Shmulevitz explains that Joseph ran out of Potiphar's house, leaving his garment behind (see *Genesis* 39:12) rather than stopping to take back his garment, for he refused to tarry for even a moment in a situation of potential spiritual

> [7] *And now, [my] children, listen to me. and do not stray from the word of my mouth.* [8] *Distance your way from her and do not come near the door of her house.* [9] *Lest you give your glory to others and your [remaining] years to the cruel one.* [10] *Lest strangers be sated with your strength and your painfully earned wealth [be] in a stranger's house.* [11] *You will groan at your [life's] end when your flesh and your body perish.*

9. פֶּן־תִּתֵּן לַאֲחֵרִים הוֹדֶךָ — *Lest you give your glory to others.* This verse warns against turning your heart to other gods by giving them glory and praise (*Rashi*).[1] These gods are referred to as "others" because they are as powerless as strangers to those who worship them (*Sifri, Eikev*).

וּשְׁנֹתֶיךָ לְאַכְזָרִי — *And your [remaining] years to the cruel one,* i.e., the שַׂר שֶׁל גֵּיהִנֹּם, *Master of Gehinnom* (*Rashi*).

Metzudos explains the verse differently. Your actions will cause the glory that was given to you from Heaven to be taken away and given to others; you will die prematurely, and be under the dominion of the Master of *Gehinnom*.

Malbim explains that הוֹד, *glory*, refers to an inner, spiritual beauty. Adultery darkens the brightness of one's mind and dims the glory of his soul. In addition, one's *years*, referring to his body, will be controlled by an אַכְזָרִי, *a cruel disease*, which afflicts the promiscuous. Metaphorically, this verse describes a heretic, who devotes his הוֹד, i.e., his spiritual and intellectual energies, to causes and concerns that not only fail to bring him lasting spiritual happiness, but hasten his physical and spiritual demise.

10. פֶּן־יִשְׂבְּעוּ זָרִים כֹּחֶךָ וַעֲצָבֶיךָ בְּבֵית נָכְרִי — *Lest strangers be sated with your strength and your painfully earned wealth [be] in a stranger's house.* Your strength refers to the wealth which you have accumulated through effort and strength; עֲצָבֶיךָ is derived from the word עִצָּבוֹן, *sorrow*, also refers to wealth, for you attained it through sorrow and toil (*Metzudos*).

Rashi interprets the *strangers* in this verse as the priests of the *Baal*, who will acquire your money through their falsehoods. Thus, the wealth you amassed through arduous work will end up in pagan temples.[2]

Metzudos explains זָרִים as *people who are alien to you* and undeserving of inheriting your money, but they will now be the ones to enjoy your wealth.

11. וְנָהַמְתָּ בְאַחֲרִיתֶךָ בִּכְלוֹת בְּשָׂרְךָ וּשְׁאֵרֶךָ — *You will groan at your [life's] end, when your flesh and your body perish.* At the end of your life — on the day of death when your flesh perishes — you will groan from heartache (*Metzudos*).

Why is it that someone who is deathly ill will not find solace in the words of Kant or Lessing, but rather in those of King David's *Psalms*? Once a person's physical powers have waned and he stands at the

danger. A nazirite, as well, is not only enjoined from drinking wine, but he must also walk around a vineyard, rather than through it, to avoid putting himself in a place where he will be exposed to the possibility of eating grapes, which are forbidden to him. In grappling with the trials of life, a person is therefore advised to flee from temptations, rather than confront them.

1. So harmful is it to cause strange gods to be praised that the Sages prohibited doing business with idol-worshipers around the period of their religious holidays, so that they should not subsequently go and thank their idols (*Avodah Zarah* 2a, *Rashi* ad loc.).

2. The Talmud (*Bava Kamma* 16b) relates that the prophet Jeremiah prayed that God punish his enemies by having their contributions go to fraudulent recipients, thus denying them the merit of giving charity to worthy causes. In a similar vein, this verse warns that a person's sins may cause his hard-earned wealth to ultimately enrich the coffers of false religions; thus his wealth ends up in the hands of aliens. A deserving person, however, will merit having his charity donations go to truly worthy causes.

יב וְאָמַרְתָּ אֵיךְ שָׂנֵאתִי מוּסָר וְתוֹכַחַת נָאַץ לִבִּי:

יג וְלֹא־שָׁמַעְתִּי בְּקוֹל מוֹרָי וְלִמְלַמְּדַי לֹא־הִטִּיתִי

יד אָזְנִי: כִּמְעַט הָיִיתִי בְכָל־רָע בְּתוֹךְ קָהָל וְעֵדָה:

טו-טז שְׁתֵה־מַיִם מִבּוֹרֶךָ וְנֹזְלִים מִתּוֹךְ בְּאֵרֶךָ: יָפוּצוּ

threshold of the World of Truth, he recognizes where the truth lies, even if he has espoused other beliefs throughout his lifetime (Chevel Nachalah).[1]

R' Eliyahu Lopian questions the apparent redundancy of the phrase *when your flesh and your body perish* after the phrase *at your [life's] end*. He explains with the tale of a pauper who, having no clothing, borrowed money on interest and purchased a garment. Since he did not have money, the interest on his debt kept accumulating. After several years, his garment wore out and had to be discarded. Now the pauper was left in a hopeless situation — he still had to repay the loan for the garment, but the clothing itself had ceased to exist.

Similarly, when a person will stand for judgment in the World of Truth, he will be heavily in debt for all the pleasures in which his body had indulged in this world, while his flesh will already have rotted and decayed in the grave. Then he will groan bitterly, bemoaning the fact that he had not heeded the lessons of *mussar* while he was still alive (v. 12); for now he must repay all the debts accrued by a body that has been consumed

in the grave (Shevivai Lev).[2]

12. וְאָמַרְתָּ אֵיךְ שָׂנֵאתִי מוּסָר וְתוֹכַחַת נָאַץ לִבִּי — *Then you will say: "How could I have hated discipline, and my heart spurned reproof?"* Mussar [discipline] is related to the word יִסּוּרִים, *afflictions*. The sinner *hated discipline*, i.e, physical punishment inflicted to make him improve. תּוֹכֵחָה, however, refers to oral admonition and therefore "hatred" is too strong a word. Rather the sinner *spurned* these words of reproof in his heart [נָאַץ לִבִּי] (Vilna Gaon).

13. וְלֹא־שָׁמַעְתִּי בְּקוֹל מוֹרָי וְלִמְלַמְּדַי לֹא־הִטִּיתִי אָזְנִי — *I have not listened to the voice of my masters, and I have not inclined my ear to my teachers.* Chevel Nachalah notes that the wicked did not even listen *to the voice* of their instructors, i.e., to the נִגּוּן, the traditional *chant* that is inseparable from Torah study. Foolishly, they fail to realize that קוֹל יַעֲקֹב, *the voice of Jacob*, sounding forth in the melody of Torah study has the power to arouse and elevate the soul.

14. כִּמְעַט הָיִיתִי בְכָל־רָע בְּתוֹךְ קָהָל וְעֵדָה — *For a pittance [of enjoyment] I was into everything evil, in the presence of congre-*

1. *R' Eliyahu Lopian* told of a Jew who had been an atheist all his life, and became critically ill. His doctors said that an operation could save his life, but might result in a permanent loss of consciousness. Having no choice, the patient consented to the operation. As the doctors were about to begin, this lifelong atheist was heard calling out: שְׁמַע יִשְׂרָאֵל ה' אֱלֹקֵינוּ ה' אֶחָד, *Hear, O Israel, HASHEM is our God, HASHEM, the One and Only!*

2. The *Dubno Maggid* explains why the sinner will express his regret by groaning [וְנָהַמְתָּ] rather than by screaming [וְצָעַקְתָּ]. This is comparable to a baker who stands in the market with a basket of delicacies to sell. A passerby, wishing to amuse himself at the baker's expense, asks him: "How much do you want for your basket of goods?" When the baker answers, "Two coins," the scoffer offers to pay in full on one condition — that the baker eat every confection in the basket under the customer's watchful eye. The baker agrees, but just as he finishes the last of the cakes, the "customer" runs off, leaving the baker empty-handed. He cannot scream in protest, for he caused the loss himself. He can only groan at his own foolishness. So, too, whatever spiritual damage a person's soul suffered in this world is his own fault. Therefore, he will groan, bemoaning the damage he has inflicted on himself by his sins (Ohel Yaakov).

¹² Then you will say: "How could I have hated discipline, and my heart spurned reproof? ¹³ I have not listened to the voice of my masters, and I have not inclined my ear to my teachers. ¹⁴ For a pittance [of enjoyment] I was into everything evil, in the presence of congregation and assembly!"

¹⁵ Drink water from your own cistern and flowing water from your own well. ¹⁶ [Then] your springs will spread outward;

gation and assembly. There is a fine line separating me from *Gehinnom* (*Rashi*).[1]

I am now suffering for the seemingly small infraction of not listening to my teachers. Had I only been obedient to them, this would not have happened to me! (*Rashi*, quoting *R' Yosef Kara*).

Metzudos explains כְּמְעַט as *for a modicum*, for the smallest amount of pleasure [which I enjoyed from sinning]. Because of that, I am now suffering from evil in the presence of an entire assembly.

The sinner bemoans the superficial and fleeting pleasure he derived from gratifying his desires in this world, as a result of which he is now suffering publicly (*Malbim*); and he has forfeited his reward in the Hereafter, which lasts for eternity (*Ibn Nachmiash*).

According to the *Vilna Gaon*, this verse deals with the modes of retribution for different transgressions. Punishment for violating negative commandments is meted out amidst a *congregation*, denoting the general populace who scrupulously observe these negative commandments, whereas punishment for disregarding positive commandments is visited upon the individual in the company of an *assembly*, referring to the righteous, who are punctilious in fulfilling positive precepts, as well.

15. שְׁתֵה־מַיִם מִבּוֹרֶךָ וְנֹזְלִים מִתּוֹךְ בְּאֵרֶךָ — *Drink water from your own cistern and flowing water from your own well.* A *cistern* contains water that is collected from an outside source (such as rain water), while a *well* is a natural source of water. *Rashi* explains this verse and verse 16 as a metaphor for Torah study: A person must first drink the waters collected in his cistern — i.e., he must study the Torah which the Holy One, Blessed is He, gave him as his portion. Then his Torah knowledge will become like well water, for it will begin to flow of itself.

This is in direct contrast to idolatry, which is compared to a broken cistern, incapable of containing water [see *Jeremiah* 2:13] (*Malbim*).

The *Sifri* (*Parshas Eikev*) notes that water and Torah share many qualities. Both cleanse a person's impurities; both restore the soul; both are everlasting; and both are in abundant supply and readily

1. In Messianic times, God will slaughter the Evil Inclination in front of both the righteous and the wicked, and they will all cry. The righteous will cry because the Evil Inclination will appear to them as a tall mountain — i.e., they will be amazed that they could have conquered such a great power. The wicked will cry because the Evil Inclination will appear to them as but a חוט הַשַּׂעֲרָה, a *hairsbreadth*. The wicked will lament, "How could we not have conquered this hairsbreadth!" R' Yosi explains that the Evil Inclination first presents itself as a spider's thread. However, once a person allows himself to be drawn after it, it soon becomes as thick as the ropes that harness an ox to a plow (*Succah* 52a).

The sages of *mussar* teach that even a minor thing can determine whether a person will be found worthy of Paradise or, God forbid, *Gehinnom*. In the words of Rabbi Simcha Zissel Ziev, the *Alter* of Kelm, אֵין בֵּין גַּן עֵדֶן לְגֵיהִנּוֹם אֶלָּא כְּחוּט הַשַּׂעֲרָה, *The difference between Gan Eden and Gehinnom is but a hairsbreadth*. Therefore, explains R' Yechezkel Levenstein, a person needs constant introspection to evaluate whether his deeds are proper, for a hairsbreadth's deviation can cause enormous harm.

Similarly, even the slightest change in following the exact dictates of a *halachah*, even a minor omission or addition to the words of Torah, even an almost imperceptible misinterpretation of the words of the Sages can begin the process that can snowball into complete wickedness.

יז מַעְיְנֹתֶיךָ חֻוּצָה בָּרְחֹבוֹת פַּלְגֵי־מָיִם: יִהְיוּ־לְךָ
יח לְבַדֶּךָ וְאֵין לְזָרִים אִתָּךְ: יְהִי־מְקוֹרְךָ בָרוּךְ
יט וּשְׂמַח מֵאֵשֶׁת נְעוּרֶךָ: אַיֶּלֶת אֲהָבִים וְיַעֲלַת חֵן
דַּדֶּיהָ יְרַוֻּךָ בְכָל־עֵת בְּאַהֲבָתָהּ תִּשְׁגֶּה תָמִיד:

available to all who wish to partake of them.

Metzudos interprets the metaphor of this verse differently. The cistern and the well refer to someone's wife. He should be loyal to her, rather than be enticed by the forbidden woman.

R' Hirsch expounds upon this metaphor. A cistern contains waters collected through human efforts; a well's source of water is a natural one. So too, a successful marriage is comprised of two parts: the efforts invested in it by the husband and wife, and the elements contributed by Divine Providence.

16. יָפֻוצוּ מַעְיְנֹתֶיךָ חֻוּצָה בָּרְחֹבוֹת פַּלְגֵי־מָיִם — *[Then] your springs will spread outward; streams of water in the thoroughfares.* The streams of your water will spread out in the city squares; i.e., you will have many students; you will render Torah instruction publicly and achieve fame as a Torah sage (*Rashi*).

The *Vilna Gaon* elaborates on the metaphor of the three sources of water mentioned in these two verses. The cistern refers to a student learning from his teacher, for he is gathering wisdom from an outside source, just as the cistern collects water from outside. He then progresses to the second stage, where he can increase his Torah knowledge by studying himself; just as a well has its own natural source of water, so will he now be able to expound his own novel ideas of Torah thought. The third stage is when the student is able to teach others from his wealth of Torah knowledge, which is then comparable to the flowing waters of a spring. [The three metaphors of בּוֹר, בְּאֵר and מַעְיָן thus correspond to *chochmah, binah* and *daas*.]

The two portions of this verse refer to two ways through which a sage's Torah knowledge will spread outward: יָפֻוצוּ מַעְיְנֹתֶיךָ חֻוּצָה, *your springs will spread*

outward, refers to students whom you yourself teach; בָּרְחֹבוֹת פַּלְגֵי־מָיִם, *[your] streams of water in the thoroughfares*, are those students who did not study directly from you, but who hear your Torah as it spreads in the streets and they learn from it vicariously from you (*Vilna Gaon*).

Ibn Ezra and *Metzudos* explain: A person who remains loyal to his wife will merit to have many children, whose fame will spread afar.

17. יִהְיוּ־לְךָ לְבַדֶּךָ וְאֵין לְזָרִים אִתָּךְ — *They will be yours alone, strangers not sharing with you.* You will be esteemed for your Torah knowledge, and no one will share this honor with you. This is in direct contrast to v. 10, which states that one who approached an adulteress will have his hard-earned wealth usurped by strangers (*Rashi*).

This verse responds to people who might say: "I have toiled so hard to attain Torah knowledge; should I now go and teach it to others who have not toiled for it?" However, the reward for the effort you invested in achieving *chochmah* will be yours alone (לְבַדֶּךָ); no one can share it with you (*Vilna Gaon*).

Even though one who teaches Torah to others is like a stream of water flowing in thoroughfares (v. 16), the Torah that he teaches remains his, for it will be quoted in his name, and he alone will enjoy the reward for his wisdom (*Malbim*).

R' Chanina bar Chana (*Taanis* 7a) notes the seeming contradiction between verse 16, יָפֻוצוּ מַעְיְנֹתֶיךָ חֻוּצָה, *your springs will spread outward*, and verse 17, יִהְיוּ־לְךָ לְבַדֶּךָ, *they will be yours alone*; verse 16 instructs one to teach Torah to others, while verse 17 implies that one should keep his knowledge to himself. *R' Chanina bar Chana* reconciles the verses by explaining that if the student is worthy, teach him Torah; if not, keep the Torah to yourself.

streams of water in the thoroughfares. [17] They will be yours alone, strangers not sharing with you. [18] Your source will be blessed, and you will rejoice with the wife of your youth. [19] A beloved hind inspiring favor, her breasts will sate you at all times, you will always be intoxicated with her love.

Rashi (ad loc.) explains that this stipulation refers only to the secrets of Torah, which may be revealed only to qualified students.

The phrase *strangers not sharing with you* can also be read as a directive. You should not put extraneous subjects on a par with the study of Torah. Similarly, on the verse in *Shema*, וְדִבַּרְתָּ בָּם, *and you should speak of them* (Deuteronomy 6:7), *Rashi* comments, עֲשֵׂם עִיקָר וְאַל תַּעֲשֵׂם טָפֵל, *make them [i.e., the words of Torah] of prime importance; do not make them of secondary importance.* A person should not say, "I have studied the *chochmah* of Israel; now, I will go and study of the wisdom of Greece" (*Sifri, Vaeschanan*).[1]

18. יְהִי־מְקוֹרְךָ בָרוּךְ וּשְׂמַח מֵאֵשֶׁת נְעוּרֶךָ — *Your source will be blessed, and you will rejoice with* [lit. *from*] *the wife of your youth.* This verse refers to the Torah you studied in your youth (*Rashi*); or, literally, the wife whom you married in your youth, who will be dear to you and beloved in your eyes (*Metzudos*). [See *Sanhedrin* 22a about the special relationship between a husband and the wife of his youth.]

Malbim explains that the מָקוֹר, which is the *source* from which waters start flowing underground, applies metaphorically to a person's שֵׂכֶל, *common sense*, which will be Divinely blessed (*Malbim*).

19. אַיֶּלֶת אֲהָבִים וְיַעֲלַת חֵן — *A beloved hind inspiring favor.* A hind is very beloved to the male and finds favor in his eyes. This endearment continues, always remaining

as strong as it was initially. So, too, the words of Torah are most beloved to those who study them, and continuously remain so. The Torah also brings favor upon its students, for they become respected for their Torah knowledge (*Eruvin* 54b, and *Rashi* ad loc.).[2]

Our translation of יַעֲלַת חֵן as *inspiring favor* follows that of the Talmud (ibid.). *Malbim* explains it differently, as *a female mountain goat*, [וְיַעֲלֵה חֵן] which finds favor. Just as a hind and a mountain goat run swiftly on the mountain, so, too, wisdom comes to people from on high, and will be beloved and find favor in their eyes.

דַּדֶּיהָ יְרַוֻּךָ בְכָל־עֵת — *Her breasts will sate you at all times.* As long as a baby nurses from its mother, there will be milk. So, too, as long as a person immerses himself in the study of Torah, he will find nourishment in its words (*Eruvin* 54b).

Generally, familiarity breeds contempt, rather than love towards the other party (See 25:17, הֹקַר רַגְלְךָ מִבֵּית רֵעֶךָ), but this is not true in the case of Torah study. A person who constantly sates himself with the nourishment of Torah will find his love for it ever increasing (*Binah L'Itim*).

בְּאַהֲבָתָהּ תִּשְׁגֶּה תָמִיד — *You will always be intoxicated* [lit. *engrossed*] *with her love.* This interpretation follows that of R' Moshe HaDarshan, as quoted by *Rashi*, who explains that תִּשְׁגֶּה comes from Arabic and means *to be engrossed.* Alternatively, *Rashi* explains this word according

1. The *Netziv* headed the famed yeshivah in Volozhin, which boasted an enrollment of four hundred Torah students. When the Czarist government decreed that the yeshivah introduce secular studies and sharply cut back its Torah studies, the *Netziv* closed the institution rather than comply. He wrote to his son, Rabbi Chaim Berlin, "Do not be anguished that this matter will bring about my departure from this world . . . for it is well worth the sacrifice of my life." As he feared, he died shortly afterwards (quoted in *Lekach Tov, Shemos* 1, p.15). See *Menachos* 106b.

2. At times a Torah scholar may become so engrossed in his studies that he will not pay attention to his food or his clothing, yet he will still find favor in the eyes of his beholders in the merit of his Torah study (*Maharsha, Eruvin* 54b).

וְלָמָּה תִשְׁגֶּה בְנִי בְזָרָה וּתְחַבֵּק חֵק נָכְרִיָּה: כִּי
נֹכַח ׀ עֵינֵי יהוה דַּרְכֵי־אִישׁ וְכָל־מַעְגְּלֹתָיו מְפַלֵּס:
כב עֲווֹנוֹתָיו יִלְכְּדֻנוֹ אֶת־הָרָשָׁע וּבְחַבְלֵי חַטָּאתוֹ
כג יִתָּמֵךְ: הוּא יָמוּת בְּאֵין מוּסָר וּבְרֹב אִוַּלְתּוֹ יִשְׁגֶּה:

to the Sages (*Eruvin* 54b), who relate it to the word מִשְׁגֶּה, *an oversight*. This verse would then mean that for the sake of love of Torah, a person can even err and neglect worldly matters, for the merit of Torah will safeguard him. This is illustrated by the case of R' Elazar ben Pedas who left his cloak in the upper marketplace of Tzippori and went to study Torah in the lower marketplace. Once, a man came to steal the cloak, and found a snake wrapped around it (i.e., protecting it from harm).[1]

R' Bachya interprets the phrase as a play on words: If you have loved Torah and are constantly immersed in it, it is as if you have brought the תָּמִיד, *daily continual offerings*.

Metzudos continues the metaphor of the wife of one's youth, explaining this verse in reference to her: She will be as beloved to you as a hind is to its mate, and she will find favor in your eyes. Yet, even such a relationship must have limits. If the companionship between man and wife is *constant* and unrestrained [תָּמִיד], *it will be accounted as an error* [תִּשְׁגֶּה]. [See *Avos* 1:5, וְאַל תַּרְבֶּה שִׂיחָה עִם הָאִשָּׁה, בְּאִשְׁתּוֹ אָמְרוּ. . .]

20. וְלָמָּה תִשְׁגֶּה בְנִי בְזָרָה וּתְחַבֵּק חֵק נָכְרִיָּה — *Why then, my son, should you err with a strange woman and embrace an alien bosom?* If, as the previous verse concludes,

inordinate preoccupation with one's own wife is an error, then how much more is this true regarding a strange woman. The *mishnah* (*Avos* 1:5, see citation from previous verse) concludes: בְּאִשְׁתּוֹ אָמְרוּ קַל וָחוֹמֶר בְּאֵשֶׁת חֲבֵרוֹ, *they said this even about one's own wife; surely it applies to another's wife* (*Ibn Ezra*).

Malbim explains that the *strange woman* refers to fields of knowledge that mislead a person. Why should he engross himself in such studies when the knowledge of Torah is available to him? *An alien bosom* refers to heresy and apostasy, which someone may subsequently embrace.

21. כִּי נֹכַח עֵינֵי ה' דַּרְכֵי־אִישׁ וְכָל־מַעְגְּלֹתָיו מְפַלֵּס — *For a man's ways are opposite HASHEM's eyes, and He weighs all his courses.* God is aware of man's actions and weighs his course, knowing his sins and merits (*Rashi*).[2]

Metzudos renders: Hashem *aligns an individual's ways* with the exact measure of reward and punishment, i.e., He pays the person measure for measure, so that he will realize that what befalls him is not by chance, but in direct reciprocation for his actions.

A person should never think that God does not see all his actions. Based on this verse, the Sages teach, דַּע מַה לְמַעְלָה מִמְּךָ עַיִן רוֹאָה וְאֹזֶן שׁוֹמַעַת — *Know what is*

1. The Sages had such a burning love for Torah that they were often oblivious to worldly matters. Their Torah study protected them, and, as a result, they suffered no harm.

The *Chazon Ish* recounted that in post-World War I Russia, anarchy reigned and youths were being grabbed off the streets and sent away to serve in the army. The *Chazon Ish* was so engrossed in reviewing the tractate *Eruvin* that he walked through the streets of the town despite the precarious situation. Finally, becoming aware of the danger he was in, he rushed home. All the way home he noticed that the Russian officials seemed not to see him, as if he had become invisible (From דרכיו והנהגותיו של בעל קהילת יעקב).

2. *Rambam* (*Hilchos Teshuvah* 3:2) explains that the accounting of a person's sins and merits is not quantitative, but qualitative. There may be one merit which counterbalances several sins; a certain sin may override several merits. This evaluation is done solely according to the intelligence of God, Who knows how to evaluate merits and sins.

20 Why then, my son, should you err with a strange woman and embrace an alien bosom? ²¹ For a man's ways are opposite HASHEM's eyes, and He weighs all his courses. ²² His own iniquities will ensnare the wicked one and he will be suspended in the cords of his sins. ²³ He will die for refusing discipline, and because of the abundant foolishness with which he erred.

above you — *a watchful Eye and an attentive Ear* [Avos 2:1] (*Yalkut Shimoni*).

Since this verse follows verse 20, *embrace an alien bosom*, which implies an errant action done secretly, its purpose is to warn a sinner that no action is hidden from God's eyes. Even a sin committed in the most-hidden chambers is known to Him (*Ibn Nachmiahs*).

The *Alshich* comments that this verse addresses those who think that they will not be punished for sinning. Since God knows what a person's actions will be, such a sinner assumes that he is forced to sin and is, therefore, not liable for his actions, for what is Divinely proclaimed cannot be changed. To dismiss such a spurious claim, the verse acknowledges that a person's actions are always before God's eyes, and He knows if one's actions and intentions are good or bad. However, וְכָל־מַעְגְּלֹתָיו מְפַלֵּס, *and he* [referring to the person] *weighs all his courses.* The *person himself* can weigh and determine which way his course will ultimately run by exercising his own Free Will [and therefore will be punished for choosing the wrong course].

22. עֲווֹנוֹתָיו יִלְכְּדֻנוֹ אֶת־הָרָשָׁע — *His own iniquities will ensnare the wicked one.* Often, the sin itself brings about the downfall of the wicked (*Ralbag*). The lawless man is ensnared by his own devious ways (*R' Hirsch*).

Just as someone spreads out a net and captures fish, so a person's sins spread out like a net to ensnare him (*Yalkut Shimoni*).

וּבְחַבְלֵי חַטָּאתוֹ יִתָּמֵךְ — *And he will be suspended in the cords of his sins*, i.e, the wicked man will be hanged, for such a person is suspended by the ropes with which he was hung (*Rashi*).

According to *Metzudos*, the metaphor means that the sin he committed will testify against him and bring punishment upon him.

23. הוּא יָמוּת בְּאֵין מוּסָר — *He will die for refusing discipline.* The wicked person will die because he did not accept *mussar* (*Rashi*).

וּבְרֹב אִוַּלְתּוֹ יִשְׁגֶּה — *And because of the abundant foolishness with which he erred.* This translation follows *Metzudos*.

R' Hirsch renders: *and because of the excess of his delusion, he is caught.* A sinner may reach the point where he will even reject *mussar*, i.e., the afflictions which God sends to punish and frighten him. This results when one is involved with אִוֶּלֶת, *delusion.*

An אֱוִיל (related to אוּלַי, *maybe*; see 1:7) is skeptical about everything. He will not even accept *mussar*, i.e., Divinely inflicted punishment, for he will ascribe all his misfortunes to happenstance, since he does not recognize the Divine hand directing the world. Thus, *his skepticism* (אִוַּלְתּוֹ) about Divine Providence is what causes him to reject *mussar* (*Malbim*).

VI

The following chapter is divided into several subtopics. *Meiri* comments that verses 1-5 warn one to avoid commitments that may cause him losses. The moral of these verses is not to discourage people from lending money or doing other acts of kindness. Rather they are a warning that one should do so in a manner that will not bring him to ruin. The previous chapter warns against physical temptation that can drag someone to physical ruin; this chapter warns that one should not bring oneself to financial ruin by

בְּנִי אִם־עָרַבְתָּ לְרֵעֶךָ תָּקַעְתָּ לַזָּר כַּפֶּיךָ: נוֹקַשְׁתָּ
בְאִמְרֵי־פִיךָ נִלְכַּדְתָּ בְּאִמְרֵי־פִיךָ: עֲשֵׂה זֹאת אֵפוֹא ג
בְּנִי וְהִנָּצֵל כִּי בָאתָ בְכַף־רֵעֶךָ לֵךְ הִתְרַפֵּס וּרְהַב רֵעֶיךָ:

foolishly accepting responsibility for unsound loans. One *should* help others secure loans, but not at the cost of jeopardizing one's own financial security.

The Halachah has safeguards to protect the lender, such as his right to demand a מַשְׁכּוֹן, *security*, when making a loan; demanding collateral or cosigners; and documenting transactions in writing, as opposed to making oral commitments, so that they will be enforceable in a *beis din*. But if someone failed to be prudent, and is caught in a situation such as those described in these verses, he should extricate himself from it as soon as possible.

◈§ Avoid commitments that are beyond your abilities

1. בְּנִי אִם־עָרַבְתָּ לְרֵעֶךָ — *My child, if you have been a guarantor for your friend.* These verses (1-5) deal with עֲרַבוּת מָמוֹן, a *cosigner guarantee* (*Rashi*).

תָּקַעְתָּ לַזָּר כַּפֶּיךָ — *If you have given your handshake for a stranger.* A handshake confirms the guarantee (*Meiri*).

The verse refers to one who became a guarantor for his friend the lender, agreeing to pay a stranger's loan in case of default. The guarantor stands to gain no personal benefit, yet has obligated himself to pay someone's debt (*Ralbag*).

According to the *Vilna Gaon*, the verse speaks of two kinds of guarantees: עָרַבְתָּ לְרֵעֶךָ, *you have been a guarantor for your friend*, refers to a guarantor who pledges to pay back a loan if the borrower defaults. *You have given your handshake* refers to an עָרֵב קַבְּלָן, *a guarantor who has accepted unconditional obligation*, which is an even stronger commitment than an ordinary guarantor [for he obligates himself to pay the loan on the due date, without the lender even having to approach the actual borrower].

Metaphorically, this refers to the leaders of Israel who were made responsible for the nation (see *Deuteronomy* 1:13, וָאֲשִׂימֵם, *Rashi* ad loc.). There are two types of leaders: the elders, who teach Torah, and the judges. The teachers are like ordinary guarantors, who are obligated to educate and explain the Torah's laws so that people will be guided along the proper path and not err. Judges are like uncondi-

tional guarantors, for through their decisions, they take money from one person against his will and give it to another.

Malbim explains the verse as referring to a case where someone made a commitment to his friend, and also made a conflicting commitment to a stranger. For example, he guaranteed to sell his friend a house or a field, and then guaranteed to sell the very same property to a stranger. Accordingly, תָּקַעְתָּ לַזָּר כַּפֶּיךָ would mean: "*and afterwards you shook hands* [i.e., unconditionally guaranteed] *to the stranger.*"

2. נוֹקַשְׁתָּ בְאִמְרֵי־פִיךָ נִלְכַּדְתָּ בְּאִמְרֵי־פִיךָ — *You have been trapped by the words of your mouth, snared by the words of your mouth.* Once a promise has been made, it remains binding and may well prove to be a self-set trap (*Ibn Yachya*).

R' Hirsch explains these verses as a warning to avoid a situation where an individual commits himself to something over which he has no control. Of course, at the time of his commitment, he assumed that no harm would befall him, thinking that the lender would certainly repay his debt. However, facts may prove that he has made a costly error in judgment, in which case he will have to pay the consequences. Therefore, a person should seriously consider the possible consequences and avoid entering into such obligations.

3. עֲשֵׂה זֹאת אֵפוֹא בְּנִי וְהִנָּצֵל כִּי בָאתָ בְכַף־רֵעֶךָ — *Do this, therefore, my child, and be rescued; for you have come into your fellow's hand.* Since you have com-

¹ **M**y child, if you have been a guarantor for your friend, if you have given your handshake for a stranger, ² you have been trapped by the words of your mouth, snared by the words of your mouth. ³ Do this, therefore, my child, and be rescued, for you have come into your fellow's hand: Go humble yourself [before him], and let your fellow be superior.

mitted yourself and become responsible for the lender, do this and save yourself from your predicament (*Metzudos*).

לֵךְ הִתְרַפֵּס — *Go humble yourself [before him]*. Subjugate yourself before him and let him trample you (*Ibn Ezra, Metzudos*). הִתְרַפֵּס is related to בְּרַגְלַהּ רָפְסָה, *it trampled with its feet* (*Daniel 7:7*)

וּרְהַב רֵעֶיךָ — *And let your fellow be superior.* Plead with him to be lenient with you and to give you more time (*Meiri*). Strengthen your friend and give him dominion over yourself (*Meiri; Metzudos.*).

Metzudos explains רְהַב as *strengthen* [see יִרְהֲבוּ הַנַּעַר בַּזָּקֵן, *the youth will strengthen himself over the elder* (*Isaiah* 3:5)], rendering the phrase *strengthen your friend* and give him dominion over you.[1]

The Sages (*Bava Metzia* 115a) explain that verses 1 and 2 refer to two different problems: Either you became a guarantor for your friend (verse 1); or you have angered him with harsh words even though you owe him no money (verse 2). Verse 3 offers solutions to help extricate oneself from each of these situations: The unfortunate guarantor is told, הַתֵּר לוֹ פַּס יָד, *open the palm of your hand to him* and pay him his money; the word הִתְרַפֵּס is rendered as a contraction of הַתֵּר פַּס. The one who spoke harshly is told, רְהַב רֵעֶיךָ, *send many friends* to ask him to forgive you.[2] The letters of the word וּרְהַב may be

transposed to form the word הַרְבּוּ, *send many* (*Meiri*).

Minchas Shai points out that this is the only place in *Proverbs* where רֵעֶיךָ, meaning *your fellow* (in the singular), is written with a *yud*, a spelling which suggests the plural form — *your friends*. The interpretation, *send many friends*, follows this reading. *Minchas Shai* also quotes *R' Bachya*, who gives a different reason for the plural form. The guarantor must humble himself before two people: the lender, whom he asks for more time, and the borrower, whom he asks to pay the debt, thus freeing the guarantor from his commitment.

These verses can also be understood metaphorically. *Rashi* explains: My son, you have become committed to the Holy One, Blessed is He, Who is referred to as רֵעַ, *your Friend* (see *Shir HaShirim* 5:16: זֶה דוֹדִי וְזֶה רֵעִי, *This is my Beloved and this is my Friend*), and you twice accepted an oath to keep His commandments: at Mount Sinai and in the Plains of Moab. Then you turned away from His ways, and attached yourselves to heretics (לַזָּר), and became ensnared through your association with such strangers. Since you have a prior commitment to God, you must now do the following to save yourself: לֵךְ הִתְרַפֵּס, *humble yourself [before Him]* like the threshold of a door which is trampled upon; וּרְהַב רֵעֶיךָ, *and send many friends* to pray for you before Him.[3]

1. Even though חֲנִיפָה, *flattery*, causes much harm and is condemned by the Sages, there are three exceptions where they permit it, one of which is to placate a creditor (see *Orchos Tzaddikim*).

2. This verse serves as the source for the Sages' teaching that a person who vexes his friend in public is obligated to appease him, which may necessitate sending many people to him to beg his forgiveness. If the aggrieved person has died, one must bring ten people to his grave and ask for forgiveness (*Yoma* 87a).

3. *Fellows* refers to the righteous people of the generation whose prayers can change the Attribute of Justice to the Attribute of Mercy (see *Genesis* 8:1).

ד-ה אַל־תִּתֵּן שֵׁנָה לְעֵינֶיךָ וּתְנוּמָה לְעַפְעַפֶּיךָ: הִנָּצֵל
ו כִּצְבִי מִיָּד וּכְצִפּוֹר מִיַּד יָקוּשׁ: לֵךְ־אֶל־נְמָלָה עָצֵל
ז רְאֵה דְרָכֶיהָ וַחֲכָם: אֲשֶׁר אֵין־לָהּ קָצִין שֹׁטֵר וּמֹשֵׁל:

According to *Malbim*, the metaphor also refers to the commitment a person has made to safeguard the sanctity of his soul. Yet, he subsequently committed himself to the Evil Inclination and was attracted by materialistic desires to act in a fashion contrary to his original commitment. Since he already accepted responsibility to protect his soul from the snares of the Evil Inclination, he must now subjugate this materialistic drive (לֵךְ הִתְרַפֵּס) and uplift and strengthen his soul, which is his friend (וּרְהַב רֵעֶיךָ).[1]

4. אַל־תִּתֵּן שֵׁנָה לְעֵינֶיךָ וּתְנוּמָה לְעַפְעַפֶּיךָ — *Give not sleep to your eyes, nor slumber to your eyelids.* Do not be lazy in this matter (*Metzudos*). After humbling yourself before the lender, do not rest until you have paid the debt (*Ibn Ezra*).

תְנוּמָה is a light sleep. Thus, do not sleep or even relax temporarily [until you have extricated yourself from this situation] (*Malbim*).

5. הִנָּצֵל כִּצְבִי מִיָּד וּכְצִפּוֹר מִיַּד יָקוּשׁ — *Be rescued like a deer from the [hunter's] hand, and like a bird from the fowler.* Extricate yourself quickly from your predicament, like a deer escaping from a hunter (*Rashi*) and a bird from a trap (*Meiri*).

The Midrash (*Yalkut Shimoni*) applies these verses to a scholar who has been appointed as a Torah authority for the community. He becomes an עָרֵב, *guarantor*, for that community, i.e., because he is in a position to correct them, he becomes responsible for their actions and will be blamed and punished for their shortcomings. Such an authority must take care lest he become ensnared by his words and rule that what is unpure is pure, or what is pure

is unpure. What should he do? He must immerse himself in the study of Torah, for the word זֹאת, *this*, in verse 3 alludes to the Torah, as in וְזֹאת הַתּוֹרָה, *and "this" is the Torah* (*Deuteronomy* 4:44). He must accept someone as his own rav, and humble himself before his impartial judgment.

Alshich explains that *anyone* in a position to exert influence over others is under the same obligation as the aforementioned Torah authority. As the Sages teach, since the time of the giving of the Torah at Mount Sinai, כָּל יִשְׂרָאֵל עֲרֵבִים זֶה בָּזֶה, *all Jews are responsible for one another* (*Shevuos* 39a). Therefore, every person must do his utmost to influence his fellows to improve themselves. He must give his friend strength and elevate him from his sins (וּרְהַב רֵעֶיךָ) by influencing him to repent.

[Cf. *Shabbos* 54b. כָּל מִי שֶׁאֶפְשָׁר לִמְחוֹת לְאַנְשֵׁי בֵּיתוֹ וְלֹא מִיחָה נִתְפָּס עַל אַנְשֵׁי בֵּיתוֹ, *Whoever can protest to his household (to prevent them from sinning) but did not, is punished for the sins of his household; (if he can protest to) his fellow citizens, he is punished (for the sins) of his fellow citizens; (if he can protest to) the whole world, he is punished for the whole world.*]

According to *Midrash Shocher Tov*, בְּנִי אִם־עָרַבְתָּ לְרֵעֶךָ, *My child, if you have been a guarantor for your friend* (v. 1), refers to the giving of the Torah at Mount Sinai, when God appointed the children as guarantors that the nation of Israel would fulfill the Torah they were about to receive.

◈§ Diligence in deed

Verses 6-11 teach a person to be diligent in his actions and, while he is still young, to prepare for his old age (*Meiri*).

1. *Sfas Emes* interprets this verse as relating to the quest for truth, and notes that it can succeed through sincere effort and an earnest desire to grasp the Torah. As the Sages say, "Delve into [the Torah] and continue to delve into it . . ." (*Avos* 5:26). Whenever Jews search for the truths of the Torah, if we *humble ourselves*, we can become *strengthened* and *saved*.

⁴ *Give not sleep to your eyes, nor slumber to your eyelids;* ⁵ *be rescued like a deer from the [hunter's] hand, and like a bird from the fowler.*

⁶ *Go to the ant, you sluggard; see her ways and grow wise.*

⁷ *Though there is neither officer nor guard nor ruler over her,*

❧ From an ant, learn to be industrious

6. לֵךְ־אֶל־נְמָלָה עָצֵל רְאֵה דְרָכֶיהָ וַחֲכָם — *Go to the ant, you sluggard; see her ways and grow wise.* According to the *Vilna Gaon*, this verse alludes to three qualities that can be learned from the ant: its good deeds, its fine attributes and its wisdom.

(1) If someone is sluggish in performing good deeds, he should learn from the diligence of an ant, who gathers much more than it needs for its survival. The Sages (*Devarim Rabbah* 5:2) teach us that an ant lives only six months and needs only a kernel and a half of wheat to sustain itself, yet throughout the summer it is busy gathering whatever it finds, whether it be wheat, barley, or lentils. Why does the ant do so? Its instinct dictates, "Maybe the Holy One, Blessed is He, will decree that I will live longer, and thus I must prepare what I will need for my sustenance [during the winter months]." R' Shimon bar Yochai relates that he once found a vast quantity of wheat stored in an anthill.

(2) רְאֵה דְרָכֶיהָ, *see her ways.* "Ways" refers to characteristics. Even though the ant is eager to collect a large amount of food, it will not touch something which belongs to another. The Midrash (ibid.) recounts that an ant once dropped a grain of wheat. All the other ants realized from its scent that it was not theirs. No ant took it until the original ant returned and retrieved its wheat.

(3) וַחֲכָם, *and grow wise.* A person can learn wisdom from the way an ant stores its food. According to the Midrash (ibid.), ants makes three compartments in their hill. They do not store food in the upper compartment for fear that it will be ruined by rain, nor in the lower compartment because the underground moisture may spoil it. Instead, they store food in the middle section. Similarly, a person should choose the correct path for himself (*Vilna Gaon*), and take all necessary precautions to ensure that his actions are secure and enduring (see *Eitz Yosef*, to *Devarim Rabbah* 5:2).

All the forces found in creation are also implanted in the soul of man. Man should realize that every trait he observes in the myriad of creatures is also present in his own being. Certain creatures possess instincts that are not necessary for their survival, but are inherent in them to serve as a lesson to human beings. Thus, R' Yochanan states, אִילְמָלֵא לֹא נִיתְּנָה תּוֹרָה הָיִינוּ לְמֵידִין צְנִיעוּת מֵחָתוּל וְגֵזֶל מִנְּמָלָה וַעֲרָיוֹת מִיּוֹנָה דֶּרֶךְ אֶרֶץ מִתַּרְנְגוֹל, *Had the Torah not been given, we would have learned modesty from a cat, [not to commit] theft from an ant, [not to commit] adultery from a dove, the proper manner of conduct [towards one's mate] from a rooster* (*Eruvin* 100b). Hashem endowed the ant with diligence so that man may learn from its example not to be sluggish in his quest for wisdom (*Malbim*).

Nevertheless, there is an important distinction between the traits found in creatures, and the corresponding traits in mankind. The former is but instinct, whereas the latter is a rational decision on the part of man to behave in a certain manner. That is why the verse does not instruct the person to go see the ways of an ant, and then וַעֲשֵׂה, *and do likewise,* but rather, וַחֲכָם, *grow wise,* i.e., to learn to apply them wisely. An ant's diligence in collecting much more than it needs should not be misapplied to amassing material wealth, but rather to amassing spiritual wealth (*Kol Omer Kera*).

7. אֲשֶׁר אֵין־לָהּ קָצִין שֹׁטֵר וּמֹשֵׁל — *Though there is neither officer nor guard nor ruler over her.* An ant has no one to rebuke it, to encourage it to be diligent, or to take back what it may have stolen from its fellow

ח תָּכִין בַּקַּיִץ לַחְמָהּ אָגְרָה בַקָּצִיר מַאֲכָלָהּ:
ט עַד־מָתַי עָצֵל ׀ תִּשְׁכָּב מָתַי תָּקוּם מִשְּׁנָתֶךָ: מְעַט

ant. Nevertheless, it gathers and prepares its food (see next verse) and does not steal (*Rashi*).

The three terms in this verse correspond to the three praiseworthy traits of the ant referred to in the previous verse: קָצִין, *an officer*, is one who teaches wisdom to others; שֹׁטֵר, *an overseer*, is one who makes sure that the proper actions are taken and the verdict of the court is carried out; and מֹשֵׁל, *a ruler*, is one who corrects behavior and makes sure there is no theft or violence in the city. Even though the ant has none of these superiors to direct it, it still possesses wisdom, good deeds and fine character (*Vilna Gaon*).

Officer, overseer or ruler. Rabbeinu Bachye comments on the triple usage of administrators in this verse. He explains that the intent of the verse as indicating that the ant acts without any intelligence, whatsoever. All her actions are natural and instinctive. Yet, because intelligence has three appellatives, *chochmah, tvunah* and *daas*, all of which are in the same class and found only in human beings, Shlomo HaMelech recounted three authority figures, also of the same class, for comparison.

If an ant acts this way without the benefit of a superior, how much more is demanded of the Jewish people who have Divinely appointed judges and overseers? Israel should certainly heed their teachings! (*Devarim Rabbah* 5:2).

8. תָּכִין בַּקַּיִץ לַחְמָהּ — *She prepares her bread in the summer*. Each ant prepares and gathers its own food, and one does not steal from the other (*Rashi*).

אָגְרָה בַקָּצִיר מַאֲכָלָהּ — *And gathers her food in the harvest time*. Just as an ant instinctively prepares its sustenance when food is available in the fields, so, too, a person must make his preparations when it is in his power to do so (*Metzudos*).

Malbim explains: An ant prepares its bread in the summer [קַיִץ] after having gathered its food during the harvest [קָצִיר] in late spring. Once summer arrives and the kernels are no longer available in the fields, the ant concentrates its efforts on preparing and storing food for the upcoming winter.

"Harvest" and "summer" are metaphors for youth and old age. During one's youth, a person must "harvest" a large amount of Torah knowledge. Afterwards, in old age, one takes the accumulated knowledge and attempts to comprehend it fully (*Vilna Gaon*).

The Midrash recounts that in the future, the wicked will ask God for a chance to repent. The Holy One, Blessed is He, will reply: "Fools! You lived in a world compared to Sabbath eve, whereas the World to Come is compared to the Sabbath. One who has not prepared before the Sabbath will have no food to eat on the Sabbath. This world is like dry land; the Hereafter, like the sea. If one neglects to take food from shore before embarking on his journey, will he have food to eat at sea? You should have learned this lesson from the ant!" (*Yalkut Shimoni*).

The same principle applies to Torah study — one must invest his wholehearted effort to acquiring Torah knowledge in this world, so that he may enjoy its benefits in the Hereafter (*Meiri*).

Alshich points out that if an ant is so diligent even though its life span is so short, how much more necessary is it for a person to be diligent both in his youth and in his old age to continuously amass merits for his everlasting life in the World to Come. He must take advantage of the short seventy-year life span allotted him to accumulate enough merits to last for eternity.[1]

1. The Sages give several examples of this concept, based on *Ecclesiastes* 11:6: בַּבֹּקֶר זְרַע אֶת־זַרְעֶךָ
וְלָעֶרֶב אַל־תַּנַּח יָדֶךָ, *In the morning sow your seed and in the evening do not be idle.*
R' Yehoshua said that if one lost the wife of his youth, one should remarry. And if one had children when young, one should continue to have children in one's old age. R' Akiva said that

8 she prepares her bread in the summer and gathers her food in the harvest time. 9 How long will you recline, O sluggard? When will you arise from your sleep? 10 A little

9. עַד־מָתַי עָצֵל תִּשְׁכָּב — *How long will you recline, O sluggard?* "Reclining" implies laziness in *performing* good deeds, but the person may still be thinking about Torah at the time (*Vilna Gaon*).[1]

מָתַי תָּקוּם מִשְּׁנָתֶךָ — *When will you arise from your sleep?* However, a person in a state of *sleep* is devoid of even thoughts of Torah (*Vilna Gaon*).

Alshich comments that a lazy person remains in bed and rests, even after he has awakened; only after a prolonged period does he finally get up. Therefore, the verse asks, *When will you arise from your sleep* — i.e., when will you get out of bed as soon as you wake up?[2]

Malbim explains that the *sluggard* is a metaphor for one who sleeps through his youth, i.e., he does not realize his purpose in life. When he finally wakes up to the

if one had disciples in youth, one should also have disciples in old age (*Yevamos* 62b). R' Akiva exemplified this teaching, for his 24,000 students died between Pesach and Shavuos, but he started again and taught in his old age.

Derech Chaim relates the verse to charity. One should be charitable in the *morning*, when one is affluent. But even if one became impoverished, one should still contribute whatever possible. One can never know which is more pleasing to God.

1. The *Vilna Gaon* was legendary for his total immersion in Torah study. For more than fifty years, he slept only two hours a day, in four thirty-minute segments, three during the night and one during the day. Even when he slept, his lips would constantly murmur words of Torah.

Once he was forced to leave Vilna for a period of time, and he spent some time in the town of Meretz. Its residents were overjoyed to have such a holy person in their midst, and the wealthiest man in town placed the second floor of his home, at the *Gaon's* disposal, with the promise that he could study undisturbed. The townspeople, however, longed to see this human "angel," and they devised a scheme to do so without disturbing him. They erected a tall ladder outside his study window, and took turns climbing it to watch him study.

Once after midnight, the *Gaon* awoke with a start from his short sleep. He had overslept by ten minutes — forty minutes instead of thirty — and was anguished that he had lost ten precious minutes of Torah study. He was heard to remark, "It seems that sleep comes easily in Meretz." A deep gloom descended on the townspeople at the thought that this "tragedy" had happened in their midst.

Some time later, the *Gaon* was able to return to Vilna, and he once again stayed overnight in Meretz, at the same home. This time, he woke up ten minutes earlier than usual, thus retrieving the ten lost minutes. Gloom turned to happiness, as both he and the people of Meretz rejoiced that he had been able to make amends for the lost minutes of Torah study.

2. *Kitzur Shulchan Aruch* 1:4 teaches: It is everyone's duty to make himself strong as a lion and immediately upon awakening to arise quickly to serve the Creator, Blessed is He, before the Evil Inclination overcomes him with excuses and dissuades him from rising.

Torah sages, who value every waking moment as an irreplaceable opportunity for Torah study, were a living embodiment of this principle. Among the קַבָּלוֹת, *resolutions*, that the *Alter of Kelm*, R' Simcha Zissel Ziev, accepted upon himself, was to arise from bed immediately upon awakening. When this saintly man lay dying, he forced his frail and sick body to rise from bed in order to stand while reciting the *Minchah* prayer. When his students protested that in his condition he was permitted to pray in bed, the Alter replied, "Yes, that is halachically correct, but I suspect that it is laziness that tempts me to pray in bed!" With that, he arose and prayed. After *Minchah*, he returned to bed and passed away.

In a lighter vein, when the Rebbe, Reb Heschel, was still a young boy, his father came to wake him up in the morning remarking, "Heschele, why don't you learn from your Evil Inclination? Even at this early hour he is already hard at work, for you see how he is succeeding in keeping you in bed!"

"True, Father," answered the young genius. "But it is not a fair comparison, for my *yetzer hara* does not have a *yetzer hara* to deter it from its task."

שְׁנוֹת מְעַט תְּנוּמוֹת מְעַט ׀ חִבֻּק יָדַיִם לִשְׁכָּב:

יא-יב וּבָא־כִמְהַלֵּךְ רֵאשֶׁךָ וּמַחְסֹרְךָ כְּאִישׁ מָגֵן: אָדָם

יג בְּלִיַּעַל אִישׁ אָוֶן הוֹלֵךְ עִקְּשׁוּת פֶּה: קֹרֵץ

יד בְּעֵינָיו מֹלֵל בְּרַגְלָו °בְּרַגְלוֹ מֹרֶה בְּאֶצְבְּעֹתָיו: תַּהְפֻּכוֹת ׀

טו בְּלִבּוֹ חֹרֵשׁ רָע בְּכָל־עֵת °מדנים °מִדְיָנִים יְשַׁלֵּחַ: עַל־כֵּן

°בְּרַגְלָיו ק

°מִדְיָנִים ק

need for Torah study, his ingrained laziness prevents him from actively pursuing spiritual growth. Thus, both his "harvest" and "summer" have passed, and he has accomplished nothing.

10. מְעַט שְׁנוֹת מְעַט תְּנוּמוֹת מְעַט חִבֻּק יָדַיִם לִשְׁכָּב — *A little sleep, a little slumber, a little folding of the hands to recline.* *Metzudos* explains: Should a person think, "I will sleep a little, then I will slumber a little, and then I will lie with my hands folded and rest just a little [for one who lies down to rest folds his hands]," the result will be as expressed in verse 11.

11. וּבָא־כִמְהַלֵּךְ רֵאשֶׁךָ — *And your poverty will come like a traveler.* If a person acts in such a manner described in verse 10, then his poverty will come upon him immediately like one who walks hurriedly (*Rashi*).

Metzudos renders: His poverty will come upon him suddenly like an unexpected guest who is traveling on the road and arrives without any prior warning at his host's home.

וּמַחְסֹרְךָ כְּאִישׁ מָגֵן — *And your loss like a shield-bearer.* His loss will come upon him like a shield-bearer who rushes to protect his master. Metaphorically, these verses refer primarily to those who are too lazy to engage in Torah study (*Rashi*).

Our Sages stress the speed with which spiritual poverty can beset a person if he is negligent in Torah study. *Meiri* cites *Sifrei* (*Eikev* 11:22), quoting the *Yerushalmi*, אִם תַּעַזְבֵנִי יוֹם יוֹמַיִם אֶעֱזָבֶךָ, *If you leave me for one day, I will leave you for two* — i.e., if you neglect Torah study for even a short time, you will soon find yourself far removed from Torah (*Talmud Yerushalmi, Berachos* 9:4). This is comparable to two people who meet one another, and

then each travels a distance of one *mil* in opposite directions from their meeting point. In the end, they will find themselves a distance of two *mil* apart.

The *Vilna Gaon* explains that רֵאשֶׁךָ refers to *your poverty* in the performance of *mitzvos*. This will come upon the person כִּמְהַלֵּךְ, *like one who walks* toward his friend — he does not run, but gradually approaches the latter. So, too, the poverty in *mitzvos* will accumulate gradually, as the person neglects to perform each of the commandments in its respective time. However, מַחְסֹרְךָ, *your loss* in Torah will come like an אִישׁ מָגֵן, a *shield-bearer*, who runs to save his friend when the latter is under attack. The loss in the area of Torah study will be swift and immediate, since the obligation to study Torah is a constant and continuous one.

Alshich interprets these verses (9-11) allegorically. Certain circumstances in life may cause a person to arouse himself from the stupor of materialism in this world and inspire him to repent from his past sins and pursue spirituality. He will then make Torah his primary goal, and his periods of "sleep" — i.e., the time and effort he invests in the affairs of this world — will diminish accordingly. As he immerses himself more and more in spiritual matters, he will quickly realize how impoverished and wanting he is in *mitzvos*, but the process will be gradual, and he will still be forced to contend with the residual effects of his past sins. However, if he attains the highest level of spiritual resurgence and reaches the level of תְּשׁוּבָה מֵאַהֲבָה, *repentance that stems from the love of God*, then even the sins that have created destructive forces to harm him will become an אִישׁ מָגֵן, a *shield-bearer to protect him*. As the Sages teach, such repentance

sleep, a little slumber, a little folding of the hands to recline,
¹¹ and your poverty will come like a traveler, and your loss like
a shield-bearer.

¹² The lawless person is a man of iniquity: He engages in
distortion of the mouth; ¹³ he winks with his eyes, shuffles
with his feet, points with his fingers; ¹⁴ perversities in his
heart, he plots evil all the time; he incites strife. ¹⁵ Therefore,

changes even intentional sins to merits and creates angels that protect the former sinner (*Yoma* 86b).

~§ Dishonest people will be undone

Verses 12-15 warn of the dangers of certain undesirable charecter traits that can lead to grave transgressions (*Meiri*).

12. אָדָם בְּלִיַּעַל אִישׁ אָוֶן הוֹלֵךְ עִקְּשׁוּת פֶּה — *The lawless person is a man of iniquity: He goes forth with distortion of the mouth.* בְּלִיַּעַל, *lawless*, is a combination of the words בְּלִי עוֹל, *without a yoke*, i.e., he casts off the sovereignty of God. Such an individual is iniquitous, for he perverts his mouth with a slanderous intent (*Metzudos*).

This is a person who casts off the sovereignty of both God and man; he does whatever evil he sees fit to do. The three parts of this verse correspond to three aspects of evil: אָדָם בְּלִיַּעַל, *a lawless man*, refers to man's evil deeds, for he perpetrates evil and fears no one; אִישׁ אָוֶן, *a person of iniquity*, refers to man's evil thoughts, for although he speaks nicely, he harbors thoughts of iniquity in his heart; עִקְּשׁוּת פֶּה, *distortions of the mouth*, refers to man's evil speech (*Vilna Gaon*).

13. קֹרֵץ בְּעֵינָיו מֹלֵל בְּרַגְלָיו מֹרֶה בְּאֶצְבְּעֹתָיו — *He winks with his eyes, scrapes with his feet, points with his fingers.* קֹרֵץ, מֹלֵל, and מֹרֶה are all terms which indicate, signaling or hinting. They all describe wicked people (*Rashi*). According to *Metzudos*, they all refer to hints of לָשׁוֹן הָרַע, slander.

14. תַּהְפֻּכוֹת בְּלִבּוֹ — *Perversities in his heart.* His heart's thoughts are to transform things from what they really are (*Metzudos*).

He says, "Yes," but in his heart he thinks the opposite (*Ibn Nachmias*).

חֹרֵשׁ רָע בְּכָל־עֵת — *He plots evil all the time.* Just as plowing prepares the soil for seeding, so evil thoughts are the prelude to evil deeds. (See *Rashi* 3:29.)

מִדְיָנִים יְשַׁלֵּחַ — *He incites strife.* *Rashi* explains that he causes fights between man and his Creator.

He constantly plots evil and he incites quarrels among people. These verses demonstrate that once a person rejects God's sovereignty (אָדָם בְּלִיַּעַל), then he will surely perform all the evil activities which follow (*Metzudos*).

Thus, according to *Malbim*, verses 12-14 enumerate seven characteristics by which the אָדָם בְּלִיַּעַל, *a lawless person*, who flaunts commandments between man and his Creator, and who is also an אִישׁ אָוֶן, *a man of iniquity*, who disregards commandments between man and his fellow man, is recognized:

1. Through his speech — *he engages in distortion of the mouth* (v. 12) against the dictates of *chochmah*.

2. With his eyes — *he winks* (v. 13) and disregards the Torah precept, *You shall not turn after your eyes* (*Numbers* 15:39).

3. With his movements — *he scrapes with his feet* — (v. 13) in readiness to do evil deeds.

4. With his hands — *he points with his fingers* (v. 13).

5. With his thoughts —(v. 14) *perversities in his heart* — he harbors heretical thoughts.

6. *He plots evil at all times* (v. 14) and also in his thoughts towards his fellow men.

7. *He incites strife* (v. 14) — among others.

פִּתְאֹם יָבוֹא אֵידוֹ פֶּתַע יִשָּׁבֵר וְאֵין מַרְפֵּא:

שֵׁשׁ־הֵנָּה שָׂנֵא יהוה וְשֶׁבַע °תּוֹעֲבוֹת נַפְשׁוֹ: עֵינַיִם   °תּוֹעֲבַת ק טז-יז

רָמוֹת לְשׁוֹן שָׁקֶר וְיָדַיִם שֹׁפְכוֹת דָּם־נָקִי: לֵב חֹרֵשׁ   יח

מַחְשְׁבוֹת אָוֶן רַגְלַיִם מְמַהֲרוֹת לָרוּץ לָרָעָה: יָפִיחַ   יט

כְּזָבִים עֵד שָׁקֶר וּמְשַׁלֵּחַ מְדָנִים בֵּין אַחִים: נֹצֵר   כ

15. עַל־כֵּן פִּתְאֹם יָבוֹא אֵידוֹ פֶּתַע יִשָּׁבֵר וְאֵין מַרְפֵּא — *Therefore, his misfortune will come suddenly: he will be broken in an instant, without healing.*

פִּתְאֹם and פֶּתַע are both terms which imply immediacy. פִּתְאֹם denotes *immediacy of time*, whereas פֶּתַע denotes *swiftness of action* (*Malbim*). He will not be aware of his imminent downfall (*Rashi*) and there will be no remedy for it (*Metzudos*).

Since he constantly harbored evil thoughts against others, his calamity will come suddenly and allow him no time to plan an alternative course of action to save himself (*Alshich*).

He will have no remedy, for he will not repent (*Malbim*).

According to *Midrash Mishlei*, these verses (12-15) refer to the habitual speaker of לָשׁוֹן הָרָע, *slander*. This sin is as severe as idol-worship, murder and adultery (see *Arachin* 15b). In this verse King Solomon curses such a person.

⧫§ God hates those who incite strife

After describing the ways of the lawless person in verses 12-15, verses 16-19 explain the root cause behind these actions — arrogance (*Meiri*).

16. שֵׁשׁ־הֵנָּה שָׂנֵא ה' וְשֶׁבַע תּוֹעֲבַת נַפְשׁוֹ — *HASHEM hates these six, but the seventh is the abomination of His soul*, i.e., the seventh is also included with them (*Rashi*). The seventh thing is an abomination to Hashem, i.e., it is hated even more than the others (*Metzudos*).

According to *Meiri* the seventh most abhorrent trait is the one which is mentioned first — that of arrogance (עֵינַיִם רָמוֹת, *haughty eyes*, see next verse). It is

the cause of the six hated things that follow. *Malbim* explains that the seventh and worst thing is the last one mentioned: inciting strife among people (verse 19).

The seven things are enumerated in the following three verses:

17. עֵינַיִם רָמוֹת לְשׁוֹן שָׁקֶר וְיָדַיִם שֹׁפְכוֹת דָּם־נָקִי — *Haughty [lit. "exalted"] eyes, a false tongue and hands shedding innocent blood.*

1. עֵינַיִם רָמוֹת, *haughty [lit. "exalted"] eyes*, refers to the trait of arrogance, for one who is arrogant lifts his eyes towards Heaven, as opposed to the humble, who cast their gaze downward (*Metzudos*).[1]

2. לְשׁוֹן שָׁקֶר, *a false tongue*, in other words, false speech.

3. וְיָדַיִם שֹׁפְכוֹת דָּם־נָקִי, *and hands shedding innocent blood*, i.e., a murderer (*Ibn Ezra*).

The *Vilna Gaon* explains this verse as describing the full gamut of the evil person's wickedness: in his thought — he is arrogant (עֵינַיִם רָמוֹת); in his speech — he is a deceiver [לְשׁוֹן שָׁקֶר]; and in deed — he sheds innocent blood [וְיָדַיִם שֹׁפְכֹת דָּם נָקִי].

18. לֵב חֹרֵשׁ מַחְשְׁבוֹת אָוֶן רַגְלַיִם מְמַהֲרוֹת לָרוּץ לָרָעָה — *A heart plotting iniquitous thoughts, feet hastening to run to evil.*

This verse includes two more of the seven evil traits:

4. a heart devising ways to harm people (*Ralbag*);

5. feet rushing to perform evil acts, before one has time to have any thoughts of regret (*Metzudos*);

19. יָפִיחַ כְּזָבִים עֵד שָׁקֶר — *A false witness spouting [lit. blowing] deceptions.*

6. people who testify falsely in court;

---

1. The *Ramban*, in his famous *Iggeres HaRamban*, advises the individual how to accustom himself to acting humbly: *Let your words be spoken gently; let your head be bowed; cast your eyes downward and your heart Heavenward.*

his misfortune will come suddenly; he will be broken in an instant, without healing.

¹⁶ H ASHEM *hates these six, but the seventh is the abomination of His soul:* ¹⁷ *haughty eyes, a false tongue, and hands shedding innocent blood,* ¹⁸ *a heart plotting iniquitous thoughts, feet hastening to run to evil,* ¹⁹ *a false witness spouting deceptions; and one who incites strife among brothers.*

וּמְשַׁלֵּחַ מְדָנִים בֵּין אַחִים — *and one who stirs up strife among brothers.*

7. The last trait is that of causing strife among people who should love one another.

According to *Malbim*, verses 16-19 parallel the seven traits enumerated in verses 12-14 [though not in the same order], but these seven are even more reprehensible: *Haughty eyes,* corresponding to one who *winks with his eyes,* refers to intellectual rejection of Torah faith; *false tongue,* corresponding to *one who engages in distortion of the mouth,* refers to the twisting of logic that produces heresy; and *hands shedding innocent blood* is the outcome of *one who points with his fingers. A heart plotting iniquitous thoughts* corresponds to *he plots evil all the time. Feet hastening to run to evil* corresponds to *shuffles with his feet. A false witness spouting deceptions* in a matter of faith corresponds to *perversities in his heart;* and *one who incites strife*

among brothers corresponds to *he incites strife.*

Malbim explains that the incitement of strife among people is worse than the other six sins, for it brings about the destruction of society.

When there is unity in Israel, God's Holy spirit rests among the people. However, should there be *strife among brothers,* Hashem despises them (*Vilna Gaon*).[1]

Metzudos comments that a person causes strife by spreading gossip and slander. This is why the seventh sin is more severe than the other six, for one who slanders kills three people: himself, the listener (who accepted it) and the person about whom it was spoken (see *Arachin* 15b).[2]

The *Chafetz Chaim* enumerates the consequences that result from slander and incitement to strife. He warns that these sins empower Satan to prosecute the Jewish people in Heaven. On the other hand, if there is harmony in Israel, and there are no

1. Peace is such a potent force that it can even outweigh the most severe sins. *Rashi* (*Genesis* 11:9) asks: Which sin is more severe, that of the generation of the Flood or that of the generation of the Dispersion? The former did not rebel against God, while the latter did, yet the generation of the Flood was completely destroyed, while the generation of the Dispersion was not. The generation of the Flood was noted for robbery, which caused disputes and discord, and that is why they were completely destroyed. The generation of the Dispersion, on the other hand, lived in peace and harmony (see ibid., 11:1), and were therefore spared a more severe punishment, despite the evil of their plans. This teaches us how hateful is dispute, and how great is peace in God's eyes! (cf. *Bereishis Rabbah* 38:6).

Peace is such a great virtue that even if Jews worship idols, but live in peace and harmony, God says, as it were, "I have no power to punish them since there is peace among them" (*Bereishis Rabbah* 38:6).

2. *Midrash Shocher Tov* (*Psalms* 52) expounds *lashon hara* is a more serious transgression that the cardinal sins of idolatry, adultery and murder. Whereas a murderer kills only one person, one who speaks *lashon hara* kills three: the speaker, the listener and the person about whom it was spoken. We learn this from the case of Doeg, who told King Saul that the Kohen Gadol Achimelech was a supporter of David (see *I Samuel* 22:9-10). Subsequently, all three were killed: Saul, who believed Doeg, was killed in battle with the Philistines (*I Samuel* 31:6); Achimelech, the subject of the slander, was executed by command of King Saul (*I Samuel* 22:16); and Doeg, the slanderer, died at a young age and lost his share in the World to Come (see *Sanhedrin* 106b).

כא בְּנִי מִצְוֺת אָבִיךָ וְאַל־תִּטֹּשׁ תּוֹרַת אִמֶּךָ: קָשְׁרֵם
כב עַל־לִבְּךָ תָמִיד עָנְדֵם עַל־גַּרְגְּרֹתֶךָ: בְּהִתְהַלֶּכְךָ |
תַּנְחֶה אֹתָךְ בְּשָׁכְבְּךָ תִּשְׁמֹר עָלֶיךָ וַהֲקִיצוֹתָ
כג הִיא תְשִׂיחֶךָ: כִּי נֵר מִצְוָה וְתוֹרָה אוֹר

---

talebearers among them, then Satan is neutralized and cannot condemn them even for such a severe sin as idolworship.[1]

◄§ Seek ways to keep the commandments

20. נְצֹר בְּנִי מִצְוַת אָבִיךָ וְאַל תִּטֹּשׁ תּוֹרַת אִמֶּךָ. — *Heed [lit. guard] my child, the command of your father and do not forsake the teaching of your mother.* Commandments can be fulfilled only at their designated times or when the opportunity presents itself. Therefore, in reference to *mitzvos*, the verse states נְצֹר, *guard*, i.e., preserve them until the opportunity to perform them arises. Torah, however, should be studied always. Hence, the warning אַל־תִּטֹּשׁ, *do not forsake* Torah study for even one minute (*Vilna Gaon,* cf. verse 11 and 2:1).

The word מִצְוָה connotes a command, implying the dictates of a superior, such as a father's command to his child or a master's to his servant. *Torah,* on the other hand, refers to *instruction,* teaching in the areas of faith, ideology and ethics. *Mitzvah* is associated with the father [the authority figure who chastises and forces one to heed his dictates], for one must heed the commandments of Torah, even if they go against one's natural instinct. If he does so, he will automatically not abandon the ideology of Torah [וְאַל־תִּטֹּשׁ תּוֹרַת

אִמֶּךָ], for the soul is innately attracted to it. Only when a person rejects a commandment will his defense mechanism lead him to justify himself by denying the fundamentals of faith (*Malbim*).

Alshich interprets *the command of your father* as a reference to תּוֹרָה שֶׁבִּכְתָב, *the Written Law,* and תּוֹרַת אִמֶּךָ, *the teaching of your mother,* as תּוֹרָה שֶׁבְּעַל פֶּה, *the Oral Law.* We were given the Written Law at Mount Sinai, and from then, not even a letter was added to it. This is comparable to the father's role in the child's conception: After the child is conceived, the father's role is over. The Oral Law is compared to the mother's role, because each succeeding generation draws upon the unbroken chain of Torah knowledge from previous generations, just as a child nurses from its mother.

According to *Ralbag, the command of your father* refers to the Torah, which God, your *Father,* commanded you to heed. *The teaching of your mother* refers to the stories recounted in the Torah, which elevate a person and convey the spiritual legacy of the Patriarchs. The forefathers are like a "mother" *vis-a-vis* God, the "Father."

21. קָשְׁרֵם עַל־לִבְּךָ תָמִיד עָנְדֵם עַל־גַּרְגְּרֹתֶךָ — *Tie them on your heart always; entwine them upon your neck.* The heart signifies thought, while the neck signifies

---

1. *Midrash Shocher Tov* (Psalms 7) cites a case in point. The generation of Ahab worshiped idols, yet his army was always victorious, because there were no talebearers among them. No one informed King Ahab that Obadiah had hidden one hundred prophets, thus saving them from certain death at the hands of the king and Queen Jezebel (see *I Kings* 18:4ff.). On the other hand, the great and righteous King David suffered occasional defeats, because there was strife and talebearing in his time.

Hashem responds to a person's deeds measure for measure. If he controls himself and refrains from slander, the Heavenly Accuser is unable to prosecute Israel. But one who slanders another and thereby enables Satan to bring the sins of Israel before God is abhorrent to Him, for now He must accede to Satan's demands and punish His beloved children, simply because this person chose to slander his friend (*Shemiras Halashon, Shaar Hazechirah* 2).

 20 Heed, my child, the command of your father and do not forsake the teaching of your mother. 21 Tie them on your heart always; entwine them upon your neck. 22 As you go forth, it will guide you; as you recline, it will protect you; and when you awake, it will converse with you. 23 For a commandment is a lamp and the Torah is light;

speech (*Vilna Gaon*).

קָשְׁרֵם, *bind them,* implies that the commandments are foreign to human instinct. One must therefore bind them to his heart with ropes, so to speak, i.e., subjugate his heart to follow their dictates. To assure that these *mitzvos* are not forgotten afterwards, *entwine them* around your neck and throat, i.e., speak about them constantly, for that will help you remember (*Malbim*).

By constantly recounting and delving into the stories of the forefathers (see previous verse), a person will begin to comprehend their meaning and realize the remarkable wisdom they contain (*Ralbag*).

22. בְּהִתְהַלֶּכְךָ תַּנְחֶה אֹתָךְ בְּשָׁכְבְּךָ תִּשְׁמֹר עָלֶיךָ וַהֲקִיצוֹתָ הִיא תְשִׂיחֶךָ — *As you go forth, it will guide you; as you recline, it will protect you; and when you awake, it will converse with you.* Metzudos explains the verse in the literal sense: The Torah will lead you on the straight road, protect you from robbers who attack at night, and when you wake up, it will speak with you like a good friend who entertains you.

According to *Rashi, as you go forth* is during your lifetime; *as you recline* is in the grave; and *when you awake* refers to the Resurrection of the Dead to answer for their actions in life, at which time הִיא תְשִׂיחֶךָ, *it will speak up on your behalf* to defend you (see *Sotah* 21a).[1]

בְּשָׁכְבְּךָ — *When you lie down,* in the grave. When someone dies, the merit of Torah will protect his body so that worms and maggots will have no effect on it. Such was the case with R' Elazar bar R' Shimon (*Bava Metzia* 84b), Achai bar Yoshia (*Shabbos* 152b) and other such righteous people (*Alshich*).

וַהֲקִיצוֹתָ — *When you awake* for the Resurrection of the Dead, *it* (the Torah) *will speak for you,* i.e., a person will be resurrected in the merit of his Torah study. The Sages explain (*Kesubos* 111b) that a person who made use of the light of Torah in his lifetime will be resurrected by it.[2]

23. כִּי נֵר מִצְוָה וְתוֹרָה אוֹר — *For a commandment is a lamp and the Torah is light.* The merit of a *mitzvah* is just temporary, like the flame of a lamp. The merit of Torah study, however, is

1. R' Yose ben Kisma was once offered a fortune as an inducement to move to another city. He replied, "Even if you would give me all the wealth in the world, I would reside only in a place of Torah." When a person departs from this world, neither silver, gold, nor precious stones escort him. Only his Torah and good deeds remain with him, as taught in our verse (*Avos* 6:9).

In a similar vein, *Yalkut Shimoni* explains that a person has three friends: his family, his money and his good deeds. As he departs from the world, a person gathers his family and asks them, "Please save me from this evil decree of death," but they are powerless to help him. The same is true of his wealth. His good deeds, however, respond, "Before you come, we will proceed you [in the Hereafter], as the verse states: וְהָלַךְ לְפָנֶיךָ צִדְקֶךָ, *your righteous deed will precede you*" (*Isaiah* 58:8).

2. The *Chafetz Chaim* explains that a person's soul will delight in Paradise in the merit of his good deeds in life, but only in the merit of Torah study can his body, which has already turned to dust, be resurrected. He emphasizes this point with the following metaphor: Even though the chances of fire are slim, a person understands the need to have fire insurance, so that he can rebuild in case it happens. Likewise, he must assure himself of the means to "rebuild" his body, which is absolutely *certain* to be destroyed at his death. This is only possible if he has guaranteed himself a share in Torah study while still alive.

כד וְדֶרֶךְ חַיִּים תּוֹכְחוֹת מוּסָר: לִשְׁמָרְךָ מֵאֵשֶׁת רָע
כה מֵחֶלְקַת לָשׁוֹן נָכְרִיָּה: אַל-תַּחְמֹד יָפְיָהּ בִּלְבָבֶךָ

everlasting, like the light of the sun (Rashi).[1]

Malbim explains that sunlight comes from above; so, too, the light of Torah emanates from above and is part of a person's spiritual being, his Divine soul. Its light is eternal and continues to shine for the righteous even after their souls depart from their bodies. The light of a lamp is dependent on the physical properties of oil and a wick in order to give light. So, too, a mitzvah is connected to the physical part of one's being and is limited, as it were, by the existence of the body.

The Talmud (Sotah 21a) illustrates this verse with a parable. A man walking in the dark of night feared the thorns, thistles, pits, wild animals and robbers along the way. Moreover, he did not know where he was headed. He found a torch that enabled him to avoid the thorns, thistle and pits, 7but he still feared the wild animals and robbers, and he still did not know his way. Once the light of dawn appeared, he was saved from the wild animals and the robbers as well, but still uncertain about his direction. Only when he reached a crossroads was he relieved of that fear, as well.

Rashi (ibid.) explains the parable. Someone who performs a mitzvah is only partially saved from punishments. Once he has the merits of Torah study, he is saved from both sin and affliction. However, there is still a danger that his Evil Inclination will overcome him and stop him from studying Torah. Thus, only when he gets

to a "crossroads" is he safe and secure from all danger.

The Sages interpret the "crossroads" in various ways. Either it refers to his day of death, for only then can a scholar be sure that his Evil Inclination has neither led him astray nor influenced him to abandon the Torah. Or, it refers to a scholar who has acquired the fear of sin, for his Torah knowledge teaches him what is required and what is prohibited, and his fear of sin restrains him from chasing after his Evil Inclination.

The Midrash teaches that both the soul and the Torah are likened to a lamp, referring to this verse and to 20:27: נֵר ה׳ נִשְׁמַת אָדָם, A man's soul is the lamp of HASHEM. The Holy One, Blessed is He, says: נֵר בְּיָדְךָ וְנֵרִי בְּיָדִי, My lamp [i.e., the Torah] is in your hands, and your lamp [i.e., your soul] is in Mine — if you watch over Mine, I will watch over yours.

This is comparable to two people. One lived in the Galilee and owned a vineyard in Judea, and the other lived in Judea and owned a vineyard in the Galilee. As each one traveled to tend his vineyard, they met. One said to the other, "Instead of traveling here to tend your vineyard, stay at home and tend mine, and I will do the same for you." So, too, God says to Israel: "If you safeguard My Torah, I will watch over you" (Yalkut Shimoni).

According to R' Yosef Kara, this verse elaborates upon verse 20, which exhorts one to heed his father's command and his mother's instruction. The command of a

1. The great merit of Torah study is reiterated many times in the teachings of our Sages. The Mishnah enumerates the mitzvos whose "fruit" a person enjoys in this world, but whose principal reward is reserved for the World to Come. The Mishnah concludes: וְתַלְמוּד תּוֹרָה כְּנֶגֶד כֻּלָּן, and the study of Torah is equivalent to them all. According to one view, the entire universe is not equivalent to one word of Torah study; according to another view, all the commandments combined are not equivalent to one word of Torah study (Yerushalmi Peah 1:1).

The Sages also teach (Sotah 21a), עֲבֵירָה מְכַבָּה מִצְוָה וְאֵין עֲבֵירָה מְכַבָּה תוֹרָה, a sin extinguishes a mitzvah, but a sin does not extinguish Torah. Rashi explains that a sin extinguishes the reward for a mitzvah, but it cannot extinguish the reward of one who had previously occupied himself with Torah study.

Midrash Shocher Tov (17:8) expounds: מִצְוָה בִּפְנֵי תוֹרָה כְּנֵר בִּפְנֵי חַמָּה, a mitzvah is to Torah as is a lamp to the sun.

and reproving discipline is the way of life, [24] *to guard you from an evil woman, from the smoothness of a foreign woman's tongue.* [25] *Do not covet her beauty in your heart,*

father is like a lamp. If one obeys his father's command, it is as if he took a lamp to illuminate the darkness. Anything he may have lost will now be found with its help. The same is true of one who heeds his mother's instruction; it is a source of light for him.[1]

The Sages (*Shabbos* 23b) point out that there is a direct connection between kindling a candle and meriting the light of Torah: הָרָגִיל בְּנֵר הֲוַיִין לֵיהּ בָּנִים תַּלְמִידֵי חֲכָמִים, *A person who is accustomed to kindling (Sabbath and Chanukah) candles will have children who are Torah scholars.* Quoting our verse, *Rashi* explains that through the lamp of such commandments as the Sabbath and Chanukah, one will be able to acquire the light of Torah. *R' Bachya* points out that since prayers are more readily accepted when they are offered during the performance of a *mitzvah*, a woman should pray for children who will enlighten the world in Torah when she kindles her Sabbath candles.[2]

וְדֶרֶךְ חַיִּים תּוֹכְחוֹת מוּסָר — *And reproving discipline is the way of life.* Since *mussar* rebukes incline a person to [a proper and productive] life, they are *the way of life* (*Rashi*).

Even if someone has a lamp to illuminate his way, he still must be sure that he is going on the proper path, or else the light will be of no benefit. The force that leads him along this path is *reproving discipline* (*Malbim*).

R' Shimon bar Yochai explains that the Holy One, Blessed is He, gave three precious gifts to Israel, and all were given only through affliction. They are Torah, the Land of Israel and the World to Come. We learn that the World to Come is bestowed through affliction from the words, וְדֶרֶךְ חַיִּים תּוֹכְחוֹת מוּסָר, which can be rendered, *the way to life [in the World to Come] is attained through affliction* (*Berachos* 5a; cf. 10:17, citation from *Vilna Gaon*).[3]

24. לִשְׁמָרְךָ מֵאֵשֶׁת רָע — *To guard you from an evil woman.* Torah will protect you from a woman of evil behavior, which *Rashi* interprets as a reference to idol-worship, whose severity is equivalent to all other transgressions (cf. 2:16, *Rashi* ibid.). Otherwise what is the great praise and reward for Torah — merely that it protects one from an adulteress?

[Idolatry is likened to adultery because it is a betrayal of the One to Whom a Jew owes his loyalty.]

מֵחֶלְקַת לָשׁוֹן נָכְרִיָּה — *From the smoothness of a foreign woman's tongue.* *Rashi* renders: from an alien tongue that seals one's eyes. [The glibness of idolaters and heretics covers a person's eyes and blinds him to the truth.]

Metzudos renders this phrase, *from the smooth persuasions of the alien woman.*

1. *One who curses his father or mother, his lamp [i.e., his soul] will flicker out in the deepening darkness* (20:20). If someone's lamp flickers out when he does not heed his parents' command, it follows that if he heeds their commands, his lamp will burn light (*R' Yosef Kara*).

2. *Likutei Yehudah* relates that the *Chiddushei HaRim* once instructed his *chassidim* to study Torah immediately after kindling the Chanukah lights, *For a mitzvah is a lamp and Torah is light.* The *Chiddushei HaRim* explained with certainty that fulfilling a *mitzvah* illumines the light of Torah, how much more so when the *mitzvah* itself lights up the world.

In a similar vein, the *Maggid of Koznitz* would always encourage people to make time to study directly after *davening.* For, after asking the Almighty to "Endow us graciously from Yourself with wisdom, insight and discernment" (*Amidah*), we should see that we are now able to understand that which was previously unclear to us. After performing a *mitzvah* with proper intent, it creates a light for our Torah understanding.

3. *Maharsha* (ibid.) explains that the righteous will attain their reward in the World to Come through the afflictions they suffer in this world, which serve to cleanse them of their sins. We can understand this concept with the following illustration. A person was invited to attend a wedding, but until he removed all the spots and stains from his suit, he could not enter to enjoy the festivities.

כה וְאַל־תִּקָּחֲךָ בְּעַפְעַפֶּיהָ: כִּי בְעַד־אִשָּׁה זוֹנָה עַד־
כו כִּכַּר לָחֶם וְאֵשֶׁת אִישׁ נֶפֶשׁ יְקָרָה תָצוּד: הֲיַחְתֶּה
כז אִישׁ אֵשׁ בְּחֵיקוֹ וּבְגָדָיו לֹא תִשָּׂרַפְנָה: אִם־
כח יְהַלֵּךְ אִישׁ עַל־הַגֶּחָלִים וְרַגְלָיו לֹא תִכָּוֶינָה: כֵּן
כט הַבָּא אֶל־אֵשֶׁת רֵעֵהוּ לֹא יִנָּקֶה כָּל־הַנֹּגֵעַ בָּהּ:
ל לֹא־יָבוּזוּ לַגַּנָּב כִּי יִגְנוֹב לְמַלֵּא נַפְשׁוֹ כִּי יִרְעָב:
לא וְנִמְצָא יְשַׁלֵּם שִׁבְעָתָיִם אֶת־כָּל־הוֹן בֵּיתוֹ יִתֵּן:

25. אַל־תַּחְמֹד יָפְיָהּ בִּלְבָבֶךָ וְאַל־תִּקָּחֲךָ בְּעַפְעַפֶּיהָ — *Do not covet her beauty in your heart, and do not let her captivate you with her eyelids.* Do not let her take your wisdom from you with her winking eyelids (*Rashi*).[1]

26. כִּי בְעַד־אִשָּׁה זוֹנָה עַד־כִּכַּר לָחֶם — *Because, for the sake of a licentious woman, [one may beg] for a loaf of bread.* A harlot may cause someone to become impoverished and lack all good things (*Rashi*), until he may even have to beg for a loaf of bread (*Metzudos*) (cf. 29:3, וְרֹעֶה זוֹנוֹת יְאַבֶּד־הוֹן, *but the companion of harlots will lose a fortune.* See also *Sotah* 4b).

The *Vilna Gaon* explains that this refers to a person who pursues his desires. He will forget his Torah knowledge and be reduced to such a state of poverty in Torah that he will not know even a single law (for לֶחֶם, *bread,* is a metaphor for Torah (see 9:5). The Sages foretell that Torah knowledge will be forgotten in Israel to such an extent that in the future a woman will take a loaf of *terumah* (bread made from the *Kohen's* tithe, which must be kept ritually pure) and go from study hall to study hall to ascertain if it is pure or impure, and no one will have sufficient understanding to answer her.

וְאֵשֶׁת אִישׁ נֶפֶשׁ יְקָרָה תָצוּד — *An adulterous woman can ensnare a precious soul.* Through her smooth talk, this adulteress will ensnare a soul that was precious and free of sin (*Metzudos*), i.e., the soul of a philanderer (*Ibn Ezra*), and bring it to total destruction (*Meiri*).

Meiri explains that every soul is a נֶפֶשׁ יְקָרָה, *a precious soul,* for it is carved from the Divine Rock. Alternatively, these words point out that an adulteress can ensnare even a highly respected person.

Quoting the *mishnah* that one who converses excessively with a woman causes evil to himself, neglects Torah study and will eventually inherit *Gehinnom* (*Avos* 1:5), R' Yonah warns of the dangers of associating with an evil woman. The *mishnah* implies that excessive conversation with a woman will lead to more serious transgressions until one reaches *Gehinnom.* The temptations of an evil woman can be worse than death (see *Ecclesiastes* 7:27), for death causes one to lose this world, but such a woman causes the destruction of one's soul for all eternity. A man can become ensnared in her trap; seeing something that his heart covets, he is blinded to the dangerous consequences. R' Yehudah HaLevi expressed this poetically: יוֹנָה פּוֹתָה הוֹלֶכֶת בַּמִּדְבָּר, וְרוֹאָה אֶת הַבָּר וְאֵינָה רוֹאָה אֶת הַמִּכְמָר, *A foolish dove in the desert goes; it sees the grain, but not the net.*

27. הֲיַחְתֶּה אִישׁ אֵשׁ בְּחֵיקוֹ וּבְגָדָיו לֹא תִשָּׂרַפְנָה — *Can a man draw fire into his bosom without his clothes being burned?* *Rashi* renders חֵיק as *the lower part of one's clothing,* and relates יַחְתֶּה to חֹתִיּת גֶּחָלִים, *raking coals.* Thus he renders the verse,

---

1. A person must particularly beware of the influences that affect his heart and his eyes, as the Torah states: וְלֹא תָתוּרוּ אַחֲרֵי לְבַבְכֶם וְאַחֲרֵי עֵינֵיכֶם, *and do not explore after your heart and after your eyes* (*Numbers* 15:39). The heart and the eyes are the spies of the body that seek out sins (see *Rashi*, ibid.).

and do not let her captivate you with her eyelids, ²⁶ because, for the sake of a licentious woman, [one may beg] for a loaf of bread; an adulterous woman can ensnare a precious soul. ²⁷ Can a man draw fire into his bosom without his clothes being burned? ²⁸ Can a man walk on coals without his feet being scorched? ²⁹ So is one who consorts with his fellow's wife; anyone who touches her will not be exonerated.

³⁰ A thief is not [overly] scorned if he steals to satisfy his soul when he is hungry. ³¹ When he is found, he would even pay sevenfold; even give all the wealth of his house!

Can a person rake burning coals with the lower part of his clothing without burning them?

Meiri explains that these verses refer not only to one who associates with an adulteress, but also to one who pursues any unbefitting materialistic excess. This hinders one from perfecting his character traits, which are referred to as *his clothes.*

28. אִם־יְהַלֵּךְ אִישׁ עַל־הַגֶּחָלִים וְרַגְלָיו לֹא תִכָּוֶינָה — *Can* [lit. *If*] *a man walk on coals without his feet being scorched?* Just as these two cases are impossibilities, so is it impossible for someone who is involved in adultery to avoid receiving a terrible punishment (see next verse) (*Ralbag*).

29. כֵּן הַבָּא אֶל־אֵשֶׁת רֵעֵהוּ — *So is one who consorts with his fellow's wife.* In addition to its literal meaning, this verse also refers to idol-worshipers (*Rashi*).

לֹא יִנָּקֶה כָּל־הַנֹּגֵעַ בָּהּ — *Anyone who touches her will not be exonerated,* from an appropriate punishment (*Metzudos*).

30. לֹא־יָבוּזוּ לַגַּנָּב כִּי יִגְנוֹב לְמַלֵּא נַפְשׁוֹ כִּי יִרְעָב — *A thief is not [overly] scorned if he steals to satisfy his soul when he is hungry. Rashi* explains that verses 30-32 are connected. One who steals because he is hungry should not be scorned like the person who commits adultery.

31. וְנִמְצָא יְשַׁלֵּם שִׁבְעָתָיִם אֶת־כָּל־הוֹן בֵּיתוֹ יִתֵּן — *When he is found, he would even pay sevenfold; even give all the wealth of his house!* Stealing is not as bad as immorality, for the thief may have stolen only because he was hungry. Furthermore, when a thief is caught, he can make amends for his crime by returning or paying for the stolen goods. Even if the only way to pacify his victim is to pay many times over, even up to fifty times the amount of the theft, money can smooth things over. (The number seven often signifies "many" rather than literally "seven." See *Psalms 12:7, Radak* ibid.)

Sevenfold may refer to a case where one steals an ox and its utensils, and slaughters the ox. He must repay five cattle for the ox (*Exodus* 21:3-21:37) and כֶּפֶל, *double repayment*, for the utensils, totaling seven in all. Even if he must sell all his possessions to repay what he owes, at least he has means of rectifying his sins. And initially, the theft was motivated by hunger (*Rashi*).

The most he would have to repay is his net worth. But he will not have to suffer a plague on his soul [as the adulterer will; see verse 33] (*Metzudos*).

These verses point out two aspects in which the thief is better than the adulterer:
1) The thief stole out of necessity, because he is hungry.
2) There is a limit to his punishment (*Malbim*).

Rashi quotes a Midrashic interpretation of these verses: *They will not scorn the thief* refers to one who "steals away" from his friends and goes to the study hall of Torah and immerses himself in study. *When he is found he would pay even sevenfold,* i.e., eventually he will be appointed a judge and instruct others in Torah. The word שִׁבְעָתָיִם, *sevenfold,* alludes to the Torah, for we find the words of Hashem described as מְזֻקָּק שִׁבְעָתָיִם, *refined sevenfold* (*Psalms 12:7*).

לב נֹאֵף אִשָּׁה חֲסַר־לֵב מַשְׁחִית נַפְשׁוֹ הוּא יַעֲשֶׂנָּה:

לג-לד נֶגַע־וְקָלוֹן יִמְצָא וְחֶרְפָּתוֹ לֹא תִמָּחֶה: כִּי־קִנְאָה

לה חֲמַת־גָּבֶר וְלֹא־יַחְמוֹל בְּיוֹם נָקָם: לֹא־יִשָּׂא פְנֵי

א כָל־כֹּפֶר וְלֹא־יֹאבֶה כִּי תַרְבֶּה־שֹׁחַד: בְּנִי

ב שְׁמֹר אֲמָרָי וּמִצְוֹתַי תִּצְפֹּן אִתָּךְ: שְׁמֹר מִצְוֹתַי

ג וֶחְיֵה וְתוֹרָתִי כְּאִישׁוֹן עֵינֶיךָ: קָשְׁרֵם עַל־

---

32. נֹאֵף אִשָּׁה חֲסַר־לֵב — *But he who commits adultery with a woman is lacking an [understanding] heart.* An adulterer is devoid of understanding, for he was not forced to sin by hunger (*Rashi*).

מַשְׁחִית נַפְשׁוֹ הוּא יַעֲשֶׂנָּה — *A destroyer of his soul will do this,* i.e., commit the sin of immorality (*Rashi*).

33. נֶגַע־וְקָלוֹן יִמְצָא — *Plague and shame will he find.* Plagues come for the sins of idolatry and adultery (*Rashi*).

An adulterer will receive a plague from Heaven and be disgraced among people (*Metzudos*).

He will be severely wounded by the betrayed husband (*Alshich*).

וְחֶרְפָּתוֹ לֹא תִמָּחֶה — *And his disgrace will not be erased.* It will not be forgotten (*Metzudos*).

A thief pays for his crime only with money, while a philanderer suffers a plague. Whereas one does not scorn a thief for his crime (verse 30), the philanderer will be the object of shame; and whereas the thief's disgrace ends when he makes the proper retribution, the philanderer's disgrace is never erased (*Malbim*).

His disgrace is never erased for this sin cannot be rectified. The Sages (*Chagigah* 9a) explain that one who had relations with a married woman and begot a child is an example of מְעֻוָּת לֹא־יוּכַל לִתְקֹן, a *twisted thing cannot be made straight* (*Ecclesiastes* 1:15), because the child born of such a union carries an eternal stigma.

On the other hand, a thief or a robber can return what was stolen and thereby rectify his sin (*Binah L'Ittim*).

34. כִּי־קִנְאָה חֲמַת־גָּבֶר וְלֹא יַחְמוֹל בְּיוֹם נָקָם — *For jealousy ignites a husband's wrath, and he will not have mercy on the day of revenge.* The feeling of vengeance will arouse the wrath of the husband of the adulteress. He will have no mercy on the adulterer when the opportunity arises for revenge.

According to *Rashi*, גָּבֶר refers to the Holy One, Blessed is He, who is the גִּבּוֹר עַל הַכֹּל, *the Mighty One over all.* The wrath of Hashem will be kindled to take revenge and punish the adulterer, and He will have no compassion on the day of revenge.

[קִנְאָה refers to the *kindling of anger to take revenge for something.* (See *Numbers* 25:11, בְּקַנְאוֹ אֶת־קִנְאָתִי, *Rashi* ibid.)]

35. לֹא־יִשָּׂא פְּנֵי כָל־כֹּפֶר — *He will not be appeased by any ransom.* The husband will not accept any form of ransom to appease his anger [against the adulterer] (*Metzudos*).

Rashi continues: Hashem will not accept any money to atone for a person's having denied Him and cleaved to idolatry.

וְלֹא־יֹאבֶה כִּי תַרְבֶּה־שֹׁחַד — *Nor will he consent though you give many bribes.* He will not agree to forgive even if you give many bribes (*Metzudos*).

Unlike the sin of theft, this sin will not be appeased with money (*Ralbag*).

VII

1. בְּנִי שְׁמֹר אֲמָרָי — *My child, heed my words. Heed my words* constantly. This refers to Torah study, which is obligatory at all times; review the words of the Torah

constantly so that you will not forget them (*Vilna Gaon*).

"Words" refers to the ethical teachings and philosophical insights of the Torah,

6/32-35 ³² *But he who commits adultery with a woman is lacking an [understanding] heart; a destroyer of his soul will do this.* ³³ *Plague and shame will he find, and his disgrace will not be erased.* ³⁴ *For jealousy ignites a husband's wrath, and he will not have mercy on the day of revenge.* ³⁵ *He will not be appeased by any ransom, nor will he consent though you give him many bribes.*

7/1-3 ¹ *My child, heed my words and treasure my commandments with yourself.* ² *Heed my commandments and live, and [heed] my Torah like the apple of your eyes.* ³ *Bind them on*

which the individual must recognize and accept as the truth (*Malbim*, cf. 2:1).

וּמִצְוֹתַי תִּצְפֹּן אִתָּךְ — *And treasure my commandments with yourself.* Many commandments can be performed only at particular times. *Treasure* them with yourself, i.e., be ready to perform them at their appropriate time (*Vilna Gaon*).

2. שְׁמֹר מִצְוֹתַי וֶחְיֵה — *Heed my commandments and live.* Because of them, you will live (*Metzudos*). You will attain eternal life (*Ralbag*).

R' Bachya divides the commandments into three categories:

1) מִצְוֹת מְקֻבָּלוֹת, *received commandments.* Such commandments had to be received from God, for a person could never deduce them through his own understanding. Among these are such commandments as *tefillin*, *tzitzis*, circumcision, *succah*, *shofar*, the Four Species of Succos, the Sabbath, *Shemittah* (Sabbatical year) and *Yovel* (Jubilee year). The Torah refers to them as עֵדוֹת, *testimonies*, for they testify to God's Divinity and His creation of the world.

2) מִצְוֹת מוּשְׂכָּלוֹת, *logical commandments.* These are the commandments that mankind would have deduced through their own understanding, had the Torah not been given. Included in this category are the prohibitions against robbery, theft, murder and deceit. The Torah refers to them as מִשְׁפָּטִים, *civil laws*, or *ordinances*; they are the laws that make it possible for organized society to function without degenerating into strife and violence.

3) מִצְוֹת שֶׁאֵין טַעֲמָן נִגְלָה וּמְבוֹאָר, *com-* mandments *whose reason is not revealed and clarified*, such as כִּלְאַיִם, forbidden mixtures; the prohibition against cooking milk with meat; the he-goat sent to Azazel on Yom Kippur, and the Red Cow. They are referred to as חֻקִּים, *decrees.*

Verses 1 and 2 refer to these three categories: *heed my words* refers to received commandments; *heed my commandments and live* refers to the logical commandments for they allow people to live and societies to exist in peace; *treasure [תִּצְפֹּן] my commandments* refers to the commandments whose reasons are hidden [צָפוּן].

וְתוֹרָתִי כְּאִישׁוֹן עֵינֶיךָ — *And [heed] my Torah like the apple of your eyes.* Rashi explains that אִישׁוֹן is the black part of the eye, relating it to אִישׁוֹן לַיְלָה, *the blackness of night* (see verse 9).

Metzudos relates the term to the word אִישׁ, *a man* for when someone looks a man in the eye, he is reflected in the pupil of the eye.

Just as a man zealously protects his eyes so that he should not become blind, so, too, he should heed the Torah, the intellectual "eye" which provides him [spiritual] illumination (*Malbim*). In this sense, the Sanhedrin is called the "eyes of the congregation" (see *Leviticus* 4:13).

The Midrash relates that King David requested of Hashem, שָׁמְרֵנִי כְּאִישׁוֹן בַּת־עָיִן, *Guard me like the pupil of the eye (Psalms 17:8)*, to which God replied, שְׁמֹר מִצְוֹתַי וֶחְיֵה, *Heed My commandments and live.* This teaches that if one heeds the commandments, God will protect him. [See 6:23, citation from *Yalkut Shimoni*.]

ד אֶצְבְּעֹתֶיךָ כָּתְבֵם עַל־לוּחַ לִבֶּךָ: אֱמֹר לַחָכְמָה

ה אֲחֹתִי אָתְּ וּמֹדָע לַבִּינָה תִקְרָא: לְשָׁמָרְךָ מֵאִשָּׁה

ו זָרָה מִנָּכְרִיָּה אֲמָרֶיהָ הֶחֱלִיקָה: כִּי בְּחַלּוֹן בֵּיתִי בְּעַד

ז אֶשְׁנַבִּי נִשְׁקָפְתִּי: וָאֵרֶא בַפְּתָאיִם אָבִינָה בַבָּנִים נַעַר

ח חֲסַר־לֵב: עֹבֵר בַּשּׁוּק אֵצֶל פִּנָּה וְדֶרֶךְ בֵּיתָהּ יִצְעָד:

A case in point is the commandment to recite the *Shema*. This prayer contains a total of 248 words, corresponding to the 248 organs in a person's body. Hashem promises that if one recites *Shema* properly, He will protect that person's organs (*Yalkut Shimoni* to 4:4).

3. קָשְׁרֵם עַל־אֶצְבְּעֹתֶיךָ — *Bind them on your fingers*, i.e., make reminders for yourself in a visible place, so that you should always remember them (*Meiri*).

After the exhortations to heed the Torah and its commandments, this verse addresses the individual who is preoccupied with physical labor. Lest he feel that his toil precludes the observance of commandments, this verse instructs him to *bind them on your fingers*, i.e., in every step of your work (symbolized by the fingers), be conscious of the relevant commandments. When you work your field using two oxen or two donkeys to pull your plow, bear in mind that you are doing so because the Torah forbids one to harness together two different species of animals (*Deuteronomy* 22:10). When you plant, do so with the intent to avoid the prohibition of כִּלְאַיִם, *forbidden mixtures* (ibid. 22:9), such as planting grain and vegetables together. When you reap, have in mind that you will perform the commandments of helping the poor by leaving לֶקֶט, *gleanings* (*Leviticus* 19:9), שִׁכְחָה, *forgotten sheaves* (*Deuteronomy* 24:19), and פֵּאָה, *the edge of the field* (*Leviticus*, ibid.). In doing business, have in mind that you will give a portion of the profits to support the poor, rather than only thinking of enriching yourself. In this way, you are binding a

mitzvah onto your every action. Our Sages compare the ten forms of labor needed to produce bread to a person's ten fingers and the ten commandments one can fulfill during the course of growing and baking. This is why one should place all ten fingers on the piece of bread when reciting the *Hamotzi*, a blessing that contains exactly *ten* words (*Alshich*).

כָּתְבֵם עַל־לוּחַ לִבֶּךָ — *Inscribe them on the tablet of your heart. Fingers* signify deeds; *heart* signifies thought. Make the words of Torah indelible in your consciousness, so that they will control your emotions, desires and action (*Malbim*).

4. אֱמֹר לַחָכְמָה אֲחֹתִי אָתְּ וּמֹדָע לַבִּינָה תִקְרָא — *Say to wisdom, "You are my sister," and call understanding a kinsman.* Draw *wisdom* and *understanding* close to you always (*Rashi*).

Be as familiar with *wisdom* as a person is with his sister (*Metzudos*).[1] Love *wisdom* (*Ralbag*).

A person should sacrifice himself for Torah just as people are willing to sacrifice their lives for a sister, as may be seen from the actions of Simeon and Levi (Jacob's sons) on behalf of their sister Dinah (*Genesis* 34) (*Shaarei Chaim*).

R' Hirsch explains that we are to call wisdom *our sister*, for she is our Father's daughter. As we are indebted to Him for our physical existence, we are also indebted to Him for wisdom that He placed at our side as a helping sister, like Miriam, who watched over the infant Moses and arranged for his own mother to nurse him. With wisdom as our sister, we can also stride towards Divine truth, and be pro-

1. Rabbi Avraham Mordechai Alter of Gur interprets this portion of the verse homiletically: Close though you are to your sister, intimacy with her is forbidden. Similarly, although a person should cultivate his own intelligence and judgment, he should beware of too much reliance on his mental prowess. The wisdom of the Torah must always supersede his own wisdom.

your fingers; inscribe them on the tablet of your heart. [4] *Say to wisdom, "You are my sister," and call understanding a kinsman,* [5] *that they may safeguard you from a forbidden woman, from a foreign woman who makes her words glib.* [6] *For I have looked out from the window of my house, through my lattice,* [7] *and I saw among the simpletons, I discerned among the youths, a lad who lacked [an understanding] heart* [8] *passing through the marketplace near her corner, and he strode toward her house,*

tected from errors that may estrange us from God.

וּמֹדָע לַבִּינָה תִקְרָא — *And call understanding a kinsman. Kinsman* refers to a niece or nephew. *Understanding* is compared to such a *relative,* for it is "born" from *wisdom,* your sister (*Alshich*).

5. לִשְׁמָרְךָ מֵאִשָּׁה זָרָה מִנָּכְרִיָּה אֲמָרֶיהָ הֶחֱלִיקָה. — *That they may safeguard you from a forbidden* [lit. *alien*] *woman; from a foreign woman whose words are glib.* Be familiar with *wisdom* (previous verse) so that it will save you from a woman who is forbidden to you (*Metzudos*).

Forbidden woman refers to a Jewish woman other than one's wife. *Foreign woman* refers to a gentile woman (*Malbim*) (cf. 2:16, citation from *Vilna Gaon*).

According to the *Vilna Gaon, forbidden woman* refers to the sin of חֶמְדָּה, *coveting,* and *foreign woman* refers to the sin of תַּאֲנָה, *lust* (c.f. 2:16).

6. כִּי בְּחַלּוֹן בֵּיתִי בְּעַד אֶשְׁנַבִּי נִשְׁקָפְתִּי — *For I have looked out from the window of my house, through my lattice.*

In the following verses, King Solomon describes how a harlot entices men with glib talk. In order to impress the listener with the seriousness and truthfulness of the warning, Solomon describes the occurrence as if he saw the proceedings himself, from his window (*Meiri*).

Though grammatically the word נִשְׁקָפְתִּי means *I was looked upon,* it is used to mean *I looked,* for one who gazes out at others is also seen by them. Metaphorically it means, "Thanks to my wisdom, I understood people's actions" (*Metzudos*).

A *window* implies seeing that which is openly visible, whereas a *lattice* implies an aperture through which hidden things

may be glimpsed (*Malbim*).

7. וָאֵרֶא בַפְּתָאיִם אָבִינָה בַבָּנִים נַעַר חֲסַר־לֵב. — *And I saw among the simpletons, I discerned among the youths, a lad who lacked [an understanding] heart.*

Looking through the window, I saw groups of gullible people, and among them I discerned a lad lacking understanding (*Metzudos*), i.e., lacking the power to control his desires (*Malbim*).

8. עֹבֵר בַשּׁוּק אֵצֶל פִּנָּה — *Passing through the marketplace near her corner.* Her corner refers to the corner of harlots and idolaters (*Rashi*).

וְדֶרֶךְ בֵּיתָהּ יִצְעָד — *And he strode toward her house.* The verse specifies *the marketplace,* since the Evil Inclination does not control a person unless he makes the first move and exposes himself to temptation. The power of the Evil Inclination is progressive. First it is compared to a traveler, someone who just passes by (הֵלֵךְ), then to a guest (אוֹרֵחַ), and finally to the master (אִישׁ) (see *Succah* 52b). This sequence is suggested in this verse: *Passing through the marketplace* refers to the initial step of sin, when the Evil Inclination influences a person's thoughts rather than his deeds. Sin begins casually; initially the sinner is like someone merely passing through the marketplace. However, once a person begins to leave the Torah, it distances itself from him. Gradually, he removes himself so far from the Torah that he comes *near her corner* — i.e., he becomes the Evil Inclination's guest. Finally, *he strode toward her house,* i.e., he became so accustomed to going there that she leads him, and it becomes *her house* — i.e., she is now the mistress of the house (*Vilna Gaon*).

ט בְּנֶשֶׁף־בְּעֶרֶב יוֹם בְּאִישׁוֹן לַיְלָה וַאֲפֵלָה: וְהִנֵּה
יא אִשָּׁה לִקְרָאתוֹ שִׁית זוֹנָה וּנְצֻרַת לֵב: הֹמִיָּה הִיא
יב וְסֹרָרֶת בְּבֵיתָהּ לֹא־יִשְׁכְּנוּ רַגְלֶיהָ: פַּעַם בַּחוּץ
יג פַּעַם בָּרְחֹבוֹת וְאֵצֶל כָּל־פִּנָּה תֶאֱרֹב: וְהֶחֱזִיקָה בּוֹ
יד וְנָשְׁקָה לּוֹ הֵעֵזָה פָנֶיהָ וַתֹּאמַר לוֹ: זִבְחֵי שְׁלָמִים
טו עָלַי הַיּוֹם שִׁלַּמְתִּי נְדָרָי: עַל־כֵּן יָצָאתִי לִקְרָאתֶךָ

9. בְּנֶשֶׁף־בְּעֶרֶב יוֹם בְּאִישׁוֹן לַיְלָה וַאֲפֵלָה — *In the twilight, as daylight wanes, in the blackness of night and darkness.* The gullible lad walks in the darkness so that people will not see him (*Metzudos*).

The word נֶשֶׁף can refer either to the darkness at the beginning of the evening, or to the darkness of the predawn hours before the day begins (see *Berachos* 3b). Therefore, the verse specifies *in the twilight, as daylight wanes* (*Malbim*).

The Vilna Gaon explains that this verse delineates four progressive stages of darkness.

1) נֶשֶׁף, *twilight*, the period when the day is waning, but it is not yet night;

2) בְּעֶרֶב, *in the evening*, when stars begin to appear and day and night are mixed (מְעוֹרָב);

3) בְּאִישׁוֹן לַיְלָה, *in the blackness of night*, refers to the middle of the night, when people can be seen only with great difficulty; and

4) אֲפֵלָה, *pitch darkness*, is the predawn hours of night when the darkness is absolute.

In a figurative sense, night refers to this world, and Torah is the light that illumi-nates it. Torah can be studied on four levels: פְּשָׁט, *the literal meaning* of the words; רֶמֶז, *the implied meaning*; דְּרַשׁ, *the expounded, exegetical meaning*; and סוֹד, *the secret, hidden* meaning.

If someone forsakes the study of Torah, first he will forget the סוֹדוֹת, *the secrets* of Torah; then the דְּרַשׁ, *the interpretations* of difficult passages; then the רְמָזִים, *the hints and allusions* of the Torah; until he reaches the stage of forgetting even the פְּשָׁט, *the literal meaning* of Torah, and will be left in total darkness (אֲפֵלָה).[1]

10. וְהִנֵּה אִשָּׁה לִקְרָאתוֹ — *Then behold, a woman approached him.* Literally, the verse refers to a woman; figuratively, to one of those who wants to entice him to sin (*Rashi*).

שִׁית זוֹנָה — *The nakedness of a harlot.* The translation follows *Rashi*; *Metzudos* renders: *bedecked as a harlot.*

וּנְצֻרַת לֵב — *And with siege in [her] heart.* Her heart is surrounded — engulfed by lewdness and foolishness (*Rashi*).

She besieges the hearts of men, to capture and control them (*Metzudos*).

11. הֹמִיָּה הִיא — *She is tumultuous.* She

1. Rabbi Elazar ben Arach was one of the greatest disciples of Rabban Yochanan ben Zakkai, who referred to him as "a spring flowing stronger and stronger" (*Avos* 2:11). His mystical interpretation of Torah was so brilliant that Rabban Yochanan once exclaimed, "Fortunate are you, our father Abraham, that from your loins sprung Elazar" (*Chagigah* 14b).

When Rabban Yochanan ben Zakkai died, most of his disciples remained in Yavneh, but R' Elazar ben Arach settled in his wife's city, Diomysous, a lovely and healthful place. Long isolation from his colleagues made his Torah knowledge deteriorate (*Koheles Rabbah* 7:15). According to the Talmud (*Shabbos* 147b), R' Elazar ben Arach was attracted to the waters of Diomysous and the lifestyle of its people. Consequently, his learning vanished.

When he returned to Yavneh, he was honored with an *aliyah* to the Torah. In Talmudic times, the person called to the Torah also read the Torah portion. Instead of reading הַחֹדֶשׁ הַזֶּה לָכֶם, *This month shall be unto you* (*Exodus* 12:2), he erroneously read, הַחֵרֵשׁ הָיָה לִבָּם, *Their heart was silent* — to such a degree had he forgotten his learning! The sages of Yavneh prayed for him, and his great knowledge and acumen were restored.

⁹ in the twilight, as daylight wanes, in the blackness of night and darkness. ¹⁰ Then behold, a woman approached him, the nakedness of a harlot and with siege in [her] heart. ¹¹ She is tumultuous and rebellious, her feet do not dwell at home. ¹² Sometimes in the courtyard, sometimes in the squares, she lurks at every corner. ¹³ She seized him and kissed him; she thrust forth her face and said to him: ¹⁴ "I had vowed to bring peace-offerings, and today I have fulfilled my vow. ¹⁵ That is why I went out toward you,

makes an uproar so that those seeking her should hear her voice even in the darkness (*Ibn Ezra*). By being so voluble, she demonstrates her lack of modesty (*Ralbag*).

She yearns to see the commotion and tumult of the world and therefore she goes out (*Meiri*).

וְסֹרָרֶת — *And rebellious.* She abandons the ways of propriety (*Rashi*), and speaks words of rebellion and adultery (*Metzudos*).

בְּבֵיתָה לֹא-יִשְׁכְּנוּ רַגְלֶיהָ — *Her feet do not dwell at home.* By not remaining in her home, she violates the precepts of modesty (*Malbim*) (see *Psalms 45:14*, כָּל-כְּבוּדָּה בַּת-מֶלֶךְ פְּנִימָה, *every honorable princess dwells within*).

12. פַּעַם בַּחוּץ פַּעַם בָּרְחֹבוֹת — *Sometimes in the courtyard, sometimes in the squares*, to chase after her lovers (*Metzudos*).

וְאֵצֶל כָּל-פִּנָּה תֶאֱרֹב — *She lurks at every corner*, waiting to find someone lacking understanding (*Ibn Ezra*).

13. וְהֶחֱזִיקָה בּוֹ וְנָשְׁקָה לּוֹ הֵעֵזָה פָנֶיהָ וַתֹּאמַר לוֹ — *She seized him and kissed him; she thrust forth her face and said to him.* She acts brazenly, with no shame (*Metzudos*).

Only after she sees that her initial advances were not repulsed, does she dare begin to speak to him. This, too, is the approach of the Evil Inclination: First it shows love to the person, and only then does it speak up to entice him to sin (*Vilna Gaon*).

◆§ She tries to entice her victim

14. זִבְחֵי שְׁלָמִים עָלַי הַיּוֹם שִׁלַּמְתִּי נְדָרָי — *"I had vowed to bring peace-offerings, and today I have fulfilled my vow."* Because I fulfilled my vow to bring peace-offerings, I was able to prepare a lavish banquet [and invite guests] (*Rashi*).

She speaks deceitfully (*Ibn Ezra*). [She conceals her evil intent by implying that she offers pleasures of a religious nature.]

The Evil Inclination could not ensnare a person by approaching him directly with a proposition to sin, for what decent person would listen to it? Instead, it presents the person with a *mitzvah*, and thereby draws him to sin. Using this ploy, the evil woman serves meat from peace-offerings, because such offerings are not brought to atone for sins, and it is a great *mitzvah* to partake of them and rejoice with them. Furthermore it is a *mitzvah* to eat such meat, so that it will not be left over and have to be burned [נוֹתָר; see *Leviticus* 7:16]. Having eaten and rejoiced, a person can be vulnerable to the Evil Inclination. The same is true in all areas of sin — the Evil Inclination can best succeed if it can sweeten its designs with good deeds; it seldom succeeds in total evil. A person must be particularly wary of sinning when feasting and rejoicing in a *mitzvah*, for that is the perfect breeding ground for the Satan to lull him into sin (*Vilna Gaon*).[1]

1. After his sons completed a celebratory feast, Job would call them together and sacrifice עוֹלוֹת, *elevation-offerings.* He feared that the joviality of the feast had led them to sin in their hearts, and elevation-offerings atone for sinful thoughts (see *Job 1:5, Metzudos* ibid.).

This is also a reason for the fast days of Monday, Thursday and Monday that follow the holidays of Pesach and Succos. Since these festivals are extended periods of feasting and rejoicing, one fears that the joy may have led to light-headedness and sin, which require repentance and atonement (see *Sefer HaTodaah* p. 156).

טז לְשַׁחֵר פָּנֶיךָ וָאֶמְצָאֶךָּ: מַרְבַדִּים רָבַדְתִּי עַרְשִׂי
יז חֲטֻבוֹת אֵטוּן מִצְרָיִם: נַפְתִּי מִשְׁכָּבִי מֹר אֲהָלִים
יח וְקִנָּמוֹן: לְכָה נִרְוֶה דֹדִים עַד־הַבֹּקֶר נִתְעַלְּסָה
יט בָּאֲהָבִים: כִּי אֵין הָאִישׁ בְּבֵיתוֹ הָלַךְ בְּדֶרֶךְ מֵרָחוֹק:
כ צְרוֹר־הַכֶּסֶף לָקַח בְּיָדוֹ לְיוֹם הַכֵּסֶא יָבֹא בֵיתוֹ:

15. עַל־כֵּן יָצָאתִי לִקְרָאתֶךָ לְשַׁחֵר פָּנֶיךָ וָאֶמְצָאֶךָּ —
*That is why I went out toward you, to
seek your countenance, and I have found
you! Rashi* renders וָאֶמְצָאֶךָּ as *so that I may
find you.*

I went out looking for you because I
have [sacred] meat to feed you (*Metzudos*).

I have a *mitzvah* to share, and I know
that you love *mitzvos* very much, so I went
to seek you, to enable you to do the good
deed. And I had Divine assistance, for I was
able to find you immediately (*Vilna Gaon*).

16. מַרְבַדִּים רָבַדְתִּי עַרְשִׂי — *I have decked
my bed with spreads.* She continues her
enticement, telling the unsuspecting victim
that she has prepared in anticipation of his
visit.

חֲטֻבוֹת אֵטוּן מִצְרָיִם — *Of superior braided
Egyptian linen.* She continues her description of the opulent bedspreads: They are
made of highly praised, braided Egyptian
linen (*Rashi*).

My bed poles are carved out, and bedecked with beautiful Egyptian linen ropes
(*Metzudos*).

The *Vilna Gaon* explains this metaphorically. This world is alluded to as "night,"
and its pleasures are a "bed." The Evil
Inclination says: Why should you pass up
all the delights of this world, which are as
pleasant as a bed bedecked with lovely
spreads? Egypt symbolizes earthly pleasures, for it is the source of lusts and the
breeding ground for impurities.

17. נַפְתִּי מִשְׁכָּבִי מֹר אֲהָלִים וְקִנָּמוֹן — *I have
perfumed my bed [with] myrrh, aloes and
cinnamon. Rashi* explains נַפְתִּי as *I fanned
the scent,* like a person who waves a scarf
in a perfumery in order to circulate the
scent.

נַפְתִּי may also mean *I dripped or poured,*
i.e., I have sprinkled my bed with aromatic
spices of myrrh, aloes and cinnamon to

bring a good scent (*Metzudos*).

◆§ The temptress assures him he has nothing to fear

18. לְכָה נִרְוֶה דֹדִים עַד־הַבֹּקֶר נִתְעַלְּסָה בָּאֲהָבִים —
*Come, let us sate ourselves with love
until the morning, let us rejoice with acts
of love.* The Evil Inclination continues its
persuasions, saying: We can continue our
sinful acts until morning, i.e., until your life
nears its end, and then you can repent.
Until then, however, let us delight in our
love (*Vilna Gaon*).

19. כִּי אֵין הָאִישׁ בְּבֵיתוֹ הָלַךְ בְּדֶרֶךְ מֵרָחוֹק —
*For [my] husband is not home [lit. in his
home]; he has gone on a distant journey.*
You need not fear that my husband will
discover you; he is away on a long journey
(*Metzudos*).

Rashi explains this figuratively: You
have seen that God has removed His Holy
Presence, and has been good to idol worshipers.

Ibn Ezra points out that this woman
does not even refer to her husband as אִישִׁי,
my husband, but rather הָאִישׁ, *the husband*, contemptuously disregarding him
completely, as she commits adultery with
impunity.

20. צְרוֹר־הַכֶּסֶף לָקַח בְּיָדוֹ — *He has taken
the money pouch with him.* Do not worry
that he will return tonight; he took a
bundle of money with him, and will not
return until he has used it all to purchase
merchandise (*Metzudos*).

Rashi explains *money pouch* figuratively as Israel's most valuable people: He
[i.e., God] has killed their best people.
Chevel Nachalah points out that this is a
denial of God's justice in the world. It is the
claim of לֵית דִּין וְלֵית דַּיָּן, *there is no justice
and no judge*, since God allowed the
wicked to live peacefully in this world, and

to seek your countenance, and I have found you! ¹⁶ *I have decked my bed with spreads of superior braided Egyptian linen.* ¹⁷ *I have perfumed my bed [with] myrrh, aloes and cinnamon.* ¹⁸ *Come, let us sate ourselves with love until the morning; let us rejoice with acts of love,* ¹⁹ *for [my] husband is not home; he has gone on a distant journey.* ²⁰ *He has taken the money pouch with him; he will come home on the appointed day"*

He killed the righteous ones mercilessly.

לְיוֹם הַכֶּסֶא יָבֹא בֵיתוֹ — *He will come home* [lit. *his home*] *on the appointed day.* Rashi relates כֶּסֶא to the phrase בְּכֶסֶה לְיוֹם חַגֵּנוּ, *at the time appointed for our festive day* (*Psalms* 81:4).

Had he not set an appointed time for his return, it is possible that he could return now, but he set a time for his return, and that time had not yet arrived (*Vilna Gaon*).

Ralbag explains that יוֹם הַכֶּסֶא, *the appointed day,* alludes to Rosh Hashanah, which is called "כֶּסֶה" as the verse states (*Psalms* 81:4), תִּקְעוּ בַחֹדֶשׁ שׁוֹפָר בַּכֶּסֶה לְיוֹם חַגֵּנוּ, *Blow the shofar at the moon's renewal, at the time appointed for our festive day,* i.e., Rosh Hashanah. This reference also suggests כֶּסֶא, *chair,* for on this day, God "sits on the seat of judgment" dispensing justice to the world.[1]

The *Vilna Gaon* explains that verses 19 and 20 express the Evil Inclination's persuasive powers. He makes an all-out attempt to get an individual to disregard the four major areas of Divine service: Torah study, performance of commandments, fear of God, and wisdom, as follows:

❑ *For [my] husband is not home* implies that the Holy Temple has been destroyed and God's spirit no longer rests there. Therefore, wisdom is gone, for the Temple was its source.

❑ *He has gone on a distant journey* refers to the absence of fear of God. Such fear is a product of understanding; without understanding, there is no fear of God. Now that understanding is absent (see *Isaiah* 29:14), there is no fear of God.

❑ *He has taken the money pouch with him.* The Torah is now bound up and sealed, says the Evil Inclination; even if you exert yourself and struggle, you will be unable to understand it (see *Isaiah* 8:16).

❑ *He will come home on the appointed day* alludes to the end of days, when God will return to His Temple. Since it will not be possible to perform all the commandments until then, continues the Evil Inclination, you can disregard them now.[2]

1. The Evil Inclination argues, "God ignores your deeds all year; it is only on Rosh Hashanah that He sits in judgment. That is the only time you need fear Him; at other times, you can do as you please" (*Chessed L'Avraham*).

2. The Talmud (*Sanhedrin* 96b) homiletically applies verses 19-20 to a dialogue between the nations of Ammon and Moab and King Nebuchadnezzar of Babylon. Having heard the prophecies that Jerusalem would be destroyed, Ammon and Moab sent Nebuchadnezzar, king of Babylonia, a message saying, "Come and capture the Land of Israel." Nebuchadnezzar replied, "I am afraid that God will do to me as He did to my predecessors [i.e., He will punish me just as He punished those who harmed Israel in the past]. Ammon and Moab sent back quoting this verse, כִּי אֵין הָאִישׁ בְּבֵיתוֹ, *The Master* (i.e., God, who is also referred to as אִישׁ מִלְחָמָה, *Master of War* [*Exodus* 15:3]) *is not at home.*

Nebuchadnezzar responded: "Perhaps He is nearby, and will come [when His nation is in danger]." "*He has gone on a distant journey*," replied Ammon and Moab. "Maybe they have righteous people among them who will pray to God for mercy and bring Him back," Nebuchadnezzar retorted. "*He has taken the money pouch with him*," i.e., the righteous among them died (*Rashi*, ibid.), replied Ammon and Moab. "The wicked will repent and pray for mercy and bring Him back," Nebuchadnezzar argued. Ammon and Moab replied, "*He will come home on the appointed day*" [i.e., he will not return until after the completion of seventy years of exile in Babylon (*Rashi* ibid.)].

כא־כב הֱטַתּוּ בְּרֹב לִקְחָהּ בְּחֵלֶק שְׂפָתֶיהָ תַּדִּיחֶנּוּ: הוֹלֵךְ
אַחֲרֶיהָ פִּתְאֹם כְּשׁוֹר אֶל־טֶבַח יָבוֹא וּכְעֶכֶס
כג אֶל־מוּסַר אֱוִיל: עַד יְפַלַּח חֵץ כְּבֵדוֹ כְּמַהֵר צִפּוֹר
אֶל־פָּח וְלֹא־יָדַע כִּי־בְנַפְשׁוֹ הוּא:
כד וְעַתָּה בָנִים שִׁמְעוּ־לִי וְהַקְשִׁיבוּ לְאִמְרֵי־פִי:
כה אַל־יֵשְׂטְ אֶל־דְּרָכֶיהָ לִבֶּךָ אַל־תֵּתַע בִּנְתִיבוֹתֶיהָ:
כו כִּי־רַבִּים חֲלָלִים הִפִּילָה וַעֲצֻמִים כָּל־הֲרֻגֶיהָ:
כז דַּרְכֵי שְׁאוֹל בֵּיתָהּ יֹרְדוֹת אֶל־חַדְרֵי־מָוֶת:

21. הֱטַתּוּ בְּרֹב לִקְחָהּ — *She sways him with her abundant talk.* King Solomon remarks: See how she has swayed this naive youth with all the talk she is accustomed to use to entice people. לֶקַח implies לִמּוּד וְהֶרְגֵּל, *something which is customary and habitual* (Metzudos). [Although *lekach* has been used previously in *Proverbs* to mean *a [good] teaching* (4:2), here the word seems to be used as a contrast to *chochmah*. The tempted youth has his choice of virtuous *chochmah* or vicious *lekach*.]

בְּחֵלֶק שְׂפָתֶיהָ תַּדִּיחֶנּוּ — *She thrusts him astray with the glibness of her lips.* With her smooth talk, she leads him off the right path (Rashi). Initially when she grasped him (v. 13), she just swayed him, and he could have gone either way. However, with her talk she led him totally astray (Vilna Gaon).

⇒ He rushes to his doom

22. הוֹלֵךְ אַחֲרֶיהָ פִּתְאֹם כְּשׁוֹר אֶל־טֶבַח יָבוֹא — *He follows her, unsuspectingly, like an ox going to the slaughter.* Just as an ox goes unsuspectingly to the slaughter, so does he follow the evil woman without realizing that she is entrapping him (Ibn Nachmiash).

Once she has enticed him away from the proper way of life, he follows her of his own volition, without any need of additional persuasion. Like an ox going to the slaughter, he does not suspect that his punishment is imminent, and he will have no time to repent (Vilna Gaon).

וּכְעֶכֶס אֶל־מוּסַר אֱוִיל — *Like a venomous snake to discipline of the fool.* Rashi renders עֶכֶס as אֶרֶס נָחָשׁ, *venom of a snake.* Just as a snake rushes to fulfill its God-given mission of chastising the fool who deserves Divine retribution, so, too, this person rushes after this temptress until he sins with her [and her arrow splits his liver (see following verse)].

Other commentators (Ibn Nachmiash, Ibn Ezra, Meiri) explain עֶכֶס as a *fetter*: The woman is like a fetter that binds the fool to chastise him, while he himself thinks it is an ornament. [When used with reference to a woman, the word עֶכֶס means an ornament. See *Isaiah* 3:6 (Meiri).]

Meiri explains that the *ox* and the *fetter* are both symbols of what happens to the person who follows this woman. When shown fodder, an ox hastens toward it, expecting to eat, not realizing it is just the bait to lead it to the slaughterhouse. Similarly, a sinner anticipates the pleasure awaiting him by following the woman — when actually he is bringing death and doom upon himself. Thus, the very ornament that lures him to sin will become the *fetter* to bind his feet.

23. עַד יְפַלַּח חֵץ כְּבֵדוֹ — *Until an arrow splits his liver.* [He runs after her] until he sins with her, and her arrow splits his liver, for he loses his eternal world because of her (Metzudos).

21 She sways him with her abundant talk; she thrusts him astray with the glibness of her lips. 22 He follows her, unsuspectingly, like an ox to the slaughter; like a venomous snake to discipline of the fool, 23 until an arrow splits his liver; he is like a bird hurrying to a trap, unaware that its life will be lost.

24 So now, children, listen to me, and heed the words of my mouth. 25 Let not your heart incline to her ways; do not stray in her pathways. 26 For she has felled many victims; the number of her slain is huge. 27 The ways to her house lead to the grave, descending to the chamber of death.

The *arrow* alludes to Divine retribution; he will not learn his lesson until an arrow splits his liver (*Ibn Ezra*).

כְּמַהֵר צִפּוֹר אֶל־פָּח וְלֹא־יָדַע כִּי־בְנַפְשׁוֹ הוּא — *He is like a bird hurrying to a trap, unaware that its life will be lost.* He is like a bird rushing to the snare, not knowing that the snare will take its life (*Rashi*).

Just as a bird flies to the snare to enjoy the small amount of bait, not realizing that this bit of enjoyment will cost it its life, so, too, this person will lose his eternal life, because of fleeting and temporal pleasures (*Metzudos*).

⇥ Torah urges him to reject the wiles of the temptress

25. אַל־יֵשְׂטְ אֶל־דְּרָכֶיהָ לִבֶּךָ אַל־תֵּתַע בִּנְתִיבוֹתֶיהָ — *Let not your heart incline to her ways; do not stray in her pathways.* Let your heart not veer toward the house of the harlot, and do not go astray from the right way to traverse her byways (*Metzudos*).

דֶּרֶךְ, *way,* is a main road traversed by many; נְתִיב, *pathway,* is a little path taken by an individual. The verse warns man not only to avoid her main road — i.e., not to commit the sin of adultery with her — but not even to stray in her pathways — not even to speak to her or look at her, mistakenly assuming that he can incite his Evil Inclination and then overcome its temptations and earn reward (see *Avodah Zarah* 17b) (*Malbim*).

26. כִּי־רַבִּים חֲלָלִים הִפִּילָה וַעֲצֻמִים כָּל־הֲרֻגֶיהָ — *For she has felled many victims* [lit. *corpses*]; *the number of her slain is huge.* She has already destroyed and killed many mighty people (*Ralbag*).

Do not depend on your righteousness to save you from her, for she has slain people who were mighty in Torah and fear of God, and even they could not withstand the test. Therefore, beware not to approach her at all, in any way (see 5:8) (*Malbim*).

By enticing people, the adulteress turns them into living *corpses* [חֲלָלִים]; for even though they are still physically alive, they are considered dead because of their sins (see *Berachos* 18b: אֵלּוּ רְשָׁעִים שֶׁבְּחַיֵּיהֶן קְרוּיִין מֵתִים, *these are the wicked ones who in their lifetime are called dead*). Her victims are mighty, in the sense that they are still strong and healthy in body, but are considered "slain," because of their disgraceful, sinful deeds (*Binah L'Ittim*).

27. דַּרְכֵי שְׁאוֹל בֵּיתָהּ יֹרְדוֹת אֶל־חַדְרֵי־מָוֶת — *The ways to her house lead to the grave, descending to the chambers of death.* The approaches to her house are roads to *the grave,* which descends to *the chambers of death,* for an individual can easily be enticed by her, and will lose his share in the Hereafter (*Metzudos*).

The seductive ways of the adulteress and the bitter consequences of her victims are a metaphor for the punishments that await a person who is enticed to pursue worldly desires (*Meiri*).

א הֲלֹא־חָכְמָה תִקְרָא וּתְבוּנָה תִּתֵּן קוֹלָהּ:
ב בְּרֹאשׁ־מְרוֹמִים עֲלֵי־דָרֶךְ בֵּית נְתִיבוֹת נִצָּבָה:
ג לְיַד־שְׁעָרִים לְפִי־קָרֶת מְבוֹא פְתָחִים תָּרֹנָּה:
ד אֲלֵיכֶם אִישִׁים אֶקְרָא וְקוֹלִי אֶל־בְּנֵי אָדָם:
ה הָבִינוּ פְתָאיִם עָרְמָה וּכְסִילִים הָבִינוּ לֵב:

VIII

After warning against the influences of heretics (Ch. 7), Solomon now turns to the benefits that will be enjoyed by those who recognize the importance of the Torah. Verses 1-3 introduce *Chochmah*/Wisdom as the speaker. [Throughout *Proverbs*, "Wisdom" is synonymous with Torah.] Verses 4-36 speak in the first person, as Torah describes some of its many virtues and benefits, and its pivotal role in Creation.

◦§ Wisdom invites all to learn from her

1. הֲלֹא־חָכְמָה תִקְרָא — *Surely wisdom will call out.* The Torah announces, as it were, all the ideas recorded below (*Rashi*). The virtues of wisdom are so self-evident that it is as if it calls others to follow its path (*Metzudos*).

These verses are similar to verses 1:20-21. There the Torah's proclamation is contrasted with the words of robbers, whereas here they are contrasted with those of the adulteress. Her words are shrouded in darkness and secrecy (see 7:9), but the words of the Torah are announced publicly, for there is nothing to be ashamed of (*Vilna Gaon*).

וּתְבוּנָה תִּתֵּן קוֹלָהּ — *And understanding will raise her voice.* The first few verses use four different verbs to describe the Torah's speech: *call out* and *raise her voice* (v. 1), *cries out* (v. 3), and *I will speak* (v. 6). They symbolize the four different levels of interpreting the Torah: as noted in 7:9 (*Vilna Gaon*).

2. בְּרֹאשׁ־מְרוֹמִים — *Atop the heights.* The Torah makes its words heard from afar as if it would be calling out from atop high mountains (*Metzudos*).

עֲלֵי־דָרֶךְ — *Along the way.* The Torah proclaims its message on the busy highway, from which multitudes of people branch off to their respective byways (*Metzudos*).

These two verses indicate that the Torah speaks to people wherever they may be found (*Meiri*).

בֵּית נְתִיבוֹת נִצָּבָה — *At the place where pathways diverge, she stands.* The message of the Torah is found at the crossroads, where there are many passersby, the place where they may mistakenly choose a wrong path. The Torah is found there to direct and guide them onto the correct path (*Ralbag*).

The Talmud (*Avodah Zarah* 19a) discusses the seeming contradiction between the phrases *atop the heights* and *along the way*, and applies these phrases to a person's Torah study. Initially, the Torah appears to be found only *atop the heights*, but subsequently it appears even *along the way*. *Maharsha* (ad loc.) explains that at the outset, it is very difficult to understand the Torah, but after continued exposure, one realizes that it is easily accessible and available, as if it were *along the way* where all people walk.

3. לְיַד־שְׁעָרִים לְפִי־קָרֶת — *Near the gateways of the city.* Our translation follows *Ibn Ezra, Meiri* and *Ralbag* who explain קָרֶת as קִרְיָה, *city*. *Rashi* derives קָרֶת from תִּקְרָה, *roof*. A shelter was erected over the gates, and people sat in its shade.

Ralbag explains that the Torah directs a passerby to the entrance that will lead him to his desired destination.

מְבוֹא פְתָחִים תָּרֹנָּה — *At the approach to the entrances, she cries out.* The Torah's message begins with the next verse (*Rashi*).

¹**S**urely wisdom will call out, and understanding will raise her voice. ² Atop the heights along the way, at the place where pathways diverge, she stands. ³ Near the gateways of the city, at the approach to the entrances, she cries out: ⁴ "To you, O men, do I call, and my voice is to the sons of man. ⁵ Simpletons, understand shrewdness; and fools, understand [in your] heart.

Verses 1-3 speak metaphorically. The praises of Torah are so obvious that it is as if they are being announced to all (*Metzudos*).

R' *Hirsch* explains that wisdom is neither the heritage of the privileged, nor a science or academic subject that is far removed from the strivings and activities of life. The Torah relates to the entire fullness of life on earth, including every internal and external relationship of the individual and of society as a whole. It wishes to direct us through its challenging spirit of illumination. Thus, wisdom involves itself with the vitality of life; it scales the elevations that scan our ways and goes to the centers where paths of life meet and cross. It seeks disciples at the gates of public life, at the entrance of a city's community, at the doorstep of the home and in the domestic life of individuals and families.

Malbim notes that verses 2 and 3 portray four successive levels in the study of Torah:

1) *Atop the heights along the way* refers to the literal meaning of Torah, its commandments and narratives that are disseminated to all [דֶּרֶךְ, *way*, refers to a broad road traversed by all].

2) *The place where pathways diverge* refers to the deeper teachings that are reserved for scholars, such as homiletical expositions or the reasons for commandments [נְתִיבוֹת, *paths*, imply small roads used only by individuals].

3) *Near the gateways of the city* refers to the teachings reserved for the Sanhedrin, the judges and the great Torah scholars who sit by the city gates and render decisions for the whole nation.

4) *At the approach to the entrances* refers to the hidden mystical teachings of Torah, and the secrets of Creation,

which are only revealed to a select few, taught individually.

4. אֲלֵיכֶם אִישִׁים אֶקְרָא וְקוֹלִי אֶל־בְּנֵי אָדָם — *To you, O men, do I call, and my voice is to the sons of man.* Ibn Ezra explains אִישִׁים, *men,* as a reference to the rich people, and בְּנֵי אָדָם, *the sons of man,* to the poor. Both are obligated to hear the words of Torah.

According to the *Vilna Gaon, men* are the princes, the important people who are close to Torah. They need only a call (אֶקְרָא) to bring them wisdom. However, בְּנֵי אָדָם, *sons of man,* the general populace, which is far from the Torah, must be addressed with *my voice.*

Malbim explains *men* as distinguished people who have sanctified themselves by discarding impure ideas and information that impede the absorption of *chochmah.* Its call is addressed personally to them. Lesser people, *the sons of man,* can hear the *voice* of wisdom, even though it is not personally addressed to them, for everyone can attain Torah knowledge according to his level of understanding.

5. הָבִינוּ פְתָאִים עָרְמָה — *Simpletons, understand shrewdness. Simpletons* lack the *shrewdness* to avoid being seduced by their Evil Inclination, therefore they are exhorted to *understand cleverness,* so that they will be able to see through its wiles (*Vilna Gaon;* see 1:4).

וּכְסִילִים הָבִינוּ לֵב — *And fools, understand [in your] heart.* A *fool* knows the wisdom of the Torah, but fails to apply it to his actions because he lets his evil desires and bad traits overwhelm him. His heart is unable to overcome his Evil Inclination and he disputes the dictates of wisdom because they impede him in his quest to fulfill his desires. *Wisdom* addresses the *fools,* telling them: Learn to hold your will in check and let your heart control your

שִׁמְעוּ כִּי־נְגִידִים אֲדַבֵּר וּמִפְתַּח שְׂפָתַי מֵישָׁרִים: כִּי־ ו־ז

אֱמֶת יֶהְגֶּה חִכִּי וְתוֹעֲבַת שְׂפָתַי רֶשַׁע: בְּצֶדֶק כָּל־ ח

אִמְרֵי־פִי אֵין בָּהֶם נִפְתָּל וְעִקֵּשׁ: כֻּלָּם נְכֹחִים לַמֵּבִין ט

desires so that you will be receptive to wisdom (*Malbim*).

Wisdom invites everyone to drink from its fountain before trying to solve problems and carry out tasks in public life, in the circle of one's family, or even in private. If anyone tries to fulfill his duties, whether in the role of spouse, family member, citizen, or decent human being, without previously arming his mind with the lessons of wisdom, he will ultimately be a dismal failure (*R' Hirsch*).

◆§ The Torah is supreme

6-9. In these verses King Solomon teaches how to value the words of Torah. Its every letter is perfect; nothing in it is extraneous, redundant, or irrelevant. The exact phraseology and order of each statement is vital to its understanding; even a change in the spelling of a word may imply a vital halachic determination. If someone fails to see the significance of the Torah's words, it is due to his lack of understanding (v. 9) and not to any deficiency in the Torah. That its truth and righteousness are beyond question becomes more and more self-evident the deeper one delves into it.

6. שִׁמְעוּ כִּי־נְגִידִים אֲדַבֵּר — *Listen, for I will speak noble things.* The word נְגִידִים is

derived from the word נָגִיד, *ruler*; the Torah speaks words of nobility and importance (*Rashi*). All of its words are like princes and ministers, and must therefore be heeded (*Vilna Gaon*).

R' Chananel bar Papa explains that just as a ruler has the power of life and death in his hands, the words of Torah can bring life or death (*Shabbos* 88b).[1]

The Talmud (ibid.) offers another explanation: Every utterance that emanated from God at Mount Sinai had two crowns tied to it figuratively, to commemorate Israel's two expressions of נַעֲשֶׂה וְנִשְׁמָע, *we will do and we will hear*, which represented their unquestioning acceptance of God's will. [Thus, the words of Torah are like "rulers" wearing royal crowns.]

Every word of Torah is of unfathomable significance, for the letters of the Torah can be joined in combinations that form the Names of God (*Alshich*; see also *Ramban*'s introduction to the Torah).[2]

וּמִפְתַּח שְׂפָתַי מֵישָׁרִים — *The opinion* [lit. *opening*] *of my lips will be fair words.* Whatever my lips open to utter [interpreting מִפְתַּח from פֶּתַח, *opening*] is fair and upright (*Metzudos*).

7. כִּי־אֱמֶת יֶהְגֶּה חִכִּי — *For my palate will utter truth.* I speak only the truth, as opposed to the alien woman whose words

---

1. Rava (ibid.) compares the Torah to סַם הַחַיִּים, *a life-giving potion*. To those who apply themselves wholeheartedly to learning and understanding it, it is the elixir of life, but it becomes סַם הַמָּוֶת, *a deadly poison*, to those who do not put their full effort into comprehending its sacred words.

2. The Talmud (*Bava Basra* 15a) inquires into the authorship of the last eight verses of Torah, which describe the death of Moses. Could Moses have written about his own death while he was still alive? R' Shimon's opinion is that the Holy One, Blessed is He, dictated the words of those verses, and Moses wrote them בְּדֶמַע, *with tears*. The *Vilna Gaon* explains R' Shimon differently. He renders the word בְּדֶמַע as "a *mixture* of letters." When Moses recorded the last eight verses, they did not form the combination of words as we now have them in the Torah. Rather, Moses wrote them according to the Divine Names that are hidden in these verses. Thus the verse did not read וַיָּמָת שָׁם מֹשֶׁה, *And Moses died there* (Deuteronomy 34:5), but some other combination of letters and words, according to סוֹד, *the hidden mysteries* of the Torah. Only after Moses' death was Joshua allowed to write these same verses according to נִגְלֶה, *the revealed meaning* of Torah. Thus, even though Moses did not write about his own death while he was still alive, he wrote the entire Torah; not a letter was missing.

6 Listen, for I will speak noble thoughts; the opinion of my lips will be fair words. 7 For my palate will utter truth; wickedness is an abomination to my lips. 8 All the words of my mouth are [said] with righteousness; they contain no twisting or perversity. 9 They are all correct to one who understands,

are based on falsehood (see Chapter 7) (*Chevel Nachalah*).[1]

וְתוֹעֲבַת שְׂפָתַי רֶשַׁע — *Wickedness is an abomination to my lips.* It is abhorrent to my lips to speak words of wickedness (*Metzudos*).

8. בְּצֶדֶק כָּל־אִמְרֵי־פִי — *All the words of my mouth are [said] with righteousness.* Not only is every individual law of Torah righteous, all the laws of Torah together are harmonious and consistent with each other. This contrasts sharply with man-made statutes, which are often at odds with each other (*Alshich*).[2]

אֵין בָּהֶם נִפְתָּל וְעִקֵּשׁ — *They contain no*

twisting or perversity. The words of a mortal may contain irrelevancies and mistakes. Not so the Divine words of Torah; every instance of a "missing" letter, an "extra" letter, or a change in the order of the words contains profound interpretations, deep wisdom and hidden meanings known only to those who delve to full depths of the Torah's wisdom (*Malbim*).[3]

9. כֻּלָּם נְכֹחִים לַמֵּבִין — *They are all correct to one who understands.* One who has the understanding to comprehend Torah's words will realize that they are all true (*Metzudos*).[4]

1. *Sfas Emes* explains that it is very hard to perceive the truth in this world, which is עָלְמָא דְשִׁקְרָא, *a world of falsehood.* The word עוֹלָם, *world,* is derived from the word הֶעְלֵם, *concealment*; truth is hidden under the cloak of the natural and physical. The only way to arrive at the truth is through Torah, which reveals the inner, spiritual workings of the world.

2. King David also extols the beauty of Torah, stating: מִשְׁפְּטֵי ה' אֱמֶת צָדְקוּ יַחְדָּו, *the judgments of Hashem are true, altogether righteous (Psalms 19:10),* i.e., when taken all together, they are still righteous.

3. One of many examples where an important principle is derived from a slight variation in the words of Torah is found in the laws of *tefillin.* The Torah states: *and it should be a sign* עַל־יָדְכָה, *upon your arm (Exodus 13:16).* Our Sages explain that the word יָדְךָ, *your arm,* is spelled יָדְכָה, to teach that *tefillin* are are placed on a person's יָד כֵּהָה, *weaker arm* (i.e., the left arm of a right-handed person, and vice versa).

The precision of Torah's wording often serves as a means of teaching a moral lesson. When speaking of the animals taken into Noah's ark, the verse states: וּמִן־הַבְּהֵמָה אֲשֶׁר אֵינֶנָּה טְהֹרָה, *And of the animal that is not clean (Genesis 7:8).* Rather than use the single word טְמֵאָה, *unclean,* the Torah uses three words, eight extra letters, saying אֲשֶׁר אֵינֶנָּה טְהֹרָה, *that is not clean.* R' Yehoshua ben Levi explains that this teaches us to always avoid using coarse expressions in our speech (*Pesachim* 3a).

[Even though the Torah generally uses the word טָמֵא, *unclean,* the lesson is derived from the unusual change in this verse to a more roundabout expression (*Rashi,* ad. loc.).]

4. Before He created Adam, God addressed the angels and said: נַעֲשֶׂה אָדָם, *Let us make man (Genesis 1:26).* By using the plural *let us,* as if He needed the concurrence of the angels, God taught the ethical lesson that a greater person should show lesser people the courtesy of consulting them. The Torah uses this wording despite the possibility that some may choose to find a sacrilegious implication in the plural form, and infer that there is a plurality of divinities, God forbid. A discerning person will clearly see the falseness of such an interpretation, for in the following verse we immediately find וַיִּבְרָא אֱלֹהִים, *And God created,* in the singular form, clearly indicating that God alone created man [see *Rashi* ad loc.]

As R' Yochanan said: In all passages that the heretics have misinterpreted as grounds for heresy, their refutation is found near at hand (*Sanhedrin* 38b). One who sincerely seeks the truth will see it.

יוְישָׁרִים לְמֹצְאֵי דָעַת: קְחוּ־מוּסָרִי וְאַל־כֶּסֶף
יאוְדַעַת מֵחָרוּץ נִבְחָר: כִּי־טוֹבָה חָכְמָה מִפְּנִינִים
יבוְכָל־חֲפָצִים לֹא יִשְׁווּ־בָהּ: אֲנִי־חָכְמָה שָׁכַנְתִּי
יגעָרְמָה וְדַעַת מְזִמּוֹת אֶמְצָא: יִרְאַת יהוה שְׂנֹאת
רָע גֵּאָה וְגָאוֹן | וְדֶרֶךְ רָע וּפִי תַהְפֻּכוֹת שָׂנֵאתִי:

וִישָׁרִים לְמֹצְאֵי דָעַת — *And upright to those who find knowledge.* Even mystical interpretations become clear to those who have the required level of knowledge (*Malbim*).

10. קְחוּ־מוּסָרִי וְאַל־כֶּסֶף וְדַעַת מֵחָרוּץ נִבְחָר — *Accept my discipline and not silver, [for] knowledge is choicer than fine gold.* Put your efforts into the acquisition of discipline rather than silver, and the acquisition of knowledge rather than fine gold (*Meiri*).

Ralbag renders *and knowledge is chosen over gold.*[1]

11. כִּי־טוֹבָה חָכְמָה מִפְּנִינִים — *For wisdom is better than pearls.* Pearls are valuable because they are rare and hard to find, but the hidden meanings of the Torah surpass even pearls in their rarity (*Vilna Gaon*; see 3:15).

וְכָל־חֲפָצִים לֹא יִשְׁווּ־בָהּ — *And all desires cannot compare to it.* All the things a person desires because they are so essential to him are not comparable to the Torah (*Vilna Gaon*).

The Talmud (*Moed Kattan* 9b) questions the seeming contradiction between this verse and 3:15: וְכָל־חֲפָצֶיךָ לֹא יִשְׁווּ־בָהּ, *and all* **your** *desires cannot compare to it.* *All* **your** *desires* implies that your personal needs are insignificant in comparison to Torah, and you must give them up in order to study Torah, but one may infer that one should interrupt his studies for the sake of חֶפְצֵי שָׁמַיִם, *the desires of Heaven;* i.e., performance of the commandments. Our verse — *and all desires* — implies the reverse, that Torah study takes priority over everything, even other commandments.

The Talmud resolves this conflict by explaining that when a *mitzvah* can be performed by others, Torah study takes precedence. However, if only that person himself can perform the commandment (e.g., putting on *tefillin*, eating matzah on Pesach), then he must set aside his learning for the sake of the Heavenly desire, and perform the commandment instead.[2]

1. R' Menachem Mendel Bendet, a disciple of the *Vilna Gaon*, explains why discipline is compared to silver, and knowledge to gold. Silver is used by rich and poor alike; so, too, discipline is vital to both the learned and unlearned. Gold, however, is used exclusively by the rich, just as deep knowledge of the Torah is available only to those who are already rich in Torah knowledge.

2. **Six Parts of the Torah.** According to the *Vilna Gaon*, verses 6-11 allude to six different parts of Torah: Scripture, Mishnah, Gemara, Midrash, Aggadah and *Sod*.

◄§ **Verse 6** refers to Scripture. Just as one who speaks with a נָגִיד, *ruler*, weighs each word he utters and is careful to avoid anything unnecessary, so, too, the words of the Written Law were spoken to Moses and Aaron, the nobility of the human race, and the words were precise, exact and significant. מִפְתַּח שְׂפָתַי, *the opening of my lips,* is a reference to *Genesis*, the first section of the Torah, which is called סֵפֶר הַיָּשָׁר, *The Book of the Upright*, since it speaks of our forefathers who were just and upright in their actions. From the start the Torah is מֵישָׁרִים, *fair and upright*.

◄§ **Verse 7**, which speaks of *truth*, refers to Mishnah, which gives the laws very concisely: permitted or forbidden, pure or impure, valid or invalid. Truth is what the Mishnah rules to be permitted, pure, or valid. Wickedness is what it rules to be *an abomination* — i.e., *forbidden, impure, or invalid.*

◄§ **Verse 8** refers to Gemara, which discusses and elucidates the Mishnah. The Gemara is the epitome of *righteousness*, even when the Sages state, חַסּוּרֵי מִחַסְּרָא, *words are missing*, meaning

and upright to those who find knowledge. [10] *Accept my discipline and not silver, [for] knowledge is choicer than fine gold,* [11] *for wisdom is better than pearls, and all desires cannot compare to it."*

[12] *I am wisdom; I dwell in shrewdness; I provide knowledge of designs.* [13] *Fear of HASHEM is hatred of evil. I hate pride and haughtiness, the way of evil, and a duplicitous mouth.*

◆§ Torah is the source of truest success

12. אֲנִי־חׇכְמָה שָׁכַנְתִּי עׇרְמָה — *I am wisdom; I dwell in shrewdness.* Once a person has studied Torah, he attains shrewdness in all other areas as well (*Rashi*).

The *Vilna Gaon* points out that though the Patriarch Jacob was an אִישׁ תָּם, *a man of perfect innocence*, he nevertheless had the shrewdness necessary to outwit Esau (in obtaining the blessings from Isaac) and Laban (in obtaining his well-deserved wages). This shrewdness was a direct outgrowth of Yaakov's mastery of the wisdom of the Torah.

Metzudos explains that without the Torah's wisdom, a person cannot have the shrewdness needed to outwit his Evil Inclination.

וְדַעַת מְזִמּוֹת אֶמְצָא — *I provide knowledge of designs.* Torah provides the ideas a person needs to save himself from the persuasion of his Evil Inclination (*Metzudos*).

13. יִרְאַת ה' שְׂנֹאת רָע גֵּאָה וְגָאוֹן וְדֶרֶךְ רָע וּפִי תַהְפֻּכוֹת שָׂנֵאתִי — *Fear of Hashem is hatred of evil. I hate pride and haughtiness, the way of evil and a duplicitous mouth.* These are the words of discipline that wisdom makes known to mankind (*Rashi*).

Hatred of these evil qualities is the essence of fear of God; therefore I hate them (*Metzudos*).

R' Bachya renders רָע as *an evil person,* who personifies the base traits enumerated in this verse; pride and haughtiness, an evil way, and a duplicitous mouth. A God-fearing person will hate evildoers, as King David says: הֲלוֹא מְשַׂנְאֶיךָ ה' אֶשְׂנָא, *For indeed, those who hate You, Hashem, I hate* (Psalms 139:21). [See *Pesachim* 113b.][1]

that additional words need to be inserted in order to properly explain the text. Unlike other works of disputation and dialectic, which the reader may find unacceptable because their reasoning is perverse or excessively verbose, there is no *twisting or perversity* in the discussions of the Gemara.

◆§ **Verse 9** refers to Midrashic literature that deals with halachic exegesis. Sources such as *Sifra* and *Sifre* use hermeneutic principles to render rulings which seem contrary to the literal meaning of the text, and to read additional meanings into the words of the verse. For instance, the rule of עַיִן תַּחַת עַיִן, *an eye for an eye*, is explained as monetary rather than physical revenge. Though some laws may not seem to be indicated by the plain meaning of a verse, they are nevertheless *correct*, and though some laws, such as the one cited above, may seem to be contradicted by the verse, they are clear to *one who understands*. Regarding laws that some people consider unfair, the verse responds that they are *upright to those who find [Torah] knowledge.*

◆§ **Verse 10** refers to the part of the Aggadah that teaches *mussar*, i.e., ethics and discipline. Our Sages advise that someone who wants to know more about the Creator of the World should learn the Aggadah, and our verse states that it is more precious than silver and gold.

◆§ **Verse 11** refers to the part of the Aggadah that is known as *Sod*, the mysteries of the Torah. They are precious because they are rarer than pearls and because they are needed beyond all other human desires.

1. The Talmud (*Yerushalmi Shabbos* 16:1) identifies apostates and renegade Jews whose heresy is especially virulent as those whom it is a *mitzvah* to hate. They are far more dangerous than ordinary evildoers because they attempt to poison other Jews against God.

יד-טו לִי־עֵצָה וְתוּשִׁיָּה אֲנִי בִינָה לִי גְבוּרָה: בִּי מְלָכִים
טז יִמְלֹכוּ וְרוֹזְנִים יְחֹקְקוּ צֶדֶק: בִּי שָׂרִים יָשֹׂרוּ
יז וּנְדִיבִים כָּל־שֹׁפְטֵי צֶדֶק: אֲנִי °אהביה אֹהֵב

°אֹהֲבַי ק'

The *Vilna Gaon* differentiates between גֵּאָה וְגָאוֹן, *pride and haughtiness*, A proud person regards himself as superior and the rest of the world as insignificant. A haughty person goes further, for he wishes to impose his authority over others.

Arrogance is the seminal trait of faulty character. The Sages (*Sotah* 5a) stress how much God hates an arrogant person, and they teach that the arrogant deserve to be cut down like an אֲשֵׁרָה, a tree used for pagan worship. Their bodies will not be resurrected in the Messianic era. The Holy One, Blessed is He, exclaims about such a person: אֵין אֲנִי וְהוּא יְכוֹלִים לָדוּר בָּעוֹלָם, *He and I cannot dwell together in the world.*

14. לִי־עֵצָה וְתוּשִׁיָּה אֲנִי בִינָה לִי גְבוּרָה — *Mine are counsel and wisdom; I am understanding, mine is strength.* The

Torah provides the tools through which one can conquer the Evil Inclination: the counsel that saves one from its persuasions, the ability to weaken it,[1] the understanding to repulse it and the strength to overcome it (*Metzudos*).

The *Vilna Gaon* explains עֵצָה as counsel in identifying the persuasions of the Evil Inclination and גְבוּרָה as *strength* in overcoming them once one recognizes them for what they are.

15. בִּי מְלָכִים יִמְלֹכוּ וְרוֹזְנִים יְחֹקְקוּ צֶדֶק — *Through me, kings will reign and rulers will decree righteousness.* I [the Torah] teach them laws and justice (*Rashi*). If a king follows the Torah's dictates, his reign will endure and his laws will be just and correct (*Metzudos*).[2]

All judgments and advice needed by a

1. According to *Metzudos*, the word תוּשִׁיָּה is derived from תָּשׁוּת הַכֹּחַ, *weakening of strength*, i.e., the Torah's *counsel* enables one to weaken the Evil Inclination's power.

The Talmud (*Kiddushin* 30b) derives a similar idea from the verse וְשַׂמְתֶּם אֶת־דְּבָרַי אֵלֶּה, *You shall place these words of Mine* (Deuteronomy 11:18). The word וְשַׂמְתֶּם can be understood as סָם תָּם, *a perfect potion*. The Torah's words are the perfect remedy for all evil. The Talmud illustrates this with a parable of a father who punished his son and then placed a bandage on the wound. He instructed the child that as long as the bandage remained on the wound, he may eat and drink whatever he desires and he may wash either in hot or cold water without fear. However, should he remove the bandage, the wound will fester. So too, Hashem says: בָּרָאתִי יֵצֶר הָרָע וּבָרָאתִי לוֹ תוֹרָה תַּבְלִין, *I created the Evil Inclination, but I created the Torah as an antidote to it.*

When the Sages describe Torah as מַתֶּשֶׁת כֹּחוֹ שֶׁל אָדָם, *weakening a person's strength*, this seems to contradict the fact that Torah brings strength and health to the person's body (see 3:8). However, both characteristics are true. *Rabbi Tzvi Charif Heller* explains that the degree of single-minded intensity needed to succeed in Torah study may weaken a person at first, as he struggles to plumb its depths. Once the Torah is understood, however, it brings him strength and valor. This is implied in the words of this verse: לִי־עֵצָה וְתוּשִׁיָּה, *Mine are counsel and tushiah*, i.e., when I am trying to understand the meaning of Torah, it weakens me, but אֲנִי בִינָה לִי גְבוּרָה, *I am understanding, mine is strength*, once I have discerned what the Torah teaches, then I am strengthened. (See 2:7 for other explanations of why Torah is called תוּשִׁיָּה.)

2. One of the commandments incumbent upon a Jewish king is to write his own Torah scroll and take it with him everywhere, so that he can constantly learn and practice its teachings. He should stay loyal to its teachings, לְמַעַן יַאֲרִיךְ יָמִים עַל־מַמְלַכְתּוֹ הוּא וּבָנָיו בְּקֶרֶב יִשְׂרָאֵל, *so that he will prolong years over his kingdom, he and his sons amid Israel* (Deuteronomy 17:20). The permanence of his reign is conditional upon his adherence to the Torah, as is illustrated many times in the history of the Jewish monarchy, which is related in the Prophets and Writings.

When God appeared to King Solomon in Gibeon and granted his request for wisdom, God also added other blessings that Solomon had not even requested — longevity, wealth and victory over his enemies. Those blessings were given unconditionally, but the endurance of his dynasty was conditional upon allegiance to Torah and commandments, as had been stipulated

ruler can be found in Torah (*Vilna Gaon*).

The Talmud (*Gittin* 62a) derives from this verse that Torah scholars are called *kings*.[1]

16. בִּי שָׂרִים יָשׂרוּ וּנְדִיבִים כָּל־שֹׁפְטֵי צֶדֶק — *Through me, officials will rule, and nobles, all who judge righteously* [lit. *all judges of righteousness*]. If the laws of Torah are the guidelines for the sovereign, his rule will endure (*Metzudos*).

Malbim explains that verses 15 and 16 delineate two different types of justice. Verse 16 deals with שָׂרִים, *officials*, and נְדִיבִים, *nobles*, who judge according to the established laws of the Torah; verse 15 deals with מְלָכִים, *kings*, and רוֹזְנִים, *rulers*, who have more latitude to go beyond the letter of the law (see *Rambam, Hilchos Melachim* 3:10). Yet the Torah is the basis of all justice, for it contains the guidelines

for both kings and officials to execute righteous judgment.

⊷§ The Torah is generous to those who love it

17. אֲנִי־אֹהֲבַי אֵהָב — *I love those who love me.* Wisdom loves those who love her (*Metzudos*).[2]

Rashi explains the verse according to the כְּתִיב, *the Masoretic spelling*, of the word אֹהֲבַי, which is spelled אהביה, *those who love her.* God is speaking, saying that He loves those who love the Torah.

This close relationship between God and those who study His Torah can be understood in light of our Sages' words that קוּדְשָׁא בְּרִיךְ הוּא וְאוֹרַיְיתָא חַד הוּא, *The Holy One, Blessed is He, and the Torah are one* (*Chevel Nachalah*).

Malbim explains that if an individual cherishes wisdom and cleaves to it, wis-

previously (see *I Kings* 3:13,14, *Rashi* ad loc.).

King Saul lost his throne because he did not obey the prophet Samuel. (Disregarding the words of a prophet is tantamount to disregarding the words of God.) As a result, Samuel prophesied that the kingdom would be torn away from him and given to someone more worthy (see *I Samuel* Ch. 15). Had Saul heeded Samuel's words, the kingdom would have remained in his family. As it was, after only two years as king, Saul was killed in a war with the Philistines and the monarchy passed to King David.

1. Noting that three vessels in the Tabernacle — the Altar, the Ark and the Table — were made with a זֵר, *a golden rim*, which protruded upward like a crown, R' Yochanan teaches (*Yoma* 72b): The crown of the Altar was taken by Aaron, for it symbolizes the Divine Temple Service, a task exclusively reserved for Aaron and his descendants; the crown of the Table was taken by David, for it symbolizes material success, which is the responsibilty of the monarchy to protect and nurture; but the crown of the Ark, symbolizing the glory of Torah, is available for anyone wishing to attain it. Lest we think that the crown of Torah is the lesser of the three, the Talmud quotes our verse: *Through me* [i.e., the Torah], *kings will reign.*

In a similar vein, the *Sifri* quotes a question posed by R' Shimon ben Elazar: Who is greater, one who appoints kings or the monarch himself? One who appoints officers, or an officer? Undoubtedly, the one who appoints others to a position of authority exercises the greatest power of all. The crown of priesthood and the crown of kingship are both derived from the Torah, as our verse states, בִּי מְלָכִים יִמְלֹכוּ, *Through me* [i.e., the Torah], *kings will reign.* Therefore, someone who has earned the crown of Torah is credited as if he had achieved all three crowns simultaneously. (See also *Rambam, Hilchos Talmud Torah* 3:1 and *Lechem Mishnah* ibid.)

2. The Sages (*Berachos* 55a) point out: אֵין הקב"ה נותן חָכְמָה אֶלָּא לְמִי שֶׁיֵּשׁ בּוֹ חָכְמָה שֶׁנֶּאֱמַר יָהֵב חָכְמְתָא לְחַכִּימִין, *The Holy One, Blessed is He, does not give wisdom except to one who already has wisdom, as is written: "He gives wisdom to the wise"* (*Daniel* 2:21). Since wisdom is granted by God, how does one initially attain it in order to qualify for the further blessing of even more wisdom? The *Vilna Gaon* explains that a person merits the heavenly blessing of wisdom by exhibiting a love for it.

יח וּמְשַׁחֲרַי יִמְצָאֻנְנִי: עֹשֶׁר־וְכָבוֹד אִתִּי הוֹן עָתֵק
יט וּצְדָקָה: טוֹב פִּרְיִי מֵחָרוּץ וּמִפָּז וּתְבוּאָתִי מִכֶּסֶף
כ נִבְחָר: בְּאֹרַח־צְדָקָה אֲהַלֵּךְ בְּתוֹךְ נְתִיבוֹת מִשְׁפָּט:

dom requites his love and reveals its secrets to him, just as a person confides in someone he loves. Also, wisdom will guard him from sin, like a person who protects his beloved.

וּמְשַׁחֲרַי יִמְצָאֻנְנִי — *And those who search for me shall find me.* Those who search for the meaning of the Torah's words will find many explanations and reasons by delving into its wisdom (*Metzudos*).

Rashi notes the use of an extra "נ" in the word יִמְצָאֻנְנִי, explaining that it alludes to the fifty levels of discernment [נ שַׁעֲרֵי בִינָה, see *Rosh Hashanah* 21b] that God will reveal to those who love the Torah.[1]

18. עֹשֶׁר־וְכָבוֹד אִתִּי — *Riches and honor are with me.* A person will attain riches and honor through the Torah (*Metzudos*).

Even a person who studies Torah not purely for the sake of Heaven will merit honor and wealth (see 3:16). However, someone who studies solely for the sake of Heaven and does not seek benefits in this world will have his merits accumulated אִתִּי, *with Me*, God, and they will be stored away for the World to Come (*Vilna Gaon*).

הוֹן עָתֵק וּצְדָקָה — *A powerful fortune and righteousness.* This verse advises us not to neglect Torah study in favor of pursuing worldly needs. Once an individual has acquired its wisdom, he will enjoy wealth and honor as well, for it contains all good qualities. When Solomon became king at the young age of twelve, God allowed him to request anything he desired. He requested wisdom. As his reward for choosing wisdom over everything else, God granted him not only wisdom, but wealth and honor as well (*I Kings* 3:11-13). The

Midrash compares this to a king who told his courtier: "Whatever request you make now will be granted." The man reasoned, "Let me make one request that will include everything." He said to the king, "I request your daughter as my wife." So, too, Solomon reasoned that if he had wisdom, he would have everything! (*Meiri*).

The *Vilna Gaon* explains the difference between the two words for righteousness, צֶדֶק and צְדָקָה. צֶדֶק means that a person is given only what he deserves according to the attribute of justice, whereas צְדָקָה means that he will be provided with his needs whether he is deserving or not. Thus our verse indicates that in the merit of his Torah study, a person will be treated with צְדָקָה, i.e., he will be supplied with all his needs, regardless of whether he merits them or not.

Malbim explains that the rewards of Torah study are true and everlasting. Though wealth is usually transitory, the wealth of Torah knowledge is הוֹן עָתֵק, an *enduring fortune*, which will accompany the person even in the World to Come. The honor he will earn through Torah is attained בִּצְדָקָה, *through righteous actions.* Consequently, it will also endure and remain with him in the Hereafter.

Metzudos explains the word צְדָקָה differently. The wealth attained by one who studies Torah will be given to him as צְדָקָה, *charity.* In other words, God will bless him with great fortune in this world without diminishing his eternal reward in the Hereafter (see citation from R' Aharon Kotler in commentary to 10:22).

19. טוֹב פִּרְיִי מֵחָרוּץ וּמִפָּז — *My fruits are better than refined gold, even fine gold. My fruits* refers to the reward for Torah

1. The Sages (*Avos* 6:1) seem to echo the theme of verses 14-18, stating: Whoever engages in Torah study for its own sake merits many things ... From him people enjoy counsel and wisdom, understanding and strength, as it said: "*Mine are counsel and wisdom I am binah, mine is strength*" (v. 14). [The Torah] gives him kingship and dominion, and analytical judgment (see vs. 15-16), and the secrets of Torah are revealed to him.

and those who search for me shall find me. [18] *Riches and honor are with me, a powerful fortune and righteousness.* [19] *My fruits are better than refined gold, even fine gold, and my produce [better than] choice silver.* [20] *I will lead in the path of righteousness, amid the pathways of justice.*

(*Metzudos*), which is more valuable than the finest gold.[1]

Why is it that the righteous may not enjoy wealth and honor in this world, despite the promise of the previous verse? The *Vilna Gaon* explains the since the rewards of the World to Come are far greater than the best pleasures of this world, the righteous prefer that even the *fruits* — i.e., the part of their reward that can be awarded in this world; see *Shabbos* 127a — should be saved for the World to Come. This is comparable to a traveler who passed through a country where iron was expensive and gold, cheap. The astute traveler took advantage of this opportunity by exchanging iron for gold, and hoarding it carefully. He scrimped on his own needs rather than spend any of his valuable treasure. When he returned home, he brought a fortune in gold with him from all that he had saved.

So it is with the righteous. They realize that they are just "traveling through" this world; they work hard amassing a fortune of Torah and good deeds here, living frugally in this world, for they know that *My fruits* — i.e., even the smallest part of their reward for keeping the Torah — surpasses the finest which symbolizes the finest pleasures of this world. They save their wealth to enjoy it in the World to Come.

וּתְבוּאָתִי מִכֶּסֶף נִבְחָר — *And my produce [better than] choice silver.* Produce refers to *binah*, understanding. Just as a man plants wheat and brings forth its produce through his labors, so too, an individual attains understanding by delving into the Torah's wisdom (*Vilna Gaon*).

20. בְּאֹרַח־צְדָקָה אֲהַלֵּךְ — *I will lead in the path of righteousness.* The translation follows *Metzudos*. According to the *Vilna Gaon*, צְדָקָה refers to doing kind deeds for all people. Thus, wisdom states: If a person goes on a path of kindliness, then I will go on this person's path.

בְּתוֹךְ נְתִיבוֹת מִשְׁפָּט — *Amid the pathways of justice.* A person who wants to acquire wisdom must follow the path of righteousness and justice. The verse stresses *amid* the pathways, because a person must choose the middle road, and veer neither to the right nor to the left (*Ibn Ezra*).

Malbim explains this verse as describing two ways in which God treats the righteous. When He metes out *justice*, He gives them exactly what they deserve, each individual according to his own merits. Therefore, the term associated with *justice* is נְתִיבוֹת, the small byways traversed by an individual, because each person is dealt with individually. However, when God dispenses צְדָקָה (which *Malbim* interprets as undeserved goodness), He bestows kindness beyond what individuals have earned. His charity does not depend on each individual's deeds. Thus, the channel associated with charity is אֹרַח, a broader path upon which many travel.

1. There is a similar comparison in *Psalms* 19:11, where David extols the value of the Torah's dictates over earthly treasures, declaring, הַנֶּחֱמָדִים מִזָּהָב וּמִפַּז רָב, *They are more desirable than gold — than even much fine gold. Ibn Ezra* (ad loc.) explains that people desire gold and precious stones, for they are durable and of undiminishing value, but the Torah surpasses them, for Torah learning will stand by a person not only in this world, but in the World to Come. *Radak* (ad loc.) points out that precious possessions can be stolen or lost, but nothing can deprive man of his Torah knowledge. When a person spends his money, it is no longer his; but when he shares his Torah with others, his own resources are not depleted, and the very process of teaching his students makes him wiser (see 3:14-15).

כא לְהַנְחִיל אֹהֲבַי ׀ יֵשׁ וְאֹצְרֹתֵיהֶם אֲמַלֵּא:
כב יְהוָֹה קָנָנִי רֵאשִׁית דַּרְכּוֹ קֶדֶם מִפְעָלָיו מֵאָז:

21. יֵשׁ אֹהֲבַי לְהַנְחִיל — *I have what to bequeath [to] those who love me.* I have with Me a great inheritance to give those who love Me (*Rashi*).[1] This refers to the tremendous good awaiting the righteous in the Hereafter (*R' Bachya*).

Wisdom declares: True benefit does not accrue from gold and riches; it is the fruit of wisdom (v. 19). As stated in the previous verse, wisdom leads people on the ways of duty and justice (v. 20), thus bringing its followers to the only valuable inheritance, and filling their storehouses with the treasures of truth (*R' Hirsch*).

וְאֹצְרֹתֵיהֶם אֲמַלֵּא — *And I shall fill their storehouses.* The *Chafetz Chaim* comments that when a mortal invites others to share in his bounty, the size of each guest's share is diminished as the numbers of participants increase. However, this is not true of Heavenly good. The reward of the righteous in *Gan Eden* does not lessen as the number of righteous increase. No matter how many people are deserving of eternal reward, God declares: אֹצְרֹתֵיהֶם אֲמַלֵּא, *I shall fill their storehouses,* and everyone will still receive his full measure of good.[2]

In this sense, *Gan Eden* is comparable to the courtyard of the Holy Temple, where there was always room for the hundreds of thousands of Jews who came to Jerusalem on each festival (*Avos* 5:7). Just as God is unbounded by space, His dwelling place is not limited by physical constraints.

The word יֵשׁ can also be explained as *an everlasting possession,* one that is acquired for eternity (*Ibn Ezra*).

Quoting this verse, the Sages (*Avos* 5:22) explain the difference between the disciples of our forefather Abraham and the disciples of the wicked Balaam. The disciples of our forefather Abraham enjoy

1. The *Chafetz Chaim* wonders why there is a need to reassure the righteous who love God that He has enough resources to reward them adequately. He explains that this is an indication of the enormity of the reward awaiting those who study Torah — so great is the reward that one might wonder if even God Himself, as it were, has sufficient resources to provide it to all those who devote themselves to such study. To study each individual word of Torah is a *mitzvah* unto itself, with its own commensurate reward. The term *those who love Me* describes those who study Torah constantly. Each word of their Torah study creates another angel who will greet them and reward them in the Hereafter. In one day of Torah study alone, they accumulate thousands and thousands of merits. Should one doubt that the Holy One, Blessed is He, can settle the account of the immeasurable words of their Torah study, this verse reassures us, יֵשׁ, God indeed has the ability to do so. Since God is infinite, He can allot infinite good to the righteous in the World to Come.

In this respect, we see how greatly God's power differs from that of a mortal king. If the latter were to find all his subjects deserving, he could not possibly reward them all. Even if he were fabulously wealthy, any reward he allocated would be minuscule if he divided his fortune among everyone. Furthermore, he can reward only those subjects who are alive; those who have died are beyond his realm of reward. On the other hand, God has infinite capacity to reward, even if the whole world were to be righteous. He can create many more worlds, as an inheritance for the deserving. (See *mishnah* from *Uktzin*, cited below.) And even after the righteous have died, God continues to reward them in the Hereafter.

2. This verse also reassures Torah scholars who fear that they will have less eternal reward because poverty prevents them from dispensing charity. God will fill their treasuries with the reward even for these unperformed *mitzvos*. They deserve this reward, because their poverty is a great benefit to the world at large, since everyone else receives sustenance in the merit of their suffering. The Talmud (*Berachos* 17b) relates that the whole world was sustained in the merit of R' Chanina ben Dosa, whereas he himself had only a small measure of carob to eat for the entire week. God credits the account of the righteous with the benefits they bring to others, benefits that surpass those of even the most generous benefactors (*Chafetz Chaim*).

²¹ *I have what to bequeath [to] those who love me, and I shall fill their storehouses.*

²² *HASHEM made me at the beginning of His way, before His deeds*

[the fruits of their good deeds] in this world and inherit the World to Come, as is said: *I have an everlasting possession [the World to Come] to bequeath to those who love Me, and I shall fill their storehouses [in this world].*

Based on the numerical value of the word יֵשׁ, which is 310, the Sages (*Uktzin* 3:12) teach: In the future, the Holy One, Blessed is He, will cause each of the righteous to inherit three hundred and ten worlds.[1]

◂§ The Torah preceded everything; it is the blueprint of Creation

The following group of verses (22-29) emphasizes the primacy of Torah. The speaker in these verses is Wisdom/Torah, describing how it preceded all stages of Creation. Torah is thus the essence of all that is created; the manifold facets of the universe are but manifestations of the Torah's wisdom.

To assume that the commandments are nothing more than Heavenly guidelines necessary to direct and maintain civilization is a great error. The commandments of the Torah were not promulgated to conform to the needs of society; rather, it is society that was created to conform to the dictates of Torah. The commandment to honor one's parents, for example, is not imposed upon the child because this is his duty to his elders. Rather, God ordained that children be born of parents so that they may perform the commandment of *Honor your father and your mother* (*Exodus* 20:12, cf. 3:12). It follows, then, that the continuity of Creation is contingent upon man's adherence to the Torah.

22. ה' קָנָנִי רֵאשִׁית דַּרְכּוֹ — *HASHEM made me at the beginning of His way.* God created the Torah before He created the world (*Rashi*). [Literally, קָנָנִי means *acquired me.* By creating something, God acquires it. See *Genesis* 14:19, *Rashi* ad loc.]

Torah served as a blueprint for the entire creation (see v. 30). The Sages teach הָיָה הקב"ה מַבִּיט בַּתּוֹרָה וּבוֹרֵא אֶת הָעוֹלָם, *The Holy One, Blessed is He, looked into the Torah and created the world* (*Bereishis Rabbah* 1:2). The Torah begins with the words, בְּרֵאשִׁית בָּרָא, which may be interpreted to mean, *With the Torah* [which is called רֵאשִׁית, *beginning*], *God created heaven and earth* (*Eitz Yosef* ad loc.; cf. *Rashi, Genesis* 1:1). Every detail of Creation followed a master plan designed and executed for one purpose — the Torah. (See 3:19-20.)

קֶדֶם מִפְעָלָיו מֵאָז — *Before His deeds of yore.* The Talmud (*Pesachim* 54a) teaches that seven things antedated Creation:

---

1. The commentators on the *mishnah* address the question of why the righteous are promised specifically three hundred and ten worlds as a reward.

Tosafos Yom Tov explains that in the past, the nation of Israel inherited the land of seven out of seventy nations — a mere tenth. In the future they will inherit ten times as much, for they will be the moral rulers of all the nations of the world. Similarly, when conquering the Land of Israel in the time of Joshua, the Jews overpowered and killed thirty-one kings. Since their future conquests will be ten times greater, they will then inherit a total of three hundred and ten worlds.

Alternatively, there are six hundred and thirteen commandments in Torah, and seven Rabbinic commandments, which total six hundred and twenty. God gives the righteous one world for each commandment they observe. However, this *mishnah* mentions that they will receive three hundred and ten, rather than six hundred and twenty worlds of reward, because the remaining three hundred and ten worlds belong to their wives, who deserve an equal share of their husband's reward in the World to Come (*Zechus Avos*).

Ezor Eliyahu comments homiletically that the word יְשֵׁשָׁכָר can be read יֵשׁ שָׂכָר, *there are three hundred ten worlds of reward* [שָׂכָר] *awaiting those who study Torah.* [Issachar was the tribe that personified total dedication to Torah study.]

כג-כד מֵעוֹלָם נִסַּכְתִּי מֵרֹאשׁ מִקַּדְמֵי־אָרֶץ: בְּאֵין־
תְּהֹמוֹת חוֹלָלְתִּי בְּאֵין מַעְיָנוֹת נִכְבַּדֵּי־מָיִם:
כה בְּטֶרֶם הָרִים הָטְבָּעוּ לִפְנֵי גְבָעוֹת חוֹלָלְתִּי:
כו עַד־לֹא עָשָׂה אֶרֶץ וְחוּצוֹת וְרֹאשׁ עָפְרוֹת תֵּבֵל:
כז בַּהֲכִינוֹ שָׁמַיִם שָׁם אָנִי בְּחֻקוֹ חוּג עַל־פְּנֵי
כח תְהוֹם: בְּאַמְּצוֹ שְׁחָקִים מִמָּעַל בַּעֲזוֹז עִינוֹת
כט תְהוֹם: בְּשׂוּמוֹ לַיָּם ׀ חֻקּוֹ וּמַיִם לֹא יַעַבְרוּ־פִיו

Torah, repentance, the Garden of Eden, *Gehinnom*, the Throne of Glory, the Holy Temple and the name of the Messiah. Our verse, HASHEM *made me at the beginning of His way*, is cited to prove that the Torah preceded the Creation.

According to the Midrash (*Bereishis Rabbah* 1:5), six things preceded Creation; of these the Torah and the Throne of Glory were created before the world, but the others existed only in His thought before Creation. Which of these two, Torah or the Throne of Glory, was created first? The answer lies in the verses themselves. With reference to the Throne of Glory, the verse states, נָכוֹן כִּסְאֲךָ מֵאָז, *Your throne was established from times of yore* (*Psalms* 93:2). However, regarding Torah, our verse states, **before** *His deeds of yore*, i.e., the Torah preceded the Throne of Glory, which was created *in times of yore.*

The Sages single out five possessions that God acquired for Himself in His world (*Avos* 6:10). The first of these is the Torah, as taught by our verse.[1]

23. מֵעוֹלָם נִסַּכְתִּי מֵרֹאשׁ מִקַּדְמֵי־אָרֶץ — *I have reigned since the distant past: from the beginning, from before [there was] the earth.* As one of the seven creations that preceded the creation of the world, the Torah's wisdom reigned from before Creation (*Metzudos*).

24. בְּאֵין־תְּהֹמוֹת חוֹלָלְתִּי בְּאֵין מַעְיָנוֹת נִכְבַּדֵּי־מָיִם — *When there were no depths, I was formed; when there were no springs rich with water.* [King Solomon now delineates the various stages of Creation which the Torah preceded — the sources of water (here and v. 28), the mountains (v. 25), land (v. 26), the heavens and the earth (v. 27), and the division of earth into land and sea (v. 29).]

Wisdom reigned and set guidelines for Creation even before the elements were separated (*Malbim*).

25. בְּטֶרֶם הָרִים הָטְבָּעוּ לִפְנֵי גְבָעוֹת חוֹלָלְתִּי — *Before mountains were settled, before hills, I was formed.* Wisdom was created before the mountains were sunk into the water (*Rashi*).[2]

26. עַד־לֹא עָשָׂה אֶרֶץ וְחוּצוֹת — *When He had not yet made the earth and [its] environs.* Rashi explains that אֶרֶץ refers to *the Land of Israel,* and חוּצוֹת to *all other lands.*

וְרֹאשׁ עָפְרוֹת תֵּבֵל — *Or the first dust of the [inhabited] world.* תֵּבֵל refers to the portion of the earth which is inhabited by man. Wisdom was formed before God made even the *first dust* of the inhabited part of earth (*Metzudos*).

Rashi explains that עָפְרוֹת תֵּבֵל, *the dust of inhabited land,* refers to the creation of

---

1. *Midrash Shmuel* explains that categorizing these five items as God's possessions shows us how important they are to him. Just as a person spends money to buy something that is dear to him, so God, so to speak, acquired these specific items for they are precious to Him.

2. The word טָבַע, literally *sunk into,* is related to טֶבַע, *the natural instincts* ingrained in a person from birth, and מַטְבֵּעַ, *a coin,* which has a form embedded on it (*Chevel Nachalah*). Thus all of the natural laws of Creation, from the physical to the instinctual, were ingrained into the earth and all living beings from the time of Creation.

of yore. ²³ *I have reigned since the distant past: from the beginning, from before [there was] the earth.* ²⁴ *When there were no depths, I was formed; when there were no springs rich with water,* ²⁵ *before mountains were settled, before hills, I was formed;* ²⁶ *when He had not yet made the earth and [its] environs or the first dust of the [inhabited] world.* ²⁷ *When He prepared the heavens, I was there; when He etched out the globe upon the face of the depths;* ²⁸ *when He strengthened the heavens above; when fortifying the wellsprings of the depths;* ²⁹ *when He set for the sea its limit, so that the waters would not transgress His word;*

Adam [whose body was fashioned from the earth].[1]

27. בַּהֲכִינוֹ שָׁמַיִם שָׁם אָנִי — *When He prepared the heavens, I was there.* Wisdom was present at the creation of the heavens, for it had been created before then (*Metzudos*).

בְּחוּקוֹ חוּג עַל־פְּנֵי תְהוֹם — *When He etched out the globe* [lit. *circle*] *upon the face of the depths,* i.e., when God spread the circle of the earth upon the depths, as a boundary that the water cannot overrun (*Rashi*).

In forming the world, God made the laws of Torah inherent in everything. Therefore, a person who looks at the wonders of the world with open eyes will perceive that they were fashioned to facilitate the performance of the Torah's commandments, which serve as the spiritual foundation holding up the structure of Creation. This lesson may be learned not only from living things, but from inanimate objects as well. Each of God's creations is linked to a precept of Divine wisdom. Those who seek it will find this wisdom everywhere, for it is present in all aspects of creation (*Chevel Nachalah*).

28. בְּאַמְּצוֹ שְׁחָקִים מִמָּעַל בַּעֲזוֹז עִינוֹת תְּהוֹם — *When He strengthened the heavens above; when fortifying the wellsprings of the depths.* The Torah was there at all these stages of creation.

29. בְּשׂוּמוֹ לַיָּם חֻקּוֹ וּמַיִם לֹא יַעַבְרוּ־פִיו — *When He set for the sea its limit, so that the waters would not transgress His word* [lit. *His mouth*]. When God established the boundary for the sea, so that the waters would not transgress His word by going further than the limit He ordained for them, wisdom was present (*Metzudos*).

Ibn Ezra quotes the prophet Jeremiah who exhorts the nation of Israel to learn the fear of God from the waters of the ocean, which steadfastly adhere to God's commands: אֲשֶׁר־שַׂמְתִּי חוֹל גְּבוּל לַיָּם חָק־ עוֹלָם וְלֹא־יַעַבְרֶנְהוּ, *That I have set sand as boundary against the sea, as a permanent law that cannot be broken* [i.e., its boundary of sand] (*Jeremiah* 5:22).

According to *Rashi*, when God created the Sea of Reeds, He stipulated that it must split at Moshe's command.[1]

1. This may be understood in light of the verse describing the creation of Adam, וַיִּיצֶר ה' אֱלֹהִים אֶת־הָאָדָם עָפָר מִן־הָאֲדָמָה, *And HASHEM God formed the man of dust from the ground* (*Bereishis* 2:7). *Rashi* states that the earth from which man was created was gathered from the four corners of the earth. This was to assure that no matter where man died, the earth would accept his body for burial and preserve it for the future Resurrection of the Dead.

2. The Sages derive this same teaching from a passage in the Torah. After Israel had crossed through the Sea of Reeds, וַיָּשָׁב הַיָּם לִפְנוֹת בֹּקֶר לְאֵיתָנוֹ, *and towards morning the water went back to its power* (*Exodus* 14:27). The letters of the word לְאֵיתָנוֹ, *to its power,* can be rearranged to form the word לִתְנָאוֹ, *to its stipulation* — the stipulation that God had made with the Sea of Reeds at Creation, that it would split for the nation of Israel (*Baal HaTurim* ibid.).

Or HaChaim (ibid.) explains that the condition God imposed upon the Sea applies to all of Creation. God stipulated that all creatures must be subordinate to the Torah and those who toil

לֹ בְּחוּקוֹ מוֹסְדֵי אָרֶץ: וָאֶהְיֶה אֶצְלוֹ אָמוֹן וָאֶהְיֶה
שַׁעֲשֻׁעִים יוֹם ׀ יוֹם מְשַׂחֶקֶת לְפָנָיו בְּכָל־עֵת:
לֹא מְשַׂחֶקֶת בְּתֵבֵל אַרְצוֹ וְשַׁעֲשֻׁעַי אֶת־בְּנֵי אָדָם:
לֹב-לֹג וְעַתָּה בָנִים שִׁמְעוּ־לִי וְאַשְׁרֵי דְּרָכַי יִשְׁמֹרוּ: שִׁמְעוּ
לֹד מוּסָר וַחֲכָמוּ וְאַל־תִּפְרָעוּ: אַשְׁרֵי אָדָם שֹׁמֵעַ לִי

בְּחוּקוֹ מוֹסְדֵי אָרֶץ — *When He forged the foundations of the earth.* Wisdom was present when God set the foundations of the earth (*Metzudos*).

30. וָאֶהְיֶה אֶצְלוֹ אָמוֹן — *I was a nursling beside Him.* The Torah was like God's beloved child, nurtured by Him and His source of constant delight (*Metzudos*).

The word אָמוֹן is from the word אוֹמֵן, *one who rears a child.* The Midrash (*Bereishis Rabbah* 1:2) relates the word אָמוֹן to כְּלֵי אוּמָנוּת, *tools of a trade*; i.e., the Torah was the craftsman's tool through which God fashioned the world. Just as a king builds his palace according to the directives of his architect who, in turn, follows his blueprints, so, too, God, so to speak, followed the blueprint of Torah in designing the world (see v. 22).

וָאֶהְיֶה שַׁעֲשֻׁעִים יוֹם יוֹם — *I was then [His] delight every day.* According to *Rashi*, יוֹם יוֹם means *two thousand years,* i.e., the Torah preceded the creation of the world by two thousand years [during which it alone was God's *delight*]. This interpretation is in accordance with the verse: כִּי אֶלֶף שָׁנִים בְּעֵינֶיךָ כְּיוֹם אֶתְמוֹל, *For even a thousand years are in Your eyes like a bygone yesterday* (Psalms 90:4). Since God regards a thousand years as but a single day, then two days would be two millennia. Thus the Torah preceded the

creation of the world by two thousand years (*Bereishis Rabbah* 8:2).[1]

מְשַׂחֶקֶת לְפָנָיו בְּכָל־עֵת — *Playing before Him at all times.* The Heavenly pleasure with the Torah refers to its hidden secrets, which are beyond the comprehension of mortals. However, it brings rejoicing not only to Heavenly spheres, for the Torah can be understood by flesh-and-blood creatures as well, although on a different level. Since the Torah encompasses all levels of wisdom, it brings happiness both in heaven and on earth (see following verse) (*Ohel Yaakov*).

[This verse stresses the importance of the Torah, by showing how much it is cherished by the Master of the Universe. Verse 31 continues the thought, explaining that the Torah should be cherished by mankind as well.]

31. מְשַׂחֶקֶת בְּתֵבֵל אַרְצוֹ — *Playing in the inhabited areas of His world.* The Torah brings happiness and rejoicing to the inhabitants of the earth (*Metzudos*).

Originally, the Torah was only in the Heavens (v. 30-28). Then Moses brought it down to people on earth, where it brought rejoicing to man (*Yalkut Shimoni*).

R' Shimon bar Yochai interprets תֵבֵל אַרְצוֹ homiletically. He relates תֵבֵל to the word תַבְלִין, *a spice.* Thus, *His land, Eretz Yisrael,* is especially seasoned with every-

in it. He decreed that their authority over Creation is tantamount to His own authority, for everything is through the power of the Torah. [Through Torah study and prayer, the righteous can change nature, because they represent the power of the Torah which preceded everything and was the blueprint of Creation. Thus, all creatures are subordinate to the Torah and those who embody it.]

1. The Torah is composed entirely of Divine Names formed by different combinations of its letters and words (see *Ramban's* introduction to the Torah). The *Vilna Gaon* explains that the Torah had this form for the two thousand years that it predated Creation. Once the world was created and the Torah was given to Israel, God divided the letters and words in such a way as to delineate the commandments needed for man. From then on the hidden meanings were reserved only for those who are qualified and deserving to know them.

when He forged the foundations of the earth; 30 I was a nursling beside Him, I was then [His] delight every day, playing before Him at all times, 31 playing in the inhabited areas of His world, my delights are with mankind.

32 And now, children, listen to me; praiseworthy are those who heed my ways. 33 Hearken to discipline and grow wise, and do not reject [wisdom]. 34 Praiseworthy is a person who listens to me,

thing good. Unlike other lands that may be blessed with certain resources but lacking in others, God will see to it that when His nation lives in the land according to His will, *you will lack nothing there* (*Deuteronomy* 8:9).

וְשַׁעֲשֻׁעַי אֶת־בְּנֵי אָדָם — *My delights are with mankind* [lit. *children of man*]. *Rashi* renders מְשַׂחֶקֶת as *laughing at*. The Torah laughed at all the wicked generations from Adam until Noah and from Noah until Abraham.

The Torah waited expectantly for the Generation of the Wilderness, which would receive the Torah [and delight in it] (*Rashi*). Mankind is delighted with the Torah, and the Torah with mankind (*Metzudos*).

The Torah rejoices with mankind, for in every generation there are at least thirty-six righteous men; there is even someone capable of attaining the stature of Moses. No matter how neglected the Torah may seem to be, there are always those who honor it, follow its dictates and treasure its words (*Chevel Nachalah*).

◄§ Be wise: Follow the Torah and its teachings

After depicting the Torah's effect on the cosmos, wisdom now addresses mankind. For the remainder of the chapter, wisdom addresses its "children," calling upon them to adhere to its teachings.

32. וְעַתָּה בָנִים שִׁמְעוּ־לִי וְאַשְׁרֵי דְּרָכַי יִשְׁמֹרוּ — *And now, children, listen to me; praiseworthy are those who heed my ways.* Since I, wisdom, am of such vital impor-

tance, it is only fitting that you should listen to me; and those who heed my ways are fortunate (*Metzudos*).

Children refers to the Jewish people, who are called God's children (*Deuteronomy* 14:1). *Praiseworthy are those who heed my ways* refers both to Jews who observe the Torah's commandments, and to non-Jews who follow the moral and ethical teachings of Torah (*R' Chaim Shmulevitz*).

33. שִׁמְעוּ מוּסָר וַחֲכָמוּ וְאַל־תִּפְרָעוּ — *Hearken to discipline and grow wise, and do not reject [wisdom].* Do not nullify the words of my discipline (*Rashi*).

A person must first heed discipline and become God fearing; only then will he be able to acquire the Torah's wisdom, for then his fear of God will prevent him from nullifying Torah's wisdom (*Metzudos*).

Ibn Ezra stresses that the study of discipline must precede that of wisdom. This order must not be reversed, as the verse states, וְאַל תִּפְרָעוּ, *do not nullify mussar/ discipline* as a prerequisite to embarking upon the study of wisdom. He quotes the Sages: כֹּל שֶׁיִּרְאַת חֶטְאוֹ קוֹדֶמֶת לְחָכְמָתוֹ, חָכְמָתוֹ מִתְקַיֶּמֶת, *Anyone whose fear of sin takes priority to his wisdom, his wisdom will endure* (*Avos* 3:11). [See 1:7.]

The *Vilna Gaon* explains that once you have studied both wisdom and discipline, אַל תִּפְרָעוּ, *do not nullify* them, i.e., make sure to put both into practice. *R' Hirsch* renders, אַל תִּפְרָעוּ, as *Do not become unruly*, for this is what happens when wisdom and discipline are neglected.[1]

---

1. In the words of *R' Hirsch*: The call of אַל תִּפְרָעוּ reverberates from heaven to earth and rebounds to the heavens. The deeper and more penetrating one's quest for knowledge becomes, the more distinctly the echo of אַל תִּפְרָעוּ is heard: *Do not be unruly; do not go against the rules. Do not take pride in unrestrained behavior.*

Look around you; only by unswerving obedience to a higher law has everything in nature

לִשְׁקֹד עַל־דַּלְתֹתַי יוֹם | יוֹם לִשְׁמֹר מְזוּזֹת
לה פְּתָחָי: כִּי מֹצְאִי °מֹצְאֵי חַיִּים וַיָּפֶק רָצוֹן מֵיהוָה:
לו וְחֹטְאִי חֹמֵס נַפְשׁוֹ כָּל־מְשַׂנְאַי אָהֲבוּ מָוֶת:

34. אַשְׁרֵי אָדָם שֹׁמֵעַ לִי לִשְׁקֹד־עַל־דַּלְתֹתַי יוֹם
יוֹם — *Praiseworthy is a man who listens to me, to be constantly at my doors every day.* Rashi explains לִשְׁקֹד as *to watch*, i.e. to constantly be there. A person should regularly be the first to enter the halls of Torah and the last to leave. *Ibn Ezra's* rendering is similar. According to *Metzudos* לִשְׁקֹד means *to hasten.* (This is similar to *Jeremiah* (1:12): כִּי־שֹׁקֵד אֲנִי, *for I hasten.*) Wisdom praises the person who hurries to the house of Torah [and is constantly involved in its study].

The Sages point out that those who constantly frequent the houses of prayer and Torah study will merit long life. The Talmud (*Berachos* 8a) relates that when R' Yochanan heard that there were old Jews living in Babylon he was surprised. R' Yochanan said that the Torah promises longevity only in the Land of Israel as the verse states: לְמַעַן יִרְבּוּ יְמֵיכֶם וִימֵי בְנֵיכֶם עַל הָאֲדָמָה אֲשֶׁר נִשְׁבַּע ה׳ לַאֲבֹתֵיכֶם, *In order to prolong your days and the days of your children upon the land that* HASHEM *has sworn to your forefathers* (Deuteronomy 11:21), i.e., only in the Land of Israel! However, when R' Yochanan was told that these Jews constantly frequented the house of prayer, rising early and staying late (to attend the morning and evening services), he responded, "This is what makes them deserving of long life, for so

did R' Yehoshua ben Levi instruct his sons: 'Come early to the house of prayer and stay late so that you will lengthen your lives.'" This teaching is implied by the juxtaposition of this verse with the next (v. 35) which states: *For one who finds me has found life.*

לִשְׁמֹר מְזוּזֹת פְּתָחָי — *To guard the doorposts of my entrances.* Just as a watchman is constantly at his post, so too, a person should be constantly sitting within the portals of the study house of Torah (*Metzudos*).

Wisdom praises those who show a special eagerness to frequent the study halls of Torah. They can be compared to a merchant who comes to the palace gates to sell his wares. The official in charge is occupied with other matters, so the merchant is left waiting outside. However, he eagerly waits at the gates, anticipating that at any moment he may be called and he may reap a huge profit. So too, a true servant of God eagerly stands watch at Torah's gate, waiting to seize any opportunity that may arise for him to serve God (*Yerios HaOhel*).[1]

35. כִּי מֹצְאִי מָצָא חַיִּים — *For one who finds me has found life.* One who finds Torah will obtain a blessing of חַיִּים, *life,* both for his body and for his soul (*Ibn Ezra*).[2]

come about. Whether observing the tiniest cell multiplication, or calculating the mightiest galaxy, everything in the world testifies to the fact that only by observing the laws governing them do natural entities find the energy needed for their existence and perpetuation.

Of all things created, man alone has been ennobled by spirit and will, bestowed so that he may gain the wisdom of God's law. While everything else follows God's law automatically and unconsciously, man may fulfill it by the free determination of his will.

1. The *Chiddushei HaRim* explains that we must be ready when God provides an opportunity to serve Him. When a gate opens, one must hasten to enter, as King David said, *Open for me the gates of righteousness*, and immediately afterward he said, *I will enter them and thank God* (Psalms 118:19).

2. The Sages tell of an elderly woman who complained to R' Yose ben Chalafta that she did not want to live any longer, for life had become repulsive. He asked her how she merited such longevity, to which she replied that even if she was busy with something very dear, she would leave it and go to the house of prayer every morning. R' Yose advised her not to go to the house

to be constantly at my doors every day, to guard the doorposts of my entrances. ³⁵ *For one who finds me has found life and he has elicited favor from HASHEM.* ³⁶ *But one who sins against me despoils his soul; all who hate me love death.*

וַיָּפֶק רָצוֹן מֵה' — *And he has elicited favor from HASHEM.* God will be pleased with him (*Metzudos*) and will help him with whatever he desires (*Ralbag*).

36. וְחֹטְאִי חֹמֵס נַפְשׁוֹ — *But one who sins against me despoils his soul.* Someone who despises wisdom is in essence robbing his own soul, for he is destroying it (*Metzudos*).

Ibn Ezra explains that the word חֹטְאִי can also mean *one who misses a target.* [We find this meaning in the verse, קֹלֵעַ בָּאֶבֶן אֶל־הַשַּׂעֲרָה וְלֹא יַחֲטִא, *who could sling a stone at a hair and not miss* (Judges 20:16).] It would thus be the opposite of מֹצְאִי, one *who finds me*, mentioned in the previous verse.

כָּל־מְשַׂנְאַי אָהֲבוּ מָוֶת — *All who hate me love death.* Since the Torah brings life, it follows that those who hate wisdom must love death (*Malbim*).

According to *Ibn Ezra*, חֹטְאִי refers to one who studies the Torah but misses the mark, by understanding it incorrectly. Consequently, חֹמֵס נַפְשׁוֹ, *he despoils his soul*, of the truth. מְשַׂנְאַי, *those who hate me*, however, are those who hate the Torah and refuse to study it altogether.

The Sages explain that מְשַׂנְאַי, *those who hate me*, can also be interpreted as מַשְׂנִיאַי, *those who cause me [the Torah] to be hated by others.* This refers to a Torah scholar who behaves in a manner that arouses disgust in the eyes of others and causes them to disparage his Torah knowledge. As an example, the Talmud says: A Torah sage who has a grease stain on his garment deserves death, as is said, *All those who hate me love death.* Do not read the word *those who hate me*, but rather *those who cause me to be hated* (Shabbos 114a).

IX

In the first six verses of this chapter, King Solomon describes a feast prepared by a wise woman. She sets up her house (verse 1), prepares food (verse 2) and invites guests to partake of her meal (verses 3-4). She addresses her guests and guides them on the path of life (verses 5-6). In the second part of the chapter, we find a similar feast hosted by a foolish woman (verses 13-17). However, the manner in which her invitations are extended, the fare served at her meal and the message conveyed to her guests differ radically from those of the wise woman.

R' Bachya explains that these verses contrast the benefit to those who follow the *chochmah* of Torah on the one hand with, on the other hand, the enticements of idol-worship, which ensnare the individual and lead him to his death.

According to *Meiri*, these verses are the conclusion to the themes set forth in the previous two chapters. Chapter 7 presented the potent power of the adulteress to draw a person to sin, and Chapter 8 spoke of the virtues of *chochmah* and its positive influence. This chapter restates the two positions, as a judge does when he summarizes and restates the case of the two litigants before him prior to issuing his verdict.

Other commentators understand the opening metaphors of this chapter as referring to the creation of the world (*Rashi*) and the structure of the Torah (*Rashi, Vilna Gaon, Malbim*).

of prayer for three consecutive days. The woman followed R' Yose's advice, and on the third day she died. This was in accordance with verses 34-35: *Praiseworthy is the person who listens to me . . . For one who finds me has found life* (*Midrash Yilamdeinu*).

א חָכְמוֹת בָּנְתָה בֵיתָהּ חָצְבָה עַמּוּדֶיהָ שִׁבְעָה:
ב טָבְחָה טִבְחָהּ מָסְכָה יֵינָהּ אַף עָרְכָה שֻׁלְחָנָהּ:
ג שָׁלְחָה נַעֲרֹתֶיהָ תִקְרָא עַל־גַּפֵּי מְרֹמֵי קָרֶת:

⊷ The wise woman prepares

1. חָכְמוֹת בָּנְתָה בֵיתָהּ — *Wisdom has built her house.* The syntax of the phrase is difficult, since חָכְמוֹת, *chochmos,* the subject, is plural, i.e., many forms of wisdom, but the verb, בָּנְתָה, *has built,* is singular. *Meiri* renders, *each one of the chochmos has built her house.* Alternatively, *wisdom* is referred to in the plural for the Torah encompasses all types of wisdom.

Alshich explains the plural as a reference to the Written and Oral Torah. Thus, it follows that the world was created through the combined power of the Written and Oral Torah. It is only through those people who engross themselves in the study of Torah that the world can continue to exist.

Metaphorically, this verse teaches that wisdom has everything arranged in an orderly fashion. Just as a builder must plan and arrange the construction of an edifice — first laying the foundation, then constructing the building's walls, and then adding the upper floors and finally the roof — so, too, one must study the Torah's teachings in the correct order (*Meiri*).

חָצְבָה עַמּוּדֶיהָ שִׁבְעָה — *She carved out her seven pillars.* The house is built on many pillars — "seven" is idiomatic for "many" (*Ralbag*) — each of which is carved exactly like the other, something quite appealing to behold (*Metzudos*).

Rashi explains: The Holy One, Blessed is He, fashioned the world with wisdom, i.e., Torah (cf. 3:19). The seven pillars of her house symbolize the seven days of Creation.[1]

The *Malbim* elaborates on this metaphor. At the very beginning of Creation, the entire potential of the universe — the "structure of *her house*" — was brought into being יֵשׁ מֵאַיִן, *ex nihilo.* Afterwards, *seven pillars* were carved out, i.e., on each day of the seven days of Creation, the potential of that day was brought to fulfillment and firmly established in its completed form. This is comparable to someone who plants six seeds at a time. Although they were all planted simultaneously, each one sprouts on a different day (see *Genesis* 2:1, *Rashi* and *Sifsei Chachamim*). The creation of the Sabbath, a day without physical activity, is one of the pillars of the world, for it symbolizes the principle that God can suspend the rules of "nature" and run the world miraculously.

Rashi cites an alternate metaphor to this verse. The seven pillars refer to the seven books of (the Written Law of) Torah. This follows the opinion that the Book of *Numbers* is divided into three books, for the two "nuns" surrounding the verses וַיְהִי בִּנְסֹעַ and וּבְנֻחֹה יֹאמַר (*Numbers* 10:35-36) separate them from the rest of *Numbers* and make them into a separate "book" of only two verses. Thus, the verses preceding וַיְהִי בִּנְסֹעַ are one book; these two verses are a second book; and the remaining verses of *Numbers* form a third book (see *Shabbos* 116a, *Rashi* ibid.).

The *Midrash* states that בָּנְתָה בֵיתָהּ, *has built her house,* refers to Torah as a "house," to teach that שֶׁכָּל מִי שֶׁקָּנָה לוֹ דִבְרֵי תוֹרָה קָנָה לוֹ בַּיִת לְעוֹלָם הַבָּא, *everyone who has acquired the words of Torah has acquired a house for himself in the World to Come.*[2]

---

1. The Sabbath is also considered a day of Creation, in the sense that מְנוּחָה, *rest,* was missing until the arrival of *Shabbos* (see *Rashi* to *Genesis* 2:2; see *Sanhedrin* 38a, *Tosafos* ibid.).

2. The *Chafetz Chaim* explains that a person must erect his own spiritual house for his soul through his own efforts; he will not be able to "borrow" it from others in the Hereafter. Only by toiling and laboring to study Torah in this world can one merit this reward in the next. There are, however, two ways to attain a house in this world — a person may either build one himself, or,

¹ Wisdom has built her house; she carved out her seven pillars. ² She prepared her meat, mixed her wine and also set her table. ³ She has sent out her maidens, she announces upon the wings of the city heights:

2. טָבְחָה טִבְחָה מָסְכָה יֵינָה אַף עָרְכָה שֻׁלְחָנָהּ — She prepared [lit. slaughtered] her meat, mixed her wine and also set her table. The term טָבְחָה means both slaughtered and cooked (Ibn Ezra).

She mixed her wine with water, since it was customary to dilute strong wine with water (Rashi).

Continuing the metaphor of Creation, Rashi explains that this refers to the creation of all solids and liquids. According to the Talmud (Sanhedrin 38a), this refers to the oceans and rivers, and all the needs of the world.

The Vilna Gaon and Malbim explain this verse metaphorically as referring to Torah:

According to the Vilna Gaon, prepared her meat refers to the Written Torah, mixed her wine refers to the Mishnah, where many laws mentioned in disparate places in the Pentatuch are "mixed," i.e., combined into one mishnah; and also set her table refers to the Talmud, in which the laws are arrayed like a set table.

According to Malbim, meat refers to חָכְמָה, wisdom, which is the sustenance of the soul; just as food physically sustains life, so wisdom spiritually sustains the heart, so that it will not succumb to the influence of the Evil Inclination. Wine refers to בִּינָה, understanding, for just as wine gladdens the heart and uplifts it, understanding enables a person to derive one thing from another. The set table refers to דַעַת, knowledge, for just as she sets her table with all types of food and sweets, daas includes all types of worldly knowledge.

Wisdom has prepared a full array of testimonies, laws and injunctions, each with its own unique taste, and set them out

in a proper, logical order — one preceding the other, in accordance with proper etiquette (R' Hirsch).

Everything is displayed publicly, and everyone seeking wisdom may come and partake of it (Yalkut HaMachiri).

3. שָׁלְחָה נַעֲרֹתֶיהָ תִקְרָא עַל-גַפֵּי מְרֹמֵי קָרֶת — She has sent out her maidens, she announces upon the wings of the city heights. Wings refers to the high places in the city where birds wing and soar. Through her maidens, wisdom announces at the high places of the city, so that the call will be heard even from afar (Metzudos).

According to Rashi, maidens follows the metaphorical themes of the first verse: They refer either to Adam and Eve (in the analogy to Creation); or, to Moses and Aaron (in the metaphor of the Torah).

Wisdom does not personally invite her guests; she sends messengers. This symbolizes that no individual can attain the Torah's wisdom on his own; he must receive it through the Sages, prophets and teachers, the maidens sent out in every generation to invite the populace to partake of wisdom's "feast" (Malbim).

Yalkut Shimoni quotes several Midrashic applications of these verses:

❑ These verses refer to the future when the Third Temple will be built. Gog, the monarch who will organize an alliance to attack Eretz Yisrael, will be defeated, and for seven years — seven pillars — Israel will burn and destroy the vast amount of ammunition with which its enemies had sought to wage war against it. These years will be a time of feasting for the righteous. Figuratively they will eat the meat, i.e., flesh of the strong warriors; drink the wine, i.e.,

if he is unable to do so, he may purchase one with money. The same two alternatives apply to his house in the World to Come: If he is a Torah scholar, he builds his spiritual abode through his Torah study (see Berachos 64a, אַל תִקְרֵי בָּנָיִךְ אֶלָא בּוֹנָיִךְ, do not read "your children" but your "builders," referring to Torah scholars who build eternity through their own learning). One who cannot learn himself can support Torah scholars and thereby "acquire" their words of Torah, with which he merits a house for his soul in the Hereafter.

ד-ה מִי־פֶּתִי יָסֻר הֵנָּה חֲסַר־לֵב אָמְרָה לּוֹ: לְכוּ לַחֲמוּ
ו בְלַחֲמִי וּשְׁתוּ בְּיַיִן מָסָכְתִּי: עִזְבוּ פְתָאיִם וִחְיוּ וְאִשְׁרוּ
ז בְּדֶרֶךְ בִּינָה: יֹסֵר ׀ לֵץ לֹקֵחַ לוֹ קָלוֹן וּמוֹכִיחַ לְרָשָׁע מוּמוֹ:

blood of the princes; and be satiated from the *table* that will be set before them, i.e., the spoils of the deceased enemy warriors. *Maidens* refers to Ezekiel, who prophesied the downfall of Gog (see *Ezekiel* 39:9, 17-20).

❑ The verses refer to אֹהֶל מוֹעֵד, *the Tent of Meeting*. The wisdom with which the house was built refers to Bezalel, about whom the verse states: וָאֲמַלֵּא אֹתוֹ רוּחַ אֱלֹהִים בְּחָכְמָה, *I have filled him with a Godly spirit, with wisdom* (*Exodus* 31:3). The seven pillars refers to the שִׁבְעַת יְמֵי הַמִּלֻּאִים, *the Seven Days of Inauguration* (*Leviticus* 8), during which *meat was prepared*, i.e., offerings were brought to dedicate the Tabernacle. *Her wine* refers to the wine libations; and the *set table* refers to the Showbread. *The maidens* through whom she calls alludes to Moses, our teacher, as the Torah states: וַיְהִי בַּיּוֹם הַשְּׁמִינִי קָרָא מֹשֶׁה, *It was on the eighth day, Moses summoned* . . . (*Leviticus* 9:1).

❑ These verses refer to the Torah with which God created the world. Then it was "hewn" away from the seven heavens and given to mankind. The Holy One, Blessed is He, states that someone who studies Torah is considered as if he has established the entire world.

❑ These verses refer to Queen Esther who, upon seeing the impending misfortune, arranged a feast for Ahasuerus and the wicked Haman and intoxicated them with wine. Through her deeds, Queen Esther set a table for herself in the World to Come, and in this world — for Purim will never be abolished from the Jewish people's calendar.

⋙§ **She wants to share with others**

4. מִי־פֶּתִי יָסֻר הֵנָּה — *"Whoever is a simpleton, let him turn here!"* He should come to study and become wise (*Rashi*). A person who lacks the sense to prepare his own meal should turn from his place and

come here (to eat from my bread and wine, see next verse). The same call applies to one lacking understanding; wisdom addresses his needs in verses 5-6 (*Metzudos*).

חֲסַר־לֵב אָמְרָה לּוֹ — *As for the one who lacks [an understanding] heart, she says to him:*

A פֶּתִי is a credulous person who wants to do the right thing but is easily enticed. Once he can be persuaded to *turn here*, he will see for himself that Torah is the ultimate good. For the חֲסַר־לֵב, *one who lacks an understanding heart*, however, merely being exposed to the Torah is not enough. He must be spoken to softly and sympatheticaly [אֲמִירָה רַכָּה], to soften his heart and make him receptive to the Torah's message (*Vilna Gaon*).

Malbim explains why a simpleton and one without understanding are invited to this meal. A simpleton is easily swayed because he lacks the basic tenets of wisdom; once he acquires wisdom (the לֶחֶם, *bread*, mentioned in the next verse), he will leave his foolish ways, for the Torah will provide him the shrewdness necessary to outwit his evil impulse (verse 6). *One who lacks [an understanding] heart* knows the principles of wisdom but lacks the moral strength to control his Evil Inclination and overcome his sinful desires. Once he attains understanding (the יַיִן, *wine*, referred to in verse 5) and with his newly acquired insight begins to fathom the depths of wisdom, he will free himself from the Evil Inclination and be able to follow the proper path (verse 6).

5. לְכוּ לַחֲמוּ בְלַחֲמִי וּשְׁתוּ בְּיַיִן מָסָכְתִּי — *"Come, partake of my food [lit. bread] and drink of the wine that I have mixed."* If you do not have your own food, come here and enjoy my bread and wine. In other words, the Torah's wisdom is delightful; it enlightens its students and imparts knowledge to them. All those who so desire should come and study the Torah;

4 *"Whoever is a simpleton, let him turn here!" As for the one who lacks [an understanding] heart, she says to him:* 5 *"Come, partake of my food and drink of the wine that I have mixed.* 6 *Leave [your paths], O simpletons, and live, and stride in the way of understanding."* 7 *One who chastises a scoffer acquires disgrace for himself, and he who rebukes a wicked man, [it is] his blemish.*

even if one lacks sense, the Torah will provide it to him (*Metzudos*).

The Torah is likened to bread, for just as the world cannot exist without bread, it cannot exist without Torah (*Ibn Nachmiash*).

Bread refers to the Written Law, and *wine* to the Oral Law (cf. verse 2). Just as bread is ready to be eaten, so, too, the Written Torah is ready to be studied. The Oral Torah, however, is like wine which must be mixed in order to prepare it for consumption (for a combination of laws from different sources in the Pentateuch may be combined into one *mishnah*; see verse 2). *Chochmah* has already "mixed" and prepared this "wine" (*Vilna Gaon*).

The *Chafetz Chaim* expounds on the concept of bread as a metaphor for Torah. Just as bread provides the physical sustenance for one's body, the words of Torah provide the spiritual sustenance for one's soul. Therefore, a person's attitude towards Torah study should parallel his attitude towards food. A person makes sure to eat at least once each day. Similarly, he must set aside time each day for Torah study.[1] Should one for some reason be unable to eat for a day (e.g., a fast day), he will hasten to make up for it as soon as possible so as not to deplete his strength. In the same vein, if he missed a day of Torah study, he should compensate for it immediately so that he may keep his spiritual strength from waning.

However, someone who abstains from eating for a prolonged period of time no longer feels hunger or a desire for food; he feels only a general, overall weakness. The same effect occurs in the spiritual realm. If one abstains from Torah study for a protracted period, even if he does not do it

willfully, he will lose his innate yearning for spirituality. Subsequently, it will be very difficult for him to resume a normal routine of Torah study. The danger of even the smallest lapse in one's daily Torah study routine can be severely debilitating to his soul.

According to the Midrash, *bread* symbolizes the laws of the Torah and *wine* symbolizes its secrets. [The numerical value of יַיִן, *wine*, and סוֹד, *secret*, both equal seventy (*Bamidbar Rabbah* 10:21).

[This verse alludes to wisdom's modesty; while it accomplishes much, it does not boast. Verse 2 described a lavish bouquet of meat and a set table. Yet here, wisdom speaks only of *bread* and *wine*.]

6. עִזְבוּ פְתָאיִם וִחְיוּ וְאִשְׁרוּ בְּדֶרֶךְ בִּינָה — *"Leave [your paths], O simpletons, and live, and stride in the way of understanding."* The translation follows *Rashi*. Alternatively, פְתָאיִם can be rendered as פְּתַיוּת, *foolishness*. Wisdom addresses her guests, saying: "If you want to partake of and enjoy my foods, you must forsake your foolishness" (*Meiri*).

"Leave the company of the unintelligent, and acquire understanding, and live!" (*R' Yaakov Kamenetsky*).

"Immerse yourself in a Torah environment. Constantly frequent the study hall; be content to warm yourself with the insightful thoughts of Torah scholars. Walk towards happiness upon the path of understanding." (The word אִשְׁרוּ, *stride*, is also related to אֶשֶׁר, *happiness* and *good fortune*.) (*R' Yisrael Zev Gustman*).

7. יֹסֵר לֵץ לֹקֵחַ לוֹ קָלוֹן וּמוֹכִיחַ לְרָשָׁע מוּמוֹ — *One who chastises a scoffer acquires disgrace for himself, and he who rebukes a wicked man, [it is] his blemish. Rashi* explains: If one attempts to rebuke a wicked

1. The Talmud (*Shabbos* 31a) teaches us that on the final Day of Judgment, each individual will be asked, קָבַעְתָּ עִתִּים לַתּוֹרָה, *have you designated times for Torah study?*

man, it is considered his blemish, since the latter will not only ignore the rebuke, he will insult whoever tries to correct him. This warning serves as a prohibition against speaking with those who entice others to idol-worship, not even to rebuke them or attempt to draw them nearer to the Torah. Such people are beyond the pale.

Wisdom does not attempt to admonish either the scoffer or the wicked person. By admonishing a scoffer, one disgraces himself, for the scoffer only derides and scorns him in return. By rebuking a wicked person, a person brings a blemish upon himself, for the wicked person responds insultingly, claiming that the reprover is as bad as he is. For these reasons, wisdom has no dealings with such people (*Metzudos*).

The *Vilna Gaon* explains that the לֵץ, *scoffer*, is one who is wicked in his speech; he insults and disgraces his friend. If you attempt to chastise him, he will only bring shame upon you by insulting you. A רָשָׁע, *wicked man*, does wicked deeds. If you rebuke him, you will bring a blemish upon yourself, because he will harm you. יִסֵּר, *one who chastises*, refers to administering physical afflictions to reprimand the person. מוֹכִיחַ, *one who rebukes*, refers to verbal admonishment. The לֵץ, *scoffer*, will disgrace you only if you attempt to chastise him physically, but not if he is rebuked verbally. The רָשָׁע, *wicked man*, however, will harm you even if you have only given him verbal rebuke.

8. אַל־תּוֹכַח לֵץ פֶּן־יִשְׂנָאֶךָ — *Do not rebuke a scoffer, lest he hate you,* for he considers himself to be wise and is convinced that his way is correct (*Metzudos*).

Even though the scoffer does not shame someone who rebukes him verbally, you should refrain from doing so, lest he hate you (*Vilna Gaon*).

הוֹכַח לְחָכָם וְיֶאֱהָבֶךָ — *Rebuke a wise man, and he will love you,* for he wishes to refine his character traits and wants to learn from everyone (*Metzudos*). Even though he is already wise and knows what sin is, you should still rebuke him. This may be compared to the way a woman uses a mirror. She prefers a magnifying mirror, for it makes a blemish more visible and easier to treat or remove, and thus she can perfect her appearance. Similarly, righteous people are happy when others point out and magnify their sins even if they are only the most minute infractions, so that they may purify themselves of every flaw. The more one magnifies their imperfections to the righteous, the more he becomes beloved to them (*Vilna Gaon*).

The Talmud (*Arachin 16b*) relates that R' Yochanan ben Nuri testified that there were many times he caused R' Akiva to be punished, because he would complain to R' Gamliel if he saw any improper action on R' Akiva's part. Yet, he said, "This only increased the love between us."[1]

If rebuke is to successfully effect an improvement in someone's behavior, its words and tone must be palatable and acceptable to the listener. The key to this is the way the reproof is presented. Based on this verse, the *Sh'lah Hakadosh* explains that every person is really a combination of both a לֵץ, *scoffer*, and a חָכָם, *wise man*. אַל־תּוֹכַח לֵץ, *do not rebuke* someone by labeling him *a scoffer,* i.e., by pointing out

---

1. Our Torah sages personified the trait of loving rebuke to such an extent that they sought out people to admonish them, attempting to further perfect their already exemplary conduct.

The *Maharshal*, for example, would hire a wagon driver (who was usually at the lowest rungs of the social ladder) to come and rebuke him. The sage would sit bedecked in his *tallis* and *tefillin* and eagerly drink in the words of rebuke.

The *Vilna Gaon* called the *Dubno Maggid*, R' Yaakov Kranz, to admonish him. Despite the latter's refusal to stand in judgment over such a great and holy man, the *Gaon* insisted that the *Maggid* come. In a letter to the *Maggid*, R' Avraham, the son of the *Vilna Gaon*, writes: "It will be considered a great *mitzvah* for you to revive the soul of our master, our teacher, our rebbe, my father the *gaon*" (see *Ruach Eliyahu*, p. 86).

8 Do not rebuke a scoffer, lest he hate you; rebuke a wise man, and he will love you. 9 Give [wisdom] to a wise man and he will become even wiser; make [wisdom] known to the righteous

his faults and denigrating him, פֶּן־יִשְׂנָאֶךָ, *lest he hate you.* Rather, הוֹכַח לְחָכָם, *rebuke* a person by addressing him as *a wise man,* and treating him with respect, then וְיֶאֱהָבֶךָ, *and he will love you* and accept your admonishment.[1]

This point is further emphasized by R' Chaim of Volozhin, תּוֹכָחָה שֶׁלֹּא לְדָבָר קָשׁוֹת וּדְבָרִים קָשִׁים בְּשׁוּם אֵינָם נִשְׁמָעִין רַק יֵאָמֵר בְּלָשׁוֹן רַכָּה, וְאִם אֵין טִבְעוֹ בְּשׁוּם אוֹפֶן לְדַבֵּר רַכּוֹת, פָּטוּר הוּא מְלְהוֹכִיחַ, *Rebuke takes place when one does not speak harshly, for harsh words are not accepted. Rather, it should be uttered in a gentle tone, and if a person does not have the ability to speak softly, he is absolved from the obligation to rebuke others (Kesser Rosh (113).*

R' Illai, in the name of R' Yehudah bar Shimon, teaches a guideline to be followed when giving admonition: "Just as it is a *mitzvah* for a person to say something which will be accepted, so is it also a *mitzvah* for a person not to say something which will not be accepted. R' Abba derives this from our verse: *Do not rebuke a scoffer"* (Yevamos 65b).[2]

9. תֵּן לְחָכָם וְיֶחְכַּם־עוֹד — *Give [wisdom] to a wise man and he will become even wiser.* Teach a worthy student (*Rashi*), and, through his own understanding, he will become still wiser (*Metzudos*).

Rashi cites an example. God com-

1. This teaching is illustrated by a parable of the sun and the wind, who were arguing with each other as to which was stronger. Each attempted to prove its superiority by how much damage it could cause, but neither emerged victorious, for both could be equally destructive. Finally, a test case was agreed upon: Whichever of the two could strip the traveler walking down the road of his coat would be declared the winner.

The wind took the first turn. It began to blow at the poor traveler, who responded by wrapping his coat more firmly around himself. The more fiercely the wind blew, the more adamantly the wayfarer clung to his coat. Finally, the wind gave up in defeat.

The sun now began to shine. As its warm rays beat down on the traveler, he began to relax his grip on his coat. Beads of perspiration began to form on his brow, until the traveler finally yielded to the pleasant warmth of the noontime sun and removed his coat.

The moral is that what stormy, fierce words of rebuke cannot accomplish, a few well-chosen, gentle, warm words of encouragement can.

Torah scholars were adroit at applying this principle to their students, as illustrated by the following incident. The *Alter of Slobodka* admonished a student, saying, "You are killing R' Meir Simchah of Dvinsk (author of *Or Sameach* and *Meshech Chochmah*)!" The student was taken aback, until the *Alter* explained: "You have the potential to become a leading Torah sage of the caliber of R' Meir Simchah. By not applying yourself to your Torah studies with your full capabilities, you are killing that potential in you!" (heard from *Rabbi Mordechai Gifter*).

The same guidelines hold true for parental rebuke. Parents who label their child with epithets such as "stupid" or "liar" not only insure the child's resistance to their reproof, but also reinforce such misbehavior, as if encouraging him to live up to this negative image. However, parents who say, "Such a good child would never do a thing like that," encourage the child through their reproof to live up to the positive image and high regard of the parents. Their rebuke is lovingly accepted.

2. The *Vizhnitzer Rebbe*, R' Yisrael, visited the manager of a bank, who was known for professing his "enlightened" views. Though he certainly was no follower of the Rebbe, the banker welcomed him courteously.

The Rebbe sat silently for quite a while. After a protracted silence, he got up and headed for the door. Nonplussed, the banker walked him all the way home. Finally, unable to contain himself any longer, the banker asked, "Rebbe, why did you come? And why did you leave without saying anything?"

The Rebbe replied, "I came to do a *mitzvah.*"

"A *mitzvah?*" questioned the banker surprisingly. "What possible *mitzvah* could the Rebbe have performed?"

The Rebbe replied, "I have carried out the dictum of the Sages that just as it is a *mitzvah* for

manded Noah to take seven pairs of every kosher animal into the ark (*Genesis* 7:2), though he was to take only two each of the non-kosher animals. When the Flood was over and Noah left the ark, he built an altar and brought offerings to God from the kosher animals (ibid. 8:20). Noah reasoned, "Why did God command me to take seven pairs of the kosher animals? It must be that He wants me to bring offerings from them"(*Midrash Tanchuma, Vayakhel* 6:6).

The Midrash applies this verse to Bezalel, as well. In his instructions to Bezalel regarding the Tabernacle in the Wilderness, Moses' first command was to fashion the Ark, but Bezalel understood that the Tabernacle should be made first, so that there would be a place where the Ark could be housed (see *Exodus* 38:22, *Rashi* ibid. and *Berachos* 55a).[1]

הוֹדַע לְצַדִּיק וְיוֹסֶף לֶקַח — *Make [wisdom] known to the righteous and he will add [to his] learning.* Make wisdom known to the righteous one, and from his own knowledge, he will add more teachings to what he has already heard (*Rashi*).

◄§ Fear of God is the road to blessing

10. תְּחִלַּת חָכְמָה יִרְאַת ה' — *The beginning of wisdom is fear of HASHEM. Meiri* connects this verse with the previous one. Wisdom should not be taught even to a worthy student, until the teacher has ascertained that the student has fear of Hashem, for *anyone whose fear of sin takes priority over his wisdom, his wisdom will endure* (*Avos* 3:11). Fear of Hashem is the foundation to wisdom's edifice; without a foundation, there is no building (cf.1:7).[2]

This is one of seven places in the Scrip-

a person to say something which will be accepted, so is it also a *mitzvah* for a person not to say something which will not be accepted. As it is clear that in your case my words will not be accepted, it was a *mitzvah* not to speak at all!"

"But what are the words that will not be accepted?" questioned the banker.

"That I cannot say," replied the Rebbe, "for I am sure that you will not listen to them."

The banker's curiosity was piqued. He pleaded with the Rebbe to reveal the mysterious "thing."

Finally the *Vizhnitzer Rebbe* explained: "A widow stands to lose her home to the bank, which is going to foreclose on her property. I wanted to plead with you to cancel her mortgage, but since I knew you would not agree, I did not even voice my request."

"What!" said the banker, aghast. "How could I do such a thing! It is not a personal debt to me! I am only an employee of the bank, not its owner. . . ."

"It's just as I predicted — you would not listen," said the Rebbe. Cutting him short, the Rebbe turned and left.

The Rebbe's words hit their mark. Within a few days the widow's mortgage was paid from the banker's personal funds. Her debt was canceled, and she was able to remain in her home (*Imrei Chaim*).

1. The Talmud (*Shabbos* 113b) applies this verse to the following two cases:

Ruth the Moabitess was instructed by her mother-in-law Naomi to bathe, anoint herself, don her finery and go down to the threshing floor where Boaz was spending the night (*Ruth* 3:3). Ruth decided that it was preferable for her to reverse the sequence of these instructions, and she went down to the threshing floor first, and only then did she continue to follow Naomi's bidding (ibid. 3:6).

When the prophet Samuel was a young lad, he heard a voice calling him at night. Not realizing that the Holy Presence was speaking to him, he ran to Eli, the Kohen Gadol, for direction. Eli told him to lie down again, and should he hear the voice again, he should respond: "Speak, Hashem, for Your servant is listening." However, upon hearing the voice once more, Samuel answered: "Speak, for Your servant is listening." He did not mention "Hashem" just in case it was not the Holy Presence calling.

2. The Talmud (*Shabbos* 31a-b) uses parables to illustrate the vital nature of the fear of God. *Isaiah* states (33:6): *fear of Hashem is its [i.e., wisdom's] storage house.* This is like a farmer who ordered his worker to store grain in his warehouse. Later, when the worker admitted that he had not added preservatives to the grain to prevent rot, the farmer said, "It would have been better if you had not stored the grain in the first place!" Similarly, if Torah wisdom is not preserved with sincere

ture where 'יִרְאַת ה, *the fear of HASHEM,* and חָכְמָה, *wisdom,* are mentioned together. This frequent repetition indicates the importance of the link between the two. God is the Creator of the universe and life; all wisdom emanates from Him. It is impossible to understand man's place in the design of the universe without reverential awe of God and submission to His will; indeed, it is the only starting point that will lead man to his true goal. As the *mishnah* teaches, אִם אֵין יִרְאָה אֵין חָכְמָה, *If there is no fear of God, there is no wisdom* (*Avos* 3:21). However, the very same *mishnah* teaches that אִם אֵין חָכְמָה אֵין יִרְאָה, *if there is no wisdom there is no fear of God* (ibid.). (See 2:5, אָז תָּבִין יִרְאַת ה'.) How do we reconcile these two seemingly contradictory teachings; which comes first, wisdom or fear of God?

Maharal (*Nesivos Olam, Nesiv HaTorah*) resolves this dilemma by explaining that a certain measure of wisdom is the prerequisite to fear of God. However, without fear of God, *exalted* wisdom (הַחָכְמָה הָעֶלְיוֹנָה) is impossible.

The *Vilna Gaon* explains that the determination of which comes first depends on whether we are thinking theoretically [מַחְשָׁבָה] or practically [מַעֲשֶׂה]. In the realm of theory, the goal is the primary concern, and only then does one approach the practical question of how to achieve

the goal. Man's primary goal is to attain fear of God. Our verse addresses the realm of theory, and therefore it states: *the beginning of wisdom is fear of HASHEM.* This is echoed in the *mishnah* (*Avos* 3:21), "If there is no fear [of God] there is no wisdom." In practical application, wisdom takes precedence; hence, *if there is no wisdom there is no fear of God.*

The concept that fear of God is a prerequisite of wisdom is also found above, in 1:7, and in *Psalms* 111:10, but there the word for *beginning* is רֵאשִׁית, while here it is תְּחִלַּת. Although the two words are similar, *Malbim* explains that they have different shades of meaning. The word רֵאשִׁית refers to something that is *part* of wisdom — not an outside factor that leads to it — and the *primary* component of wisdom. [The term is used similarly in the Torah, רֵאשִׁית עֲרִסֹתֵכֶם, *the first of your kneading* (*Numbers* 15:20), which gives the commandment of giving part of one's dough to a Kohen.] In the case of wisdom, this "first part" (mentioned above in *Mishlei* 1:7 and *Psalms* 111:10) refers to יִרְאַת הָרוֹמֵמוּת, reverence for God's awesome greatness, the knowledge of which is itself a component of wisdom.

The word תְּחִלַּת, on the other hand, refers to an external factor that is necessary to the concept under discussion, but is not an intrinsic part of it. In our verse, תְּחִלַּת

fear of God, it will degenerate into a distortion of His will.

A scholar without fear of God is like a treasurer who has the key to a vault, but does not have the key to the outer chamber leading to the vault. If he is barred from the outer chamber, he will never be able to enter the inner vault. The Torah is the essence of God's will, but fear of God is the prerequisite for entry into His service.

King Solomon stated: וְהָאֱלֹהִים עָשָׂה שֶׁיִּרְאוּ מִלְּפָנָיו, *And God has made it [the world] so that men should fear Him* (*Koheles* 3:14). As Rabbi Yehudah expressed it, "God created this world for the sole purpose of having men fear Him!"

Two rabbis were seated when a great sage passed by. One said, "Let us stand [out of respect] because the one who passes is God fearing!" The other said, "Let us stand because he is a brilliant Torah scholar!"

Said the first rabbi, "When I tell you that this man is worthy because he is God fearing, why do you explain to tell me that he is a scholar [for wisdom is insignificant compared to fear of God]! Indeed, Hashem cares for nothing in the world except for fear of God, as the Torah itself declares: *And now, Israel, what does Hashem, your God, ask of you? Only to fear Hashem, your God* (*Deuteronomy* 10:12). Job also states: *He said to man, "Behold, fear of the Lord is wisdom!"* (*Job* 28:28).

יא בִּינָה: כִּי־בִי יִרְבּוּ יָמֶיךָ וְיוֹסִיפוּ לְךָ שְׁנוֹת חַיִּים:
יב אִם־חָכַמְתָּ חָכַמְתָּ לָךְ וְלַצְתָּ לְבַדְּךָ תִשָּׂא:

חָכְמָה, *the beginning of wisdom*, refers to
יִרְאַת הָעוֹנֶשׁ, *fear of Divine punishment*.
One who fears retribution for his misdeeds
and worries that he will forfeit the rewards
that accrue to those who serve God is really
motivated by self-interest, rather than reverence for and love of God. Nonetheless,
this attitude is beneficial, for it impels man
to accept and integrate the principles of
wisdom.

Radak (*Psalms* 111:10) comments that
in order to acquire fear of God, one must
first divorce himself from pursuit of mundane values and concentrate on spiritual
matters. That will enable one to believe
that nothing in the world matters, except
God.

וְדַעַת קְדֹשִׁים בִּינָה — *And knowledge of the
sacred [is the essence] of understanding*.
This knowledge is the principal part of
understanding (*Rashi*).

According to *Ibn Ezra*, the word קְדֹשִׁים
alludes to God, Who is described as אֱלֹהִים
קְדֹשִׁים, *a holy God* (*Joshua* 24:19). Thus
our verse teaches that knowledge of God is
the beginning of understanding.

Tochachos Mussar renders that sanctity
results from understanding. The better one
understands the laws of the Torah, the
better he can apply them to his own life
and attain levels of holiness by avoiding
practices and pleasures that may be permissible according to the letter of the law.

R' Hirsch explains that the sum of all
fields of study is knowledge about the
essence of things, their origin, existence
and laws which determine their phenomena. Once we realize that every phenomenon has reason, regulation, purpose

and law, we must realize that the premise
that comes before all others must of necessity be the existence of a Divine Thinker,
Who has thought out these reasons and
Whose thoughts we try to follow. A thinking person attempts to follow the lines of
thought of this supremely wise Thinker,
this omnipotent First Cause, Who evoked
all forces, created all matter, set all limits,
planned all purposes and made all laws.
Thus, following דַּעַת קְדֹשִׁים, *sacred
knowledge*, leads to בִּינָה, *understanding*.

11. כִּי־בִי יִרְבּוּ יָמֶיךָ — *For through me [i.e.,
through wisdom (Metzudos)] your days
will be increased*. *Alshich* cites the example of Abaye and Rava, who were descendants of the house of Eli and were therefore destined to die at the age of eighteen
(see *I Samuel* 3:13-14). However, in the
merit of their Torah study, their days were
increased (Rava lived until 40, and Abaye
until 60. See *Rosh Hashanah* 18a).

וְיוֹסִיפוּ לְךָ שְׁנוֹת חַיִּים — *And they will add
years of life to you*, i.e., years of sustenance
and wealth (*Rashi*) (see 3:2).

An "increase" in days refers to days
which are dedicated and consecrated to the
service of Hashem. Each such day is
marked by some good deed. Such days
endure far after their actual time has
passed, for their impression remains in the
world. Therefore, for one who is involved
in Torah, his years will be *years of life*, i.e.,
the good deeds he performed in those years
will live on forever (*Kol Omeir K'ra*).[1]

Metzudos explains: As a result of a
person's involvement in *chochmah*, his
days will increase (יִרְבּוּ יָמֶיךָ). This increase

---

1. Abraham is described as זָקֵן בָּא בַּיָּמִים, *old, well on in years* (*Genesis* 24:1). בָּא בַּיָּמִים can also be
explained: Abraham *came with the days*. I.e., he came to old age with *all* of his days. Not one day
of his life was wasted; each was utilized in the performance of good deeds. The Mussar masters
perceive in this expression the teaching that, for Abraham, each day of life represented a new
challenge and a new mission. Abraham's accumulated years were days of total devotion to his
Creator.

After the funeral of the *Sfas Emes*, his eldest son, the *Imrei Emes*, remarked to his brother, R'
Moshe Bezalel: "Our father had אֲרִיכוּת יָמִים, *long days*." Surprised, his brother responded, "But
our father did not even reach the age of sixty!" "True," answered the *Imrei Emes*, "our father did
not have long years, but he did have long days. He made every day count."

understanding. [11] For through me your days will be increased, and they will add years of life to you. [12] If you have become wise, you have become wise to yourself, but if you have scoffed, you alone will bear [it].

of days in this world will afford him the opportunity to perform more good deeds, and this will add on years to his life in the World to Come (וְיוֹסִיפוּ לְךָ שְׁנוֹת חַיִּים).[1]

12. אִם־חָכַמְתָּ חָכַמְתָּ לָּךְ — *If you have become wise, you have become wise for yourself.* You will be the one to attain benefit and honor from *chochmah* (Meiri).

וְלַצְתָּ לְבַדְּךָ תִשָּׂא — *But if you have scoffed, you alone will bear [it].* If you scorn people, you alone will bear the punishment for the sin (Ibn Ezra).

We have already been warned that there are times when a scoffer should not be rebuked (verse 8). If there is no longer any obligation to rebuke such a person, then this releases a fellow Jew from any responsibility (עֲרֵבוּת) towards the scoffer alone, and therefore the scoffer alone is left with the burden of his transgressions (Turei Zahav).

Your pursuit of wisdom — and vice versa — affects *you*; it neither enriches nor diminishes God. Ibn Ezra cites Job 35:7: אִם־צָדַקְתָּ מַה־תִּתֶּן־לוֹ, *Were you to have been righteous, how would you have benefited Hashem?*

Chochmah and the values inculcated by it are absolute, not conditional on any attention which is paid or denied them. Its truth remains true even if an entire genera-

tion denies it. Whoever goes to the source of this wisdom, to draw from it purity and humility and to faithfully follow its tenets, fulfills himself. He perfects his own spiritual and ethical being; he reaches temporal happiness and eternal salvation. However, if someone rejects wisdom and derides it, he will not only forfeit its blessing, but he will suffer a bitter curse as his spiritual essence wastes away (R' Hirsch).

Every person is destined to labor and toil in this world (see Job 5:7, כִּי־אָדָם לְעָמָל יוּלָּד, *For a person is born to toil*). A person is fortunate if he toils in Torah study, for this labor is deducted from the sum total of his allotted labors, and he also receives reward for this labor. In this vein, our Sages state that אַשְׁרֵי מִי שֶׁעֲמָלוֹ בְּתוֹרָה, *fortunate is he whose toil is in Torah.* Not only that, but the Torah itself and the Almighty assist him in bearing the burden of such toil (Midrash Tanchuma: Tzav 14). Therefore, this verse states: אִם־חָכַמְתָּ, *if you have become wise,* then חָכַמְתָּ לָּךְ, *the wisdom you have attained is yours,* but the burden of the toil has been removed from you by the Divine assistance you have merited. Thus, it is as if you had acquired wisdom without toil. However, if you do not invest your labors into Torah, then not only will you fail to attain *chochmah*, but in addition to your loss, לְבַדְּךָ תִשָּׂא, *you alone will*

---

1. Torah sages value every minute of life in this world, for who more than they appreciate the priceless opportunity to use this time to the fullest in the service of their Maker? We cite a few examples:

As the *Vilna Gaon* lay on his deathbed, he held the *tzitzis* of his garment in his hand and cried, "With just a few pennies, I can buy a pair of *tzitzis* in this world. I am earning immeasurable reward in the Hereafter, for every minute I wear them," he explained. "However, in the world to which I am going, no amount of money will enable me to perform even one more *mitzvah!*"

On the last Yom Kippur of his life, R' Leib Chasman was very weak from the fast, and he left the yeshivah and returned home immediately after the *Ne'ilah* prayers. A *minyan* of students accompanied him, and sat waiting for the *Maariv* prayers to begin. R' Leib Chasman addressed them and said: "In the *haftarah* of the Yom Kippur *Minchah* prayers, we read that Jonah said to the people on the ship, 'שָׂאוּנִי וַהֲטִילֻנִי אֶל־הַיָּם, *pick me up and heave me into the sea*' (Jonah 1:12). Why did Jonah specify שָׂאוּנִי, *pick me up,* when it would have sufficed to say הֲטִילֻנִי, *heave me?* However, Jonah valued that extra moment of life which he would gain by being lifted first and, only afterwards, thrown into the sea. So, too, we should value and utilize to the fullest the remaining minute of this holy day, and not forfeit this golden opportunity (Ohr Yahel, MiToldosav).

יג אֵשֶׁת כְּסִילוּת הֹמִיָּה פְּתַיּוּת וּבַל־יָדְעָה מָה:
יד וְיָשְׁבָה לְפֶתַח בֵּיתָהּ עַל־כִּסֵּא מְרֹמֵי קָרֶת:
טו-טז לִקְרֹא לְעֹבְרֵי־דָרֶךְ הַמְיַשְּׁרִים אֹרְחוֹתָם: מִי־פֶתִי
יז יָסֻר הֵנָּה וַחֲסַר־לֵב וְאָמְרָה לּוֹ: מַיִם־גְּנוּבִים

---

bear the burden of your toil, for no one will help you carry it (*Alshich*).

◆§ The temptress is alluring

After recounting *chochmah's* words and the pleasantness of its teachings, the chapter continues and contrasts the wise words of the woman of wisdom with the rebelliousness of the woman of folly, who makes an uproar attempting to influence people towards evil (*Malbim*).

13. אֵשֶׁת כְּסִילוּת הֹמִיָּה פְּתַיּוּת וּבַל־יָדְעָה מָה — *The woman of foolishness is tumultuous, [the woman] of simpleness who does not know anything.* Ibn Ezra and Malbim explain that the verse speaks about two different kinds of women, both of whom are errant, but in different ways. *The woman of foolishness* turns away from wisdom because of her appetite for the forbidden; she is rebellious and tries to entice men to evil. *The woman of simpleness* is ignorant and naive; she does wrong because she lacks knowledge. It is conceivable that once she becomes wiser, either learning from others or by her own realization, she will relent from her attraction to evil. For an intentionally foolish person [כְּסִיל] there is little hope for improvement, whereas a simple one [פֶּתִי] can be changed for the better.

Meiri renders: A woman of foolishness makes an uproar and screams foolish things, yet she, herself, does not even know what she is saying (*Meiri*).

14. וְיָשְׁבָה לְפֶתַח בֵּיתָהּ — *She sits at the entrance of her house* to watch those who pass by (*Metzudos*).

Rabbeinu Bachya points out that it is proper for a modest woman to sit בְּיַרְכְּתֵי

הַבַּיִת, *in the inner chamber of the house* (see *Psalms* 128:3), and not at the entrance of her house, so that she will not be seen by passersby.[1]

Torah is praised with the virtue of כָּל־כְּבוּדָּה בַת־מֶלֶךְ פְּנִימָה, *The complete glory of the princess is within* (*Psalms* 45:14). In this vein, *chochmah* is described as sending her maidens out to call [שָׁלְחָה נַעֲרֹתֶיהָ, v. 3). However, this woman *herself* sits at the entrance of her house to call and shout out [thus displaying immodesty which is unbefitting for a woman] (*Vilna Gaon*).

This woman is the antithesis of the wise woman. The wise woman is industrious and builds her house and prepares her fare without any tumult. The foolish woman does not know how to do any of these things, yet she makes an uproar. She sits at the entrance of her house, in the open, for there is nothing prepared inside. Symbolically, this verse contrasts the benefits of Torah to the futility of idol-worship. Whereas Torah encompasses the totality of all that is good and beneficial and reaches out to others to guide them on the correct path, idol-worship is devoid of all good yet it extends itself to mislead others and encourages evil (*R' Bachya*).

This woman neither builds her house, prepares meat, nor mixes wine as *chochmah* did. This is symbolic of the fact that whereas a person needs preparation in order to attain *chochmah*, the same is not true of wickedness, whose essence is lack of preparation and foresight (*Ibn Ezra*).

The woman of *k'silus* does not build a house which is firmly established on pillars; her house seems to hang in the air.

---

1. When the angels visited Abraham, they inquired: אַיֵּה שָׂרָה אִשְׁתֶּךָ, *where is Sarah your wife?* To which Abraham responded: הִנֵּה בָאֹהֶל, *Behold — [she is] in the tent* (*Genesis* 18:9). *Rashi* (ibid.) explains that the angels knew where Sarah was. The purpose of their question was to draw attention to her modesty, i.e., the fact that she was *inside* the tent, thus endearing her to her husband.

¹³ *The woman of foolishness is tumultuous, [the woman] of simpleness who does not know anything.* ¹⁴ *She sits at the entrance of her house, on a chair at the city heights,* ¹⁵ *to call out to passersby who make their ways upright:* ¹⁶ *"Whoever is a simpleton, let him turn here, and one who lacks [an understanding]heart," and she says to him:* ¹⁷ *"Stolen waters*

Instead of building, she destroys the edifice of the world, which rests on pillars of wisdom. She does not prepare meat, wine, nor set the table, symbolizing that evil lacks any true good or delight to offer a person. The fact that she does not send maidens as *chochmah* did, but rather stations herself at the entrance of her house, implies that wickedness comes to the person on its own (whereas *chochmah* needs an intermediary in order to pass its teachings on to the person, see v. 3) (*Malbim*).

עַל־כִּסֵּא מְרֹמֵי קָרֶת — *On a chair at the city heights.* So that she can make her voice audible from afar (*Metzudos*).

Foolishness comes with arrogance, thus the association with *a chair atop the city heights* (*Ibn Ezra*).

15. לִקְרֹא לְעֹבְרֵי־דָרֶךְ הַמְיַשְּׁרִים אֹרְחוֹתָם — *To call out to passersby who make their ways upright.* This woman calls out to innocent people who are going on a straight path, with the intention of misleading them. This is in direct contrast to wisdom, which calls out to those who are straying, in order to straighten their ways (*Ibn Ezra*).

This is a metaphor for one's desires, which entice a person to sin by portraying the pleasures and sweetness of sin (*Metzudos*).

The *Vilna Gaon* quotes the *Zohar*, which explains that it is specifically when a person wants to repent for his sins, or when he puts his efforts into the study of Torah and the performance of commandments, that the Evil Inclination tries to lead him astray. Therefore, she calls out to עֹבְרֵי־דָרֶךְ, *those who have sinned* (for עֹבְרֵי suggests עֲבֵירָה, *sin*) and who are now attempting to *make their ways upright* by repenting.

Malbim explains עֹבְרֵי דָרֶךְ as those who are still passing on their way and have not yet reached the city. Symbolically, this

refers to those who have not yet corrected their character traits, nor attained spiritual perfection, but are trying to straighten their paths. They are the targets of the temptress, because those who struggle to repent are especially vulnerable to the enticements of the evil desires that led them astray in the first place.

16. מִי־פֶתִי יָסֻר הֵנָּה וַחֲסַר־לֵב וְאָמְרָה לּוֹ — *"Whoever is a simpleton, let him turn here, and one who lacks [an understanding] heart," and she says to him:* What the temptress says is spelled out in verse 17 (*Rashi*).

Just as wisdom admonishes people to leave their foolish ways, so too, the woman of foolishness tries to convince them to remain with their folly (*R' Bachya*).

Him refers to both the פֶתִי, *simpleton,* i.e., a creduluous person, and the חֲסַר־לֵב, *one who lacks an understanding heart.* Torah addresses these two types of people with a similar call (see verse 4). However, there is a difference: In verse 4, Torah's words are directed only to the one lacking understanding (חֲסַר־לֵב אָמְרָה לּוֹ), whereas in this verse, the words of the temptress are addressed both to the credulous one and to the one lacking understanding. The Torah need not address a credulous person. He has common sense; once he turns to the Torah, he will recognize the good inherent in it and leave his foolish ways. The temptress of this verse, however, cannot rely on the display of her wares. She has no true benefits to offer, so she must rely on verbal promises and allurements (*Vilna Gaon*).

Metzudos interprets the verse differently. To this woman, anyone who denies himself the pleasures and delights of sin is a fool. Therefore, she addresses these people with the appellation of "fools," offering them the opportunity to become enlightened by the pleasures of sin (see next verse).

These words are the same as those of

יח יִמְתָּקוּ וְלֶחֶם סְתָרִים יִנְעָם: וְלֹא־יָדַע כִּי־רְפָאִים
שָׁם בְּעִמְקֵי שְׁאוֹל קְרֻאֶיהָ:

א מִשְׁלֵי שְׁלֹמֹה בֵּן חָכָם יְשַׂמַּח־אָב וּבֵן כְּסִיל
ב תּוּגַת אִמּוֹ: לֹא־יוֹעִילוּ אוֹצְרוֹת רֶשַׁע וּצְדָקָה

wisdom's invitation in verse 4. Thus both *chochmah* and *k'silus* address credulity and ignorance with the same words, in accordance with the principle, זֶה לְעֻמַּת זֶה עָשָׂה הָאֱלֹהִים, *God has made the one as well as the other* — good with its reward and evil with its ensuing punishment — to parallel the other (*Koheles* 7:14). Yet, there is a difference between verse 4 and this verse. Here, the conjunctive letter *vav*, and, is appended to the words חֲסַר־לֵב, *one who lacks understanding*, whereas it is not present in wisdom's declaration in verse 4. This suggests that wisdom does not lump all sorts of people together; rather, it has a unique approach to each type of person, suiting its words to the person's level of understanding. Therefore, it does not equate the credulous person with the one who lacks understanding. The foolish woman, however, is only out to mislead people. She makes no distinction between these two types of people, lumping them both together in one category (*Chevel Nachalah*).

17. מַיִם־גְּנוּבִים יִמְתָּקוּ וְלֶחֶם סְתָרִים יִנְעָם — *"Stolen waters are sweet, and bread [eaten] in secret is pleasant."* Stolen waters are sweeter than water which is not stolen, and stolen bread which is eaten in secret is very pleasant; i.e., the pleasure of doing what is permissible is not comparable to the pleasure of doing that which is forbidden. Therefore, says this woman, why do you deny yourself this pleasure? (*Metzudos*).

This refers to the pleasure derived from

the sin of adultery, for whatever is forbidden and must be done furtively is more tempting (*Rashi*). This is how the credulous one and the one lacking understanding are enticed to sin (*Ibn Ezra*; see *Sanhedrin* 75a).

Torah offers a person "meat and wine" (verse 2), things which are innately good. This woman, on the other hand, has only *water* and *bread* to offer — things which are not in essence inherently good. Their appeal lies only in the fact that they are גְּנוּבִים, *stolen*, and סְתָרִים, *eaten in secret* (*Vilna Gaon*).

18. וְלֹא־יָדַע כִּי־רְפָאִים שָׁם — *But he does not know that dead men are there.* *Metzudos* explains רְפָאִים as *those who are weakened by death.* One who is attracted to her does not realize that this is the place where the dead are, i.e., someone who follows his desires will die as a result (cf. 2:18).

בְּעִמְקֵי שְׁאוֹל קְרֻאֶיהָ — *That those she invites are in the deepest grave.* Those who accept her invitation will descend to the depths of *Gehinnom* (*Metzudos*).

This is just the opposite of one who listens to *chochmah*. He will merit longevity both in this world and in the World to Come (v. 11), whereas someone who is enticed by the woman of *k'silus* will die before his time, and will descend to *She'ol* (*Omer Hashikchah*).

The guests of the foolish woman are being lured to spiritual demise, for by sinning they destroy their souls (*Malbim*).

X

The words מִשְׁלֵי שְׁלֹמֹה, *the Proverbs of Solomon*, mark the beginning of the second section of *Mishlei/Proverbs*. According to the *Vilna Gaon*, the book is divided into three parts: Chapters 1-9, 10-24 and 25-31 (see 1:1, citation from *Vilna Gaon*). In this section, we find maxims teaching *mussar/*discipline. As such, most verses in the section contain two statements that balance one another: a positive one praising or commanding good conduct, and a negative one condemning or warning against bad conduct.

Meiri observes another basic difference in the structure of the verses in the first section of *Mishlei* as compared to this second section. In the first nine chapters we find groups of

are sweet, and bread [eaten] in secret is pleasant." ¹⁸ But he does not know that dead men are there, that those she invites are in the deepest grave.

10/1-2 ¹ The Proverbs of Solomon:
A wise son gladdens a father, but a foolish son is his mother's sorrow. ² Treasures of wickedness will not avail, but charity

verses (and sometimes even entire chapters) centering on one subject or related themes. In chapters 10 through 24, the verses are, in most cases, unrelated to one another. Each verse postulates a separate point, except for the few cases where several verses expand on the same idea.

The patterns of the verses can be divided into three general categories: antithetical couplets, where the first and second half of a verse describe the effects of opposite behavioral patterns (the wise and the foolish, love and hatred, industry and sloth); single cohesive thoughts; and parallelism, in which the second clause reinforces the first clause in different words.

An examination of the verses in this section reveals that King Solomon often does not use exact antonyms in the two parts of the verse. His prophetic wisdom is illuminated by the commentators as they infer lessons to be derived from the different nuances in the phraseology of the verse and the precision of his language.

1. בֵּן חָכָם יְשַׂמַּח־אָב — A wise son gladdens a father. The father refers either to the Holy One, Blessed is He, or to his biological father (Rashi), who is gladdened when his son sits among wise men (Metzudos).

וּבֵן כְּסִיל תּוּגַת אִמּוֹ — But a foolish son is his mother's sorrow. Such a child is constantly at home with his mother, who sees his foolishness and is pained by it. Metaphorically, the "mother" refers to the Jewish people, and the foolish son is Jeroboam ben Nebat, who brought grief to his nation (Rashi).

The commentators explain why it is specifically the father who rejoices over the wise son, while it is the mother who grieves over the foolish one. A father tends to recognize the son's wisdom (Ibn Ezra), more than the mother (Ralbag). A son's waywardness, on the other hand, is usually not apparent while the father is alive, for he imposes his authority and fear on the child. Once the father dies, however, the son's wickedness is revealed, causing grief to his mother (Meiri).

The Vilna Gaon explains that when a father is in the study hall, he has the pleasure of hearing the Torah thoughts of his wise son who learns with him; a mother does not have this opportunity. However, the foolish son who does not go to the study hall and wiles away his time at home

doing nothing is a source of sorrow to his mother who constantly sees his foolishness.

According to Malbim, the wise son's success is credited to the father, who taught him and chastised him when necessary. However, the son's waywardness is attributed to the mother, whose excessive maternal compassion prevented her husband from punishing their son when required. [Thus, in Malbim's view, the "father" symbolizes the strict parent and the "mother" symbolizes the indulgent one.]

R' Hirsch finds the verse to be an implied praise of dedicated mothers. No matter how much a father does for his child, it cannot be compared to a mother's sacrifices. By the time a father directs his personal attention to the child's development, the mother has already devoted years of constant care to his physical, moral and spiritual growth. If the child turns out to be wise and successful, the father has won a big prize for a comparatively small personal investment. If the child is foolish, however, the mother's pain at the thought of her wasted years, anxious days and sleepless nights is much deeper.

2. לֹא־יוֹעִילוּ אוֹצְרוֹת רֶשַׁע — Treasures of wickedness will not avail. Illicitly gained money will not save someone from danger

ג תַּצִּיל מִמָּוֶת: לֹא־יַרְעִיב יהוה נֶפֶשׁ צַדִּיק וְהַוַּת רְשָׁעִים
ד יֶהְדֹּף: רָאשׁ עֹשֶׂה כַף־רְמִיָּה וְיַד חָרוּצִים תַּעֲשִׁיר:

when the time for his punishment arrives, for he will not be able to "ransom" his soul with money (*Metzudos*). *Rashi* cites the example of Jeroboam ben Nebat (*Hosea* 12:9), who boasted that he would lay claim to all the wealth of the ten tribes for himself.

וּצְדָקָה תַּצִּיל מִמָּוֶת — *But charity rescues from death*. Though illicitly gained wealth is of no advantage, a "loss" of money can greatly benefit a person — the merit of the money he spent on charity and other *mitzvos* will stand in his good stead, even to the extent of saving him from death (*R' Yonah*).[1]

Contrary to human logic, the true power of wealth is wielded not by those who amass it, but by those who know how to spend it properly. In a similar vein, the Talmud (*Kesubos* 66b) states: מֶלַח מָמוֹן חֶסֵּר, *the preservative of money is the lessening of it*, i.e., the best way for someone to preserve his fortune is by giving to charity and using it for other *mitzvos*.

R' Hirsch connects this verse with the preceding one, thematically. If parents wish to derive joy from their child, they must stress the spiritual aspect of his upbringing more than the material one. A child should be taught to recognize that *treasures of wickedness will not avail*; money does not guarantee true well-being.

1. The Talmud (*Bava Basra* 10a) notes that King Solomon says twice that charity rescues from death, here and in 11:4. This signifies that charity rescues its donor from two kinds of death; מִמִּיתָה מְשׁוּנָּה, *from an unnatural death*; and מְדִינָה שֶׁל גֵּיהִנּוֹם, *from the judgment of Gehinnom*. The charity of our verse, which is the one that saves from unnatural death, refers to charity given anonymously, in such a manner that neither the donor nor the recipient knows the identity of the other.

The Talmud (*Shabbos* 156b, see *Maharsha*) recounts an incident from which Shmuel derived that charity saves even from death itself. As he and the Persian astrologer Avleit were sitting, they observed a group of workers going to a swamp. Avleit pointed to one worker and said, "That man is going, but will not return, for a snake will bite him and he will die." Shmuel responded, "If he is a Jew, he will return" [for a Jew is not controlled by the stars, and his fate can be changed]. When the worker returned alive, Avleit examined his knapsack and found a snake cut in two. When Shmuel questioned the worker as to his deeds, the man explained that each day his group collected everyone's food into one basket, and then ate together. That day, one of the men had no food to contribute. To avoid embarrassing him, the worker volunteered to collect the daily food and pretended to take also from the one who was emptyhanded. Later the worker shared his own portion with that man (*Rashi* ad loc.). Thus, his charitable deed saved him from death.

The Talmud (ibid.) relates a second incident to illustrate the same point. Chaldean astrologers told Rabbi Akiva that his daughter would be killed by a serpent on her wedding day. Naturally, this concerned R' Akiva as his daughter's marriage approached. On her wedding night, his daughter removed her gold brooch and stuck it in the wall. In the morning, when she tried to remove her brooch from the wall, a dead snake came trailing with it. Unbeknown to her, when she plunged the brooch into the wall, it had penetrated the snake's eye.

"What good deed did you do yesterday?" her father asked. "A poor man came to our door in the evening," she replied, "and everyone was so busy feasting that there was no one to give him food, so I gave him my portion." Then Rabbi Akiva taught, charity rescues not merely from unnatural death, but from natural death.

The Talmud (*Bava Basra* 11a) also tells of a woman who appealed for charity to Benjamin the Tzaddik, who was in charge of charity disbursements. He had to refuse her request because the funds had been exhausted. In despair, the woman cried that she and her seven children would die of hunger. Hearing that, Benjamin supported the family from his personal funds. Some time later, when he lay dying, the angels pleaded his case, saying that someone who had saved eight lives did not deserve to die at a young age. Immediately, the decree was annulled and twenty-two years were added to Benjamin's life in the merit of his charity.

rescues from death. ³ HASHEM will not bring hunger upon the soul of a righteous one, but the destructiveness of the wicked shall batter them. ⁴ A deceitful scale makes a pauper, but the hand of the diligent brings prosperity.

If the child is trained to turn his efforts toward spiritual wealth, then he will be a source of true satisfaction to his parents.

3. לֹא יַרְעִיב ה׳ נֶפֶשׁ צַדִּיק — *HASHEM will not bring hunger upon the soul of a righteous one.* Even in a time of famine, the *tzaddik* will not want (*Ibn Ezra*). God will provide the needs of the *tzaddik* (*Metzudos*).[1]

Lest we wonder how the *tzaddik* who generally gives to charity will sustain himself, this verse reassures us that God will not let him go hungry (*Rashi*).

וְהַוַּת רְשָׁעִים יֶהְדֹּף — *But the destructiveness of the wicked shall batter them.* However, the damage the wicked do will thrust them down, i.e., the sin itself will bring punishment upon them (*Metzudos*).

No damage can result from lessening one's money by giving to charity, for God will provide for the righteous, but great harm will result if one increases one's assets dishonestly, for this sin will batter its

perpetrator (*R' Yonah*).

Ibn Nachmiash translates *and the desire of the wicked He will thrust away.*

4. רֹאשׁ עֹשֶׂה כַף־רְמִיָּה — *A deceitful scale makes a pauper.* One who uses false weights and measures will eventually become impoverished (*Ibn Ezra; Vilna Gaon*).[2]

וְיַד חָרוּצִים תַּעֲשִׁיר — *But the hand of the diligent brings prosperity.* Those who work diligently and honestly, with their own hands, will be enriched (*Ibn Ezra*).

The term חָרוּצִים denotes both זְרִיזוּת, *diligence,* and יַשְׁרוּת, *uprightness.* These are people whose every action follows a set rule, without deviation (for חֲרִיצוּת also means גְּזֵירָה וּמִשְׁפָּט, *rendering judgment*). But those who are too lazy to earn their living through hard work resort to deceit, trying to enrich themselves by taking money that is not rightfully theirs (*Meiri, Ralbag*).

1. When the fires of World War I began to consume Europe, the *Brisker Rav*, Rabbi Yitzchok Zev Soloveitchik, took refuge in Warsaw. One of the rich men of the city undertook to provide him with bread every day, which he would divide with his son. The Rav insisted on not leaving any of the meager ration over for the next day, for he felt this showed a lack of faith in God's ability to provide daily sustenance for every person.

On 8 Tishrei, the *Brisker Rav* made an exception. Because of the *mitzvah* of eating on Erev Yom Kippur, he decided to leave over some bread for the following day. On the morning of Erev Yom Kippur, the rich benefactor arrived with only challah for the Rav, explaining apologetically that fish and other foods had been prepared, but some shrapnel had fallen into the food and it all had to be discarded. His wife had only had time to bake new challos.

Upon hearing this, the *Brisker Rav* exclaimed, "I see from here that I should have trusted in God to provide me with food for Erev Yom Kippur. Had I not left that bread over, the shrapnel might not have ruined the other foods. What a lesson in בִּטָּחוֹן, *trust,* God is teaching me!"

2. The *Chafetz Chaim* used a parable to illustrate the self-defeating nature of deceit. A local farmer had arranged to sell his wheat to a wholesaler at a set price per bushel. The farmer would make daily deliveries of the bushels but receive payment at the end of the season. In order to keep count of the illiterate farmer's deliveries, a penny would be deposited in a sack for each bushel received, and at the end of the harvest the pennies would be redeemed at the set price.

One day, the farmer was alone with his sack, which by now had become quite heavy with pennies. Stealthily, he dug his hand into the sack and grabbed a fistful of pennies. The foolish farmer was elated about the small fortune he had now acquired behind the wholesaler's back, but he did not realize that, far from enriching him, his theft of pennies had actually caused him a great loss. Through his own deceit, he had actually deprived himself of a fortune in payment rightfully due him.

Similarly, deceitful people count only their fraudulent gains, without realizing that they will lose far more than they seem to be gaining.

ה אֵגֵר בַּקַּיִץ בֵּן מַשְׂכִּיל נִרְדָּם בַּקָּצִיר בֵּן מֵבִישׁ:
ו בְּרָכוֹת לְרֹאשׁ צַדִּיק וּפִי רְשָׁעִים יְכַסֶּה חָמָס:
ז זֵכֶר צַדִּיק לִבְרָכָה וְשֵׁם רְשָׁעִים יִרְקָב:

The term חָרוּצִים is used in contradistinction to both the עָצֵל, *sluggard* (13:4),
and to רְמִיָּה, *deceit* (12:24) (*Malbim*).

Rashi explains that רָאשׁ, *pauper*, refers
to someone impoverished in Torah knowledge. Such a person will disseminate false
teachings; the *diligent*, on the other hand,
are those who are straight, who "cut off"
the correct judgments truthfully and without injustice.

In this verse, the word רָשׁ, *pauper*, is
spelled with an additional letter, *aleph* —
רָאשׁ — which can be read רֹאשׁ, *head*. This
teaches that although at present, this individual appears to be at the "head" in
wealth and power, he will become impoverished (*R' Yonah*). He will learn that
indolence and deception bring poverty
and failure, while honest energetic effort
brings wealth and success (*R' Shalom
Schwadron*).

The word כַּף can also be rendered as the
palm of the hand; thus the verse speaks of
the *"palm"* of deceit and the יַד, *"hand,"* of
the diligent. Commentators offer several
explanations why כַּף, *palm*, is mentioned
in connection with deceit, while יַד, the
whole *hand*, is associated with honesty.

Relating this verse to the theme of
tzedakah, the *Vilna Gaon* comments that
someone who refuses to give charity closes
the fingers of his hands and shows only
the palm. His refusal to give *tzedakah* will
cause him to become impoverished. However, one who opens his hand and gives
tzedakah will become rich.

Additionally, explains the *Vilna Gaon*,
this verse serves as a warning to those who
try to take shortcuts in studying Torah.
Someone who studies only superficially,
without delving in depth into the topic at
hand, in order to trick others into thinking
that he knows, will become poor in Torah
(רָשׁ), for he will forget what he has learned.
One who delves deeply and studies all the
particulars of a law will become rich in
knowledge (תַּעֲשִׁיר) for he will know all.

Malbim comments that כַּף, the *palm* of
the hand, symbolizes a lazy person who
does not use his entire hand, i.e., all of his
ability, to earn a living. Such laziness
causes him to rely on deceit, and he will be
impoverished. An industrious person,
however, uses his entire יַד, *hand*, and
works diligently — his *hand* will enrich
him.

5. אֵגֵר בַּקַּיִץ בֵּן מַשְׂכִּיל נִרְדָּם בַּקָּצִיר בֵּן מֵבִישׁ
— *A wise son gleans in the summer, but a
shameful son slumbers through the harvest.* The *harvest* is in late spring, and by
the *summer* little remains in the field. The
wise son, whose wisdom and foresight are
matched by his alacrity, continues to glean
even in the summer, gathering whatever is
left. On the other hand, the *shameful son*
brings embarrassment to his family by
being lazy and shortsighted. Not only does
he not work in the summer, he sleeps even
during the harvest when an abundance of
wheat is available in the field and the lion's
share of the work must be done.

Harvest and summer are metaphors for
two phases in a person's life. The harvest
represents youth, when a person is strong
and able to gather a great amount of Torah
learning. The shameful son squanders this
golden opportunity and does not study
Torah even then. The summer of a person's life is his old age, when he is already
weak and it is difficult for him to learn
new things. Even then, the enlightened
son is still at work, reinforcing the knowledge he had previously accumulated
(*Vilna Gaon, Malbim*).

R' Shimon bar Yochai told a parable of
two brothers who shared an inheritance
from their father. One son took a coin at a
time and frittered it away. The other son
took each coin and saved it. The first
brother was soon left penniless, whereas
the second brother became rich. So, too,
one who studies even a bit of Torah at a
time — two or three chapters a week, two
or three *sidras* a month — will accumulate

⁵ *A wise son gleans in the summer, but a shameful son slumbers through the harvest.* ⁶ *Blessings [will descend] upon the head of a righteous one, but [their] violence will smother the mouth of the wicked.* ⁷ *Remembrance of a righteous one brings blessing, but the name of the wicked will rot.*

a wealth of knowledge. However, the person who always says, "Tomorrow I will learn," will be left with nothing (*Sifri*).[1]

R' Hirsch teaches that where the acquisition of knowledge is concerned, indolence amounts to culpable negligence, for laziness is a betrayal of the Almighty, Who has blessed us with strength and many capabilities. By diligently using his industry even in his youth, the *wise son* differs from the *shameful son*, whose indolence betrays the justified expectations held out for him.

6. בְּרָכוֹת לְרֹאשׁ צַדִּיק — *Blessings [will descend] upon the head of a righteous one.* God will bring blessings to the righteous (*Ibn Ezra*). The *Vilna Gaon* explains that since the righteous person is always blessing others, God will bless him in return.[2]

וּפִי רְשָׁעִים יְכַסֶּה חָמָס — *But [their] violence will smother the mouth of the wicked.* Violence will cover their mouths and kill them (*Rashi*). The sin itself will bring the punishment upon them (*Metzudos*).

According to the *Vilna Gaon*, a wicked person brings חָמָס, *violent talk*, upon himself since he curses and speaks badly of others. The same curses revert to him.

The *head* is mentioned with regard to the righteous, because a good thought is regarded as a [good] deed (*Kiddushin* 40a).

Therefore, as soon as the idea of blessing someone enters the head of a righteous person, God blesses him in return. Regarding the wicked, however, the verse speaks of the mouth, because the wicked are not punished until they utter the evil with their mouths, since God does not punish for a mere *intention* to do wrong (*Vilna Gaon*).

7. זֵכֶר צַדִּיק לִבְרָכָה — *Remembrance of a righteous one brings blessing.* One who mentions a righteous person blesses him (*Rashi*).

Ibn Ezra explains that this verse refers to a righteous person after his death. The previous verse, *blessings [will descend] upon the head of a righteous one*, applies while he is alive.

וְשֵׁם רְשָׁעִים יִרְקָב — *But the name of the wicked will rot*, because no one wants to mention the name of the wicked. Therefore, their name is automatically forgotten (*Rashi*).

The *Vilna Gaon* explains that the remembrance of a righteous person is blessed even after his death, when only his זֵכֶר, *memory*, remains. The wicked, however are cursed even when they are still alive, for the word שֵׁם, *name*, implies the name of a living person.

Malbim explains that שֵׁם refers to one's personal name and identity, whereas זֵכֶר

1. In the Talmud Torah of Kelm, a five-minute session of learning was added to the usual hours-long sessions. This was intended to hammer home the point that a scholar must value even five minutes.

Similarly, Rabbi Zelig Reuven Bengis once celebrated a *siyum*, upon completing the entire Talmud. For seventeen years, he had completed a special cycle of learning in addition to his regular schedule. He had found the time to do so by taking advantage of otherwise wasted minutes while he waited to officiate at the various functions he was obligated to attend as rabbi of the *Eidah Hachareidis* in Jerusalem.

2. The Sages teach: כָּל הַמְבָרֵךְ מִתְבָּרֵךְ, *Anyone who blesses others is blessed himself* (see *Sotah* 38b), for God will bless him in return, as God told Avraham: וַאֲבָרְכָה מְבָרְכֶיךָ, *I will bless those who bless you* (*Genesis* 12:3). So, too, when the Kohanim blessed the Jews, God blessed them, as the verse states: וְשָׂמוּ אֶת שְׁמִי עַל־בְּנֵי יִשְׂרָאֵל וַאֲנִי אֲבָרְכֵם, *Let them place My Name upon the Children of Israel, and I shall bless them* [i.e., the Kohanim (*Rashi*)] (*Numbers* 6:27).

refers to the *remembrance* of one's deeds. The good deeds of a righteous person will be remembered for generations, and he will be blessed because of them. For the wicked, however, not only will their deeds not be remembered, but neither will their name — their very essence. It will rot away and be destroyed, for there will be no remnant left of their souls.

The *Midrash* (*Bereishis Rabbah* 49:1) explains this verse as an obligation: R' Yitzchak says that anyone who mentions a righteous person and does not bless him transgresses a positive commandment, as it states, *Remembrance of a righteous one brings a blessing.* Anyone who mentions a wicked person and does not curse him transgresses a positive commandment, as it states, *But the name of the wicked will rot.*[1]

The *Talmud* (*Yoma* 38b) derives this principle from the juxtaposition of verses in the Torah. In *Genesis* 18:17, God says, הַמְכַסֶּה אֲנִי מֵאַבְרָהָם אֲשֶׁר אֲנִי עֹשֶׂה, *Shall I conceal from Abraham what I do?* The next verse states: וְאַבְרָהָם הָיוֹ יִהְיֶה לְגוֹי גָּדוֹל, *And Abraham will surely become a great and mighty nation.* Once God mentioned Abraham, He blessed him [see also *Rashi, Genesis* 6:9 concerning Noah].

Conversely, וְשֵׁם רְשָׁעִים יִרְקָב, *but the name of the wicked will rot.* When speaking of Lot, the Torah states וַיֶּאֱהַל עַד־סְדֹם, *and he pitched his tents as far as Sodom* (*Genesis* 13:13). Once the wicked city of Sodom is mentioned, the next verse states: וְאַנְשֵׁי סְדֹם רָעִים וְחַטָּאִים לַה' מְאֹד, *Now the people of Sodom were wicked and sinful toward* HASHEM, *exceedingly.*

The Sages also interpret this verse as follows. When the Name of God, Who is referred to as צַדִּיקוֹ שֶׁל עוֹלָם, *the Righteous One of the Universe,* is mentioned, those hearing it should respond by blessing His Name (*Yoma* 37a). Thus, when the Kohen

Gadol pronounced God's Name during his וִדּוּי, *Confession,* in the Yom Kippur service in the Temple, those present answered: בָּרוּךְ שֵׁם כְּבוֹד מַלְכוּתוֹ לְעוֹלָם וָעֶד, *Blessed is the Name of His glorious kingdom for all eternity.*

8. חֲכַם־לֵב יִקַּח מִצְוֹת — *The wise of heart will seize good deeds.* One who is wise of heart will search and seek opportunities to do good deeds, even when he has no immediate obligation to do so. Contemplation of how short life is, and how imminent death is, will spur him on to amass as many merits as possible for the benefit of his soul (*R' Yonah*).

A wise person [חָכָם] is one who has studied the dictates of wisdom and acts accordingly. Nevertheless, he must always battle to subdue his Evil Inclination and force it to follow the dictates of wisdom. Though his Good Inclination will eventually emerge victorious, his internal struggle between right and wrong persists. The epithet חֲכַם־לֵב, *wise of heart,* refers to someone who has internalized wisdom to such a degree that it has become second nature to him. His heart no longer inclines to do evil. This is apparent in his approach to performing *mitzvos.* An ordinary wise man will observe the commandments because he is commanded to do so, otherwise he would prefer to do otherwise. However, the wise of heart will not only perform *mitzvos* as he becomes required to do so. He will, of his own volition, pursue opportunities to do more and more of them, since this is his heart's only desire (*Malbim*).

Rashi cites the example of Moses. Immediately before leaving Egypt, all the Jews were busy gathering booty from the Egyptians, but Moses occupied himself with the *mitzvah* of removing the bones of Joseph from Egypt, in order to fulfill the oath the children of Israel had made to

1. The actual name of a wicked person will rot after his death, since it will not be reused. The Midrash [ibid.] quotes R' Shmuel bar Nachmani who asks, "Have you ever heard of a person calling his son by the name [of such wicked people as] Sisera, Sennacherib, or Pharaoh? Rather, [people are named after] Reuben or Simeon!"

⁸ *The wise of heart will seize good deeds, but one of foolish lips will become weary.* ⁹ *He who walks in perfect innocence*

Joseph before his death (see *Exodus* 13:19).[1]

The Midrash (*Bereishis Rabbah* 52:3) derives the same lesson from Abraham. After Sodom was destroyed, no more wayfarers passed by his tent, and he had no one to whom he could extend hospitality. Seeking a venue where he could continue to help others, Abraham moved his residence to Gerar. [See *Genesis* 20:1, *Rashi* ibid.]

וֶאֱוִיל שְׂפָתַיִם יִלָּבֵט — *But one of foolish lips will become weary.* The translation of יִלָּבֵט as an expression of weariness follows *Rashi*.[2]

Meiri offers four additional explanations of the term יִלָּבֵט:

1. He will become peverted in his words.
2. He will stumble in what he says.[3]
3. He will act hastily and haphazardly.
4. He will be indecisive.

This phrase may be understood in several ways:

❏ *Metzudos* renders *a fool wearies his lips* by speaking a lot, but he does nothing. This is in direct contrast to the

wise of heart, who constantly seizes the opportunity to do good deeds.

❏ The *Vilna Gaon* explains that the wise of heart performs the *mitzvos* at hand immediately and does not postpone them. In contrast to him, the *fool* just speaks with his lips about doing the *mitzvos*, but always postpones action. With such an attitude, יִלָּבֵט, *he will stumble,* and he will never do them at all.

❏ *Malbim* renders the phrase: *but one who verbalizes skepticism will become weary.* He explains that the term אֱוִיל is related to the word אוּלַי, *maybe.* Accordingly, an אֱוִיל שְׂפָתַיִם is one who believes in the truth of wisdom in his heart, but who nonetheless verbalizes doubts; he expresses his foolish doubts even as he observes the commandments. Thus, he is the antithesis of the wise of heart, for whom *chochmah* has become ingrained in his every fiber. Because the fool's lips constantly verbalize doubts, יִלָּבֵט, *he will become weary* without any gain.

9. הוֹלֵךְ בַּתֹּם יֵלֶךְ בֶּטַח — *He who walks in*

1. Rabbi Yechezkel Levenstein asks why Moses is particularly commended for seizing the opportunity to care for Joseph's remains. Since Moses had commanded the Jews to take the booty of the Egyptians, they, too, were performing a *mitzvah*. R' Yechezkel explains that there is no comparison between doing a good deed that brings instant, tangible reward, and doing a good deed that involves hardship and self-sacrifice. The Jews became rich from the booty they were gathering, whereas Moses waived that opportunity in order to fulfill the vow made to Joseph 139 years earlier.

2. The *Chafetz Chaim* uses a parable to explain why the wise of heart is so eager to do *mitzvos*, whereas the fool tires of doing them.

In the bookkeeping system of a small retail business, each entry represents only dollars in profit or loss. For a large wholesaler, the same entry might mean thousands of dollars. However, in the ledger of a huge corporation, each figure stands for millions of dollars. A knowledgeable businessman studying such a ledger would realize the significance of every number entered therein.

The same is true, in Hashem's "bookkeeping system." In His "ledger" — the Torah — each entry is of immense significance, for the existence of the whole world is based on the Torah. The wise of heart realizes that every *mitzvah* represents "millions" in reward. Therefore, he eagerly searches for opportunities to gain part of this treasure. The fool, however, does not fathom the truedepth of the words of the holy Torah. He tires easily of doing *mitzvos*, for to him they are a burden and a yoke, since he fails to comprehend their true significance.

3. In contrast to Moses, Korach is given as an example of one who stumbled. For while Moses was busy with Joseph's remains, Korach was amassing the riches that led to his downfall. His new affluence caused his foolish talk against Moses (*Maamar Mordechai*).

י יֵלֶךְ בֶּטַח וּמְעַקֵּשׁ דְּרָכָיו יִוָּדֵעַ: קֹרֵץ עַיִן יִתֵּן
יא עַצֶּבֶת וֶאֱוִיל שְׂפָתַיִם יִלָּבֵט: מְקוֹר חַיִּים פִּי צַדִּיק
יב וּפִי רְשָׁעִים יְכַסֶּה חָמָס: שִׂנְאָה תְּעוֹרֵר מְדָנִים

perfect innocence will walk securely, for he need not fear that any trouble will befall him (*Ibn Ezra*).

(See 2:7: Torah *is a shield to those who walk in perfect innocence.*)

According to *Rabbeinu Yonah*, this describes an individual who does not relinquish his way of innocence out of the fear that others will overpower him. He does not resort to wiles and subterfuge in his business dealings with others, nor does he impose his authority on them.

Rabbeinu Bachya explains that a person who *walks in perfect innocence* will be secure in the assurance that he will merit the World to Come. We find that when King David enumerates those who *"may sojourn in Your Tent"* and who *"may dwell on Your Holy Mountain,"* הוֹלֵךְ תָּמִים, *one who walks in perfect innocence*, is included among them (*Psalms* 15:1-2).

וּמְעַקֵּשׁ דְּרָכָיו יִוָּדֵעַ — *But he who perverts his ways will be broken.* One who follows a crooked path will be broken and chastised as a result [*Rashi* relates יִוָּדֵעַ to וַיֹּדַע אֹתָם אֶת אַנְשֵׁי סֻכּוֹת, *and with them he thrashed the men of Succos* (*Judges* 8:16)] (*Rashi*).

Other commentators render יִוָּדֵעַ as *will become known.* Someone who perverts his good ways will become known, for when troubles befall him, it will become obvious to others that he walked on a crooked path (*Ibn Ezra*).

According to the *Vilna Gaon*, this verse describes someone who is trying to harm his friend without letting his evil intentions become known. He must, therefore, walk a crooked path; in order to hide his wicked schemes he must feign friendship with his intended victim. In the end,

however, יִוָּדֵעַ, his schemes will *become known* to his friend, for Hashem will publicize them.[1]

10. קֹרֵץ עַיִן יִתֵּן עַצֶּבֶת — *He who winks an eye causes sadness.* According to *Rashi*, this verse describes someone who is signaling and winking to another in order to entice him to evil.

Ibn Ezra explains that he signals to do evil. He is fearful of carrying out his evil plans openly, therefore he signals furtively. In the end, he will only cause *himself* sorrow.

According to *Meiri*, one who plans evil furtively will cause sorrow to *others*, who are unaware of his sinister plans and will not take precautions to protect themselves. The Sages (*Sotah* 22b) quote King Yannai, who warned his wife: Do not fear the פְּרוּשִׁים, *those zealously faithful to the laws of the Torah*, or those who are not faithful. Rather fear those who are צְבוּעִים, *duplicitous*, i.e., insincere. In the same vein, *Meiri* quotes a *mussar* sage who prayed daily: "Protect me from my friends (i.e. those who pretend to be my friends); from my enemies I will be able to protect myself."

וֶאֱוִיל שְׂפָתַיִם יִלָּבֵט — *But one of foolish lips will be considered perverted.* This follows *Meiri*, who points out that the meaning of this phrase differs from the identical phrase in verse 8. He explains that once the person reveals his evil plans with his lips, he will be considered perverted and rotten by others, who will take precautions to protect themselves from him.

Malbim explains that קֹרֵץ עַיִן, *he who winks an eye*, describes a person who follows the path of Torah, but constantly looks towards the wrong path in indeci-

1. This is echoed in the statement סוֹף גַּנָּב לִתְלִיָּה, *in the end the robber will be hung.* Someone who plans to commit a crime secretly will eventually be caught and punished by public hanging. The same is true of any sinner. *Midrash Shocher Tov* states that Hashem does not punish an individual until he publicizes his deeds.

will walk securely, but he who perverts his ways will be broken. ¹⁰ *He who winks an eye causes sadness, but one of foolish lips will be considered perverted.* ¹¹ *The mouth of a righteous one is a wellspring of life, but the mouth of wicked ones conceals [their intended] violence.* ¹² *Hatred arouses strife,*

sion, wondering what is the correct path to take. Even though he remains on the true path, יִתֶּן עַצָּבֶת, he *causes himself sorrow*, for he awakens doubts in his own heart. וֶאֱוִיל שְׂפָתַיִם, *one who verbalizes skepticism*, traverses the right path; he does not even glance over to the crooked way. However, he expresses doubts and skepticism externally with his lips, and, therefore, he will still exhaust himself.

11. מְקוֹר חַיִּים פִּי צַדִּיק — *The mouth of a righteous one is a wellspring of life.* Torah and *mitzvos* are the lifeblood and source of vitality to all who heed them. Since the *tzaddik* teaches others to study Torah and perform *mitzvos*, his words are a source of life to all (*Vilna Gaon*).[1]

וּפִי רְשָׁעִים יְכַסֶּה חָמָס — *But the mouth of wicked ones conceals [their intended] violence.* The wicked speak smoothly. However, it is only outwardly that their words are sweet. [In the context of this verse, the clause has a different meaning than the same words in verse 6] (*Rashi*).

12. שִׂנְאָה תְּעוֹרֵר מְדָנִים — *Hatred arouses strife.* Animosity which already exists

between two people stirs up fights, for even trifles become a cause for irritability and quarrels (*Metzudos David*). R' Hirsch explains that hatred is not the outcome of a quarrel, but rather the cause of it.

The *Vilna Gaon* explains how human nature works. When one individual has a petty falling out with another, he sets it aside and does not immediately react, for it is too minor. However, when some future action of this person provokes him once again, his latent hatred is aroused. The argument that ensues is totally out of proportion to the present provocation, for it is really the past, dormant grudges that are now reawakened. It is the שִׂנְאָה, *hatred*, that he already harbors in his heart that now provokes מְדָנִים, *strife*, over an incident which would have otherwise been ignored.[2]

According to *Rashi*, this verse pertains to the sins of the Children of Israel. Hashem may seem to "forget" their transgressions, for He does not punish them immediately. However, once they have accumulated a great number of sins, Hashem's anger is aroused, and the seem-

1. The life-giving power of a *tzaddik's* words is apparent not only from his teachings, but even from his casual conversation.

The story is told of a Jew who visited the *Vilna Gaon* in his *succah*. When the visitor entered, the *Gaon* was so engrossed in his learning that he failed to notice the guest's presence or to greet him, as he would usually do. The guest was upset, assuming that the *Gaon* was angry at him for some reason. When he questioned the *Gaon*, the *Gaon* replied, "How could I be upset at someone who came to join us on this festival of our rejoicing?! May you live to one hundred years!"

The words of the *Vilna Gaon* came true. When the man reached his ninety-eighth year, he took ill. The family members wished to call a doctor, but the man refused, saying, "The *Vilna Gaon* blessed me with one hundred years of life. I still have two years left, and I am not going to give up even a single day of this *tzaddik's* blessing." On the exact day of his hundredth birthday, he passed away.

2. The Sages teach (*Rosh Hashanah* 17:1): כָּל הַמַּעֲבִיר עַל מִדּוֹתָיו מַעֲבִירִין לוֹ עַל כָּל פְּשָׁעָיו, *Whoever changes his natural characteristics* [i.e., and forgives wrongs committed against him], *[Heaven] forgives all his transgressions.* According to this verse, one can understand the great merit of such an individual. A person can usually put aside animosity temporarily. However, if he is able to erase it so completely that a future provocation cannot even reawaken it, he has successfully reframed the situation, thereby retraining himself and changing his very nature. Thus, Heaven reassesses him and changes his accountability for the transgressions he has committed (*Achar He'aseif*).)

יג וְעַל כָּל־פְּשָׁעִים תְּכַסֶּה אַהֲבָה: בְּשִׂפְתֵי נָבוֹן
יד תִּמָּצֵא חָכְמָה וְשֵׁבֶט לְגֵו חֲסַר־לֵב: חֲכָמִים
טו יִצְפְּנוּ־דָעַת וּפִי־אֱוִיל מְחִתָּה קְרֹבָה: הוֹן עָשִׁיר
טז קִרְיַת עֻזּוֹ מְחִתַּת דַּלִּים רֵישָׁם: פְּעֻלַּת צַדִּיק לְחַיִּים

ingly "forgotten" transgressions are brought to the fore.

We see this from the prophecy of Ezekiel (20:7), who chastised the Elders in Babylon about the idols which Israel had worshiped in Egypt. Though hundreds of years had passed since then, this sin had never been mentioned [for out of love for Israel, Hashem concealed it]. However, in Ezekiel's time, the sins of Israel had increased so much that God's anger was kindled and the transgressions of generations past were reawakened.

וְעַל כָּל־פְּשָׁעִים תְּכַסֶּה אַהֲבָה — *But love covers all transgressions.* When there is love between two people, even if one seriously wrongs the other, his friend will overlook it and not take offense (*Metzudos*).

Malbim explains that it is the inherent internal attitude that determines the nature of human relations. While hatred interprets all events according to its own hostility, love casts a forgiving aura on even the most injurious actions.

Even if the Jewish people commit serious transgressions against Hashem, these will be covered over and forgiven once they improve their actions and repent (*Rashi*).

The *Vilna Gaon* explains this verse in accordance with the Gemara (*Yoma* 86:2) which teaches that someone who does תְּשׁוּבָה מֵאַהֲבָה, *repentance out of love for Hashem*, will not only have his sins forgiven, but they will even be considered as meritorious acts.

13. בְּשִׂפְתֵי נָבוֹן תִּמָּצֵא חָכְמָה — *In the lips of an understanding one, wisdom will be found.* When a נָבוֹן, *an understanding one*, is rebuked for a wrongdoing, he answers wisely by admitting, "I have sinned." When the prophet Nathan chastised King David for taking Bathsheba, David responded, חָטָאתִי לַה', *I have sinned against God* (II Samuel 12:13)[1] (*Rashi*).

וְשֵׁבֶט לְגֵו חֲסַר־לֵב — *But a rod [must be used] for the back of one who lacks [an understanding] heart.* Such a person does not listen unless he is hit, like Pharaoh who did not respond to God's warnings to free the Jews until he was hit by the Ten Plagues (*Rashi*).

The heart is the controlling agent in man, directing him to act in accordance with the dictates of *chochmah*. Someone who acts with no direction whatsoever, who haphazardly follows any whim or fancy to the extent that there is no controlling power over his actions, is termed a חֲסַר־לֵב, *one who lacks heart.* Such a person needs a rod to direct him towards the proper path, just as an animal is directed on its path with a whip. His actions resemble that of an animal, in that he fails to see his free choice to decide on a course of action, and therefore must be forced by external sources to chose the right path (*Malbiim*).[2]

According to *Metzudos*, when a question is posed to an understanding person, his wise response is an implied rod of reproof to those who lack understanding

1. Because of David's response, *I have sinned*, his sin was subsequently forgiven and he retained his reign over Israel. King Saul, however, reacted differently when confronted by the prophet Samuel regarding his sin. Instead of admitting his mistake immediately, he tried to excuse himself for his actions. As a result, he lost the kingship, which was then transferred to David.

R' Yechezkel Sarna comments that the tragic consequences which resulted from Adam's eating the fruit of the Tree of Knowledge resulted from his not saying חָטָאתִי, *I have sinned*, when confronted by God about his wrongdoing.

2. The numerical value of לְגֵו, *for the back*, is thirty-nine — the same number as the lashes meted out to the sinner punished by flogging (*Ibn Nachmiash*, quoting *Parp'raos L'Chochmah*.

but love covers all transgressions. [13] *In the lips of an understanding one, wisdom will be found, but a rod [must be used] for the back of one who lacks [an understanding] heart.* [14] *The wise conceal knowledge, but the mouth of a fool [brings] ruin near.* [15] *A rich man's wealth is his citadel of strength, [but] the ruin of the indigent is their poverty.* [16] *The deed of a righteous person brings life,*

and whose deeds are sinful, for his words disgrace the latter for his wrongdoing.

14. חֲכָמִים יִצְפְּנוּ־דָעַת — *The wise conceal knowledge.* The wise guard their knowledge in their heart, watching over it lest it be forgotten (*Rashi*).[1]

R' Hirsch explains that the wise know a great deal and foresee many things, but keep them to themselves so as not to cause unnecessary anxiety.

The wise hide even their knowledge, revealing it only to those who are deserving of it. They fear that their words may become a stumbling block to those who do not fully understand them (*Metzudos*). As Avtalyon warns: Scholars, be cautious with your words, for you may incur the penalty of exile and be banished to a place of evil waters [i.e., heresy]. The disciples who follow you may drink and die, and consequently the Name of Heaven will be desecrated (*Avos* 1:11).

וּפִי־אֱוִיל מֶחִתָּה קְרֹבָה — *But the mouth of a fool [brings] ruin near.* Someone lacking in wisdom knows no discretion. He speaks words which may cause imminent damage, for he does not take into account the consequences of his words (*Metzudos*).

This verse points out the danger of associating with people lacking in wisdom. They say whatever comes to their mind, and their conversation is likely to include talebearing, derogatory information, bad advice and slander, which can harm others [*Rabbeinu Yonah*].

15. הוֹן עָשִׁיר קִרְיַת עֻזּוֹ — *A rich man's wealth is his citadel of strength.* A person's wealth protects him just as a fortified city safeguards its inhabitants

(*Metzudos*). הוֹן, *wealth*, in this verse refers to *chochmah*. A person's wealth of Torah knowledge will be a citadel of strength to him (*Rashi*).

מְחִתַּת דַּלִּים רֵישָׁם — *[But] the ruin of the indigent is their poverty.* Their poverty — in that they did not engage in Torah — is their ruination (*Rashi*).

According to *R' Yonah*, this verse describes the mistaken perception that people have about money. The rich trust in their wealth to protect them, and the poor are frightened by their poverty (for מְחִתָּה also means *fear*). However, they both err. Life and all blessings are not factors of a person's wealth. True security is assured only by a person's good deeds, and the poor need not fear their poverty as long as their ways are righteous (see the following verse).

Both the wealthy and the impoverished should realize that one's true value does not lie in the sum of his possessions, but in the way in which they were acquired (*R' Hirsch*).

16. פְּעֻלַּת צַדִּיק לְחַיִּים — *The deed of a righteous person brings life.* Whatever the righteous do — whether it be performing *mitzvos* or whether it be earning money — is all for life, as the Torah defines life. Their efforts at earning money are motivated by higher considerations: they want to avoid resorting to sinful means of sustaining themselves; they want to obtain the resources to serve God; they want to be able to dedicate themselves completely to serving Him (*R' Yonah*).

The virtuous action of a righteous person brings life (*Metzudos*).

---

1. The perseverance and diligence of our Sages in constantly reviewing the Torah they had learned is legendary. The *Vilna Gaon* would review one hundred pages of the Talmud every day, in additional to his regular schedule of learning. It is said that even in his sleep, the *Gaon's* lips were moving and reviewing his learning, so trained were they by his constant concentration on Torah every waking moment (*Oros HaGra*).

יז תְּבוּאַת רָשָׁע לְחַטָּאת: אֹרַח לְחַיִּים שׁוֹמֵר
יח מוּסָר וְעוֹזֵב תּוֹכַחַת מַתְעֶה: מְכַסֶּה שִׂנְאָה
יט שִׂפְתֵי־שָׁקֶר וּמוֹצִא דִבָּה הוּא כְסִיל: בְּרֹב

The Midrash applies this verse to the deeds of King Solomon. By building the Temple, he brought life to the whole nation of Israel, enabling them to achieve atonement for their sins (*Rashi*).

תְּבוּאַת רָשָׁע לְחַטָּאת — [*But*] *the produce of a wicked one is for sin.* All the wealth a wicked person amasses becomes an instrument of sin, even if the wealth did not come through violence and robbery [for the verse does not say חַטָּאת, *a sin*, but לְחַטָּאת, *for sin*]. The wicked person will use his wealth as a means of imposing his authority over the righteous; of strengthening the power of evildoers; of fulfilling his sinful desires. His wealth will lead to arrogance, and he will put his trust in his fortune rather than in his Creator. His wealth will cause others to honor him, thus uplifting those whom God abhors. This aphorism is in response to the indigent person who fears poverty (verse 15): If he chooses to go on the way of the righteous, then all his actions are for life, and he has nothing to fear. If he goes on the way of evildoers, then all the wealth which he desires will end up being a stumbling block to him (*R' Yonah*).

The outcome of a wicked person's actions causes his life to be shortened [חַטָּאת means חִסָּרוֹן, *deficiency*) (*Metzudos*).

In any undertaking, the goal to be achieved is the primary consideration, whereas the means of achieving it is only of secondary importance. For instance, the plowing and the planting of seeds are not the primary goal; they are only the פְּעֻלָּה, *action*, to bring about the growth of the תְּבוּאָה, *produce*, which is the main

purpose and goal.

For the righteous, not only is the outcome of their actions good, but even the means they use (פְּעוּלָה) is important, and it brings life (לְחַיִּים). Their eating, for example, serves not only as a means of sustaining their bodies, but the action of eating itself is of such holiness that it attains the sanctity of a sacrifice to God. On the other hand, when the wicked act, not only are their means wrong, but even the תְּבוּאָה, *produce*, i.e., the very purpose and goal of all they do, is sin (*Vilna Gaon*).

The fruits of the wicked person's labors, his accomplishments and even his successes, ultimately prove his undoing and become an expiation for his sins (*R' Hirsch*).

The word תְּבוּאָה can also be derived from the word הֲבָאָה, *bringing*. When King Menashe brought an idol into the Temple, it caused a sin for the nation of Israel (*Rashi*).

[One of the main benefits enjoyed by Israel while the Temple stood was the ability to bring sacrifices and atone for their sins, thereby lengthening their lives. When Menashe brought an idol into the Temple, it was the first step towards the Temple's destruction. Ultimately, this one sin of Menashe's caused a loss of the means of atonement for all the sins of the nation of Israel.][1]

17. אֹרַח לְחַיִּים שׁוֹמֵר מוּסָר — *One who heeds mussar is [on] a path to life.* One who heeds *mussar* — that is the way to life (*Rashi*). *Mussar* implies correction, discipline and even suffering. The *Vilna Gaon* explains that מוּסָר, *chastisement*, is related to the word יִסּוּרִים, *afflictions*, which may be either self-imposed or from

---

1. The Midrash (*Bamidbar Rabbah* 12, see *Eitz Yosef*) explains that pictures of trees were drawn on the golden walls of the Temple. When the trees in the fields bore fruit, the golden trees of the Temple also gave forth their crop. This demonstrated that the Temple was a microcosm of the world. The whole world flourished through the service performed in the Temple. When Menashe brought an idol into the Temple, the fruits on the walls dried out, and so did the fruit in the orchards. Once the holiness of the Temple was profaned, its power to provide bounty to the whole world was also lost.

[but] the produce of a wicked one is for sin. [17] *One who heeds mussar is [on] a path to life, but one who abandons rebuke goes astray.* [18] *One who conceals hatred has false lips, but he who utters slander is a fool.* [19] *In an abundance of*

others. If a person fights his Evil Inclination, even though hardships and suffering are involved, this will lead him to the *path of life.* He will merit life in the World to Come, for the only way to merit the World to Come is through suffering (see 6:23).[1]

וְעוֹזֵב תּוֹכַחַת מַתְעֶה — *But one who abandons rebuke goes astray.* He leads both himself and others astray (*Rashi*).

Whereas מוּסָר implies יִסּוּרִים, *afflictions,* תּוֹכָחָה is *verbal rebuke.* Someone who hates even oral reproof will not only never achieve the path to life, but will also be led completely astray. Since he hates reproof, he will have no one to guide nor admonish him; he will follow the dictates of his own heart and not even perceive that his actions are wrong (*Vilna Gaon*).

18. מְכַסֶּה שִׂנְאָה שִׂפְתֵי־שָׁקֶר — *One who conceals hatred has false lips.* A flatterer has false lips, and conceals hatred in his heart (*Rashi*).

One who harbors hatred in his heart, refusing to leave it, causes yet another transgression. He lies in order to conceal his hatred and appear as a friend (*Metzudos*). *R' Yonah* cites the words of the

prophet Jeremiah (9:7): "With his mouth one speaks peace with his fellow, but inside of him he lays his ambush."[2]

וּמוֹצִיא דִבָּה הוּא כְסִיל — *But he who utters slander is a fool.* On the other hand, someone who does not conceal his hatred, but expresses it by slandering his friend and causes him to be the subject of people's conversation, will himself be considered a fool, for one who finds fault with others is only reflecting on his own fault (*Metzudos*). [Defaming others is, in essence, a defamation of oneself, since the listener's reaction will be: He must have this fault in himself if he is so sensitive to it in others.][3]

Just as it is wrong to conceal hatred in one's heart, so it is wrong to openly malign the object of one's hatred. *R' Yonah* explains that the Torah teaches how to deal with feelings of animosity or knowledge of wrongdoing. לֹא־תִשְׂנָא אֶת־אָחִיךָ בִּלְבָבֶךָ הוֹכֵחַ תּוֹכִיחַ אֶת־עֲמִיתֶךָ וְלֹא־תִשָּׂא עָלָיו חֵטְא, *You shall not hate your brother in your heart, you shall reprove your fellow and do not bear a sin because of him* (*Leviticus* 19:17). Do not sin by rebuking him publicly and embarrassing

1. In *Even Shleimah* (Ch. 1), the *Vilna Gaon* writes: וְאִם לָאו [שְׁבִירַת הַמִדּוֹת] לָמָּה לוֹ חַיִּים? *if not for [the breaking of bad character traits], what is [the purpose of] his life?* One of the main reasons life was bestowed upon a person was to give him the opportunity to contain his Evil Inclination through *mussar.*

2. The Midrash points out a virtue of Joseph's brothers. Because they hated him inwardly, וְלֹא יָכְלוּ דַּבְּרוֹ לְשָׁלֹם, *they could not speak to him peaceably.* These words praise the brothers for not being hypocritical, speaking sweetly with their mouths while concealing hatred in their hearts. (See *Genesis* 37:4, *Rashi* ibid.)

3. The Talmud (*Kiddushin* 70b) relates that R' Yehudah proclaimed in public that a certain person was an עֶבֶד, *slave.* The accused summoned R' Yehudah to the court of R' Nachman and charged him with slander. R' Yehudah was asked to prove his contention. He answered, "I know he is a slave because he always calls other people slaves. We know that כָּל הַפּוֹסֵל בְּמוּמוֹ פּוֹסֵל, *one who finds fault in others finds fault with his own flaw.*"

The man responded, "How can you call me a slave when I am a descendant of the Hasmonean dynasty, and therefore I am of royal lineage?"

As soon as the man mentioned his ancestry, the truth of R' Yehudah's claim became apparent, because the Sages knew that the royal family of the Hasmoneans had been assassinated by King Herod. Thus, anyone claiming that royal lineage was actually a descendant of Herod, who had been a slave of the Hasmoneans.

דְּבָרִים לֹא יֶחְדַּל־פָּשַׁע וְחשֵׂךְ שְׂפָתָיו מַשְׂכִּיל:
כ כֶּסֶף נִבְחָר לְשׁוֹן צַדִּיק לֵב רְשָׁעִים כִּמְעָט:

him; however, you should admonish him privately.

The *Vilna Gaon* points out that this verse teaches a person to speak sparingly with others. If his fellow has wronged him and he responds by concealing his hatred and speaking sweetly, this is שְׂפַת שֶׁקֶר, *false lips*. On the other hand, if he responds with rebuke, his fellow will lash out, saying, "You are a fool. Compared to you, I am righteous!" The only thing he will have gained is an enemy, so the best recourse is to limit his speech as much as possible (see following verse).

19. בְּרֹב דְּבָרִים לֹא יֶחְדַּל־פָּשַׁע — *In an abundance of words, offense will not be lacking.* One who talks excessively brings on sin (*Rashi*; cf. *Avos* 1:17). The prohibitions related to the spoken word are so numerous that excessive talk is bound to include some transgression (*Metzudos*).

A person who speaks too much does not allow himself ample opportunity to properly scrutinize and weigh his words before they are spoken. Therefore he should restrain his lips from speaking until he has scrutinized what he is planning to say (*R' Yonah*).

Meiri points out that even a wise person should not speak too much, and this even when discoursing in wisdom, for the tongue is likely to sin.

וְחשֵׂךְ שְׂפָתָיו מַשְׂכִּיל — *But one who restrains his lips is wise.* Rambam (commentary on *Avos* 1:17) divides speech into four categories: (1) דִּבּוּר הָאָסוּר, *forbidden speech*; (2) דִּבּוּר הָרְשׁוּת, *optional speech*; (3) דִּבּוּר מִצְוָה, *virtuous speech*; and (4) דִּבּוּר מוּתָר, *permissible speech.* Malbim points out that most categories of speech, even דִּבּוּר הָרְשׁוּת, *optional speech*, lead to sin. Therefore, a wise person restrains his

lips, speaking words of wisdom exclusively.

The Midrash explains that King Solomon does not suggest that a person must be silent all the time. Rather, he must take care to refrain from speaking about other people.

The *Chafetz Chaim* advises us to be as stingy as possible in using our power of speech (in areas other than Torah and *mitzvos*). Just as a person pays for every word in a telegram, so, too, on the Day of Judgment he will have to account and "pay" for every word that he uttered here in this world.[1]

The Talmud (*Eruvin* 53:2) relates that R' Yose HaGlili was traveling on a road when he met Bruria, the wife of R' Meir. He asked her, בְּאֵיזוֹ דֶרֶךְ נֵלֵךְ לְלוֹד, *Which road should we take to go to [the city of] Lod?*

Bruria admonished R' Yose for speaking to her at such "length" and told him it would only have been necessary to say בְּאֵיזֶה לְלוֹד, *by which to Lod.*

20. כֶּסֶף נִבְחָר לְשׁוֹן צַדִּיק — *The tongue of a righteous person is choice silver.*

The words of the righteous who know how to reprove are like pure silver (*Rashi*).

The righteous know how to admonish others in a positive manner, without speaking harshly or embarrassing the listener. This type of rebuke is compared to silver that has no impurities and is desired by all, for sensible people are eager to hear constructive, pleasantly delivered criticism. This is exemplified by Aaron HaKohen who was אוֹהֵב שָׁלוֹם וְרוֹדֵף שָׁלוֹם, *loving* אוֹהֵב אֶת הַבְּרִיּוֹת וּמְקָרְבָן לַתּוֹרָה, *peace and pursuing peace, loving people and bringing them closer to Torah* (*Avos* 1:12). Aaron's rebuke was given in such a kindly manner that he was loved by all and his words succeeded in bringing

---

1. How careful a person must be before he even allows a syllable to escape his lips is stressed many times by the Sages. R' Shimon ben Gamliel says (*Avos* 1:17): כָּל יָמַי גָּדַלְתִּי בֵּין הַחֲכָמִים וְלֹא מָצָאתִי לַגּוּף טוֹב אֶלָּא שְׁתִיקָה, *All my days I have been raised among the Sages and I found nothing better for oneself than silence.*

words, offense will not be lacking, but one who restrains his lips is wise. [20] The tongue of a righteous person is choice silver, but the heart of the wicked is minute.

people closer to Torah (*Vilna Gaon*).[1]

The moral integrity of an individual is reflected in his speech — neither flippant nor abrasive, but measured and well thought out, refined and without dross (*R' Hirsch*).

לֵב רְשָׁעִים כִּמְעָט — *[But] the heart of the wicked is minute*, for they do not heed the rebuke of the righteous. *Midrash Tanchuma* cites an example: When the prophet Iddo chastised Jeroboam ben Nebat for his idol-worship, Jeroboam raised his hand against the prophet, and his hand became paralyzed. Even so, he did not heed the reproof, for he then requested of the prophet, "Please pray to HASHEM, *your* God, to heal me" (*I Kings* 13). He did not refer to Hashem as "my God" but as "your God." Once his hand was healed, he continued to worship idols as before (*Rashi*).

R' Yonah explains כִּמְעָט as *an instant* (see *Psalms* 81:15, כִּמְעַט אוֹיְבֵיהֶם אַכְנִיעַ, *In an instant I would subdue their foes*). The rebuke of the righteous is refined and

pure. However, the heart of the wicked hears this rebuke for just an instant.

The *Vilna Gaon* elaborates: Though the rebuke given by the righteous is flawless, their words do not improve the wicked. In no way are the righteous to blame for this. On the contrary, the fault lies totally in the heart of the wicked, which is soft and retains the effect of the rebuke for but a short while.

When a hole is bored into hard matter such as iron, even though penetrating the iron is initially difficult, once accomplished, the hole remains. On the other hand, even though a dent is easily made in soft matter, the opening soon closes up and no impression remains. So it is with the heart of the wicked. Any impression the reproof of the righteous may have made lasts but for a short while, after which the wicked return to their evil ways.

In this vein, our Sages state: כָּל תַּלְמִיד חָכָם שֶׁאֵינוּ קָשֶׁה כְּבַרְזֶל אֵינוּ תַּלְמִיד חָכָם, *Any Torah scholar who is not as hard as iron is*

---

1. Examples abound of the ability of the Sages to admonish sinners in such a positive manner that their words were accepted and effective.

When R' Yisrael Salanter lived in Memel, in present-day northwestern Poland, he became aware of flagrant desecration of Shabbos by the Jewish stevedores. In *shul* on Shabbos, R' Yisrael addressed them about the holiness of the day, and said that although they might feel compelled to load and unload ships on Shabbos, it was not necessary for them to write. The workers agreed, and from then on, ceased to write on Shabbos.

A few weeks later, R' Yisrael spoke to them again, pointing out that although they may have no alternative but to *unload* the ships on Shabbos, *loading* them could be avoided. Again the stevedores agreed, and stopped loading the ships on Shabbos. In a third address a few weeks later, R' Yisrael spoke about the prohibition of unloading ships on Shabbos. Step by step, his words eventually caused a complete turnabout in the level of Shabbos observance in the city (*Tnuas HaMussar*, p. 184).

The *Chafetz Chaim* once stopped at an inn, where one of the other patrons happened to be a Cantonist. (Cantonists were Jewish boys who were forcibly taken from their families at the young age of 8 or 9 and inducted into the Russian army, under whose authority they remained for the next twenty-five or more years. This virtually assured that all traces of their former religious way of life were eradicated.) This fellow acted in a crude manner, gulping down his food without reciting a blessing. Even when the *Chafetz Chaim* became aware of this man's background, he felt obligated to reprove the man for his behavior, despite the seeming hopelessness of the situation. He went over and greeted the man warmly, saying, "How I admire you! Despite all the efforts of the Russians to convert you, still know you are a Jew."

Upon hearing these uncritical words, the man broke down and cried. He was so moved by the *Chafetz Chaim's* love for a fellow Jew that he resolved then and there to return to the Torah's true path.

כא שִׂפְתֵי צַדִּיק יִרְעוּ רַבִּים וֶאֱוִילִים בַּחֲסַר־לֵב יָמוּתוּ:
כב בִּרְכַּת יהוה הִיא תַעֲשִׁיר וְלֹא־יוֹסִף עֶצֶב עִמָּהּ:
כג כִּשְׂחוֹק לִכְסִיל עֲשׂוֹת זִמָּה וְחָכְמָה לְאִישׁ תְּבוּנָה:

not a true Torah scholar (Taanis 4a). This trait also distinguishes the entire Jewish nation, who are described as קְשֵׁה עֹרֶף, obstinate. Their obstinacy is a virtue, for they stubbornly cling to their beliefs and cannot be moved from their convictions (Vilna Gaon).

The heart of the wicked is very small, i.e., they can understand only very little (Metzudos).

21. שִׂפְתֵי צַדִּיק יִרְעוּ רַבִּים — The lips of a righteous one will nourish many. Many people "eat" [i.e., benefit] from the prayers and merits of the righteous (Rashi).[1]

The words of the righteous, who teach others to properly follow the path of life, bring them great benefit (Metzudos).

וֶאֱוִילִים בַּחֲסַר־לֵב יָמוּתוּ — But fools will die for lack of [an understanding] heart. Fools, who do not listen to the words of the righteous, will perish as a result of their lack of understanding of these words (Metzudos).

They will die lacking understanding, or they will die as a result of a lack of understanding (Meiri).

The righteous benefit not only themselves, but others as well, like a shepherd who grazes (יִרְעוּ) his sheep. The fools, however, not only fail to benefit others, but they will bring the ultimate harm — death — upon themselves because of their lack of understanding (Ralbag).

22. בִּרְכַּת ה' הִיא תַעֲשִׁיר וְלֹא־יוֹסִף עֶצֶב עִמָּהּ — It is the blessing of HASHEM that enriches, and one need not add toil with it. When God blesses a person, he need not toil to become rich, for God's blessing will suffice (Rashi).

When a person becomes rich, he should not attribute his success to his own efforts, but he should realize that it is God Who gave him the ability and the ideas that were the cause of his success. (See Deuteronomy 8:11-17, where a person is warned not to let his prosperity mislead him into forgetting God and thinking כֹּחִי וְעֹצֶם יָדִי עָשָׂה לִי אֶת־הַחַיִל הַזֶּה, My strength and the might of my hand made me all this wealth.) He should recognize that ברכת ה', the blessing and success that came from Hashem, הִיא תַעֲשִׁיר, that is what enriches, as the verses continue (ibid., v. 18), כִּי הוּא הַנֹּתֵן לְךָ כֹּחַ לַעֲשׂוֹת חָיִל, that it was He Who gave you strength to make wealth (Meiri).

Ibn Ezra renders: When God blesses someone with wealth, God will not include any sorrow with that blessing.

The word עֶצֶב implies two things: טִרְחָה, labor, and דְּאָגָה, worry. The two meanings are essentially one, for usually when a person has to work hard to attain wealth, he is in a constant state of worry, as the Mishnah states (Avos 2:8): מַרְבֶּה נְכָסִים מַרְבֶּה דְאָגָה, the more possessions, the more worry. However, when Hashem blesses an individual, this blessing will make him wealthy, yet he will be spared the labor and worry usually associated with attaining wealth. He will have no toil or worry resulting from it, for he will sit tranquilly in his house and Hashem will send him success in all his undertakings.

This same blessing applies to spiritual wealth. When Hashem blesses a person in Torah, הִיא תַעֲשִׁיר, it enriches, for he will not forget what he has learned and he will be rich in Torah knowledge. In addition, he will not need עֶצֶב, toil, in his learning, for it will come to him naturally like a spring of flowing water (Vilna Gaon).

1. The Talmud (Berachos 17b) reveals that כָּל הָעוֹלָם כֻּלּוֹ נִזּוֹנִין בִּשְׁבִיל חֲנִינָא בְּנִי, וַחֲנִינָא בְּנִי דַּי לוֹ בְּקַב חָרוּבִין מֵעֶרֶב שַׁבָּת לְעֶרֶב שַׁבָּת, the whole world receives sustenance because of Chanina my son, and Chanina my son is satisfied with a measure of carob from one eve of Shabbos to the next eve of Shabbos. R' Chanina ben Dosa's merit was so great that his whole generation was sustained because of him, and yet he himself subsisted on the most meager diet.

²¹ *The lips of a righteous one will nourish many, but fools will die for lack of [an understanding] heart.* ²² *It is the blessing of HASHEM that enriches, and one need not add toil with it.* ²³ *It is like sport to a fool to carry out [an] evil design; and [so is] wisdom to a man of understanding.*

This verse gives us an insight into the righteous individual's perspective on wealth. He is neither anxious to amass great riches nor upset about financial losses, for he realizes that both are controlled by Heavenly decree. Worrying is superfluous in either case. For if wealth is ordained for an individual, he will receive it without worrying about it and constantly thinking about it. And if poverty is his lot, no amount of scheming will save him from it. The righteous are, therefore, content with whatever Hashem gives them and they are happy with their lot, for they realize that it is Hashem's blessing that brings wealth, and worrying will add nothing to it (*Rabbeinu Yonah*).

A righteous person enjoys the biggest imaginable blessing — he is satisfied even with the little he has. Such a person is called a rich man (see *Avos* 4:1, *Who is rich? He who is happy with his lot*) (*Ibn Nachmiash*).

R' Aaron Kotler explains that when Hashem blesses the righteous (such as our forefathers) with wealth, it is a blessing of genuine goodness. It does not bring any sadness with it, for it does not diminish the person's reward in the World to Come. On the contrary, the wealth of the righteous increases their eternal reward, for it serves as a means of sanctifying God's Name, by proving that He rewards those who fulfill His commandments. If this were not so, it would be impossible to measure the agony of the righteous who would be given wealth in this world at the expense of spiritual wealth in the World to Come (*Mishnas R' Aharon*).

The Midrash (*Devarim Rabbah* 3) relates that Shimon ben Shetach once bought a donkey from an Arab. His students found a jewel hanging on the donkey's neck, and told their Rebbi, "בִּרְכַּת ה׳ הִיא תַעֲשִׁיר", *It is the blessing of Hashem that enriches.*" But Shimon ben Shetach answered, "It is the donkey that I bought; I did not buy the jewel." [Even though halachically he was not obligated to return the jewel, Shimon ben Shetach wished to sanctify Hashem's Name.] When he returned the jewel to the Arab, the Arab cried out, "Blessed is Hashem, the God of Shimon ben Shetach."[1]

According to the Midrash (*Bereishis Rabbah* 11:1), בִּרְכַּת ה׳ הִיא תַעֲשִׁיר refers to the day of Shabbos, about which the verse states (*Genesis* 2:3), וַיְבָרֶךְ אֱלֹהִים אֶת־יוֹם הַשְּׁבִיעִי, *God blessed the seventh day.* It is a day which brings no עֶצֶב, *sorrow*, with it, for there is no public display of mourning on Shabbos. The Shabbos enriches (תַעֲשִׁיר), for in the merit of honoring the Shabbos, a person will be blessed with wealth.

23. כִּשְׂחוֹק לִכְסִיל עֲשׂוֹת זִמָּה — *It is like sport to a fool to carry out [an] evil design.* Just as it is easy to engage in sport, it is easy for the wicked to carry out their sinful plans (*Metzudos*).

וְחָכְמָה לְאִישׁ תְּבוּנָה — *And [so is] wisdom to a man of understanding.* Similarly, *wisdom is like sport* to a *man of understanding*, i.e., he finds it easy to act upon its teachings (*Rashi*).

The *Vilna Gaon* explains that שְׂחוֹק, literally *laughter*, comes upon a person suddenly; one sees something amusing, and bursts out laughing. So too, זִמָּה, which can also mean *depravity* (see *Leviticus* 18:17), comes upon the wicked person with a suddenness. Though initially he had intended only to banter with a woman, suddenly he feels driven to sin. Similarly, an original Torah thought or

1. The students applied this verse literally — that Hashem had blessed their *rebbi* with wealth — whereas Shimon ben Shetach introduced a new meaning to the verse. In his eyes, bringing about a blessing of God's Name in the world — הִיא תַעֲשִׁיר — that is real wealth!

כד מְגוֹרַת רָשָׁע הִיא תְבוֹאֶנּוּ וְתַאֲוַת צַדִּיקִים יִתֵּן:
כה-כו כַּעֲבוֹר סוּפָה וְאֵין רָשָׁע וְצַדִּיק יְסוֹד עוֹלָם:
כַּחֹמֶץ | לַשִּׁנַּיִם וְכֶעָשָׁן לָעֵינָיִם כֵּן הֶעָצֵל לְשֹׁלְחָיו:

wise idea comes suddenly to the learned.

Man is a "creature of habit"; his regular conduct, whether good or evil, becomes second nature to him. So great is the cumulative effect of his past deeds that, ultimately, his present decisions to do good or bad become almost instinctive, like laughter, which is spontaneous. Thus, sinful actions are spontaneous to the fool, and wise deeds are spontaneous to a *man of understanding* (*Malbim*).[1]

24. מְגוֹרַת רָשָׁע הִיא תְבוֹאֶנּוּ — *What a wicked one dreads will come upon him.* The Generation of the Dispersion attempted to build a tower because they feared פֶּן־נָפוּץ, *lest we be dispersed* (*Genesis* 11:4). In the end, this is exactly how they were punished: וַיָּפֶץ ה' אֹתָם, *And HASHEM dispersed them* [*Genesis* 11:8, see *Rashi* ibid.] (*Rashi*).

Similarly the Egyptians plotted against the Jews for fear פֶּן יִרְבֶּה, *lest they become plentiful.* God declared that the more the Egyptians afflicted the Jews, כֵּן יִרְבֶּה, *so they* [the Jews] *became plentiful* (*Exodus* 1:10,12).

The *Vilna Gaon* explains that the wicked fear the effect of the sins they have committed, for the sin itself brings judgment upon the sinner.

וְתַאֲוַת צַדִּיקִים יִתֵּן — *And [God] will fulfill the desire of the righteous.* The desire of the righteous will be given to them by God, the One Who has the power to give (*Rashi*).

It is God Himself Who rewards the righteous for their good deeds, for then the reward is infinite, just as He is infinite. If the reward would come only from the *mitzvah* itself (as the punishment comes from the sin itself) the reward would be limited, just as the *mitzvah* itself (as something performed by mortals with material artifacts) is limited. The verse uses the word יִתֵּן, *He will fulfill,* in future tense, to imply that the true reward does not come immediately, but will only be given at a later time [in the World to Come] (*Vilna Gaon*).

25. כַּעֲבוֹר סוּפָה וְאֵין רָשָׁע — *When the storm passes, a wicked one is no more.* The fury of a storm wind comes suddenly, and drives the wicked one from his place (*Rashi*). He will be destroyed suddenly, and will not be able to save himself from disaster (*Meiri*).[2]

Malbim explains that because the wicked one has no roots, his position is very tenuous. When things are going well he remains standing, but as soon as a storm hits he will be uprooted.

וְצַדִּיק יְסוֹד עוֹלָם — *But a righteous one is the foundation of the world.* Alternatively, he is *an everlasting foundation* (*Vilna Gaon*). A righteous person is compared to the foundation of the world, which does not move. So, too, he will be strong in times of trouble, able to protect others, like

1. Clearly, then, each person must be careful to habituate himself in doing God's will. This was the level of Divine service achieved by the righteous, as exemplified by King David, who stated: חִשַּׁבְתִּי דְרָכָי וָאָשִׁיבָה רַגְלַי אֶל־עֵדֹתֶיךָ, *I considered my ways and returned my feet to Your testimonies* (*Psalms* 119:59). He said, "Master of the Universe, every day I considered my ways and said I would go to such and such a place and to such and such a house; however, my feet would lead me to the houses of prayer and study (*Vayikra Rabbah* 35:1)." So ingrained was Torah in David's soul that his feet rebelled against taking him to any destination other than that of Torah.

2. A sudden downfall is characteristic of the punishment meted out to the wicked, just as Haman was hurriedly brought to Esther's drinking party while he was in the midst of his consultation with his wife and advisors (*Esther* 6:14). R' Yechezkel Levenstein points out that the verse states וַיַּבְהִלוּ, *and they hurried,* to emphasize that Haman's punishment began suddenly. Thus it was evident that the Divine Hand was at work, thwarting his evil plans and bringing his just retribution.

²⁴ What a wicked one dreads will come upon him, and [God] will fulfill the desire of the righteous. ²⁵ When the storm passes, a wicked one is no more, but a righteous one is the foundation of the world. ²⁶ Like vinegar to the teeth and like smoke to the eyes, so is a sluggard to those who send him.

a foundation that upholds a wall (*Meiri*).

The *Vilna Gaon* explains that even after his death, a righteous person remains a foundation of the world, for his merit protects the world.[1]

R' *Hirsch* explains that as long as all is quiet and events seem to proceed routinely, the wicked prosper and enjoy the fulfillment of their desires. However, when God ordains a purifying storm to cleanse humanity, everything rotten reveals itself and collapses. The just will weather all storms and will remain a solid foundation for future humanity, which rests in Hashem's hand.

The Midrash (*Bereishis Rabbah* 30) applies this verse to the Generation of the Flood, who were all wiped out by the sudden stormy waters. But the righteous one, Noah, was the foundation of the world, for the world continued to exist in his merit.

The Talmud (*Yoma* 38:2) derives from our verse that the world continues to exist even for one righteous person, (צַדִּיק) because he is *the foundation of the world*.

Midrash Tanchuma (*Nitzavim* 2) elucidates this principle further, stating: "You are all guarantors for one another; even if there is [only] one righteous one among you, you are all existing in his merit. Not only you [exist in his merit], but if there is one righteous one among you, the whole world exists in his merit, as it says, *But a righteous one is the foundation of the world*."

Rambam (*Hilchos Teshuvah* 3:4) instructs that a person should consider himself and the whole world as half meritorious and half guilty. If he commits even one [additional]

transgression, he tips the balance for himself and for the whole world to guilt, and causes destruction. If he performs one [additional] *mitzvah*, he tips the balance in favor of merit, and brings salvation to himself and the whole world, as the verse states: *a righteous one is the foundation of the world*, i.e., a righteous person tips the balance of the world in favor of merit and salvation.

26. כַּחֹמֶץ לַשִּׁנַּיִם וְכֶעָשָׁן לָעֵינָיִם כֵּן הֶעָצֵל לְשֹׁלְחָיו — *Like vinegar to the teeth and like smoke to the eyes, so is a sluggard to those who send him.* Just as vinegar irritates a person's teeth and smoke irritates his eyes, so a lazy person harms the one who depends upon him to fulfill a certain assignment. The sluggard's failure to do so causes harm to the sender (*Metzudos*).

If someone were to drink vinegar, the damage would be twofold. Not only would he ruin his appetite, but he would also be unable to eat because of the irritation caused to his teeth. Similarly, if a person attempted to produce light by igniting damp wood, so much smoke would be emitted that not only would there be no light, but the smoke would dim his eyes even further. So, too, when an individual sends a lazy person to fulfill an assigned task, the sender suffers a twofold loss. Firstly, the messenger will fail to carry out his mission. Secondly, the sender will become agitated and nervous, and may even suffer heartache, as he anxiously awaits the return of his messenger, only to learn that it was all in vain (*Vilna Gaon*).

R' *Yonah* explains that this verse is a metaphor for a person who is lax in

---

1. Sometimes the passing of a righteous person is in itself the merit for the preservation of the world. After the death of the renowned *tzaddik* R' Hirsch Levinson, the son-in-law of the *Chafetz Chaim*, his widow bemoaned the fact that the Heavenly judgment passed over the world's many people and struck her righteous husband. The *Chafetz Chaim* comforted her, explaining that if Heaven had not taken R' Hirsch, in his place half of the world would have had to die. Thus R' Hirsch's merit was needed to protect countless people.

כז יִרְאַת יְהוה תּוֹסִיף יָמִים וּשְׁנוֹת רְשָׁעִים
כח תִּקְצֹרְנָה: תּוֹחֶלֶת צַדִּיקִים שִׂמְחָה וְתִקְוַת
כט רְשָׁעִים תֹּאבֵד: מָעוֹז לַתֹּם דֶּרֶךְ יהוה
ל וּמְחִתָּה לְפֹעֲלֵי אָוֶן: צַדִּיק לְעוֹלָם בַּל־יִמּוֹט

carrying out the task God sent him to accomplish in this world. Someone who is lazy in fulfilling the commandments will fail to do them perfectly, and therefore cause himself untold spiritual damage.

27. יִרְאַת ה' תּוֹסִיף יָמִים — *The fear of HASHEM will increase days.* Someone who fears Hashem will merit additional days of life, beyond those normally allotted to him, for Divine Providence will protect him from happenings that would have caused his death (*Ralbag*).[1]

וּשְׁנוֹת רְשָׁעִים תִּקְצֹרְנָה — *But the years of the wicked will be shortened.* The wicked will have their allotted years of life shortened because of their sins (*Ralbag*).

R' Bachya expounds on this verse. Worry and fear usually weaken a person physically and hasten his death. In this case, however, the opposite is true. Someone who lives with the constant worry of sin and fear of God will have his life lengthened. The wicked, on the other hand, who pamper their bodies and therefore expect to enjoy good health and longevity, actually cause their lives to be shortened. This verse emphasizes that the merits or sins of a person can change the number of years allotted to him. This in essence is a hidden miracle.

He explains further that this verse is not stating an absolute, immutable rule that the righteous will live long and the wicked die young. Rather, it teaches that sometimes God lengthens the life of the righteous such as King Hezekiah, and shortens the life of the wicked, such as Ben Hadad, the king of Aram. If this does not happen to every righteous or wicked individual, it is probably because the righteous are not absolutely righteous, and the wicked not absolutely wicked. Another factor may be that Hashem wishes to increase the reward for the righteous and the punishment of the wicked in the World to Come.

In any case, the lengthening or shortening of lives is a miracle that is hidden from people, who perceive it as only the "natural" course of nature. One of Torah's basic principles is that all that transpires is based on hidden miracles; there is no such thing as "nature" or an ordinary course of events (אֵין לָהֶם טֶבַע וּמִנְהָג שֶׁל עוֹלָם), neither for the individual nor for the general public. Rather, a *mitzvah* brings reward, and a transgression brings destruction [cf. *Exodus* 13:16, *Ramban* ibid.] (*R' Bachya*).

The direct correlation between merit and longevity is illustrated by comparing the lifespan of the *Kohanim Gedolim*, the High Priests, in the First and Second Temples. R' Yochanan states (*Yoma* 9:1) that throughout the 410 years of the First Temple, there were only 18 *Kohanim Gedolim* [who generally served as long as they lived]. Because they were righteous, their days were prolonged. However, during the 420 years of the Second Temple, there were more than 300 *Kohanim*

---

1. R' Shimon ben Chalafta was at the circumcision of a baby. At the meal, the father of the newborn served seven-year-old wine and remarked, "I am putting the rest of this wine away for a future celebration of my son." After the meal, which lasted well into the night, R' Shimon ben Chalafta left to return home. On his way, he met the Angel of Death, who was very upset. When R' Shimon ben Chalafta asked why, the Angel of Death explained, "I am perturbed because of the way people talk — they make plans for the future without even knowing the day of their death. This father who said he will keep wine for his son's future celebration is destined to die after thirty days." R' Shimon asked the angel when he was destined to die, but the angel answered, "I have no power over you or those like you. At times, the Holy One, Blessed is He, likes your good deeds and adds life onto you, as it says, *The fear of HASHEM will increase days*" (*Devarim Rabbah* 9:1).

²⁷ The fear of HASHEM will increase days, but the years of the wicked will be shortened. ²⁸ The expectation of the righteous is gladness, but the hope of the wicked will go lost. ²⁹ The way of HASHEM is a stronghold for the innocent, but a ruin to workers of iniquity. ³⁰ A righteous one will never falter,

---

Gedolim. Of these, Shimon *HaTzaddik* served for 40 years, Yochanan *Kohen Gadol* for 80 years, Yishmael ben Pavi for 10 years and R' Elazar ben Charsum for 11. Deducting these terms from the total of 420 years, we find that the remaining *Kohanim Gedolim* did not even complete one year of service, as the verse states, שְׁנוֹת רְשָׁעִים תִּקְצֹרְנָה, *the years of the wicked will be shortened.*[1]

28. תּוֹחֶלֶת צַדִּיקִים שִׂמְחָה — *The expectation of the righteous is gladness.* The hope of the righteous will eventually be fulfilled and they will rejoice (*Rashi*).

וְתִקְוַת רְשָׁעִים תֹּאבֵד — *But the hope of the wicked will go lost,* for it will not be fulfilled (*Rashi*).

A person's longings for wealth or honor often bring disappointment and heartache. However, the righteous one's hope brings happiness, for he does not depend on his own strength or wisdom to attain his desires, but places his trust in God's kindness. Even if his expectations are not immediately fulfilled, he still rejoices at having had the opportunity to put his continuous trust and hope in God. The more prolonged his expectation, the greater the reward for his hope. Thus, even if his original hope was not realized, his trust in God will bring him ultimate reward and great kindness from Him, which will far surpass any benefit he would have enjoyed had his original hope been fulfilled (*R' Yonah*). [See *Psalms* 32:10, וְהַבּוֹטֵחַ בַּה' חֶסֶד יְסוֹבְבֶנּוּ, *but the one who trusts in Hashem, kindness surrounds him.*]

According to the *Vilna Gaon,* the expec-

tation [תּוֹחֶלֶת] of the righteous is for a long-awaited desire, whereas the hope [תִּקְוָה] of the wicked is for something anticipated in the immediate future. The righteous do not look for an immediate reward for their good deeds in this world; rather, they await the good they will receive in the World to Come. Their hopes will be realized, and they will rejoice with their eternal reward. However, the wicked people's yearning for immediate pleasure is in vain, for their way will perish (*Vilna Gaon*).

29. מָעוֹז לַתֹּם דֶּרֶךְ ה' — *The way of HASHEM is a stronghold for the innocent.* God's way will strengthen the innocent one, who goes on His path i.e., it will defend him [in the Heavenly Court] (*Metzudos*).

וּמְחִתָּה לְפֹעֲלֵי אָוֶן — *But a ruin to workers of iniquity.* God's way is a ruin to evildoers who flout it, and it brings retribution upon them (*Rashi*). It prosecutes them [in the Heavenly Court] (*Metzudos*).

The *Vilna Gaon* refers to the verse: כִּי־יְשָׁרִים דַּרְכֵי ה' וְצַדִּקִים יֵלְכוּ בָם וּפֹשְׁעִים יִכָּשְׁלוּ בָם, *For the ways of HASHEM are straight; the righteous will walk in them and sinners will stumble over them* (*Hosea* 14:10).

It is because the wicked adopt methods opposed to Hashem that they have such a disastrous end (*Malbim*).

30. צַדִּיק לְעוֹלָם בַּל־יִמּוֹט — *A righteous one will never falter.* Even if the righteous falter, their fall will not last forever, for they will rise again (*Rashi*). [Cf. 24:16, כִּי שֶׁבַע יִפּוֹל צַדִּיק וָקָם, *even if a righteous man falls seven times, he will rise up.*] His

---

1. *R' Aharon Kotler* explains that even though the Talmud labels the *Kohanim Gedolim* of the Second Temple as wicked, this term is not meant literally. Rather, they fell short of the spiritual perfection demanded of someone who would have to enter the Holy of Holies on Yom Kippur and witness the revelation of the Divine Presence. The fact that each year another *Kohen* was eager to assume the position, knowing that his predecessor had died after a short term in office, attests to the willingness of these *Kohanim* to sacrifice their lives for Divine Service.

לא וּרְשָׁעִים לֹא יִשְׁכְּנוּ־אָרֶץ: פִּי־צַדִּיק יָנוּב חָכְמָה
לב וּלְשׁוֹן תַּהְפֻּכוֹת תִּכָּרֵת: שִׂפְתֵי צַדִּיק יֵדְעוּן רָצוֹן
א וּפִי רְשָׁעִים תַּהְפֻּכוֹת: מֹאזְנֵי מִרְמָה תּוֹעֲבַת יהוה

children will remain after his death (*Ibn Ezra*).

R' Yonah connects this verse with the previous one: The *tzaddik* will not falter because God will be his stronghold at the time of his misfortune.

A *tzaddik* is like a tree. Even if the winds blow its branches back and forth, the roots underground are steadfast, and the tree returns to its upright position. So, too, despite the storms of life, the righteous remain firm, for they are anchored by their strong roots (*R' Hirsch*).

וּרְשָׁעִים לֹא יִשְׁכְּנוּ־אָרֶץ — *But the wicked will not dwell [tranquilly] in the land.* The wicked will not endure in the land for long. Their success in this world is only temporary (*Metzudos*). The memory of the wicked, as well as their children, will perish (*Ibn Ezra*).

31. פִּי־צַדִּיק יָנוּב חָכְמָה — *The mouth of a righteous one will speak wisdom.* Rashi relates יָנוּב to נִיב שְׂפָתַיִם, *speech of the lips* (Isaiah 57:19). *Ibn Ezra* relates it to תְּנוּבָה, *produce.* Thus, the words of the righteous will *produce the fruits of wisdom*.

A righteous person is compared to a tree [*He shall be like a tree deeply rooted alongside brooks of water, which yields*

its *fruit in due season and whose leaf never withers* (*Psalms 1:3*)]. A tree produces both leaves and fruit. Though fruit is its main product, the leaf serves a function by providing shade to protect the fruit from heat. So, too, a righteous person produces both leaves and fruit. The "leaves" represent his speech in everyday, mundane matters. Like the *leaf that never withers*, such speech is of great value, since, as the Sages explain (*Succah 21b*), even the mundane conversation of Torah scholars requires study. The "fruit" represents the speech of the righteous in Torah, which is of primary importance, just as the fruit is the primary product of the tree. A righteous person has so accustomed himself to speak wisdom that it issues from his mouth like fruit (*R' Bachya*).

וּלְשׁוֹן תַּהְפֻּכוֹת תִּכָּרֵת — *But a tongue of perversities will be cut off.* The tongue of the wicked, who pervert the truth of Torah's *chochmah* into heresy, will be cut off (*Metzudos*).

32. שִׂפְתֵי צַדִּיק יֵדְעוּן רָצוֹן — *The lips of a righteous one know how to appease.* The righteous know how to placate and appease God,[1] and also know how to appease their fellow men by making peace

1. We find numerous examples of how the righteous, through their words of prayer and supplication, appeased Hashem's wrath at the sins and thereby averted harsh decrees. When those who worshiped the Golden Calf aroused God's anger, Moses appealed for Divine mercy to save the nation from annihilation (see *Exodus 32:9-14*). After the sin of the Spies, Moses' entreaties again protected the Jewish nation from the full brunt of Divine wrath (*Numbers 14:11-20*). The Talmud also abounds with cases where righteous people appeased God's anger and attained the Heavenly blessing sought by the Jews (e.g., see *Taanis 19a* regarding Choni Hame'agal and his prayers in time of drought).

Torah scholars in all generations were also blessed with the Divinely inspired wisdom to enable them to find favor with God and appease His displeasure. R' Levi Yitzchak from Berdichev was famous as an advocate for Jews, always finding a favorable way to present their case to the Heavenly court. Once he saw a Jewish wagon driver who was busily greasing his wagon wheels while still wearing his *tallis* and *tefillin* and praying. Instead of berating this fellow for his disrespectful attitude towards prayer, R' Levi Yitzchak turned his eyes heavenward and exclaimed, "Hashem, look how closely your people are attached to You. Even when doing their menial tasks, they cannot stop praying to you for a minute."

but the wicked will not dwell [tranquilly] in the land.
³¹ The mouth of a righteous one will speak wisdom, but a
tongue of the perversities will be cut off. ³² The lips of a
righteous one know how to appease [God], but the mouth
of the wicked [knows] perversities.

¹ Deceitful scales are an abomination of HASHEM,

between them.[1]

Rabbeinu Yonah connects this verse to the previous one: Even though *the mouth of a righteous one will speak wisdom* and he speaks only truth, he will bend the truth for the sake of bringing peace among people. This is in line with the dictum of the Sages (*Yevamos* 65b), מוּתָּר לוֹ לְאָדָם לְשַׁנּוֹת בִּדְבַר הַשָּׁלוֹם, *it is permissible for a person to alter* [the exact truth] *for the sake of peace*. The mouth of the wicked, on the other hand, constantly sides with falsehood, favoring the guilty party in an argument and supporting his lies.

וּפִי רְשָׁעִים תַּהְפֻּכוֹת — *But the mouth of the* wicked [knows] perversities. *Ibn Ezra* renders: The righteous know how to say that which finds favor, and the mouth of the wicked ones knows how to speak perversities. *Metzudos* adds that they know how to distort Hashem's words, for this is what they are accustomed to doing.

A *tzaddik* who has wronged someone knows how to appease the person and ask his forgiveness.[2] He regrets his wrongdoing and expresses his apology so sincerely that the person forgives him immediately. However, when the wicked person comes to appease the one he has wronged, he speaks perversities, i.e., lies and insincerities (*Vilna Gaon*).

XI

1. מֹאזְנֵי מִרְמָה תּוֹעֲבַת ה׳ — *Deceitful scales are an abomination of HASHEM*. These are scales that are weighted in such a way as to cheat customers (*Metzudos*).

1. Aaron *HaKohen* personified this trait of making peace between man and wife and between feuding Jews. He is praised for (*Avos* 1:12) אוֹהֵב שָׁלוֹם וְרוֹדֵף שָׁלוֹם, *loving peace and pursuing peace*. *Avos D' Rav Nosson* 12 describes how Aaron brought about a reconciliation between two parties: Upon meeting the first party, he said: "Your friend is distraught about how he wronged you! He is even too embarrassed to approach you!" Aaron then approached the second party with the very same statement. When the two subsequently met, they hugged and kissed.

Torah scholars often utilized unconventional means to make peace between the disputants who came before them. It is told that the *Noda B'Yehudah*, Rabbi Yechezkel Landau, rav of Prague, was asked to adjudicate a case about the disputed ownership of a certain gravesite. After hearing the claims of the two litigants, each of whom claimed that the plot belonged to him, the *Noda B'Yehudah* stated that in order to settle the case, he must see the property in question. At the gravesite, R' Yechezkel bent down and put his ear to the ground. The surprised litigants asked the Rav what he had heard. The *Noda B'Yehudah* responded, "Both of you are claiming that this gravesite is yours. But the earth is saying, 'Both of you are mine.'" Abashed, the two litigants quickly settled their dispute themselves.

2. In his later years, the *Steipler Gaon*, R' Yaakov Yisrael Kanievsky, rarely attended celebrations outside of the family. His appearance at the *bar mitzvah* of a boy to whom he was not related was therefore a surprise to those present. The Steipler asked to speak to the boy privately. He explained that six years earlier he had seen this boy in the Lederman Shul on Yom Kippur holding a large *sefer*. The Steipler reprimanded the boy for learning at a time when he should be praying. However, the boy held up his *sefer* and showed that it was actually a *siddur* that resembled a Gemara. The Steipler wished to apologize immediately, but according to Jewish law, a minor does not have the capacity to forgive. The Steipler made a mental note of the boy's *bar mitzvah* date, and hastened to ask his forgiveness as soon as it was halachically possible.

ב וְאֶבֶן שְׁלֵמָה רְצוֹנוֹ: בָּא־זָדוֹן וַיָּבֹא קָלוֹן וְאֶת־צְנוּעִים
ג חָכְמָה: תֻּמַּת יְשָׁרִים תַּנְחֵם וְסֶלֶף בּוֹגְדִים °וׁשַׁדֵּם:
ד לֹא־יוֹעִיל הוֹן בְּיוֹם עֶבְרָה וּצְדָקָה תַּצִּיל מִמָּוֶת:

°יְשָׁדֵּם ק'

וְאֶבֶן שְׁלֵמָה רְצוֹנוֹ — *But a perfect* [i.e., honest] *weight is His desire.* The Torah warns against possessing false weights both in *Leviticus* — *You shall not commit a perversion in justice, in measures of length, weight or volume. You shall have correct scales, correct weights, correct dry measures, and correct liquid measures* (15:35,36); and again in *Deuteronomy* — *You should not have in your pouch a weight and a weight — a large one and a small one. And you shall not have in your house a measure and a measure — a large one and a small one. A perfect and honest weight shall you have . . .* (25:13-15).

The *Chinuch* (*Mitzvah* 259) explains that the retribution for false weights and measures is more severe than for most other offenses, because the sinner is usually unaware of those whom he has cheated, and therefore cannot make restitution.[1]

Deceitful scales are so abhorrent to God that it is forbidden to own them, even if they are not being used for measuring (*Bava Basra* 89b).

This verse follows the last verses of the preceding chapter, which condemn the false words of the wicked. The juxtaposition teaches us that just as deceitful scales are loathsome even before they are put to use, for they are meant to cheat, so, too, God hates a person who prepares to speak falsehood, even if his words have not yet caused actual harm. His readiness to speak evil makes him hateful to Hashem (*R' Yonah*).

The *Vilna Gaon* applies this verse to spiritual matters as well. *Deceitful scales* would describe the person who rules leniently for himself, but strictly for others; or one who chooses the lenient rulings of

both the House of Hillel and the House of Shammai. A *perfect weight* refers to a person who is consistent in observing the rulings of either house, both the leniencies and restrictions. The person who chooses only the restrictions of both houses, however, is a fool, for this is not God's desire.

Malbim explains that there is no neutral value between proper and improper. The very avoidance of that which is abhorrent to God is a positive action, which delights Him.

2. בָּא־זָדוֹן וַיָּבֹא קָלוֹן — *[When] a willful sinner comes, disgrace comes.* A willful sinner brings shame with him, for his actions disgrace his fellow man (*Metzudos*). [זָדוֹן, literally an intentionally committed sin, is explained by the commentators as אִישׁ זָדוֹן, *a person who is a willful sinner.*]

וְאֶת־צְנוּעִים חָכְמָה — *But with modest ones [comes] wisdom. Malbim* explains that a *willful sinner* is one who arrogantly and publicly disputes God's word, contemptuously transgressing it. Such behavior tends to be accompanied by extreme haughtiness, leading him to mock words of wisdom and the Sages (see 21:24 זֵד יָהִיר לֵץ שְׁמוֹ, *a malevolent, haughty man, scoffer is his name*). The צְנוּעִים, *modest ones,* on the other hand, accept the words of the Sages; therefore, they are the ones who can attain wisdom.

The *Vilna Gaon* explains a זָדוֹן as an arrogant person who studies to be disputatious, rather than to find the truth. Such a person brings embarrassment to the serious students in the study hall. Wisdom can be attained only by צְנוּעִים, *modest ones,* i.e., those who sit silently and absorb the words of their teacher, rather than rushing

1. As a young man, the *Chafetz Chaim* earned his livelihood by keeping a store. His wife generally took care of the business, and the *Chafetz Chaim* himself would take time from his learning to come to the store daily and inspect the weights and measures, lest they be inaccurate and cause a customer to be cheated. His first published work was a booklet on the importance of having honest weights and measures.

but a perfect weight is His desire. ² [When] a willful sinner comes, disgrace comes, but with modest ones [comes] wisdom. ³ The innocence of the upright will guide them, but the corruption of the faithless will despoil them. ⁴ Wealth will not avail in a day of wrath, but charity rescues from death.

to voice their own opinion. For this reason the human being was created with two eyes, two ears, but just one mouth. His two eyes should be utilized for pursuing the words of the Written Law; his two ears, for absorbing the words of the Oral Law; but his speech should be limited. Thus, the Talmud teaches: מִלָּה בְּסֶלַע מַשְׁתּוּקָא בִּתְרֵין, *[if] a word is worth one coin, then silence is worth two (Megillah 18a).*

Midrash Tanchuma comments that when a generation possesses false weights, ultimately it will be afflicted by a harsh government. This is implied by the juxtaposition of the first two verses of this chapter: *Deceitful scales are an abomination of Hashem. . . . When a willful sinner comes, disgrace comes* [i.e. an outgrowth of deceitful scales is that the government will bring shame upon the Jews]. The Torah, too, alludes to this, because the prohibition against false weights and measures (*Deuteronomy* 25:13-15) is followed by the reminder of Amalek's attack against Israel in the desert (ibid. 17, see *Rashi*).

3. תֻּמַּת יְשָׁרִים תַּנְחֵם — *The innocence of the upright will guide them.* The perfect innocence of the upright will lead them on a road that is good for them (*Metzudos*).[1]

R' Yonah compares the terms תֹּם, *innocence,* and יוֹשֶׁר, *uprightness.* He explains that these two are very similar and are usually used jointly. The word תֹּם refers to "perfection." In an animal, it means that there is no physical blemish, since this is its perfection. In human beings, which are defined in terms of their character, pere-

fection refers to refinement of מִדּוֹת, *character traits,* while a "blemished" person is one with an evil or base character. A יָשָׁר, *just person,* is someone who loves justice and chooses what is correct. In order to do so, he must clearly recognize what is upright. In addition to a natural propensity to uprightness, he must also retain and redirect his desires towards this goal. This verse explains that the perfection of their character traits, which the upright achieve, guides them to act properly in all situations, and protects them from stumbling in any of their actions.

וְסֶלֶף בֹּגְדִים יְשָׁדֵּם — *But the corruption of the faithless will despoil them.* The traitors' crookedness will rob them of their life (*Metzudos*).

4. לֹא־יוֹעִיל הוֹן בְּיוֹם עֶבְרָה — *Wealth will not avail in a day of wrath.* In peacetime, riches are of value (see 10:15); but in times of wrath, when God brings pestilence or war, wealth will be of no avail (*Malbim*).

If God is angry at a person, his wealth will not redeem him from misfortune, for his enemy will scorn his riches (*Metzudos*).

וּצְדָקָה תַּצִּיל מִמָּוֶת — *But charity rescues from death.* By contributing to charity, a person can save himself from death (*Metzudos*), and from the judgment of *Gehinnom* (*Bava Basra* 10a). [See commentary to 10:2, where the identical phrase appears.]

In 10:2, when saying that money cannot save one from misfortune, King Solomon speaks of אוֹצְרוֹת רֶשַׁע, *treasures of*

---

1. The Talmudic sage Rava was once so engrossed in study that he did not notice that he was injuring his hand. A Sadducee reproached him, "The Jewish nation was impetuous, and you still retain this bad quality. You put your mouth before your ears, for you accepted the Torah before you even heard what it contained," i.e., when God offered them the Torah, the Jews said נַעֲשֶׂה, *we will do,* before נִשְׁמַע, *we will hear.* Rava replied, "Our approach was one of perfect innocence and love of God. We trusted that He would neither mislead us nor demand the impossible of us, and in such cases the verse promises: *the innocence of the upright will guide them*" (*Shabbos* 88a).

ה צִדְקַת תָּמִים תְּיַשֵּׁר דַּרְכּוֹ וּבְרִשְׁעָתוֹ יִפֹּל רָשָׁע:
ו צִדְקַת יְשָׁרִים תַּצִּילֵם וּבְהַוַּת בֹּגְדִים יִלָּכֵדוּ:
ז בְּמוֹת אָדָם רָשָׁע תֹּאבַד תִּקְוָה וְתוֹחֶלֶת אוֹנִים
ח אָבָדָה: צַדִּיק מִצָּרָה נֶחֱלָץ וַיָּבֹא רָשָׁע תַּחְתָּיו:
ט בְּפֶה חָנֵף יַשְׁחִת רֵעֵהוּ וּבְדַעַת צַדִּיקִים יֵחָלֵצוּ:

wickedness, teaching that wealth attained dishonestly will not rescue someone from misfortune. Our verse goes further, saying that even righteously attained wealth will not rescue a person in time of wrath. The merit one earns by giving charity is the only fortune that can save a person from wrath, evil decrees and even death. In that case, his money will not only rescue him from death in this world, but will also earn him greater rewards in the World to Come (*R' Yonah*).

5. צִדְקַת תָּמִים תְּיַשֵּׁר דַּרְכּוֹ — *The righteousness of an innocent one straightens his path.* The righteousness that a person does leads him on the straight path, and this is of great benefit to him (*Metzudos*).

וּבְרִשְׁעָתוֹ יִפֹּל רָשָׁע — *But a wicked one shall fall in his own wickedness.* He will fall victim to the very same evil he plotted to bring upon his fellow man (*Metzudos*).

The *Vilna Gaon* explains that when a wicked person errs in Torah and falls, it is a result of the evil deeds that he had previously committed. Our Sages explain (*Chagigah* 15b) that Doeg and Achitofel, two outstanding Torah scholars of their generation, sinned and died because wickedness was buried in their hearts from before. According to *Tosafos* (ibid) they approached Torah learning without the fear of God.

6. צִדְקַת יְשָׁרִים תַּצִּילֵם — *The righteousness of the upright will rescue them,* from distress (*Ibn Ezra*).

Conscientious observance of God's commandments provides, in itself, protection from many ills (*R' Hirsch*).

וּבְהַוַּת בֹּגְדִים יִלָּכֵדוּ — *But the faithless will be trapped in the destruction [they perpetrate].* Traitors will be caught in the destructiveness they perpetrate (*Rashi*).

Or, they will become trapped by the destructiveness they had planned for others (*Metzudos*; cf. 26:27).

7. בְּמוֹת אָדָם רָשָׁע תֹּאבַד תִּקְוָה — *When a wicked man dies, hope is lost,* i.e., the hope of all those who trusted in him (*Rashi*).

R' Bachya explains why particularly in this verse the wicked person is referred to as an אָדָם רָשָׁע", *a wicked "man."* The word אָדָם, *man,* is related to the word אֲדָמָה, *earth,* because Adam, the first man, was fashioned from the earth. An individual who is drawn after "earthly" concerns and expends all his efforts in pursuing his physical lusts and desires is considered wicked. All expectations perish with him, for all his hopes were for physical, rather than spiritual, gratification; with his death, nothing remains.

וְתוֹחֶלֶת אוֹנִים אָבָדָה — *And the expectation of [his] offspring perishes.* אוֹנִים refers to *offspring,* for they come from the person's אוֹן, *strength* (*Metzudos*). Their *expectation* is lost, for they receive no benefit in their father's merit. When the righteous die, however, their children can rely on their parents' righteousness (*Rashi*).

The word תִּקְוָה, *hope,* implies immediacy, while תּוֹחֶלֶת, *expectation,* is a long-range hope for the future (see 10:28). The wicked person expects good for himself personally, and he expects it immediately, and this is lost as soon as he dies. His long-range hope for the future good of his children, and their hopes of benefiting from their father's actions, will also perish with his death (*Vilna Gaon*).

8. צַדִּיק מִצָּרָה נֶחֱלָץ וַיָּבֹא רָשָׁע תַּחְתָּיו — *A righteous one is extricated from trouble, but a wicked one comes in his place.* If a misfortune is decreed upon a righteous

⁵ The righteousness of an innocent one straightens his path, but a wicked one shall fall in his wickedness. ⁶ The righteousness of the upright will rescue them, but the faithless will be trapped in the destruction [they perpetrate]. ⁷ When a wicked man dies, hope is lost, and the expectation of [his] offspring perishes. ⁸ A righteous one is extricated from trouble, but a wicked one comes in his place. ⁹ With [his] mouth, a flatterer corrupts his fellow, but the righteous are extricated through knowledge. ¹⁰ The city

man and, due to his good deeds, he is spared, the decree is visited upon a wicked man in his stead. The Heavenly Attribute of Judgment is not appeased unless someone else comes in his stead (*Metzudos*) (see 21:18).[1]

As examples of this, when Mordechai was saved from Haman's wicked schemes, Haman himself became the victim in his stead (*Esther* 9:25). Chananyah, Mishael and Azaryah were saved from the burning furnace, and those who had thrown them in were consumed in their place (*Daniel* 3:22) (*Vilna Gaon*). [Similarly, when Daniel was saved from the lion's den, those who had slandered him were thrown in and devoured instead (*Daniel* 6:25).]

R' Menachem Mendel Bendet, a disciple of the *Vilna Gaon*, explains that the word נֶחֱלָץ, *is extricated*, is also derived from the word יַחֲלִיץ, *will strengthen* (*Isaiah* 58:11). Not only will the righteous be extricated and saved from the distress threatening them, but they will also be strengthened and elevated as a result. Mordechai, Daniel, Chananyah, Mishael and Azaryah all attained high positions as a direct outcome of the troubles which threatened them.

Rashi connects this verse to the previous one: when the wicked man dies, the righteous man is saved from distress.

R' Hirsch comments that there are situations when attractive and advantageous but evil schemes may be presented to a righteous person, who rejects them out of hand. Instead, a lawless person carries them out, thereby causing his own destruction. Thus, the righteous person escaped unharmed from the results of that evil.

9. בְּפֶה חָנֵף יַשְׁחִת רֵעֵהוּ — *With [his] mouth, a flatterer corrupts his fellow.* A flatterer who convinces his friend to go on an evil path destroys him with his glib mouth (*Rashi; R' Yonah*).

The *Vilna Gaon* renders the verse: בְּפֶה חָנֵף, *with a flattering mouth*, he destroys his friend.

וּבְדַעַת צַדִּיקִים יֵחָלֵצוּ — *But the righteous are extricated through knowledge.* The righteous will be extricated from the flatterer's effect thanks to their Torah knowledge, for Scripture adjures, לֹא תֹאבֶה לוֹ וְלֹא תִשְׁמַע אֵלָיו, *You shall not accede to him and not hearken to him* (*Deuteronomy* 13:9) [referring to the מֵסִית וּמַדִּיחַ, *one who entices someone to worship idols*] (*Rashi*).

The flatterer destroys his friend by praising him for his wicked deeds, thereby encouraging him to continue in his wickedness.[2] The righteous, however, do not deceive themselves; they do not let

1. A wicked person gets not only his portion in *Gehinnom*, but his friend's portion as well (*Chagigah* 15a). Thus, the righteous one is rescued from *Gehinnom*, and the wicked one suffers in his place.

2. A person who sees his friend sinning is obliged to reprove him. One who flatters the sinner arouses God's anger — indeed, flatterers are one of the four groups that will not merit the Divine Presence (*Sotah* 13a).

How careful Torah scholars are to avoid even a tinge of flattery may be seen by the example of the *Chafetz Chaim*, when he had to raise money to rebuild the fire-ravaged city of Radin. He wanted to appeal for funds through newspapers, but he was in a quandary as to whether or not

י בְּטוּב צַדִּיקִים תַּעֲלֹץ קִרְיָה וּבַאֲבֹד רְשָׁעִים רִנָּה:
יא בְּבִרְכַּת יְשָׁרִים תָּרוּם קָרֶת וּבְפִי רְשָׁעִים תֵּהָרֵס:
יב בָּז־לְרֵעֵהוּ חֲסַר־לֵב וְאִישׁ תְּבוּנוֹת יַחֲרִישׁ:

such praise go to their heads. The Sages advise (Niddah 30b) that even if the entire world tells you that you are righteous, you should still consider yourself a wicked person (Rabbeinu Yonah).[1]

A wicked person who wishes to entice others away from God's service will approach them with flattery and sweet talk. Consequently most heretics are good natured, thus gaining their friends' confidence and subsequently misleading them. Only the righteous, who are constantly involved with commandments and know God's ways, can recognize the danger in their enticing words and be saved from them (Vilna Gaon).

10. בְּטוּב צַדִּיקִים תַּעֲלֹץ קִרְיָה — The city exults in the good of the righteous. When God gives good to the righteous, the people of their city are happy (Ibn Ezra), for the righteous share their bounty with others (Metzudos).

וּבַאֲבֹד רְשָׁעִים רִנָּה — And when the wicked perish there is glad song, since they had harmed others during their lifetime (Metzudos).

Since the righteous are beloved by all, people rejoice when they are successful. The opposite is true of the wicked. People are unhappy when they prosper, and rejoice at their downfall (Ralbag).

According to the Vilna Gaon, the two parts of this verse are sequential. When saving the nation of Israel from their enemies, God first redeems His nation and bestows good upon them, and afterwards He punishes their enemies. For instance, God first took Israel out of Egypt, and only afterwards did He drown the Egyptians in the Sea of Reeds. Similarly, Mordechai was elevated and honored [see Esther 6:10], and subsequently the wicked Haman was hanged (Esther 7:10). In this way, the wicked person himself witnesses the Omnipotence of God and the honor He gives Israel. When He brings good to the righteous, תַּעֲלֹץ קִרְיָה, the city exults; however, they still do not joyously praise God. But once God takes revenge upon the wicked and they perish, there is רִנָּה, glad song.

R' Yonah explains that rejoicing at the downfall of the wicked does not contradict the commandment of לֹא־תִשְׂנָא אֶת־ אָחִיךָ בִּלְבָבֶךָ, do not hate your brother in your heart (Leviticus 19:17), for a wicked person is not included in the category of אָחִיךָ, your brother.

The Talmud applies this verse to the joy that was felt at the death of the wicked Ahab, king of Israel. This raises a question. Can the Holy One, Blessed is He, rejoice at the downfall of the wicked? Didn't He enjoin the angels from singing His praises when the Egyptians drowned in the Sea of Reeds? R' Yose bar Chanina answers that although God Himself does not rejoice when the wicked perish, as they, too, are His handiwork, He permits

to insert an ad in a newspaper whose editor was a heretic. On one hand, substantial monies could be raised, but, on the other, the Chafetz Chaim feared that the wording of his request might flatter the editor, which is prohibited. He agonized for several days before arriving at wording that would appeal to the editor without flattering him (retold in the name of R' Elchonon Wasserman).

1. Although the Sages teach that, despite all this flattery, one should regard himself as wicked, they also state and do not judge yourself to be a wicked person (Avos (2:18). This teaches us the obligation of self-esteem. Do not consider yourself to be so wicked and beyond help that you lose hope for Divine mercy. As for the harmful effect of flattery and the danger that it may blind one to the need for self-examination and self-improvement, with continued prayer and proper perspective, you will counteract the destructive forms of flattery heaped upon you and will not be led astray (Likkutei Yehudah).

exults in the good of the righteous, and when the wicked perish there is glad song. [11] When the upright are blessed, a city is exalted, but through the mouth of the wicked — it is torn down. [12] He who scorns his fellow lacks (an understanding) heart, but a man of discernment will remain silent.

others to rejoice (*Sanhedrin* 39b).

11. בְּבִרְכַּת יְשָׁרִים תָּרוּם קָרֶת — *When the upright are blessed, the city will be uplifted.* *Metzudos* explains קָרֶת as קִרְיָה, *city.* When blessing comes to the righteous [and they are in power (*Metzudos*)] they lead the inhabitants of the city on a proper course, and the whole city is thus elevated (*Vilna Gaon*).

Rashi renders קָרֶת as תִּקְרָה, *ceiling.* Through the blessing of the upright, the ceiling will be kept high and not fall; i.e., as long as the Judean kings were righteous, their prayers kept the Holy Temple standing.

וּבְפִי רְשָׁעִים תֵּהָרֵס — *But through the mouth of the wicked, it is torn down.* The city is destroyed as a result of the mouth of the wicked, i.e., their talebearing, their inclination toward strife, their glorification of falsehood and their denigration of truth (*Rabbeinu Yonah*).

When the wicked are in power and their dictates control the city, the city is destroyed as a result.[1] The verse associates the word "blessing" with the upright and "mouth" with the wicked, following the principle that, *A good thought is regarded as a [good] deed... but the Holy One, Blessed is He, does not regard a bad thought as a deed* (*Kiddushin* 40a). As soon as the righteous "bless" the city with their *thoughts* of guiding them on the right path, Hashem already uplifts the city, because God reckons with the worthy thoughts of the righteous. On the other hand, God puts no value in the mere *thoughts* of the wicked. Therefore, our verse states that destruction comes about only through their *mouth*, which represents their tangible attempt to bring their evil designs to fruition, through speech and deed (*Vilna Gaon*).

Many commentators (*Ibn Ezra, Ralbag, Malbim*) connect verses 10 and 11, explaining that the reason for rejoicing when the righteous have good [v. 10] is the benefit they bring to the city by being in power [v. 11].

R' Hirsch notes that the righteous person's acts are not only salutary for his own existence and for the progress of his descendants, but are also the source of good fortune and gain for the community at large. The wicked, on the other hand, undermine the well-being of the community, preventing goodness and human dignity from even raising their heads.

12. בָּז־לְרֵעֵהוּ חֲסַר־לֵב — *He who scorns his fellow lacks [an understanding].* According to *Rabbeinu Yonah*, the term חֲסַר־לֵב describes one who lacks good character traits and *mussar*, as well as one who lacks understanding. One who scorns his friends proves that he is lacking both *mussar* and understanding.

וְאִישׁ תְּבוּנוֹת יַחֲרִישׁ — *But a man of discernment will remain silent.* Even when the one lacking in understanding embarrasses him, he keeps silent. We find such a case when Saul, newly anointed as king, was ridiculed by some wicked men. They refused to offer him a gift, and scorned his choice as monarch, yet, וַיְהִי כְּמַחֲרִישׁ, *and he was like one who is mute* (*I Samuel* 10:27) (*Rashi*).

The man of discernment will suffer the scorn in silence. He will neither embarrass his friend in return nor respond to him (*Ibn Ezra*).

He does not reply when someone lacking in understanding scorns him, for he

1. *Shevet M'Yehudah* cites the example of our forefather Jacob. When he came to Egypt, the famine ended, for the Nile River was blessed, and the waters rose to his feet. On the other hand, the country was destroyed by the mouth of the wicked, i.e., Pharaoh, who said defiantly, לִי יְאֹרִי, *the river is mine* (*Ezekiel* 29:3).

יג הוֹלֵךְ רָכִיל מְגַלֶּה־סּוֹד וְנֶאֱמַן־רוּחַ מְכַסֶּה דָבָר:
יד בְּאֵין תַּחְבֻּלוֹת יִפָּל־עָם וּתְשׁוּעָה בְּרֹב יוֹעֵץ:
טו רַע־יֵרוֹעַ כִּי־עָרַב זָר וְשֹׂנֵא תֹקְעִים בּוֹטֵחַ:

realizes the type of person with whom he is dealing. It is beneath his dignity to respond, for to answer would put him on par with the person who had embarrassed him (*Rabbeinu Yonah*).

Malbim notes that the term לְהַחֲרִישׁ, *to remain silent*, means more than just not talking. It implies not answering in a case where an answer may be indicated. When a man of discernment is the object of scorn, though he can very well respond, he chooses not to do so.[1]

King David personified this trait throughout the many trials he endured during his lifetime. When he was fleeing for his life during his son Absalom's rebellion, he was accosted by Shimi ben Gera, who cursed and stoned him. Avishai ben Tzruyah, one of David's generals, wanted to behead Shimi; but David refused, saying: "Let him curse. He curses me thus because Hashem is the One Who told him to curse me. O that Hashem should see my tears and repay me with good because of the insult I suffered today" (*II Samuel* 16:5-12).

13. הוֹלֵךְ רָכִיל מְגַלֶּה־סּוֹד — *He who reveals a secret is a talebearer* [lit. *goes talebearing*]. Revealing someone's secret is in essence talebearing. [*R'chilus*, talebearing, by definition means reporting to someone what others have done or spoken against him.] Even though initially the information was not discussed in the subject's presence (but rather to a third party, i.e., a friend), another friend will receive the

information and eventually it will get back to the subject himself (*Metzudos*). (See *Bava Basra* 28b: *Your friend has a friend, and your friend's friend has a friend.*)

וְנֶאֱמַן־רוּחַ מְכַסֶּה דָבָר — *But one faithful of spirit conceals a matter.* Someone whose spirit is faithful to Hashem will conceal any matter, even one which was not told to him as a secret (*Metzudos*).

The *Ralbag* applies this verse to one who reveals Torah secrets to those who are unworthy of learning them. This can cause them great harm. A person of faithful spirit, however, will be careful of doing something which is likely to cause others to sin. He will keep *chochmah* concealed from those who are not deserving of studying it.

The Talmud (*Sanhedrin* 31a) applies the prohibition against revealing secrets to anyone who is a member of the panel which adjudicates a case. He may not leave the courtroom and say, "I wished to acquit you but my fellow judges found you guilty, and they outnumbered me." A student was rumored to have divulged some information from a court case which took place twenty-two years before, and R' Ami removed this student from his yeshivah.

R' Hirsch exclaims: Where conscience orders silence, even an honest word can become a serious offense.

14. בְּאֵין תַּחְבֻּלוֹת יִפָּל־עָם — *Without strategies a nation will fall.* If a nation does not

---

1. Our Sages extol one who can suffer insults in silence. The Talmud (*Shabbos* 88b) praises those who are the subject of insults but do not answer in kind, who are embarrassed but do not respond. Those who lovingly and happily accept this suffering are described as וְאֹהֲבָיו כְּצֵאת הַשֶּׁמֶשׁ בִּגְבֻרָתוֹ, *let them that love him be as the sun when it comes out in its might* (*Judges* 5:31).

Torah scholars throughout the generations were subjected to scorn and derision, only to prove time and time again their silent acceptance of the Divine Will. Once R' Chaim Volozhin and his brother R' Zalman were traveling, and stopped at an inn to spend the night. The innkeeper verbally abused them and refused them a place to stay, so the two righteous brothers were forced to continue traveling into the night. As they journeyed on, R' Chaim noticing R' Zalman crying and asked, "Why are you crying for nothing? You see I completely ignored the insults they heaped upon us." His brother replied, "I am not crying because of the insults to which we were subjected. What bothers me is that in my heart I felt some pain. This proves that I fell short of what the Sages state, that one must happily accept suffering (of being insulted). This is truly a cause for tears."

plan strategies for a war, they will fall to their enemies (*Metzudos*). If trouble comes to the Jewish nation and they do not try to understand, fast or repent, they will fall (*Rashi*).[1]

Malbim explains that, metaphorically, the verse refers to the internal battle being fought, i.e., every man's attempt to defeat the Evil Inclination.

וּתְשׁוּעָה בְּרֹב יוֹעֵץ — *But there is salvation with many advisors* [lit. "advisor"]. The *Vilna Gaon* explains why the verse uses the word רֹב, *many*, which is plural, in conjunction with the word יוֹעֵץ, *advisor*, which is singular. It is not ideal for an army to have a sole commander, who makes all the decisions, for he is only human and may err. On the other hand, if there are many officers and advisors leading the army, there would be a lack of consensus as to which move to make, and the army would be ineffective. The ideal situation is when many counselors express their advice and opinions, and one commander-in-chief chooses what he feels to be the best of their suggestions and implements it. Hence victory comes בְּרֹב, *with many* who give their suggestions, but with only one יוֹעֵץ, *advisor*, who chooses among their proposals and takes charge.

This verse is directed to those who have become so accustomed to embarrassing others, to flattery, to weighing with false scales, lying, corruption, deception and fraud that they feel there is no way to extricate themselves from these sins. This is not so. A nation accustomed to living in peace and not being attacked by an enemy will not despair and surrender just because it is not accustomed to war. People will seek every means at their disposal to defeat the enemy. So, too, a person involved with sin must seek strategies to save himself from the enemy within; otherwise he will surely be defeated. His victory will come only if he turns to others to advise him and teach him the correct path (*Chevel Nachalah*).

15. רַע־יֵרוֹעַ כִּי־עָרַב זָר — *An evil man will be broken for having guaranteed for a stranger. Rabbeinu Yonah* explains the verse as referring to surety on monetary matters. רַע, *an evil person*, יֵרוֹעַ, *will be broken*, for having guaranteed for a זָר, *stranger* (cf. 6:1-2). A "stranger" refers to someone he does not know and who has not proven his trustworthiness to him. If this stranger should decide not to repay the loan, or if he lacks the funds with which to pay, one of two possibilities will result: either the lender will blame the guarantor for not repaying the borrower's loan and much discord will result; or the court will force him to pay and he will countersue the borrower. In either case, the result will entail argument, disagreement and financial loss. This is true if the guarantor is an evil person. However, if the guarantor is a good person this will not occur. His initial intention when assuming this responsibility is unquestioningly to repay the loan, should the borrower be unable to pay. He will not argue or fight with the lender. He will avoid quarrel and conflict, for he is a person who hates discord and seeks peace.

Rashi explains the verse metaphorically: A wicked person who pledged his heart to the worship of strange gods will be broken.

וְשֹׂנֵא תֹקְעִים בּוֹטֵחַ — *But a hater of handshakes will be secure.* Someone who hates

---

1. Only proper spiritual strategy is effective in attempting to defeat the enemy. As every distress befalling the Jewish people is a result of their sins, their only successful defense is to repent from these sins and increase their merits. Unfortunately, there are those who defy the advice of the Torah sages and pursue military might as their security. Tragically, they ignore the lessons which fill the annals of Jewish history of the bitter consequences of such a course of action.

טז אֵשֶׁת־חֵן תִּתְמֹךְ כָּבוֹד וְעָרִיצִים יִתְמְכוּ־עֹשֶׁר:
יז גֹּמֵל נַפְשׁוֹ אִישׁ חָסֶד וְעֹכֵר שְׁאֵרוֹ אַכְזָרִי:

to guarantee transactions with a handshake will be secure and avoid any damage (*Metzudos*). He will be secure and not fear the lender (*Ibn Ezra*).[1]

Rabbeinu Yonah explains that the only way a person can be secure with his money is if he *hates* (שׂנֵא) guaranteeing for others. Otherwise he will eventually be talked into it, for he will not be able to resist those pleading with him and begging him to be a guarantor.

R' Hirsch explains that this verse and the first five verses of Chapter 6 not only caution us against guaranteeing of another's debts, but also warn us of taking upon ourselves obligations with a broader concept of עֲרֵבוּת, *security*, in situations where we cannot exert influence. For once a promise has been made, it is binding and may prove to be a self-imposing trap.

Metaphorically, תֹּקְעִים are *people who extend a handshake* to those who entice them to sin and follow their advice (*Rashi*).

16. אֵשֶׁת־חֵן תִּתְמֹךְ כָּבוֹד — *A woman of grace upholds honor.* A woman who finds favor because of her worthy deeds wants to maintain her status of honor. She does so by performing more good deeds (*Metzudos*).

According to *Rashi*, this refers to the people of Israel who always draw near to the honor of the Almighty and His Torah.

Metaphorically, the good woman who finds favor through her worthy deeds, refers to the precious, wise soul (*Malbim*).

וְעָרִיצִים יִתְמְכוּ־עֹשֶׁר — *But mighty men uphold wealth.* Mighty men "support" their riches by taking steps to assure that

they will not lose it (*Metzudos*).

Rabbeinu Yonah explains that עָרִיצִים are *those who cast their fear on others* [relating it to לֹא־תַעַרְצוּן וְלֹא־תִירְאוּן, *do not be broken and do not fear* (Deuteronomy 1:29).] Such people "support" wealth, i.e., their only concern is to increase their wealth, so that they can wield even greater power over others by intimidating them. They will even resort to theft and violence to increase their wealth. However, they are making a grave mistake. These people erroneously think that by intimidating others with their wealth, they will gain honor. They fail to realize that only good deeds and humility truly bring honor; for only then does one become truly beloved and admired by all because of his worthy actions.

17. גֹּמֵל נַפְשׁוֹ אִישׁ חָסֶד — *A man of kindness brings good upon himself.* Rashi renders נַפְשׁוֹ as *his relatives*: A benevolent man acts kindly to his relatives.

A person's first obligation in dispensing charity is to his family. The Talmud (*Bava Metzia* 71a) derives this from the verse אִם כֶּסֶף תַּלְוֶה אֶת־עַמִּי אֶת־הֶעָנִי עִמָּךְ, *When you lend money to My people, to the poor person who is with you* (Exodus 22:24). עִמָּךְ, *with you*, implies the poor people from your family, for they are closest to you (see *Rashi* ibid.); they take precedence over all other needy people.

Similarly, when speaking of charity, Isaiah exhorts וּמִבְּשָׂרְךָ לֹא תִתְעַלָּם, *and do not hide yourself from your kin* (Isaiah 58:7). *Radak* (ibid.) explains that it is obligatory to feed and clothe any Jew; but for a relative, the obligation extends further. A person should not wait until his poor relative comes to ask for help. He must anticipate the family member's need, lend him money and find ways to enable him to earn a living.[2]

1. Noting that the word תֹּקְעִים comes from תְּקִיעָה, *sounding the horn, Likutei Yehudah* explains that this verse refers to an individual who is שׂנֵא תֹּקְעִים, who *hates to blow his horn.* A person who is not used to observing *mitzvos*, but finally performs one, broadcasts it because he wants it to be known, to be his עָרֵב, *guarantor.* But שׂנֵא תֹּקְעִים, the one who does not publicly announce his performance of *mitzvos* and good deeds, בּוֹטֵחַ, *trusts* and relies upon Hashem and performs these acts only for His honor and glory, not for public acclaim.

2. The importance of this precept was brought home to one of the followers of the late Kapitchinitzer Rebbe. When the Rebbe appeared in his office one day, the surprised *chassid*

Based on our verse, we are taught that concentration in prayer is considered an act of kindnesss, for one who prays sincerely is bestowing goodness upon himself (*Shabbos* 127b, see *Rashi* ad loc.).

וְעֹכֵר שְׁאֵרוֹ אַכְזָרִי — *But a cruel person troubles his flesh.* A cruel person harms his relatives (*Rashi*).

According to *Metzudos*, this verse speaks about the way a person relates to his personal needs. If he makes sure that he has enough food, drink and rest to remain alive and well, he may be expected to be generous to others, for just as he caters to his own needs, so, too, he may tend to the needs of others. However, someone who mortifies his own flesh, who starves himself and jeopardizes his health because he prefers to accumulate money will certainly be cruel to others.

R' Yonah delineates the middle road in dealing with the needs of the body. An אִישׁ חֶסֶד, *a kind man*, weans himself away from lusts and desires, but takes care to provide his body with its needs. If he starves himself and ruins his body, he is just as cruel as a person who harms his fellow man, for by destroying his own body, he weakens his soul to the point where he can no longer attain wisdom and is thus unable to serve God properly. [See *Rambam, Hil. Deios* Ch. 4, and *Kitzur Shulchan Aruch* Ch. 32 for halachic rulings regarding care for bodily health.][1]

Those who assume that they are doing the will of God by causing pain and suffering to their body are in error. This is the opposite of God's desire, for only on Yom Kippur does the Torah command that some pain be inflicted on the body. Man's physical strength is a necessary tool to serve his intellect; this is only possible when mind and body are healthy. Someone who weakens or sickens his body is thus ruining the Creator's intention (*Ralbag*).[2]

quickly ushered him in and eagerly awaited the Rebbe's bidding. The Rebbe explained that he had come to raise funds for a family whose father was ill and out of work, and whose mother, blessed with many children, was unable to take a job. Upon hearing the sad plight of the family, the Jew quickly wrote out a check for a sizable sum, and asked the Rebbe, "To whom should I make out the check?" To which the Rebbe replied, "Your brother" (*Around the Maggid's Table*).

1. Torah sages are so exacting in heeding the commandment of וְנִשְׁמַרְתֶּם מְאֹד לְנַפְשֹׁתֵיכֶם, *and You shall greatly beware for your souls* (*Deuteronomy* 4:15), which refers to health habits, that many doctors regard them as model patients.

R' Yisrael Salanter's students once saw him standing outside in the evening, gazing at the stars. He explained that he was ill, and the doctor had ordered him to refrain from studying Torah for three days until he regained his strength. This was the end of the third day, and R' Yisrael was looking to see if the third star had already appeared in the sky, signifying the beginning of the next day (which is counted from the night before). If he were to begin studying Torah before the third star appeared, he would be transgressing the commandment of caring for his health. On the other hand, if he were to delay his learning until after three stars appeared, he would be guilty of the transgression of wasting time from Torah study. Therefore, he was waiting to determine exactly when the third day had ended and he could resume his Torah study.

R' Boruch Ber Leibowitz, Rosh Hayeshivah of Kamenetz, was ill and did not deliver his usual Torah lecture in the yeshivah one day. When he failed to appear the next day as well, his students went to find out the reason for his absence. R' Boruch Ber told them, "I stayed home an additional day in order to heed the wording of this commandment, which states, וְנִשְׁמַרְתֶּם מְאֹד, *And you shall* **greatly** *beware for your souls.*"

2. The *Rambam* (*Hilchos Deios* 3:1) labels one who avoids the pleasures of this world, thinking that this is the highest level of Divine service, as a חוֹטֵא, *sinner*. He cites the example of the Nazarite, who avoided *one* of the pleasures of this world — wine — and must therefore bring a sin-offering (see *Numbers* 6:11 and *Nedarim* 10a). A person should follow the restrictions imposed by the Torah, and not impose further restrictions in areas which the Torah permitted.

רָשָׁע עֹשֶׂה פְעֻלַּת־שֶׁקֶר וְזֹרֵעַ צְדָקָה שֶׂכֶר אֱמֶת: כֵּן־צְדָקָה לְחַיִּים וּמְרַדֵּף רָעָה לְמוֹתוֹ: יט תּוֹעֲבַת יהוה עִקְּשֵׁי־לֵב וּרְצוֹנוֹ תְּמִימֵי דָרֶךְ: כ

The *Vilna Gaon* gives an additional interpretation of this verse: Someone who does kindness with others is, in a sense, doing kindness to himself [גוֹמֵל לְנַפְשׁוֹ], for the others will reciprocate and the Holy One, Blessed is He, will also repay him in kind. On the other hand, someone who is cruel to others harms himself [עֹכֵר שְׁאֵרוֹ], for others will be cruel to him in return. Furthermore, if a person's intentions are always geared to doing kindness and performing *mitzvos*, then even when he eats or takes care of his other personal needs (גוֹמֵל נַפְשׁוֹ), it is considered a good deed, for all his intentions are for the sake of Heaven. His eating, for example, is elevated to the status of an offering. However, if he indulges in physical pleasures only for personal gratification, not only is this not considered a good deed, but he is harming his flesh (עֹכֵר שְׁאֵרוֹ), for his behavior will cause it to deteriorate after death.[1]

18. רָשָׁע עֹשֶׂה פְעֻלַּת־שֶׁקֶר — *A wicked one performs a false act.* The action of the wicked person deceives him. He thinks it will bring him lasting success, but all will

be lost (*Rashi*).[2]

A wicked person exerts all his efforts to amass enough money to pamper his body or to glorify himself. His actions are *false*, in the sense that his body will decay after his death and all his efforts will have been wasted (*R' Yonah*).

וְזֹרֵעַ צְדָקָה שֶׂכֶר אֱמֶת — *But one who sows righteousness has a true* [i.e., lasting] *reward.* צְדָקָה refers to both *righteousness* (צֶדֶק) and *charity. Ibn Ezra* renders: One who *sows righteousness*, i.e., performs good deeds, will receive a true reward from God. *Targum, Ibn Ezra, R' Yonah* and *Vilna Gaon* all render שֶׂכֶר as שָׂכָר, *reward.*

Rashi related the word שֶׂכֶר to עֹשֶׂה, שֶׂכֶר, *all who dammed calm pools* [in order to gather fish] (*Isaiah* 19:10). He renders the verse: *one who sows righteousness deems truth*, meaning that just as a dam confines fish in a small area, guaranteeing that many will be caught, so, too, one who acts righteously is performing a *true* deed, for his success is assured.

R' Yonah notes that acts of kindness are listed among the *mitzvos* whose fruit a person enjoys in this world but whose

1. The students of Hillel the Elder once asked him where he was going. He replied, "To do a mitzvah." They asked him which *mitzvah*, and he answered that he was going to the bath-house. He explained that just as a statue of the emperor must be cleaned, and the person who maintains it is rewarded for his efforts, so, too, it is important for a person to take care of his body, which was formed in God's image. *Eitz Yosef* (ad loc.) explains that Hillel's motivation in providing for his body's needs was not to indulge himself in physical pleasures, but rather to take proper care of the King's likeness.

Similarly, Hillel once departed from his students and told them that he was on the way to do a kindness to a guest in his house. "Do you have guests in your house every day?" asked one of his students [for the same exchange recurred several times, *Eitz Yosef*]. Hillel explained, "Isn't my soul a guest in my body, for today it is here, but tomorrow it is gone?" (*Vayikra Rabbah* 34:3).

Eitz Yosef explains that Hillel did not answer, "I am going to eat," but rather spoke of caring for his "guest," in order to teach his students a lesson. A guest is anxious to continue traveling. When he stops to eat, he does so hastily, just grabbing a bite and continuing on his journey. The same attitude should apply to each person. When stopping to take care of his physical needs, he should not linger, but rather provide for them as quickly as possible and then hasten to resume his "journey" in this world.

2. The deceitful Laban ended up losing all his wealth. After taking leave of Jacob, וַיָּשָׁב לָבָן לִמְקֹמוֹ, *and Lavan . . . returned to his place* (*Genesis* 32:1). The Midrash expounds that he returned to his former "place," i.e., his original state of poverty, for he lost the possessions he had accumulated in the merit of Jacob's presence in his household.

¹⁸ *A wicked one performs a false act, but one who sows righteousness has a true reward.* ¹⁹ *Sincere charity brings life, but one who pursues evil [is consigned] to his death.* ²⁰ *The perverse of heart are an abomination to HASHEM, but His desire is for those whose way is wholehearted.*

principal remains intact for him in the World to Come (*Shabbos* 127a).

R' *Bachya* explains that this verse speaks of the great reward for giving charity. When a person sows, he does not know if his labors will necessarily yield a crop, because his success depends on the weather. However, a person who sows charity is guaranteed a "true" reward, for the "principal" of his deed remains an everlasting source of benefit in the World to Come.[1]

The *Vilna Gaon* explains how a פְּעוּלָה, *action*, differs from זְרִיעָה, *sowing*. An action does not entail any loss. For example, when a merchant buys wares, he receives merchandise in return for his money. When he sells, he parts with the merchandise, but receives money. Yet, the profit on each transaction is small. When a person sows, he sustains a loss, for he receives no immediate return for the seeds he deposits in the ground and for his work; even the seeds soon disintegrate. However, when his crop ripens he realizes a great profit. In the same way, the wicked enjoy an immediate reward in this world, but even that is illusory, for it has no lasting substance. On the other hand, giving charity is compared to sowing. The giver receives nothing immediate; his reward comes much later, but it is *true*, for it will last forever.

The comparison of charity to sowing also suggests that just as a farmer covers

the seeds completely with earth, so too, a person who gives *tzedakah* should conceal his action [מַתָּן בְּסֵתֶר] (*Alshich*).

19. בֵּן־צְדָקָה לְחַיִּים וּמְרַדֵּף רָעָה לְמוֹתוֹ — *Sincere charity brings life, but one who pursues evil [is consigned] to his death.*

Metzudos explains that "sincere" charity is given לִשְׁמָה, *for its own sake*, i.e., without any ulterior motive. Such charity earns life. However, if one uses charity to *pursue evil*, i.e., to fool others into thinking that he is righteous, such deeds will not only not be considered meritorious, but will be regarded as faults.

The *Vilna Gaon* explains בֵּן as a *base*, as in אֶת הַכִּיּוֹר וְאֶת כַּנּוֹ, *the Laver and its base* (*Exodus* 38:8). Someone who makes himself a base to charity, by assisting those who give charity, will also merit life.

R' *Yonah* renders the verse: Just as charity definitely brings life, so will one who pursues evil be pursued by that very evil onto death. Pursuing evil (מְרַדֵּף רָעָה) refers to one who constantly seeks opportunities to harm others.

20. תּוֹעֲבַת ה' עִקְּשֵׁי־לֵב — *The perverse of heart are an abomination to HASHEM.* This refers to someone who is outwardly righteous, but whose thoughts are perverse (*Metzudos*).

וּרְצוֹנוֹ תְּמִימֵי דָרֶךְ — *But His desire is for those whose way is wholehearted.* God craves people whose conduct is perfect,

1. King Monbaz depleted his royal treasuries in order to provide for his people during a drought. His brothers and father's family protested, "Your fathers hoarded their wealth and added to the fortune of their forefathers, but instead of increasing our family riches you are wasting them." In reply, Monbaz enumerated the advantages of giving charity over hoarding wealth: "My fathers hoarded wealth on earth down below, but by giving charity I have hoarded merit above in Heaven. My fathers hoarded their wealth in an insecure place, but I have hoarded my "wealth" in a secure place. My fathers hoarded something that does not produce fruit, but I have hoarded something that does produce fruit. My fathers hoarded stores of money, and I have hoarded stores of souls. My fathers hoarded their wealth for others, but I have hoarded the reward for my charitable deeds for myself. My fathers hoarded wealth for this world and I have hoarded merits for the World to Come" (*Bava Basra* 11a).

כא יָד לְיָד לֹא־יִנָּקֶה רָּע וְזֶרַע צַדִּיקִים נִמְלָט:
כב נֶזֶם זָהָב בְּאַף חֲזִיר אִשָּׁה יָפָה וְסָרַת טָעַם:
כג תַּאֲוַת צַדִּיקִים אַךְ־טוֹב תִּקְוַת רְשָׁעִים עֶבְרָה:

whose hearts are consistent with their exterior (*Metzudos*).

R' Yonah explains that those with bad character traits are *an abomination* to God, while the *wholehearted* are those who have perfect character traits, whether naturally or by subordinating their traits to the dictates of their intellect. Since God desires such people, a person must exert himself to remove his faulty traits and thereby become desirable to God.

Yalkut Shimoni comments that the *perverse of heart* are those who stubbornly refuse to repent.

21. יָד לְיָד לֹא־יִנָּקֶה רָּע — *[From] hand to hand, evil will not be exonerated.* Punishment will come from God's hand to the hand of the sinner, and he will not be cleansed from the evil he perpetrated (*Rashi*).

One who does evil will be repaid מִדָּה כְּנֶגֶד מִדָּה, *measure for measure* (*Vilna Gaon*).

Targum Yonasan renders: Someone who stretches out a hand against his friend will not be exonerated from punishment.

There are various Midrashic interpretations based on the term *hand to hand:*

❑ Someone who does a good deed in this world and expects to be rewarded immediately (*hand to hand* denotes immediacy) will not be cleansed. He is wicked, for he does not leave any merits for his children. Had our forefathers requested reward in this world, would any merit be left for their descendants? (*Vayikra Rabbah* 36:3).

❑ *Midrash Mishlei* teaches that if someone steals with one hand and gives charity with the other, he will not be cleansed from evil in the Hereafter.

R' Yochanan illustrates this with the example of someone who sinned with a prostitute. As he left her, he was approached by a beggar. He reasoned, "Had the Holy One, Blessed is He, not

intended to atone for my sin, He would not have sent me this opportunity to give charity." The Almighty tells him, "Wicked man, do not think thus. You should learn from the wisdom of Solomon, who says that [from] *hand to hand, evil will not be exonerated.*

וְזֶרַע צַדִּיקִים נִמְלָט — *But the offspring of the righteous will escape.* The descendants of the righteous escape misfortune due to the meritorious deeds of their fathers (*Ibn Ezra*).

The progeny of the righteous are protected from doing evil and from suffering misfortune, following the Talmud dictum that "A righteous person for whom things are good [is] a righteous person the son of a righteous person; a righteous person for whom things are bad [is] a righteous person, the son of a wicked person" (*Berachos* 7a). Even though a righteous person may not have sufficient merits of his own to save him from distress, our verse teaches that *the offspring of the righteous will escape* harm; he will be saved through the merit of four generations of righteousness (*Vilna Gaon*).

22. נֶזֶם זָהָב בְּאַף חֲזִיר אִשָּׁה יָפָה וְסָרַת טָעַם — *[Like] a golden ring in the snout of a pig, [so] is a beautiful woman [whose] good sense has departed.* If a nose ring were to be put on a pig, not only would the pig not be beautified, but it would besmirch the ornament in filth. The same is true of a woman who has beauty but is devoid of reason and wisdom; she will use her beauty for sin. This verse also speaks metaphorically of someone who is blessed with wisdom, but rather than applying it to the Torah, uses it to deceive people and for other sinful actions (*Metzudos*).

Rashi explains the verse as symbolizing a Torah scholar who subsequently forsakes the way of Torah.

An adornment adds beauty only to something inherently beautiful; otherwise,

²¹ *[From] hand to hand, evil will not be exonerated, but the offspring of the righteous will escape. ²² [Like] a golden ring in the snout of a pig, [so] is a beautiful woman [whose] good sense has departed. ²³ The yearning of the righteous is only for good; the hope of the wicked is wrath.*

the adornment itself is debased. So, too, physical beauty does not embellish a woman who is ugly in her טַעַם, i.e., her character traits and mannerisms, which reveal the inner qualities of her soul. If her speech and actions reveal a debased character, not only will her external beauty be of no value, but her bad nature will sully her physical beauty. The same is true of one who has acquired intellectual beauty, but whose character traits and actions are corrupt. His Torah knowledge is debased. As the Talmud states (*Yoma* 86a), one who studies Torah, but is dishonest in business and does not speak nicely with others, causes people to decry those who have taught him Torah (*Malbim*).

God invested man with abilities and utensils that are more precious than gold, such as senses and intelligence. Therefore, he should use them to serve God and fulfill His commandments. When he uses these abilities for other things, it is like *a golden ring in the snout of a pig* (*Sfas Emes*).

The Sages derive another lesson from this verse. Rabbi Yehoshua ben Levi taught (*Avos* 6:2) that whoever does not occupy himself with the Torah is called נָזוּף, *rebuked*. The word נָזוּף is a *notarikon* (abbreviated shorthand), formed by the initials of נֶזֶם זָהָב, which are combined with the last letter of_ בְּאַף to form נזף, *rebuke* (*Machzor Vitry, Rashi* ad loc.).

HaChassid Yaavetz explains: Just as a swine's ugliness and stench are not camouflaged by the golden ring in its snout, so a woman's physical beauty cannot conceal her moral blemishes. In the same way, man created in God's image should be ashamed if he does not nurture that image by studying Torah. Nothing can disguise the spiritual ugliness of a wasted soul.

23. תַּאֲוַת צַדִּיקִים אַךְ־טוֹב — *The yearning of the righteous is only for good.* Of all

desires, the righteous choose only to do good, and forsake all other desires (*Metzudos*). The word אַךְ is a term that indicates exclusion. In this case, it excludes all other desires (*Ibn Ezra*).

A person cannot be considered righteous until he has completely eradicated all negative desires from his heart — desires for evil, for physical pleasures, for acquiring positions of authority — and only the desire to do good remains. King David expressed this, saying, נֶגְדְּךָ כָל תַּאֲוָתִי, *before You is all my yearning* (Psalms 38:10). You know that there is no desire for bad included among my yearnings (*R' Yonah*).

תִּקְוַת רְשָׁעִים עֶבְרָה — *The hope of the wicked is wrath.* The hope of the wicked is to find an opportunity to become enraged at someone (*Metzudos*).

According to *Rashi, wrath* refers to *Gehinnom* (see 11:4). The wicked are assured of and hope for *Gehinnom*.

The word תִּקְוָה refers to a hope for something immediate (see verse 7). The wicked look for immediate gratification in this world. However, even in this world their expectation brings them wrath, for they will not attain their desires (*Vilna Gaon*).

This verse warns a person not to get caught up in the pursuit of wealth. A person who pursues his desires will never be completely satisfied, as the Sages state: *a person does not leave the world with even half his desires in hand* (*Koheles Rabbah* 1:34). The limitation אַךְ, *only*, in our verse implies that the righteous seek to provide themselves only with the basic necessities for life; they do not try to amass a fortune. Since the wicked desire more and more, they are never satisfied, so their desires cause them anger and frustration and they can never enjoy life (*Chevel Nachalah*).

כד יֵשׁ מְפַזֵּר וְנוֹסָף עוֹד וְחוֹשֵׂךְ מִיֹּשֶׁר אַךְ־לְמַחְסוֹר:
כה-כו נֶפֶשׁ־בְּרָכָה תְדֻשָּׁן וּמַרְוֶה גַּם־הוּא יוֹרֶא: מֹנֵעַ
בָּר יִקְּבֻהוּ לְאוֹם וּבְרָכָה לְרֹאשׁ מַשְׁבִּיר:
כז שֹׁחֵר טוֹב יְבַקֵּשׁ רָצוֹן וְדֹרֵשׁ רָעָה תְבוֹאֶנּוּ:

24. יֵשׁ מְפַזֵּר וְנוֹסָף עוֹד — *There is one who scatters and more is added.* There is a case where people scatter money, yet even more is added to their fortunes. This is true of money given to *tzedakah* (*Rashi*). Hoarded wealth does not make one rich. But money which is spent on pursuits pleasing in God's sight brings additional wealth (*R' Hirsch*).

וְחוֹשֵׂךְ מִיֹּשֶׁר אַךְ־לְמַחְסוֹר — *While one who refrains from what is proper, only for a loss.* If one holds himself back from giving what is right, it will be a loss only to him (*Rashi*). One who withholds his money and does not give the proper amount to *tzedakah* does not preserve his money, but, rather, causes its loss (*Metzudos*).

Where there are two opposite traits, the ideal is to choose the middle road (see *Rambam, Hilchos Deios* 1:4). נְדִיבוּת, *benevolence*, is the ideal compromise between the extremes of כִּילוּת, *stinginess*, and פַּזְרָנוּת, *extravagance*. People would assume that if one were to veer towards either of these two extremes, the better choice would be to lean towards stinginess, for this would at least preserve a person's wealth. However, the opposite is true. There are cases where extravagance increases wealth, such as giving charity and using one's riches to perform commandments, whereas stinginess can never benefit an individual and will only cause him a loss in the long run (*Malbim*).[1]

The Talmud (*Berachos* 63a) applies this verse to teaching Torah. Hillel states, if

you see that the generation is eager to study Torah, פַּזֵּר, *spread out* its teachings. *Midrash Mishlei* continues: If the generation is eager to learn and you refrain from teaching them, your Torah knowledge will diminish for by teaching others, a person gains knowledge for himself. *Ralbag* comments that the more one teaches others, the more one adds to one's own knowledge, as Rabbi states (*Makkos* 10a), from my students [I learned] more than from anyone.

25. נֶפֶשׁ־בְּרָכָה תְדֻשָּׁן — *A benevolent soul will grow fat.* The verse refers to one who gives out his money very easily to help others (*Rashi*); or one who wants others to have maximum good, who will himself enjoy good (*Metzudos*).

Hearing good tidings makes a person rejoice and his bones expand (*cf.* 15:30). Thus a person who constantly blesses others and desires their benefit, who is not jealous of their good fortune and therefore gladdens their hearts with his blessing, thereby fattens their bones. Therefore, he himself *will grow fat.* His trait is the opposite of jealousy, about which King Solomon states (14:30), *jealousy is the rot of bones* (*Vilna Gaon*).

The person who is happy to give to others and help them out in their distress enjoys a sense of gratification far greater than the happiness of the recipient (*R' Hirsch*).[2]

וּמַרְוֶה גַּם־הוּא יוֹרֶא — *And one who sates [others] will himself be sated.* One who

1. The *Vilna Gaon* illustrates this with an incident described in the Midrash. A man gave away his last coin to a pauper in a time of drought, and was left with nothing for himself. Having no food to eat, he went to the synagogue and collected all the ownerless *esrogim*. He set out to sea, and reached a place where they had proclaimed that anyone who had an *esrog* should bring it to the king and he would be handsomely rewarded. The man thus became rich.

2. As the sages comment, more than the donor does for the poor person, the poor person does for the donor. The donor provides the poor person with food, but by accepting the donation, the poor person gives the donor merits that will save him in the World to Come (*Ruth Rabbah* 5:9).

feeds the poor will himself be sated with good (*Rashi*). God will bless the food in his innards, providing him with a feeling of satiety and nourishment. He will enjoy this blessing in addition to the wealth he will merit for giving charity (*Vilna Gaon*).

Targum Yonasan renders that one who teaches others will himself learn.

Whoever heartens a languishing soul, as the rain moistens a parched field, feels in that moment an even greater freshness in himself, as if he himself were like rain (*R' Hirsch*).

26. מֹנֵעַ בָּר יִקְּבֻהוּ לְאוֹם — *One who withholds produce, the nation will curse him.* One who refuses to sell his grain when it is needed [during a famine, *Ibn Ezra*] — for he is hoarding it, waiting for the price to go up — will be cursed by his nation (*Metzudos*).

This refers to one who withholds his Torah knowledge and does not teach others (*Rashi*). He is cursed for refusing to share the good that God bestowed upon him (*Ralbag*) (c.v. 3:9).

וּבְרָכָה לְרֹאשׁ מַשְׁבִּיר — *But blessing [will be] on the head of a provider.* One who sells his grain when it is needed will be blessed by the people. This is a metaphor for one who disseminates his wisdom to others (*Metzudos*).

As grain is an essential food supply, so is Torah knowledge essential to the spirit. Hence these items must always be available and dispensed as needed, never hoarded or saved for a more profitable time (*R' Eliyahu Lopian*).

27. שֹׁחֵר טוֹב יְבַקֵּשׁ רָצוֹן — *One who seeks good [for others] seeks [God's] favor.* One who seeks to direct others on the correct path, and admonishes and rebukes them,

wants God to be pleased with them and be reconciled with them (*Rashi*).

One who seeks good for others will thereby find favor in God's eyes and God will act favorably toward him (*Metzudos*).

Midrash Mishlei states that if someone speaks well of his friend then the angels above speak of his merits to the Holy One, Blessed is He.

The *Vilna Gaon* applies this principle to man's relationship with God. When a person gives priority to observing the commandments, which are called טוב, *good*, thus foregoing his personal desires in order to do those of God, God will fulfill his desires, as the Mishnah states, *Nullify your will before His will, so that He will nullify the will of others before your will* (*Avos* 2:4)

וְדֹרֵשׁ רָעָה תְבוֹאֶנּוּ — *But he who searches out evil [for others], it will come upon him.* R' Bachya explains that this verse instructs the person always to seek the welfare of others and never their detriment, for he will be repaid measure for measure. One who seeks good for his friend and prays on his behalf solicits God's favor, as the Talmud states: He who prays for another and is in need of the same thing is answered first (*Bava Kamma* 92a). This happened to Job, for God restored his fortune because he had prayed for his friend (*Job* 42:10). One who prays for others benefits himself, as King David said, וּתְפִלָּתִי עַל חֵיקִי תָשׁוּב, *may my prayer return upon my own bosom* (*Psalms* 35:13). A leader has a special obligation to pray for his people; if he does not, he will be punished. On the other hand, someone who tries to bring harm upon his fellow will have that evil revert upon himself.

Malbim differentiates between שֹׁחֵר and

כח בּוֹטֵחַ בְּעָשְׁרוֹ הוּא יִפֹּל וְכֶעָלֶה צַדִּיקִים יִפְרָחוּ:
כט עוֹכֵר בֵּיתוֹ יִנְחַל־רוּחַ וְעֶבֶד אֱוִיל לַחֲכַם־
ל לֵב: פְּרִי־צַדִּיק עֵץ חַיִּים וְלֹקֵחַ נְפָשׁוֹת חָכָם:

דְּרֹשׁ. Both mean *seeking* or *searching*, but שַׁחֵר — related to שַׁחַר, *morning*, which comes day in and day out — implies continual seeking. Since it is human nature to do evil, for such desires have been ingrained in him since infancy, he can easily succumb to his senses and his desires. Therefore, to succeed, he must שַׁחֵר, *constantly seek* to do good, whereas to do evil, it is sufficient just to דְּרֹשׁ, *search for*, the bad. To attain this sought after good he must also *seek out willingness* [וִיבַקֵּשׁ רָצוֹן] to do good. Such a willingness does not come naturally; one must dig deep within one's soul to uncover the good impulses buried there. To sin, however, no such search is necessary, for evil comes upon him of itself (תְּבוֹאֶנּוּ), since that is one's natural inclination. The term יְבַקֵּשׁ also connotes prayer, i.e., one must seek God's help to enable him to carry out his good intentions, as the Talmud teaches us, הַבָּא לִיטַּהֵר מְסַיְּעִים אוֹתוֹ, *one who comes to purify himself is assisted*. Evil, on the other hand, will come of itself to one who seeks it, as the Talmud continues: בָּא לִיטַּמֵּא פּוֹתְחִין לוֹ, *if one comes to defile himself, he is given an opening*, i.e., he is permitted to do as he wishes, but is not helped (*Shabbos* 104a).

28. בּוֹטֵחַ בְּעָשְׁרוֹ הוּא יִפֹּל — *He who trusts in his wealth — he will fall*, i.e., his wealth will not help him (*Metzudos*).

He will fall as a result of his wealth. Similarly, עֹשֶׁר שָׁמוּר לִבְעָלָיו לְרָעָתוֹ, *riches hoarded by their owner to his misfortune* (*Ecclesiastes* 5:12) Or, as punishment for trusting in his wealth, he will lose it suddenly and fall (*R' Yonah*).

R' Bachya connects this verse to the preceding one. Usually a person who seeks harm for others is one who trusts too much in his wealth. As a result of his financial standing, he becomes haughty and harbors thoughts of evil and revenge. Therefore, he falls as a result of his wealth.

וְכֶעָלֶה צַדִּיקִים יִפְרָחוּ — *But the righteous will flourish like foliage* [lit. *a leaf*]. The righteous, who trust in God [and not in their wealth, *Ibn Ezra*], will flourish (*Metzudos*).

Just as a leaf grows more quickly than the fruit and is fully developed in a short time, so, too, the righteous will be saved quickly from their troubles, in reward for their trust in God. Because of his trust in his wealth, the person will suddenly lose it and fall, whereas the righteous who trust in God will be rescued swiftly from their distress (*R' Yonah*).

Riches are of primary importance to a wealthy man, but wealth is never stable, as the Talmud puts it, גַּלְגַּל הוּא שֶׁחוֹזֵר בָּעוֹלָם, *it is a wheel that revolves in the world* (*Shabbos* 151b). Once he loses his wealth, he himself will topple, since wealth was his mainstay. To the righteous, however, wealth is but the leaf to a tree, i.e., it is an insignificant part of the total picture. A leaf falls from the tree in the autumn, but it grows again in the spring. So, too, even if the righteous fall like a leaf, יִפְרָחוּ, *they will flourish* (cf. 24:16) (*Vilna Gaon*).

29. עוֹכֵר בֵּיתוֹ יִנְחַל־רוּחַ — *One who troubles his household will inherit wind*. One whose misbehavior troubles his family will be left with nothing worthwhile (*Ibn Ezra*). According to *Ralbag*, the *household* is a metaphor for the person himself; he is lazy and *troubles* his intellect and organs by not using them for anything worthwhile.

Rashi inverts the order of the phrase: A lazy person who constantly *inherits the wind*, by toiling neither in Torah nor in work, will eventually ruin his household, for they will have nothing to eat (*Rashi*).

Metzudos explains רוּחַ as *contention*, and renders the verse according to the sequence of the words: A sluggard ruins his household through his laziness, because he will not earn the means to provide

for them. As a result, fights and anger abound, and it is as if he inherits the spirit of anger.

וְעֶבֶד אֱוִיל לַחֲכַם־לֵב — *And a fool will become a servant of the wise of heart.* Ultimately, this fool will have to become a slave to the wise of heart in order to sustain himself (*Metzudos*).

R' Yonah applies the verse to a stingy person. He harms his household and makes them suffer, and he withholds the money necessary to pay for someone to teach them Torah or a profession or trade. His wealth will dissipate, and he will be left only with *wind*. Even if his children inherit his wealth, they will lack the wisdom to benefit from it, because their father made no effort to teach them properly. And a fool — even one with wealth — is just a slave to the wise at heart. The best inheritance a father can leave his children is a wealth of Torah and *mussar*.

30. פְּרִי־צַדִּיק עֵץ חַיִּים — *The fruit of a righteous one is a tree of life.* The reward for the deeds of the righteous is a tree of life for the world (*Rashi*).

The deeds of the righteous are like a tree that brings life to the world (*Metzudos*). Something beneficial grows from his every deed, giving life to his surroundings (*R' Hirsch*).

Righteous people raise children, their *fruit*, according to the Torah, and by their teachings and example they are imbued with eternal life (*R' Yaakov Kamenetsky*).

וְלֹקֵחַ נְפָשׁוֹת חָכָם — *And a wise man acquires souls.* Rashi explains that by teaching people the proper way to live, *a wise man "acquires"* them, as the Torah says of Abraham and Sarah, וְאֶת־הַנֶּפֶשׁ אֲשֶׁר־עָשׂוּ בְחָרָן, *and the people* [lit. *souls*] *they had acquired in Charan* (*Genesis* 12:5).

Metzudos interprets that one who acquires souls by directing them on the straight road is considered a wise man.

The *Vilna Gaon* explains that פְּרִי צַדִּיק, *the fruit of a righteous one,* refers to his children, for someone who dies and leaves a son to fill his place is not considered dead; thus they are his *tree of life.* He *acquires souls* of his students, his spiritual children, to whom he teaches *Torah*.

Malbim differentiates between a *tzaddik* and a *chacham*. A *tzaddik* is outstanding in his righteous deeds; a *chacham* has amassed Torah knowledge from his teachers. Each has a positive influence in a different way. A *tzaddik* is like a fruit-bearing, life-sustaining tree. The "fruits" of a righteous person are his deeds and the personal example he sets. Those who "eat his fruit" by following his example merit life. A wise man, on the other hand, attracts people [לֹקֵחַ] through his words and his teachings.

The Midrash applies this verse to Noah. What is the fruit of a righteous man? His *mitzvos* and good deeds, as the verse states: *These are the offspring of Noah — Noah was a righteous man* (*Genesis* 6:9). [The "offspring" mentioned in this verse are not his children, but his deeds. (See *Rashi* ibid.).] *A wise man acquires souls* refers to Noah, for he fed and sustained all the creatures in the ark for a full twelve months (*Genesis Rabbah* 30:6). Each creature in the ark had to be fed at a specific time. Hence, Noah is praised as a wise man for knowing the correct feeding time for each (*Eitz Yosef*).

Midrash Tanchuma states that *the fruit of a righteous one is a tree of life* applies to Sarah. All the infants she nursed (see *Genesis* 21:7, *Rashi* ibid.) later became converts. [Thus, even one contact with such a righteous woman had an enormous life-giving impact on these children.]

לא הֵן צַדִּיק בָּאָרֶץ יְשֻׁלָּם אַף כִּי־רָשָׁע וְחוֹטֵא:

א-ב אֹהֵב מוּסָר אֹהֵב דָּעַת וְשֹׂנֵא תוֹכַחַת בָּעַר: טוֹב

ג יָפִיק רָצוֹן מֵיהוָה וְאִישׁ מְזִמּוֹת יַרְשִׁיעַ: לֹא־יִכּוֹן

ד אָדָם בְּרֶשַׁע וְשֹׁרֶשׁ צַדִּיקִים בַּל־יִמּוֹט: אֵשֶׁת־חַיִל

31. הֵן צַדִּיק בָּאָרֶץ יְשֻׁלָּם אַף כִּי־רָשָׁע וְחוֹטֵא — *If a righteous one is punished on earth, surely a wicked one and a sinner.* How can a wicked person trust in his good fortune in this world? He sees that a righteous person gets paid while still in this world for any sin he has committed, so surely, the wicked will be punished for their evil, whether during their lifetime or after death (*Rashi*). As Yose ben Yoezer said: *If this [suffering] is so for those who do His will, how much more so for those who anger Him* (*Bereishis Rabbah* 65:18).

The Midrash applies this verse, like the previous one, to Noah. Though he faithfully took care of all the animals in the ark for a full year, Noah was immediately punished for one small infraction. Once he was late in bringing the lion its food, and the lion struck him. As a result, Noah was limping when he emerged from the ark and was not fit to bring an offering to God. His son Shem brought the sacrifice instead. (See *Rashi* to *Genesis* 7:23). If such a righteous person was immediately requited for a small wrongdoing, how much more so the sinful Generation of the Flood (*Bereishis Rabbah* 30:6).

The *Vilna Gaon* comments that one may question why the wicked have a good life in this world, while the righteous suffer. In reply, our verse states that *a righteous person must become perfect* [יְשֻׁלָּם from שָׁלֵם, *complete*] in this world. Even righteous people must have sinned, since *there is no man so wholly righteous on earth that he [always] does good and never sins* (*Ecclesiastes* 7:20). These sins must be atoned for through suffering in this world. If this is true of the righteous, then surely the wicked will suffer.

XII

1. אֹהֵב מוּסָר אֹהֵב דָּעַת — *One who loves discipline loves knowledge.* One who loves the ethical teachings and discipline of *mussar* loves *knowledge*, for by listening to *mussar*, he will attain a level of knowledge previously unknown to him (*Metzudos*).[1]

If a person has been misled by temptation, but is pleased to hear words of reproof, that indicates that he is essentially a man of knowledge, but that he has sinned only because his desires have gotten the best of him. His love of knowledge leads him to love *mussar*, for he hopes that the admonition he receives will help him overcome the persuasions of his Evil Inclination (*R' Yonah*).

וְשֹׂנֵא תוֹכַחַת בָּעַר — *But one who hates reproof is boorish.* One who hates reproof has no sense, for he will remain with his folly. The word בָּעַר is related to וּבְעִירֵנוּ, *and our animal*, (*Numbers* 20:4), for such a person is comparable to an animal (*Metzudos*), in that his soul is drawn after his desires (*R' Yonah*).

R' Hirsch explains בָּעַר as *burning*, which describes a person who is ablaze with instinctual desires that he cannot control. He heeds only the sensual fires of his flesh and totally disregards his mind, thus becoming devoid of sensibility.

Mussar is related to the word יִסּוּרִים,

1. Great Torah scholars, in their quest for even higher levels of perfection in God's service, hungered for *mussar*. The *Maharshal* went so far as to assign someone to rebuke him at regular intervals. He instructed this person to treat him as if he were an ordinary Jew, and not to stint in his reproof. When this person entered the *Maharshal's* room, the *Maharshal* would immediately wrap himself in a *tallis* and wait, trembling, to hear the words of rebuke (quoted in *Mutzal Me'Eish*).

³¹ *If a righteous one is punished on earth, surely a wicked one and a sinner.*

¹ One who loves discipline loves knowledge, but one who hates reproof is boorish. ² A good person draws forth favor from HASHEM, but a scheming man causes wickedness. ³ A person will not be steadfast through wickedness, but the root of the righteous will not falter. ⁴ An accomplished woman

afflictions. Our Sages teach that Torah is one of three valuable gifts bestowed upon the Jewish nation, which can be acquired only through afflictions (*Berachos* 5a). Therefore, it is not possible for a person to excel in Torah knowledge unless he lovingly accepts afflictions. On the other hand, a person who hates even תוֹכָחָה, *verbal admonition,* will remain a fool (*Vilna Gaon*).

2. טוֹב יָפִיק רָצוֹן מֵה' — *A good person draws forth favor from HASHEM.* A good person brings out God's pleasure to bring good to the world (*Rashi*).

וְאִישׁ מְזִמּוֹת יַרְשִׁיעַ — *But a scheming man causes wickedness.* A person who indulges in evil schemes makes others blameworthy, thus causing them to suffer punishment. Similarly, in *Ecclesiastes* 9:18 we find: וְחוֹטֶא אֶחָד יְאַבֵּד טוֹבָה הַרְבֵּה, *but a single sinner can ruin a great deal of good* (*Rashi*). He condemns the whole world because he tips the balance to the guilty side (*Metzudos*).[1]

According to *Rashi* and *Metzudos*, the term יַרְשִׁיעַ means *he brings blameworthiness upon others.* R' Yonah and Ibn Ezra explain it as: *He [Hashem] will find him guilty.* If someone harbors evil thoughts, God will judge him guilty and not show him leniency, for such a person is hateful to God.

The term מְזִמָּה refers to *deep thoughts.* When it is mentioned in relation to wisdom, it means deep thoughts of wisdom (see 1:4). However, when it is used in other contexts, it

usually means plotting against one's fellows (*Malbim*).

A man who overestimates his own cleverness and thinks his ways are acceptable dares to act against Divine law. Such actions not only offend God but prepare the greatest vexation for the individual, because God transforms him into a merciless cause of harm to himself (*R' Hirsch*).

3. לֹא־יִכּוֹן אָדָם בְּרֶשַׁע — *A person will not be steadfast through wickedness.* A person's wicked deeds — i.e., sinfully accumulated wealth — will not enable him to remain well established (*Metzudos*).

There is no כֵּן, *firm base,* under the wicked person. Although things may go well for him now, it is only temporary. Lacking a firm foundation, his prosperity will not last (*Vilna Gaon*).

וְשֹׁרֶשׁ צַדִּיקִים בַּל־יִמּוֹט — *But the root of the righteous will not falter.* Even if the righteous fall, their root will not falter — and as long as the root remains in the ground, a plant can grow again. Therefore, when the righteous fall, it is only temporary (*Vilna Gaon*), and they will rise again (*Metzudos*) (cf. 10:30 and 24:16).

According to *Ibn Ezra,* the root of the righteous refers to their children who remain after their death.

A כֵּן, *base,* and a שֹׁרֶשׁ, *root,* differ. A base is a separate entity supporting the object resting upon it, like the כֵּן, *stand,* that supported the כִּיּוֹר, *Laver,* in the Tabernacle. A root, on the other hand, is an intrinsic part of the plant. Man is

1. In the ethical perspective, every individual must view himself as being the deciding factor in the world's righteousness or guilt. The Talmud (*Kiddushin* 40b) explains that a person should consider the sum total of his and the world's deeds as exactly equal: half meritorious and half guilty. Therefore, if he commits only one transgression, it may be the deciding factor in tipping the scales for himself and the entire world towards guilt (thereby causing the whole world to lose much good).

עֲטֶרֶת בַּעְלָה וּכְרָקָב בְּעַצְמוֹתָיו מְבִישָׁה:
ה מַחְשְׁבוֹת צַדִּיקִים מִשְׁפָּט תַּחְבֻּלוֹת רְשָׁעִים
ו מִרְמָה: דִּבְרֵי רְשָׁעִים אֱרָב־דָּם וּפִי יְשָׁרִים
ז יַצִּילֵם: הָפוֹךְ רְשָׁעִים וְאֵינָם וּבֵית צַדִּיקִים יַעֲמֹד:

compared to an inverted tree with roots on top, for his head is like a root planted in the heavenly spheres, from which he draws spiritual sustenance. A wicked person has cut himself off from his spiritual root, his body resting solely on a material base in this world. This base lacks stability, however; it will eventually collapse, i.e., since his wealth was obtained illicitly, it will not endure. The righteous, however, cleave to their holy roots, and therefore, even if they slip — even if their body is drawn toward the impurities of this world — their roots remain firmly planted in spirituality and eventually their bodies will also return to their roots (*Malbim*).

In the midst of life's storms, the righteous still have an inner support holding them firm and straight. The wicked lack this root and are unable to replace it with artificial superficialities (*R' Hirsch*).

4. אֵשֶׁת חַיִל עֲטֶרֶת בַּעְלָה — *An accomplished woman is the crown of her husband.* Her husband glories in her deeds (*Metzudos*). Like a crown, she becomes his source of dignity and pride in the eyes of others. [See 31:23 נוֹדָע בַּשְּׁעָרִים בַּעְלָה, *Her husband is known in the gates*] (*Malbim*).

The term אֵשֶׁת חַיִל used to describe an accomplished woman has many complimentary connotations.

❏ It describes a woman who is diligent (זְרִיזָה) and just in her actions (*Metzudos*).

❏ The term חַיִל is related to wealth (see *Deuteronomy* 8:17 and *Jeremiah* 15:13,

et al.). A woman who can acquire wealth is her husband's crown. He is honored for her sake, just as a king is honored because of his crown (*Ibn Ezra*).

❏ She protects her husband so that no bad befalls him (*Vilna Gaon*). (This suggests similar terms such as אִישׁ חַיִל or גִּבּוֹר חַיִל, *a man of strength, a warrior*).

Targum renders, אִתְּתָא כְשֵׁרְתָּא, *a virtuous woman.*

וּכְרָקָב בְּעַצְמוֹתָיו מְבִישָׁה — *But a shameful one is like rot in his bones.* An evil woman whose deeds are shameful is like a worm that enters a person's bones and grinds them up (*Rashi*); there is no cure for this malady (*Ibn Ezra*).

A wife is considered part of her husband's bones [since Eve was created from Adam's bone: see *Genesis* 2:23, עֶצֶם מֵעֲצָמַי, *a bone of my bones*]. Therefore, when she acts shamefully, it is as if part of his body is rotted away, for half of him — his wife — is rotted, and this rot will invade the other half and rot it away as well (*Malbim*).

This verse warns man to investigate carefully and not choose a shameful wife. He should not be attracted by the riches she may offer (*R' Yonah*).[1]

5. מַחְשְׁבוֹת צַדִּיקִים מִשְׁפָּט — *The thoughts of the righteous are just*, i.e., to do true justice and save the oppressed from their oppressors (*Metzudos*).

This trait is personified by Moses, our teacher, who came to the aid of Jethro's

1. When R' Yechezkel Levenstein was seeking his partner in life, his rebbe recommended a girl from a rather wealthy home as a possible match for him. When R' Chatzkel turned down this proposal, his rebbe asked him, "Don't you want this rich match?" To which R' Chatzkel replied, "I would be agreeable to a wealthy father-in-law, but as for the daughter of a wealthy father — to that I am not agreeable." R' Chatzkel subsequently married an orphan from a very poor home and, with her help, proceeded to devote his life to Torah until he passed away at the age of 90.

is the crown of her husband, but a shameful one is like rot in his bones. ⁵ The thoughts of the righteous are just, but the strategies of the wicked are deceit. ⁶ The words of the wicked lie in ambush for blood, but the mouth of the upright will rescue them. ⁷ The wicked are overturned and are no more, but the house of the righteous will endure.

daughters when the shepherds chased them away and would not let them water their sheep (*Exodus* 2:17).

The mental processes of truthful people are straightforward and artless, and are directed toward justice (*R' Hirsch*).

תַּחְבֻּלוֹת רְשָׁעִים מִרְמָה — *But the strategies of the wicked are deceit.* They plot stratagems to facilitate deceit (*Metzudos*).

Thoughts enter a person's mind as he considers various possibilities. *Strategies* are a combination of various ideas intertwined and woven together to form a plan of action (see *Malbim* to 1:5, who relates תַּחְבֻּלוֹת to חֶבֶל, a *rope*, for both are made of intertwined strands). Even the ordinary thoughts of the righteous are just; therefore, they do not need schemes. The wicked, however, plan and plot devious ways to cheat, extort and steal from their victims; hence, their need for complicated stratagems (*Malbim*).

6. דִּבְרֵי רְשָׁעִים אֱרָב־דָּם — *The words of the wicked lie in ambush for blood.* The wicked advise murder, either to shed blood with their own hands or through their false testimony (*Rashi*), as Jezebel brought about the murder of Navoth through false testimony (*I Kings* 21). They spread gossip and slander, thus destroying their victim (*Malbim*).

וּפִי יְשָׁרִים יַצִּילֵם — *But the mouth of the upright will rescue them.* When upright people hear the plans of the wicked, they come to the aid of the intended victims and rescue them, either by warning them of the danger or by testifying against the wicked (*Rashi*).

Even if wicked people speak sweetly, it is just a cover-up for the sinister plans in their hearts. This is comparable to one who hides in ambush until he can catch a

victim and shed his blood. Just people also speak deceptively at times, but their intention is only to save would-be victims from the *words of the wicked.* For example, when Hushai the Archite seemed to advise Absalom about how to vanquish King David, in reality, he intended to undermine Ahitophel's strategy and save David's life (see *II Samuel* 17:7-13) (*Vilna Gaon*).

7. הָפוֹךְ רְשָׁעִים וְאֵינָם — *The wicked are overturned and are no more.* The wicked are overthrown in an instant and are completely destroyed, like Sodom (*Rashi*). They cease to exist and their memory is obliterated (*Metzudos*).

This verse is the outcome of the preceding two verses: Since the wicked anger God in both thought (v. 5) and action (v. 6), they will be completely destroyed (*R' Yonah*).

וּבֵית צַדִּיקִים יַעֲמֹד — *But the house of the righteous will endure.* Even when the righteous die, their house, i.e., their children, will endure (*Vilna Gaon*).

This verse is exemplified time and again: by the Generation of the Flood, which was totally destroyed, while Noah and his family were saved (*Genesis* 7:21- 8:15); by Sodom which was overthrown, while Lot and his daughters survived (*Genesis* 19:25); by the Egyptians who all drowned in the Sea of Reeds, while Israel was saved (*Exodus* 14:28); by Babylon which had neither remnant nor posterity, while the exiled Israel was renewed (*Isaiah* 14:22). As King David exclaims: *There they fell, the practitioners of iniquity; they were thrust down and are unable to rise* (*Psalms* 36:13). However, *Klal Yisrael* endures, for even if they fall, they rise again (*Midrash Tanchuma*).

ח לְפִי־שִׂכְלוֹ יְהֻלַּל־אִישׁ וְנַעֲוֵה־לֵב יִהְיֶה לָבוּז:
ט טוֹב נִקְלֶה וְעֶבֶד לוֹ מִמִּתְכַּבֵּד וַחֲסַר־לָחֶם:
י יוֹדֵעַ צַדִּיק נֶפֶשׁ בְּהֶמְתּוֹ וְרַחֲמֵי רְשָׁעִים אַכְזָרִי:

8. לְפִי־שִׂכְלוֹ יְהֻלַּל־אִישׁ — *According to a man's wisdom will he be praised.* A person will receive his reward according to how much wisdom he achieved, whether little or much (*Rashi*).

וְנַעֲוֵה־לֵב יִהְיֶה לָבוּז — *But one of distorted heart will be put to shame.* One who has moved his heart completely away from the Torah will be subject to contempt (*Rashi*).

When one's heart is pure, his intellect becomes his greatest glory; when one's heart is perverse, it corrupts his insights and intellect, and is eventually despised (*Malbim*).

Even if a God-fearing person studies Torah away from the public eye, and his vast Torah knowledge is not revealed, he will still be praised, because God will reveal his Torah knowledge to others, and "his Torah will herald him on the outside" (see *Moed Kattan* 16b). On the other hand, someone who harbors evil thoughts in his heart but does not reveal them to anyone else will still be despised, for God will publicize his shame (*Vilna Gaon*).

9. טוֹב נִקְלֶה וְעֶבֶד לוֹ מִמִּתְכַּבֵּד וַחֲסַר־לָחֶם — *Better off is a lowly one who serves for his keep than a pompous one who lacks bread.* It is better for a person to hold himself in low esteem and be his own slave [working even at a servile job (*Vilna Gaon*)] than to consider himself so honorable that it is beneath his dignity to work, so that he ends up lacking food (*Rashi*).

The Sages (*Bava Basra* 110a) advise a person to get paid for skinning an animal in the marketplace and not consider himself an important person, i.e., he should even resort to menial labor or coarse work if that provides a source of livelihood, and not think it is beneath his dignity.

The *Vilna Gaon* figuratively applies this verse to Torah study. It is preferable that a person embarrass himself by asking question and consulting anyone who can help him, thus "being a slave to himself," than to be too pompous, pretending to understand everything, and in the end knowing nothing.

10. יוֹדֵעַ צַדִּיק נֶפֶשׁ בְּהֶמְתּוֹ — *A righteous one knows [the needs of] his animal's soul.* A righteous man attends to the needs of his animals and the members of his household (*Rashi*).

A righteous man is attentive even to his animal's needs and fulfills its desires, for he has acquired the trait of compassion (*Metzudos*).

Just as a righteous person performs all the mitzvos personally, not delegating them to others, he is concerned with the poor and attends them personally. This concern extends even to his animals, for he takes care to feed them in a timely manner. The Sages derive from the Torah that a person may not eat any food himself until he has fed his animals (*Gittin* 62b). Being cruel to animals is a negative trait, for man must emulate the traits of God, about Whom it is written, וְרַחֲמָיו עַל־כָּל מַעֲשָׂיו, *and His mercies are on all His creatures* (*Psalms* 145:9). Just as Heavenly mercy is extended not only to humans, but also to creatures, a person must also show mercy to all creatures (*R' Yonah*).

According to the Sages, צַעַר בַּעֲלֵי חַיִּים, causing needless suffering to living creatures, is a Biblical prohibition (*Shabbos* 128b).[1]

וְרַחֲמֵי רְשָׁעִים אַכְזָרִי — *But the mercies of the wicked are cruel.* The "compassion" which the wicked appear to have in reality is a mask for their inner cruelty. Their

1. The Talmud (*Bava Metzia* 85a) recounts how Rabbi (Rabbi Yehudah HaNasi) suffered thirteen years of pain because he failed to show compassion for a calf being taken out to slaughter. After all the years of suffering, it was only when Rabbi instructed the maid not to chase a litter of baby weasels out of the house, explaining that God shows mercy to all His creatures and so must we, that God had mercy on him and took away his afflictions..

8 *According to a man's wisdom will he be praised, but one of distorted heart will be put to shame.* 9 *Better off is a lowly one who serves for his keep than a pompous one who lacks bread.* 10 *A righteous one knows [the needs of] his animal's soul, but the mercies of the wicked are cruel.*

mercy is insincere; in their hearts they are not compassionate (*Metzudos*).

Even if a wicked person gives charity to a poor man, he is still cruel, because he may do it in such a way as to embarrass the pauper or show off at his expense. For instance, he may seat a poor man in an insignificant place at his table, or only grudgingly give him a handout, or fail to speak to him encouragingly. The Talmud (*Kiddushin* 31a) applies the same principle to the commandment of honoring one's parents. Though a child may feed his father fine foods, he will be punished if he does so begrudgingly and disrespectfully (*R' Yonah*).

The *Vilna Gaon* explains that the righteous man attends to the needs of his livestock, but does not overfeed or overwork them. However, the wicked who give more food than necessary to their animals are really cruel, for they are doing so to make their beasts ride faster or carry heavier loads, overtaxing their abilities. This verse also speaks metaphorically of the human being as he relates to his body. A righteous man is conscious of his נֶפֶשׁ הַבְּהֵמִית, his *animal instincts*, i.e., his physical desires. He does not indulge such cravings nor succumb to every physical desire; he eats only enough to sustain his health. The wicked are more "merciful"; they neither break their desires nor curb their appetites. They cater to their bodily needs with the greatest compassion. This is truly cruel, for their increased flesh will lead to increased maggots (see *Avos* 2:7) and their actions cause them to descend to *Gehinnom*.

R' Bachya renders the word יוֹדֵעַ as *breaks* or *subdues*, relating it to the verse וַיָּדַע בָּהֶם אֵת אַנְשֵׁי סֻכּוֹת, *and with them he thrashed* [lit. *broke*] *the men of Succos* (*Judges* 8:16). A righteous person subdues his animal desires, thereby allowing his intellectual soul to become elevated. The wicked, however, have mercy on their body and fulfill all its lusts, but they exhibit cruelty to their intellect, for physical desires are the obstacles that block the intellect from attaining true wisdom.

R' Hirsch explains that Torah educates us to be mindful even of the needs of animals that depend on man, to spare their strength and provide for their wants. By being kind to animals, we will realize how much more we must be considerate of our fellow human beings. By contrast, when someone's cares, concerns, feelings and mercy are not rooted in Torah, but derive from inclination, an individual can just as easily become cruel as compassionate, depending upon his mood, momentary state of mind, or any presumptive notion.[1]

1. History has illustrated time and again that mercy, as defined by human perception, is often a masquerade for cruelty. Many "civilized" and "merciful" nations have ended up perpetrating heinous crimes upon those whom they perceive as their "enemies." The culture which was heralded as the model of civility and gentility, Germany, nurtured a cruel viper unmatched in the annals of mankind. Those who pity the plight of criminals turn a deaf ear to the anguish of their next victim. The slogan of "choice" masks a lack of concern for the sanctity of life.

Only the Torah can prescribe the exact balance between mercy and cruelty. The execution of a murderer who was been tried according to Jewish law in the time of the Sanhedrin was not cruelty, but rather was merciful both to the sinner and to society at large. The laws of *shechitah* (ritual slaughter) are not inhumane, but elevating. The circumcision of a newborn is not a cause for tears, but for rejoicing, as this newborn enters a covenant with the Almighty. When the human mind perverts the merciful command of God to its own understanding of "compassion," then only tragedy can result. (See *I Samuel* 15 for the results of Saul's misplaced mercy for King Agag of Amalek, who became the progenitor of Haman.)

יא עֹבֵד אַדְמָתוֹ יִשְׂבַּע־לָחֶם וּמְרַדֵּף רֵיקִים חֲסַר־לֵב:
יב־יג חָמַד רָשָׁע מְצוֹד רָעִים וְשֹׁרֶשׁ צַדִּיקִים יִתֵּן: בְּפֶשַׁע
יד שְׂפָתַיִם מוֹקֵשׁ רָע וַיֵּצֵא מִצָּרָה צַדִּיק: מִפְּרִי
פִי־אִישׁ יִשְׂבַּע־טוֹב וּגְמוּל יְדֵי־אָדָם °יָשׁוּב לוֹ:

°יָשִׁיב ק'

11. עֹבֵד אַדְמָתוֹ יִשְׂבַּע־לָחֶם — *He who works his soil will be sated with bread.* This refers either literally to tilling the soil, or metaphorically to one who constantly reviews his learning so that it should not be forgotten (*Rashi*).

Malbim compares the soul to a plot of land that can produce crops. Just as one must tend the soil, remove the weeds, plant seeds and water them, so, too, a person must remove the faulty elements in his nature and implant within it seeds of wisdom and discipline, and "water" it with intellect and knowledge until it produces beautiful fruits. If a person invests spiritual labor, he will reap spiritual fruits that will nourish his soul.

וּמְרַדֵּף רֵיקִים חֲסַר־לֵב — *But he who pursues vanities lacks an [understanding] heart.* One who pursues things of no value lacks understanding, for he should rather use the time to till the soil (*Metzudos*).

R' Yonah points out that one who does not work to support himself will not only lack bread (see verse 9), but also lack understanding. The Sages warn that הַבַּטָלָה מֵבִיאָה לִידֵי שֶׁעֲמוּם, *idleness leads to idiocy* (*Kesubos* 59b). In addition, his inactivity causes him to associate with others who are empty and idle, and he begins to learn from their base character traits.

12. חָמַד רָשָׁע מְצוֹד רָעִים — *A wicked person craves the prey of evildoers.* A wicked person desires to attain his livelihood from the prey of the wicked, who prey on others with robbery and violence (*Rashi*).

Metzudos renders מְצוֹד as מִבְצָר, *a fortress.* A wicked person desires to sit in the fortress of evil people, where they strengthen themselves to do violence.

According to *R' Bachya*, verses 11 and 12 are a continuation of the same theme:

how one must avoid the sin of חֶמְדָּה, coveting. One who invests effort into earning a living will be satiated with all good. However, one who pursues empty things and just sits idly will come to covet the wealth of evil men. A person who covets is termed a *wicked person*, for one is prohibited from coveting someone else's money, all the more so if the money was obtained through robbery and violence. Work has the power to protect a person from coveting by assuring that he will have provided for his own needs, and he will not need gifts nor become impoverished. The same is true of Torah study — one who exerts himself to study Torah will be satiated with its knowledge, and he will not covet the wealth of others since he will be satisfied with what he has.

Yalkut Shimoni applies this verse to Esau, who coveted and stole Nimrod's elegant clothes (see *Rashi* to *Genesis* 27:15).

וְשֹׁרֶשׁ צַדִּיקִים יִתֵּן — *But the root of the righteous will provide [for them].* Their root will produce what is fit for them to yield, which is the fruit (*Rashi*). Similarly, King David teaches that the righteous one *will be like a tree deeply rooted alongside brooks of water that yields its fruit in its season* (*Psalms* 1:3).

The righteous will not need outside sources of help, for their own roots produce fruit; i.e., they are self-motivated to strengthen themselves to do good (*Metzudos*).

The *Vilna Gaon* explains that *the root of the righteous* refers to one who is not only righteous himself, but also comes from righteous "roots," i.e., ancestors. Good is so intrinsically ingrained in his nature that his only desire is יִתֵּן, *to constantly give* to others.

13. בְּפֶשַׁע שְׂפָתַיִם מוֹקֵשׁ רָע — *In the sin of the lips lies a snare of evil.* When someone

12/11-14   [11] *He who works his soil will be sated with bread, but he who pursues vanities lacks an [understanding] heart.* [12] *A wicked person craves the prey of evildoers, but the root of the righteous will provide [for them].* [13] *In the sin of the lips lies a snare of evil, but a righteous person escapes travail.* [14] *From the fruit of a man's mouth he will be sated with good, and the recompense of a man's handiwork will be returned to him!*

transgresses with his lips and speaks in a rebellious manner, he is ensnared by evil (*Metzudos*). Imprudent talk ends up ensnaring the person himself, as stated below: *The mouth of a fool [brings] ruin to him, and his lips are a snare to his soul* (18:7) (*Ibn Ezra*).

וַיֵּצֵא מִצָּרָה צַדִּיק — *But a righteous person escapes travail.* Through his pleasant words, a righteous person escapes this imminent distress (*Metzudos*).

Because the Generation of the Flood spoke against God, claiming that there was no benefit in serving Him (*Job* 21:15), an evil snare came upon them, but the righteous Noah was saved from this distress (*Rashi*).

The tongue and the mouth are the biggest potential sources of trouble for a person. The righteous guard their tongues and remain silent, and are therefore saved from distress (cf. 18:21 and 21:23) (*Meiri*).

14. מִפְּרִי פִי־אִישׁ יִשְׂבַּע־טוֹב וּגְמוּל יְדֵי אָדָם יָשִׁיב לוֹ — *From the fruit of a man's mouth he will be sated with good, and the recompense of a man's handiwork will be returned* [lit. *He will return*] *to him.* Those who are occupied with Torah study enjoy the fruit of their labor by receiving good in this world, while the principal of their reward is saved for them in the World to Come (*Rashi*). See *Peah* 1:1: *These are the precepts whose fruits a person enjoys in this world, but whose principal remains*

intact for him in the World to Come ... and the study of Torah is equivalent to them all.

A person should seek to earn merits both through his speech and his deeds, for he can earn as great a reward through his speech as through his deeds. An individual should garner his powers of speech to give good advice to others; he should sanctify God's Name with his words; he should influence others to stop sinning and do good. If a person's speech has yielded "fruit" by affecting others for the good, he will share equally in the reward they earn through their subsequent good deeds. As the Sages declare (*Bava Basra* 9a), "One who causes others to give [charity] is greater than one who gives himself" (*R' Yonah*).[1]

The *Vilna Gaon* comments that a person should always reprove his friend, if his behavior warrrants rebuke, even if he does not know if the reproof will be heeded. If the rebuke is successful, then the one who delivered it will be rewarded for his friend's subsequent *mitzvos*, as if he himself had done those good deeds. If the rebuke goes unheeded, he will at least have fulfilled his obligation to the sinner, and will be rewarded for that *mitzvah*. The *Arizal* teaches that if one rebukes a wicked person and the latter ignores it, all the good that the sinner has done is reckoned as if it had been done by the one who administered the rebuke. Thus, our verse states,

1. When Rabbi Boruch Ber Leibowitz was fourteen years old, he delivered a Torah discourse with a clarity, depth and sharpness that astounded all who heard it. Nine-year-old Yechiel Michel Rabinowitz was so impressed by it that he resolved to dedicate himself to Torah study until he would attain such a high level of scholarship. He carried out his resolution and eventually became an outstanding Torah sage and the author of *Afikei Yam*. R' Boruch Ber was heard to proudly claim, "דער אפיקי ים איז מיינער, the *Afikei Yam* is really mine," by which he meant: Since I was instrumental in motivating R' Yechiel Michel to excel in Torah wisdom, his scholarly work is really to my credit.

דֶּרֶךְ אֱוִיל יָשָׁר בְּעֵינָיו וְשֹׁמֵעַ לְעֵצָה חָכָם: אֱוִיל
טו
בַּיּוֹם יִוָּדַע כַּעְסוֹ וְכֹסֶה קָלוֹן עָרוּם: יָפִיחַ אֱמוּנָה
טז
יַגִּיד צֶדֶק וְעֵד שְׁקָרִים מִרְמָה: יֵשׁ בּוֹטֶה
יז
כְּמַדְקְרוֹת חָרֶב וּלְשׁוֹן חֲכָמִים מַרְפֵּא: שְׂפַת־
יח
אֱמֶת תִּכּוֹן לָעַד וְעַד־אַרְגִּיעָה לְשׁוֹן שָׁקֶר:
יט

From the fruit of a man's mouth who rebukes the sinner, even if his words go unheeded, *he will be sated with good*, for he will be given all the good done by the one he has reproved. On the other hand, if the rebuke is heeded, then the *recompense of a man's handiwork* — all the good deeds that the other person will subsequently do — *will be returned to him*, as if he had performed those good deeds, and he will be rewarded for them.

R' Yonah comments that the second half of the verse alludes to the punishment meted out to a sinner for his deeds. This explains the קְרִי וּכְתִיב, *written form and pronounced form*, found in this verse. Bad does not emanate from God; it results from a person's actions. Therefore it is not God Who is responsible for bringing [יָשִׁיב] bad upon a person; but, rather, the bad deed itself that the sinner did [יָשׁוּב] *will return* to him and punish him.

15. דֶּרֶךְ אֱוִיל יָשָׁר בְּעֵינָיו — *The way of a fool is just in his eyes*, for he considers himself to be wise (*Metzudos*), and therefore will not ask others for advice (*Ralbag*), nor believe someone who rebukes him (*Ibn Ezra*).

וְשֹׁמֵעַ לְעֵצָה חָכָם — *But the wise man heeds counsel*. One who is already a *chacham* and could rightfully rely on his own knowledge listens to the advice of others (*Ralbag*).

A *fool* is misled by his desires and leaves the way of wisdom. He should suspect that his decisions may be prejudiced by temptations that blind him to the truth, and therefore should seek the counsel of others to set him straight. He does not think so,

however, for his way *is just in his eyes* and he relies on his own knowledge to guide him. A wise man, on the other hand, constantly fears that he may err because of his personal wants and desires. Therefore, even though many others rely on him to guide them, in his personal matters he seeks advice from others (*R' Yonah*).

Metzudos renders: only one who listens to the advice of others who will be considered wise.

16. אֱוִיל בַּיּוֹם יִוָּדַע כַּעְסוֹ — *A fool's anger will become known on that very day*. On the very day he becomes angry, the fool makes his anger known by quarreling with his friend and berating him in public. He does not restrain his anger (*Rashi*); he becomes instantly enraged and vindictive (*Malbim*).

וְכֹסֶה קָלוֹן עָרוּם — *But a clever man conceals disgrace*. A shrewd person conceals his shame and does not rush to fight with others. According to the Midrash, this verse alludes to Adam. On the very first day of his creation, his misdeeds became known [for he sinned by eating from the Tree of Knowledge]. But in His wisdom, the Holy One, Blessed is He, did not want to destroy His creations. Therefore, He concealed Adam's shame and deferred His decree of death from Adam's day to His day, which is one thousand years (*Rashi*).[1]

17. יָפִיחַ אֱמוּנָה יַגִּיד צֶדֶק — *One who [always] spouts the truth* [lit. *faith*] *will give righteous testimony*. One who speaks in good faith will testify righteously in court in order to justify the innocent party (*Rashi*). If he is accustomed to be truthful

1. Adam was warned not to eat from the Tree of Knowledge, for *on the day you eat of it, you shall surely die* (*Genesis* 2:17). God changed this "day" of Adam's to His day, which is a thousand years, as we are taught in *Psalms* (90:4): *for a thousand years in Your eyes are like a bygone yesterday*. Adam actually died at the age of 930 — close to a thousand years after his sin.

¹⁵ *The way of a fool is just in his eyes, but the wise man heeds counsel.* ¹⁶ *A fool's anger will become known on that very day, but a clever man conceals disgrace.* ¹⁷ *One who [always] spouts the truth will give righteous testimony, but a witness saying falsehoods [personifies] deceit.* ¹⁸ *There is one who speaks [harshly] like piercings of a sword, but the tongue of wise men heals.* ¹⁹ *True speech will be established forever, but a false tongue is only for a moment.*

in all that he says, he certainly will testify truthfully in court (*Ralbag*). His testimony is reliable (*R' Yonah*).

וְעֵד שְׁקָרִים מִרְמָה — *But a witness saying falsehoods [personifies] deceit.* The translation follows *R' Yonah, Ralbag* and the *Vilna Gaon*, who explain that a deceitful person, who is accustomed to lie, will testify falsely when called upon as a witness, for he loves falsehood and injustice.

The *Vilna Gaon* explains why עֵד, a *witness*, is in the singular form while שְׁקָרִים, *falsehoods*, is in the plural. Someone who is out to deceive others will include *many* falsehoods in *one* testimony, for he will say one thing to one person and a different thing to the other, since he wants to ingratiate himself to everyone.

According to *Targum Yonasan* and *Ibn Ezra*, the verse reads, *But a false witness is a deceitful person.*

18. יֵשׁ בּוֹטֶה כְּמַדְקְרוֹת חָרֶב — *There is one who speaks [harshly] like piercings of a sword.* A person's speech can stir up arguments among people and cause them to kill (*Rashi*). *Psalms* 120:4 likens slander to the sharpened arrows of the mighty, which can harm from afar.

וּלְשׁוֹן חֲכָמִים מַרְפֵּא — *But the tongue of wise men heals.* The words of wise people, which bring peace between man and his fellow man, are the antidote to harsh talk (*Rashi*).

Someone who slanders or defames an-

other can cause as much harm as if he had actually stabbed someone with a sword. The words of the wise, however, can heal, for their sweet words can convince a person to repent from the evil that he spoke, and this repentance is his cure (*Metzudos*).

Wise people will nullify the damage brought about through slander by rebuking and denouncing those who spoke evil, and making known the punishment of those who accept and believe slander (*R' Yonah*).

The tongue of the wise heals, for the Sages (*Arachin* 15b) cite Torah as the remedy for gossip and slander [see 15:4] (*Vilna Gaon*).

19. שְׂפַת־אֱמֶת תִּכּוֹן לָעַד — *True speech* [lit. *lip of*] *will be established forever.* Truth will endure (*Rashi*). If a person is careful to speak truthfully, his words will be accepted and believed, and others will be eager to hear his words (*R' Yonah*).

וְעַד־אַרְגִּיעָה לְשׁוֹן שָׁקֶר — *But a false tongue is only for a moment.* Falsehood perishes in a short moment, for it has no feet upon which to stand (*Rashi*).[1] The duration of a falsehood is momentary; it lasts only for the time it is said. Afterwards, the truth comes out (*Metzudos*).

Falsehood will soon be revealed, and the liar will be entrapped in his own words. People will not listen to him, for whatever he says will be suspect. In a similar vein, the Sages state (*Sanhedrin* 69b) that the punishment for a liar is that no one be-

1. The Talmud explains how the structure of the words אֱמֶת, *truth*, and שֶׁקֶר, *falsehood*, depicts the actual qualities of these traits. The letters of falsehood ש, ק, ר appear next to one another in the Hebrew alphabet; while the letters א, מ, ת are far apart, with א as the first letter, מ as the middle letter and ת as the last letter. This shows that falsehood is very common, whereas truth can be isolated and hard to find. The letters ש, ק, ר have only one foot upon which to stand (i.e., the letters are shaped so that each ends with only one point on the bottom), whereas the letters א, מ, ת have a firm base beneath them (for instance, א has two wide "feet" for balance). This symbolizes that truth lasts, while falsehood does not (*Shabbos* 104a).

כ מִרְמָה בְּלֶב־חֹרְשֵׁי רָע וּלְיֹעֲצֵי שָׁלוֹם שִׂמְחָה:
כא לֹא־יְאֻנֶּה לַצַּדִּיק כָּל־אָוֶן וּרְשָׁעִים מָלְאוּ רָע:
כב תּוֹעֲבַת יְהוָה שִׂפְתֵי־שָׁקֶר וְעֹשֵׂי אֱמוּנָה רְצוֹנוֹ:
כג אָדָם עָרוּם כֹּסֶה דָּעַת וְלֵב כְּסִילִים יִקְרָא אִוֶּלֶת:

lieves him even when he tells the truth (*R'
Yonah*).

שְׂפַת, literally, *a lip of*, symbolizes casual,
superficial speech, such as conversation
that has little or no significance. לָשׁוֹן, a
tongue, which is inside the body, implies
serious, meaningful speech. In speaking of
truthful people, our verse says *the lip of*,
because even the unimportant words of
such a person will be established and
endure forever. However, even the most
serious words of a liar last only a short
time, for his falsehoods are soon revealed
(*Vilna Gaon*).[1]

20. מִרְמָה בְּלֶב־חֹרְשֵׁי רָע — *Deceit [lurks] in
the heart of those who plot* [lit. *plow*] *evil*.
Devising evil schemes resembles turning
over the earth for planting (*Ibn Nachmiash*). (Cf. אַל־תַּחֲרֹשׁ עַל רֵעֲךָ רָעָה 3:29.)

Since such people are occupied with
thoughts of deceit, they have no happiness
(*Rashi*).

R' Yonah warns that if someone advises
you to take revenge upon your friend,
claiming that he wants to protect your
honor, do not believe him. There is deceit
in the heart of those who plot evil; their
bad advice does not stem from love, but
from hatred. If they really meant your
good, they would never advise you to
harm someone else and increase his hatred,
since a person never knows when his
enemy will be in a powerful position [and
be able to retaliate].

וּלְיֹעֲצֵי שָׁלוֹם שִׂמְחָה — *But for those who
counsel peace, [there is] gladness*. Those
who plot evil and harbor deceitful
thoughts in their heart are constantly worried and anxious lest their plots be discovered. However, those who counsel peace
do not worry — on the contrary, they even
rejoice if their thoughts become known
(*Metzudos*).

Malbim points out that evil and peace
are opposites. Evil includes anything
which destroys the world; while peace
encompasses anything that preserves the
world. This refers to any good, whether
personal, communal or political.

The Midrash quotes *R' Zeira*, who applies this verse to someone who lies in bed
at night and thinks to himself, "Tomorrow, I will get up and do a favor for
so-and-so." Such an individual will enjoy
the happiness destined for the righteous in
the future (*Yalkut Shimoni*)

21. לֹא־יְאֻנֶּה לַצַּדִּיק כָּל־אָוֶן — *No iniquity
will befall the righteous person*. A righteous person will not inadvertently stumble into sin (*Rashi*).

Malbim notes that the word יְאֻנֶּה implies something that happened as a result
of a previous act, as in *Exodus* 21:13. This
follows the principle that one good deed
leads to another and one bad deed leads to
another, so that a previously committed
sin often becomes the trigger for the next
sin. In the normal course of events, this
means simply that one who develops the
habit of doing good will continue to do
good, and vice versa. Therefore, those who
follow the path of righteousness will not
sin, even inadvertently. [In a deeper sense,
one who is zealous about acting righteously earns as his reward that God assist
him in avoiding sin in the future.][2]

1. Great people scrutinized every sound that crossed their lips to be sure it met the highest
standards of truthfulness. The *Kotzker Rebbe* emphasized that even a *krechtz*, a sigh of com-
plaint, must be truthful. If the *krechtz* exaggerates the sufferer's pain, it is considered false.

2. The *Beis HaLevi* (R' Yosef Dov Soloveitchik) once visited R' Yehoshua Leib Diskin. When the
Beis HaLevi was ready to return home, his host gave him some provisions for the journey. Some
hours later, the maid in R' Yehoshua Leib's house came to him with a question concerning the

God protects the righteous from mistakes and helps them overpower their Evil Inclination. A person must restrain himself from sinning once and then a second time, but from then on God will protect him from sinning, as Hannah prophesied (*I Samuel* 2:9), *He guards the steps of His devout ones* [See also *Yoma* 38b.] (*R' Yonah*).

וּרְשָׁעִים מָלְאוּ רָע — *But the wicked are filled with evil.* The wicked are unceasingly filled with evil as one sin leads to another (*Metzudos*). See *Avos* 4:2, וַעֲבֵרָה גוֹרֶרֶת עֲבֵרָה, *and one sin leads to another.*

R' Yonah cites the Talmud (*Yoma* 86b) that once a person has committed a sin, and then repeats it a second time, נַעֲשֵׂית לוֹ כְּהֶיתֵּר, he begins to regard it as a permissible act. [Thus, the wicked continuously sin with no scruples of conscience to stop them.]

22. תּוֹעֲבַת ה' שִׂפְתֵי־שָׁקֶר — *False lips are an abomination to* HASHEM. This refers to one whose lips speak lies (*Metzudos*) or one who is a false witness (*Ibn Ezra*).

The Talmud (*Sotah* 42a) lists כַּת שַׁקְרָנִים,

a group of liars, as one of the four groups that will not merit being in God's Presence in the World to Come (*R' Yonah*).[1]

וְעֹשֵׂי אֱמוּנָה רְצוֹנוֹ — *But those who act in faith are His desire.* Regarding אֱמוּנָה, *faith*, the verse stresses action — עֹשֵׂי, *those who act* — rather than speech (שִׂפְתֵי, *the lips of*), as it does in the first half of the verse, for it is insufficient for a person to say the right things if his actions are inconsistent with his words (*Ralbag*).

Chevel Nachalah explains that when a person becomes sick and feels pain in various parts of his body, a good doctor attempts to identify and treat the root cause of all the symptoms. Once he has successfully treated the cause of the many maladies, then all the other symptoms will disappear. Similarly, if someone is spiritually ill and is suffering from faulty character traits, he should work on the root cause of all his maladies — שֶׁקֶר, *falsehood*.[2]

23. אָדָם עָרוּם כֹּסֶה דָּעַת וְלֵב כְּסִילִים יִקְרָא אִוֶּלֶת — *A clever person conceals knowledge, but the heart of fools proclaims foolishness. A wise person* is discreet even

kashrus of a chicken, and R' Yehoshua Leib ruled that it was not kosher. He immediately instructed that someone be sent to catch up with the *Beis HaLevi* and inform him that the chicken that had been included in his provisions was not kosher. R' Yehoshua Leib explained, "Even though I am sure that the *Beis HaLevi* did not eat the chicken, I am still obligated to warn him that it is not kosher." And so it was — when the messenger reached the *Beis HaLevi* and informed him of the development, R' Yosef Dov remarked, "I did not eat the chicken, as it didn't 'smell' good to me."

1. The prophet Michahyahu (*I Kings* 22:19-22) recounts how the Heavenly tribunal sat in judgment on the wicked King Ahab. God asked, "Who will go and persuade Ahab to fight Aram so that he will fall in battle?" Navos' spirit volunteered to put a false prophecy in the mouth of the prophets; they would predict Ahab's victory, thereby convincing him to go to battle. God answered, תְּפַתֶּה וְגַם תּוּכָל צֵא וַעֲשֵׂה־כֵן, *[with this] you will convince and you will succeed, go out and do so.* The Talmud (*Sanhedrin* 102b) questions what is meant by צֵא, *go out.* Ravina explains, *"Leave my presence* for דּוֹבֵר שְׁקָרִים לֹא יִכּוֹן לְנֶגֶד עֵינָי, *one who tells lies will not be established before my eyes."* (*Psalms* 101:7).

2. A story is told of a thief who wanted to repent from his life of crime. He came to the *Ramban* for guidance, and the latter advised that he must commit himself never to lie again. The thief did not understand how this alone would suffice to bring him back from his wickedness, until the

כד יַד־חָרוּצִים תִּמְשׁוֹל וּרְמִיָּה תִּהְיֶה לָמַס:
כה דְּאָגָה בְלֶב־אִישׁ יַשְׁחֶנָּה וְדָבָר טוֹב יְשַׂמְּחֶנָּה:

about his wisdom, so he certainly will conceal foolish things. A *fool*, however, loudly proclaims his foolishness (*Rashi*).

R' *Simchah Zissel Ziev* maintains that by concealing his wisdom, an individual is privileged to derive full benefit from it (*Chochmah U'Mussar*).

R' *Yonah* comments that the modesty of the righteous causes them to conceal good deeds that could be a source of pride and honor to them. This is in line with the verse וְהַצְנֵעַ לֶכֶת עִם אֱלֹהֶיךָ, *and walk humbly with your God* (*Michah* 6:8).[1]

A wise man reveals wisdom only to those who are worthy of it (*Metzudos*). *Ibn Ezra* explains that he conceals wisdom so that he should not forget it. (Cf. 10:14 חֲכָמִים יִצְפְּנוּ דָעַת.)

According to *Meiri*, this verse teaches a person not to be hasty in putting thought into action. A person must patiently and deliberately analyze his thoughts until he has refined them, and only then act upon them. A wise man conceals even thoughts based on knowledge, and not motivated by anger or revenge, until they are completely refined. A fool, on the other hand, announces what is on his mind, even if it is foolish and not thought through; he immediately verbalizes it and plans to execute it.

Malbim explains the difference between the two kinds of fools, an אֱוִיל [*evvil*] and a כְּסִיל [*k'sil*]. An *evvil* is skeptical about wisdom and questions its validity; he does not believe in it because he does not understand it. A *k'sil*, on the other hand, knows the correctness of true wisdom, but forsakes it because of the persuasions and

temptations of his Evil Inclination. He knows he is wrong and even fears punishment. In order to rationalize and defend his misdeeds, יִקְרָא אֻוֶּלֶת, *he will proclaim skepticism*, i.e., he uses skepticism to camouflage his evil, casting doubt on the validity of wisdom in order to excuse his own wickedness.

24. יַד חָרוּצִים תִּמְשׁוֹל — *The hand of the diligent will rule. Rashi* explains that חָרוּצִים are *just people*, who will become rich (cf. 10:4). *Ralbag* explains that through their industriousness and righteousness they will acquire much wealth, which will bring them power.

The term חָרוּץ implies diligence and scrupulousness. Such a person is neither lazy nor deceitful. He does not aim for instant riches, but tries to accumulate wealth gradually, through his industriousness, and thereby become powerful (*Malbim*).

וּרְמִיָּה תִּהְיֶה לָמַס — *But deceit will melt.* The hand of those who rely on deceit to gain wealth will become lowered and will melt away (*Metzudos*). רְמִיָּה is explained either *the hand of deceit* (*Meiri*), or as a *deceitful person* (R' *Yonah*).

Malbim renders לָמַס as *paying tribute*. The traits of deceitful people are the exact opposite of those of the diligent. Instead of working, they are lazy and depend on their deceit to provide them with a living. Rather than being upright and just, they are deceptive. They will end up being subservient to the diligent who have become wealthy and powerful, like servants who pay tribute (מַס) to their masters.

next time he stole. Immediately, he began to worry, "What if I am caught? Since I've promised not to lie anymore, how will I answer my accusers?" With this reasoning he returned the stolen item, and eventually repented fully from his life of crime. So, too, if a person perfects himself in the area of falsehood, he cures the root cause of his problems and thus avoids all faulty character traits, for in essence, they are all false. Thus, עֹשֵׂי אֱמוּנָה, *those who act faithfully*, רְצוֹנוֹ, will eventually do whatever is *His desire*.

1. Rabbi Gershon Zaks recalls that he was once studying Torah late into the night with his father, Rabbi Mendel Zaks, when there was a knock at the door. R' Mendel instructed his son to quickly put away all the *seforim* they were studying before opening the door, so that the visitor would not think, 'Oh, how diligent R' Mendel is in his Torah studies, that he learns so late at night.'

25. דְּאָגָה בְלֶב אִישׁ יַשְׁחֶנָּה — *When there is worry in a man's heart, he should suppress it.* Worry is never beneficial; it can only cause harm. Therefore, should worry enter a person's heart, he must attempt to subdue it. An intelligent person should realize that anxiety about something which is only transitory is שִׁגָּעוֹן, *insanity.* Rather than worry about it, a person should trust in God (*Ralbag*).[1]

Rashi offers two explanations for the word יַשְׁחֶנָּה: Either יְסִיחֶנָּה מִדַּעְתּוֹ, *he should remove it from his mind,* i.e. he should divert his attention from it; or יְשִׂיחֶנָּה לַאֲחֵרִים, *he should tell it to others* (see *Yoma* 75a).

Metzudos relates the term יַשְׁחֶנָּה to שְׁחִיָּה וְהַשְׁפָּלָה, *bowing and bringing down.* Should a person worry, he should "lower" and minimize his concern.

Malbim explains that if a person begins to visualize worrisome images, his anxiety becomes all-encompassing and can destroy his entire body. For instance, a person enjoying wealth and tranquility may begin to worry that his house will be destroyed, his wealth will be lost, his children will die, and he will be in a constant state of anxiety. Therefore he must subdue these worries and take his mind off of them.

If a person suffering misfortune or affliction does not share his concerns with someone else, his worries and anxieties will probably overcome him. But if the man is an אִישׁ, whom our Sages define as a man of outstanding stature (see *Numbers* 13:3, *Rashi* ibid.), then even if the worry remains in his heart, יַשְׁחֶנָּה, he will use his intelligence to *minimize* his concern (*Alshich*).

The above commentators explain יַשְׁחֶנָּה, *he should suppress it,* as referring to the worry. *R' Yonah* and *Vilna Gaon* explain *it* as referring to the heart, i.e. if there is worry in a person's heart, it "lowers" his heart.

וְדָבָר טוֹב יְשַׂמְּחֶנָּה — *And let a good thing convert it to gladness.* He should involve himself in Torah and this will change his worry to happiness (*Rashi*).

King David, whose life epitomized the suffering of the righteous, exclaimed, *Had Your Torah not been my preoccupation, then I would have perished in my affliction* (*Psalms* 119:92).

The *Vilna Gaon* elaborates, explaining that *good* alludes to Torah, the greatest good (see *Avos* 6:3). He who accepts the yoke of Torah is relieved of his worries. Thoughts of sword, hunger, adultery and the Evil Inclination are removed from one who inscribes the words of Torah into his heart (see *Avos D'Rabbi Nosson* 20:1).

According to the view that the first half of the verse counsels one to share his concerns with others, the verse concludes that it is good if his friend can comfort him and transform his worry into happiness (*Rashi*)

As friends of an anxious or worried person, we should also realize that an apt word can bring a balm of consolation, healing and calm to our agitated neighbors (*R' Hirsch*).

A person should not worry about untoward events nor be upset by them. Realizing the futility of this world, he should neither rejoice excessively at his successes nor be overly anxious about his failures. If worries overcome him because of his weak nature, he must attempt to subdue them, and turn the worry into happiness with a דָבָר טוֹב, *good thing* — i.e., by reflecting upon, and immersing himself in, the ways of God (*Meiri*).

Metzudos renders: It is good if one is able to change the worry to gladness by realizing that whatever happens is for the good.

1. R' Simchah Zissel Ziev quotes the following quatrain: — הֶעָבָר אַיִן, הֶעָתִיד עֲדַיִין, הַהֹוֶה כְּהֶרֶף עַיִן, דְּאָגָה מִנַּיִן? "The past is no more, the future is yet to be, the present is like the blink of an eye — why should there be worry?"(*Chochmah U'Mussar*).

כו-כז יֶתֵר מֵרֵעֵהוּ צַדִּיק וְדֶרֶךְ רְשָׁעִים תַּתְעֵם: לֹא־
כח יַחֲרֹךְ רְמִיָּה צֵידוֹ וְהוֹן־אָדָם יָקָר חָרוּץ: בְּאֹרַח־
צְדָקָה חַיִּים וְדֶרֶךְ נְתִיבָה אַל־מָוֶת:

א-ב בֵּן חָכָם מוּסַר אָב וְלֵץ לֹא־שָׁמַע גְּעָרָה: מִפְּרִי

26. יֶתֵר מֵרֵעֵהוּ צַדִּיק וְדֶרֶךְ רְשָׁעִים תַּתְעֵם —
*The righteous one excels over his fellow,
but the [successful] way of the wicked
leads them astray.* A righteous person is
vastly superior to his non-righteous fellow,
but when the wicked are successful, their
success leads them astray to continue in
their wickedness, and they ignore the
superiority of the righteous (*Metzudos*).

Meiri explains that this verse encourages one to appreciate the virtues of the
righteous. Even though they suffer hardship and the wicked seem to prosper, one
should not deny the superiority of the
former nor cleave to the latter. The average
person is enticed by the success of the
wicked; it misleads him and dissuades him
from leaving their evil ways.

The *Vilna Gaon* relates the word יֶתֵר to
וַיָּתֻרוּ אֶת אֶרֶץ כְּנַעַן, *and they should spy out
the Land of Canaan* (Numbers 13:2). Since
a *righteous person* keeps his good deeds
hidden (see *R' Yonah* to v.23), one must
"spy" out his actions in order to emulate
them.[1]

According to *Rashi*, a righteous person
is מְוַתֵּר, *gives in* to others, overlooking the
wrongs done him. However, the way of
the wicked, which is habitually evil, leads
them astray.

Chevel Nachalah offers a different
explanation for this verse. He cites *Ramban's* advice to his son: If you are in some
way superior to your friend, you must
realize that this imposes a greater obligation on you to be superior in your service

of God. Thus, the verse states: יֶתֵר מֵרֵעֵהוּ,
someone who *excels over his fellow*, (יֶתֵר)
צַדִּיק, must also be [more] righteous.

Alshich connects this verse with the
previous one. What דָּבָר טוֹב, *good thing*,
can be said to one who is suffering in order
to make him happy? He should be told
that he is a righteous person who has an
advantage over his sinful companion, and
God chose him as the recipient of afflictions because ה' צַדִּיק יִבְחָן, *HASHEM examines the righteous one* (Psalms 11:5). God
chastises the righteous in order to purify
them (*Rashi*, ibid.). One who is suffering,
therefore, should not spurn his afflictions,
but rather, value them, for they are the
means by which he will merit the World to
Come. Should someone wonder why God
seems to shower good upon the wicked
and not upon him, this verse responds: דֶרֶךְ
רְשָׁעִים, *the way of the wicked* who have
material success in this world, תַּתְעֵם, *leads
them astray*, for their wealth will cause
them to rebel against God. This realization
will bring him joy [וְיִשְׂמְחָנָה] because he
will visualize the eternal happiness that
awaits him because of his present suffering.

27. לֹא־יַחֲרֹךְ רְמִיָּה צֵידוֹ — *He will not roast
his prey of deceit.* Rashi sees this as a
continuation of the previous verse.

According to *Rashi*, רְמִיָּה refers to the
prey gained through deceit. The wicked
person of verse 26 will not roast the prey of
his deceit, i.e., he will not succeed with his
deceit (for a successful hunter captures

---

1. R' Shlomo Bloch, a disciple of the *Chafetz Chaim*, was determined to hear the *Chafetz Chaim*
recite the וִדּוּי, *confession*, on Yom Kippur. Knowing that the *Chafetz Chaim* returned to the study
hall on Yom Kippur night, after everyone was home and asleep, to confess in private, R' Shlomo
hid in a closet and awaited the return of the *Chafetz Chaim*. The *Chafetz Chaim* returned and
checked to make sure no one was present, even going so far as to look into the closets. When he
reached R' Shlomo's closet, the *Chafetz Chaim* did not open the door. Hiding in great fright, R'
Shlomo listened in as the *Chafetz Chaim* recited the confession. Later he remarked, "I yearned a
whole lifetime to attain the fear of heaven that I reached just hearing the *viduy* from the mouth
of the *Chafetz Chaim*!"

12/26-28 ²⁶ *A righteous one excels over his fellow, but the [successful] way of the wicked leads them astray.* ²⁷ *He will not roast his prey of deceit, but the wealth of an honest person is precious.* ²⁸ *In the way of charity there is life; in the way of its path there is no death.*

13/1-2 ¹ A *wise son [desires] a father's discipline, but a scoffer has not heard chastisement.* ² *From the fruits of*

birds and roasts them in the fire).

A deceitful person [רְמִיָּה] will have no enjoyment and no success from the wealth he obtained illicitly (*R' Yonah*), for it will be stolen from him (*Ibn Ezra*).

Metzudos explains that when a hunter succeeds in catching birds he singes their wings so that they cannot fly away. A deceitful person, however, does not singe their wings, for he wants the birds to look nice, so that he can more easily cheat his customers. As a result, he will lose his prey, for the birds will fly away. This verse is also a metaphor for someone who is too stingy to give charity. He will lose *all* of his money.

וְהוֹן־אָדָם יָקָר חָרוּץ — *But the wealth of an honest person is precious.* The translation follows *Rashi*, who inverts the order of the Hebrew, and explains חָרוּץ as an *honest person* (cf. 10:4). The wealth of such a person is *precious.*

Metzudos explains חָרוּץ as *fine gold* (see 8:19). The fortune of a precious man who distributes *tzedakah* is comparable to precious gold. Just as such gold does not become corroded like other metals, so, too, his fortune will endure.

28. בְּאוֹרַח־צְדָקָה חַיִּים — *In the way of charity there is life.* Many times, years will

be added onto a person's life in the merit of his charity (*R' Yonah*). See 10:2 and 11:4, that charity can rescue one from death.

By following the path of righteousness (צֶדֶק) and justice in one's character traits and ideologies, a person will attain Eternal Life (*Ralbag*).

וְדֶרֶךְ נְתִיבָה אַל־מָוֶת — *In the way of its path there is no death.* On the road of charity, one will not find death (*Metzudos*). He will not die a spiritual death (*Ibn Nachmiash*).

Most certainly, the life of one who gives charity will not be shortened, for it will protect him (*R' Yonah*).

R' Bachya elaborates: Everyone is allotted a set amount of years to live, but the number may change according to his deeds. The power of charity is twofold: It guarantees that the donor's allotted years will not be shortened and it may even add additional years to his life. This is referred to in the two halves of this verse. First the verse states that the merit of charity can add years to a person's life, even if he was destined to die (as in the case of Binyamin the Tzaddik, see *Bava Basra* 11a). If so, then certainly one who traverses the road of charity will not die before living his allotted years.

XIII

1. בֵּן חָכָם מוּסַר אָב — *A wise son [desires] a father's discipline.* The Hebrew text of this phrase does not have a verb. *Rashi* explains that the implied verb is that a wise son *desires* his father's discipline; or, alternatively, that he *is* wise thanks to his father's discipline.

Malbim explains that a father must admonish his son while the latter is still

young in order to enable him to control his natural instincts and accept wisdom. If the youth indeed becomes wise, it is a testimony to the effectiveness of his father's discipline and training.

וְלֵץ לֹא־שָׁמַע גְּעָרָה — *But a scoffer has not heard chastisement.* The translation follows *Ibn Ezra*, who comments that while a father rebukes his wise son since he knows

ג פִּי־אִישׁ יֹאכַל טוֹב וְנֶפֶשׁ בֹּגְדִים חָמָס: נֹצֵר פִּיו
ד שֹׁמֵר נַפְשׁוֹ פֹּשֵׂק שְׂפָתָיו מְחִתָּה־לוֹ: מִתְאַוָּה
וָאַיִן נַפְשׁוֹ עָצֵל וְנֶפֶשׁ חָרֻצִים תְּדֻשָּׁן:
ה דְּבַר־שֶׁקֶר יִשְׂנָא צַדִּיק וְרָשָׁע יַבְאִישׁ וְיַחְפִּיר:
ו צְדָקָה תִּצֹּר תָּם־דָּרֶךְ וְרִשְׁעָה תְּסַלֵּף חַטָּאת:

the rebuke will be accepted and appreciated, a scoffer has never heard his father raise his voice, because the father understands that his words will neither be accepted nor heeded.

This son does not accept rebuke (*Rashi*), and that is why he became a scoffer (*Metzudos*).

Ralbag cites the example of Adoniyahu ben Haggith, who was never admonished by his father, King David (*I Kings* 1:6) [and who subsequently tried to usurp the throne and was killed (cf. v.24)].

R' Yonah points out that parents must carefully attend to their children, correcting and guiding them always, chastising them should they scorn or speak slander, for habits acquired · in youth persist throughout life.

2. מִפְּרִי פִי־אִישׁ יֹאכַל טוֹב — *From the fruits of man's speech he will enjoy* [lit. *eat*] *good*. As a reward for his Torah study, a person will enjoy good in this world, and the principal of that reward will remain intact for the World to Come (*Rashi*, cf. 12:14). (See *Peah* 1:1.)

וְנֶפֶשׁ בֹּגְדִים חָמָס — *But the desire of the faithless is violence*. This translation follows *Rashi* who explains נֶפֶשׁ as *desire*: The desire of the faithless is violence.

R' Yonah, connecting this verse with the previous one, explains that since the wicked desire violence, how can they chastise their children? Since they desire evil, they are not upset when their children exhibit evil traits. Even if they rebuke their children, their words will be ignored, for they are insincere.

According to *Metzudos*, just as a good person will be satiated with Torah both in this world and in the World to Come, so too, the soul of traitors will be sated with

the recompense for their violence (*Metzudos*).

According to the *Vilna Gaon*, חָמָס means *violent talk*. A person who spoke violently to others, cursing and embarrassing them, will "eat," i.e., suffer, from his verbal violence, both in this world and the World to Come. The verse specifies נֶפֶשׁ, *the soul of* traitors, since the punishment of the wicked is primarily that their soul will suffer in the World to Come. In this world, only minimal suffering is meted out to them.

3. נֹצֵר פִּיו שֹׁמֵר נַפְשׁוֹ — *One who guards his mouth* [from saying forbidden things (*Metzudos*)] *protects his soul*.

One who will not say anything unless his heart has sanctioned it protects his soul (*R' Yonah*).

פֹּשֵׂק שְׂפָתָיו מְחִתָּה־לוֹ — [*But*] *one who opens his lips wide, that is his ruin*. One who opens his lips wide to say anything he pleases (*Rashi*) will thereby bring ruination upon himself (*Metzudos*). A fool speaks thoughtlessly without calculating the consequences. Then he is alarmed to see what he has brought about and his own responsibility for it (*R' Hirsch*).

Malbim explains that "mouth" is used to symbolize *inner* expression, i.e., speech that follows considered thought and wisdom. "Lips," however, symbolizes external, superficial speech. One who *guards his mouth* — exercising constant discretion even when speaking about Torah or other important matters — *protects his soul*. Certainly someone who *opens his lips wide* to speak slander and gossip will bring ruin not only to his soul, but even to his body.

4. מִתְאַוָּה וָאַיִן נַפְשׁוֹ עָצֵל — *The soul of a sluggard lusts and has nothing*. A lazy

man's speech he will enjoy good, but the desire of the faithless [is] violence. ³ One who guards his mouth protects his soul, [but] one who opens his lips wide, that is his ruin. ⁴ The soul of a sluggard lusts and has nothing, but the soul of the diligent will be fattened. ⁵ A righteous person despises a false matter, but a wicked person sullies and insults. ⁶ Righteousness will guard one who is perfect in his way, but wickedness will corrupt the sinner.

person may desire all good things, but has naught (*Rashi*), for his laziness prevents him from attaining anything (*Metzudos*).

Metaphorically speaking, this verse alludes to the Hereafter, when the lazy person will see the great honor accorded the Torah scholar and will desire it for himself, but he will not achieve it (*Rashi*), because a person can earn such reward only through his deeds in life.

R' Yonah interprets: מִתְאַוָּה נַפְשׁוֹ וָאַיִן, *Someone whose soul desires something but has nothing,* עָצֵל, *is surely a lazy person.* As the Sages teach: If someone tells you I labored in the study of Torah but did not succeed, do not believe him (*Megillah* 6b).[1]

וְנֶפֶשׁ חָרֻצִים תְּדֻשָּׁן — *But the soul of the diligent will be fattened.* The *diligent* are just people who will enjoy the fruit of their labors (*Rashi*).

Although a diligent person wearies his body from constant toil and effort, נַפְשׁוֹ, *his soul,* will be gratified, for he will have obtained his desire. In the spiritual sense, a person who wearies his body through diligent pursuit of wisdom will have his soul satiated and gratified from the bounty of Heaven (*Malbim*).

5. דְּבַר־שֶׁקֶר יִשְׂנָא צַדִּיק וְרָשָׁע יַבְאִישׁ וְיַחְפִּיר — *A righteous person despises a false matter, but a wicked person sullies and insults.* A righteous person hates to accept lies and slander; a wicked one believes them and then despises and disgraces the object of this slander (*Metzudos*).

A wicked person will make his enemy or the person he envies appear odious in

the eyes of others by spreading lies about him (*R' Yonah*).

The wicked try to reinforce their evil deeds with falsehood. When the righteous attempt to expose their lies or express skepticism and disbelief, the wicked heap curses upon them. The righteous are sometimes intimidated into silent acquiescence with the wicked. King Solomon therefore advises the righteous to hate (יִשְׂנָא) the falsehoods of the wicked, and neither to agree with them nor heed them. The wicked will only try to make their opponents seem odious and humiliate them; therefore their words should be ignored (*Alshich*).

6. צְדָקָה תִּצֹּר תָּם־דָּרֶךְ — *Righteousness will guard one who is perfect in his way.* His righteous actions will protect him from any ensuing harm (*Meiri*). His merits will protect him from sinning (*R' Yonah*).

Most commentators explain צְדָקָה as *righteousness,* contrasting it to רִשְׁעָה, *wickedness,* mentioned in the second part of the verse. *Metzudos,* however, renders צְדָקָה as *charity*: Charity will speak up in defense of one who is perfect in his ways and will guard him. "Perfection" in charity refers to giving charity with the best motives, and not for honor and glory.

וְרִשְׁעָה תְּסַלֵּף חַטָּאת — *But wickedness will corrupt the sinner* [lit. *sin*]. Since this person is completely wicked, he is labeled חַטָּאת, the embodiment of *sin.* His wickedness will *corrupt* him and cast him down (*Rashi*).

Wickedness will ruin the sinner for [וַ]עֲבֵרָה גוֹרֶרֶת עֲבֵרָה . . . וּשְׂכַר עֲבֵרָה עֲבֵרָה, *[And] one sin leads to another sin....and*

---

1. However, as the Talmud (ibid.) goes on to explain, this applies only to achievements in the field of Torah study. In business, one's success is dependent on assistance from heaven [סִיַּיעְתָּא דִשְׁמַיָּא]. [Perhaps this is also implied by the word נַפְשׁוֹ, *his soul,* i.e., if the desire is a spiritual one.]

ז יֵשׁ מִתְעַשֵּׁר וְאֵין כֹּל מִתְרוֹשֵׁשׁ וְהוֹן רָב:
ח כֹּפֶר נֶפֶשׁ־אִישׁ עָשְׁרוֹ וְרָשׁ לֹא־שָׁמַע גְּעָרָה:
ט אוֹר־צַדִּיקִים יִשְׂמָח וְנֵר רְשָׁעִים יִדְעָךְ:

---

the consequence of a sin is a sin (*Avos* 4:2) (*R' Yonah*).

The sinner's wickedness will bring punishment and Heavenly revenge upon him (*Meiri*).

The wickedness itself will lead the sinner on a crooked path so that he will stumble there (*Metzudos*).

7. יֵשׁ מִתְעַשֵּׁר וְאֵין כֹּל מִתְרוֹשֵׁשׁ וְהוֹן רָב — *Some pretend to be rich and have nothing, while others act poor and have great wealth.* Rashi offers three explanations for this verse: A person may feign wealth, yet have nothing. A person may achieve great wealth even though he begins with nothing, yet he can also fall from great wealth into poverty. A person who enriches himself by stealing from the poor will end up with nothing, and a person who becomes impoverished by distributing much money to the destitute will eventually be rewarded with great wealth.

According to *Meiri*, neither feigning wealth nor feigning poverty is a virtue, and both should be avoided. If a person feigns wealth and really has nothing, he will cause himself needless expenses until he becomes so impoverished that he will no longer be able to conceal it. If he feigns poverty, on the other hand, he will be overly stingy and fail to fulfill his charitable obligations.

Ralbag, however, comments that it is better to feign poverty than to feign wealth, for that can save one from the troubles and problems that usually beset the wealthy, as the next verse states, *the poor hear no chastisement.*

Wealth is illusory; it is not an intrinsic part of man's soul, and therefore there is no true, lasting bond between him and his acquisitions. He may easily lose his fortune or die and leave it behind. Therefore, a person may seem to be rich, but in essence וְאֵין כֹּל, *have nothing*, since his material success is unrelated to his soul. However, a person who distributes his money and uses it for charity and good deeds (see verse 8) has utilized his fortune to perfect his soul, which is eternal. He will have a הוֹן רָב, *great wealth*, for he will have succeeded in transforming his fortune into everlasting spiritual wealth in the World to Come (*Malbim*).

The *Chafetz Chaim* explains this verse as follows: A person may possess much wealth, but have nothing in the World to Come, for he is using up all his merits in this world. God rewards the wicked immediately, so that they will have no claim to a share in the Hereafter (see *Deuteronomy* 7:10, Rashi, ad loc.). On the other hand, a person may have nothing in this world and even be considered a "failure"; yet, he will have a great fortune awaiting him in the World to Come, for his suffering in this world atoned for his sins, and left his reward intact for the Hereafter.

Ralbag and the *Vilna Gaon* explain that this verse also applies to Torah study. There are people who present themselves as great scholars, but actually know nothing;[1] while there are others who feign ignorance in Torah, but really possess a wealth of Torah knowledge.[2]

---

1. The Talmud (*Yerushalmi, Makos* 7:2) teaches that when the townspeople want to honor a visiting Torah scholar for knowing *two* tractates and he knows only one, he must admit that he knows only one.

2. *Rabbi Yitzchak Blazer*, known as R' Itzel Peterburger, was once at a meeting with many great Torah sages, including the renowned author of *Beis HaLevi*, R' Yosef Dov Soloveitchik. The *Beis HaLevi* raised a Talmudic difficulty and presented two answers: his own, and that of his son R' Chaim. There followed a lively debate among the assembled scholars, except for R' Itzel, who remained silent throughout the discussions. The *Beis HaLevi* was puzzled by his silence. Why

⁷ *Some pretend to be rich and have nothing, while others act poor and have great wealth.* ⁸ *A man's wealth may redeem his soul, but only if the poor hear no chastisement.* ⁹ *The light of the righteous will rejoice, but the lamp of the wicked will flicker out.*

8. כֹּפֶר נֶפֶשׁ־אִישׁ עָשְׁרוֹ וְרָשׁ לֹא־שָׁמַע גְּעָרָה —
A man's wealth may redeem [lit. *be a redemption for*] *his soul, but only if the poor hear no chastisement.* A person can ransom his soul from misfortune through the money he gives to charity, but this is true only if the donor helps the poor person without insulting him (*Rashi*).

This verse teaches the rich person two things: He should give a fitting amount of money to the needy; and he should be careful not to abuse them verbally. The Talmud (*Bava Basra* 9b) explains that someone who gives a coin to a poor person is blessed with six blessings, whereas one who appeases and comforts the poor person with nice words merits eleven blessings (*Meiri*).

The *Vilna Gaon* explains that at times, God may give a person wealth so that he will have the means to ransom himself from imminent misfortune by giving away his money instead of his life. A poor person, however, will not be beset by such troubles, because he does not have the money to save himself from distress, and God does not impose unfair challenges. Not only will a pauper not suffer afflictions, he will not even hear a גְּעָרָה, *chastisement*; i.e., he will not even be threatened by misfortune. He will be tranquil and peaceful.

This verse can also be explained metaphorically. *Rashi* explains that someone's wealth of Torah knowledge will be a ransom for his soul. On the other hand, someone who is poor in Torah knowledge לֹא־שָׁמַע גְּעָרָה, *hears no chastisement*; i.e., he does not avoid evil because he lacks the knowledge of what is wrong.

Rashi also quotes a Midrash that applies this verse to the mitzvah of מַחֲצִית הַשֶּׁקֶל, *the half-shekel coin*, that was donated annually by every Jew to purchase animals for communal offerings. [Thus, this money was a ransom for the person's soul, since the offerings atoned for his sins.] Rich and poor are equal in this *mitzvah*, for everyone must contribute the same amount. As a result, a poor person never hears a rich man boasting, "I have a greater share than you in the communal offerings."

An individual's true wealth is the money he has used for the benefit of his soul. Whatever one accumulates, he eventually forfeits, yet that which is used in accordance with the *mitzvos* is his forever [see *Psalms 49:7-9*] (*R' Hirsch*).

9. אוֹר־צַדִּיקִים יִשְׂמָח וְנֵר רְשָׁעִים יִדְעָךְ — *The light of the righteous will rejoice, but the lamp of the wicked will flicker out.* The soul of the righteous will rejoice in *Gan Eden*, but the soul of the wicked will be extinguished and not shine (*Metzudos*).

The word יִדְעָךְ literally means *will jump.* It describes a flame which jumps away from the wick — i.e., flickers — as it is extinguished (*Rashi*).

Light and *lamp* are metaphors for a person's soul, which emanates from the Divine Light. (See 20:27, נֵר ד' נִשְׁמַת אָדָם, *the soul of man is* HASHEM's *lamp.*) The soul of the righteous is compared to *the light* of the sun, which constantly shines; while the soul of the wicked is like a *lamp*, whose light is only temporary and finite, for their souls will expire prematurely (*Ibn Ezra*).

R' Yonah elaborates further: Both the soul of the righteous and the sun are everlasting, and are dependent solely on the Master of the Universe. The soul of the righteous always rejoices. It rejoices in this world when performing *mitzvos*, and it will certainly rejoice in the eternal bliss of the World to Come. Even if God brings

did he not participate in the discussion?

Upon returning to Brisk, the *Beis HaLevi* asked to see a copy of *Pri Yitzchak*, the writings of R' Itzel. While perusing the book, the *Beis HaLevi* was astounded to find the very question he himself had raised at the meeting, along with the very same two answers!

suffering upon the body, the soul accepts it with happiness. This is like the sun which also constantly and joyously fulfills the will of its Creator, as the verse states, יָשִׂישׂ כְּגִבּוֹר לָרוּץ אֹרַח, it [the sun] *rejoices like a powerful warrior to run the course* (*Psalms* 19:6). The wicked, on the other hand, are compared to a lamp, which can burn only as long as it has fuel. So, too, the soul of the wicked is dependent on the body. It may enjoy happiness in this world, as long as the physical body is still active. Once the body of the wicked one perishes, however, the happiness of their soul is also lost, as it is doomed forever.

The *Vilna Gaon* explains that a *lamp* [נֵר] is a metaphor for the merit of a *mitzvah*, while *light* [אוֹר] is a metaphor for the even greater merit of Torah study (see 6:23). The merits of a person who is constantly engrossed in Torah study are comparable to ever-increasing sunlight. Therefore, even if he occasionally sins, his light will still shine, as our Sages state, עֲבֵירָה מְכַבָּה מִצְוָה וְאֵין עֲבֵירָה מְכַבָּה תּוֹרָה, *A sin can extinguish [the reward for] a mitzvah, but a sin cannot extinguish [the reward for] Torah study* (*Sotah* 21a). On the other hand, a wicked person does not study Torah. Though he may fulfill a commandment and thus light a *lamp*, its light *will flicker out*, due to the multitude of his sins.

10. רַק־בְּזָדוֹן יִתֵּן מַצָּה — *Only by willfulness is strife fomented.* When people act willfully and impetuously, strife and fights are the result (*Ibn Ezra*).

A person whose actions are only sinful and evil will cause fights among people (*Metzudos*).

וְאֶת־נוֹעָצִים חָכְמָה — *But wisdom is with*

those who take counsel. Wisdom will be with those who act advisedly (*Rashi*), only after careful consideration and deliberation, for no strife results from such actions (*Metzudos*).

The *Vilna Gaon* explains נוֹעָצִים as *those who constantly consult with others*. They will become wise, as Ben Zoma teaches, Who is wise? He who learns from every person (*Avos* 4:1).[1]

Ralbag interprets the verse as a reference to the company with whom one associates. One who associates with willful sinners will learn from them to cause strife. On the other hand, one who associates with thoughtful people will learn wisdom from them.

Malbim explains that the verse speaks of an intentional sinner who publicly disputes the wisdom of the Torah and does not subjugate his opinions to the teachings of the Sages. When a difference of opinion arises among people, it can usually be settled peaceably by airing the various opinions and choosing the one that best conforms to the teachings and advice of Torah scholars. However, when a party to such a dispute rejects the rulings of the Torah, the outcome is מַצָּה, *strife*, which leads to physical harm. Such was the case when Korach instigated his followers against Moses and God (see *Numbers* 16).

11. הוֹן מֵהֶבֶל יִמְעָט — *Wealth gained by vanity will diminish.* Wealth that comes not from honest labor, but from *vanity*, i.e., through robbery and violence, will dwindle and will not last (*Metzudos*).

Rashi explains homiletically that this verse applies to someone who makes his Torah study חֲבִילוֹת חֲבִילוֹת, *bundles*, i.e., he learns a great deal at once, so that he

1. God Himself set the example of consulting with others. Before creating man, God said, נַעֲשֶׂה אָדָם, *Let us make man* (Genesis 1:26) in the plural, as if, so to speak, He was consulting with the angels. The Torah used this phraseology to teach the ethical lesson that even someone of higher standing should consult with those of lower standing.

¹⁰ *Only by willfulness is strife fomented; but wisdom is with those who take counsel.* ¹¹ *Wealth gained by vanity will diminish, but what one gathers by hand will increase.* ¹² *A drawn-out hope sickens the heart, but desire attained is a tree of life.*

does not allow himself sufficient time for review. (See *Avodah Zarah* 19a, *Rashi* ibid.). Such Torah knowledge יְמָעָט, will be forgotten מְעַט מְעַט, *little by little*.

Meiri explains that, for the purpose of this elucidation, the word הֶבֶל, *futility*, can be read as חֶבֶל, *bundle*, by interchanging the letter *hei* with the letter *ches*.

וְקֹבֵץ עַל־יָד יַרְבֶּה — *But what one gathers by hand will increase.* However, if a person gathers wealth through the labor of his hands, it will increase (*Metzudos*). Homiletically, if he learns a small amount at a time, he will increase his knowledge. (See *Avodah Zarah* 19a and *Eruvin* 54b.)

The *Vilna Gaon* explains that wealth gained from futile means, and not through labor, will decrease, for "easy come, easy go" (כְּמוֹ שֶׁבָּא לוֹ בְּקַל כֵּן יֵלֵךְ מִמֶּנּוּ בְּקַל). However, someone who gathers things little by little through honest work will increase his wealth. The same is true of the study of Torah. When someone acquires a "wealth" of Torah knowledge, obtained quickly through "futility," and not through effort and toil, this Torah knowledge diminishes, for it is soon forgotten. However, someone who toils and labors in his study of Torah, even if he is able to learn only a little at a time, increases his Torah knowledge, for whatever he studied will remain with him.

Alshich explains the use of the expression עַל־יָד, lit., **above** *a hand* rather than בְּיָד, **by** *hand*. Wealth is not secure; it may leave a person at any moment. However, one who gathers wealth עַל־יָד, *above the grasp of a human hand*, by investing his

money in *mitzvos* and thus earning himself "wealth" in the World to Come, will have his wealth endure.[1]

12. תּוֹחֶלֶת מְמֻשָּׁכָה מַחֲלָה לֵב — *A drawn-out hope sickens the heart.* This refers to someone who promises to help a friend, but does not do so. The friend becomes sick at heart as he waits and waits in vain for the help that does not come (*Rashi*).

When a person expectantly awaits something that is delayed in coming, he suffers heartache (*Metzudos*).

וְעֵץ חַיִּים תַּאֲוָה בָאָה — *But desire attained is a tree of life.* *Rashi* explains the verse by inverting the words: תַּאֲוָה בָאָה, understanding it to mean *a desire attained* is like *a tree of life* to the person. *Metzudos* adds: and his heartache is healed. Thus, *Meiri* expounds, a person should try to fulfill his promises to others immediately. The person making the request is very anxious to have it fulfilled, and dreads being embarrassed or being pushed off with some lame excuse. The longer he has to wait, the more heartache he suffers. If his request is fulfilled in a timely manner, it is like a tree of life to him.

Rashi also explains this verse homiletically as an allusion to the relationship between God and Israel: God promised great benefits to Israel, if they would but repent. He hoped that they would repent, but they did not mend their ways, and the unfulfilled hope brought them heartache. When His desire is fulfilled — that they do His will — it will be a tree of life for them.

1. King Monbaz, a Hasmonean king who was the son of Queen Helena, depleted his treasuries and the treasuries of his forebears to feed the poor during a famine. Answering familial objections that he was destroying the efforts of those who had amassed a fortune over generations, Monbaz answered, "My fathers hoarded their wealth in a place which is controlled by the hand of others, but I have hoarded my wealth in a place that no hand can control." He explained that the merit of charitable deeds will gaze down from Heaven to bestow reward. Furthermore, although no one's fortune is truly safe from loss or destruction in this world, the merit of charitable deeds is concealed under the foundation of God's throne, a most secure repository (*Bava Basra* 11a, *Rashi*).

בָּז לְדָבָר יֵחָבֶל לוֹ וִירֵא מִצְוָה הוּא יְשֻׁלָּם: תּוֹרַת חָכָם

טו מְקוֹר חַיִּים לָסוּר מִמֹּקְשֵׁי מָוֶת: שֵׂכֶל-טוֹב יִתֶּן-חֵן

R' Yochanan (*Berachos* 32b) applies this verse to someone who expects God to fulfill his requests merely because his prayers are lengthy. He will be frustrated and heartsick if his expectations are not met. The Sages continue that the remedy is, "Let the person involve himself in the study of Torah, as is written, *but desire attained is a tree of life.*" *Tree of life* is a reference to the Torah (cf. 3:18).

The *Vilna Gaon* explains why prayer may cause heartache, while Torah study will bring one his desire. Prayer is for something transitory, for it pertains to a person's needs in this world. Torah, however, provides eternal life and is the path to the World to Come. Thus, one who studies Torah is assured that his desire will be attained.

The Midrash applies the verse to a marriage. One who becomes engaged, but delays marriage unduly, causes himself heartache; but if the marriage is not delayed, such a *desire attained* is *a tree of life* (*Yalkut Shimoni* quoting *Pesikta*).

13. בָּז לְדָבָר יֵחָבֶל לוֹ — *He who scorns a word will himself be harmed.* One who scorns any of God's commandments will cause himself harm (*Metzudos*). According to *Rashi*, ultimately the word of Torah will castigate him and he will be taken as collateral for it. [In this view, the word יֵחָבֶל is derived from לַחְבֹּל, *to take a*

pledge for a loan, as in *If you take your fellow's garment as security* (*Exodus* 22:25).][1]

A person should never scorn advice or reprimands given to him by his elders or superiors. Doing so will cause himself harm. Some Egyptians heeded Moses' warning and brought their cattle indoors before the plague of hail. Their animals remained alive, but those who ignored Moses' warning lost all their cattle in this plague [*Exodus* 9:20-21, 25] (*Meiri*).

Rabbeinu Bachya applies this principle to other areas, as well. If a person scorns something and makes light of it, he will ultimately become obligated because of it. This is what happened to Abimelech, who harassed Isaac; to Joseph's brothers, who scorned Joseph; and to the inhabitants of Gilead, who scorned Jephtah. Subsequently, they all had to ask for the help of the person they had scorned. A person must beware of scorning or belittling anything, as the Sages teach: *Do not be scornful of any person and do not be disdainful of any thing* (*Avos* 4:3).

וִירֵא מִצְוָה הוּא יְשֻׁלָּם — *But he who reveres a commandment will be rewarded.* Someone who reveres a *mitzvah* and makes its value greater in his own eyes will be rewarded for this [besides the reward for the actual performance of the *mitzvah*] (*Metzudos*).[2]

1. *Rashi* cites *Midrash Tehillim*, which applies this verse to King David, who questioned why God created madmen. God answered, "You yourself will eventually need madness." While fleeing from Saul, David found himself in mortal danger from King Achish of Gath, who suspected him of being a sworn enemy. David prayed for help and feigned madness, writing on the doors of the gates and letting his saliva drool on his beard. This show of madness protected him from certain death at the hands of Achish, who expelled him unharmed. Thus, David's life was saved by the very thing he had scorned — madness (*I Samuel* 21:14-16).

2. The members of the illustrious Soloveitchik family of Brisk were living legends for meticulous care in the proper performance of *mitzvos*. When Rabbi Yosef Dov Soloveitchik, the *Beis HaLevi*, baked his matzos for the upcoming Passover holiday, he was scrupulous to feed large pieces of wood into the oven so that it would heat up as soon as possible, assuring that the matzos would bake quickly and not become leavened.

One year, the *Beis HaLevi's* grandson accompanied him to the bakery. He lay on his makeshift bed that night and observed his grandfather, who though thoroughly engrossed in studying the laws of matzah baking, interrupted his studies every half hour to feed the oven's fire with more

¹³ *He who scorns a word will himself be harmed, but he who reveres a commandment will be rewarded. ¹⁴ The teaching of a wise man is a source of life, to turn [him] away from the snares of death. ¹⁵ Good sense provides grace,*

The *Vilna Gaon* explains יְשֻׁלָּם as a derivative of שָׁלֵם, *complete*. There are 248 organs in a person's body, corresponding to the 248 positive commandments in Torah. Each commandment gives life to another organ, so that anyone who scorns a commandment actually injures himself, for he will be missing the life-giving power of that *mitzvah*. One who reveres all the *mitzvos* and is careful not to neglect any of them, יְשֻׁלָּם, *will be complete* in all his organs.

Ibn Ezra, *Meiri* and *Ralbag* render יְשֻׁלָּם as *he will be tranquil*.

R' Hirsch comments that even little things can be important. Even a pin should not be disdained, for some day one may need it. Similarly, one should not consider any duty too insignificant to fulfill. A God-fearing person will also pay attention to the smallest detail of God's laws and will be richly rewarded for his conscientiousness.

14. תּוֹרַת חָכָם מְקוֹר חַיִּים לָסוּר מִמֹּקְשֵׁי מָוֶת — *The teaching of a wise man is a source of life, to turn [him] away from snares of death.* The Torah of a wise man teaches him to avoid the snares of death (*Rashi*),

i.e., it teaches him to avoid sins, which are the snares which cause death (*Metzudos*).[1]

The *Vilna Gaon* explains that while the commandments strengthen all the organs (verse 13), the Torah is the very essence of life. It is is מְקוֹר חַיִּים, the *source of life*, which gives life to all the commandments and all organs of the body.

Just as a spring of water flows constantly, so the rebuke and the advice of a wise man is constantly renewed according to each situation and person. Those who listen to his advice will always be helped to avoid the snares of death (*R' Yonah*).

15. שֵׂכֶל־טוֹב יִתֶּן־חֵן — *Good sense provides grace.* If a person uses his sense to do good, this sense will gain him favor in the eyes of God and his beholders (*Ibn Ezra*).

Someone who has both שֵׂכֶל, *sense*, i.e., Torah, and טוֹב, *good character traits*, will find favor in everyone's eyes. The Talmud (*Yoma* 86a) notes that such people evoke the remark, "How fortunate is his father who taught him Torah! How fortunate is his rebbe who taught him Torah! This individual who studied Torah — how pleasant are his ways!" (*Vilna Gaon*).

wood. The child eventually drifted off to sleep. In the morning, he found the *Beis HaLevi* still fueling the oven and asked, "Is this really so necessary — isn't the oven hot enough already?" The *Beis HaLevi* replied, "For my grandfather, R' Chaim Volozhiner, they would heat the oven this way for seventy-two hours before the baking. As we are unfortunately a weak generation, just one night of pre-heating the oven will have to suffice" (*Haggadah shel Pesach MiBeis Levi*).

1. In the city of Luban, in the former Soviet Union, there was a Jew who became an informer to ingratiate himself with the local authorities. Shortly before his death, he instructed the *Chevra Kadisha*, the burial society, that he wished to be buried face down. The members of the *Chevra Kadisha* were in a quandary: Were they obligated to fulfill the request, or were they bound by the requirement of Jewish law to bury a person face up? They referred the question to their rabbi, Rabbi Moshe Feinstein. He ruled that the deceased be buried face up, as Torah law prescribes.

Two weeks later, the local authorities came to Rabbi Feinstein, demanding that the informer's grave be opened, because they had received a letter from the deceased before his death alerting them that the local Jewish community might take revenge upon him by disgracing his body and burying it face down. The grave was opened and the charges were proven false. R' Moshe's strict adherence to Torah law had saved himself and his community from criminal charges.

טז וְדֶרֶךְ בֹּגְדִים אֵיתָן: כָּל־עָרוּם יַעֲשֶׂה בְּדָעַת
יז וּכְסִיל יִפְרֹשׂ אִוֶּלֶת: מַלְאָךְ רָשָׁע יִפֹּל בְּרָע
יח וְצִיר אֱמוּנִים מַרְפֵּא: רֵישׁ וְקָלוֹן פּוֹרֵעַ מוּסָר
יט וְשׁוֹמֵר תּוֹכַחַת יְכֻבָּד: תַּאֲוָה נִהְיָה תֶּעֱרַב
כ לְנָפֶשׁ וְתוֹעֲבַת כְּסִילִים סוּר מֵרָע: °הָלוֹךְ

°הוֹלֵךְ ק'

וְדֶרֶךְ בֹּגְדִים אֵיתָן — *But the way of traitors is harsh*, harsh for himself and for others (*Rashi*). The way of the wicked is so stubborn that even a person of good sense, who usually finds favor in people's eyes, is unable to persuade them to abandon their wicked ways (*Ibn Ezra*).

This verse emphasizes the importance of heeding a wise man and accepting his rebuke, because he has attained such a level of knowledge that he finds favor in everyone's eyes. One who does not do so is called a *traitor*, for not fulfilling his obligation to listen to someone greater and wiser than himself. The way of a traitor is *harsh*, i.e., it is too hard for him to change (*Meiri*).

Malbim explains אֵיתָן as *harsh earth*, which is unsuitable for planting and does not become saturated from the water of a wellspring. So, too, traitors, who conduct themselves on the way of death, are as harsh as such earth and do not deserve to be nourished from the wellspring of life (v. 14).

16. כָּל־עָרוּם יַעֲשֶׂה בְדָעַת — *Every clever person acts with knowledge.* A wise person acts with forethought and purpose, even if this is not understood by all (*Metzudos*).

A clever person will not undertake an action if there is any doubt about its pro-

priety (*Vilna Gaon, Malbim*).

וּכְסִיל יִפְרֹשׂ אִוֶּלֶת — *But a fool broadcasts [his] stupidity.* A fool does the first thing that comes to his mind, which will inevitably be foolish. Not only does he do it, he even publicizes it to everyone (*Vilna Gaon*), even if people would normally want to conceal such deeds (*R' Yonah*).[1]

17. מַלְאָךְ רָשָׁע יִפֹּל בְּרָע — *A wicked agent will fall into evil.* A wicked messenger, who alters his mission for the bad, will himself suffer from that very evil (*Metzudos*).

Rashi associates this phrase with Balaam, whom God permitted to go with Balak's messengers. However, he acted wickedly and advised Balak to use the daughters of Moab to lure the Israelites into sin (*Numbers* 22:20). As a result of his wickedness, he fell by the sword (ibid., 31:8).

וְצִיר אֱמוּנִים מַרְפֵּא — *But an emissary of the faithful brings healing*, even to those who sent him, by bringing about the fulfillment of the latter's desire (*Meiri*).

Metzudos renders: An emissary of a faithful person even heals the message; if he perceives some flaw in the message, he will improve it with the sweetness of his words.[2]

1. *Rashi* cites the contrast between King David and King Ahasuerus. When David's servants suggested, *Let them seek for my master the king a young virgin* (I Kings 1:2), they acted with forethought by announcing that the king sought only one maiden. Every father eagerly offered his daughter to the servants, hoping that she would be the one to find favor in the king's eyes.

On the other hand, when Ahasuerus sought a new queen, he foolishly commanded that all the maidens of the kingdom be gathered to him, even though he would marry only one maiden and all the others would be rejected. Therefore, all the fathers hid their daughters from him (*Megillah* 12b, see *Rashi* ad loc.).

2. When Reb Zussia traveled to his master, the Maggid of Mezritch, people would send along *kvitlach*, notes requesting that the *Rebbe* pray for them. During the course of his journey, R' Zussia himself would pray for these people. When the Maggid read the requests, he commented, "These requests have already been prayed for!"

but the way of traitors is harsh. ¹⁶ *Every clever person acts with knowledge, but a fool broadcasts [his] stupidity.* ¹⁷ *A wicked agent will fall into evil, but an emissary of the faithful will bring healing.* ¹⁸ *Poverty and disgrace [befall] one who spurns discipline, but he who heeds reproof will be honored.* ¹⁹ *Desire attained is sweet to the soul, but turning from evil is an abomination to fools.* ²⁰ *One who walks*

This verse refers to Moses (*Rashi*), about whom it is written, בְּכָל־בֵּיתִי נֶאֱמָן הוּא, *In my entire household, he is faithful* (*Numbers* 12:7). Moses transmitted the Torah, which heals the nation of Israel [see 3:8] (*Ibn Nachmiash*).

A wicked messenger will fall into evil when confronted with a situation where there is a possibility of error. However, a faithful emissary, i.e., one who has proven faithful from previous missions, will be able to remedy the evil caused by the wicked messenger. This was the case of Caleb and Phineas, the faithful spies sent by Joshua to gather information about Jericho (see *Joshua* 2). They corrected the damage caused by Moshe's spies who fell into evil by saying: *it is a land that devours its inhabitants* [*Numbers* 13:22] (*Vilna Gaon*).

This verse also speaks metaphorically of the human soul, which is God's emissary to this world. If this agent is wicked and does not fulfill its mission here, then it will earn the punishment of *Gehinnom*. However, a faithful emissary can return to its Master and report, "I have fulfilled Your bidding." It will then bask in the healing rays of the sun which will shine for the righteous, as Malachi (3:20) declares: *A sun of righteousness will shine . . . with healing in its rays* (*Malbim*).

18. רֵישׁ וְקָלוֹן פּוֹרֵעַ מוּסָר — *Poverty and disgrace [befall] one who spurns discipline.* Without accepting rebuke, it is difficult for a person to develop honorable character traits or to acquire diligence, which brings wealth (see 10:4, *the hand of the diligent will enrich*). Thus, by spurning rebuke the person invites poverty and shame (*R' Yonah*).

וְשׁוֹמֵר תּוֹכַחַת יְכֻבָּד — *But he who heeds*

reproof will be honored. *Ibn Ezra* explains that if one heeds rebuke, he will be honored not only by people but by God, as is written: כִּי מְכַבְּדַי אֲכַבֵּד, *For I honor those who honor Me* (*I Samuel* 2:30, also see *Avos* 4:1).

19. תַּאֲוָה נִהְיָה תֶּעֱרַב לְנָפֶשׁ וְתוֹעֲבַת כְּסִילִים סוּר מֵרָע — *Desire attained is sweet to the soul, but turning from evil is an abomination to fools.* Since a person enjoys having his desire gratified, a wicked person who finds pleasure in his evil pursuits finds it abhorrent to turn away from them. The verse can also mean that the Holy One, Blessed is He, desires that Israel do His will, and when that desire is fulfilled, it is sweet to Him (*Rashi*).

R' Yonah points out that the verb נִהְיָה is in the present tense. A *desire* is sweet only in the present, while a person is enjoying it, but once he has sinned and the desire is spent, the pleasure is gone. Because of the ephemeral pleasure that evil offers, the wicked person despises any effort to turn him away from it, and he chooses to ignore the eternal consequences he will suffer as a result of succumbing to this fleeting pleasure.

According to other commentators, נִהְיָה means *is broken* (see *Daniel* 8:27, נִהְיֵיתִי וְנֶחֱלֵיתִי). The *Vilna Gaon* explains: When a person is able to overcome and break his desires, even though this may be distressing to him now, his soul will have immense pleasure later on. Fools, however, not only fail to control their desires and curb themselves from actions that may be technically permissible but are improper; they do not even turn away from sin, which is an unquestionable evil. Not only is avoidance of evil not a pleasure to them, they consider it abominable! In relation to

יג/כא-כב ׳יְחֲכָּם ק אֶת־חֲכָמִים °וחכם וְרֹעֶה כְסִילִים יֵרוֹעַ:
כא חַטָּאִים תְּרַדֵּף רָעָה וְאֶת־צַדִּיקִים יְשַׁלֶּם־טוֹב:
כב טוֹב יַנְחִיל בְּנֵי־בָנִים וְצָפוּן לַצַּדִּיק חֵיל חוֹטֵא:

desire, the verse uses the word נֶהְיָה, which also means *attained*. When a person suppresses his desire in order to act according to the Torah, God fulfills that person's wishes. The Mishnah states: *Nullify your will before His will, so that He will nullify the will of others before your will* (*Avos* 2:4). Thus, when a person's desire נֶהְיָה, *is broken*, in essence his true, noble desire נֶהְיָה, *will be attained*, for God will fulfill it.

20. הוֹלֵךְ אֶת־חֲכָמִים יֶחְכָּם — *One who walks with the wise will become wise*, for he will learn from them (*Metzudos*).

וְרֹעֶה כְסִילִים יֵרוֹעַ — *But one who befriends fools will be broken*. One who befriends fools will be broken (*Rashi*), for he will learn from them and be repaid according to his actions (*Metzudos*). [רֹעֶה, according to these commentators, is derived from the word רֵעַ, *a friend*.]

King Solomon points out the benefit derived from associating with righteous people and the harm which results from befriending the wicked. Therefore, a person must take great care in choosing his social companions (*R' Bachya*).[1]

A person cannot become a friend of a wise person easily; he must be his follower

and walk humbly behind him (הוֹלֵךְ אֶת־ חֲכָמִים). However, one can immediately become the equal and friend of the wicked (רֹעֶה כְסִילִים). Similarly, wisdom is hard to attain, whereas it is easy to become wicked (*Malbim*).

R' Yonah and Vilna Gaon explain רֹעֶה as *one who becomes the leader*, in the sense of a רֹעֶה, *shepherd*.

The Sages advise: וֶהֱוֵי זָנָב לַאֲרָיוֹת וְאַל תְּהִי רֹאשׁ לְשׁוּעָלִים, *and better be a tail to lions and not a head to foxes* (*Avos* 4:20). This can be inferred from our verse. With reference to the wise, the verse indicates that one should follow and subordinate himself to them. He will become wise for he will hear them and observe their conduct, for a person is influenced by those with whom he associates (see following citation from *Rambam*). However, one who becomes the leader of fools will suffer with them when God administers punishment. Alternatively, יֵרוֹעַ can be rendered *he will become [רַע] evil*, like them (*Vilna Gaon*).[2]

The Midrash cites several examples to illustrate the far-reaching effects of a person's associations:

❑ Those who associated with Abraham became wise. However, Lot left Avra-

1. The Midrash compares one who associates with the wise to someone who enters a perfumery. Even if he buys no perfume, a pleasant scent will linger on his clothing when he leaves. But one who associates with wicked people is like someone who enters a leather tannery. When he leaves, his clothing will have a foul odor. So, too, when a person associates with the wise, people will say, "If he were not wise himself, the *chacham* would not be associating with him!" The same applies to those who join the wicked (*Yalkut Shimoni*).

2. *Rambam* comments that by nature a person is drawn after his friends and compatriots. Therefore, he must live near righteous people so that he will learn from their good deeds, and distance himself from the wicked so that he will not be influenced by them. It may be necessary for a person to leave his native country and move elsewhere, or to completely isolate himself from society, or even to dwell in caves and deserts, in order to avoid the evil influence of his environment.

Furthermore, it is a positive Torah commandment to cleave to the wise in order to learn from their good deeds, as the verse states: וּבוֹ תִדְבָּק, *to Him you shall cleave*. How is it possible to cleave to God? This means that one should cleave to Torah scholars. One should try to marry the daughter of a Torah scholar and marry his daughter to a Torah scholar, to eat and drink with Torah scholars, to do business for them and to associate with the wise in every possible way. Regarding this, our Sages instructed (*Avos* 1:4) *and sit in the dust of their feet* (*Hilchos Deios* 6:1-2).

with the wise will become wise, but one who befriends fools will be broken. [21] *Evil pursues sinners, but He will reward the righteous with good.* [22] *A good person will bequeath to grandchildren, but wealth of a sinner is secreted for the righteous person.*

ham and settled in Sodom (*Genesis* 13:12). As a result, all his possessions were captured in the war of the Four Kings and the Five Kings (*Genesis* 14:12, *Rashi* ibid.).

❑ In the Generation of the Flood, not only was Noah saved because of his righteousness, but in his merit God saved all the animals with him in the ark (*Genesis* 8:1). On the other hand, not only were the wicked people of that generation destroyed in the Flood, but all animals and other living things also perished on their account (*Genesis* 7:23).

❑ In Korach's dispute with Moses, not only did Korach and the two hundred fifty leaders who accompanied him perish, but all their possessions were swallowed up with them (*Numbers* 16:32)

❑ When Chananyah, Mishael and Azaryah were saved from the burning furnace, not only were their bodies untouched by the fire, but even their clothing remained intact (*Daniel* 3:27). If the clothing attached to the righteous was saved in their merit, then certainly Jewish people, who are attached to the Eternal God, will be saved from the fires of *Gehinnom* (*Yalkut Shimoni*).

21. חַטָּאִים תְּרַדֵּף רָעָה — *Evil pursues sinners.* A wicked person will be pursued by his own wickedness until he is destroyed (*Rashi*). His evil deeds will accuse him (*Metzudos*).

The evil perpetrated by the wicked pursues them and makes them stumble into even more serious transgression, so that they will be completely destroyed (*R' Yonah*).

וְאֶת־צַדִּיקִים יְשַׁלֶּם־טוֹב — *But He will reward the righteous with good.* God will reward the righteous for their good deeds with good (*Ibn Ezra, Meiri, Vilna Gaon*).

The good deeds of the righteous will benefit them by preventing them from stumbling into transgression. (See 12:21.)

The Sages (*Yoma* 38b) teach that once a person has twice resisted the temptation to sin, God helps him resist sin (*R' Yonah*).

The *Vilna Gaon* explains that the reward of the righteous will be that they will be given the opportunity to do more *mitzvos*, for the commandments are called טוב, *good.* This follows the principle that *the consequence of a mitzvah is [another] mitzvah* (*Avos* 4:2).

Metzudos explains that the merit of the righteous will repay them, for it will speak up in their behalf.

The punishment for a transgression is inherent in the nature of the sin itself. It is not that God must inflict a punishment; rather, the corrupting influence of the deed will pursue the sinner until his downfall. The reward for a *mitzvah*, however, comes from God Himself. In addition to the good inherent in the *mitzvah* itself, God will reward the one who performed it.

This may be illustrated with a parable: A king once commanded his servants not to eat from a certain poisonous fruit, and to eat another fruit which was nutritious. Those who disregarded his command and ate the forbidden fruit died from its poison. Those who heeded the king's decree and ate the nutritious fruit not only benefited from the fruit's healthful qualities, but were also rewarded for obeying the royal command (*Malbim*).

22. טוֹב יַנְחִיל בְּנֵי־בָנִים וְצָפוּן לַצַּדִּיק חֵיל חוֹטֵא — *A good person will bequeath to grandchildren, but wealth of a sinner is secreted for the righteous person.* A good person bequeaths his merits and wealth to his grandchildren. [It will be passed on not only to his children, but even to his grandchildren (*Ralbag*).] The sinner, however, leaves no inheritance [not even to his children (*Ralbag*)]; for his wealth is hidden away to be given to the righteous, as is the case of Haman, whose house and wealth were given to Mordechai (*Esther* 8:2).

כג רַב־אֹכֶל נִיר רָאשִׁים וְיֵשׁ נִסְפֶּה בְּלֹא מִשְׁפָּט:
כד חוֹשֵׂךְ שִׁבְטוֹ שׂוֹנֵא בְנוֹ וְאֹהֲבוֹ שִׁחֲרוֹ מוּסָר:

Meiri finds this idea expressed by Koheles: וְלַחוֹטֶא נָתַן עִנְיָן לֶאֱסֹף וְלִכְנוֹס לָתֵת לְטוֹב לִפְנֵי הָאֱלֹהִים, *But to the sinner He has given an urge to gather and amass — that he may hand it on to one who is pleasing to God* (Ecclesiastes 2:26).

Malbim points out that the previous verse teaches that the wicked will be pursued by their evil, and the righteous will be rewarded for their good. Why then do righteous people suffer, while the wicked enjoy a peaceful life? This verse explains that the reward due the righteous is stored as an inheritance that God will bestow upon his progeny in future generations. On the other hand, the wealth enjoyed by the wicked is but temporary, for in reality they are amassing riches that are destined for the righteous in the future.

Every person is allotted a share in *Gan Eden* and a share in *Gehinnom*. If he is worthy, he will inherit his share and his friend's share in *Gan Eden* (see *Chagigah* 15a). Thus, the חַיִל, *wealth* — i.e., the share in *Gan Eden* — of a sinner is stored away for the righteous person (*Alshich*).

23. רַב־אֹכֶל נִיר רָאשִׁים וְיֵשׁ נִסְפֶּה בְּלֹא מִשְׁפָּט — *Much food [grows from] the furrows of the poor, but substance may be swept away for lack of justice.* Much grain is produced through the plowing of poor people, but their grain may suffer if its owner fails to separate the required tithes and gifts to the poor (*Rashi*).

Poor people work hard for the landowners who enjoy the fruits of their labor, while they themselves remain poor, with little to eat. Yet, if the rich do not provide for the poor and give them what they deserve, their wealth will be swept away (*HaMachiri*).

Ibn Ezra explains that there will be an abundance of food for the poor, as long as they plow and till the earth properly (see 12:11), but a person may perish if he does not know the best way to plow and plant. In this case, מִשְׁפָּט connotes *the proper way* of working the land.

Rashi also explains this verse figuratively, as referring to Torah learning. Much Torah results from students [i.e., those impoverished in wisdom] for through their debate and inquiry, their teachers deepen their own knowledge. Many students may lose their lives, however, if they do not act properly.[1]

This verse underscores the obligation to give charity to the poor. A person should not say, "If God wants the poor to be provided for, why doesn't He provide for them Himself?!" (See *Bava Basra* 10a, where the Roman governor Turnos Rufus posed a similar question to R' Akiva.) The rich should realize that the world needs poor people, for without them there would be no laborers to work for others. Most of the world has food to eat only because of the tillage of the poor. In other words, the poor labor and suffer for the entire generation, and it is in the merit of their suffering that everyone has food. Not only that, but the rich should provide for the poor because God will take away their lives [וְיֵשׁ נִסְפֶּה] if they do not provide the just amount [בְּלֹא מִשְׁפָּט] to the needy (*Vilna Gaon*).

Continuing from the previous verse, this verse addresses the question of why God does not reward the righteous person himself with good. Why is it that the righteous person, whose merit sustains the whole generation with food, suffers deprivation? This is compared to the poor who produce an abundance of food through their toil, while they often go hungry, or even die of

---

1. R' Chanina said: I have learned much Torah from my teachers, and from my colleagues even more than from my teachers, *but from my students even more than from them all* (*Taanis* 7a). This is because students ask more questions than colleagues, who in turn ask more questions than teachers; and questions prompt further discussion, study and proper elucidation (*Maharsha*). On the other hand, twelve thousand pairs of R' Akiva's students died during a thirty-three-day period because they did not act respectfully toward one another (*Yevamos* 62b).

 ²³ *Much food [grows from] the furrows of the poor, but substance may be swept away for lack of justice.* ²⁴ *He who spares his rod hates his child, but he who loves him disciplines him constantly.*

starvation. Similarly, while the merits of the righteous allow the blessings of Heaven to flow more freely to others, they themselves lead a life of deprivation. As ironic as these situations may appear to us, God knows that were the poor to become affluent, they would no longer work the land. And were the righteous to become wealthy, their merit would no longer be able to affect such a flow of Heavenly blessings upon the world.[1] All of God's ways are just, though they remain beyond our comprehension (*Malbim*).

24. חוֹשֵׂךְ שִׁבְטוֹ שׂוֹנֵא בְנוֹ — *He who spares his rod hates his child.* In the end he will hate his child, for he will see the child fall into bad ways (*Rashi*). It is considered as if he hates him, for eventually the child will fall into bad company and die a result of his sins (*Metzudos*).[2]

One who withholds discipline from his child hates him, for by doing so he denies perfection to his child (*Meiri*).

The parent who lets pity for his child override the need to chastise him in essence loves himself and hates his child; for the pain he feels at chastising his child is more important to him than the benefit his child would get from the discipline and the acquisition of *chochmah* (*Malbim*).[3]

וְאֹהֲבוֹ שִׁחֲרוֹ מוּסָר — *But he who loves him disciplines him constantly.* According to

Rashi and *Meiri*, שִׁחֲרוֹ, which is derived from שַׁחַר, *dawn*, implies that the *mussar* is given constantly, every morning. *Metzudos* interprets שַׁחַר as *youth* (i.e., the dawn of life). One who loves his child gives him *mussar* in his youth, when it is possible to mold him in the proper way. *Ralbag* adds that one who loves his child disciplines him in his youth, training him according to his nature.

According to the *Vilna Gaon*, שִׁחֲרוֹ means *he seeks out* even the slightest infraction of his son and chastises him for that (cf. 11:27). The *Vilna Gaon*, quoting *Akeidas Yitzchak*, explains this with the metaphor of a woman who beautifies herself using a mirror that magnifies her imperfections. With all her blemishes visibly enlarged, she can identify and attend to every flaw, removing even the slightest blemish so that her appearance will be all the more beautiful. Similarly, the more a person loves his child, the more exacting he is of him, so that he will not repeat his errors.

R' Hirsch points out that educating a child is not an easy task, and it requires both a great dead of patience and constant serious application. Though the task is hard, the knowledge that one has given his child a sound upbringing is most gratifying.

Yalkut Shimoni teaches how this verse

1. *Malbim* cites the example of R' Chanina ben Dosa, in whose merit the whole generation received sustenance. R' Chanina himself, however, subsisted on only a small measure of carob from one Sabbath eve to the next (*Berachos* 17b). *R' Chaim Shmulevitz* explains this as cause and effect; because R' Chanina satisfied himself with so little, therefore his merit sufficed to sustain his whole generation.

2. Sometimes, the verb שׂוֹנֵא is used to mean *not love* (*Genesis* 29:31, *Deuteronomy* 21:15, *Malachi* 1:2), rather than *hate*. In this case, however, the commentators agree that the father not only fails to display love for his child, but by overlooking his faults and failing to correct him he actually causes him harm, as in the case of King David and his son, Adoniyahu ben Haggith (see 13:1).

3. Someone once entered the room just as Rabbi Chaim Soloveitchik spanked his young son, Yitzchak Zev. The visitor protested, "Yitzchak Zev is such a weak child; how can you hit him?" R' Chaim ignored the remark. A week later, the same visitor was present as Yitzchak Zev told his father an original Torah thought with great erudition. All those present were astounded at the brilliance of the young child. R' Chaim then turned to his critic and said, "Last week's spanking produced this original Torah thought."

כה צַדִּיק אֹכֵל לְשֹׂבַע נַפְשׁוֹ וּבֶטֶן רְשָׁעִים תֶּחְסָר:
א חַכְמוֹת נָשִׁים בָּנְתָה בֵיתָהּ וְאִוֶּלֶת בְּיָדֶיהָ תֶהֶרְסֶנּוּ:

applies in the relationship between God and man. Since God loves the righteous, He chastises them with afflictions in this world, so their sins may have an atonement.

25. צַדִּיק אֹכֵל לְשֹׂבַע נַפְשׁוֹ — *A righteous person eats to satisfy his soul.* It appears to the righteous one that he is satisfied (*Rashi*).

A righteous person does not eat to fill his stomach, but to satisfy *his soul* — i.e., he eats only what is necessary to sustain himself. [Thus, even his physical needs are provided for out of spiritual considerations (*R' Hirsch*).] The pleasures of this world are insignificant to the righteous, whose main enjoyments are the pleasures of the Hereafter. That is why R' Chanina ben Dosa was satisfied with only a measure of carobs from one Friday to the next. It was enough for him, and he desired no more (*Malbim*).

The *Zohar* explains that a righteous person eats only after satisfying his soul with prayer and the reading of Torah (*Yalkut Me'am Loez*).

The Midrash applies this verse to Ruth. She ate leftovers in the field, yet the verse says of her, וַתֹּאכַל וַתִּשְׂבַּע וַתֹּתַר, *and she ate and she was satisfied and she left over* (*Ruth* 2:14). The Sages teach that God blesses the righteous so that even though they consume just a little food, they feel sated.[1]

וּבֶטֶן רְשָׁעִים תֶּחְסָר — *But the stomach of the wicked will [always] lack.* It does not seem to the wicked that they are satisfied (*Rashi*).

The righteous do not desire delicacies. They eat only to satisfy the soul. On the other hand, the wicked treat themselves to sweets and delicacies. Therefore, their stomachs always feel empty, for there is always room to fill it with more sweets (*Metzudos*).

The *Vilna Gaon* explains that a righteous person eats only enough to satisfy his hunger and sustain his life. The wicked, on the other hand, seem to be "missing a stomach," because they want to eat so much that their stomachs are too small to contain it all. Also, eating habits are a reflection of a person's trust in God. The righteous trust that God will provide for them, and therefore they eat a full meal (see 10:3). The wicked are always worried that they will not have enough for tomorrow. Whatever they have does not seem sufficient. Since they have no trust in God, they are stingy with their food, and therefore, their stomachs always feel want.

This verse also applies to a person's attitude to Torah study. A righteous person studies Torah in order to satisfy his soul. It is inconsequential to him whether he has covered much material or little, as long as he understands his studies well, for then his knowledge will endure. The wicked, who study in order to show off their knowledge, try to "grab" a great deal of Torah at once. However, since they cannot possibly digest all this knowledge at one time, their "stomachs" are empty, for none of their Torah will endure.

The wicked rely on robbery to sustain them; therefore, they will feel want (*Ralbag*).

According to *Yalkut Shimoni*, צַדִּיק אֹכֵל לְשֹׂבַע נַפְשׁוֹ, *A righteous person eats to satisfy his soul,* refers to King Hezekiah of Judea, who ate two bundles of greens and one liter of meat every day. On the other hand, וּבֶטֶן רְשָׁעִים תֶּחְסָר, *but the stomach of the wicked will [always] lack,* refers to Pekach ben Remalyahu, king of the Ten Tribes, who would consume three hundred chicks for dessert.[2]

1. This blessing was repeated for many Torah scholars. The *Vilna Gaon*, for example, ate only two olive-sized pieces of bread daily, yet he was full.

2. *Midrash Mishlei* records the following incident: R' Meir related, A Cuthean in my city made a feast for all the townspeople, and I, too, was invited. He served everything that God made during the Six Days of Creation. The only food missing from his table was a type of nut. What did he do?

²⁵ *A righteous person eats to satisfy his soul, but the stomach of the wicked will [always] lack.*

¹ **T**he *wise among women, each builds her house, but a foolish one tears it down with her hands.* ² *One who*

XIV

1. חַכְמוֹת נָשִׁים בָּנְתָה בֵיתָהּ — *The wise among women, — each builds her house.* Noting the unusual plural form of חַכְמוֹת, Rashi translates this phrase as, "*the wise among women* build their houses," i.e., it is because of such women that their homes endure. Such was the case with the wife of On ben Peleth, whom the Midrash credits with saving his life, by persuading him to sever his association with Korach and his followers at the time of their confrontation with Moses.[1]

The opening phrase of this chapter presents textual and grammatical difficulties. The term חַכְמוֹת is usually translated as the plural of חָכְמָה, *wisdom*, i.e., varieties of wisdom. *Rashi* points out, however, that since here the vowelization is חַכְמוֹת (with a *patach*, as opposed to a *komatz*), the translation is the *wise among women*.

A wife is actually the builder of the home, a responsibility so complex that wisdom alone is not sufficient. She needs חַכְמוֹת, a combination of knowledge, in-

sight, abilities and skills, as well as moral and spiritual excellence, to execute her task. Her wise or unwise handling of seemingly minor relationships in domestic life can be decisive for the comfort, prospering, and happiness of the home (*R' Hirsch*).

The *Vilna Gaon* explains this verse metaphorically. An individual's soul is called his wife, and his house refers to the permanent abode of his soul in the World to Come. Thus, *the wise among women*, i.e., someone with a good soul, *builds her house*, i.e., builds a worthy abode in the Hereafter.

וְאִוֶּלֶת בְּיָדֶיהָ תֶהֶרְסֶנּוּ — *But a foolish one tears it down with her own hands.* Rashi applies this part of the verse to Korach's wife.[2]

By casting doubts on the laws of wisdom, skepticism destroys what wisdom builds (*Malbim*).

The Sages attribute great power and

[He was so upset that] he took his table, which was worth six talents of gold, and broke it. When I asked him why, he replied, "You claim that this world belongs to us and the World to Come belongs to you. If we don't eat now in this world, when will we eat?" To such a person, R' Meir applied the verse, *but the stomach of the wicked will [always] lack* (13:25).

1. The Talmud (*Sanhedrin* 109b) relates that On's wife reasoned with her husband, saying, "What have you to gain by supporting Korach in his attempt to become *Kohen Gadol*? Your position will be the same, no matter who is the *Kohen Gadol*." On conceded that she was right, but explained that he could not disengage from Korach's assembly as he had sworn to join them.

On's wife assured him that she would take care of the matter, and contrived a plan to rescue him from disaster. She realized that the men of Korach's assembly would not approach her if her appearance was immodest. She gave On an intoxicating drink and put him to sleep inside their tent. She sat near the entrance of her tent and let down her hair. All those who came to call On to the assembly recoiled at the sight of a woman whose head was uncovered, and turned back. While On was safe at home, Korach and his followers were swallowed up by the earth.

2. The Talmud (*Sanhedrin* 110a) recounts her conversation with Korach. She told her husbnd: "Look at what Moses did. He is the king; he made his brother the *Kohen Gadol*, and his nephews — the ordinary *Kohanim*. If someone comes with *terumah* (the priestly tithe), Moses says to give it to the *Kohen*. And as for the tithes you as Levites are entitled to, Moses tells you that a tenth of it must go to the *Kohanim*. Not only that, but Moses has also shaved off all your hair (see *Numbers* 8:7 for the procedure that sanctified Levites for service in the Tabernacle). He treats you like excrement. He doesn't want you to look as nice as he does."

With these and other spurious arguments, Korach's wife "tore down her house" and destroyed it, for Korach's rebellion caused his household to be destroyed (see *Numbers* 16:32).

ב הוֹלֵךְ בְּיָשְׁרוֹ יְרֵא יהוֹה וּנְלוֹז דְּרָכָיו בּוֹזֵהוּ:
ג בְּפִי־אֱוִיל חֹטֶר גַּאֲוָה וְשִׂפְתֵי חֲכָמִים תִּשְׁמוּרֵם:
ד בְּאֵין אֲלָפִים אֵבוּס בָּר וְרָב־תְּבוּאוֹת בְּכֹחַ שׁוֹר:

ability to the wife. A virtuous wife can influence a wicked husband to be good; while a wicked wife can cause a righteous husband to become bad. This verse teaches that a wise woman can rebuild her house, even if it was destroyed through her husband's wickedness. A foolish woman, however, destroys her house with her own hands. Though her house is well-established, and her husband is righteous, her foolish actions will tear it down (*Alshich*).

The Midrash (*Bereishis Rabbah* 17:12) emphasizes this concept. A pious man was married to a pious woman, but as they did not have children, they decided to divorce. He took a wicked woman as his new wife, and she made him become wicked. The pious woman married a wicked man, whom she made righteous. Thus, the determining factor in the family is the woman.

Meiri comments that this verse teaches a person to investigate carefully and choose a virtuous wife with fine character traits. He should not be misled by wealth, for a poor woman who is sensible is far more desirable than one of high rank, who is full of folly. The Sages of *mussar* express this poetically: אַל תִּקַּח אִשָּׁה לְעוֹשֶׁר אוֹ לְיוֹפִי כִּי הַכֹּל יֵלֵךְ וְיִשָּׁאֵר הַדוֹפִי, *Do not take a wife for her wealth or her beauty, for all this is vain. Eventually these will leave her, and only her faults will remain.*

2. הוֹלֵךְ בְּיָשְׁרוֹ יְרֵא ה׳ — *One who walks in his uprightness fears HASHEM.* That one follows the straight path is an indication that he is a person who fears God (*Metzudos*).

A righteous person fears God continuously, even as he follows the straight path, for he is concerned lest he has not fulfilled

all of his obligations to the fullest (*Binah L'Ittim*).[1]

The *Vilna Gaon* explains why the verse states הוֹלֵךְ בְּיָשְׁרוֹ, *One who walks in **his** uprightness*, rather than *one who walks in uprightness*. Each person must walk a path that suits his own nature. Since no two natures are alike, each individual has his own temptations to sin, and must determine for himself what precautions will protect him from these situations. One may need to take precautions in a certain area while his friend needs none at all, or vice versa. The person who follows a path that is proper for him is the one who fears God, even though others may look at him askance, as they do not realize his specific needs and nature.

וּנְלוֹז דְּרָכָיו בּוֹזֵהוּ — *But he who is perverse in his ways scorns Him.* One whose conduct is perverse scorns God by the way he acts (*Rashi*).

R' Yonah notes that the term בּוֹזֵהוּ, *scorns Him*, is used in contrast to יְרֵא ה׳, *fears HASHEM*, implying that one honors God by fearing Him.

Alshich and *Metzudos* render בּוֹזֵהוּ as *scorns him*, i.e., the person who turns away from the straight road scorns a God-fearing person and considers him a fool.

According to *Meiri*, someone who becomes involved in evil to such an extent that he is unable to repent will scorn perfection, as he despairs of ever attaining it (cf. 1:7).

3. בְּפִי־אֱוִיל חֹטֶר גַּאֲוָה — *In the mouth of a fool is a staff of pride.* A fool's arrogance protrudes like a staff (*Metzudos*).

Rashi cites the pride and arrogance of Pharaoh, who exclaimed, "Who is Hashem that I should hearken to His voice?" (*Exodus* 5:2).

1. When the leader of his generation, R' Yochanan ben Zakkai, was close to death, he cried. When asked why he wept, he explained, "There are two paths before me — one to *Gan Eden* and one to *Gehinnom* — and I do not know down which of these two paths I will now be led!" (*Berachos* 28b).

walks in his uprightness fears HASHEM, but he who is perverse in his ways scorns Him. ³ In the mouth of a fool is a staff of pride, but the lips of the wise will protect them. ⁴ Where there are no oxen, the trough is clean; but an abundance of crops [comes through] the strength of an ox.

Ibn Ezra explains that the tongue in a fool's mouth is like a stick, with which he hits others with arrogant words.

וְשִׂפְתֵי חֲכָמִים תִּשְׁמוּרֵם — *But the lips of the wise will protect them.* The lips of the wise will prevent them from speaking arrogantly (*Metzudos*).

The root of the fool's arrogance is in his heart; its branch is in his mouth. Just as a branch produces fruit, so a fool's mouth spews forth words of pride and scorn. Arrogance is so entrenched in a fool's heart and mouth that he cannot guard his lips from giving forth their "fruits." Arrogant words come naturally to him, as if a branch of pride were implanted in his mouth. Wise people, on the other hand, would never consciously speak with arrogance. Their lips protect them from even inadvertently blurting out haughty thoughts that may have entered their heart. Their lips are so well trained to speak humbly, that they cannot even tolerate haughty speech (*R' Yonah*).

The *Vilna Gaon* explains that a fool arrogantly threatens to hit those who disobey him with his "stick." However, wise people protect themselves from his threats by closing their *lips* and not countering his threats. Thus they give him no excuse to strike them.

4. בְּאֵין אֲלָפִים אֵבוּס בָּר — *Where there are no oxen, the trough is clean.* If there are no oxen [to work the land and produce grain (*Vilna Gaon*)], then the feeding trough is cleaned out and empty, for even straw is not available in the house. This alludes to a place where there are no Torah scholars, which results in a lack of proper Torah instruction (*Rashi*).

The word אֶלֶף means both *oxen* [as in שְׁגַר אֲלָפֶיךָ, *the offspring of your oxen* (*Deuteronomy* 7:13)] and *teaching or training* [as in וַאֲאַלֶּפְךָ חָכְמָה, *and I will teach you wisdom* (*Job* 33:33)]. *Malbim*

connects both meanings, rendering אֲלָפִים as *oxen that were trained* to plow and work the land.

וְרָב־תְּבוּאוֹת בְּכֹחַ שׁוֹר — *But an abundance of crops [comes through] the strength of an ox.* Much grain is produced through the ox's strength as it plows the field. So, too, someone who takes the yoke of Torah upon himself like an ox will benefit from a great deal of Torah knowledge (*Metzudos*).

The *Vilna Gaon* explains as follows: If there are no students with whom to learn, then the *trough*, which refers to the person himself, will become empty. However, an abundance of Torah knowledge comes from the strength of an *ox*, i.e., a worthy student. Just as an ox can use its horns to gore, so, too, a worthy student can help his teacher clarify and explain an issue, through the probing questions and answers in the give-and-take of Torah study (*Cf.* 13:23).

Malbim interprets the verse differently: אֲלָפִים are *oxen who are trained to work* in the field. They need not be fed in a *trough*, because they will graze in the fields. Not only does their presence in the field provide them with food, but their work results in much grain being produced. On the other hand, an ox that is not trained to work will remain by the trough eating its fill. Not only will it not produce crops, it will use up the grain already stored in the manger. (בָּר here is translated as *grain*. The first phrase reads: בְּאֵין אֲלָפִים אֵבוּס בָּר, *When there are no trained oxen there is [no] grain in the trough.*) Metaphorically, this refers to a person who must plow the fields of wisdom and understanding, for he will produce an abundance of "grain," i.e., the fruit of his soul and his intellect. Through the tireless efforts of his body, which has been trained to serve God, his soul will enjoy its produce in *Gan Eden.*

ה-ז עֵד אֱמוּנִים לֹא יְכַזֵּב וְיָפִיחַ כְּזָבִים עֵד שָׁקֶר: בִּקֶּשׁ־
ז לֵץ חָכְמָה וָאָיִן וְדַעַת לְנָבוֹן נָקָל: לֵךְ מִנֶּגֶד לְאִישׁ
ח כְּסִיל וּבַל־יָדַעְתָּ שִׂפְתֵי־דָעַת: חָכְמַת עָרוּם הָבִין
ט דַּרְכּוֹ וְאִוֶּלֶת כְּסִילִים מִרְמָה: אֱוִלִים יָלִיץ אָשָׁם

However, the skeptic, who disputes wisdom, does not tend its field. He is busy fattening himself at the *trough* with the pleasures of this world, while ruining the spiritual "grain" of *chochmah*.

5. עֵד אֱמוּנִים לֹא יְכַזֵּב — *A trustworthy witness will not deceive.* An individual who is truthful in his testimony does not deceive others even in his daily conversation, for he has trained himself to speak only the exact truth (cf. 12:17) (*R' Yonah*).

Metzudos renders: A person who always speaks honestly will certainly not be deceitful in his testimony.

וְיָפִיחַ כְּזָבִים עֵד שָׁקֶר — *But a spouter of deceptions is a false witness.* A person who has become accustomed to speak deceptively, even if it is in areas of little significance, has habituated himself to speak falsely. Therefore, he will not hesitate to testify falsely, and his testimony should be thoroughly investigated (*Metzudos*).

According to the *Vilna Gaon*, this verse refers to the recitation of the *Shema*, which is our testimony to God's unity. In the first verse of *Shema*, the letter "ע" in the word שְׁמַע and "ד" in the word אֶחָד are enlarged. Together, they spell the word עֵד, *witness*, for when we recite this verse, we bear witness to Hashem's unity. The words in the middle of this verse, ה' אֱלֹהֵינוּ, *Hashem is our God*, correspond to the first two of the Ten Commandments — אָנֹכִי ה' אֱלֹהֶיךָ, *I am Hashem your God*, and לֹא־יִהְיֶה לְךָ אֱלֹהִים אֲחֵרִים עַל־פָּנַי, *You shall not recognize the gods of others in My presence* — which encompass all the positive and negative commandments in the Torah. By reciting the *Shema*, therefore, we accept upon ourselves the fulfillment of all the positive and negative commandments. Thus, a *faithful witness* is one who *will not deceive*, for he will be sure to heed all the commandments. On the other hand,

one who is *a spouter of deceptions*, i.e., one who has no intention fulfilling the commandments, is a *false witness* when he recites the *Shema*.

6. בִּקֶּשׁ־לֵץ חָכְמָה וָאָיִן — *The scoffer seeks wisdom yet there is none.* When he needs wisdom he does not find it in his heart (*Rashi*).

A scoffer may try to learn wisdom, but he will be unable to, because he is involved in mockery (*Ibn Ezra*).

A לֵץ is one who is engrossed in idle chatter, who scoffs at others and mocks their words and actions. Such behavior can stem only from the absence of fear of God and from casting off His yoke. Such a person will never be able to attain wisdom because he associates with idle people and because he lacks reverence, which is a prerequisite for the study of Torah. Rebbe advised his son (*Kesubos* 103b), "Cast fear into the students" for wisdom is found only in those who study it with trepidation (*R' Yonah*).

וְדַעַת לְנָבוֹן נָקָל — *But knowledge will come easily to an understanding one.* He will find it quickly, for he is accustomed to it (*Metzudos*).

Of the three levels — *chachmah* (wisdom), *tvunah* (understanding or discernment) and *daas* (knowledge) — *daas* is the highest achievement. A scoffer cannot even reach the first level. However, since the discerning one and has achieved the level of understanding, then knowledge will be easily attainable, for one leads to the next. Having attained *binah* (understanding), he has trained himself to analyze and choose the correct opinions and reject the faulty ones. Our Sages refer to this when they say: אם אין בינה אין דעת, *If there is no understanding there is no knowledge* (*Avos* 3:21) (*R' Yonah*).

7. לֵךְ מִנֶּגֶד לְאִישׁ כְּסִיל וּבַל־יָדַעְתָּ שִׂפְתֵי־דָעַת

⁵ *A trustworthy witness will not deceive, but a spouter of deceptions is a false witness.* ⁶ *The scoffer seeks wisdom yet there is none, but knowledge will come easily to an understanding one.* ⁷ *Go far away from a man who is a fool, lest you not know the lips of knowledge.* ⁸ *The wisdom of a clever person is to understand his way, but the folly of fools is deceit.* ⁹ *A guilt-offering will intercede for fools,*

— *Go far away from a man who is a fool lest you not know the lips of knowledge.* Do not associate constantly with a fool, or you will eventually not attain wisdom (*Rashi*). Either distance yourself from him, or you may end up being like him (*Metzudos*).

R' *Yonah* explains that this verse instructs one to stay far away from a person who is known to be wicked, as well as from a person who you are not sure possesses *lips of knowledge.* [The letter "ל" of לְאִישׁ כְּסִיל also refers to the second half of the verse, rendering it וּלְבַל־יָדַעְתָּ, *and from one who you did not know* [to have] *lips of knowledge.*] Do not associate with the latter until you have ascertained that he is careful not to reveal another's secrets, and not to shame or embarrass others as a result of his anger or arrogant nature. As long as there are any doubts about him, avoid his company, for it is dangerous to associate with such people.

Meiri adds another interpretation to the words בַּל־יָדַעְתָּ: וּבַל־יָדַעְתָּ שִׂפְתֵי־דָעַת, *To admit that you did not know,* is שִׂפְתֵי־דָעַת, *lips of knowledge.* Therefore, a person should always train himself to admit: "I do not know."

R' *Hirsch* renders this verse: " 'Go away from the presence of a conceited fool, and do not know him,' so say the *lips of knowledge.*" There is nothing more annoying than meeting a person who lacks proper perception, but considers his opinions to be irrefutably correct. A sensible individual stays far away from such a person.

8. חָכְמַת עָרוּם הָבִין דַּרְכּוֹ — *The wisdom of a clever person is to understand his way.* He displays his wisdom by weighing his paths (*Rashi*); he analyzes his way so that he does not act by impulse (*Metzudos*).

A person must be shrewd in his fear of

God. Just as the primordial snake was shrewd in entrapping Eve into sin, so, too, a person needs shrewdness to recognize these entrapments and, taking into account his own nature and tendencies, carefully guard himself from any way that may lead him to sin. Thus, חָכְמַת עָרוּם, *the wisdom of a shrewd person* is הָבִין דַּרְכּוֹ, *to understand his way* — his nature — in order to avoid any chance of sinning (*Vilna Gaon*).

וְאִוֶּלֶת כְּסִילִים מִרְמָה — *But the folly of fools is deceit.* The folly of fools is the deceit they harbor in their hearts; ultimately this deceit brings them to act foolishly (*Rashi*).

Meiri explains that a shrewd person's wisdom will help him understand which road he should take, whereas the folly of fools will teach them only evil and deceit.

Just as a shrewd person's actions are based on forethought and not on impulse, so, too, the aim of fools is to execute the deceit in their hearts; they do not act impulsively (*Metzudos*).

According to *Malbim*, the fool of this verse is someone who recognizes true wisdom, but consciously refutes it because of his desires. He feigns אִוֶּלֶת, *skepticism,* but what he claims to be intelligent analysis is really מִרְמָה, *deceitful* and untrue. He uses skepticism only as a pretense to allow him to follow the dictates of his heart, claiming that his doubts force him to disbelieve the claims of wisdom. This is actually deceit, however, for he has no doubts — he will not yield to wisdom, for he hates it (see 1:22) (cf. *Malbim* 12:23).

9. אֱוִלִים יָלִיץ אָשָׁם — *A guilt-offering will intercede for fools.* Those who sin against people must make financial restitution to the party they have wronged. This money serves as a guilt-offering to defend them.

י וּבֵין יְשָׁרִים רָצוֹן: לֵב יוֹדֵעַ מָרַת נַפְשׁוֹ וּבְשִׂמְחָתוֹ לֹא-
יא יִתְעָרַב זָר: בֵּית רְשָׁעִים יִשָּׁמֵד וְאֹהֶל יְשָׁרִים יַפְרִיחַ:
יב יֵשׁ דֶּרֶךְ יָשָׁר לִפְנֵי-אִישׁ וְאַחֲרִיתָהּ דַּרְכֵי-מָוֶת:

For example, when the Philistines were stricken by God for having captured the Holy Ark, they wanted to return the Ark and admit their guilt to Him. Along with the Ark, they sent a gift of gold to honor God and appease His anger, thereby mitigating their punishment (see *I Samuel* 6:4,5) (*Rashi*).

וּבֵין יְשָׁרִים רָצוֹן — *But [HASHEM's] favor is among the upright*, i.e., He is pleased with them (*Rashi*).

The guilt-offering brought by fools will protect them by atoning for their wrongdoing. However, God's favor is among the upright, even without an offering (*Metzudos*).

Ibn Ezra renders the word יָלִיץ as יִתְלוֹצֵץ, *will scoff*. Fools scoff at the idea of bringing a guilt-offering and refuse to do so, claiming that it is to no avail. Similarly, they scoff at all the decrees of the Torah. On the other hand, God is pleased with the guilt-offering of the upright, for it atones for their sins. Alternatively, this verse means that fools scoff at the concept of sin; therefore, they do not hesitate to steal, rob, or cause others to transgress. However, the upright desire only to do what is pleasing to God and to man.

Meiri explains יָלִיץ as *will make sweet*, as in מַה נִּמְלְצוּ לְחִכִּי, *how sweet to my palate* (*Psalms* 119:103). When a fool sins, he makes his wrongdoing sweet and pleasant by claiming that what he did was proper. For the upright, however, only a good deed is sweet and pleasant. [Good deeds are called רָצוֹן, *desire*, for they are the desire of the just.]

10. לֵב יוֹדֵעַ מָרַת נַפְשׁוֹ וּבְשִׂמְחָתוֹ לֹא-יִתְעָרַב זָר — *A heart knows its own bitterness, and no stranger will share in its joy.* No outsider can fathom the depth of a heart's sorrow, nor can he measure its joy (*R' Hirsch*).

A person's own heart knows his toil and labor for Torah. Therefore, when he

receives his reward in the future, no stranger will share his reward. The verse also alludes to the Jewish people, who have suffered the bitterness of exile and accept death for the sanctification of God's Name. In the future, therefore, when they achieve their time of happiness, no stranger will have a share in it (*Rashi*).

According to the *Vilna Gaon*, when a person teaches Torah to others, he should not feel that he is giving away the fruit of his exertion to someone who did not work hard at it, but who will be equally rewarded for it. This is not so. Only the person who endured hardship for the sake of Torah will be rewarded for his toil; no outsider will share it (cf. יִהְיוּ לְךָ לְבַדֶּךָ 5:17).

According to *Meiri*, this verse advises a person who is plagued by adversity to try to strengthen himself and conceal his suffering from others. [*Chovos Halevavos* describes a pious person as one "whose joy is on his face and whose grief is in his heart."] In the same vein, when he merits financial success or acquires wealth, he should neither publicize it nor draw unnecessary attention to his status; he should handle his affairs with privacy and modesty. Thus, as far as is possible, לֵב, only *his own heart* should know the bitterness of his soul. Similarly, *in his joy* he should also refrain from publicizing his affairs to others, for the more something is well known, the greater the chance that it will cause harm. As our Sages have taught: אֵין הַבְּרָכָה מְצוּיָה אֶלָּא בַּדָּבָר הַסָּמוּי מִן הָעַיִן, *Blessing is not found except in something that is hidden from the eye* (*Taanis* 8b).

Excessive happiness can cause transgression, for Satan immediately intervenes and influences the person to sin (see *Job* 1:5 regarding Job's offerings to atone for his sons, so they would not sin in their happiness.) However, לֵב יוֹדֵעַ מָרַת נַפְשׁוֹ, *if a person's heart* constantly *knows the*

but [HASHEM's] favor is among the upright. ¹⁰ A heart knows its own bitterness, and no stranger will share in its joy. ¹¹ The house of the wicked will be destroyed, but the tent of the upright will blossom. ¹² There is a way that seems right to a man, but its end are the ways of death;

bitterness of his soul, i.e., the sins that defiled his soul, then even when he is happy, his joy will not be excessive. Therefore, a זָר, *stranger,* which refers to Satan, will not intervene in his happiness and cause him to sin, for a person who constantly keeps his transgressions in mind has achieved a high level of repentance (*Alshich*).

The Sages (*Yoma* 83a) refer to this verse when ruling about a sick person who may have to eat on Yom Kippur. In ruling on whether a sick person must eat on Yom Kippur, a rabbi must give serious consideration to the patient's assessment of his own condition, for he *knows the bitterness of his soul.*

11. בֵּית רְשָׁעִים יִשָּׁמֵד — *The house of the wicked will be destroyed.* Even though their house is a strong edifice, it will be destroyed, for God will not protect it from misfortune. The wicked person himself brings great misfortune upon himself as a result of his wicked deeds (*Ralbag*).

וְאֹהֶל יְשָׁרִים יַפְרִיחַ — *But the tent of the upright will blossom.* The righteous do not desire houses as do the wicked. They scorn the desires and lusts of the world and prefer to dwell in modest homes, like

tents. God will establish these righteous people like a flourishing tree (*Ibn Ezra*).

This world is the בַּיִת, *permanent home,* of the wicked, for it is of primary importance to them, but it will be destroyed. To the righteous, however, this world is just an אֹהֶל, *a tent,* i.e., a temporary abode; nevertheless, it will flourish (*Vilna Gaon;* cf. 3:33).

12. יֵשׁ דֶּרֶךְ יָשָׁר לִפְנֵי־אִישׁ וְאַחֲרִיתָהּ דַּרְכֵי־מָוֶת — *There is a way that seems right to a man, but its end are the ways of death.* He commits a sin and says, "There is no transgression involved" (*Rashi*).

The way seems straight to the person but it ends up being one of the ways of death (*Metzudos*).[1]

A person may assume that the way before him is דֶּרֶךְ יָשָׁר, a single straight way. Ultimately, however, it turns out that this way branches out into many ways, all of which lead to death (דַּרְכֵי־מָוֶת). Therefore, a person must be very cautious and search out the proper way, for what appears to him to be certainly straight may in reality lead to death. This is true even of an אִישׁ, *a Torah scholar* (אִישׁ denotes a man of importance), who must also be wary and not rely on his own reasoning (*Vilna Gaon*).[2]

---

1. *Baal HaTurim* (*Numbers* 31:8) quotes this verse in reference to Balaam. The first letters of the words יֵשׁ דֶּרֶךְ יָשָׁר have the numerical value of 24 (10 + 4 + 10). The final letters of these words (ש - כ - ר) form the word שָׂכָר, *reward.* Balaam came to Midian to claim שָׂכָר, *reward,* for the twenty-four thousand Jews who had been killed as a result of his advice; yet the consequence was his own way of death, for he was slaughtered when Israel waged war against Midian.

2. The Midrash applies the words *There is a way that seems right* to Aaron, who was commanded to bring offerings on the eighth day of the inauguration of the Tabernacle (*Leviticus* 9:2), and was praised for it. *But its end are ways of death* refers to Nadab and Abihu, who brought an unbidden incense offering in the Tabernacle and died (*Leviticus* 10:1-2). This is comparable to a king who asked a member of his household to bring him food. The person brought the food to the king, and the king enjoyed it. When others saw that the king enjoyed the food, they also brought him bowls of food. The king was angered and commanded, "Those who brought food without permission are to be punished." So, too, Nadab and Abihu meant to please God, but they were punished for bringing their own incense without Divine permission. [Thus what may seem logically correct and pleasing may actually be a punishable offense] (*Yalkut Shimoni*).

יג גַּם־בִּשְׂחוֹק יִכְאַב־לֵב וְאַחֲרִיתָהּ שִׂמְחָה תוּגָה:
יד מִדְּרָכָיו יִשְׂבַּע סוּג לֵב וּמֵעָלָיו אִישׁ טוֹב:
טו פֶּתִי יַאֲמִין לְכָל־דָּבָר וְעָרוּם יָבִין לַאֲשֻׁרוֹ:

God presents a person with a choice of two paths. One seems smooth and straight to the beholder, but winds up being full of thorns, pits and obstacles. The second is initially narrow and covered with thorns, but it turns into a beautifully landscaped path. Similarly, each person is presented with two options in this world. He is either attracted to physical pleasures and temptations, which eventually lead to sin and *Gehinnom*; or, he may ignore these temporal delights and dedicate himself to amassing treasures for the Hereafter. A person can easily be fooled into choosing the former way, for it appears to be straight. However, he must distance himself from it, for it branches into a multitude of ways — i.e., many sins, such as robbery and adultery — which will bring him to his ultimate death in *Gehinnom* (*Alshich*; cf. 4:18-19). See *Daas Zekeinim MiBaalei Tosafos*, to *Deuteronomy* 11:27.

13. גַּם־בִּשְׂחוֹק יִכְאַב־לֵב וְאַחֲרִיתָהּ שִׂמְחָה תוּגָה — *Even in sporting the heart may ache, and the end of joy may be sorrow.* Even excessive laughter will grieve the heart; for although one may not have directly committed a transgression, one has sinned by turning his heart to idleness. Thus, ultimately his joy will turn to sorrow (*Metzudos*).

Laughter and empty merrymaking are dangerous pastimes, for they make the person prey for serious transgressions, as the Sages said, *Mockery and levity accustom a man to immorality* (*Avos* 3:17).

The Sages teach that it is forbidden for a person to fill his mouth with laughter in this world, i.e., to experience unadulterated merriment, for the verse states (*Psalms* 126:2), אָז יִמָּלֵא שְׂחוֹק פִּינוּ, *Then* [only in the future, when there is a general recognition of God's love for Israel] *our mouth will be filled with laughter* (*Berachos* 31a).

One will never achieve true happiness through the pursuit of worldly pleasures. It can be attained through Torah study and the performance of commandments, as King

Solomon states, וְשִׁבַּחְתִּי אֲנִי אֶת־הַשִּׂמְחָה, *So I praised enjoyment* (*Ecclesiastes* 8:15), which our Sages explain as שִׂמְחָה שֶׁל מִצְוָה, *the joy of performing a mitzvah* (*Shabbos* 30b).

Though God may seem to revel with idol worshipers in this world and allow them to enjoy a happy life, their hearts will ache in the World to Come (*Rashi*).

The *Vilna Gaon* explains that a person does not have any true happiness in this world. What greater joy does a parent have than his children? Yet raising them involves very great suffering. The more the value of any joy, the more the grief that can result from it; for if something should mar the source of this joy, the resulting grief is felt all the more keenly. *Sporting* is of even less value than *gladness*, for at least at the time of *gladness* the person may feel completely happy, albeit temporarily, but even in the midst of *sporting*, one's heart may ache inwardly at the very same time. *The end of both sporting and gladness may be sorrow.*

This verse proves the previous one: That which a person considers good may actually be detrimental. The pleasures of this world may seem to bring laughter and happiness to people, but ultimately they may lead to heartache (*Sefer Halkarim*).

Alshich interprets this verse rather differently, connecting it to the previous one. Even in times of merriment, a righteous person's heart should ache to a degree, so that giddiness will not lead to sin. In this way, he will avoid an end which is a way of death, and instead, אַחֲרִיתָהּ שִׂמְחָה תוּגָה, *joy will be the end of his grief*, for God will exchange his worry for tremendous joy.

14. מִדְּרָכָיו יִשְׂבַּע סוּג לֵב — *One with dross in his heart will be sated from his own ways*, for he will be repaid according to his actions (*Metzudos*).

The translation of סוּג לֵב as *one with*

¹³ *Even in sporting the heart may ache, and the end of joy may be sorrow.* ¹⁴ *One with dross in his heart will be sated from his own ways, but above him is a good man.* ¹⁵ *A simpleton believes anything, but a clever person understands his steps.*

dross in his heart follows *Rashi* and the *Vilna Gaon*, who explain that סוּג לֵב is a wicked person, relating סוּג to the word סִיג, *dross.* [סִיג is the dross and סוּג is the silver mixed with the dross (*Rashi*).]

Alternatively, סוּג לֵב is a *wayward heart*, a heart that turns away from God, relating the word סוּג to וְהֻסַּג אָחוֹר מִשְׁפָּט, *and justice was turned back* (Isaiah 59:14; *Metzudos*); or a heart which turns away from *reason* (*Meiri*).

וּמֵעָלָיו אִישׁ טוֹב — *But above him is a good man.* A righteous man will be superior to a wicked one (*Rashi*).

Ralbag renders that when a wicked person receives his retribution, a good person will separate himself from him [מֵעָלָיו] in order not to be punished together with him. *Meiri* cites the example of Korach and his followers, about whom Moses warned, *turn away please, from upon the tents of these wicked people* (Numbers 16:26), lest you perish because of their sins.

R' Yonah explains that סוּג לֵב is one who stubbornly clings to his own opinions and refuses to consider those of others. He never stops to think that he may be mistaken, for he consults with no one but himself. He is always *satisfied with his own ways* (יִשְׂבַּע מִדְּרָכָיו); he never sees his shortcomings; he never takes advice or heeds the counsel of others who may point out flaws in his thinking. Such a person makes snap decisions without weighing or analyzing his course of action. An אִישׁ טוֹב, *a good man*, on the other hand, is not stubborn. He readily listens to others. He will distance himself from the company of stubborn people, in order to avoid arousing their hatred, for they will resent any advice he gives them. *Ibn Ezra* and the *Vilna Gaon* render this phrase quite differently, explaining מֵעָלָיו as *from his leaves* (עָלָיו being derived from עָלֶה, a *leaf*).

The *Vilna Gaon* explains that a righteous person who does good to others is rewarded with the *fruits* of his good deeds, in this world (see *Isaiah* 3:10) [while the קֶרֶן, *principal*, is stored for the World to Come]. Whenever possible, even the "fruits" are stored away to be enjoyed with the principal in the World to Come, for even the smallest reward in the Hereafter is immeasurably greater than any good in this world. Consequently, in this world a righteous person partakes only "from his leaves." On the other hand, a wicked person has earned no "fruits" at all. When he is rewarded in this world for his occasional good deeds, he takes the entire reward, leaving nothing for the Hereafter. Hence, a wicked person will be sated מִדְּרָכָיו, *from his [entire] ways,* i.e., from the קֶרֶן, *the principal part,* of the reward.

R' Hirsch summarizes the message of the last few verses: Anything based on mere external gratification collapses and crumbles, just as material prosperity is itself transitory. The contentment of a righteous individual stems from inner, Divinely blessed roots. The evil actions of a wicked person are his own enemy; though he seems to enjoy his activities, he proceeds to destruction and ruin. A person whose heart is not morally sound looks for satisfaction only in attaining exterior goals, while a good person seeks fulfillment in his internal achievements.

15. פֶּתִי יַאֲמִין לְכָל־דָּבָר וְעָרוּם יָבִין לַאֲשֻׁרוֹ — *A simpleton believes anything, but a clever person understands his steps.* A credulous person believes talebearers. A clever person, however, refrains from reacting and waits until the truth of the matter has been determined (*Rashi*).

אֲשֻׁרוֹ literally means *his steps* (*Rashi*); he understands which is the proper path (*Vilna Gaon*).

A credulous person can be convinced to

חָכָם יָרֵא וְסָר מֵרָע וּכְסִיל מִתְעַבֵּר וּבוֹטֵחַ: קְצַר־ טז-יט

יח אַפַּיִם יַעֲשֶׂה אִוֶּלֶת וְאִישׁ מְזִמּוֹת יִשָּׂנֵא: נָחֲלוּ פְתָאיִם

יט אִוֶּלֶת וַעֲרוּמִים יַכְתִּרוּ דָעַת: שַׁחוּ רָעִים לִפְנֵי טוֹבִים

do anything, since he does not analyze the situation to see if it is fitting to do the action or not. A clever person, on the other hand, understands what should be done and how to go about it (*Ralbag*). An intelligent person should be discriminating about what he believes (*Meiri*).

A credulous person believes his Evil Inclination as it attempts to persuade him, "You can sin, for the Holy One, Blessed is He, will forgive you" (see *Chagigah* 16a). He does not think about the consequences of his actions. A shrewd person, on the other hand, who understands the shrewdness of the Evil Inclination, does not believe its claims that it is a *mitzvah* to do such and such action. He has an innate understanding of right and wrong, and he carefully weighs his course (*Vilna Gaon*).

While a gullible person believes the wicked indiscriminately, the shrewd person tests and assesses everything to see if it will be for his spiritual benefit. Thus, *the wisdom of a shrewd person is to understand his way* (14:8); *and every clever person acts with knowledge* (13:16) (*Malbim*).

The cleverness inherent in the shrewd person is his astute observation of everything going on around him and his monitoring of his own steps (*R' Hirsch*).

16. חָכָם יָרֵא וְסָר מֵרָע — *A wise man fears and turns away from evil.* A wise man fears punishment and turns away from the evil (*Rashi*).

He fears that which is theatening and takes precautions to protect himself (*Ralbag*).

וּכְסִיל מִתְעַבֵּר וּבוֹטֵחַ — *But a fool becomes enraged and is confident.* The translation follows *Ralbag*, who explains: A fool becomes enraged [מִתְעַבֵּר from עֶבְרָה, *rage*] and provokes the one whom he should fear. He is confident that no bad will befall him from this, but in reality impetuosity brings him much harm.

R' Yonah explains: A wise man turns away from evil with all his might, but still fears that he has fallen short of his obligation. [This follows the Midrashic interpretation, which renders the verse: חָכָם וְסָר מֵרָע יָרֵא, *a wise man, while turning away from evil, fears.* See *Tanchuma Lech Lecha* 15].[1] On the other hand, even though a fool draws nearer to evil, he is confident that he will not sin and that his way is pure. In particular the negative trait of anger is mentioned because it causes fights, hatred and much harm, and yet a fool remains confident and is not apprehensive that any harm or sin will result.

According to *Rashi*, a fool strengthens himself to *transgress* [מִתְעַבֵּר], but he *slips and falls* [בוֹטֵחַ] (as in *Jeremiah* 12:5). *Rashi* also offers a second explanation: A fool בוֹטֵחַ, *trusts*; he is complacent, confident that no harm will befall him. Or, explains the *Vilna Gaon*, after sinning, he erroneously trusts that God will forgive him (see *Chagigah* 16a אַל תִּבְטְחוּ בְאָלוּף).

17. קְצַר־אַפַּיִם יַעֲשֶׂה אִוֶּלֶת — *A short-tempered person acts foolishly.* A short-tempered person rushes to seek revenge (*Rashi*).

וְאִישׁ מְזִמּוֹת יִשָּׂנֵא — *And a person of evil designs will be hated.* Examples of מְזִמּוֹת,

1. Careful scrutiny and meticulous self-evaluation is characteristic of the righteous. The Talmud recounts the righteousness of King Josiah. Fearing that he may have erred in his verdicts during his early years as monarch (from the age of eight until the age of eighteen), he used his own funds to repay any monies he had made the guilty parties pay in each case (*Shabbos* 56b).

This meticulousness in judgment was emulated by many Torah scholars. Before the Brisker Rav died, he called his son, R' Berel and להבחל"ח, Rabbi Eliezer Menachem Schach, and reviewed the decisions and positions he had taken during his lifetime, so that they could scrutinize them and tell him if in their opinion, he had acted properly.

¹⁶ *A wise man fears and turns away from evil, but a fool becomes enraged and is confident.* ¹⁷ *A short-tempered person acts foolishly, and a person of evil designs will be hated.* ¹⁸ *Simpletons have inherited folly, but the shrewd make knowledge a crown.* ¹⁹ *Evildoers will grovel before good people,*

evil designs, include seeking evil, hatred, gloating over someone else's misfortune, arrogance, choosing evil and refuting good. All these are the harmful consequences of anger (v. 16). (*R' Yonah*).

According to *Metzudos*, אִישׁ מְזִמּוֹת is a *capricious person*, who follows the thoughts of his heart without considering whether they are good or bad. Such a person will be hated by both God and man.

Ralbag explains that the two halves of this verse describe two opposite traits. A קְצַר־אַפַּיִם [which literally means quick of desire or endeavor, *R' Hirsch*] is one who acts impulsively, analyzing matters hastily and superficially. On the other hand, an אִישׁ מְזִמּוֹת, *a person of many thoughts,* deliberates endlessly before acting. He will be hated by others, for only after much hardship and strenuous effort will they be able to get him to fulfill their requests. A person who spends so much time pondering and analyzing becomes confused and is not able to take action, even in his own best interests. [See *Ecclesiastes* 11:4: *One who watches the wind will never sow, and one who keeps his eyes on the clouds will never reap.*] Therefore, a person must be careful neither to act too hastily nor to excessively prolong his deliberations.

18. נָחֲלוּ פְתָאיִם אִוֶּלֶת — *Simpletons have inherited folly.* Foolishness is their inheritance (*Ibn Ezra*), because they accept the words of fools and skeptics indiscriminately, as an heir would accept an inheritance (*Malbim*).

They hold on to their foolishness like a person holds on to an inheritance (*Metzudos*).

וַעֲרוּמִים יַכְתִּרוּ דָעַת — *But the shrewd make knowledge a crown* for their heads (*Rashi*). Wise people hold on to knowledge, making it a crown on their heads, and glorifying themselves with it (*Metzu-*

dos).

R' Yonah offers an alternate explanation. Shrewd people place a crown of glory upon wisdom, for their wise demeanor makes wisdom beloved to others. *Meiri* adds that when people see the actions of the wise, they praise wisdom and knowledge, as noted in the Talmud (*Yoma* 86a): When an individual conducts himself with propriety, people say of him, "How fortunate is his father who taught him Torah! How fortunate is his teacher who taught him Torah!... See how pleasant are his ways, how correct are his actions."

R' Hirsch looks at the previous four verses as one unit. An individual who does not think independently is dependent upon others. One with a clear mind is capable of evaluating his duties according to the reality of the moment — weighing and judging each action before he takes it. A person who possesses true wisdom does not have unlimited confidence in his own recognition of right, but a conceited fool is overconfident and oversteps his bounds. King Solomon advises us not to exaggerate to either extreme in matters of judgment and decision making. Combining a lucid mind with knowledge and comprehension is the successful prescription which will yield man the crowning achievement of recognition for the true wisdom of the spirit.

19. שַׁחוּ רָעִים לִפְנֵי טוֹבִים — *Evildoers will grovel before good people.* Both *Rashi* and *Ibn Ezra* see this verse as a continuation of the previous one. The wise will make knowledge a crown for their heads and eventually, in the future, evildoers will grovel before good people (*Rashi*). The *evildoers* are the *simpletons* of the previous verse, whereas *good people* are the aforementioned *shrewd people.* The good people will attain the crown of knowledge and achieve greatness, and, consequently,

כ וּרְשָׁעִים עַל־שַׁעֲרֵי צַדִּיק: גַּם־לְרֵעֵהוּ יִשָּׂנֵא רָשׁ וְאֹהֲבֵי
כא עָשִׁיר רַבִּים: בָּז־לְרֵעֵהוּ חוֹטֵא וּמְחוֹנֵן °עֲנִיִּים אַשְׁרָיו:
כב הֲלוֹא־יִתְעוּ חֹרְשֵׁי רָע וְחֶסֶד וֶאֱמֶת חֹרְשֵׁי טוֹב:
כג בְּכָל־עֶצֶב יִהְיֶה מוֹתָר וּדְבַר־שְׂפָתַיִם אַךְ־לְמַחְסוֹר:

°עֲנָוִים ק

fools will be subordinate to them (*Ibn Ezra*).

R' Yonah explains that לִפְנֵי טוֹבִים means בְּעֵינֵי טוֹבִים, *in the eyes of the good people.* Although the wicked are successful in this world and are accorded honor by many, they are despised in the eyes of the righteous.

וּרְשָׁעִים עַל־שַׁעֲרֵי צַדִּיק — *And the wicked at the gates of a righteous one.* Ultimately the wicked will have to come beg for bread at the gates of the righteous (*Metzudos*).

Malbim explains that even though evil opposes good, once a wicked person comes into the presence of a righteous person, he will submit to the latter. Evil will eventually give way to good, just as darkness gives way to light.

20. גַּם־לְרֵעֵהוּ יִשָּׂנֵא רָשׁ — *A poor person will be hated even by his fellow.* This refers to one ignorant in Torah, who does not know how to act properly (*Rashi*; cf. 19:7).

וְאֹהֲבֵי עָשִׁיר רַבִּים — *But the lovers of a rich man are many.* Both the poor and the rich are friends of the rich man (*Metzudos*).

A rich person does not only retain his old friends, but continues to acquire new ones (*Meiri*) (cf. 19:4, *Wealth adds many friends.*)[1]

Even though people tend to be friends with people in similar circumstances, the rich man and the pauper are exceptions to this rule. A poor person is hated even by רֵעֵהוּ, *his fellow pauper,* whereas the rich man is beloved by the poor, though they

are not his equals (*Alshich*).

A Torah scholar is beloved by all, for everyone glories in him (*Vilna Gaon*).

21. בָּז־לְרֵעֵהוּ חוֹטֵא — *He who scorns his fellow is a sinner.* This verse is connected to the previous one. It is wrong for the rich man to scorn the poor man, even though the rich have many friends and the poor are hated even by their companions (*R' Yonah*).

Alshich points out that this verse does not refer to one who verbally embarrasses his friend, for it is understood that such an action is sinful. Furthermore, the verse would then have used the transitive verb form, מְבַזֶּה. Rather, the verse means that he scorns him in his heart and looks down on him. Such a person is a sinner, for he has already transgressed the commandment of וְאָהַבְתָּ לְרֵעֲךָ כָּמוֹךָ, *You shall love your fellow as yourself* (*Leviticus* 19:18).

Vilna Gaon renders חוֹטֵא as *missing.* One who scorns a friend will lose him as a friend.

וּמְחוֹנֵן עֲנָוִים אַשְׁרָיו — *But praiseworthy is one is who is gracious to the humble.* Humble refers to those who are poor and lowly (*Meiri*).

R' Yonah explains the difference between חוֹנֵן and מְחוֹנֵן: חוֹנֵן refers to one who shows favor and is merciful to another; מְחוֹנֵן refers to one who makes an effort to think favorably of someone. The verse is praising a person who refuses to scorn the poor, for he recognizes the virtue of their humility.[2] The natural tendency of people is to agree that piety and humility are more

---

1. The Torah alludes to this when Jacob declares to Esau, *I have acquired oxen and donkeys, flocks, servants and maidservants* (*Genesis* 32:6). Jacob was thus describing his great wealth, and riches bring friends (*Likutei Yehudah*). This theme also appears in the Talmud, as Rav Papa taught: "At the gate of the shop (where many things may be obtained), there are many brothers and friends; at the gate where there is loss (where one must pay or at a toll gate), there are neither brothers nor friends" (*Shabbos* 32a).

2. This is why the word עֲנָוִים, humble, in this verse, is spelled עֲנִיִּים, poor (*R' Yonah*).

and the wicked at the gates of a righteous one. [20] *A poor person will be hated even by his fellow, but the lovers of a rich man are many.* [21] *He who scorns his fellow is a sinner, but praiseworthy is one who is gracious to the humble.* [22] *Will the plotters of evil not go astray? But those who plan goodness [will reap] kindness and truth.* [23] *In all toil there will be gain, but talk of the lips brings only loss.*

important than wealth and honor, but all the same, since a poor person is looked down upon by others, most people will not accord him the respect he deserves. On the other hand, someone who knows the value of humility and how pleasing it is to God, and will therefore uplift and honor the poor person despite his poverty, and will look upon him favorably, is truly deserving of the accolade אַשְׁרָיו, *he is praiseworthy.*

According to the *Vilna Gaon,* מְחוֹנֵן means *he makes others act favorably of the humble.*

R' Hirsch renders אַשְׁרָיו as *he strides towards happiness.*

22. הֲלוֹא יִתְעוּ חֹרְשֵׁי רָע — *Will the plotters* [lit. *plowers*] *of evil not go astray?* One who causes his friend to sin will ultimately stumble and sin as well (*R' Yonah*).

The *Vilna Gaon* explains that an individual who plots evil against his friend will himself stray and fall in that very evil. Such was the case with Haman, whose evil plots against the Jews and against Mordechai backfired upon himself.

וְחֶסֶד וֶאֱמֶת חֹרְשֵׁי טוֹב — *But those who plan goodness [will reap] kindness and truth.* Truth refers to repayment in exact accordance with one's action, and *kindness* refers to an additional, extra payment (cf. 3:3, *Vilna Gaon's* explanation of חֶסֶד and אֱמֶת). Those who constantly seek to do good will be repaid by God not only with exact recompense [*truth*], but with even more [*kindness*]. Also, the Talmud (*Berachos* 6a) explains that if a person wished to perform a *mitzvah,* but was prevented from doing so, he is credited as if he had done it. In such a case, God rewards the individual both for the good intention and

the good deed, because God reckons the sincere desire to do good as if it had been carried out (*Vilna Gaon*). Thus, Hashem rewards those who plan to do good with both *truth* [i.e., for the good intention] and *kindness* [i.e., for the deed, though it never came to fruition].

According to *Malbim,* "plowing" connotes scheming or acting secretly. When one strays off the road in the presence of others, they can redirect him unto the correct path. However, those who secretly scheme to do evil will go astray, for there is no one to see and correct them. On the other hand, those who are secretive about their *good* actions do so in order to avoid public adulation, shunning all recognition and reward. They are inspired by *kindness* and *truth* — because they acted without thought of reward or praise.

Those who plot against others are in error. They plan harm for others, but it will befall them. However, those who eagerly seek another's welfare will themselves be treated with *kindness,* and their good plans for others will be realized, i.e., *truth* (*Metzudos*).

23. בְּכָל־עֶצֶב יִהְיֶה מוֹתָר וּדְבַר־שְׂפָתַיִם אַךְ־לְמַחְסוֹר — *In all toil there will be gain, but talk of the lips brings only loss.* In all toil there will be a gain, but empty words cause only a loss (*Rashi*).

This verse points out the importance of זְרִיזוּת, *alacrity.* Any toil which a person invests, whether in wisdom or labor, is beneficial (*R' Yonah*). Even if he earns nothing from this toil, he still gains from it because he did not sit idle, and idleness causes depression and disintegration. On the other hand, frittering away the day with idle talk always causes a loss, for *In an abundance of talk, transgression*

כד עֲטֶרֶת חֲכָמִים עָשְׁרָם אִוֶּלֶת כְּסִילִים אִוֶּלֶת:
כה מַצִּיל נְפָשׁוֹת עֵד אֱמֶת וְיָפִחַ כְּזָבִים מִרְמָה:
כו בְּיִרְאַת יהוה מִבְטַח־עֹז וּלְבָנָיו יִהְיֶה מַחְסֶה:

will not be lacking (10:19) (*Talmidei R' Yonah*).

This is also true with regard to Torah and good deeds. When a person attempts to perform a *mitzvah* without delay, as soon as the opportunity arises, he will realize a gain. However, if someone speaks of doing a *mitzvah* at some later time [or if he boasts about the deed he plans to do, attributing it to his own abilities instead of to God (*R' Yonah*)], he incurs a loss. Such chatter causes his plans to be nullified, and his good intentions never materialize (see *Sanhedrin* 26b, ספר מחשבות ערומים, second explanation *Rashi* ad loc.) (*Vilna Gaon*).

The word עֶצֶב can also be rendered as *sorrow*. There is a benefit in sorrow, for it restrains one from being overly joyful and attracted to the pleasures of this world. This does not mean that a person should try to be sad, for sorrow is like an illness that hampers a person's proper service of God. The ideal is that a person should be neither joyful nor sad, but rather, achieve an even balance between the two (*Talmidei R' Yonah*).

According to *Malbim*, this verse describes one's reaction when beset with misfortune. A person should feel sorrow in his heart for the sins that caused this suffering, and he should repent. In this way, the *sorrow* will bring a *gain*. However, if he expresses his sorrow only with his lips, i.e., he complains about the misfortune without doing anything to improve himself, then it will only cause him loss. After the death of his two sons, Aaron was silent (*Leviticus* 10:3), and for this silence he was rewarded (see *Rashi* ibid.). Similarly, our Sages explain (*Berachos* 6b) that mourners are rewarded for their silence. [The mourning period is to enable the bereaved to contemplate their loss and return to God.] A person will be rewarded for the investment of any toil and sorrow in order to

attain higher spiritual levels, especially if he keeps quiet and does not publicize his acts of special piety to others. For if he speaks about it with others, he detracts from the perfection of his deed and stands to lose all (*Binah L'Ittim*).

24. עֲטֶרֶת חֲכָמִים עָשְׁרָם — *The crown of the wise is their wealth.* Wise people become glorified when they attain wealth, for it reveals their benevolence to all, as they use this wealth generously and willingly to help the poor (*Metzudos*).

Wise people benefit from their wealth because it gives them the freedom to study and contemplate wisdom (*Ralbag*).

The crown of the wise is that they are wealthy in Torah (*Rashi*).

אִוֶּלֶת כְּסִילִים אִוֶּלֶת — *But the foolishness of fools is but foolishness.* Their foolish deeds reveal the folly in their hearts. Since all their actions are foolish, it is obvious that even more folly is embedded in their hearts and will be revealed as soon as the occasion arises (*Metzudos*).

Their folly cannot be remedied by wealth, for wealth cannot remove their foolishness (*Ibn Ezra*).

The ruination of fools is that they were too lazy to study wisdom (*Rashi*).

R' Yonah treats *their wealth* as the subject of the second half of the verse also, rendering it: *[and] the wealth of fools is their folly.* [The word אִוֶּלֶת is repeated to strengthen the statement.] Wealth is both a crown for *the wise*, who use it well, and a prime cause of foolish behavior for *fools*. If a Torah scholar is poor, then his wisdom may be scorned and his words disregarded, but when the wise attain wealth, they have the power to inspire more fear of God in the world — to weaken the wicked and strengthen the power of truth. Should fools become wealthy, they become haughty, and people begin respecting them and emulating their ways. Wealth

²⁴ *The crown of the wise is their wealth; but the foolishness of fools is but foolishness.* ²⁵ *A truthful witness saves souls, but one who spouts deceptions [is a man of] deceit.* ²⁶ *In fear of HASHEM is a powerful stronghold, and for his children it will be a refuge;*

also enables them to sin and transgress to their heart's content.

R' Bachya compares this to the light of the sun, which causes two opposite results: It bleaches the laundry but it darkens the face of the launderer, for the effect of sunlight depends on the nature of the recipient. So, too, wealth is a crown to one type of person but folly to another. The word אִוֶּלֶת, *folly*, is repeated twice to show that wealth in a fool's hand is doubly evil — it is detrimental to his body and destructive to his soul. A wise man, on the other hand, is careful lest wealth lead him astray. He uses it to benefit both body and soul, for he realizes that the true function of wealth is to enable the soul to attain wisdom.

25. מַצִּיל נְפָשׁוֹת עֵד אֱמֶת — *A truthful witness saves souls.* A truthful witness saves lives, for if he testifies against a murderer who deserves to be put to death, he saves potential victims. And if he testifies that the accused is not guilty, then he saves the life of the defendant (*Metzudos*).

A truthful witness saves two souls: the victim from the robber, and the robber from the punishment of *Gehinnom.* Saving the robber is even greater than saving his victim, for the latter recoups only his money, while the former regains his soul. The Talmud explains that when the court orders a person's garment to be taken from him [in order to pay back what he owes another], the defendant should sing for joy. [Since this was a true judgment, he did not lose anything; only the object to which he was not entitled was taken from him (*Sanhedrin* 7a, *Rashi* ad loc.).] He was thereby redeemed from the sin of robbery.[1] Moreover, a truthful witness saves

the souls of both the robber and his victim from additional suffering after death. If someone robbed a victim and did not return the item while both were still alive, then both souls must return to this world in a גִּלְגּוּל, *transmigration of souls* (*Vilna Gaon*).

וְיָפֵחַ כְּזָבִים מִרְמָה — *But one who spouts deceptions [is a man of] deceit.* A witness who is accustomed to lying is a person of deceit (*Ibn Ezra*).

Ralbag renders: A person of deceit will testify falsely, thus causing lives to be destroyed.

According to *Metzudos*, one who spouts deceptions "saves" the *person of deceit,* by helping him with false testimony.

26. בְּיִרְאַת ה' מִבְטַח־עֹז וּלְבָנָיו יִהְיֶה מַחְסֶה — *In fear of HASHEM is a powerful stronghold, and for his children it will be a refuge.* A person's fear of God provides him with strength, as well as a refuge for his children, who will be protected in his merit (*Metzudos*). God said of Abraham, *for now I know that you are a God-fearing man,* and then promised him *for I will surely bless you* and your offspring (*Genesis* 22:12,17, see *Rashi* ad loc.) (*Rashi*). Thus, Abraham's fear of God was the reason for the Divine blessing to both him and his offspring.

Ibn Ezra and *Ralbag* explain יִהְיֶה as *He will be;* i.e., God will be a refuge for the children of the God fearing, and protect them from all ills in the merit of their parents.

The *Vilna Gaon* explains that there are two aspects to בִּטָּחוֹן, *trust.* One is when God promises to bring specific benefits to

1. King David is described as עֹשֶׂה מִשְׁפָּט וּצְדָקָה לְכָל־עַמּוֹ, *administering justice and charity to his whole people* (II Samuel 8:15). The terms seem contradictory, for *justice* implies strict dispensation of the law while *charity* implies leniency. The Sages explain that David meted out justice to one litigant and charity to the other; i.e., justice to the victim by returning the money that was stolen from him and charity to the robber by removing the stolen goods from his possession (*Sanhedrin* 6b).

כז יִרְאַ֣ת יְהוָ֭ה מְק֣וֹר חַיִּ֑ים לָ֝ס֗וּר מִמֹּ֥קְשֵׁי מָֽוֶת׃
כח בְּרׇב־עָ֥ם הַדְרַת־מֶ֑לֶךְ וּבְאֶ֥פֶס לְ֝אֹ֗ם מְחִתַּ֥ת רָזֽוֹן׃
כט אֶ֣רֶךְ אַ֭פַּיִם רַב־תְּבוּנָ֑ה וּקְצַר־ר֝֗וּחַ מֵרִ֥ים אִוֶּֽלֶת׃

individuals, such as His promise to enrich Abraham (*Genesis* 12:2). Another aspect of trust is when God does not make a promise, but an individual places trust in Him. This is called חִסָּיוֹן, *taking refuge*, as we find in the verse, צוּר חָסָיוּ בוֹ, *the rock in whom whey sought refuge* (*Deuteronomy* 32:37). A rock shelters a person even though the rock never promised to protect him. This is the meaning of the verse, טוב לַחֲסוֹת בַּה׳ מִבְּטֹחַ בָּאָדָם, *It is better to take refuge in HASHEM than to trust in man* (*Psalms* 118:9), i.e., it is better for a person to throw his burden on God even though He did not specifically promise to help him than to put his trust in a person who promised to help him. Our verse states that as a result of being God fearing, a person will reach the point where Hashem will promise to do good to him. Such a Divine promise is a *powerful stronghold*. Even *for his children*, who did not receive this Divine promise, God will be a *refuge* and protect them as well.

Malbim explains that wisdom without fear of God is not secure. Even when a person is learned, his wisdom is vulnerable to attack by his desires and temptations, which can lead him astray. Only when he possesses fear of God to restrain his natural impulses and to keep himself in check can he be sure that his wisdom will be secure. As the Sages taught, *Anyone whose fear of sin takes priority to his wisdom, his wisdom will endure* (*Avos* 3:11). Thus, with fear of God, he has *a powerful stronghold* for his wisdom, as well as a *refuge* for his children.

27. יִרְאַת ה׳ מְקוֹר חַיִּים לָסוּר מִמֹּקְשֵׁי מָוֶת — *Fear of HASHEM is the source of life, to turn one away from the snares of death*. Fear of God is the source from which eternal life emanates (*Meiri*).

Fear of God is the source of life, for fear of God results in wisdom, through which a person can attain eternal life (*Ralbag*).

Just as the force of the current in a flowing stream of water washes away all obstacles in its path, so, too, fear of God will remove all the snares of death from a person. Needless to say, if the snares of death are removed, then, certainly, fear of God will protect one from lesser pitfalls and other obstacles as well (*Alshich*).

Fear of God is the wellspring of life because it warns a person to turn away from sins and transgressions, which are the snares of death (*Metzudos*; cf. 13:14).

The *Vilna Gaon* explains that the previous verse refers to *mitzvos*, and this verse speaks about Torah. This is inferred from the first words of the respective verses. בְּיִרְאַת (verse 26) has the numerical value of תרי"ג (613), corresponding to the total number of *mitzvos*. יִרְאַת (verse 27) has the numeric value of Torah, תור"ה (611). *Mitzvos* relate to the physical body, while Torah relates to the soul. Therefore, verse 26 mentions *a trust*, and *a refuge*, for the body, whereas our verse speaks of a *wellspring of life*, for the soul.

28. בְּרׇב־עָם הַדְרַת־מֶלֶךְ — *In a multitude of people is a king's glory*. It is a king's splendor to have a multitude of people, for he will be able to strengthen himself with them against his enemies (*Ralbag*).

The splendor of the king is evident because of the multitude of people who are with him (*Metzudos*).

וּבְאֶפֶס לְאֹם מְחִתַּת רָזוֹן — *But without a nation, rulership is broken*. If a ruler does not have the loyalty of his subjects, it will bring him ruination. It is very likely that he has no nation because he lacks fear of God (*Ibn Ezra*).

R' Yonah connects this verse to the previous one. One who is God fearing is much more secure and tranquil than a king, for a God-fearing person does not place his trust in people, whereas a mortal king puts his trust in his subjects, for his splendor depends on them.

[27] *fear of HASHEM is the source of life, to turn one away from the snares of death.* [28] *In a multitude of people is a king's glory, but without a nation, rulership is broken.* [29] *Slowness to anger [shows] much understanding, but a quick-tempered person elevates foolishness.*

R' Bachya adds that this is why God did not want the Jewish people to have a mortal king. A nation places its trust in its king, and the trust of a king is in his nation; whereas all the trust and fear of Israel should rightfully be directed only to God.

Rashi explains that *King* is a metaphor for the Holy One, Blessed is He. When the multitude is righteous, that is God's splendor, but if the people do not cleave to Him, then it diminishes His majesty, for it appears as if He allow others to usurp his authority. *Metzudos* adds that it is God's splendor when a multitude of people perform a *mitzvah*.[1]

29. אֶרֶךְ אַפַּיִם רַב־תְּבוּנָה — *Slowness to anger [shows] much understanding.* Someone who does not get angry is very wise (*Vilna Gaon*).

וּקְצַר־רוּחַ מֵרִים אִוֶּלֶת — *But a quick-tempered person elevates foolishness.* He chooses folly as his lot (*Rashi*).

Meiri offers several explanations of the word מֵרִים. It can be related to the word תְּרוּמָה, the portion that was separated and given to the priest. Hence, in this verse, he separates for himself the portion of folly. It may also mean he reveals and publicizes foolishness; he elevates foolishness; or, he causes people to revolt (see *I Kings* 11:26 וַיָּרֶם יָד בַּמֶּלֶךְ). This verse is connected to

1. The Sages cite many examples illustrating the principle that it is a greater glory to Hashem when a multitude of people are involved in the performance of a *mitzvah*. This is true even in a case where the commandment can be performed just as well by an individual, or even when the multitudes are present merely as passive observers. The very fact that Jews have congregated to do His Will brings honor to God.

❑ The Talmud (*Succah* 52b) describes how a *Kohen*, the son of Marta bas Beisos, was able to carry two thighs of a large ox by himself to the Altar, but the other priests did not allow him to do so. They insisted that all the sacrificial parts of the ox be divided among twenty-four *Kohanim* to be brought to the Altar because *a multitude of people is the King's glory.*

❑ In the case of a large group of people in a study hall at the end of the Sabbath, all of whom must recite or hear *Havdalah*, the blessing marking the conclusion of the Sabbath, the academy of Hillel ruled that it is preferable that one person recite it on behalf of the entire group, so that the *mitzvah* should be performed by the entire group together (*Berachos* 53a).

❑ When the High Priest read a portion of the Torah in the Yom Kippur service, it was considered a *mitzvah* to be present among the many listeners (*Yoma* 70a).

❑ R' Yonah condemns those who separate themselves from the congregation for the service of God, for a large assemblage constitutes a sanctification of the Holy Name. Those who separate themselves profane the Divine service, scorn God's word and are included in the category of those who cause the public to sin (*Shaarei Teshuvah* 168).

❑ It is preferable to hear the *Megillah* read on Purim in a house of prayer, among a large assembly of people (*Mishnah Berurah* 690:62).

❑ Even though a person who studies Torah alone fulfills the commandment of Torah study, it is preferable to enhance the *mitzvah* by studying together with a group, for it is a greater sanctification of God's Name when many Jews gather together to serve Him (*Chafetz Chaim*).

The Midrash expounds on this concept. R' Chama bar Chanina says that this demonstrates the praise and greatness of God. For even though He has myriads of ministering angels to serve and praise Him, He desires the praises of Israel, for עָם, *people*, refers to the Nation of Israel. R' Shimon says that God's name is elevated in His world when Israel gathers together in houses of prayer and houses of Torah and expresses God's praise and greatness. R' Yishmael states that when Israel hears a Torah discourse and answers, אָמֵן יְהֵא שְׁמֵהּ רַבָּא מְבָרַךְ, *Amen, May His great Name be blessed* (in the *Kaddish* prayer), God is joyful. He says to His angels, "Come and see the nation I created — how much they praise Me" (*Yalkut Shimoni*).

ל חַיֵּי בְשָׂרִים לֵב מַרְפֵּא וּרְקַב עֲצָמוֹת קִנְאָה:
לא עֹשֵׁק דָּל חֵרֵף עֹשֵׂהוּ וּמְכַבְּדוֹ חֹנֵן אֶבְיוֹן:
לב בְּרָעָתוֹ יִדָּחֶה רָשָׁע וְחֹסֶה בְמוֹתוֹ צַדִּיק:

the previous one. It is in a king's interest to see to it that his nation loves him and is eager to do his will. A king who is slow to anger at his nation is a person of great understanding. However, if he angers quickly, he may cause the people to rebel.

Someone who gets angry not only acts foolishly, but also elevates his folly by publicizing it for all to hear (*Vilna Gaon*).

Someone who is quick to anger elevates *foolishness* above *understanding*, for his wisdom will leave him as a result of his anger. By becoming angry, he shows his preference for folly over wisdom (*Metzudos*).

R' Yonah explains how the trait of controlling one's anger leads to great understanding. If a person is slow to anger, he neither reacts immediately nor takes revenge. Instead he waits until he is calm and can consider the matter rationally. A quick-tempered person is not likely to analyze a matter thoroughly and weigh all possible angles of a question with seriousness and proper deliberation. He will act hastily, choosing the first option that comes to mind, with little regard for its propriety. When he encounters something that is initially hard to grasp, he immediately rejects it without delving into it. On the other hand, one who is slow to anger will be deliberate and level headed. He will listen and analyze an issue until he has fathomed its depths.

Anger and short-temperedness thus confuse the mind and prevent a person from penetrating the depths of an issue, as our Sages teach us, כָּל אָדָם שֶׁכּוֹעֵס, אִם חָכָם הוּא, חָכְמָתוֹ מִסְתַּלֶּקֶת מִמֶּנּוּ, *when a man becomes angry, if he is wise — all his wisdom departs from him* (*Pesachim* 66b).

Things always occur that may anger and upset a person. Therefore a person must try to uproot love of this world from his heart, so that he will not be unduly upset by its inevitable hardships, nor will he be excessively joyful in its pleasures. By purifying his heart from reacting angrily to the futilities of the world, he will be able to dedicate himself to seek wisdom and will attain great understanding.

Malbim differentiates between the two types of quick-tempered people: the קְצַר־אַפַּיִם of verse 17 and the קְצַר־רוּחַ of this verse. Verse 17 speaks of someone who immediately takes revenge against the person who angered him and he *acts foolishly* as a result. Our verse speaks of someone who appears calm externally, but inwardly seethes with resentment and plans to take revenge when the opportunity presents itself. Thus he *elevates foolishness* from the depth of his soul to occupy his thoughts.

30. חַיֵּי בְשָׂרִים לֵב מַרְפֵּא — *A tender heart is the life of the flesh.* A soft heart that can heal the bad and forgive wrongs is the life of Hashem's creations, who are flesh and blood [and must have that sort of sensitivity and compassion] (*Rashi*).

R' Yonah explains that a *healing heart* is patient and tolerant, and it heals both body and soul of anger and sorrow. It also heals others with its pleasant talk (see 15:1). While most medicines heal some limbs of the body but harm others, a tolerant heart brings life to *all* the limbs of the body [for בְשָׂרִים means אֵבָרִים, *limbs*].

Meiri renders לֵב מַרְפֵּא as *a soft heart*, deriving מַרְפֵּא from רִפְיוֹן, *weakness*.

An even temperament that accepts all things calmly produces a tranquil heart that heals both body and soul. Such a heart prolongs life and insures continued sustenance to all organs (*Rabbi Y. Z. Gustman*).

וּרְקַב עֲצָמוֹת קִנְאָה — *But envy [brings] rotting of the bones.* *R' Yonah* renders קִנְאָה as *envy*, explaining that *envy* will not only ruin a person's flesh, but even rot the strength of his עֲצָמוֹת, *bones*. The trait of envy is the opposite of *a healing heart*, for the former brings life to the limbs and the latter rots the bones.

R' Bachya elaborates on why לֵב מַרְפֵּא, *a*

³⁰ *A tender heart is the life of the flesh, but envy [brings]*
rotting of the bones. ³¹ *One who robs the poor disgraces his*
Maker, but one who is gracious to the destitute honors
Him. ³² *In his evil, a wicked one is cast off [from God], but he*
who takes shelter [in Him] remains righteous in death.

healing heart, and קִנְאָה, *envy,* are opposite traits. One who has a good heart and does not envy anyone will have a pleasant life, free of jealousy, strife and hatred. It will be חַיֵּי בְשָׂרִים, *the life of the flesh,* i.e., a source of healing to all his limbs. An envious person will constantly worry and strive to acquire what his friend has. If he succeeds in his quest, this will lead him to seek honor and power; and if he does not achieve his goal, his life will be miserable. His envy is compared to a rot of the *bones,* for rotting flesh can regenerate, but rotting bones are incurable, just as there is no cure for the trait of envy. Our Sages infer from this verse that the bones of an envious person will rot (after his death) (*Shabbos* 152b).

A person who is constantly angry rots everyone's bones (*Rashi*). The term קִנְאָה can refer to both *envy* ([וַתְּקַנֵּא רָחֵל], *and Rachel became envious of her sister* [*Genesis* 30:1]) and *anger* (יַקְנִאֻהוּ, *they angered Him with strange gods* [*Deuteronomy* 32:16]) (*Meiri*).

Someone who hardens his heart and harbors anger will cause his bones to rot because of his constant anxiety (*Metzudos*).

A cheerful disposition is a great treasure. It fosters health and helps people deal with adversity; conversely, envy is detrimental to health. Thus King Solomon praises the warm heart that does not begrudge others, brings optimism, brightens one's outlook and even keeps the body healthy. He decries the discontented, envious heart, which weakens the limbs and paralyzes activity (*R' Hirsch*).

31. עֹשֵׁק דָּל חֵרֵף עֹשֵׂהוּ — *One who robs the poor disgraces his Maker.* One who exploits a poor person shames God. He chose this particular victim because of his weakness, thinking that the One Who created him [and Who decreed his poverty (*Ibn Ezra*)] cannot come to his aid and save him from his exploiter (*Metzudos*).

וּמְכַבְּדוֹ חֹנֵן אֶבְיוֹן — *But one who is gracious to the destitute honors Him.* By showing kindness to a poor man, one honors the One Who created him (*Metzudos*).

One who gives to a poor man does not expect to be repaid by anyone except God; thus he gives honor to Him (*Ralbag*).

One who exploits a destitute person and withholds what is rightfully due him causes him to humiliate his Maker with complaints about his poverty. Thus one who supports a poor person brings honor to God by "making peace" between God and him, by quieting the pauper's complaints (*Vilna Gaon*).

The purpose of man's creation is for his good. Just as God provided all creatures with food and the means to attain it, so too, He has provided for man's needs. For those who find it hard to obtain their sustenance, and for destitute people who have no sustenance at all, God intended that people help one another. The דָּל, *poor man,* can work for the rich man and thereby earn wages; and the אֶבְיוֹן, *destitute* person, can receive charity from the rich. But if the employer does not pay his poor laborer he humiliates Hashem, for by withholding the wages he makes it seem as if Hashem created the poor without means of sustenance. On the other hand, one who gives charity to the destitute honors God, for it soon becomes apparent that the rich and the poor were both created for a reason: so that the rich can fulfill the *mitzvah* of giving *tzedakah* to the needy (*Malbim*).

R' Hirsch explains that not giving charity to the poor is עוֹשֶׁק, *denial of justice.* The word *tzedakah* [charity] has the connotation of צֶדֶק, *justice,* for the gift given the poor is really owed and rightfully due him.

32. בְּרָעָתוֹ יִדָּחֶה רָשָׁע וְחֹסֶה בְמוֹתוֹ צַדִּיק — *In his evil, a wicked one is cast off [from God], but he who takes shelter [in Him] remains righteous in death.* One who trusts in God can be sure that he will enter

יד/לג־לה לג־לד בְּלֵב נָבוֹן תָּנוּחַ חָכְמָה וּבְקֶרֶב כְּסִילִים תִּוָּדֵעַ: צְדָקָה
לה תְרוֹמֵם־גּוֹי וְחֶסֶד לְאֻמִּים חַטָּאת: רְצוֹן־מֶלֶךְ

Eden upon his death (*Rashi*).

Ibn Ezra connects this verse to the previous one, explaining that because of the evil he plotted against the poor [by exploiting them], the wicked man will be thrust away and fall. *At the time of* [the wicked man's] *death*, the righteous one will have trust in Hashem. Alternatively, the righteous one will still trust in Hashem at the time of his own death.

The *Vilna Gaon* interprets the verse to mean that the wicked person will be brought down by very same evil he planned to perpetrate against the righteous, as happened to Haman, who was hanged on the gallows he prepared for Mordechai (*Esther* 7:10). A righteous person is protected by his righteousness even when he dies, and his righteousness continues to be a refuge to his children even *after* his death (see v. 26).

Metzudos renders: If one trusts in God even when he is close to death, he is considered a righteous person. Alternatively, a wicked person is pushed to additional transgressions because of the evil that he already did, because one sin leads to another. However, when the Evil Inclination tries to persuade a righteous person to sin, he takes refuge in the thought of *his death*, to keep from being persuaded to sin. The Talmud (*Berachos* 5a) advises that if all else fails, the final tactic to overcome temptation is to remind oneself of the day of death (see *Psalms* 4:5)

R' Yonah and *Ralbag* render בְּרָעָתוֹ as *in his adversity*. When adversity befalls a wicked person, he blames his misfortune on Heaven and loses faith in God. However, a righteous person does not lose his faith. He trusts in Hashem even at his death (*Ralbag*).

The wicked person will collapse in the face of extreme adversity [in contradistinction to the righteous person, who rises from his falls. Cf. 24:16]. Even when facing death, a righteous person trusts in God to save him. Isaiah prophesied to King

Hezekiah that he would die of his illness, yet the king still prayed to God to heal him (see *II Kings* 20). The Sages teach (*Berachos* 10a) that King Hezekiah taught that even if a sharp sword has already been placed on a person's neck, he should not give up hope of Heavenly mercy (*R' Yonah*).

33. בְּלֵב נָבוֹן תָּנוּחַ חָכְמָה — *Wisdom will reside in an understanding heart.* Wisdom will rest quietly and tranquilly in the heart of a discerning person (*Rashi*).

His wisdom will remain hidden in his heart, because a truly wise person will not seek fame. He will not speak of it except when necessary, and even then he will do so guardedly. He takes into account to whom, what, how and when he is speaking (*Meiri*).

He will not reveal his wisdom to those who are not worthy of hearing it (*Metzudos*).

וּבְקֶרֶב כְּסִילִים תִּוָּדֵעַ — *But within fools it will be publicized.* Rashi explains that a fool will loudly proclaim the little bit of wisdom he possesses. As the Sages put it (*Bava Metzia* 85b), אִסְתְּרָא בְּלָגִינָא קִיש קִיש קַרְיָא, *a single coin in a pitcher calls out "kish kish,"* i.e., it rattles and makes a lot of noise. But if the vessel were filled with coins, it would not make any noise (*Rashi, ad loc.*).

R' Yonah adds another interpretation to this verse. Even though a wise person keeps his wisdom hidden, not revealing it except to the right people and at the right time, his wisdom becomes apparent when he is surrounded by fools. He does not join in their foolish laughter, does not take part in their evil and slanderous talk, nor is he attracted to their ways. The contrast between him and the fools will clearly show his wisdom, just as the scent of myrrh is more strikingly evident in an area of foul smells.

R' Hirsch explains that a wise person knows that man is vulnerable to human error. He examines and re-examines his

33 Wisdom will reside in an understanding heart, but within fools it will be publicized. 34 Charity will uplift a nation, but the kindness of regimes is a sin. 35 The favor of the king

thoughts, trying to perfect them before expressing them. In his conceit, the fool thinks that his thoughts are wonderful and cannot be improved, and is unable to rest until he blurts out his thoughts to all.

34. צְדָקָה תְרוֹמֵם־גּוֹי וְחֶסֶד לְאֻמִּים חַטָּאת — *Charity will uplift a nation, but the kindness of regimes is a sin.* The *nation* is Israel (*Rashi*), which becomes exalted as a result of its charity (*Metzudos*). The *regimes* are idolaters whose kindness is sin, because they rob from one and give to the other (*Rashi*).[1]

Regimes, in the plural, refers to all the nations of the world, whereas *nation* in the singular, designates Israel, the one, unique nation (*Meiri*).[2]

R' Yochanan ben Zakkai taught that charity atones for the nations, rendering the verse: *the kindness of nations* [is like] *a chatas-offering* (*Bava Basra* 10b).

The *Vilna Gaon* explains חַטָּאת as a

deficiency. When any nation gives charity, it becomes exalted. Yet such acts of kindness also cause a deficiency for Israel, since it lessens the latter's merits, because God must now reward that nation for its good deeds, and that reward is tremendous. A case in point is Nebuchadnezzar who took three steps to honor Hashem. As a result, Hashem made him a world power, enabling him to destroy the Holy Temple and murder pious Jews. All this resulted in order to fulfill the Divine will and to reward Nebuchadnezzar in full. (See *II Kings* 20, *Yalkut Shimoni* ibid.)

In a different vein, *Chevel Nachalah* points out that indiscriminate kindness can actually be a sin. Kindness to a murderer and failure to enforce the death penalty is a sin to the rest of humanity, for it will result in the proliferation of wickedness and murder.[3]

1. The Talmud (*Bava Basra* 10b) cites several opinions as to why the kindness of the nations is sinful:
- ❏ R' Eliezer states that the nations perform their acts of kindness only to live longer (see *Maharsha* ad loc.).
- ❏ R' Yehoshua explains that their good deeds are performed only to enforce their dominion and extend their reign.
- ❏ R' Gamliel points out that their acts of kindness are done only to glorify themselves.
- ❏ R' Eliezar HaModai states that the nations of the world are motivated to do acts of kindness with which to taunt and humiliate Israel.
- ❏ In an opinion preferred by the Talmud, R' Nechunya ben Hakaneh attaches the word *kindness* to the first half of the verse: *Charity exalts a nation as does kindness*; thus both attributes apply to Israel, *but* [the attribute of] *the nations is sin*.

2. Kindness is an inherent trait of the Jewish people, embedded deeply in every Jewish soul, as the Talmud states, Jews have three characteristics: They are merciful, they feel shame and they do kind deeds (*Yevamos* 79a). These traits must be nurtured and developed continuously, but the seeds are there. This is not true for the nations of the world whose beneficence is but an outgrowth of their self-interest, a mask which they think veils their ulterior motives. Therefore, any kindness they display is suspect.

3. R' *Hirsch* sheds a unique light on this verse through an explanation of the terms צְדָקָה and חֶסֶד.
Tzedakah, righteousness, denotes justice under which all people are guaranteed certain rights and entitlements. When such a system is implemented fully and fairly, it promotes equality, and a national community. Every member of the nation is equal in both rights and obligations, and the full benefit of *tzedakah* is extended to everyone.
Chesed, favor or lovingkindness, can by its nature be practiced only by individuals for the benefit of individuals. For a country to do so, however, through special dispensations and grants, would constitute favoritism, and should be avoided.
An individual has privileges belonging exclusively to him and can use them according to his own private judgment, but states have no private means at their disposal. Their means and rights

א לְעֶבֶד מַשְׂכִּיל וְעֶבְרָתוֹ תִּהְיֶה מֵבִישׁ: מַעֲנֶה־
ב רַךְ יָשִׁיב חֵמָה וּדְבַר־עֶצֶב יַעֲלֶה־אָף: לְשׁוֹן
חֲכָמִים תֵּיטִיב דָּעַת וּפִי כְסִילִים יַבִּיעַ אִוֶּלֶת:
ג בְּכָל־מָקוֹם עֵינֵי יהוה צֹפוֹת רָעִים וְטוֹבִים:

35. רְצוֹן־מֶלֶךְ לְעֶבֶד מַשְׂכִּיל וְעֶבְרָתוֹ תִּהְיֶה מֵבִישׁ — *The favor of the king will be upon a wise servant, but his wrath will be [upon] a shameful one.* God desires only those who serve Him and perform His commands out of love and fear. He does not desire those who adhere to His commands only to glorify themselves, or those whose Divine service stems from force of habit and training, although such people will receive the due reward for their good deeds (*R' Yonah*).

The *Vilna Gaon* explains that if God gets angry, He can be appeased [רָצוֹן] by a *wise servant* (i.e., a righteous person), but the decree that had originally been intended for the righteous person will now befall the *shameful one*, i.e., the wicked person who has earned God's hatred (cf. 11:8).

XV

1. מַעֲנֶה־רַךְ יָשִׁיב חֵמָה — *A gentle reply turns away wrath.* When the butt of anger responds with a gentle word, he will defuse this wrath[1] (*Metzudos*).

וּדְבַר־עֶצֶב יַעֲלֶה־אָף — *But a galling word incites anger.* However, if one answers with a distressing remark, he stirs up even greater anger[2] (*Metzudos*).

The power of speech has tremendous potential to cause either benefit or harm (cf. 18:21, מָוֶת וְחַיִּים בְּיַד־לָשׁוֹן, *Death and life are in the power of the tongue*). Speech is the very essence of man and the factor that distinguishes him from all other creatures. [See *Onkelos* to *Genesis* 2:7.] Since speech has the ability to bring both destruction and salvation, King Solomon advises man to train himself to

speak softly, for a gentle word can dispel wrath and even dissolve a monarch's fury (see 16:14) (*R' Bachya*).

The *Vilna Gaon* explains that אָף, *anger,* refers to the initial stages of anger, which are expressed in thought and in words. חֵמָה, *wrath,* is the final stage of anger, and is expressed through action. A *gentle reply* can appease the wrathful actions that were about to be performed or have already been performed, whereas *a galling word* arouses anger even where it did not previously exist.

Chevel Nachalah notes that the first half of the verse refers to *a reply*, while the second half refers to *a word.* The reply is in response to a previous provocation; whereas a word is initiated by the speaker.

belong to the population collectively. Thus, the state cannot award individual grants or dispensations without doing an injustice to others. Consequently, the mercy or kindness of states is a sin, for the state cannot practice custom-tailored kindness without perpetrating a sin.

1. A case in point is the reply of the judge Gideon to the people of Ephraim. After his victory over Midian, the Ephraimites were angry that he had not called upon them to join him until the very end of the battle. Gideon answered: "*What have I now done compared to you?* טוֹב עֹלְלוֹת אֶפְרַיִם מִבְצֹר אֲבִיעֶזֶר, *Are not the gleanings of Ephraim better than the vintage of Abiezer?* I.e., Ephraim's capture of the enemy leaders, at the end of the battle, was more important than the victory of my family Abiezer at the beginning of the battle." With these words, Gideon calmed their anger (*Judges* 8:1-3).

2. The unfortunate outcome of a harsh reply is illustrated by the case of the judge Jephtah. When the tribe of Ephraim reproached him for not calling them to join him in the battle against Ammon, Jephtah lashed out against them. A civil war between the tribes of Ephraim and Menasheh erupted, and 42,000 Ephraimites were killed (*Judges* 12:1-6).

will be upon a wise servant, but his wrath will be [upon] a shameful one.

¹ **A** *gentle reply turns away wrath, but a galling word incites anger.* ² *The tongue of the wise will enhance knowledge, but the mouth of fools will utter foolishness.* ³ *The eyes of* HASHEM *are everywhere, observing the evil and the good.*

Alshich explains that this verse speaks of the relationship between God and Israel. If His anger is aroused by a generation's sins, then the gentle words of a righteous person can appease His anger. So, too, Moses' prayers appeased Hashem's anger even after such a severe sin as that of the Golden Calf (see *Exodus* 32:11-14). When punishment has already befallen the Jewish people, if an individual does a דְּבַר־עֶצֶב, *something that shows he is saddened*, that will suffice to dissipate God's anger. (Thus, according to *Alshich*, the second half of the verse is not the opposite of, but complementary to, the first half of the verse.)

A case in point is that of R' Yehudah. Once, during a drought, R' Yehudah removed one shoe. [Removing one's shoes is one of the afflictions practiced on the Day of Atonement. R' Yehudah wished to afflict himself because of the suffering that the drought brought upon the community. (See *Maharsha* ad loc.)] As soon as he removed his shoe, rain began to fall (*Taanis* 24b).

This is true not only of a righteous person. Even when a wicked person performs an act of contrition, God's anger is removed from the generation. When the wicked King Ahab showed signs of submission to God, God informed Elijah that his prophecy of punishment would not be realized in Ahab's days, but rather in the time of his successors (*I Kings* 21:29).

2. לְשׁוֹן חֲכָמִים תֵּיטִיב דָּעַת — *The tongue of the wise will enhance knowledge.* Wise people enhance knowledge because they speak clearly and concisely, so that their wise words are comprehensible (*Metzudos*). The Sages advise that one should teach his students in a concise manner (*Pesachim* 3b).

Wise people are not satisfied just to convey their knowledge to others by saying: "This is the correct way, follow it!" Their tongue also beautifies knowledge by explaining the reasons for the Torah's precepts and expounding upon them in the most beautiful terms. Thus the listener finds pleasure in what he hears and he accepts it (*R' Yonah*).

וּפִי כְסִילִים יַבִּיעַ אִוֶּלֶת — *But the mouth of fools will utter foolishness.* The word יַבִּיעַ is related to מַעְיָן נוֹבֵעַ, *a flowing spring* (*Ibn Ezra; Meiri*). The foolishness in their mouth never ceases (*Ibn Ezra*). Fools speak endlessly, pouring out their words like a flowing spring (*Metzudos*).

3. בְּכָל־מָקוֹם עֵינֵי ה' צֹפוֹת רָעִים וְטוֹבִים — *The eyes of* HASHEM *are everywhere, observing the evil and the good.* God's eyes refers to His understanding and His knowledge (*Ibn Ezra*).

Even if an individual tries to hide, God's eyes are everywhere, observing the deeds of the good and the bad. Nothing is hidden from Him (*Metzudos*).

This verse refers to Divine Providence, which encompasses everything in general and each individual in particular. Everything that occurs in the world is an outgrowth of this knowledge (*Ralbag*).

The term צוֹפֶה implies *long-range vision*. A person should not wonder why the wicked prosper, for Hashem's eyes see the end result of both wicked and good people. Therefore, He may allow the wicked person to enjoy well-being, for He sees that he will have good offspring. Or, He may give a wicked person his reward now for whatever good deeds he has performed, and thus eliminate the need to reward him in the World to Come (*Vilna Gaon*).

ד מַרְפֵּא לָשׁוֹן עֵץ חַיִּים וְסֶלֶף בָּהּ שֶׁבֶר בְּרוּחַ:
ה אֱוִיל יִנְאַץ מוּסַר אָבִיו וְשֹׁמֵר תּוֹכַחַת יַעְרִם:
ו בֵּית צַדִּיק חֹסֶן רָב וּבִתְבוּאַת רָשָׁע נֶעְכָּרֶת:

4. מַרְפֵּא לָשׁוֹן עֵץ חַיִּים — *A soothing tongue is a tree of life.* A *soothing tongue* refers to words of *mussar*, or discipline, that heal the "illness" of foolishness. Just as one who eats the fruits of the tree of life will enjoy longevity, so too, one who learns *mussar* will live (*Ibn Ezra*).

R' Yonah comments that whereas medicine may or may not cure a disease, the words of *mussar* always benefit the listener, like a tree of life whose fruits always heal. When *mussar* is presented to one who is worthy of accepting it, it enters the listener's heart, and eventually will effect either a complete or at least a partial improvement in his behavior. Thus, one who rebukes others should not despair, nor should the recipient tire of listening, for the *mussar* will surely benefit him. This applies only when dealing with an individual who is interested in change and welcomes admonition, just as a tree of life benefits only those who pluck its fruit. It will not help those who scorn reproof (cf. 9:7-8). In addition, while medicine may cure a disease, it cannot add to a person's allotted years. The healing words of *mussar*, however, can add to one's life by directing the person to the proper path of life (see 6:23, *and reproving discipline is the way of life*).

R' Bachya explains that the tongue can heal spiritual ailments by influencing people to serve Hashem, thus making them worthy of eternal life. Our forefather, Abraham, possessed this trait, for he drew the people of his generation under the aegis of God's wings. His *soothing tongue* was a *tree of life* for them. Similarly, Moses influenced Jethro to convert by telling him of the miracles that God had performed for the Jews.

Ralbag and *Metzudos* render מַרְפֵּא לָשׁוֹן as a *soft tongue*, relating מַרְפֵּא to רִפְיוֹן, *weakness*, (see 14:30). If one has a "soft tongue," i.e., he speaks gently, it will be like a tree of life for him. Should someone

threaten to harm him, he will be able to appease his adversary by speaking softly (*Ralbag*).

וְסֶלֶף בָּהּ שֶׁבֶר בְּרוּחַ — *But corruption of it is destruction of the spirit.* If someone distorts his tongue to speak folly, his spirit will be broken, with no remedy for it (*Ibn Ezra*).

Just as the tongue can be a most potent medicine, it can also cause the most lethal disease. Words can break someone's רוּחַ, *spirit*, which is potentially more dangerous than a disease that attacks his body, for if the body is broken, it can be sustained by the spirit, but if the spirit is broken, what can sustain it? (see 18:14). The disease caused by the tongue is disparagement and mockery, and the disgrace one feels when being embarrassed in public. That is why the Sages say (*Bava Metzia* 59a), הַמַּלְבִּין אֶת פְּנֵי חֲבֵירוֹ בָּרַבִּים אֵין לוֹ חֵלֶק לָעוֹלָם הַבָּא, *He who publicly puts his fellow to shame has no portion in the World to Come* (*R' Yonah*).

Rashi renders רוּחַ as *a wind.* When someone uses his tongue perversely, he ultimately brings ruin upon himself. The destruction will come with the east wind, which is used to punish the wicked, as happened at the Splitting of the Sea of Reeds (*Exodus* 14:21; see also *Jeremiah* 18:17 and *Psalms* 48:8).

According to *Metzudos*, רוּחַ is *desire.* Someone who distorts his tongue to speak harshly will cause his own desire to be broken, for his words will not be heeded and his wishes will not be fulfilled.

The Talmud (*Arachin* 15b) quotes this verse in reference to the sin of speaking לְשׁוֹן הָרַע, *lashon hora*, slander. R' Chamma bar Chaninah asks: What is the remedy for slander? A Torah scholar should occupy himself with the study of Torah, as our verse states: *the remedy for the tongue is the tree of life*, a reference to the Torah, which *is a tree of life to those*

⁴ *A soothing tongue is a tree of life, but corruption of it is destruction of the spirit.* ⁵ *A fool despises his father's discipline, but he who harbors reproof will become clever.* ⁶ *The house of the righteous one is of enduring strength, but with the arrival of a wicked one it becomes sullied.*

---

who grasp it (3:18). An ignorant man should break his spirit (i.e., humble himself); as our verse continues: שֶׁבֶר בְּרוּחַ , he should *break [his] spirit.* R' Acha bar Chaninah disagrees. He maintains that this verse advises how to avoid speaking *lashon hara* from the outset; but once spoken, there is no correction for it.[1]

A perverse tongue that utters slander is a symptom of a troubled individual (שֶׁבֶר בְּרוּחַ), for speech is an integral expression of the total human being. Such a serious malady in one's spirit can be remedied only through Torah study (*Malbim*).

5. אֱוִיל יִנְאַץ מוּסַר אָבִיו — *A fool despises his father's discipline.* A fool spurns and refuses to accept discipline (*Metzudos*).

Not only does a fool scorn *mussar*, but he even scorns it from his father, the one who raised him and guided him and benefited him more than any other person (*Meiri*).

This verse is connected to the previous one. A fool will not benefit from the healing powers of discipline, for he disdains it and refuses to heed it. Just as a tree of life benefits only the person who willingly takes from its fruits, so, too, *mussar* can only help those who are willing to hear and heed its words (*R' Yonah*).

וְשֹׁמֵר תּוֹכַחַת יַעְרִם — *But he who harbors reproof will become clever.* Someone who desires to hear *mussar* is excluded from

the category of *fool.* However, he will not fulfill his obligation completely until he harbors the reproof in his heart, lest he forget it, i.e., he observes and carries out its dictates. Such a person will attain wisdom (*R' Yonah*).

6. בֵּית צַדִּיק חֹסֶן רָב — *The house of a righteous one is of enduring strength.* It is very strong and will not be destroyed (*Metzudos*).

Rashi renders: The Holy Temple which the righteous King David built [for he planned it, laid its foundation and assembled the finances and materials for its construction] is a bulwark for the Jewish people.

וּבִתְבוּאַת רָשָׁע נֶעְכָּרֶת — *But with the arrival of a wicked one it becomes sullied.* The translation follows *Ralbag*, who explains that when the wicked one enters such a house, it becomes destroyed.

Rashi renders תְּבוּאַת as *the bringing.* When King Menasheh brought an idol into the Holy Temple, it was ruined [for the subsequent destruction of the Temple resulted from this sin (see *Jeremiah* 15:4 and *II Kings* 24:3; cf. *Mishlei* 10:16, *Rashi* and footnote)] (*Rashi*).

A righteous man may accumulate great and lasting wealth. However, should his son become wicked and scorn his father's discipline and try to increase his wealth through illicit means, he will lose even his father's righteously acquired treasure. The

---

1. The *Chafetz Chaim* explains that speaking *lashon hara* is comparable to drinking poison and then searching for an antidote. No antidote can be effective until one stops consuming more poison. The antidote for *lashon hara*, which is called *death* (see 18:21, *Metzudos* ibid.), is Torah, which is *a Tree of Life* — but only if one desists from further slander.

The *Chafetz Chaim* further explains how the Torah prevents one from speaking *lashon hara*, as R' Acha bar R' Chaninah taught. A human being continuously uses the Divine gift bestowed upon him — the power of speech. His mouth and tongue never tire; unlike other organs, they need no encouragement to execute their job. God created man this way so that he could constantly be occupied in Torah study. If his tireless mouth is not occupied with Torah, however, he will speak of other things and almost inevitably sin. Therefore, an individual's best recourse to avoid forbidden speech is to occupy himself with Torah study.

שִׂפְתֵי חֲכָמִים יְזָרוּ דָעַת וְלֵב כְּסִילִים לֹא־כֵן: ז

זֶבַח רְשָׁעִים תּוֹעֲבַת יהוֹה וּתְפִלַּת יְשָׁרִים רְצוֹנוֹ: ח

תּוֹעֲבַת יהוֹה דֶּרֶךְ רָשָׁע וּמְרַדֵּף צְדָקָה יֶאֱהָב: ט

Talmud (*Kesubos* 66b) recounts the case of a very wealthy woman who had inherited fortunes from both her father, who did not give enough charity, and her father-in-law, who was charitable. She mingled the assets, and ended up losing everything. She explained that the improperly used money caused the other money, as well, to be lost (*R' Yonah*).

The house of the righteous is strong and lasting, for it is built on a foundation of righteousness. However, if a righteous person joins the wicked in his ventures and the produce of the wicked [תְּבוּאַת רָשָׁע] is brought into his house, the house will be ruined, for the gain of the wicked, which comes through fraud and theft, and will destroy everything. As we find in *Chronicles* (II 20:37): *"Because you have allied yourself with Ahaziah, HASHEM has wrecked your undertakings"* (*Malbim*).

R' Hirsch renders חֹסֶן רַב as *a rich treasure.* No matter what possessions a righteous person may have, his home is always full of treasures. His *mitzvah* observance and Torah way of life represent meaningful and lasting values, because they are used for God's aims. Thus his domestic gains neither rise nor fall with the stock market; they are not exposed to devaluation. But when a wicked person brings home the harvest of his transgressions, he and other shortsighted onlookers believe that he has found happiness. Yet his home becomes troubled, for there can be no serenity and happiness where the fruits of lawlessness are eaten.

7. שִׂפְתֵי חֲכָמִים יְזָרוּ דָעַת — *The lips of the wise spread knowledge.* The translation follows *Meiri* and *Ralbag.* The wise spread knowledge by teaching it to others. *Metzudos* explains that יְזָרוּ is related to יְזֹרֶה, *will be scattered* (*Job* 18:15).

Rashi relates יְזָרוּ to זֵר, *crown* (see *Exodus* 25:11); he renders *the lips of the wise crown* [or *adorn*] *knowledge.*

The *Vilna Gaon* explains that wise people take the knowledge they have received and adorn it by expressing themselves with clarity and directness. Their teachings are sweet and pleasant to all who hear them (cf. 14:18, 15:2).

וְלֵב כְּסִילִים לֹא־כֵן — *But not so the heart of fools.* They do not know how to spread and teach knowledge [as do the wise] (*Ibn Ezra*).

They do not want to learn, in contradistinction to the wise, who want to teach (*Metzudos*).

לֹא־כֵן can also be explained as *not true* (*Rashi, Ralbag, Meiri*). *Meiri* renders: In contrast to the wise, who scatter knowledge to others, fools spread deceptive and untrue things.

R' Yonah explains that יְזָרוּ is derived from זוֹרֶה, *winnowing* (see *Ruth* 3:2). The lips of the wise — i.e., even words they utter spontaneously — are free of any error. They filter mistakes from their speech, making sure there is nothing distorted in it, just as one winnows grain to remove the straw. A fool, however, has not trained himself to recognize the truth. Therefore, even with thought and analysis, his heart cannot distinguish knowledge from falsehood.

Midrash Tanchuma applies the words *lips of the wise* to the nation of Israel who declare God's kingship morning and evening. On the other hand, fools deny the sovereignty of God, claiming that the world runs by itself. To such people, God says, "I created the world, as the verse states: 'וַיְהִי כֵן, *and it was so'* (*Genesis* 1:7), and you claim לֹא־כֵן, *[it is] not so!* By your life, עַל כֵּן לֹא יָקֻמוּ רְשָׁעִים בַּמִּשְׁפָּט, *therefore the wicked shall not be vindicated in judgment'* (*Psalms* 1:5)" (*Yalkut Shimoni*).

⁷ The lips of the wise spread knowledge, but not so the heart of fools. ⁸ The offering of the wicked is an abomination to HASHEM, but His desire is the prayer of the upright. ⁹ The way of a wicked person is an abomination to HASHEM, but He loves a pursuer of righteousness.

8. זֶבַח רְשָׁעִים תּוֹעֲבַת ה' — *The offering of the wicked is an abomination to HASHEM.* It is an abomination if they have not as yet repented from their wickedness and have not prayed for forgiveness (*Metzudos*).

God abhors their offerings because they bring them from stolen goods (*Ibn Ezra*).

The *Vilna Gaon* explains that זֶבַח refers to שְׁלָמִים, *peace-offerings* (see *Leviticus* 3:1). Such an offering is very desirable to God, for it is not motivated by the need to atone for a sin, as is a guilt-offering [but rather as a voluntary expression of closeness to God]. However, even the peace-offering of the wicked is abominable to God, for they have rebelled against His will.

וּתְפִלַּת יְשָׁרִים רְצוֹנוֹ — *But His desire is the prayer of the upright.* Prayer was instituted as a replacement for offerings. In essence, the offerings are of greater significance, but God prefers the prayers of the righteous to the offerings of the wicked (*Alshich*).

The main purpose of bringing an offering is not the sacrificial service of the animal itself, but the intention of the one who offers it. He pours out his soul in prayerful contrition as the service is performed. The wicked who do not repent, but rely instead on the offering, to assuage God's wrath, are committing an action that is abominable to Him. On the other hand, an upright person does not even need to bring the offering; God is pleased with his prayer alone, even without an offering (*Malbim*).

This concept is expressed many times by the prophets: *Behold, to obey is better than a choice offering* (I Samuel 15:22); *Why do I need your numerous offerings, says HASHEM* (Isaiah 1:11); *For even if you offer up to Me elevation-offerings . . . I will not be appeased* (Amos 5:22).

The offering of wicked alludes to the sacrifices of Balak and Balaam [which were brought to enable Balaam to succeed in cursing the Jewish people (see *Numbers* 23:1)]. *The prayer of the upright* refers to Moses (*Rashi*).

Through prayer, a sagacious individual may gain clarity of thought, purity of intention and strength for fulfillment of good purposes (*R' Hirsch*).

9. תּוֹעֲבַת ה' דֶּרֶךְ רָשָׁע — *The way of a wicked person is an abomination to HASHEM.* One who pursues evil, even if he has yet to execute his wicked act, is an abomination to God (*Metzudos*).

Not only does God despise a wicked deed, He is even more revolted by the דֶּרֶךְ רָשָׁע, *the way in which a wicked one goes,* i.e., the pattern of behavior that leads him to wickedness. He is arrogant, vengeful, cruel and desirous of evil. These are the outgrowth of bad character traits, which emanate from his soul, and thus are even more abominable than the actual wicked deeds that his body executes. The Sages (*Yoma* 29a) teach: הִרְהוּרֵי עֲבֵירָה קָשׁוּ מֵעֲבֵירָה, *thoughts of sin are worse than the sin itself* (*Malbim* 29a).

וּמְרַדֵּף צְדָקָה יֶאֱהָב — *But He loves a pursuer of righteousness.* The verse refers to someone who is constantly searching for opportunities to perform good deeds. [צְדָקָה refers to *righteous deeds* in general or to *acts of charity.*] This is his main concern in life; his livelihood is only of secondary importance to him (*R' Yonah*).

Even if circumstances beyond his control prevent him from executing a good deed, he is beloved to God for making the sincere effort (*Metzudos*).

Ibn Ezra notes that מְרַדֵּף is a transitive verb, and explains it as *one who causes his heart to pursue righteousness,* or *one who*

יי־יד מוּסָר רָע לְעֹזֵב אֹרַח שׂוֹנֵא תוֹכַחַת יָמוּת: שְׁאוֹל
יב וַאֲבַדּוֹן נֶגֶד יהוה אַף כִּי־לִבּוֹת בְּנֵי־אָדָם: לֹא יֶאֱהַב־
יג לֵץ הוֹכֵחַ לוֹ אֶל־חֲכָמִים לֹא יֵלֵךְ: לֵב שָׂמֵחַ יֵיטִב
יד פָּנִים וּבְעַצְּבַת־לֵב רוּחַ נְכֵאָה: לֵב נָבוֹן יְבַקֶּשׁ־דָּעַת

causes others to pursue righteousness.'
Hashem loves such a person.

God loves a person who inspires and
even pursues others, imploring them and
arguing with them to give charity (*Vilna
Gaon*).[1]

The Sages praise one who inspires
others to give charity more than the
individual who gives charity himself [גָּדוֹל
הַמְעַשֶׂה יוֹתֵר מִן הָעוֹשֶׂה; see *Bava Basra*
8b,9a] (*Chevel Nachalah*).

10. מוּסָר רָע לְעֹזֵב אֹרַח — *Stern discipline
(awaits) one who forsakes the path.*
Harsh afflictions await one who transgresses the path of the Holy One, Blessed
is He (*Rashi*).

שׂוֹנֵא תוֹכַחַת יָמוּת — *One who hates
reproof will die.* Such a person is worse
than one who forsakes the right path. The
latter succumbed to the persuasion of his
Evil Inclination, but in his heart does not
hate reproof; therefore, God will afflict
him to make him repent from his bad
ways. Someone who hates rebuke, however, will die, for there is no way to correct
his actions (*R' Yonah*).

Rambam (*Hil. Teshuvah* 4:2) lists *one
who hates rebuke* as one of the twenty-
four hindrances to repentance. A person
with this trait will have no way of
repenting and will therefore die (*Ibn
Nachmiash*).

11. שְׁאוֹל וַאֲבַדּוֹן נֶגֶד ה' אַף כִּי־לִבּוֹת בְּנֵי־אָדָם
— *The grave and perdition are exposed to
HASHEM; surely the hearts of men.* If
everything in the grave and in *Gehinnom*
is revealed to Hashem, then certainly He
knows the thoughts in the hearts of men
(*Rashi*).

God constantly examines a person's
heart; therefore, one should be ashamed to
harbor evil thoughts in his heart and
should seek to purge such ideas (*R'
Yonah*).

One should not think that since God's
eyes are Holy, He cannot see man's evil
deeds, and He is too sanctified to extend
His Providence to places of impurity.
Nothing escapes His view. If *the grave*
and *perdition*, the places of greatest impurity, are before His eyes, surely the hearts
of mankind are visible to Him as well
(*Vilna Gaon*).

R' Hirsch explains that Hashem cares
even for the grave and decay, which men
consider the end of existence, beyond
which human vision cannot reach. From
the grave He awakens new life, and from
decay, resurrection. Surely, therefore, living, pulsing hearts, however near or far
they may be from moral goodness, also
benefit from God's care. They can be
revived from moral decay to moral health,
and from the grave of immorality to a life
of moral purity.

12. לֹא יֶאֱהַב־לֵץ הוֹכֵחַ לוֹ אֶל־חֲכָמִים לֹא יֵלֵךְ
— *A scoffer does not like his being
reproved; he will not go to the wise.* Since
a scoffer does not like to hear reproof, he is
afraid to go to wise men (*Metzudos*).

Not only does a scoffer fail to study
Torah, he does not even go to those who
could teach him. He even forfeits the
benefit of הוֹלֵךְ וְאֵינוּ עוֹשֶׂה, *one who goes*
[to the house of study] *but does not study*
(*Avos* 5:17), who is at least rewarded for
going (*Vilna Gaon*).

Anything ethical or sacred, which
relates to God, is the target of the scoffer's

1. The word *pursuer* can also refer to someone who chases others with the intention of harming
them. In the case of our verse, someone who coerces others to give charity may appear bothersome
and harmful, but in reality is a great benefactor, affording his "victims" the opportunity to
perform a noble precept.

¹⁰ *Stern discipline [awaits] one who forsakes the path; one who hates reproof will die.* ¹¹ *The grave and perdition are exposed to HASHEM, surely the hearts of men.* ¹² *A scoffer does not like his being reproved; he will not go to the wise.* ¹³ *A glad heart cheers the face, but a despondent heart [causes] a broken spirit.* ¹⁴ *An understanding heart will seek knowledge,*

---

ridicule. He fears and even hates to be reproved, because he lacks self-confidence and is afraid to be taught better. Therefore, he never goes to wise people, for he cannot bear opposition to the opinions he holds so dear and exhibits so proudly (*R' Hirsch*).

13. לֵב שָׂמֵחַ יֵיטִב פָּנִים — *A glad heart cheers the face.* The happiness in a person's heart enhances the appearance and radiance of his face (*Metzudos*).

Ralbag comments that joy is commendable, for the prophet Elisha commanded that a musician play for him to make his heart rejoice, and only then did the prophetic spirit rest upon him (*II Kings* 3:15). On the other hand, all the years that Jacob was broken hearted over the loss of his son Joseph, the Divine Spirit did not reveal itself to him (*Genesis* 45:27; see *Rashi* ibid.).

וּבְעַצְּבַת־לֵב רוּחַ נְכֵאָה — *But a despondent heart [causes] a broken spirit.* Sadness of heart breaks a person's spirit, and his self-esteem is lowered (*Metzudos*).

This verse teaches us that one should be happy with his lot and not chase after riches, for happiness will enhance his appearance. If he is sad, his spirit will be broken; and when one's spirit is broken, his face will look troubled (*Meiri*).

Rashi explains the verse metaphorically. If we gladden God's heart by following His ways, then He will show us a cheerful countenance by fulfilling all our desires. However, if we sadden Him, He will manifest a spirit of fury toward us.

This verse highlights the fallacy of the popular opinion that neither benefit nor harm result from thoughts alone; only actions count. This is certainly not true, and is evidenced by the tremendous impact the heart has on the body. If the heart is happy, the entire body feels pleasure; if the heart is sad, a person's spirit is broken, and a broken-spirited person cannot enjoy physical pleasure. It follows, then, that a person whose heart rejoices in sin and wickedness will be severely punished, for he derives physical pleasure from evil, as is reflected in his cheerful countenance. On the other hand, one who rejoices in the performance of *mitzvos* and is distressed by sin will be greatly rewarded. The wicked rejoice in sin (see verse 21), whereas the righteous rejoice in serving Hashem, as King David exclaims, (*Psalms* 119:162), שָׂשׂ אָנֹכִי עַל־ אִמְרָתֶךָ, *I rejoice over Your word* (*R' Yonah*).

In various verses throughout *Mishlei*, King Solomon teaches that a cheerful disposition is an inestimable treasure (cf. 14:30, 17:22, 18:14). It preserves health, promotes convalescence and helps us cope with adversity. A discontented, dissatisfied heart weakens the limbs and paralyzes activity, while good cheer brightens one's outlook and strengthens his body (*R' Hirsch*).

Sfas Emes explains this verse as a behavioral lesson. Since, *A glad heart cheers the face,* we must try to maintain this state even in times of calamity. Especially then, one should feel trust in God and keep a cheerful face.

14. לֵב נָבוֹן יְבַקֶּשׁ־דָּעַת — *An understanding heart will seek knowledge.* He searches for it until he attains it (*Meiri*).

R' Yonah explains this verse as a continuation of the previous one. The heart of a discerning person will seek knowledge since his happiness is attained through wisdom, and this happiness is evident on his face. His Torah knowledge makes his face shine, as the verse states (*Ecclesiastes* 8:1): חָכְמַת אָדָם תָּאִיר פָּנָיו, *a*

טו ‏°וּפְנֵי כְסִילִים יִרְעֶה אִוָּלֶת: כָּל־יְמֵי עָנִי רָעִים ‏°וּפִי ק' טו

טז וְטוֹב־לֵב מִשְׁתֶּה תָמִיד: טוֹב־מְעַט בְּיִרְאַת

יז יהוה מֵאוֹצָר רָב וּמְהוּמָה בוֹ: טוֹב אֲרֻחַת

יָרָק וְאַהֲבָה־שָׁם מִשּׁוֹר אָבוּס וְשִׂנְאָה־בוֹ:

man's wisdom lights up his face.

A discerning person searches for knowledge. He infers, inquires and reflects to discover the inner meanings of laws as he adapts his life to them (*Malbim*).

וּפִי כְסִילִים יִרְעֶה אִוָּלֶת — *But the mouth of fools will befriend folly.* A fool makes foolishness his friend for he associates with it constantly (*Metzudos*).

Meiri explains יִרְעֶה as יִרְצֶה, *desires*, (for the *Targum* of רָצוֹן is רְעוּא), or *thinks* (as in the word רַעְיוֹן, *a thought*). In contrast to the understanding one, who seeks knowledge, *fools* seek foolishness in their desires and in their thoughts. The first part of the verse is singular, and the end is plural, implying that there are few discerning people, while fools abound. The word *heart* is used only in conjunction with a discerning person, since it implies reasoning and analysis, traits that are not associated with fools.

15. כָּל־יְמֵי עָנִי רָעִים — *All the days of a poor man are wretched.* Even if he has his basic needs, his days are wretched because he envies the rich man and begrudges him his wealth (*Metzudos*).

The *Vilna Gaon* elaborates: The Mishnah defines a rich man as one who is happy with his lot — אֵיזֶהוּ עָשִׁיר הַשָּׂמֵחַ בְּחֶלְקוֹ, "Who is rich? He who is happy with his lot" (*Avos* 4:1). Consequently, the poor man of our verse refers to one who is not satisfied with what he has. He will *never* be able to attain all that he desires, as the Sages state: אֵין אָדָם יוֹצֵא מִן הָעוֹלָם וְחֲצִי תַאֲוָתוֹ בְּיָדוֹ, *a person does not leave the world with even half of his desires in*

his hand (*Koheles Rabbah* 1:34); therefore, all his days are wretched.[1]

In his letter *Alim Litrufah*, the *Vilna Gaon* compares this world to one who drinks salty water — he expects it to quench his thirst, when in reality it makes him thirstier than ever.

Rashi explains that all the days of the poor are wretched, even the Sabbath and holidays, for the Talmud teaches that a change of routine is the beginning of intestinal disorder (*Sanhedrin* 101a). *Rashi* (ad loc.) explains that even a poor person eats delicacies on the Sabbath and festivals, but since this is not his usual fare and he is unaccustomed to eating so much, it causes intestinal disorder. Therefore, even festive days are "bad" for him.

וְטוֹב־לֵב מִשְׁתֶּה תָמִיד — *But a good-hearted person has a perpetual feast.* If someone is satisfied with his wealth [and not envious (*Metzudos*)], all his years seem festive to him. This verse teaches that a person should be happy with his lot (*Rashi*).

The Talmud (*Sanhedrin* 100b-101a) presents several interpretations of this verse. Among them are: Someone's days are wretched if he has an evil wife; if he is too fastidious; or if he is short tempered. Conversely, the latter part of the verse refers to a man who has a good wife; to a man of tolerance; and to one who is forbearing.

16. טוֹב־מְעַט בְּיִרְאַת ה' מֵאוֹצָר רָב וּמְהוּמָה בוֹ — *Better a little [gained] through fear of HASHEM than a great treasure accompanied by turmoil.* It is better to have less riches that were obtained through just and God-fearing means than to have a great

---

1. The *Rama* concludes *Shulchan Aruch Orach Chaim* with this phrase. He opens the work with the verse שִׁוִּיתִי ה' לְנֶגְדִּי תָמִיד, *I have set HASHEM before me always* (*Psalms* 67:8). The *Chasam Sofer* connects the two verses. One who sets God before him at all times will merit a life which is a perpetual feast.

but the mouth of fools will befriend folly. [15] All the days of a poor man are wretched, but a good-hearted person has a perpetual feast [16] Better a little [gained] through fear of HASHEM than a great treasure accompanied by turmoil. [17] Better a meal of greens where there is love than a fattened ox where there is hatred.

treasure with turmoil, i.e., where it is accompanied by the voices of people screaming that it was accumulated through robbery and oppression (*Rashi*). The former will be successful and lasting, but the latter will be destroyed and lost (*Ralbag*).

This verse also applies to Torah study. It is better that a person study the limited level of Torah which he can comprehend and be God fearing than to delve deeply into levels of Torah study that are beyond his grasp [מֵאוֹצָר רָב] and which will only cause him confusion and turmoil [וּמְהוּמָה בּוֹ], and may even cause his soul to lose eternal life. King Solomon alludes to this same point when he warns against eating too much honey (25:16). Though eating a small amount of honey is pleasant, should one consume excessive amounts, he may eventually regurgitate it all, and lose even the little bit he had eaten before (*R' Bachya*).

The *Vilna Gaon* explains that a person may study a great deal of Torah, but be motivated by pride, arrogance, deceit and other base reasons. Within this large quantity of Torah study, however, there

may be מְעַט בְּיִרְאַת ה', *a small amount* that he studied purely *with fear of HASHEM*. This small amount is better than the whole treasure of knowledge that he accumulated with the turmoil of untoward motives.

17. טוֹב אֲרֻחַת יָרָק וְאַהֲבָה־שָׁם מִשּׁוֹר אָבוּס וְשִׂנְאָה־בוֹ — *Better a meal of greens where there is love than a fattened ox where there is hatred.* It is better to give a poor man a meal of vegetables and to show him a happy face than to feed him fat meat and show him an angry face (*Rashi*), and embarrass him with harsh words (*Meiri*).[1]

The Sages (*Bava Basra* 9b) teach that one who gives a penny to a poor man is blessed with six blessings, whereas one who comforts him with kind words merits eleven blessings. This important principle applies to other precepts as well. In fulfilling the *mitzvah* of honoring one's parents, a son may feed his father luscious meat, yet inherit *Gehinnom*, while another may make his father grind the millstone and merit *Gan Eden* (*Kiddushin* 31a). The Sages (*Rashi ad loc*, quoting *Yerushalmi Peah* 1) illustrate this dictum with the story of two sons. One son fed his father the meat of a fattened bird, a tasty delicacy. When his

1. *Midrash Mishlei* recounts that King Solomon uttered this verse reflecting his own personal experiences. As he wandered from place to place seeking food when he had (temporarily) been dethroned as king of Israel, a person invited him for a meal. He served him a fattened ox and other delicacies, but as the king was eating, his host reminded him of former times, remarking, "Do you remember that when you were king you did such-and-such on that particular day?" Upon hearing this, Solomon burst out crying. He was unable to taste the feast laid out before him, and his tears continued unabated until he rose and departed.

The next day, someone else invited the king. Initially, King Solomon refused, fearing that yesterday's episode would repeat itself. His would-be-host explained that he was poor, and if the king accepted his offer, he would have to be content with a meal of meager greens. When King Solomon accepted his invitation and accompanied the poor man to his house, his host washed the king's hands and feet, and brought him a small portion of greens. The host then began comforting the king, telling him that Hashem swore to King David that the monarchy would always remain in his family. Therefore, even if God is temporarily reprimanding his son, He will certainly return King Solomon to his throne. Upon hearing these words, the king's spirit was calmed. He ate his meager meal happily, rejoiced and left feeling satisfied and in good spirits.

When Solomon was restored to his throne, he said: "Better the dinner of greens that I ate at the poor man's house that left me feeling satisfied, than the fattened ox that the rich man fed me, while constantly reminding me of my sorrow."

יח אִישׁ חֵמָה יְגָרֶה מָדוֹן וְאֶרֶךְ אַפַּיִם יַשְׁקִיט רִיב:
יט דֶּרֶךְ עָצֵל כִּמְשֻׂכַת חָדֶק וְאֹרַח יְשָׁרִים סְלֻלָה:
כ-כא בֵּן חָכָם יְשַׂמַּח־אָב וּכְסִיל אָדָם בּוֹזֶה אִמּוֹ: אִוֶּלֶת

father asked him, "Where did you get this?" the son replied, "Old man, why do you care? Just chew and eat," thus showing that he begrudged his father the food. Another son earned a difficult livelihood grinding flour with millstones. When the king drafted his elderly father to come and serve him, the son suggested, "Father, you grind flour instead of me, and I will go serve the king in your stead, for that is a labor that has no end." This son merited paradise.

Rashi applies this verse to the small קוֹמֶץ, *handful*, which is brought from the flour-offering to be placed on the Altar of the Temple. A poor man's handful is more beloved to God than a wicked person's ox brought as a *sin-offering*.

Metzudos renders: It is better for one to eat a meal of greens where he is loved than to eat a fattened ox where one is hated.

Affection makes even a small meal sweet, while hatred turns a lavish feast into a bitter experience (*Malbim*).

Metaphorically, this verse teaches that a small amount of Torah study done with love of God and with true belief in Him is better than extensive Torah knowledge if it comes with hatred of God, i.e., the denial of true belief in Him (*Meiri*).

If people prefer eating a smaller meal in the company of friends to eating delicacies in the company of enemies, then certainly a person should prefer having fewer worldly pleasures for the sake of greater love and fear of God (verse 16). His love is more precious than the company of friends. A person should not desire the good which the wicked enjoy in this world, for they are the subjects of God's hatred (*R' Yonah*).[1] This teaches one to be satisfied with his lot. He must avoid

greed and not put his trust in his wealth, nor make gold and silver the focal point of his belief (*R' Bachya*).

18. אִישׁ חֵמָה יְגָרֶה מָדוֹן—*A wrathful man incites strife*. A person who cannot control his temper and be slow to anger will instigate quarrels (*Rashi*).

וְאֶרֶךְ אַפַּיִם יַשְׁקִיט רִיב — *But one slow to anger calms a quarrel*. If one is slow to anger and does not rush to quarrel and take revenge, the quarrel will quiet down and end of its own accord (*Rashi*).

מָדוֹן refers to the beginning stage of a quarrel, and רִיב is the midst of the quarrel. A wrathful person will incite a quarrel even where no dispute existed before, whereas one who is slow to anger will be able to quiet even an ongoing conflict (*Vilna Gaon*).

19. דֶּרֶךְ עָצֵל כִּמְשֻׂכַת חָדֶק — *The way of a sluggard is fenced with thorns* [lit. *like a hedge of thorns*]. A lazy person feels as if the road before him is obstructed and hedged in by a fence of thorns (*Rashi*). Instead of trying to improve himself, a lazy person fantasizes that a barricade obstructs him, and he finds excuses to block any progressive action (*Metzudos*). [Cf. 26:13.]

Rashi cites the Midrash that Esau's way is like a thorn entangled in a woolen fleece; if one tries to lift it out on one side, it becomes re-entangled on the other. The edicts of the nations against us are like thorns in wool. No matter how we try to escape them, their libels and schemes follow us. One cannot escape Esau's evil plots without paying large sums of money. [Historically, Jews often had to pay large ransoms in order to save them-

1. The verse can be interpreted according to the principle that God makes the righteous suffer in this world so that they will have only good in the Hereafter, whereas the wicked have good in this world so that they lose any claim to good in the World to Come. Thus: *Better a meal of greens* [in this world] *where there is love* [in the World to Come] *than a fattened ox* [in this world] *where there is hatred* for the wicked [in the World to Come] (*Shevet M'Yehudah*).

18 *A wrathful man incites strife, but one slow to anger calms a quarrel.* 19 *The way of a sluggard is fenced with thorns, but the path of the upright is paved.* 20 *A wise son gladdens a father, but a foolish person shames his mother.* 21 *Folly*

selves from evil decrees.]

וְאֹרַח יְשָׁרִים סְלֻלָה — *But the path of the upright is paved.* Their path is trodden and clear (*Rashi*). They find the means to remove any obstacle standing in their way (*Metzudos*).

The *Vilna Gaon* explains that דֶּרֶךְ refers to a *wide road*, whereas אֹרַח describes a *narrow path.* A person has a choice of two courses. One begins as a wide road but ends up full of thorns, while the other is initially narrow and hard to traverse but eventually becomes wide and paved. The course chosen by a lazy person begins on the wide road (דֶּרֶךְ), but it soon becomes overgrown with thorns and thistles (חָדֵק). On the other hand, the upright choose a path that is initially troublesome, but ends up being a wide, well-paved road (see *Eruvin* 53b וְזוֹ אֲרוּכָה וּקְצָרָה, *this road is long but short*, i.e., though the distance is longer, this road leads to the entrance of the city, *Rashi* ibid.). [Cf. 4:18,19 and citations from *Bereishis Rabbah* and *Alshich*.]

Malbim explains this verse metaphorically, using דֶּרֶךְ to mean the well-traversed highway of wisdom. A sluggard finds it difficult to traverse this road, because he cannot overcome his desires, but an upright person traverses even side roads easily, i.e., his desires do not stand in the way of his piety and righteousness, because his heart is pure.

The term יְשָׁרִים, *upright*, describes individuals whose thoughts are directed exclusively to the goal that their sense of duty has established. Such a person can easily overcome difficulties because of his vision of life. His path is always even and his social relationships lead him continually upward (*R' Hirsch*).

20. בֵּן חָכָם יְשַׂמַּח־אָב — *A wise son*

gladdens a father. When his father sees him seated among the wise, he rejoices (*Metzudos*). His father can evaluate and appreciate his outstanding Torah scholarship better than his mother (*Ralbag*).

וּכְסִיל אָדָם בּוֹזֶה אִמּוֹ — *But a foolish person shames his mother.* He causes his mother to be scorned (*Rashi*).

He scorns his mother when she criticizes his ways (*Malbim*).

Ralbag explains that the mother is more to blame for his bad discipline because the son was constantly at her side when he was young.

Since women tend to pity their children and refrain from disciplining them, people will scorn the mother of such a son, saying that she is to blame for bringing up such a son (*Metzudos*).

The *Vilna Gaon* points out that even when the *wise son* is young, he brings joy to his father, for he stays near him in the study hall. A fool, however, even when he is already an אָדָם, *a grown person*, brings scorn to his mother, even when he is far away from her, for people curse the one who gave birth to and raised such a son. This verse differs from verse 10:1 which states, *but a foolish son is his mother's sorrow.* That verse refers to him when he is still a child, who stays by his mother's side and is a constant source of grief to her personally. This verse refers to the fool when he is grown and lives elsewhere. Even then, his conduct brings shame upon her.[1]

R' Hirsch renders this part of the verse differently: *but the most unwise among men is one who despises his mother.* Once parental esteem disappears, and a child begins to look upon his parents with disdain and arrogance, a brutal deterioration of values follows.

---

1. The Torah does not explicitly recount the death of Rebecca. It only alludes to the event so that people would not curse the mother who gave birth to Esau (see *Genesis* 35:8, *Rashi* ibid.).

שִׂמְחָה לַחֲסַר־לֵב וְאִישׁ תְּבוּנָה יְיַשֶּׁר־לָכֶת:
כב הָפֵר מַחֲשָׁבוֹת בְּאֵין סוֹד וּבְרֹב יוֹעֲצִים תָּקוּם:
כג שִׂמְחָה לָאִישׁ בְּמַעֲנֵה־פִיו וְדָבָר בְּעִתּוֹ מַה־
כד טּוֹב: אֹרַח חַיִּים לְמַעְלָה לְמַשְׂכִּיל לְמַעַן
כה סוּר מִשְּׁאוֹל מָטָּה: בֵּית גֵּאִים יִסַּח ׀ יהוה

21. אִוֶּלֶת שִׂמְחָה לַחֲסַר־לֵב — *Folly is joy to one lacking [an understanding] heart.* If a wise person does something foolish, he regrets and bemoans his folly, but one who lacks understanding rejoices in his folly (*Vilna Gaon*).

וְאִישׁ תְּבוּנָה יְיַשֶּׁר־לָכֶת — *But a man of understanding [will rejoice] when he walks uprightly.* He rejoices when he finds the proper way to go (*Vilna Gaon*).

Ibn Ezra renders, he seeks a straight way in which to walk.

R' Bachya comments that joy is folly for someone who lacks understanding. When such a person enjoys happiness and tranquility, he indulges in foolishness. On the other hand, the same happiness and tranquility will influence a man of understanding to act with propriety and refine his character traits.

22. הָפֵר מַחֲשָׁבוֹת בְּאֵין סוֹד — *Thoughts are frustrated for want of counsel.* Without advice, a person's designs will not be realized (*Rashi*).

The verse refers to counsel not as עֵצָה, but as סוֹד, literally *a secret*, to indicate that if one reveals his plans, they will be frustrated (*Vilna Gaon*).

וּבְרֹב יוֹעֲצִים תָּקוּם — *But through an abundance of advisors they will be established.* Through the advice of many, a person's designs will be realized (*Metzudos*).

This verse teaches one to act with deliberation, consulting others before acting. He should not be hasty in putting plans into action, for a person may regret his rash actions when it is too late to retract them

anymore (*Meiri*).

According to *Malbim*, a person should keep his ideas secret, because בְּאֵין סוֹד, *for lack of secrecy*, they can be frustrated or nullified by one's enemies and the plan will fail. Should that happen, he will need many advisors, so that if one idea fails, there will be other options, and one of the plans will prevail.

23. שִׂמְחָה לָאִישׁ בְּמַעֲנֵה־פִיו — *A man has joy through the reply of his mouth.* A person who replies softly and gently will be loved by people (*Rashi*).[1]

וְדָבָר בְּעִתּוֹ מַה־טּוֹב — *And how good is a word in its [appropriate] time.* Even though a person is happy to say something accurate, he should take another factor into account before speaking: Is it a *word in its appropriate time?* Though a person is naturally inclined to say any truism that comes to mind, he should restrain himself and say only what is fitting for the occasion (*R' Yonah*). As *R' Bachya* points out, a discussion of happy matters would be incongruous in a house of mourning, as mournful topics would be in a place of rejoicing.

The two halves of the verse refer to situations in which a Torah scholar is fortified by his knowledge: (1) If others ask him to render a halachic ruling or a discourse in Torah, and he is able to reply, then he will rejoice; and (2) if he himself realizes the necessity of pertinent speech relevant to each season as it comes (*Vilna Gaon*).

The Sages (*Eruvin* 54a, see *Rashi* ad loc.)

1. *Rav Yisrael Zev Gustman* notes that man was given the ability to organize his thoughts, but the power of expression is a gift of God. King Solomon teaches: *To man belongs the arrangement of [thoughts in] his heart, but from HASHEM comes the tongue's reply* (see 16:1). Thus, where the gifts of rhetoric and oratory are found, it indicates that God is helping a person express his appropriate ideas. Realizing this, one rejoices and is happy with the mouth's utterances.

is joy to one lacking [an understanding] heart, but a man of understanding [will rejoice] when he walks uprightly. ²² Thoughts are frustrated for want of counsel, but through an abundance of advisors they will be established. ²³ A man has joy through the reply of his mouth, and how good is a word in its [appropriate] time. ²⁴ A path of life [waits] on high for the intelligent one, so that he will turn away from the grave below. ²⁵ HASHEM will uproot the house of the arrogant,

apply the verse to someone who has the answer when a question of *halachah* is put to him; he rejoices in his knowledge. It is especially good when he can respond regarding the laws of Passover and Succos in their appropriate season (*Rashi*).

24. אֹרַח חַיִּים לְמַעְלָה לְמַשְׂכִּיל לְמַעַן סוּר מִשְּׁאוֹל מָטָה — *A path of life [waits] on high for the intelligent one, so that he will turn away from the grave below.* The path of life is prepared and arranged before the wise person. The term לְמַעְלָה לְמַשְׂכִּיל is similar to מִמַּעַל לוֹ, *above, at his service* [*Isaiah 6:2*] (*Rashi*).

The path of life for the soul of the enlightened person ascends לְמַעְלָה, *upwards*, so that it may return to God, the Source from which it was hewn, and not descend to *Gehinnom* (*Metzudos*).

Realizing that this world is transient, an intelligent person knows that the path of life is above [אֹרַח חַיִּים לְמַעְלָה], in the everlasting World to Come and therefore he turns away from the physical desires of this world [לְמַעַן סוּר מִשְּׁאוֹל מָטָה]. This may be compared to a person who temporarily lives in one place, but decides to establish his permanent residence elsewhere. He will no longer invest in property and furniture in his present locale, since his intention is to settle elsewhere. So, too, an enlightened person, who realizes that there is a path of life above, will not struggle to satisfy his body's material desires in this world, except for whatever is necessary to maintain the body to execute God's service. He realizes that the Hereafter is his permanent abode and this world is only a temporary one.

For this reason, his way is called an אֹרַח חַיִּים, *path of life*, rather than דֶּרֶךְ חַיִּים,

road of life, for אֹרַח alludes to the word אוֹרֵחַ, *a guest*. In other words, a wise person considers himself a guest in this world. Like a guest at an inn, he realizes that his sojourn is temporary; he knows that he will be moving on shortly, and his soul yearns to return and re-attach itself to its eternal source of life (*R' Bachya*).

A human being is referred to as a הוֹלֵךְ, *one who goes*, for he is in a constant state of spiritual flux, while an angel is termed an עוֹמֵד, *one who stands still*, since his spiritual stance is fixed and immutable. A human being must continuously ascend from one level to another, for if he does not ascend, he will, God forbid, descend, for a human being cannot remain stagnant. Thus, an enlightened person chooses the path that leads upward, so that he will be saved from *Sheol*, the spiritual grave (*Vilna Gaon*).

A person is a composite of earthly matter and spirituality. He is comparable to a ball that someone hurls upward with all his might. It goes higher and higher as long as the force of the thrust lasts. Once its force is spent, however, the object does not rest in midair, but immediately falls to the ground. So, too, the force of a person's intelligence can propel him to spiritual heights in Torah and fear of God. Yet, as soon as his zeal weakens, he plummets downward. Therefore, one who pursues a path of life that leads constantly upward reaps a double benefit: He reaches new heights, and he avoids falling into the depths of *Sheol*, which would be unavoidable should his upward thrust cease even for a moment (*Chevel Nachalah*).

The Midrash renders מַשְׂכִּיל as מִי שֶׁמִּסְתַּכֵּל לְמַעְלָה, *one who turns his gaze upward*; such a person will attain the path of life. One who constantly focuses his

כו וְיַצֵּב גְּבוּל אַלְמָנָה: תּוֹעֲבַת יהוה מַחְשְׁבוֹת רָע
כז וּטְהֹרִים אִמְרֵי־נֹעַם: עֹכֵר בֵּיתוֹ בּוֹצֵעַ בָּצַע
כח וְשׂוֹנֵא מַתָּנֹת יִחְיֶה: לֵב צַדִּיק יֶהְגֶּה לַעֲנוֹת

perspective towards Heaven will be forgiven for his sins and saved from misfortune (*Yalkut Shimoni, Psalms* 32:1).

25. בֵּית גֵּאִים יִסַּח ה' — *HASHEM will uproot the house of the arrogant.* According to R' Yonah, this verse is a continuation of the previous one. The *arrogant* refers to those who make life in this world their primary focus and concentrate on the transient and ephemeral, as the Psalmist says: *in their imagination their houses are forever* (*Psalms* 49:12). They pride themselves on their success and become arrogant, because they dwell in tranquility within the safety of their homes. Therefore, measure for measure, God will uproot their homes.

וְיַצֵּב גְּבוּל אַלְמָנָה — *But He will uphold the boundary of a widow.* In place of the house of the arrogant, God will firmly establish the boundary of the widow, even though she herself is weak and helpless (*Metzudos*).

If the dwelling of the proud is built on the boundary of the widow, who lacks the strength to protest, and has no one to stand up for her, then God will fight her battle. He will uproot that dwelling and reestablish her boundary. This verse emphasizes the fundamental principle of faith in Divine Providence, which will correct injustices where mortals cannot intervene (*Malbim*).[1]

Divine Providence strides towards its goal over the ruins of the temples of haughtiness. It levels the structures of

those who have been misled by their proud fortunes. But God cares for the humble, lonely widow, and He establishes her in a position of self-sufficient independence (R' Hirsch).

R' Yonah renders: God will establish the boundary of אוּמָה אַלְמָנָה, *a widowed nation,* i.e., one which has become desolate and debased to dust.

One who sees dwellings inhabited by Jews, which were reestablished after a period of exile [for example, during the Second Temple era (*Rashi*)], should recite: *Blessed is He Who upholds the boundary of a widow.* One sees a house inhabited by idol worshipers, should recite: *HASHEM will uproot the house of the arrogant* (*Berachos* 58b).

Quoting the above passage, the *Vilna Gaon* explains that *the house of the arrogant* applies to Edom. When God destroys Edom in the Messianic era, the boundary of Israel will expand [וְיַצֵּב גְּבוּל אַלְמָנָה], and according to the Sages (*Sifri, Deuteronomy* 1:1), Jerusalem will reach Damascus.

26. תּוֹעֲבַת ה' מַחְשְׁבוֹת רָע וּטְהֹרִים אִמְרֵי־נֹעַם — *Thoughts of evil are an abomination of HASHEM, but words of pleasantness are pure.* God abhors a person who speaks sweet, pure words with his lips, but harbors evil thoughts in his heart. It is proper the pleasant words should be pure and unadulterated by evil intentions (*Metzudos*).

Alternatively, *thoughts of an evil man*

1. When the Chafetz Chaim was a young man, a shocking incident occurred in his town. A widow too poor to pay her rent was threatened with eviction in the middle of a bitterly cold winter. The widow protested, but her pleas fell on deaf ears. The landlord, seeing that his threats did not produce the desired payment, resorted to his next tactic: He literally removed the roof over the widow's head! Despite the outcry of the townspeople at such cruelty, the landlord proceeded with his plans, and chased the helpless widow out into the wintry streets.

Hearing of this wickedness, the Chafetz Chaim was sure that Divine retribution would follow. After several years had passed with no overt sign of justice being done, he remarked, "It is impossible that this heinous act will go unpunished for the verse specifically states (*Exodus* 22:21-23), *You shall not cause pain to any widow .... My wrath shall blaze and I shall kill you.*"

Some ten years later, the landlord was bitten by a mad dog. He died a painful death shortly afterwards.

but He will uphold the boundary of a widow. ²⁶ *Thoughts of evil are an abomination of* HASHEM, *but words of pleasantness are pure.* ²⁷ *One who gains through robbery sullies his home, but one who hates gifts will live.* ²⁸ *The heart of a righteous person will consider what to answer,*

are the abomination, for an evil man is constantly involved in wickedness.[1] However, the thoughts of טְהֹרִים, *pure people,* become words that will be pleasant and sweet to God (*Ralbag*).

R' *Hirsch* explains טְהוֹרִים אִמְרֵי־נֹעַם as *only pure words are pleasant words.*

27. עֹכֵר בֵּיתוֹ בּוֹצֵעַ בָּצַע וְשׂוֹנֵא מַתָּנֹת יִחְיֶה — *One who gains through robbery sullies his home, but one who hates gifts will live.* Since he hates gifts, then all the more so does he hate robbery (*Rashi*).

One who robs in order to increase his wealth destroys his house, for his ill-gotten gains will ruin that which he already has (cf. v. 6 citation from R' *Yonah*). However, one who puts his trust in God and hates to receive gifts will be rewarded with life, something that no human can give (*Metzudos*).

R' *Yonah* explains that one who resorts to theft has inculcated the very essence of the trait of חֶמְדָּה, *lust,* while one who hates gifts has gone to the opposite extreme, in order to distance himself from lust. His desires to attain his sustenance only from Heaven and the labor of his own hands. R' *Bachya* adds that *will live* is a Divine promise that this individual will live without accepting gifts. A person cannot achieve the spiritual level of hating gifts unless he has trust in God. Consequently, God will provide his sustenance, and he will not be dependent on others.

The *Vilna Gaon* points out that a person who anxiously awaits gifts is likely to be disappointed when an anticipated gift does not materialize. Therefore, one who hates gifts *will live,* i.e. he will enjoy life, as opposed to the one who loves gifts and so cannot enjoy his life [cf. *Beitzah* 32b שְׁלֹשָׁה חַיֵּיהֶן אֵינָם חַיִּים וְאֵלּוּ הֵן הַמְצַפֶּה לְשֻׁלְחָן חֲבֵירוֹ ..., "There are three types of individuals whose life lacks flavor: One who awaits to be invited to his friend's table. . . ."].

One who earns an honest living and wants nothing from others will neither die of hunger nor become ill from overwork. On the contrary, *he will live,* for all is dependent on Divine Providence (*Malbim*).

The Talmud (*Chullin* 44b) recounts how careful the Sages were to avoid accepting gifts. When R' Elazar was sent a gift from the house of the *Nasi,* or leader of Israel, he did not accept it. When he was invited to eat there, he did not go, saying, "Don't you want me to live?!," for the verse says, *but one who hates gifts will live.* When R' Zeira was sent a gift, he also refused it, but he accepted an invitation to dine, explaining: "They are honored by my presence at their meal, and it gives them pleasure; therefore, it is not I who is receiving a gift, but rather, they (see *Rashi,* ad loc.).[2]

28. לֵב צַדִּיק יֶהְגֶּה לַעֲנוֹת — *The heart of a righteous one will consider what to answer.* A righteous person reflects and

1. The members of a certain congregation wanted to institute a new custom and recite the Priestly Blessing daily during the morning service (as is the custom among Sephardic Jews and in *Eretz Yisrael* today). They approached R' Yaakov Emden for his approval. Initially, he was agreeable to the idea, but he asked who had initiated the suggestion. Upon hearing that the person was a suspected follower of the false Messiah Shabsai Tzvi, R' Yaakov Emden angrily responded, "God forbid that we should heed the suggestion of an evil man. Even though the idea is essentially a good one, because it was proposed by a wicked person nothing good can result from it." Thus, מַחְשְׁבוֹת רָע, *the thoughts of an evil man,* even if they appear to be cogent and good, are still abhorrent to God (*Toras Bar Nash*).

2. The great lengths to which the righteous go in not accepting gifts, even those rightfully deserved, is personified by the two great leaders, Moses and Samuel. In rebutting the false charges leveled against him by Dathan and Abiram, who claimed that Moses sought to dominate the

כט וּפִי רְשָׁעִים יַבִּיעַ רָעוֹת: רָחוֹק יְהוה מֵרְשָׁעִים
ל וּתְפִלַּת צַדִּיקִים יִשְׁמָע: מְאוֹר־עֵינַיִם יְשַׂמַּח־לֵב

ponders how to answer before he speaks (*Rashi*). Since the righteous deliberate before they reply, their words are few (*Metzudos*).

וּפִי רְשָׁעִים יַבִּיעַ רָעוֹת — *But the mouth of the wicked will utter evil.* The mouth of the wicked, however, is like a flowing spring (יַבִּיעַ as in נַחַל נוֹבֵעַ, *a flowing spring*). The wicked utter many evil things, for they say whatever comes to mind without considering the consequences (*Metzudos*).

A righteous person does not rush to reply until he has carefully considered whether his response will cause anguish to the listener. Even when forced to answer, he will ponder as to how he should respond so that he may spare the listener shock, pain, or fright. Especially when imparting bad news, he finds a way to allude to the information and let the listener divine the true meaning himself.

An example of this is in the Talmud (*Pesachim* 4a). Rav and R' Chiya spoke to one another regarding relatives, without specifically mentioning that they were no longer alive. Because of the delicate man-

ner of the discussion, each understood that the relatives had passed away. For this reason the verse uses the word *heart* when referring to a righteous person. A righteous person uses his heart to consider his friend's feelings and avoid shocking him, but a wicked person has no *heart* to feel his friend's pain. He relates bad tidings without considering the consequences (*Toras Bar Nash*).

A righteous individual not only deliberates *how* to respond, but also considers whether he should reply at all. King Solomon warns [26:4], אַל תַּעַן כְּסִיל כְּאִוַּלְתּוֹ, *do not reply to a fool according to his foolishness*. Similarly, the Sages enjoin: מִצְוָה עַל אָדָם שֶׁלֹּא לוֹמַר דָּבָר שֶׁאֵינוֹ נִשְׁמָע, *it is a mitzvah for a person not to say something that will not be accepted* (*Yevamos* 65b). Therefore, a righteous person will not respond before deliberating the matter carefully in his heart (*Malbim*).

According to R' Bachya, the verse portrays how the righteous and the wicked are the antithesis of each other, so that we try to emulate the former and distance ourselves from the latter. The righteous individual practices humility,

nation for his own benefit, Moses said: "I have not taken even a single donkey of theirs" (*Numbers* 16:15). *Rashi* (ad loc.) explains that even when Moses returned from Midian to Egypt to rescue the nation of Israel, and he brought his wife and infants on a donkey, he used his own donkey [i.e. even though he was performing a duty for the Jewish people, he did not take the reimbursement due him]. When the prophet Samuel rebuked his generation, he asked them to bear witness if he had ever taken an ox or a donkey from anyone (*I Samuel* 12:3). Again, though Samuel traveled from city to city for the sake of the people in order to adjudicate disputes, he used his *own* donkey, even though he rightfully should have used public funds (see *Rashi* ad loc.).

Throughout the generations, God-fearing people scrupulously avoided any financial dealings that might make them recipients rather than givers. Boruch Kudowitz, a survivor of World War II, recounts the following incident: Divine Providence guided young Boruch during the war years, as he found refuge with partisans in the Polish forests. After the war ended, he returned to his native Baranovich to see if any of his relatives had survived. He found none, but a gentile neighbor recognized him and told him that there was a letter for him at the post office. A very skeptical Boruch went to the post office and, to his surprise, there was a year-old letter, postmarked 1944, addressed to his father. It was from Rabbi David Witzel, the rav of Baranovich, who had been deported to Siberia, where he subsequently died. Boruch opened the letter. It contained a crumpled ruble and a brief note. In 1938, Rabbi Witzel had borrowed a zloty from Boruch's father. Finding himself in Siberia and not knowing if he would ever be able to repay his debt in person, Rabbi Witzel was sending the ruble in lieu of the zloty, so that he would not remain financially obligated to anyone.

but the mouth of the wicked will utter evil. ²⁹ HASHEM is
far from the wicked, but He will hear the prayer of the
righteous. ³⁰ *Enlightened eyes will gladden the heart; good*

and the wicked exudes arrogance. The
heart of a righteous person is constantly
focused on thoughts of submission and
humility. [לַעֲנוֹת is associated with לֵעָנֹת
מִפָּנָי *to be humbled before Me* (*Exodus*
10:3); see *Rashi* and *Targum* ad loc.] Since
the thoughts of a righteous person center
on humility, it is certain that his speech
will be humble as well, for speech reveals
the hidden recesses of his heart. The
mussar sages teach that הַלָּשׁוֹן קוּלְמוּס הַלֵּב,
the tongue is the quill of the heart. The
opposite is true of the wicked person. Not
only does he harbor wicked thoughts and
arrogance in his heart, but through his
excessive verbiage, he publicizes them to
all.

29. רָחוֹק ה׳ מֵרְשָׁעִים — *HASHEM is far from
the wicked.* He does not hear their prayers
(*Metzudos*).

A major Torah theme is taught here.
The juxtaposition of good and evil is an
impossibility. God is the source of pure
goodness and no evil can emanate from
Him; evil begins when man attempts to
limit God's sphere of influence. When
human beings try to push Him out of their
lives, they invite misfortune, for the absence of God is synonymous with misery
(*Rabbi Avigdor HaLevi Nebenzahl*).[1]

וּתְפִלַּת צַדִּיקִים יִשְׁמָע — *But He will hear the
prayer of the righteous.* God is so close to
the righteous that He hears their prayers,
as the Sages state (*Yerushalmi Berachos*
9:1): Hashem is as near to the righteous as
the mouth is to the ear (*Vilna Gaon*).

R' *Yonah* explains this verse as a
continuation of the previous one. God
hears the prayers of the righteous, who are
always submissive to Him. A similar
thought is expressed by the Psalmist: קָרוֹב
ה׳ לְנִשְׁבְּרֵי לֵב, *HASHEM is close to the*

brokenhearted (*Psalms* 34:19), and תַּאֲוַת
עֲנָוִים שָׁמַעְתָּ ה׳, *The desire of the humble
You have heard,* HASHEM (ibid. 10:17).

Malbim points out that Divine Providence responds to man in accordance with
his deeds. If a person distances himself
from God, then God is far from him; if
someone strives to come close to God, then
God is close to him and heeds his prayers.
[See *Psalms* 145:18: *Hashem is close to all
who call upon Him.*] This does not mean
that He "changes" His position, in accordance with man's prayers. Rather, it is
the person who can either bring himself
closer or distance himself from God (*Malbim*).

According to *Meiri*, verses 27-29 all
address one theme: how careful a judge
must be in order to assure that justice is
achieved. *One who hates gifts* (v. 27) refers
to a judge who hates bribes. Verse 28 urges
a judge to be very patient and deliberate,
carefully considering the issue before him,
in order to execute a true verdict. Finally,
verse 29 assures that God will accept a
righteous judge's prayer for Divine guidance to avoid mistaken verdicts. (See *I
Kings* 3:9, where King Solomon made this
very requuest of God.)

30. מְאוֹר־עֵינַיִם יְשַׂמַּח־לֵב — *Enlightened
eyes* [lit. *enlightenment of the eyes*] *will
gladden the heart.* *Rashi* explains the
verse two ways. Literally, the verse refers
to anything which is a desirable sight for
the eyes, such as a garden or a flowing
river. These items gladden the heart and
cleanse it of sorrow. Midrashically, if one's
eyes are enlightened in Torah, his heart
will rejoice (see *Psalms* 19:9), for when he
is approached with a query in Torah, he
will know what to answer.

According to *Metzudos*, eyes are *en-*

1. The Sages teach that God never allows His Name to be mentioned in connection with evil. For
example, His Name is not mentioned either in connection with the creation of darkness (*Genesis*
1:5) or in the last five of the Ten Commandments, which refer to heinous crimes (*Exodus* 20).
Tosafos (*Taanis* 3a) likens this to a king who built a magnificent palace and had the royal coat
of arms painted in the entrance of every room, with the exception of the lavatory.

lightened when doubts are resolved. This gladdens the heart, for אֵין בָּעוֹלָם שִׂמְחָה כְּהַתָּרַת הַסְּפֵיקוֹת, there is no joy in the world like the resolution of doubts.

שְׁמוּעָה טוֹבָה תְּדַשֶּׁן־עָצֶם — Good news will fatten a bone. Enlightened eyes bring happiness only to the heart, but good news goes even further and "fattens a person's bones."[1] This is one of the ways in which the benefits of hearing surpass those of sight. In this vein, the Sages rule that one who blinds a person pays him for the loss of his eyesight, whereas one who causes a person to become deaf must pay his total value (see Bava Kamma 85b). This verse emphasizes the importance of using our sense of hearing to serve God due to the ear's great significance. Its proper use is listening to admonition, as the next verse explains (R' Yonah).

R' Bachya (Kad Hakemach: Znus Halev) explains that the human body is likened to a palace, in which the soul is the king. The soul is above the limitations of the body, although it is "housed" within it, just as God is infinitely beyond the world, though He rests His Presence upon it. One of the wonders of man's Creation is that God provided five ways for him to have contact with the outside world: the eyes, the ears, the nose, the tongue and the hands. Three of these senses — sight, hearing and smell — are spiritual ones, — while the remaining two — taste and touch — are physical. The three spiritual senses are so important that they are even used in descriptions of God: HASHEM saw (Exodus 3:4); HASHEM heard (Deuteronomy 5:25); and HASHEM smelled (Genesis 8:21). However, the two physical senses are never associated with Hashem; nowhere do we find Hashem tasted, or Hashem touched. As important as the sense of sight is, the sense of hearing supersedes it, for the sense of hearing is purer and more refined than the sense of sight. Therefore, the necessity of utilizing this sense in the service of Hashem is most imperative.

According to Metzudos, good news refers to a novel interpretation in Torah.

The Vilna Gaon explains that the Written Torah is referred to as seeing, for one must read it to study it; the Oral Law is termed hearing, for one must hear it from his rebbe.

31. אֹזֶן שֹׁמַעַת תּוֹכַחַת חַיִּים בְּקֶרֶב חֲכָמִים תָּלִין — The ear that hears life-giving reproof will abide in the midst of the wise. An ear that attends to the reproof that brings life will be eager for reproof and will come to abide among wise people, in order to hear their words of wisdom. [The word תָּלִין indicates constancy.] (Metzudos).

This is in direct contrast to the לֵץ, scorner, who does not like being rebuked and avoids the wise [see v. 12.] (Yalkut Me'am Loez).

Just as it is appropriate for those well versed in wisdom to be in the company of

1. The Talmud (Gittin 56b) recounts a case where a good tiding literally caused one's bones to swell. As Rabban Yochanan ben Zakkai was speaking with the Roman general Vespasian in his attempt to save the Jewish nation from total destruction, a messenger arrived from Rome with the news that Vespasian had been selected as the new caesar. At that moment, Vespasian was wearing only one shoe. To his consternation, he found that he could neither fit into his second shoe, nor remove the one he was already wearing. R' Yochanan ben Zakkai told him: "Do not worry, it is the result of the good news which you heard; as the verse states: good news will fatten a bone. The sage further advised: "If you have an enemy brought in front of you, it will depress your spirit, and your bones will dry up" (see 17:22, a broken spirit dries up a bone). Vespasian followed this advice and it worked. He was so impressed with R' Yochanan ben Zakkai's wisdom that he promised to fulfill the latter's requests. Thus, the city of Yavneh and its sages, the family of Rabban Gamliel the prince, and the ailing and pious R' Tzaddok were saved at the time of the destruction of the Second Temple.

Torah scholars, so, too, it is fitting for one who listens to reproof to be in such company. Scholars enjoy the company of such a person, for even if he does not fathom the depths of wisdom, he is eager to hear their words of reproof, and through them, attains admirable character traits. See next verse (*R' Yonah*).

R' Chaim Shmulevitz explains that even a הֶדְיוֹט, *layman*, who listens to the life-giving reproof from the wise attaches himself to them, and his soul is bound up with theirs, to the extent that he is counted among them.

The *Vilna Gaon* finds in this verse two reasons that it is advantageous to go to the *beis midrash*, even if one does not possess sufficient acumen to study: 1) He will hear *life-giving reproof* from those who study Torah; and 2) he will be *in the midst of the wise*, and it is good to be in the company of such people. [Cf. *Vilna Gaon* on verse 12.] [1]

Alshich contrasts this verse with the previous one. Though a person derives pleasure from seeing or hearing good things in this world, such pleasure is only temporal. However, if he hears words of admonition, even though they are harsh and unpleasant, they benefit him greatly. Thanks to them, when he leaves this world he will rest among the righteous in *Gan Eden*. The verse uses the term תָּלִין, *will rest*, to describe the passing of the righteous, since in essence they do not "die" but rather "rest" in the dust (יְשֵׁנִי עָפָר).

Binah L'Ittim derives a different lesson from this verse. Someone who hears תוֹכַחַת חַיִּים, *life-giving reproof*, not only

studies written words of rebuke, but merits hearing them from a live teacher who infuses his admonition with emotion and inspiration, thus giving the rebuke a much greater impact on him. Such words will penetrate deeply into his heart and not be easily forgotten.

There are several Midrashic applications of the verse:

❏ Every Torah scholar who turns his ear to rebuke merits sitting in the assembly of the wise (*Midrash Mishlei*).

❏ Anyone who comes to the house of prayer and hears words of Torah merits sitting among the wise in the Hereafter (*Devarim Rabbah*).

❏ Since Reuven, Shimon and Levi received rebuke from their father (see *Genesis* 49:3-7), they merited having their lineage listed together with that of Moses and Aaron [*Exodus* 6:14-26, see Rashi v. 15] (*Pesikta*).

32. פּוֹרֵעַ מוּסָר מוֹאֵס נַפְשׁוֹ — *He who rejects discipline despises his soul.* One who rejects reproof despises his soul, for he cannot perfect his character without it (*Ralbag*).

Mussar entails afflicting and restricting oneself in order to fulfill the will of one's Master (see 1:2). If one serves God with such dedication, He will fulfill the person's will, as the Sages teach: בַּטֵּל רְצוֹנְךָ מִפְּנֵי רְצוֹנוֹ כְּדֵי שֶׁיְּבַטֵּל רְצוֹן אֲחֵרִים מִפְּנֵי רְצוֹנֶךָ, *Nullify your will before His will, so that He will nullify the will of others before your will* (*Avos* 2:4). Therefore, one who rejects *mussar* despises his own soul, for as a result God will not fulfill his will, just as he did not forego his will in order to serve God (*Vilna Gaon*).

1. The tremendous benefit of just being in the proximity of wise men and hearing their words of Torah, even without fully comprehending them, is illustrated by R' Yehoshua ben Chanania, whom R' Yochanan ben Zakkai praised as *praiseworthy is she who bore him* (*Avos* 2:11). The Talmud (*Yerushalmi Yevamos* 1:6) notes that R' Dosa ben Hurkinos recalled that R' Yehoshua's mother would bring his cradle to the house of prayer, so that his ears should absorb the words of Torah. In other words, even as an infant, R' Yehoshua's mother exposed him to the words of Torah, and as a result he grew up to be a great Torah scholar.

וְשׁוֹמֵעַ תּוֹכַחַת קוֹנֶה לֵב — *But he who listens to reproof acquires [an understanding] heart.* For by listening to rebuke, he will know which is the correct road to follow (*Vilna Gaon*).

Heart refers to wisdom (*Targum Yonason*); to admirable character traits (*R' Yonah*); or to knowledge and fear of God (*Ibn Ezra*).

33. יִרְאַת ה' מוּסַר חָכְמָה וְלִפְנֵי כָבוֹד עֲנָוָה — *Fear of HASHEM is the discipline of wisdom, and humility precedes honor.* Fear of God is the force that chastises a person to hearken to wisdom. Thus, fear of God precedes wisdom and leads to it, just as humility leads to honor (*Metzudos*).

Knowing about God, and as a result of this knowledge, subordinating oneself to Him, is what is meant by *fear of HASHEM*. King Solomon has already taught that *the fear of HASHEM is the beginning of knowledge* (1:7). Now he instructs that *fear of HASHEM* is the discipline that enables one to reject folly and attain wisdom (*R' Hirsch*).

The *Vilna Gaon* explains that *fear of HASHEM* brings one to *discipline of wisdom*; in contradistinction, those who do not fear God despise discipline and wisdom (see 1:7). Yet, the *Gaon* notes that this verse is written in an ambiguous way, and lends itself to two possible interpretations: 1) Fear of God leads to *discipline of wisdom*, or 2) fear of God results from

who listens to reproof acquires [an understanding] heart. [33] Fear of HASHEM is the discipline of wisdom, and humility precedes honor.

discipline of wisdom. Essentially, both are true [see *Avos* 3:21: אם אין חָכְמָה אֵין יִרְאָה אם אֵין יִרְאָה אֵין חָכְמָה, *if there is no wisdom, there is no fear of God; if there is no fear of God, there is no wisdom*], i.e., יִרְאַת הָעוֹנֶשׁ, *the fear of punishment*, leads to wisdom, and, in turn, wisdom leads to יִרְאַת הָרוֹמְמוּת, *the fear of His sublimity*.

Ralbag renders, *The fear of Hashem will lead to accepting mussar wisely*.

וְלִפְנֵי כָבוֹד עֲנָוָה — *And humility precedes honor*. Humility causes honor to come in its wake (*Rashi*).

The *Vilna Gaon* continues: כָּבוֹד, *honor*, however, can result *only* if it is preceded by עֲנָוָה, *humility*.[1]

1. The Sages reiterate and reemphasize that humility brings honor to an individual. For three years, the Academy of Hillel and the Academy of Shammai each maintained that the *halachah* followed their respective views. A Heavenly voice proclaimed that each was an expression of the Living God. But which of the two should be followed? A Heavenly Voice decreed that the *halachah* was to be established according to the Academy of Hillel. The Sages explain that the Academy of Hillel merited this because its members were humble, to the point of quoting the opinion of the Academy of Shammai before their own. This teaches that if one lowers himself, the Holy One, Blessed is He, raises him up: Whoever flees from prominence, prominence searches for him.

This volume is part of
THE ARTSCROLL SERIES®
an ongoing project of
translations, commentaries and expositions
on Scripture, Mishnah, Talmud, Halachah,
liturgy, history, the classic Rabbinic writings,
biographies and thought.

For a brochure of current publications
visit your local Hebrew bookseller
or contact the publisher:

Mesorah Publications, ltd.

4401 Second Avenue
Brooklyn, New York 11232
(718) 921-900